d'Hereus, Lyskamm, Dent Blanche, Taschorn and Weisshorn, while the Matterhorn, the Dom, and Monte Rosa, though among the loftiest summits, are only "second-class." It will thus be evident that it is no easy matter to satisfy the conditions of membership in the English Club, and quite out of the reach of most Scotsmen. We must therefore found a club of our own. The charm of the Swiss mountains is almost beyond description, but a very fair substitute may be found nearer home, namely, by climbing the Grampians in winter or spring. In fine frosty weather such ascents are most enjoyable, and afford good practice for subsequent "Scrambles amongst the Alps." If conducted with ordinary common sense they are free from danger, but the party ought to be provided with hob-nailed boots, a rope, and an ice-axe for cutting steps. Hoping that some of your readers may be interested in the subject,—I am, &c.

WILL. W. NAISMITH.

Glasgow Herald, January 10, 1889.

A SCOTTISH ALPINE CLUB.

SIR,—The proposal by Mr Naismith to start a Scottish Alpine Club is one worthy of consideration.

The Alpine part is of no present interest to the writer, but the Highland one is.

Such a club might be of great service, not only as a rallying point for enthusiasts, but in spreading wider the interest which unfortunately is confined to comparatively few, and in giving advice and information to intending climbers.

The proposed basis of membership might perhaps with advantage be modified, as height is no real index to the "class" of the mountain. For instance, the 3500 ft. limit would include Lochnagar and Ben Nevis, two very "cheap" ascents, and would exclude all the peaks of the Coolins, which are the stiffest work in Scotland.

My record is not yet up to Mr Naismith's proposed limit, so that in the meantime an outsider.—I am, &c.,

[Gil

Glasgow Herald, January 14, 1889

SCOTTISH ALPINE CLUB.

SIR,—The suggestion contained in the letter from your correspondent "Cairn," in reply to mine in last Thursday's *Herald*, to the effect that the proposed limit of height to qualify for membership should be lowered so as to include the Cuchullins is a good one. On the other hand, all mountains up which there is a pony track might be excluded. The greatest difficulty, I fear, however, will not be to fix the qualification, but to find a sufficient number of enthusiastic climbers to form a club. Perhaps "Cairn" will kindly take the matter in hand?—I am, &c.,

WILL. W. NAISMITH.

Glasgow Herald, January 18, 1889.

A CENTURY OF

SCOTTISH MOUNTAINEERING

An anthology from the
Scottish Mountaineering Club Journal

Edited by
W.D. BROOKER

THE SCOTTISH MOUNTAINEERING TRUST

PUBLISHED BY THE SCOTTISH MOUNTAINEERING TRUST 1988
© THE SCOTTISH MOUNTAINEERING TRUST 1988

Reprinted 1993

A Century of Scottish Mountaineering:
Anthology of the Scottish Mountaineering
Club Journal, 1888-1988
I. Brooker, William D. II. Scottish
Mountaineering Club III. Scottish
Mountaineering Trust IV. Scottish
Mountaineering Club Journal
796.5' 22' 09411

ISBN 0-907521-21-5

Front cover illus: Centre Peak, Cobbler   D.J. Bennet
Rear cover illus.: Stob Binnein   P.H. Hodgkiss

Typeset by Bureau-Graphics, Glasgow
Origination by Arneg, Glasgow
Printed by Martins of Berwick
Bound by Hunter & Foulis, Edinburgh
Distributed by Cordee, 3a DeMontfort Street, Leicester, LE1 7HD

CONTENTS

IV

ILLUSTRATIONS

FOREWORD

By G.J.F. Dutton, Hon. Member S.M.C.

I felt much honoured when asked to write this foreword to Bill Brooker's selection from The *Scottish Mountaineering Club Journal* over the last (or, rather, the first) 99 years.

He has done, very well, such a difficult job. How difficult can best be understood by those who, at earlier possible stances on this long ascent — at maybe some 21, 25, 50, 75, 80 years — unthinkingly thought of so worthwhile a task; and after papering desk, table and carpet gave up with sorrowful relief. There was so much to choose from, so much, excellent; and all fascinating. They became dizzy, surveying that sweep backwards; and the exposure increased every year. No, it was not *yet* a really suitable time, all his predecessors agreed...

But you can't climb on past a Centenary. Brooker as the then *Journal* editor, had to stop and obey an official command to Compile. He was even handed the title (as a very psychological belay) — *A Century of Scottish Mountaineering*. Now, Scottish mountaineering has been going on, in and out of Gaelic verse, for much longer than a century, as *Journal* articles have long made clear, and one must emphasise that the centenary is rather that of the Scottish Mountaineering *Club*. It is natural therefore to ask why the history of mountaineering in Scotland should apparently be considered synonymous with 100 years of one particular club — and not the oldest at that (the Cairngorm Club is several months its senior).

The answer lies in the S.M.C. *Journal* itself, which is unique in offering a continuous overall view of the sport as practised in Scotland throughout this period. Founded by Stott in 1890, it aimed to provide 'information about the hills of Scotland and their exploration.' When the exploration was exhausted, a speedy and merciful release was foretold. Exploration has since then been exhausting itself tirelessly — it has broken out into Guides and, still more exhaustingly, into an infinity of New Routes; and the *Journal* has become increasingly valuable for providing information of wider import than mere topography. Its own decease was postponed simply because those of its contributors and their society could not be: as one by one the early Scottish climbers passed away, the only permanent, reasonably objective, record of their quirks, quarrels and remarkable adventures, and of the whole Scottish mountaineering environment, remained in the *Journal*.

Only in those pages can we now venture, alpenstocked and cautious with Thomson and Naismith — and their coil of window sash-cord — on to a convincingly virginal Buachaille; appreciate with Munro the difficulties of cutting steep steps up snow in a strong wind when encumbered with the contemporary Laird's issue of Inverness Cape; enjoy that supreme Victorian event, the Yacht Meet at Easter '97 with its desperate race back off the hill before the Presidential yacht sirened finality and proceeded, majestic with port, cigars and servants' bagpipes, out of Loch Hourn. And again, who now, dodging and cursing caravans, caravettes and three-storey Continental Leisure Cruisers up the A82, can forget those first Motoring Meets — the triumphant gleam of brass and goggles, the hisses of steam and satisfaction — as the Renault and Arrol-Johnston of Gibbs and Inglis Clark breasted the heathery terrors of General Wade and drew up beneath a startled and vulnerable Bidean? Nor the jeers of the 50-mile-pedallers, the tweed-wrapped horse-tail-viewers and the railway-timetable-clutchers at this new, this Edinburgh, Artificial Aid to decent clean climbing? Or how that most decorously dashing conveyance of Parties to a Meet, the 'Tortoise Sporting Waggon' of '93, gave way to the half-hitched lorries and Morris vans of the '30s and '40s and to those diesel-reeking Prairie Schooners (the otherwise-unemployable successors to The School Bus) that carried us all to J.M.C.S. and countless other ragamuffin meets in the petrol-rationed '50s? And what well-tailored renegade, adjusting safety-bindings above a trussed and prostrate Cairn Gorm, will not feel a twitch of conscience to recall Naismith's slidings in '92 across the Campsies and his grave prediction that 'it is not unlikely that the sport may eventually become popular'?

The early *Journals* take us back to climbing in hills subtly different. We are still in post-glacial Scotland: but the ice has just gone. Corries are new and mysterious; peaks virtually un-trodden. Official heights are debated and counter-debated with industrious asperity, maps corrected. New summits are spied out with trembling monoculars. A fresh wind blows everywhere.

The climbers are quite recognisable. A slip in the burn and a wet doup provoked the same reactions then as they do now, and the dubious characters — the sonorous drone, the glory-boy, the record-grabber, the whistle-blowing incompetent — are solemnly described, or describe themselves, as clearly and entertainingly as today. But the society in which they operated, in which we operate, changed greatly through the century. You realise this as you read the articles, and their fascination deepens. For the story of the S.M.C. is of interest to more than mountaineers; like any living organism it has to dodge, parry and exploit its environment or go under. It has not gone under; and its manoeuvres as a self-perpetuating community riding this social avalanche are well worth reading about. Other Scottish Climbing Clubs have suffered or enjoyed similar contortions, and recounted many of them in the *Journal* (which, despite time-honoured disbelief, cannot be thought exclusive to the S.M.C....) Of course, whatever the club, earlier years are easy to savour; there we see ourselves absurd in yesterday's zoo. It is more difficult with contemporary selections, for we are too near the bars to see the cage of the 1970s and '80s; our successors will be more conveniently placed.

Yet in one important respect the articles from the '50s onward are more enthralling. This period has witnessed a dramatic growth in the status of Scottish winter climbing. Until then it had developed slowly, from being agreeable minor practice for next year's Alps into a craft with unique skills and traditions. Since then, Scotland in winter has become one of the world's centres for Hard Ice climbing; and provides practice, now, rather for Andean and Himalayan faces. One can trace hints of this destiny far back, but Murray's splendidly independent postwar books clearly indicate that gleeful explosion of Marshall, Smith, Haston, and the rest: a technical outburst paralleled by a similarly unrestrained spree among the dust-sheets of the Club itself and — reinforcing earlier vital incursions by the Creag Dhu, the Deargies, Scrubbernut, Peaheid and others — also shaking up Scottish climbing generally. Naturally this exciting time had correspondences elsewhere in Europe and in the U.S.A., on the hills and off them; but its study is particularly instructive, as I have stressed, when condensed at one spot by a *Journal* such as this. In fact, I find the full run of the S.M.C. *Journal* as illuminating as that of the *Alpine Journal*. The A.J. scores by its wider scale of time, space and celebrities; the S.M.C.J. by its greater comprehensibility and cohesion.

You will discover that Brooker's selection illustrates all these points. It cannot be as he admits, pure History; that, though well represented here, deserves a volume of its own and, without his keen eye, could have elbowed itself intolerably across a compilation designed also to give a Good Read.

So, have a good read, and the historical background will declare itself as you turn the pages. Brooker is refreshingly undidactic and his selection runs easily and informally. Of course, we could all — at first glance — have made a slightly different selection, and no doubt of course a slightly better one. A second glance shows how little different, and how much less good, it would have been. Each choice reflects its compiler's view of the scene. Brooker's is wide, sensible and firmly based on practical mountaineering in Scotland, to which he himself has notably contributed on rock and ice and with ski. His balance allows him a range of contributors from Salvationist to Ultramontane; and the earlier vigilance of successive *Journal* editors (no doubt) has kept their prose reasonably above the damper manifestations of the period's literary climate — those late-Victorian storms of ecstacy and the late-Elizabethan drizzle of four-letter words.

When you have finished, remember that much more — 49/50ths according to Brooker — of this unique commentary on the past century of mountaineering as seen in Scotland, remains on the shelf: enough to have allowed worthy selections for at least a couple more volumes like this one, or to engender some dozen Ph.D. theses next century. Bill Brooker deserves well of us for successfully completing the daunting task of distilling his own one-fiftieth, and allowing a hundred years to climb so entertainingly and instructively past.

INTRODUCTION AND ACKNOWLEDGEMENTS

In preparing this anthology I have had the help of many people.

First of course there are the authors of the original *Journal* material. Many are no longer with us and I trust that those that are will approve even if they were not consulted about the re-use of their work. Then there are the Scottish Mountaineering Club members who responded to invitations to suggest items for inclusion. Among these I am particularly indebted to Geoff Cohen, Jim Donaldson, Peter Hodgkiss, Victor Russell, Malcolm Slesser, Alex Small and Iain Smart. Geoff Dutton, Robin Campbell and Ken Crocket gave valuable advice from the wisdom and experience gained as past and present editors of the SMC *Journal*, while the first added the benison of his generous foreword to the anthology.

In preparing the text, huge volumes of keyboard work were carried out by Ailsa Forbes and Kay Duggan while Peter Hodgkiss managed the printing operation and coped with editorial procrastination with forbearance and understanding.

Photographs are an important part of this book and since production realities procluded the direct use from the *Journal* itself it was necessary to go elsewhere. In this the Club library and slide collection were obvious sources and the help of Colin Stead and Derek Pyper was appreciated, as were contributions from Douglas Scott, Alex Small and Tom Weir. The main credit for the illustrations lies, however, with that master of mountain photography Donald Bennet, who found time in a busy Presidential year, not only to search his own collection, but also to select and collate from all the pictures considered. Others have been involved in making photographs available and to them I extend my thanks. In a few cases photographs are not attributed by caption because their origin could not be readily ascertained. Apologies are tendered where appropriate.

Finally, I would like to thank my wife Margaret for the tolerance and understanding she has displayed during the last few months.

Even with so much help I am all too aware that the final choice is a compromise between three different objectives: to present a history of the SMC in its Centenary year, to give an account of Scottish Mountaineering over the hundred years, and to provide a Good Read. Like any compromise it will not completely achieve any of these targets but I hope it will provide an adequate flavour of each.

Although this anthology contains items drawn from all but four of the 34 volumes of the SMCJ it contains only about one-fiftieth of the total content. As I became increasingly familiar with the riches in the *Journal* the more I regretted the necessary omission of so much good material, material quite well enough endowed with literary quality, wit, acumen, technical interest and historical significance to merit inclusion in this anthology. There is no doubt that were I to do this job a second time I would make changes — and if a third time there would be more changes still. Production realities preclude continued alteration of content, and omissions will have to remain just that — at least until another edition. However, I cannot resist listing some of the articles which I think deserved inclusion had space allowed. Many readers will have access to past volumes and may wish to read them.

Chalk Climbing on Beachy Head — A.E. Crowley	Vol III (1895)
Sgurr na Ciche — A Climb Against Time — H.C. Boyd	Vol III (1897)
The Ben Nuis Chimney — L.J.O. Oppenheimer	Vol VII (1902)
Courage in Climbing — W.W. Naismith	Vol X (1909)
The Brack — Elephant Gully — H. Raeburn	Vol XII (1912)
Bidean Choire Sheasgaich — J.A. Parker	Vol XV (1919)
Ski Running — H MacRobert	Vol XXI (1938)
Days on Ben Nevis — G.C. Williams	Vol XX (1935)
New Year Howffs — B. Humble	Vol XXV (1952)
Missing the Last Post — N Tennent	Vol XXVII (1960)
Beanntan Glaschu — J. MacKenzie	Vol XXX (1973)
The Forgotten Corrie — C.M. Dixon	Vol XXV (1952)
All the Way — R. Sharp	Vol XXX (1973)
Modern Scottish Winter Climbing — J.R. Marshall	Vol XXVII (1961)
Winter Dreams — K.V. Crocket	Vol XXX1(1976)
The Winter Mitre — Greg Strange	Vol XXXI (1976)
Freestyle on Creag an Dubh Loch — D. Cuthbertson	Vol XXXI (1979)

And these are only some; further articles by authors like Murray, Patey, and Robin Smith are always rewarding to read again, as are the many 'Doctor' tales by Dutton. Nor have I been able to include even a selection of the interesting technical material, the analysis of accidents, weather phenomena, the New Climbs, the historical articles on places and names or the battles with Bureaucracy like 'The Coruisk Affair'. Expedition reports can be dull but inspiring accounts of activities in the Alps, Greenland and the greater ranges abound and there are plenty of lively pieces in 'SMC Abroad', from Naismith's ascent of the second Pyramid in 1914 — in bare feet at the age of 58 — to the antipodean adventures of A.L. Cram in 1984.

But I could go on and on — so there is nothing for it but to recommend that you go to libraries or your own bookshelves and do it for yourselves.

W.D. Brooker, October 1988

THE FIRST PHASE

IN THE BEGINNING

In the Jubilee Number of the Journal in Volume XXII (1939) appeared an article called 'The Club in Retrospect' , The first part of this was by A. Ernest Maylard

THE ORIGIN AND GROWTH OF THE CLUB.

In October 1881 I came to Glasgow from Guy's Hospital in London, where I was a Demonstrator in Anatomy, to teach the same subject in a new extra-mural school which was being started on the lines of Minto House Medical School In Edinburgh. I hadn't a friend in the city, and being fond of the country and of walking I frequently spent my free days, which were usually Saturdays, in tramps about the surrounding country. The winter walks had much attraction for me, especially on the hills. One very memorable tramp was from Aberfoyle to the top of Ben Venue in deep snow. On another very similar occasion I revelled in fighting a blinding snowstorm, trying to get to the top of the Campsie Fells from Strathblane; the wind was so strong that my cap blew off, refusing to proceed any further, taking its own course downwards and compelling me to follow. I used to delight in these winter expeditions, and often expressed my surprise that I never met a soul; so I suggested to my newly made acquaintances that the citizens of Glasgow knew little of the beauties of the country around them in winter

It was with these feelings, arising, as will appear later, from a too limited experience and also a too hasty judgment, that I read one morning in the *Glasgow Herald* a letter from a writer unknown to me expressing sentiments with which I was in full sympathy. This letter was signed by W.W. Naismith, and it was followed by another signed by 'Cairn' (subsequently known to be D.A. Archie in collaboration with Gilbert Thomson) supporting the views ventilated by the former writer. I replied by a letter to the *Glasgow Herald* expressing full sympathy With the opinions of these two correspondents, and at the same time indicating in what way I thought some action might be taken. I turned to my friend Professor F.O. Bower, who was also a comparative newcomer to the City, but the existence of mutual friends in the South brought us together. Like myself, he too was a lover of walks in the country, frequently leading his students on botanising expeditions to the hills, often in search of high alpine plants. We thought that a public meeting should be advertised if a sufficient number of replies to my letter, favourable to the proposal, were received. As this proved to be the case, a notice was inserted in the *Herald* indicating date

1

and place and inviting all who sympathised with the project. We agreed that no better man could be found to preside at the meeting than Professor George Ramsay, who was himself a member of the Alpine Club. The meeting took place in the rooms of the Christian Institute, Bothwell Street, Glasgow, on 11th February 1889. This day, therefore, may be considered the birthday of the Club. All those present who wished to be so, although they might be only sympathisers with the project, were constituted 'Original Members'. This accounted for about thirty or forty, but it was subsequently arranged that the number of original members should be extended to the first hundred of those who joined the Club. In the 1893 list of members there were seventy two such. At the present time, when the Club is celebrating its Jubilee, there are only nine.'

THE FORMATION OF THE S.M.C

A long article in Volume IV (1896) by G.G. Ramsay allows the sequence of events in 1889 to be set out thus:

1889 January 10th. Letter by W.W. Naismith appeared in the *Glasgow Herald*.

14th. Reply by 'Cairn' suggesting a Scottish Alpine Club (Gilbert Thomson and D.A, Archie) supporting the proposal but objecting to the term 'Alpine'

18th. Naismith replied sympathetically.

19th. E.A. Maylard came in with a supportive letter suggesting the name Scottish Mountaineering Club and offering 'to receive the name of any gentleman or lady who might feel interested.' Another letter from Maylard said there was plenty of support and indicated that the proposed Club should embrace all Scotland and not just Glasgow. Maylard consulted Prof. G.G. Ramsay of Glasgow University and an advertisement was placed in the *Herald* for a meeting

February 11th. A 'very hearty' meeting was held with an attendance of about 40. A subcommittee was formed and met several times

March 11th. The Scottish Mountaineering Club was formally constituted wlth G.G. Ramsay as its President and A.E. Maylard, Gilbert Thomson, and W.W. Naismith respectively being appointed as Honorary Secretary, Librarian and Treasurer,

The 94 Original members represented a commendably wide geographical distribution; Glasgow and the West of Scotland 52; Edinburgh 17; England 12; Other East of Scotland 13. No fewer than 17 were already members of the Alpine Club

THE FIRST ANNUAL DINNER   Vol 1 (1890)

This took place in the Grand Hotel Glasgow on December 12th 1889 after tbe AGM. Some thirty members were present. It must have been quite an eloquent occasion for apart from 'the usual loyal toasts' no fewer than seven toasts were proposed and replied to. The main one was that of 'the Club' as it still is today, and the president's Address to it by G.G Ramsay is the first article in the first issue of the *Journal*. An extract is given here.

"Gentlemen, I have observed that on occasions like the present the Chairman generally begins his speech by saying that he rises with much diffidence. I beg to state at once, gentlemen, that I rise, on this occasion, with no diffidence at all. Not that I feel any, even the smallest, confidence that I can do justice to my theme; for my theme is such that there is probably no man living who could do full justice to it. But we are here to night as exponents of a great cause; we are here to express our common attachment to one of the purest and simplest and highest of human pleasures; We are forming an association to keep alive and spread our own love of the choicest of God's gifts to man, and that form of healthful effort which will enable us to make those gifts our own, And from the keenness with which our idea has been taken up, from the Spirit which animates you here to-night, as well as the absent remnant of that chosen hundred who are the original members of our Club, I feel assured of its success. I feel confident that this Club will not only enable us to extend and gratify our love of the mountains, but that from the basis of that common love this night will prove the beginning of a personal friendship and intimacy amongst its members which will be, I trust, as fresh and bracing, might we add everlasting, as the hills themselves.

Gentlemen, this is an historic occasion. It is not often that at the birth of a great man, or at the beginning of a great empire, either man or empire is conscious of the greatness that lies before them. But it is otherwise with us. In the very moment of our birth we can foresee our future. We know that our Club will live to be a famous Club."

Then, as befits an SMC Dinner, comes a bit of nationalism together with a friendly dig at our southern neighbours.

"Gentlemen, the marvel is not that our Club is formed, but that it was not formed before. The mountains of Scotland are not new; they have been frequently looked at; frequently admired; sometimes even climbed before. The love of scenery and of hills is implanted in the heart of every Scot as part of his very birthright; our mountains have been the moulders of our national character. And yet it was in England that grew up the first Alpine Club in Europe - not without some good Scots in it, however, amongst whom I may be permitted to name as an original member my own brother, a rare cragsman, who made a well known first ascent of Mont Blanc from the Courmayeur side in 1854. But why were the English first in the field, or rather on the tops? Perhaps their own dull flats drove them in sheer desperation to seek for heights elsewhere; perhaps the very paucity of their climbers drove them for self-defence into combination: whereas in Scotland, every man has his hill or mountain at his door; every man is potentially a mountaineer; and a mountaineering Club, in its simple sense, must thus have included nothing less than the entire nation. But the fact is that mountaineering has received an altogether new development at the hands of the Alpine Club. It is now a science of a highly complex character, cultivated by trained experts, with a vocabulary, an artillery, and rigorous methods of its own

Nay it has solved the great philosophical problem of finding the Many in the One; for whereas of old it was thought that every mountain had but one top, and that there was but one way, and that the easiest way, to the top of it, the Alpine Club has discovered that the number of ways to the top of any given mountain is infinite, and that that way only is to be discarded which is easiest."

> Ramsay enlarged on the theme of mountains and the different kinds of interest they fostered and went on…and on…and on…for about seven more pages. He was, after all, a Victorian academic. It was all grand stuff, liberally embellished with Alpine examples and classical illusions, He concluded…

"Resorting to a free paraphrase, we may say of mountains what Cicero says of books:—"
They belong to every clime and country; no race, no age, but has felt their influence. They apply to our youth a spur of active exertion; they afford to old age the peaceful soothing pleasures of contemplation. They add a new elation to our hours of strength; they supply a refuge and recruiting ground in our moments of bitterness and depression. They are the ornament of our native land; they are our first object of interest in foreign countries, We delight to look at them from our firesides ; they are as companions to us when we walk abroad. They beckon us to adventures on distant shores, and add a beauty and a tenderness indescribable to the prospect from our country homes.

THE GUIDE BOOK   A. E. Maylard.

Next to the practical indulgence in the sport of mountaineering itself must be regarded the series of excellent Guide Books that the Club has issued within the last few years ; and I may incidentally remark how deeply indebted are the non-contributory members of the Club to those who are responsible for their compilation. These well bound volumes have found a market not only among the members themselves, but are now frequently used as reference guides by visitors to the Highlands. They serve the inestimable purpose of indicating to all and sundry the beauty of Nature in some of her grandest manifestations. Of course, when the project was originally suggested of producing these 'Guides', finance was a serious initial consideration. But here a little incident occurred which I trust I may be pardoned for introducing, as it involves a slight personal effort in furtherance of the project. From some intimate friends I learnt of the former existence of a club which had been extinct for some years, whose members had now nearly all passed away, only two or three surviving. One of these was Professor Ramsay, our first President. There was a certain kinship between this club and our own; it had the suggestive name of 'The Gaiter Club'

I learnt that there was a considerable amount of capital and accumulated interest in the bank belonging to the Club. For this there was now no outlet, as the Club, like most of its members , was extinct. Fortunately for us, we had an interested survivor, Professor Ramsay. It was to him, therefore, that I appealed for some of this dormant accumulation of the Gaiter Club's wealth for our proposed Guide Book. After consultation with one or two of his co-survivors of the Club, the appeal resulted in our receiving £100. This contribution very materially helped in furthering our project, and with what excellent results; for at present there are no fewer than eight volumes profusely and beautifully illustrated.

The list is now of course much longer and includes at least a couple of dozen titles. The Club now publishes through the Scottish Mountaineering Trust arrangements.

THE JOURNAL

The Scottish Mountaineering Club Journal itself came into being in January 1890 at the suggestion of Joseph Gibson Stott who having joined the Club during its initial year of existence became founder and first Editor of the *Journal*. It is to Stott that the concept and style of the *Journal* were due but his departure to New Zealand meant that he had to leave after 7 numbers had been issued. Sadly, Stott died ln 1938 just before the 50th anniversary of the Club but he wrote these words from Melbourne as a contribution to the Jubilee Number of the *Journal* .

"...I well remember that afternoon in Glasgow when half a dozen of us debated the pros and cons of a Journal. There was a good deal of opposition, the main reason advanced being that Scotland was too small to provide material for more than a few numbers. I strongly objected, and for the first time (I believe) ventured my belief that there were not less than 300 mountains in Scotland whose height exceeded 3,000 feet

Well, they gave me the Journal: and its life of nigh half a century, and still going strong, proves the truth of all that I claimed for it. Read my preface to the first number. If you want a message from me why not reprint that preface? Many of our members can never have seen it...

The preface is too long for full reproduction but here are the first three paragraphs:

PREFACE

"Although the value of a Club Journal as a means of circulating information must be so apparent to members as to render editorial introduction almost unnecessary, it may not be out of place in this the first number, to indicate briefly one or two points in connection with it.

Probably it will surprise many readers to learn that there are more than three hundred mountains in Scotland whose height exceeds 3,000 feet above sea-level! Even were our explorations to be restricted to mountains of no lesser altitude, here truly is a formidable undertaking. Their very names might furnish us with philological study for considerable time to come, without trenching upon the more scientific aspects of their botany, zoology, and climatology; and even if we content ourselves with them from a topographical or a climbing point, it will be long indeed before they are exhausted. But fine walks, hard climbs, and magnificent scenery are by no means restricted to the higher mountains.

It is probably not too much to say that some of our Scottish summits have never been ascended; that others have only seen the adventurous climber at long intervals, and then only in the shape of the forester, the shepherd, or the sportsman, who have climbed them in pursuit of their avocation, and not in search of the picturesque or the difficult. And if they are known to these visitors, they are wholly unknown to the world at large, for many of them have never been described at all, and the only account of others is as old as the days of Pennant and MacCulloch. The field that lies before the Club is therefore a large one; and when our members have climbed all the peaks, and explored all our beautiful glens and passes, we shall still have the excellent advice of Mr Pilkington, a Vice President of the Alpine Club, to fall back upon: for he tells us that when we have found all the easy ways up our hills, we must turn our attention to conquering the difficult ways. This it is that has largely maintained the interest of the 'Alpine Journal' , full as its numbers have been, of recent years, of old friends presented under new aspects in the way of ascents and explorations by routes hitherto unattempted.

> We must remember that in 1890 the Highlands were sparsely known from a mountaineering viewpoint. Nobody even knew how many mountains there were and existing guide books only mentioned about thirty. It was to this situation that the Club and its *Journal* addressed itself, The first two volumes of the *Journal* witnessed a surge in hillwalking exploration of the Scottish hills by SMC members. Descriptive material is prominent both in the form of articles and of lesser items in the 'Notes and Queries' sections. Hugh T. Munro was a frequent contributor and one fruit of his ubiquitous activity was the inclusion in No 6 (1891) of his now famous 'Tables giving all the Scottish Mountains exceeding 3,000 ft in Height.' Munro identified 538 'Tops' and allocated 'Mountain' status to 283 of them. Later editors of the Tables have amended these and today they stand at 516 and 277 respectively. The task must have been enormous and Stott has been credited with 'successfully keeping Munro's nose more to the grindstone'
>
> In 1892 Stott's mantle was assumed by William Douglas who continued as Editor for nearly eighteen years and produced the remarkable number of 53 issues. His successor, F.S Goggs, wrote in the Jubilee Number (1939) :

"As the Club progressed in age and numbers, hill walking naturally developed into mountaineering in its two departments of snow and rock, and Douglas , a lover of the mountains , equally sympathetic to the salvationist and the ultramontane, saw to it that the *Journal* was representative of all sections. In this connection it is interesting to note that the rope and axes first appeared on the cover of the *Journal* in January 1898 (No. 25), and there they have continued until this day.

Douglas put through the *Journal* the 'S.M.C. Guide Book', the precursor of the elaborate Guide Books which have since appeared. It was started in No. 34, January 1901 and ran on to No. 57, September 1907. This number taken in conjunction with an article by him in No. 29, May 1899, entitled 'Early Descriptions of Skye' shows Douglas in his threefold capacity as a scholar, a bookman, and a mountaineer"

> Goggs had impressed upon him by Douglas the need to be particular about the correct spelling of Gaelic hill names. This has been based upon the Ordnance Survey usage although its accuracy has not always been as high as it is in today's maps. Other embargoes such as 'no articles on climbs abroad' and 'no poetry' have come to be relaxed over the years. Goggs edited the *Journal* for ten years and brought out 30 numbers. He continued... .

"Tbe Club must be counted fortunate in having only three editors over a period of thirty one years — in the next fifteen it had five.

E.P. Buchanan, of a younger generation, put in good work for four years, and was succeeded by G.B. Green, an old Oxford running 'blue' and senior classical master at the Edinburgh Academy for thirty-three years. A lover of the hills, his editorship gave him much pleasure and the Club satisfaction. He was only responsible for five numbers, and his sudden death in June 1927 necessitated George Sang the Club's Honorary Secretary, stepping into the breach and producing No. 104, November 1927. The editorial chair was then graced for five years by a Paisley man, J. MacRobert, who did his work with the thoroughness one anticipates from a member of the legal profession. Thus owing to Green's death Vol. XVIII had the names of three editors on its title-page — a unique experience for the Club. In 1933 the penultimate editor, C.W. Parry, came on the scene. He produced six interesting numbers ', but as he lived in Surrey he found that he could not keep in that close touch with the Club's activities which is essential ' so in 1936 he handed over his office to J.H.B.Bell, D.Sc. — a Fifer, though now resident in Clackmannan. His enthusiasm for the hills, his comparative youth, a fine climbing record, and the six numbers he has already issued give the Club sound reasons for wishing that he will substantially lengthen the somewhat meagre mean of the editorial term of office since 1921

> These hopes were to be fulfilled handsomely as Bell was to look after the *Journal* for 25 years and carry it through and beyond the difficult years of the 1939-45 war as well as a period of social and technical change in mountaineering. Bell's character and stature as a climber helped him to develop the *Journal* as a publication which served Scottish mountaineering and not just the interests of its parent club
> G.J. Dutton took over from Bell in 1960. Dutton was himself a talented writer and it was during his period in office and that of his later co-editor and eventual successor R.N. Campbell that the *Journal* reached its highest levels of readability and reputation as mountain writing. Articles from this fourteen year period are commonly to be found in mountaineering anthologies

The next eleven years saw the editorial chalr occupied by W.D. Brooker and changes occurred in response to alterations in the nature and tempo of mountaineering in Scotland.

Growth in the numbers of mountain accidents, the Munroist cult and of New Climbs meant that an Assistant Editor and three successive New Routes Editors gave invaluable help with the editorial task. There is no reason to suppose that the rate of change in the mountain world will slow and the current editor K.V. Crocket is well aware of the Journal's need to reflect this change while retaining the qualities it has maintained throughout its hundred years life — a daunting task but one in which the spirits of all his predecessors will be with him.

LIST OF JOURNALS AND EDITORS

Schedule of Journal Editors	First Number	Last Number
J.G. Stott	1 : Jan 1890	7 : Jan 1892
W. Douglas	8 : May 1892	60 : Sept 1909
F.S. Goggs	61 : Feb 1910	90 : Oct 1920
E.P. Buchanan	91 : April 1921	98 : Nov 1924
G.B. Green	99 : April 1925	103 : April 1927
G. Sang	104 : April 1928	— —
J. MacRobert	105 : April 1928	114 : Nov 1932
C.W. Parry	115 : April 1933	120 : Nov 1935
J.H.B. Bell	121 : April 1936	150 : 1959
G.J.F. Dutton	151 : 1960	156 : 1965
GJFD/RNC	157 : 1966	162 : 1971
R.N. Campbcll	163 : 1972	166 : 1975
W.D. Brooker	167 : 1976	177 : 1986
K.V. Crocket	178 : 1987	still in office

INDEXES

An index has been issued with each volume. Ten-volume indexes have been produced as follows

Volumes	Numbers	Years
1-10	1- 60	1890-1909
11-20	61-120	1910-1935
21-30	121- 165	1936-1974

Although the Journal has had thirteen dlfferent Editors during its hundred year life it has had only two *printers*. The first was The Darien Press of Edinburgh from 1890 to 1964. The second was Culross the Printers of Coupar Angus, from 1965 to date.

THE CAIRNGORM CLUB

The S.M.C. is not of course the oldest Scottish Mountaineering club. This distinction belongs to the Cairngorm Club of Aberdeen, which had its birth under the Shelter Stone of Loch Avon in 1888. To have been forestalled — and that by a provincial outlier — may not have gone down too well. This early reference to the Cairngorm Club in Vol. I (1891) is certainly patronising.

"We notice, with pleasure, from its second annual report, the flourishing condition of this Club. As its name implies, it exists for the purposes of exploring, and fostering a love of the Cairngorm mountains. The members number 141, presided over by Mr James Bryce, M.P., and Mr Chas. Ruxton, Advocate; and Mr A. I. McConnochie, whose writings are well known to readers of this Journal, is the Hon. Secretary. Although the summer excursions of the Club, which partake much of the nature of well-arranged mountain picnics, probably form the extent of the acquaintance of most members with the mountains, much good work has been done on the hills at all seasons of the year by several gentlemen, and some valuable information collected. The publications issued by the Club (one of which is noticed below) are interesting contributions to mountain literature; and another satisfactory feature is the love of mountains and mountain scenery diffused amongst people who might not otherwise be drawn towards them."

However, there were members common to both clubs and pamphlets on various hills published by the Cairngorm Club were given complimentary reviews. And then in Vol. II (1893) we find this review by A.E. Maylard of the first Cairngorm Club Journal:

THE CAIRNGORM CLUB JOURNAL   Edited by Alex. Inkson McConnochie.
No. 1, July 1893

"It will come with no little surprise to some to find that a second Journal has been started, and so much in the lines of our own that but for the name and the colour of the cover, it would be impossible to distinguish the one from the other. Were it not so much in the heart of every mountaineer and lover of mountain scenery to greet with true hearty fellowship every kindred endeavour to further the aims and interests of everything that pertains to mountains, it might prove a somewhat tempting question to ask, why, when there already exists a Journal which welcomes worthy contributions from all parts of Scotland, and which we believe fairly fulfils all the requirements of the case, it should be deemed needful to publish a second periodical on, so far as can be judged, precisely similar lines? Far be it from us, however, to cast any disparaging reflections, or to withhold that hand of fellowship and goodwill, which, as we have said, we would desire to extend; but we must confess to a feeling of curiosity to understand, why a member of the Scottish Mountaineering Club, a member of the Executive, and a worthy contributor to its Journal, should have thought fit to edit what is practically a facsimile."

> Maylard goes on in similar vein at length, then reviews the content, and cannot resist a final dig by referring to the concluding article.

"...on the Blue Hill, an eminence of 467 feet in height, situated in the neighbourhood of Aberdeen and apparently in the enjoyment of considerable local veneration."

> The Cairngorm Journal still flourishes to this day and has run to 100 issues. A.I. McConnochie continued as its Editor until 1911 but although he had two articles in each of the first two volumes and a lengthy notice in the third, he made no further contributions to the S.M.C. Journal. He died in 1936 and his obituary notice which appeared in both the C.C.J. and the S.M.C.J. states that he was not a member of the S.M.C. He had actually been one of the original members and was on the Club Committee in 1892 and 1893.

NOTES AND QUERIES
Vol I (1890)

Members desirous of meeting at any convenient centre during next year, should send their name, mention centre they desire to visit and the probable date, to the Editor of the Journal, before the Annual Meeting. The groups for the different centres selected, could talk the matter over at the Annual Meeting and arrange preliminaries as to tents, &c.; or, if in sufficient number, and the terms admit, by Tortoise Sporting Waggon.

Those availing themselves of this method would have secure accomodation, avoid much needless walking, and accomplish more work. There might also be looked for that pleasure derivable from meeting with kindred spirits, and that romance inseparable from camping out.

D. M'K.

CORRIE VASSIE OR THE CORRIE OF THE WOLF (Extract)
Vol II (1892) by Charles Stuart

A hearty shout from an enthusiast proclaimed the next glorious find, Saxifragra cœspitosa (true), which had not been gathered in Scotland since Dr Martin Barry found it fifty years before near the summit of Ben Avon! All sense of fatigue, hunger, and thirst vanished, and I may also state the feeling that we were gathering specimens on dangerous ground. Some of our friends had scrambled still higher in the mist, sending down pieces of rock and stones at such a pace that, had any one been struck, would have seriously injured if not killed them. Owing to the inclination of the rocks, to get out of the way was easier said than done. A naval friend who was near me, and who had served in the trenches with the Naval Brigade, shouted, "Confound it! this is worse than the cannon balls in the Crimea; unless we remove beyond the elevation of our friends we shall get killed."

OH, MY BIG HOBNAILERS!
Vol. II (1892) and III (1894)   by J.G. Stott

One of the eccentricities of the SMC Annual Dinner is that 'the Club Song' — often
with modern variations — is actually sung with enthusiasm by the whole company.
Here is most of it as it appeared in the Journal, Vol. II, (1893) and Vol. III, (1894).

AIR — *The Golden Slippers*

Oh, the big ice axe, it hangs on the wall,
With the gaiters, and the gloves, and the rope, and all;
But we'll polish off the rust, and we'll knock out all the dust,
    When we go up to the mountains in the snow.
Then our raiment stout shall the cold keep out,
And the good old axe shall again cut tracks,
And the frozen slope shall call for the rope,
    When we go up to the mountains in the snow.

Chorus — Oh, my big hobnailers! Oh, my big hobnailers!
    How they speak of mountain peak,
    and lengthy stride o'er moorland wide!
    Oh, my big hobnailers! Oh, my big hobnailers!
    Memories raise of joyous days
    Upon the mountain side!

Then our cragsmen bold shall swarm up the shoots,
And shall win their way up unheard-of routes;
While others, never flagging, the tops and peaks are bagging,
    When we go up to the mountains in the snow,
Though the hailstones rattle, like the shot in battle,
And the whirlwind and blizzard freeze the marrow and the gizzard,
Though it thunder and it lighten, still our hearts it cannot frighten,
    When we go up to the mountains in the snow.
                                                    — Chorus

Let the Switzer boast of his Alpine host;
But the Scotsman kens of a thousand Bens -
Oh! their names are most supernal, but you'll find 'em in the 'Journal'.
    As compiled by that enthusiast, Munro.
The Salvationist takes his pick from the list,

And the agile Ultramontane finds the exercise he's wantin'
Each gets climbing that'll please him, as the mood may chance to seize him.
    When we go up to the mountains in the snow.

                                   — Chorus

From the sunrise flush, when the hill-tops blush,
Till the moonbeams quiver on the ice-bound river,
'We push attack and foray, over ridge and peak and corrie,
    When we go up to the mountains in the snow.
When the long day's done, and the vict'ry's won,
And the genial whisky toddy cheers the spirit, warms the body,
Then the ptarmigan and raven, far aloft above our haven,
    Hear our chorus faintly wafted o'er the snow.

                                   — Chorus

"Oh! my big hob. nailers a reminiscence. 13/12/92   F.C.

1. *W.W. Naismith, the father of the Scottish Mountaineering Club*

2.   The SMC Meet at Tarbet, New Year 1895

3.   The SMC Meet at Loch Awe, New Year 1897

4. *Oh My Big Hobnailers! William Inglis Clark at rest*

5. *Stravagers and Marauders
   beware! The keeper at Kernsary
   in 1905 (above) and A Warning
   to tired climbers (below)*

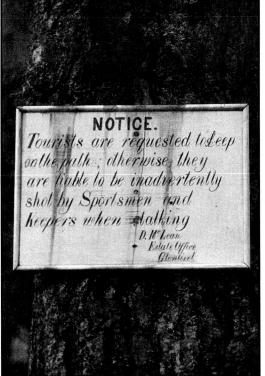

NOTICE.
*Tourists are requested to keep
on the path ; otherwise they
are liable to be inadvertently
shot by Sportsmen and
keepers when stalking*
            D. McLean
              Estate Office
               Glenuisel

BEN NEVIS Notes and Queries
Vol. I (1891)

The following proposals for the 'Improvement' of Ben Nevis may amuse our Members. They are taken from the *Glasgow Herald*:-

1. Edinburgh, 8th May 1891.

Sir, — The steamers occasionally treat their passengers, when time permits, to a run for a mile or two up some of the beautiful Highland sea lochs in the west. Among others, Loch Nevis and Loch Hourne are well worth seeing. The name of the former, being interpreted, means the Celestial Loch, and the latter its opposite, from the dark surrounding mountains. We shall suppose that Ben Nevis partakes of the character of the former. It is the highest mountain in Scotland and the British Islands, being 4,406 feet in height. It is unfortunate that instead of being of a shapely contour like Ben Lomond, Schihalion, Ben More, and others, it is of a rounded and lumpish form, and though it is seen in its whole height from the sea level at Loch Lynne its appearance is somewhat disappointing. Its upper part is composed of a mass of small stones of two or three feet in length in the form of a great cairn. It would not be difficult to follow up this idea of a cairn by blasting with dynamite some of the neighbouring hills, where the excavation would not be noticed, and obtaining a supply of similar stones to be piled up to form a more lofty and graceful summit to the hill, bringing it to the full height of 5,000 feet, and giving the British tourist a finer mountain to look at and to ascend; the view would be superb.

On the Continent there are several railways to the top of the principal mountains, and the construction of perpendicular tunnels to admit of lifts, to the summit of hitherto quite inaccessible mountain tops has even begun. Thousands of travellers are thus induced to make the ascent of these hills. With regard to Ben Nevis, there might be a great cavern of 100 feet diameter, and covered with a semi-globular roof in stone and cement to keep out the damp, constructed over the present Observatory, which could be rebuilt afterwards on the new summit. This cavern should have small chambers entering from it consisting of bedrooms and lavatories to accommodate travellers. There might also be a roomy lift built (likewise in stone and cement) to the top of the cairn. The expense of the whole, perhaps, would not exceed that of tunnelling through the solid rock, and the whole could be achieved with ease by such engineers as founded the piers of the Forth Bridge 200 feet below high water.

The cairn might be held as a memorial to the thousands of Highland soldiers who have died in the maintenance of the British Empire in its many wars.

The North British Railway Company is making a line to Fort William, which is but a small place for a terminus. Such a scheme as this is worthy of consideration by the company as a means of bringing a great accession of travellers over their lines to the Fort-William terminus at the foot of Ben Nevis. There can be little doubt that a large proportion of the visitors to Scotland would make a point of making the ascent of the hill were it thus made easily accessible, — I am, &c.,

Loch-ma-ben.

P.S. — An iron tower of some 1,100 feet in height is being made in London, another at the Isle of Man, and again at Chicago. The view from Ben Nevis would be finer than any of these.

> Even if Loch-ma-Ben is merely eccentric and not having a bit of fun the writer of the next letter is surely extending what he sees as a joke.

II. Glasgow, 12th May 1891

Sir, — I have no doubt that many of your readers, like myself, were delighted with the proposal made by a correspondent in yesterday's Herald as to the improvement and further utilisation of Ben Nevis, and sincerely trust that steps wil be taken without delay to get the scheme carried out. I think, however, that a better plan than that of using dynamite on the neighbouring hills in order to procure material for the cairn on the summit, would be to alter the shape of the mountain itself, which it appears is not at all what it should be. Could not the Exhibition surplus and the money subscribed for General Booth's scheme be used for this purpose? I find that the circumference of Ben Nevis at the base is about thirty-six miles, so that the work necessary would give employment for a considerable period to the unemployed, a great army of which could easily be transferred from London and other large centres to the scene of operations, huts erected for their accommodation, and with the aid of steam navvies and explosives, and an artist as superintendent, the shape of the mountains could be made beautiful for ever. The great quantity of debris could then be carted to the summit, and the proposed cairn erected — care of course being taken that the work of the Observatory is not interfered with in any way. After the completion of the railway, should the funds permit, a picture gallery and concert hall might be built on the top; and, to crown all, an iron tower 1,000 feet in height, with apartments in the lantern for consumptive patients, who would derive considerable benefit from the pure atmosphere. Hoping that immediate steps will be taken to start a Ben Nevis Improvement Fund, to which I would have no objection to contribute a small sum.

J.L.

> Mind you it could hardly be worse than the unsavoury mess that greets the summer visitor to the summit of Ben Nevis today!

STRAVAGERS AND MARAUDERS
Vol. XXX (1975)   by Robert Aitken

The quality of access to the mountains which we enjoy today should not be taken for granted. It was hard won - and its winning was not by the Founding Fathers of the S.M.C., but was a vital prelude to the mountaineering exploration of the Highlands.

Stravaig, stravague: a roaming about, an aimless casual ramble, a stroll
— Concise Scots Dictionary

'I and my friends had no desire to see the proposed Club mixed up with any attempt to force rights-of-way. We did not desire the Club to become a stravaging or marauding Club, insisting on going everywhere at every season ... .'
Professor Ramsay, S.M.C.J., iv, p.88.

One of the endearing features of the *Journal* is the way it evokes the flavour of the mountain scene in Scotland - if not at the time, then thirty years on. Bygones become bygones, and the truth emerges - or something like it: the rowdy, reprobate and reckless of the last generation come out, blinking nervously, into the daylight of retrospective respectability, and Peaheid and Scrubbernut take up their niche in the hall of fame at last; the cause of history is served, the record put right.

There was a time, though, long before the dawn of the Duttonian enlightenment, when such broad-mindedness was much less evident. In the days of Ramsay, the bourgeois academic, and of that land-owning reactionary, Munro, the activities and the achievements of a whole class of hillmen — a feature of the Scottish hills for half a century — went more or less unremarked. These were the advocates and exponents of Rights of Way and Access to Mountains, the deer-disturbers and signpost-erectors who walked outwith the pale of S.M.C. constitutional precept: '...respect propriety and sporting rights, and endeavour to obtain the co-operation of proprietors.' These bolshies of the Golden Age, in the heyday of the deer forest, as well as of early mountaineering in Scotland, have rested largely in obscurity ever since. Perhaps it is time to rehabilitate some of them.

The task need not be a serious one, since there is no tradition of self-important solemnity in the Rights of Way movement; one of the prime movers was in fact noted for his sense of humour, and his contribution was almost clownish. John Hutton Balfour is now remembered chiefly as professor of botany at Edinburgh University between 1845 and 1879, and for his work in the design and development of the Edinburgh botanic gardens, but in his time he was known as an entertaining and humorous lecturer, and held the incongruous post of Punster to Lord Cockburn's Bonaly Friday Club. He was particularly energetic in conducting field excursions with his students to all parts of Scotland — the kind of excursions on which the first S.M.C.meets were modelled. His contribution to the

Rights of Way movement came in August 1847, when he and seven of his students encountered the Duke of Athole in Glen Tilt. Sir Douglas Maclagan, a friend and contemporary of Balfour, commemorated the event in some of the most unforgettably excruciating doggerel of the time:

> The gerse was poo't, the boxes fill't,
> An' syne the hail clamjamphrie
> Would tak' the road by Glen o' Tilt,
> Awa' to what' they cam' frae.
> The Duke at this put up his birse;
> He vowed, in English and in Erse,
> > That Saxon fit
> > Su'd never get
> > A'e single bit
> > Throughout his yett,
> Amang the Hielan' hills, man.

After a protracted argument with the Duke and his ghillies about the disputed right of passage, the botanical party ended the deadlock and circumvented the opposition by scrambling over a wall. This, the so-called 'Battle of Glen Tilt,' generated enormous publicity and led to a prolonged lawsuit in which the Edinburgh Association for the Protection of Public Rights of Roadways in Scotland, through various agents, established the public right on this ancient drove-road, and did much to clarify the law to their advantage: it was a vital precedent for what was to become the Scottish Rights of Way Society.

It has long been tacitly assumed that Balfour and his students were the innocent and inadvertent objects of the Duke's wrath. All the evidence, though circumstantial, suggests otherwise. There is the Professor's character; the fact that he had previously on the same excursion run the gauntlet of the Earl of Fife's keepers to ascend Ben MacDhui by the forbidden Luibeg route; and the singular coincidence that less than six weeks before Balfour set out, the Edinburgh Association had held a meeting at which they explicitly stated their intention of taking up the cause of Glen Tilt, and indeed asked that pedestrians hindered in their passage should contact them. Not only was this meeting reported in the Edinburgh press, but there was also at least one close friend of Balfour's, Patrick Neill, on the committee of the Association. It is difficult to imagine that Balfour could have remained ignorant of these circumstances; it is easy to picture the impish anticipation with which he probably set off on his stravaiging excursion.

Such anticipation would certainly have been justified, for it was a time of general feeling against landowning Dukes, and there could hardly have been a more appropriate subject than the sixth Duke of Athole (the change of spelling from Atholl was quite characteristic of the man). He was a litigious, irascible romantic who squandered vast sums in lawsuits to prohibit his neighbours from shooting his deer when they crossed to adjoining estates, in entertaining Queen Victoria on her Highland jaunts from Balmoral, and in equipping his Athole Highlanders with Lochaber axes and other antique arms. After Balfour, things went from bad to worse with the Duke: in August 1850 he was involved in a brawl with two Cambridge students walking through Glen Tilt, and in October of the same year at Perth Station he more or less assaulted the Provost, who had been active in raising local sentiment, not to say local money, for the case against the Duke. Even the *Times* was moved to suggest that 'it would be doing the public a service to bring this hot-headed foolish man to his senses,' while *Punch* was merciless in mock-Ossianic style on the black eye the Duke had collected in the fray with the undergraduates:

> 'Lament; for the visual organ of Atholl is darkened. Raise the sound of wail upon a thousand bagpipes! Closed is the eye of him who would close Glen Tilt to the traveller. Ken ye not the Chieff of Clan Atholl — the tourist-baffling Duke of the impassable glen?'

Probably nobody enjoyed all this more than J.H. Balfour. It is sad, then, that he should so rarely get the credit for starting it: Sir Henry Alexander mentioned the 'Battle' in the 1928 S.M.C. Cairngorms Guide, but made the mistake of ascribing it to Balfour's son, and the error has been perpetuated through the editions until the 1975 edition, by Adam Watson, Jnr.

Twenty years on, in 1867, it fell to one of Balfour's colleagues to show how far the deer forest and its exclusiveness had spread. In August of that year John Stuart Blackie, professor of Greek at Edinburgh, and passionate champion of the Highland people, ventured to climb Buachaille Etive Mor against the wishes of the proprietor, who also, interestingly enough, refused to provide him with a guide. It is pleasant to record the sequel: 'Arrived at Fort William, he called upon the Fiscal, who, along with a hearty welcome and some glasses of excellent port, gave him the information that he had received instructions to have him prosecuted for climbing Buachaill-more. Professor Tyndall was at Fort William ...' (visiting the Parallel Roads of Glen Roy) 'and joined him in a hearty laugh at the baffled deer-stalkers, whose attack expired in this letter.'

The continued extension of the deer forests and the gradual decline in use of the great drove roads combined in a threat to the hill rights of way which became acute in the 1880's, especially where the proprietor or shooting tenant was an outsider. Such was the American, Walter Louis Winans, who controlled over 200,000 acres of jealously guarded stalking country in Affric and Kintail, paying nearly £10,000 in rents for the privilege. 'And for all this extravagance, he could not be called a true sportsman,' it is alleged; 'He believed in drives of deer and grouse, and in sumptuous hill pic-nics.'

Such too was Duncan Macpherson, who purchased the estate of Glen Doll with capital acquired in Australia. In 1885 he was the first proprietor visited by a notable stravaiging 'deputation' which toured the Central Highlands on behalf of the revived Scottish Rights of Way Society. This expedition neatly combined the impudence of the Balfour tradition with a very Victorian logistical thoroughness: the party carried signposts previously prepared to mark disputed footpaths, which they erected in the appropriate place; obstructing gamekeepers were then intimidated by the 'taking of instruments' — an obscure and no doubt impressive legal process made much easier by the presence in the party of a notary public. The passage of the deputation led to a prolonged and ruinous lawsuit over Jock's Road in Glen Doll, in which the Society was at last successful in the House of Lords, and precipitated a decade of hectic activity in claiming and forcing rights of way, activity which abated only when the Local Government (Scotland) Act of 1894 made the maintenance of rights of way a local authority responsibility. One of the leading spirits in the deputation was Walter A. Smith, who was later to become an original member of the S.M.C. and the sponsor of notable Edinburgh members such as William Douglas; he seems to have gone back over Jock's Road fairly often — it probably gave him as much satisfaction as a new route would to a different kind of mountaineer.

In fact, the S.M.C. drew several of its early adherents from the ranks of the stravaigers. Professor Veitch, J. Parker Smith, and Hely Almond, headmaster of Loretto and the original Salvationist, were members, and C.E.W. Macpherson, secretary of the Rights of Way Society. But the hard core of the Club was composed of Alpinists — often abroad in the critical months of stalking, and doing most of their Scottish climbing in winter and spring. And most were Glaswegian, with easy access by rail to hills noted more for their rocks and roughness than for their qualities as deer forest; almost without exception, the great right of way cases were fought in the eastern Highlands. It is not, then, surprising to find that the Cairngorm Club had its origins in a tradition altogether more radical than that of the S.M.C. The political background of the North-East was Liberal; the members, hillmen rather than mountaineers, were usually afoot on the Cairngorms during the stalking season; and the founders included Alexander Inkson McConnochie — a member of the Rights of Way Society — Alexander Copland, and Thomas Gillies. Under the unlikely pseudonyms of 'Dryas Octopetala' (the mountain avens) and 'Thomas Twayblade,' these last two chronicled in the Aberdeen Journal of the 1880's their early expeditions across the High Cairngorms: expeditions notable not only for their adventurous bivouacs and cuisine on the tops, but also for their encounters with, escapes from, and diatribes against stalkers, ghillies and lairds. Copland gave us the name Angel's Peak for Sgor an Lochain Uaine of Cairntoul, to offset the Devil's Point, itself a euphemistic translation of the Gaelic; and he was first Chairman of the Cairngorm Club, which he regarded as '... in some sense a reserve force in questions affecting rights-of-way to and on mountains.' Gillies, his son-in-law, was an advocate who acted as local agent for the Rights of Way Society in the Glen Doll case, mustering ancient drovers and couthy shepherds to give evidence of historic use of Jock's Road.

In electing their first President, however, the Cairngorm Club demonstrated that their stravaiging aspirations ran to more than mere footpaths; he was James Bryce, M.P., later

Viscount Bryce, the originator of the campaign for Access to Mountains. Bryce is perhaps the least known of the great Scottish mountaineers of the late Victorian period; this may well be because most of his prodigious climbing experience was gained overseas. For he was the most travelled of mountaineers, and it is unlikely that many people have climbed more widely, even in these days. The Alps, Pyrenees, Norway, Etna, Cauacasus, Andes, Rockies, Tatras, Hawaii, Ararat, Himalaya, Sinai, Iceland, Mashonaland, were all grist to his mill. He contributed a short chapter on 'Mountaineering in far-away countries' to Clinton Dent's Badminton Library volume on mountaineering, was a friend of Leslie Stephen and Freshfield, and was president of the Alpine Club between 1899 and 1901. Nevertheless, his ascents seem to have been almost identical to other interests, such as history, law, education, and botany, and to his political career, first as a Liberal Member of Parliament from 1880 to 1906, and latterly as Ambassador to the United States from 1907 to 1913, a role in which he achieved singular success and popularity, including honorary membership of the American Alpine Club. He was never a member of the S.M.C., though he was almost an exact contemporary of Ramsay; indeed, they were both successful competitors for fellowships at Trinity College, Oxford, in 1857, when Ramsay described Bryce as 'that awful Scotch fellow who outwrote everybody.'

It was mainly during his period as member for South Aberdeen, from 1885 to 1906, that Bryce waged his long campaign for free access to mountains for recreation, a concept of striking originality in Britain at that time. He did assist with the Parliamentary cause of Rights of Way, but his addresses to the Cairngorm Club, as well as his speeches in the House of Commons, show a very modern awareness of the need for a real, rather than simply linear access: '... we are by no means content to be kept to a specified limited path in the centre of a mountain.' As long as he was in the House, Bryce took every opportunity, and used every artifice of parliamentary procedure, to present and press his Bills; but while his often eloquent argument occasionally succeeded in carrying a resolution, detailed proposals were never given time. There was considerable support among Scottish M.P.s, but the opposition included many such as J. Parker Smith, who represented Partick, and who was, as mentioned earlier, a member of both the Rights of Way Society and the S.M.C. A piece by Smith in *Blackwood's Magazine* for August 1891 examines the access question, coming down heavily on the 'amicable agreement' policy of the Club — not surprisingly, since Ramsay, Munro, Veitch, and Gilbert Thomson contributed 'evidence' for the article. Not surprisingly, too, Stott gave it a very favourable notice in the *Journal* (S.M.C.J., i, 328). John Stuart Blackie, by contrast, broke into verse as he took Bryce's side:

> 'Bless thee, brave Bryce! all Scotland votes with thee,
> All but the prideful and the pampered few,
> Who in their Scottish homes find nought to do
> But keep our grand broad-shouldered Grampians free
> From tread of Scottish foot ...'

The radical simplicity of Bryce's proposals for Access to Mountains has tended to obscure the breadth and the farsightedness of his concern for the countryside. He watched with dismay the extension of the railway network into the Highlands, and its impact on the scenery of such areas as Killiecrankie and Loch Earn, while he recognised another potent threat in the destruction of the Falls of Foyers to create Scotland's first hydro scheme. To counteract these and similar future developments, he outlined a system of controls that closely foreshadowed much of our present planning legislation.

Bryce's experience of the United States also gave him an almost uncanny foresight of the motorcar era - in the days when Ford and his fellows were just tooling up for mass-production. As ambassador, he urged the Americans to keep cars out of the Yosemite National Park, in terms that were entirely unequivocal: 'Do not let the serpent into Eden at all.' It is intriguing to reflect that by 1912 Bryce was thoroughly familiar with the national park concept, as realised in the United States, Australia, and New Zealand, but he seems never to have considered importing the idea, on the grounds that private ownership of the land had rendered it impossible in Britain. At is was, Bryce returned from Washington only in time for the First World War, and died in 1922 at the age of 84. The parliamentary cause of Access to Mountains, carried forward by Sir Charles Trevelyan and others, merged imperceptibly at last into the national park movement in England and Wales: but there was no such momentum in Scotland. Perhaps Bryce had too many irons in the fire; perhaps he was essentially too restrained and self-effacing. Queen Victoria had said of him: 'I like Mr Bryce. He knows so much and is so modest'; while Freshfield, a much more astute and less amenable critic, saw in him '... a simplicity of character, an honesty, a breadth of outlook ...' This most respectable of radicals remains a prophet almost without honour in his own country; the conservation of scenery he urged so strongly is now an accepted objective, but the problems he sought to avoid still await solution.

Shortly after Bryce's death those problems were emphatically restated by Ernest Baker, leader of the notoriously dramatic climb of the Ben Nuis Chimney on Arran in 1901, in the introduction to his book, *The Highlands with Rope and Rucksack* of 1923.Republished a year later in pamphlet form as *The Forbidden Land*, and dedicated to Bryce, it is an exhiliaratingly comprehensive polemic against the Clearances, the deer forests, and every form of landlordism and access restriction, with an apologium worthy of Haston thrown in for good measure: '... we were not imbued with any superstitious reverence for legal rights. Under stress of circumstances we committed some lawless things — even a burglary on one occasion ...' The *Journal* review of Baker's book (S.M.C.J., xvi, 320) is sympathetic on the whole, but coyly declines to join battle on the content of that lively first section — Baker was, after all, a member of the Club, even if his stravaiging tendencies were rather too evident.'

No such complaint could be levelled against Arthur Russell or A.E. Robertson, whose credentials as S.M.C. men were unimpeachable. Russell, whose death in 1967 closed seventy-one years of membership, served for fourteen years in various Club offices and was closely involved with Unna and the National Trust for Scotland in the acquisition of

Glencoe and Dalness - these services concealing his sterling work as secretary of the Rights of Way Society for many years. Robertson was even more successful, plodding the Coffin Roads of the north and west with resurrectionist zeal, while doing all the Munros for light relief, and to establish his bona fides — achieving this so effectively that he became President of both the Club and the Society: and though the first to do so, he has not been the last — such schizophrenia seeming to be chronic, if not particularly malignant.

In fact, a relationship has always existed between the S.M.C. and the stravaiging faction, however little acknowledged it may have been; the Club may have done its best to ignore them, but they have patently not gone away, though the radical passions of last century have subsided. Perhaps now they can all, earnest or impish, be permitted to come forth from the shades of obscurity to which the scurrilous scribe Stott and his successors have condemned them. They're not so very wicked, after all.

(The writer wishes to acknowledge the assistance of the Scottish Rights of Way Society Ltd., and of its Secretary, Mr D.H. MacPherson, in making available the Minutes and Sederunt Books of the Association for the protection of public rights of roadways in and around Edinburgh, and the Newspaper Cuttings books of the Scottish Rights of Way Society).

THE AONACH EAGACH   by A. Fraser (Jnr)
Vol IV (1897)

This prosaic note refers to what was probably the first traverse of this mountain ridge.

In August last Messrs A.R. Wilson, A.W. Russell, and A. Fraser spent several days among the Glencoe hills, choosing Clachaig Inn as headquarters. Aonach Eagach, the north ridge of the glen, was the chief attraction, as it looked particularly inviting from below, and no record could be found in the Journal or the hotel book of any party having been along it. On the first day the ridge was gained by leaving the road a quarter of a mile below Loch Triochatan, and going nearly directly up, the ascent being easy, though long and tiresome. On the ridge itself there is no difficulty till it narrows, and there is a steep drop of fifty feet with a corresponding rise on the other side to a small peak just short of the summit. Just beyond the summit there is another dip to two little pinnacles. At this point the party left the ridge, descending by a stone shoot which, after some time, ended in a burn and a high waterfall. To escape this, another smaller burn to the right had to be crossed, and a descent made down a steep bit of cliff, on which the holds were neither so frequent nor so good as could have been wished. The rocks here, and all along the ridge, are very rotten and loose, at this point especially none could be found strong enough to trust the rope to. The rest of the descent was simple. Another day Messrs Russell and Fraser went along the whole ridge. The only difficulty on the remaining part of it was in getting on to the eastern top, which rises steeply after a dip in the ridge.

A CLIMB OVER SUILVEN (extracts)
Vol. I (1890)   by Lionel W Hinxman

> Hinxman was an original Member of the S.M.C. and since he was on the Geological
> Survey in Scotland he made a valuable contribution to the mountain exploration and
> description which was such an important part of the early Journals. Much of his writing
> is still instructive. This is especially true of an article in Vol V (1899) on The Geology
> of the Scottish Mountains from a Climbing Point of View which included a Table of
> Mountains and Rock Types.

For the benefit of those who are unacquainted with Suilven, a brief description of the form
of the mountain may here be given.

Rising steeply from a comparatively even base, it sweeps up rapidly in successive ledge
and precipice, presenting an almost unbroken wall of rock save where the mountain
torrents have cut deep gashes down its side. In fact, looking at the mountain from a little
distance either on the north or south, it appears as if these formidable-looking couloirs
were the only possible means by which the top could be reached. The crest of the
mountain forms a ridge about a mile and a half in length, divided by deeply-cut clefts into
three peaks of unequal height. These are known respectively as Meall Bheag (little hill),
Meall Mheadhonach (middle hill), and Casteal Liath (the grey castle). The latter forms
the western extremity of the ridge, overlooking Loch Inver, and is the highest of the three,
the Ordnance cairn giving the summit as 2399 feet above sea-level. Meall Mheadhonach
is about 100 feet lower, while Meall Bheag barely reaches 2000 feet.

The clefts — to which the striking appearance of the mountain, when seen in flank,
is chiefly due — mark the position of two faults which cut through the ridge from north
to south, letting down the sandstone strata in each instance to the west, though the forces
of denudation have long since obliterated all difference of level at the summit, which at
the present time is in each case actually lower on the upthrow, or unmoved side, of the
line of fracture. A probable explanation of this fact may be found by supposing that a band
of harder rock was successively let down a step, and thus the wasting and wearing down
process went on more rapidly in the softer strata on the upper or easter side of each line
of fault. The natural drainage of the hill, taking advantage of the course of these faults,
has cut deep gullies filled with loose debris down the talus slopes. This debris is inclined
at so steep an angle, that a touch of the foot is often sufficient to set the whole mass in
motion. Where, however, the lines of fracture cross the ridge, one side of each cleft forms
a more or less perpendicular wall of rock, the other a steep broken slope; and it is in
crossing these nicks that the only real difficulty of the climb is found.

The mountain is composed throughout of red gritty sandstone, which generally gives
good foothold, and, though apt to crumble in places, is never slippery. The sandstone lies
in almost horizontal beds of nearly uniform thickness, which can be traced, like lines of
masonry, along the sides of the hill, and are carved along the wind-swept crest into a

thousand forms of bastion, turret, and pinnacle, thus giving that architectural appearance which is so characteristic of these sandstone mountains.

The western peak is symmetrically dome-shaped, and plunges down at its farther extremity in an almost perpendicular precipice to the talus slope, which sweeps out, in bold parabolic curves, from the foot of the cliff to the gneiss plateau below.

Meall Bheag, though formidable enough, is less precipitous on its outer side, and, rising from a considerably higher level to considerably lesser altitude, cannot compare in grandeur with the great mural precipices of Caisteal Liath.

To reach the top of Meall Bheag was now our aim, and, after reconnoitring it on all sides, we determined to attack the peak at the south-east corner, where the first slopes seemed less steep than elsewhere.

A tolerably easy scramble up the grassy incline, strewn with fallen blocks of sandstone of all sizes, brought us to the foot of the escarpment, where the real climb might be said to begin. Precipitous though this part of the hill appears when seen from a distance, it is yet so broken into ledge and terrace by the unequal weathering of the sandstone courses, that to a firm foot and steady eye it presents no greater difficulty than that involved in going up a somewhat steep and irregular staircase, with steps varying from one to three feet in height. Occasionally, however, a higher step of six feet or more blocked the way, and had to be followed along until a break, or a succession of convenient crevices, was found, by which it could be surmounted. In this way, by a system of judicious zig-zagging, we soon reached the top, which forms a nearly flat plateau, covered with scanty grass and loose sandy debris.

Crossing to the western end, where it overlooks the cleft between Meall Bheag and Meall Mheadhonach, we became aware that between us and our next goal there was indeed a great gulf fixed. The cliff on the east side of this gully is not only vertical, but actually overhangs, as can be distinctly seen from any point on the south side of the mountain; and to get down on to the narrow saddle that bridges the chasm between the two peaks seemed at first an impossibility.

Of course we could have solved the problem by going down again to the foot of Meall Bheag, and ascending Meall Mheadhonach by means of the dividing cleft. But this was an ignominious way out of the difficulty not to be entertained for a moment. We had come out to climb Suilven from end to end, and climb him we would.

So, after craning over the horrid gulf for some little time, and examining the rocks on all sides, we came to the conclusion that nothing but a goat could get down there, and that the position must be turned in flank, or not at all.

Crossing over, then, to the northern side of the peak, we let ourselves cautiously over the edge of the cliff, gradually worming our way down from ledge to ledge wherever a good opportunity for a drop occurred, but always working westwards towards the cleft, until we found ourselves almost immediately underneath the overhanging rock from which we had just before looked down. This was a bit of work requiring great caution and a steady head, for at nearly every point the cliff fell sheer down to a depth of several hundred feet, and a slip at any time would have been fatal. Otherwise the foothold was good, and the ledges always sufficiently broad to enable one to move along with comparative safety, though here and there we had to crawl on hands and knees, the shelf above projecting too far to allow of walking upright. However, all went well, and, one after another, we crept round the last corner, and established ourselves on the narrow neck of porphyry which connects the two peaks.

Looking down the tremendous gash, through which the wind was sweeping with fearful force, we saw the distant landscape set, as it were, in a narrow frame of perpendicular walls that plunged down on either side. The entire absence of middle distance, and the immense extent of atmosphere through which one looked to the country beneath, gave a very curious and striking character to this mountain picture, enhanced by the startling contrast between the dark walls of the cleft and the sunny landscape far below.

In spite, however, of the wonderful view, this was too draughty a spot in which to linger, and we were soon attacking the farther side of the chasm.

The first few feet surmounted, leading from the neck to the slope above, the rest was not difficult, this side of Meall Mheadhonach sloping at an easy angle compared with the face that we had just come down. A climb of about 400 feet brought us to the crest of the middle peak, which forms a narrow ridge, in places less than a yard in width, and falling abruptly on either hand to the edge of the cliffs that flank each side of the mountain. So narrow was the path, and so furious the wind that swept across it, that we found it advisable to descend a little on the leeward side, and thus escape the fierce gusts that threatened at times to sweep us off our feet.

At the highest point of the ridge there is a shepherd's cairn, and round this were scattered many eagles' casts, — oval concretions of wool, hair, and feathers mixed with fragments of bone, which the eagle, like all birds of prey, throws up, after assimilating the more digestible parts of its food. We also found a few feathers, which we carried off as trophies, though we were not fortunate enough to see any of the birds, a pair of whom at that time had their eyrie in a high rock in the glen below. Golden eagles are still tolerably plentiful in this part of Sutherland, and being preserved are believed to be increasing in numbers. My friend P - - - -, who a few days before our expedition had observed the birds leave the eyrie, has seen as many as four eagles, probably a pair with their young, hunting together in Glen Canisp; and I have watched them sailing in lazy circles for hours together round the topmost point of Quinag.

The sea eagle is now much more rare, but a pair used to build regularly on the cliffs near Cape Wrath, and another near the Whitten Head.

At the western end of the ridge we came to another rather nasty bit, — a drop of over several feet of perpendicular rock on to the slope that leads down to the Bealach Mor, as the col between Meall Mheadhonach and Caisteal Liath is called. This however, I believe, might have been avoided by going a little farther down the ridge on the south side, and working round the corner as we had previously done on Meall Bheag.

The rest of the descent to the Bealach was easy enough, and having reached the ruined wall that here crosses the ridge, — put up at the time when Glen Canisp was a sheep farm to prevent the sheep from straying on to the dangerous parts of the mountain, — we called a welcome halt for luncheon.

Half-an-hour sufficed for this and the necessary pipe, and climbing leisurely up the slope at the western end of the col, we were soon standing on the dome-shaped eminence that crowns the great cone of Caisteal Liath.

Here, for the first time, we stopped to take a long look at the magnificent prospect that lay before us. Beneath our feet, as we looked out to the west, lay the houses of Lochinver, fringing the sheltered bay, beyond which the wide Atlantic stretched away to where the long blue line of the Outer Hebrides lay like a cloud along the western horizon.

On the north, the long wall of Canisp cut off much of the view, but we could see on the left the great precipices of Quinag, and the wide rolling expanse of hill and valley, studded with innumerable lochans, which stretches away from the northern shores of Loch Assynt to the low bare promontories of Stoer and Ardvar.

To the east, the sharp peak and great corrie of Ben Dearg showed above the smooth contours of the Cromalt Hills; and farther away, against the south-eastern horizon, rose the beautiful cones of An Teallach in Dundonnel, the highest of the sandstone mountains. ·

Turning to the south, we looked across the lonely waters of Loch Veyattie straight into the profound depths of Corrie Dubh, that magnificent amphitheatre carved out of the northern face of Coul Mor. Beyond the narrow winding shores of the Fionn Loch, and the line which marked the deep valley of the Kirkaig, lay the broad expanse of Loch Shianaskaig, dotted with wooded islets and backed by the graceful cone of Coul Beag and the splintered spires and pinnacles of Stack Polly. Behind them rose the long ridges and needle-like peaks of Ben More Coigach and the Fiddler; while far away to the south-west stretched the Rhu Coigach and the scattered archipelago of the Summer Isles.

The atmosphere was not clear enough for a very distant view, but beyond the faint line that showed where the Cailleach Head and Greenstone Point stretched into the Atlantic, we could just catch the dim outlines of the hills of Gairloch and Loch Maree.

But we had now to think about turning homewards; and while C - - - - - sat down to make a sketch, H - - - - - and I went to prospect the farther end of the peak, fired with the wild idea of climbing down the western face, and thus really traversing the mountain from end to end. But after scrambling down for some distance, we found ourselves brought up suddenly by a sheer wall of rock plunging straight down for several hundred feet, which effectually put an end to our hopes in that direction. So rejoining C - - - - - on the top, we determined to take the first practicable gully on the north side, and trust to chance that it would lead us to the foot of the hill.

Down we went, the loose debris clattering and sliding under our feet, and in a very short space of time — by dint of glissading with the stones, when practicable, and clinging to the rocky side of the cleft at the steepest parts — found ourselves within twenty feet or so of the foot of the cliff. Here our progress was barred by a miniature waterfall, trickling over the nearly vertical rocks, green and shiny with moss and liverworts, and making a very unpleasant, if not impossible, place to get down. However, retracing our steps for a little way, we found a branch gully, which afforded an easy path down to the foot of the precipice.

Our hard work was now over, and, rattling down the talus slope, a rough walk of half-an-hour brought us to Glen Canisp, and crossing the stream just above Loch-an-alltain Duich, we struck the forest path at Suileag.

Suilven can also be reached very easily from Lochinver, the route taken being by Glen Canisp Lodge and the forest path to Suileag. There is no difficulty whatever in reaching the top of Caisteal Liath (the western peak) by going up the Bealach Mor, either from the north or south side, and it is only in crossing the gap between the eastern and middle peaks that any real difficulty or danger is to be found.

"A Perfect Matterhorn!"

THE CLIMBER'S GUIDE TO THE PRONUNCIATION OF THE GAELIC TONGUE
Vol. IV (1897)   by L.W.H.

Oh, a terrible tongue is the tongue of the Gael,
And the names of his mountains make Southrons turn pale;
It's ill to pronounce them, to spell them is worse,
And they're not very easy to hitch into verse.

A mountain's a mountain in England, but when
The climber's in Scotland, it may be a Beinn,
A Creag or a Meall, a Spidean, a Sgor,
A Carn or a Monadh, a Stac, or a Torr.

For he goes up Beinn Dothaidh
In the ice and the snothaidh,
And nothing will staim
From climbing Sgor Mhaim;
If he's long in the leagaidh
May tackle Creag Meagaidh,
Or, job that is hardhoire,
The 'posts' of Corr'Ard Dhoire.
He strolls up Beinn Eighe
By the easiest weighe
If he's wise - but Sgurr Dubh,
Will make him look blubh.
Very grand is the vuidhe
Will get from Meall Buidhe,
But more will he sithe
From Bruach na Frithe.
Then for sport that is raoghal

He hies to Beinn Laoghal,
And surely will straidheimh
To ascend Beinn a'Chlaidheimh,
And gaze from afarr
On Beinn Airidh a'Charr.
To get up Stob Gabhar
Takes more that an abhar,
But considerably leas
The ascent of Carn Eas.
Now one cannot conciol
That the slopes of Beinn Sgriol
Are hardly as sheur
As the crags of Carn Bheur,
Nor can one mainteadhoin
That the view from Beinn Meadhoin
Surpasses the vaoigh
Observed from Beinn Laoigh.

And besides the above there are dozens which I'm
Unable at present to put into rhyme;
Whilst most of these hills, it's no libel to say,
Are easier climbed than pronounced, any day!

BEINN BHAN OF APPLECROSS
Vol. II (1892)   by Lionel W Hinxman

This was almost certainly the first ascent of the splendid ridge that leads up over A'Chioch of Beinn Bhan.

"It has every attribute of hell except its warmth," was the verdict passed on Beinn Bhan by one seeing it for the first time on a wild day of wind and rain in early spring. And savage grandeur is indeed the characteristic of the long line of precipice and corrie that forms the eastern face of the mountain, and frowns above the soft green slopes and hanging birchwoods of Glen Kishorn.

It was a glorious July morning when I left Shieldaig by the mail-gig at 7 a.m., with the intention of surveying the corries, and if possible, getting to the top of the central ridge of Beinn Bhan.

The sun, even at that early hour, was already powerful; the clegs were rampant, and everything promised an exceptionally fine, hot day. Leaving the "machine" and the road at the Allt Coultrie, I struck across the lower slopes of Beinn a' Chait, and, crossing the deep gorge of the Allt Meall na Gobhar, soon reached Allt Lochan na Ganeimh, a large burn flowing out of a troutful loch, and fed by the numerous streams that fall from the eastern corries of Beinn Bhan. Following the course of the largest of these, a climb of 700 feet brought me to the shores of Loch Coire na Poite, at the mouth of the corrie of that name.

The scene from the shore of this lonely loch is very impressive. On either hand two great spurs run out at right angles to the mountain face. These terminate in huge rounded masses of rock, known as a'Chioch and a'Phoit, whose perpendicular sides and horizontal lines of stratification — like courses of Cyclopaean masonry — suggest the idea of Titanic castles, habitations for the giants of whom legend survives in the name of the next corrie to the north — Coire nan Fheamhair (the giants' corrie).Some little way above the loch a rock terrace, over which the burn tumbles in a series of cascades, connects the two spurs, and forms the lip of the inner corrie, on whose ice-worn floor lie two little Alpine tarns of green water, crystal-clear.Immediately behind the highest of these rises the mountain wall, — 1,200 feet of purple sandstone, — broken here and there by narrow green ledges, and seamed with dark rifts, out of which pour streams of stony debris. The talus slopes are carpeted with a luxuriant growth of parsley-fern, to which succeeds a zone of delicate-fronded oak-fern; while the lower ledges, dark with dripping moisture, are lit up by the bright blossoms of the globe-flower and the sea-green fleshy leaves of the rose-root.

My work in the corrie finished, I turned to consider the best way to the top.The wall in front was quite impossible. The grassy ridge running out to a'Phoit on the right was easy enough, but from it the cliff rose sheer to the mountain top. Evidently a'Chioch, on the left, was the only chance. I could at least gain the ridge, and chance that the arete would

6. *The North-east Buttress of Ben Nevis at the head of the Allt a' Mhuilinn*

7. *The Inaccessible Pinnacle, from the west (above) and from the east (below)*

8. The guide John Mackenzie (right) with a client on Sgurr nan Gillean, looking towards Bla Bheinn

9. John Mackenzie (left) and W.W. Naismith in the Cuillin

10. *The SMC Easter Meet, 1897, cruising in Loch Hourn on the steam yacht 'Erne'*

go. A rough scramble over the talus slope, and up the side of a stone shoot hardly steep enough to be called a couloir, soon brought me to the narrow col, almost a knife edge, that joins a'Chioch to the main ridge, and separates Coire a'Phoit from Coire a'Fheola on the south.

Intent on the climb, it was not until I reached this point that I noticed the changed aspect of the day. The sunshine was gone; dense black clouds were rolling up from the sea; and the closeness of the air, and the heavy drops that were already falling, made me unpleasantly aware that a thunderstorm was fast coming up. It now became important to get to the top while I could still see the way; and, turning to the rocky arete that leads from the col to the highest point of the mountain, I lost no time in beginning to ascend. This arete is very steep. The general angle of the slope, taken from a distance by clinometer, was found to be at least 60°, while several bits are perpendicular, and had to be negotiated with the aid of friendly cracks and projections in the rock.

While at about the most difficult bit of the climb, the storm broke, almost overhead, and it seemed prudent to lie low till the worst of it had passed; so, crawling along a narrow ledge to a place where the shelf above projected sufficiently to keep off some of the rain, I lay curled up against the rock, watching the white sheet of rain rushing down past me for a thousand feet into the corrie below. The flashes were unpleasantly near; but the reverberations of the thunder, as the echoes flapped from cliff to cliff, and the intense purple gloom in the corries, where the mist was beginning to form in ragged wreaths about the crags, were grand and impressive enough to make one feel that the experience of a thunderstorm among the mountains was well worth a certain amount of risk and discomfort.

The worst of the storm being over, I found I could only get out of my present position by crawling cautiously backwards, the ledge below being too narrow, and that above too low, to admit of my turning round or standing up. The mist was now covering the highest part of the arete, and what lay before me was an unknown quantity, — there might be an impassable bit. Anyhow I felt I must go on, and hope for the best, for it was very doubtful if I could get down again by the way I had come up. However, after a nasty bit or two, the slope eased off, and I was soon standing on the main ridge close to the highest point of the mountain (2,936 feet).

The top of Beinn Bhan is an extensive plateau, covered with grass and weathered slabs of sandstone, and sloping away from the crest westwards to the sea. The clouds were so thickly down that little could be seen beyond fifty yards' distance, so, taking a hasty glance at the map - now rapidly being reduced to pulp, — I steered a compass course along the ridge, giving the precipices as wide a berth as possible.

At the head of the Giants' Corrie I came upon two shepherds, from Applecross, sitting waiting for the mist to clear. They were up gathering sheep, had little English, and seemed much surprised at seeing any one on the hill on such a day.

The clouds now lifted a little, enabling me to see where I was; but ominous grumblings all round warned me that it would be well to get off the mountain before the storm - which was evidently circling the hills - came round again. In the next corrie to the north I found a fairly easy way down by a long scree slope, and, following the course of the corrie burn to the head of Loch Lundie, crossed Beinn a'Chait, and reached Shieldaig just as the second edition of the storm came up.

Of course I saw nothing from the top. The view must, however, be particularly fine, as Beinn Bhan stands farther out to the westward than any hill on the mainland north of the Sound of Sleat.

NAISMITH'S RULE   by W.W. Naismith
Vol II (1892)

> W.W. Naismith contributed a brief entry in 'Notes and Queries' recording a traverse he had made of Cruach Ardrain, Stobinian and Ben More on 2nd May. The 'simple formula' came to be known as 'Naismith's Rule' and is still widely applied, although modified to suit the circumstances. In the current S.M.C. Guide 'The Munros' the formula used is one hour for every $4^1/_2$ km. and 1 minute for every 10m of ascent.

Distance, ten miles; total climb, 6,300 feet; time, six and a half hours (including short halts). This tallies exactly with a simple formula, that may be found useful in estimating what time men in fair condition should allow for easy expeditions, namely, an hour for every three miles on the map, with an additional hour for every 2,000 feet of ascent.

FROM 'BIDEAN AND THE BUCHAILLES'   by Gilbert Thomson
Vol. I (1890)

…Our climbing gear was made up of a dozen yards of light rope (window sash cord in fact, which was calculated to be sufficiently strong for a party of two), an ice axe carried by Naismith, and an alpenstock carried by the writer. The latter had its spike broken off the day before, and rejoiced now in a large nail with the head filed off….

…Our expedition would certainly have been more or less a failure but for the axe, and it is doubtful if, without the rope as well, we would have ventured on the slope which we traversed with its assistance.

ASCENT OF BEN NEVIS BY THE N.E. BUTTRESS
Vol. III (1895)   by W. Brown

This well illustrates the kind of marathon climbing weekend that had to be undertaken
by the early pioneers before the days of easy road travel.

The mountaineer who makes his way up the Allt a' Mhuilinn, under the stern north
precipices of Ben Nevis, sees before him, high up at the head of the valley, a steep black
ridge jutting out against the sky, which seems grander and more precipitous than any of
its neighbours. This is the N.E. Buttress, the finest object on the mountain, and one of the
last to engage the attention of the climber.

It was the last Easter Meet that brought this ridge into fame. From being an unnamed
and unhonoured incident upon the cliff-face, it became an object of ambition to a large
circle of climbers, the chief topic of the smoke-room at nights, and the focus of many
critical glances during the day. It would also have been climbed had the ice upon the rocks
not forbade the attempt; but though spared at Easter, it stood marked in the intentions
of several parties, of which Tough and I formed one.

We had reconnoitred it from Carn Mor Dearg, and had come to the conclusion that,
in spite of its formidable appearance in profile, and the presence of a sheer cliff one-third
of the way up, it was less inaccessible than it was reputed to be. This, however, was more
of a pious opinion than a reliable conclusion, for the ridge was enormously steep, and
undoubted difficulties beset the path of the climber. Once on the ridge proper, however,
above the bottom buttress, it seemed likely that the rest would go.

And there the matter rested till the Queen's birthday arrived, the date of our projected
expedition. The day seemed auspicious. It would be a graceful compliment to the
Sovereign to open up a new slice of her dominions, and peradventure the heart of the
West Highland Railway might be softened to a cheap fare. These thoughts were very
stimulating while they lasted, but they 'fled full soon'. Cheap fares are only for Glasgow
men. When we came to make our arrangements, that zest which is said to consist in
triumphing over obstacles was vouchsafed to us in most bountiful measure. It was either
Tough or the West Highland Railway that refused to fit in — the point is still in dispute.
But at any rate, owing to our utter inability to find a suitable train, it soon became manifest
that if the ridge was to be climbed by us it must be done as the American ship-captain did
St Peter's. That historical personage, as we all know, reached Rome in the morning, drove
straight to St Peter's Piazza, went to the top of the dome, and returned by the first train
after lunch to his vessel at the Civita Vecchia. His example is not usually commended for
its strict conformance to the canons of mountaineering, but Tough and I had reached a
frame of mind when, like good temper at 3 a.m., the canons had ceased to be binding. So
we drew up the following original programme, which, as the more candid of its joint
authors remarked, would have been utterly repulsive as applied to anything but the N.E.

Buttress. It was arranged that we should travel to Kingussie by the night express on Friday, 24th May, bicycle thence to Fort-William, climb our mountain on arrival, and return by the same route, reaching town on Sunday evening. There was a certain gloomy satisfaction that we were doing something quite out of the common, which deepened in gloom as our arrangements waxed in originality. But I am anticipating.

Very grey and miserable was Kingussie when we reached it at 3.50 a.m. on Sunday morning. Rain was falling dismally, and a dense white mist hung low down on the sodden hillsides. Underwheel the roads were a fell compound of mud and newly-laid metal, over which eight miles an hour was superlative progress. Under beetling Creag Dhu, past Clunie, past lone Laggan Bridge, and I may skip forward to the point when, after one or two hours' weary pedalling, we were crossing the watershed of Scotland. Here the sun was making a feeble demonstration, but its rays passed almost unnoticed in the moral gloom which now fell upon the expedition.

It came about in this way. We had just topped a stiff brae, when a sudden report, resembling the simultaneous opening of six bottles of 'Bouvier', was followed by Tough's despairing cry, "Your tyre's punctured." It was too true, and, what was still more exasperating, nothing would mend it. To this day my Norfolk tells of the cementing abilities of a sticky confection, which Tough produced from his rucksack, and of the lavishness with which we applied it. Very sorrowfully, after an hour's abortive tinkering, I pushed my now useless machine to the Loch Laggan Hotel (three miles), whither Tough had already preceded me, and where we expected to find a horse and trap to carry us on to Fort-William. Vain expectation! The zoological resources of Loch Laggan Hotel are rich in midges, but include nothing distantly resembling a horse; so we had to face a walk of thirteen miles to Inverlair, under a sun which was now something more than genial. I believe I could make literary capital out of that walk — out of the glory of the sunshine, as it fell upon the blue sparkling loch, the fluttering birch trees, and the gaunt grey corries of Creag Meaghaidh, — but our whole souls were fixed, not upon these splendid sights, but on an ingenious contrivance we had hit upon for saving time and muscle. Tough mounted the remaining bicycle, with a pyramid of ropes, axes, and rucksacks piled up on his shoulders, while his fellow-traveller half-walked, half-trotted alongside. In this order, with an occasional change of parts, when the pedestrian became (or said that he was) exhausted, we straggled to Inverlair, and completed the rest of the journey comfortably by train.

The day was close and sultry when, after a hurried lunch at the Alexandra, we left Fort-William at 1.12, and swinging past Bridge of Nevis and Claggan farm, breasted the steep grass slopes of Carn Dearg — those grass slopes of painful memory. The extraordinary behaviour of even the best mountaineers upon a steep grass slope has often been remarked. They breathe heavily as if their lungs were in difficulties; from their foreheads well fountains of moisture that has been mistaken for sweat; they watch each other furtively, and when one sits down to admire the view, down flops the other as if he were glad of the rest; the trouble of adjusting a bootlace seems more tolerable to them than all the joys of ascending. Almost you would think they were not enjoying themselves.

Tough and I, it must be confessed, exhibited some of these above-noted symptoms, which continued more or less uninterruptedly till we began the descent into the great cleft of the Allt a'Mhuilinn. Here we sat down for the hundredth time, and made an earnest study of our ridge, which descended in profile before us little more than a mile distant. It was a sight to rejoice the heart of the most blase ridgebagger. Seen from this standpoint, the lower portion appears to consist of an almost perpendicular bastion, which terminates in a well-marked platform, to which a steep gully leads up on the west side. Above the platform the rocks rise practically sheer for several hundred feet, and then ease off to a slope of about 45°, which continues, with a tendency to increase, till the foot is reached of another straight pitch, about a third of the height of the previous one. From certain points this pitch actually overhangs, but from others it shows an angle which is not greater than 60° or 70°. The top portion is an easy slope, merging almost imperceptibly in the summit plateau.

From what we now saw, the views formed at Easter were for the most part confirmed, except that the ridge seemed steeper than our recollection of it, and the straight pitches more absolutely perpendicular. Perhaps, however, this was partly due to the sudden approach of bad weather, which threw the black rocks into yet blacker gloom, and made them tower up at an angle which was positively fearsome.

Loud peals of thunder had been rolling harmlessly among the hills since noon, but now the blackness that had been lying in the horizon rose high towards the zenith and threatened to cover it. The Red Mountains were still clear and sunny, but round the flanks of Carn Dearg the mist came stealing, - at first in mere wisps of vapour, then in great smoke-like masses, which mounted to the topmost crag, and blotted out nearly the whole mountain. In ten minutes there was scarce anything to be seen but the scree slope on which we stood, and a black swirling mass straight ahead, where the storm clouds were eddying round the crags of the four great ridges.

The walk up the Allt a'Mhuilinn is grand and impressive under any circumstances, but in such weather as this it is unspeakably weird. We passed jutting headlands of black naked rock, and receding rifts in the cliff-face from which the winter snow gleamed cold and ghastly out of the gloom. The stream we were following dashed in cataracts over its stony bed, fed by torrents the far-off murmur of which came floating down from unknown heights upon our right. Next we entered a wilderness of stones and boulders, littered with the Observatory debris - tin cans, biscuit boxes, and paraffin barrels. Beyond is the steep frowning basement of the north-east buttress, and this we reached at 5.30. The weather had now reached what Mr Campbell (quoting Milton) describes as 'in the highest heights a higher height'. Even a native might have praised it. For ten minutes the rain descended with a straightness that would have been creditable in furrows at a ploughing match. Then the mist that had been scudding gaily among the higher crags came down to share in the fun. Crouching behind a stone we saw our visible world fade away into a murky circumference of twenty feet broad, beyond which the wall of the buttress, not fifty yards off, was totally concealed. Early in the day there had been some awful penalties laid upon the man who should even breathe the word "retreat", but now we shamelessly discussed it in all its bearings. Providence, however, had a better, or at least a higher, fate in store for us. Quite suddenly the deluge of rain ceased to drench us, and the mist, having bamboozled us long enough, betook itself to higher realms, showing our climb towering, crag over crag, above us — an inspiring sight. There was no longer any talk of retreating, though we could see that the enormous quantity of rain that had fallen would greatly increase the difficulty of the climb. Not even in Skye have I seen rocks so wet. There was quite a respectable waterfall coming off the ridge, and innumerable smaller ones that in England would draw hosts of worshippers.

We had the choice of attacking the bottom bastion either from the east or west, but we unhesitatingly chose the eastern route, which is quite simple, and seemed to offer a convenient approach to the greater difficulties above the first platform. Up to that point it is literally a walk, but when we had crossed to its extreme south-west corner the real climbing began. We put on the rope (time 6.15 p.m.), and for sixty or seventy feet followed the broken crest of a nice little ridge which abuts against the steep face of the buttress, just underneath a lofty and, as we thought then, unclimbable tower. Here there is a choice of routes. To the right runs a broad ledge (in Cumberland a rake), while to the left a long straight stone-shoot follows the line which in our previous reconnaisances we had judged to be best. We therefore followed the stone-shoot, which led us through a succession of small chimneys and gullies, and out upon a sloping grass ledge, till we could climb up to the right to a level space (called the second platform), where we built a small stone man. Crossing this platform, which is a mere cup scooped out of the rock, we struck the ridge proper immediately above the unclimbable tower, and commemorated the fact with another modest cairn

Here the really interesting work may be said to begin, for the ridge is fairly narrow, and, besides being very steep, is broken into all the delightful incidents of this form of mountain architecture. There are little towers up which the leader had to scramble with such gentle impetus as could be derived from the pressure of his hobnails upon his companion's head. There are ledges (not very terrible) where it is convenient to simulate the grace of the caterpillar. A sloping slab we found too, where the union of porphyry and Harris tweed interposed the most slender obstacle to an airy slide into the valley.

On the whole, I believe the rocks to be comparatively easy; but under the then conditions, what with the rain and the wearied state in which we approached them, they seemed distinctly difficult. It was most exasperating to find, whenever a friction grip was necessary, how persistently one's sodden knickers and boots kept slipping on the wet bossy rocks, and how unreliable was the hold thus obtained.

Nowhere was this more apparent than when, having climbed up as we thought to within a few hundred feet of the top, a steep little bastion, with rounded top and smooth unbroken face, loomed up out of the mist. It was crowned by an erection which in the fog, which was again closing thickly round us, might have been the Eddystone lighthouse, but which I have reason to believe is a 'peeler' of very moderate dimensions. Under ordinary circumstances we would have got up it I think without special difficulty, but a small crack about ten feet up (which is the natural hold) was at that moment extemporised for the descent of a miniature shower-bath. The result was that, perhaps without giving the crack a fair trial, we preferred to try the slabby rocks on the left. 'Twas a most dismal error. These slabby rocks are the man-trap* of the ridge. They look quite simple, and are quite the reverse. I stood in the gap under the bastion, and paid out the rope, while Tough, as leader, amused himself among them for nearly three-quarters of an hour. Judging by the movements of the rope, and the vigorous adjectives that reached my ears, the game was more energetic than amusing. At length, after a period of indefatigable energy, Tough rejoined me. The rocks would not 'go'; and if ever a charge of positive immorality was brought against a rock problem, it was involved in the emphasis with which the chief guide described how he had innocently swarmed up a nice little gully, and become spread-eagled for ten minutes on a smoothly sloping slab that looked positively alluring from below.

Meanwhile the daylight had been ebbing slowly away. It was now 9.45. Over the gaunt-grey rocks the darkness of night had settled down, rendering our position inexpressibly weird and eerie. To me it seemd that the only alternative was to bivouac where we stood; but the chief guide, while frankly admitting that two inches of nose represented his own limit of vision, drove me at the point of his axe to explore the rocks on the right. They 'went' quite easily. Up a short gully we raced and panted to the foot of a steep smooth corner about 40 feet high, formed by the junction of two rock slabs. Here, when I mildly suggested the absence of reliable holds, the inexorable guide gave me the choice of going up at the point of his ice-axe, or by pure traction at the end of the rope, along with the luggage. I chose the former; and such was the mute eloquence of that pick end, pointing upwards out of the gloom, that I succeeded at length in struggling to the top, although the holds are not exactly suited to sustain in the darkness the gravity of $11\frac{1}{2}$ stones over a nearly perpendicular precipice. At the top we could see the way stretching easily before us, and a dim black object standing up against the darkened sky that looked every inch the top. Abandoning the ridge to save time, we dashed into a stone-shoot on the left, and went rapidly up it to the foot of a final line of crags about twenty feet high. Again we thought we were stuck, but a friendly gully, running up the centre, extricated us from our difficulties, and brought us out at the summit of the mountain, almost level with the Observatory.

Volumes have been written upon the sensations of mountaineers upon finishing a stiff

---

*The name 'Man Trap' has stuck. — Ed

climb; but we simply gave a long shout of triumph, which was taken by our friends the meteorologists as a warning that some very noisy trippers were approaching, and marched for the Observatory.

This we reached at 10.5, and were received with the overflowing hospitality the Club has always received from Mr Rankin and his staff. Very grateful was the warmth and shelter, the glowing stove, the steaming coffee, after the long battle on the porphyry crags. All too short, however, was the hour of sleep, which we snatched between twelve and one, undisturbed by even a thought of what we had passed through. Then came the descent to Fort-William, under a sky which was now calm and serene. The misty curtain was drawn aside, and all around lay the slumbering hills. What mattered it that Bidean nam Bian was indistinguishable from Buchaille Etive, and that the most resolute attempt to identify Stob Ban resulted in mental entanglement among the corries of Sgor a Mhaim. We took it on trust that Bidean was there, with his darkened crest thrust through the sea of mist which lay fathoms deep in the valleys, forming islands and archipelagos, capes and peninsulas, out of the spurs and ridges of the hills. Lower down we plunged into the mist ourselves, and when we emerged from it again the morning sun was shining upon the houses of Fort William and the waters of Loch Eil. It was the dawn of another day, the third since we had left Edinburgh. At 4 a.m. the mail-gig for Kingussie numbered us among its passengers. Speyside saw us five and a half hours later; and Edinburgh and the Editor welcomed us at 6.15 p.m. after forty-five hours of continuous travelling.

NOTE — Since the above article was written a note in the current number of the Alpine Journal recording an ascent of the buttress by Messrs J.E. and B. Hopkinson, on the 6th September 1892, has come under my notice. No particulars are given, but it appears that the ascent formed one of several made by the same party, including the ascent and descent of the Tower Ridge and the outlying pinnacle at its base. It is only necessary to add, with reference to certain statements contained in the foregoing article, that no suspicion that the ridge was other than a virgin peak ever occurred to us, or any one in the district, or having knowledge of the mountain, with whom we conversed. Subsequent to our ascent the ridge has been climbed several times. It was ascended, eight days later, by Messrs Geoffrey Hastings, Howard Priestman, and Cecil Slingsby, who were likewise ignorant of the previous ascents till they encountered our first cairn. This party introduced a difficult variation below the first platform, gaining that point from the west by a steep gully, which, being much in need of cleaning, gave considerable trouble. On 8th June, the buttress was again ascended by Messrs Napier and Green, who patented still another variation by forcing a way up the steep rocks to the left of Slingsby's couloir. Both parties seem to have turned the unclimbable tower by the broad ledge, or rake, on the west side of the ridge.

THE COOLINS IN '96 (extract)
Vol. IV (1897) by W. Brown

The Coolins, like the Alps, have a magnet-power to draw climbers year after year to their summits. The climate, it must be admitted, is the wettest in Scotland. Good days are rare as the gratitude of editors, and experience shows that a climbing holiday in the central or eastern Highlands is far more healthful than a sojourn in the Isle of Mist.

Yet the Coolins are the most popular hills in Britain; and they are popular because they yield the finest climbing, contain the finest rocks, the shapeliest peaks, and the wildest corries. The ideal of the sport is to be found amongst them in perfection — the combination of all the essentials on which a keen sportsman could insist. It is a place where tyro and the expert find themselves equally at home, for the climbing is of every variety. Most of the climbs look more difficult than they are, which is an agreeable deception. The climbing, too is mostly safe, because the rocks are nearly everywhere sound. The views are superb, both near and distant. A constant feast of colour and of striking scenes is before the climber's eyes. He goes out in the morning, and the mountain tops, just piercing the mist, are red with the rising sun. At mid-day, when the morning vapours have floated up the dark mountain sides, the black jagged peaks stand out still and clear against the blue sky, and the corries, bathed in shadow, lie black at their bases, adding height and grandeur to their appearance. As the afternoon fades away, the sun sinks behind some distant isle, the shining plain of the sea is spread out beneath, and Rum, Mull, Canna and Eigg sleep peacefully on its surface, drawing graceful curves across the evening sky. There is no sight like this in all Scotland; and Nicolson is probably right in saying that there is nothing finer in the 'Isles of Greece'.

The Coolins lie at the southern extremity of the island and consist of two groups, the Red and the Black Coolins, divided from each other by Glen Sligachan. The Reds are round and uninteresting in shape, and are formed of granite. The Blacks, on the other hand, are of wonderfully bold outline, and are made of gabbro. They form a crescent or horseshoe of irregular outline, divided into two unequal portions by a low-lying ridge, on one side of which is Loch Coruisk, and on the other Harta and Lota Corries. Sgurr Alasdair and Sgurr Dearg are the giants which dominate the larger or western section, and Sgurr nan Gillean, with its five splendid needles, towers over the other. Blaven lies detached from its Black brothers at the south-west end of the Reds, with which, however, it has no connection other than a geographical one. Bidein Druim nan Ramh, though the lowest of all the peaks, is, from its position at the junction of the ridges, the keystone to the whole fabric, and is the most central and easily identified summit in the whole range.

From Sgurr na h-Uamha in the north Gars-bheinn in the south, the Coolins form a continuous chain, the highest summits being linked together by high ridges, which, though broken into many bealachs, rarely fall much below 3,000 feet. On each side of the main chain there are short lateral ridges, between which lie the corries, nine in number, including the huge hollow of Coruisk. Neither in the corries nor on the tops is there much trace of vegetation; the summits of bare and naked rock, blue-black in colour, while the corries contain the debris torn off from the peaks above, and tossed into a state adequately measured by its deadly effect upon shoe leather. On account of their chain-like formation, the Coolins have always lent themselves to the form of climbing known as 'ridge wandering'. It is said that the whole ridge has been traversed from end to end in one day; but ordinary climbers will agree that this is a feat for the gods, who can step from mountain top to mountain top. Three long summer days would ordinarily be required to complete the circuit.

The development of rock-climbing in Skye has followed for the most part the line of the ridges. These are so full of material, so bristling with obstacles of every kind, that hitherto climbers have been content to travel along the obvious routes. Of course, when Nicolson made his first ascents of Sgurr Alasdair and Sgurr Dubh, the latter was reputed 'inaccessible', a halo of awe and reverence protected the hill from casual visitors, and the ordinary ascents were mentioned in very respectful tones. As for the 'Inaccessible Pinnacle', the brothers Pilkington had not yet ascended its eastern edge, and Nicolson hazarded the reluctant opinion that 'with rope and irons it might be possible to get to the top', but, he added, 'it would be a useless achievement'. The present-day climber who runs over the 'Pinnacle Route' smiles at those sentiments, and goes off to scale some 'inaccessible' face; but it would be easy to show that Nicolson's climbs were relatively as difficult as, say Alasdair from Coire Labain by the rocks, when the moral effect exercised by unexplored and traditionally dangerous peaks is taken into account. And when we find a distinguished climber like Mr Pilkington traversing round the central peak of Bidein Druim nan Ramh instead of climbing straight up its north-eastern face, and an ex-President of the Alpine Club pronouncing the Alasdair Dubh ridge 'impracticable', the achievement of Nicolson in getting down the Coruisk face of Sgurr Dubh by midnight, and with a plaid for a rope, is extremely creditable.

There comes a time, however, even at the richest centres, when the search for new climbs has to be conducted through a microscope. The Alps have reached that stage long ago, but the best instance in point are the mountains round Wastdale. At Christmas and Easter men assemble there in scores, and not the most lurking crack nor the most faintly marked wrinkle on the mountain face can for long escape their vigilance. This minute form of the sport has not hitherto been necessary in Scotland, where N.E. corries and unclimbed faces exist in all the Highland counties; but the historian of the future will no doubt record the fact that it began in Skye in the summer of 1896.

A large muster of the mountaineering clan filled Sligachan from June to September; and as the weather was so good that all the old smoking-room jokes, made at its expense, had to be carried out and buried, a large amount of new climbing was done....

THE INACCESSIBLE PINNACLE
Vol. XXII (1939)   by Lawrence Pilkington

I first visited Skye in 1880 with my brother Charles. We had only one day's climbing there as we were on our way to fish in the Hebrides with an older brother who did not climb. We had an Ordnance Map with us; on it was marked "The Inaccessible Pinnacle." We made the first ascent. I shall always remember that as the noisiest climb I ever had. There was a foot or more of loose rock which had been shattered by the lightning and frost of ages. This formed the edge of the pinnacle and had to be thrown down as we climbed up. The noise was appalling; the very rock of the pinnacle itself seemed to vibrate with indignation at our rude onslaught.

After that we went on to the Hebrides to fish, but the weather proved too dry for any but sea-fishing. We stayed at Tarbert for a week, then caught the steamer at Stornoway and went home. Such an opportunity lost! Most maddening!

My next visit to Skye was in 1883 when Horace Walker, Eustace Hulton, and I made the third ascent of the pinnacle — but how different! Not a single loose rock on the ridge; thick mist all round; 3,000 feet below, the sea visible through a rift in the cloud; nothing nearer to be seen. The cloud stretched away and away all round us, a silver sea with the tops only of the highest peaks standing out like black, rocky islands. No sound! I shall never forget the contrast of those two ascents.

and in Vol II (1892) Walter Brunskill writes:—

Sgurr Dearg Pinnacle, Skye. — We believe in one respect, as compared with the pinnacles or rock summits well known to climbers in Great Britain, the pinnacle of Sgurr Dearg is absolutely unique. It forms an actual mountain summit, being in fact the highest point of one of the two highest peaks in the Coolin range.

It stands quite alone, having no companion points, or ridge of rock, and is a survival of the fittest of the range, being a hard slab of trap which has more successfully than the rest of the mountain withstood the weathering action of the elements. It is fixed into the east side of the mountain summit, its western end forming a point topping the mountain; while running down to the east, a long sloping edge falls for some hundreds of feet at a somewhat similar inclination to the mountain side, until becoming more steep, it terminates in the mountain side.

It is now usually crossed, and indifferently from E. to W. or W. to E. The climb by the west end is really quite short, and its chief difficulty consists in passing a few feet of steep rock, which offers no secure foot or hand hold. Commencing at the north corner, a few reaches bring you on a level with a narrow piece of trap, sloping down. Standing on this there is a steeply sloping shelf of rock, about the height of the shoulder, on to which it is necessary to get, when climbing it the usual way. There is little hand-hold, and it is a place to take very carefully, and it is well to make use of all the friction a close hugging of the rock allows. The difficulty is not lessened by too long a search for holds. A slow pull, a wriggle or two, the difficulty is passed, and the rest is easy. Dr Norman Collie found that this end could be climbed by keeping closer to the north-west corner, and good holds all the way.

The east edge is a much longer climb, but it is less steep, and offers little difficulty: all the same the edge is so narrow, and at such a height from the mountain side, that, as Mr Pilkington says, it is a finer and more sensational climb than the west end. To those who first climbed this edge, the difficulty must have been infinitely greater than now, as it is very rotten, and bears unmistakable evidence of having been very thoroughly cleaned. It is necessary to try every hold before trusting to it, but so well has the work of cleaning the edge been done, that on a recent descent, not a single stone was removed.

CLACH GLAS FROM BEALACH BETWEEN RUADH STAC AND GARBH BHEINN

ON A MOUNTAIN RIDGE Vol XXXIII (1984)

Two contrary impressions share
In our experiences there:
One is of rock and one of air.
Yet in a sense the two agree,
For they together hold the key
To what we feel and what we see.
With all the world reduced to this
A narrow crest, a vast abyss
There is no need for emphasis.

Feet firmly planted on the ground,
Our gaze is free to range around,
Alert to every sight and sound.
So, as we test each step with care,
We move in space, at once aware
Of solid rock and empty air.
This is the balance climbing brings:
In air our fancy spreads its wings,
On rock we touch enduring things.

D.J.F.

LOCHNAGAR BY THE CLIFFS
Vol. IV (1896) by William Tough

Lochnagar has, for various reasons, long held a high place in popular favour among the mountains of Scotland. Some of these reasons there are, such as the ease of the ordinary routes of ascent, and the example of Royalty, which, while doubtless appealing strongly to the bulk of visitors, do not at all influence the true mountain worshipper. But the principal reason is one which affects all classes; drawing upwards with varying power of fascination both the professed lover of high places and the tyro to whom the cult of the mountaineer is as one of the divine mysteries. For even among the lower orders — if I may use the expression without any reference to distinctions in the social scale — it will be acknowledged that the compelling attraction of Lochnagar is that magnificent crescent of cliffs which encircles the head of the great corrie and towers above the waters of the small dark loch, stern and sheer to the level of the summit plateau. One does not need to be a mountaineer to appreciate the grandeur of this range of precipices. Indeed, if the feeling of reverent awe is to be taken into account in analysing the emotions excited by such a scene, it is questionable whether the ordinary sensitive man or woman has not a distinct advantage over the trained mountaineer — especially if the latter be of the cliff-climbing variety on the hunt for a first ascent.

Strangely enough no serious attempt to test the accessibility of the Lochnagar cliffs seems to have been made previous to the time of our visit, if we except the gully climb attempted by Messrs Gibson and Douglas, and described by the latter in the second volume of our Journal. Their local reputation perhaps had something to do with this. "Why don't you climb the cliffs of Lochnagar?" I was asked in Aberdeen the day before this very ascent. "They would try your mettle and give you something to talk about — if you succeeded". The irony of the remark was obvious, and the smile that accompanied it that of the man who has made his point. But I kept my own counsel. My reputation for sanity had already suffered during a previous visit for suggesting the feasibility of such an undertaking, and I had no wish again to bring upon me the fate of the irreverent innovator.

It was a forenoon early in August when Brown and I dismounted at the gate of the small farmhouse of Inchnabobart. We had cycled up from Ballater without meeting with any of those exciting incidents which only prove their value in the period of reminiscence and description. The day, our only one, was well enough suited to our purpose. The higher summits, it is true, were all invisible, and as we topped the ridge we saw the black brows of the great frowning cliffs swathed in bands of fleecy mist. But below all was clear, and the work we had taken in hand lay plain before us.

A pretty exhaustive survey of the cliffs both from above and below had been made by my companion some weeks before, with the result that much time was probably saved on the present occasion. It had seemed to him that the most feasible line of attack was to be found on the precipice forming the central buttress of the N.W. division of the corrie. Here the cliffs attain about their greatest range in altitude and while presenting a tempting appearance of accessibility give promise of quite that degree of sensationalism which renders rock-climbing one of the most fascinating pastimes in the world.

The position of our climb is easily found in the ordinary photographs of Lochnagar corrie, as the buttress stands in the very centre of the picture, its base descending well down towards the loch in the form of a gigantic V. And now having made our selection we spent no time in wider investigation, but resolved to risk our solitary day on this one hazard.

With vivid recollections of the corries of Skye, and fresh from the boulder-strewn slopes at the head of the Coire Beith in Glencoe, we found the walk over the screes of Lochnagar gentle and easy to a degree. Passing above the lower range of rocks which continue the wall of separation between the two divisions of the corrie almost down to the water's edge, we quickly reached the beginning of our climb and at once put on the rope.

The part of the precipice we had chosen is, as we now saw, divided by two shallow water-worn gullies into three vertical sections of very unequal width. The principal of these, that most to the west, shows a very decided ridge on its extreme right running straight to the top. Our selected route lay up this ridge. But a very short examination showed us that any attempt to reach it by a perpendicular climb from the base of the cliff was out of the question. The most clearly indicated, possibly the only available, line of ascent at first, and for a considerable distance, lies up the face of the more easterly of the above-mentioned gullies.

For the first hundred feet or so we made excellent progress, although from the smoothness of the rocks and the downward dip of the stratification the whole of this first part of the climb was distinctly more difficult than its appearance from below had led us to expect. The rock was nowhere shattered or weathered so as to give a firm footing. There were none of those slight projections round which a cast of the rope gives such a sense of security. Every fissure capable of holding the most infinitesimal quantity of soil had been taken advantage of to form a strip of green, so that, altogether, we had an exceedingly favourable opportunity of testing the various merits of the frictional method.

After crossing the first gully and establishing our position well up on the central section, we at length seemed to see our way stretching clearly before us. The plan we now adopted was to climb straight up and cross the gully No. 2 at a point where the cliff retreats more sharply backwards, and a series of slight ledges appear to offer a comparatively easy route to the crest of the main ridge. The idea was good, but it wanted carrying out, and this, as we shortly found, was a task rather beyond our powers. For a short distance indeed Fortune seemed to bestow on our efforts her most propitious smile; then, having lured us on sufficiently far to suit her malevolent purpose, she abandoned us in a manner which I can now describe as utterly heartless, though another adjective would perhaps more clearly express my feelings at the time. It was a series of great slabs, steep, smooth, and fitted so closely together as to defy both finger-tip and toe, that barred our way. Even the trustworthy footing I always confidently look to find on Brown's head in cases of more than ordinary emergency failed me here. The support he would have had here was altogether too "moral" in its nature to enable him to bear the double strain, and nothing was left for us but to descend. I need hardly say that the process of climbing down loses none of its usual humiliating characteristics when the physical is added to the figurative significance of the act.

As is always the case on very steep rocks the descent cost us both more time and trouble than the ascent. But it was managed at last, and then we crossed the gully easily enough. The place where we did so was somewhat lower than the point we had reached where we went to waste precious time on the smooth face of the precipice, and was as nearly as we could judge about 150 feet from its base. Of course we had seen this route from the first, but as the other appeared more direct and easier we had chosen it, thus falling into the trap which stands ever open for the unfortunate rock-climber and which no amount of experience seems to enable him to avoid.

After we had crossed the gully we encountered a very dirty and disagreeable scramble by the side of the trickling stream, over rocks plashing with water and covered with a most objectionable slippery green slime. Then came a further traverse to the right, which landed us on a wide grassy ledge crossing the face of the precipice with a moderate upward slant, and leading straight in the direction we wished to go.

It was here that our second great disappointment met us full in the face. The upper end of the ledge terminated in a new series of slabs. These projected over each other in a manner that was perfectly hopeless, and besides were covered with patches of loosely adhering moss which came away on the slightest touch, and seemed rather to be placed upon the rock than growing on it. We did indeed make a trial of these rocks, but almost as soon as Brown removed his hands from the soles of my boots I simply stuck ingloriously, and had to be helped down again.

We had already seen that it was manifestly useless to make any attempt to force a way up from the bottom end of the ledge, so that things now began to look rather blue. About half-way up the ledge, however, we had noticed a narrow, irregular kind of rocky shelf running some distance athwart the face of the cliff above us. As it seemingly led to nowhere in particular, and was a most unlikely place in every respect, we had never thought of tackling it. But the last few minutes had put a different complexion on things, and we resolved to give it a trial. Clambering on to it, we crept across only to find that it suddenly ended round a projecting corner in a small grassy patch. Above was an overhanging brow of rock, showing no crack or crevice for a distance of several feet. There was no longer any choice of routes with us; we had either to get up there or abandon the climb for the time being. The game was worth a last effort, and we determined to make one. As it was impossible to climb the place without aid, Brown came to my help, and it is certainly due to his efficient backing that the place was conquered. With considerable difficulty, for I was in front and Brown close up to me, there being barely standing room for two, I managed to scramble from his knee to his shoulder. But even when mounted on this lofty pedestal I failed to reach the necessary hold by a good couple of feet. For a minute or two I remained helplessly spread-eagled on the face of the cliff, almost despairing of ever getting up, and not at all clear as to how I should ever get down from my awkward perch, when suddenly the thing was done. How he managed it, considering the position he was in, I don't know; but with a supreme effort Brown shot me upwards the required distance by a sudden powerful jerk. My outstretched fingers caught the welcome crack, and mounting rapidly I found safe anchorage about forty feet above one of the most awkward places it has ever been my fortune to tackle successfully. Our delight was naturally great, and in the cast of one of us at least showed itself in a very practical manner, not unconnected with the use of the rope. For the way in which the heavy man of the party now came up those rocks, his finger-tips playing upon the face of the cliff with a delicacy of touch that would have moved the envy of a professional pianist, and his every movement suggestive of the bounding lightness of the airy thistledown, was a treat to see.

We had besides another source of satisfaction, though of rather a grim kind, in what we had done. There was now no turning back for us. We had crossed the Rubicon, burned our ships, been guilty of any and every act which metaphorically expresses the absolute necessity of reaching the top of our cliff. But fortunately we came on nothing afterwards which could at all compare in difficulty with the place we had just passed, though more than once we found the way seriously threatening to close in upon us. Forced slightly to the left as we fought our way upwards, we almost immediately encountered one or two bits where a slight impulse from behind, if not exactly needed, was nevertheless received with gratitude, and where just the gentlest suggestion of traction was followed by no outburst of indignant protestation.

Our course, somewhat devious certainly, but strictly marked out for us, next led to a series of broad ledges bearing strongly to the right, and separated from each other by steep pitches of rock and grass. The ledges themselves were invariably covered with a growth of grass or grey moss, and we found the most convenient way to negotiate them was to run rapidly up them on all-fours. The slope was generally pretty considerable, and the smallest stop caused the treacherous stuff to yield beneath our feet. It promptly slid if we tried to sit on it, and more than once induced in us that feeling of utter helplessness in the face of possible disaster which is surely the high-water mark of mountaineering misery.*

But when we at length reached the edge of the long-looked-for ridge, the nature of the climbing underwent a sudden and delightful change. It still continued for some distance excessively steep, but in place of the smooth slabs on which up to this point a good hold

---

* North East climbers will recognise here the typical inability of climbers from the Central Belt to appreciate the quality and reliability of the vegetation found on granite cliffs like these! — Ed.

11. *Harold Raeburn*

12. *The traverse from Abraham's Ledge on the Crowberry Ridge, Buachaille Etive Mor*

13. The old Glen Coe road at Achtriochtan

13a. A.E. Robertson going to the hills in style, chauffeur driven to the Mamores

14. *A' Chioch of Sgurr a' Chaorachain*
    Inset: G.T. Glover and W.N. Ling fifty years after their climb of A' Chioch

had been a rarity and a slip a contingency to be guarded against most carefully, we found the rock so broken and shattered that the numerous projections seemed by comparison to form a huge natural staircase.

There was only one thing now to disturb our serenity, and that was the appearance of a deep notch in the upper horizontal part of the ridge which looked as if it might still cut us off from the top. But none of the plans that were formed for circumventing that notch were brought into operation for us, very happily indeed considering the nature of some of them. The place when we came to it proved to be a mere shallow depression, over which we walked with our hands in our pockets on to the summit plateau. We had spent just three hours on the rocks.

Our first business was to build the usual commemorative stone man at the top of our ridge. But I much fear that long ere now his various members have gone to increase the screes at the foot of the precipice. The habit of hurling stones over the cliffs seems to flourish on Lochnagar as it can do only there and on Ben Nevis, and I really think attention ought to be called on it. These falling stones form a very real danger to every visitor to Lochnagar Corrie. We had a slight experience of it while on the cliff. The sudden crash of a large stone, which seemed to be coming straight down upon us, broke on our ears. As it happened, we were not in a line with it, but the numerous reverberations made it impossible for us to say where it was until we accidentally saw it rushing past far below. Had it been coming straight towards us, we could certainly have done nothing to get out of its way, and an accident would probably have resulted. Our shouts stopped the discharge of any further missiles, but surely none but idiots need to have it pointed out to them that Lochnagar is far too much frequented a mountain to make such a practice permissible under any circumstances whatever.

On the top of the mountain we found a strong wind blowing, and as the mist did not allow of any distant view, we only stayed long enough to make a few notes of possible climbs for future occasions, and then scudded gaily down before the breeze to Alltnaguibhsaich. There we were received with the usual bountiful hospitality, and found awaiting us one of those teas which live in the memory. I certainly tried hard to do it justice, but Brown... that, however, might be the subject of a separate paper.

LOCHNAGAR CLIFF

AUGUST AT SLIGACHAN (extracts)
Vol. V (1898) by G. Bennet Gibbs

> In this article dealing with a very active exploratory month in Skye the two remaining problems on the main ridge were solved. One of them by King's Chimney on Sgurr Mhicoinnich and the other the almost direct ascent to the Bhasteir Tooth by Naismith's Route. Both are now trade routes but even today many find the latter an intimidating prospect, especially if encountered toward the end of the Main Ridge Traverse. The centre piece of the article was the account of the ascent of the Bhasteir Nick Gully (King's Cave Route) which took twelve hours and occupied five pages of text and two full page diagrams. This complex and largely subterranean route is rarely climbed these days.

...The month of August 1898 was phenomenal at Sligachan, both for the number of members of the S.M.C. who foregathered there, and the number of fine days enjoyed.From the second to the last day of the month, no day passed without two members at least being present at dinner; and during the same period there were only five or six days on which the weather was so bad that no expedition beyond the neighbouring boulders could be attempted....

...On the 8th, Douglas, King, and Naismith ascended Sgurr Sgumain by a gully from the lochan in Corrie Labain, and gained the top by a short climb, probably new.Crossing the screes, they climbed into the Alasdair-Dubh gap, did both sides of the gap, and King did a new variation at the foot of the long side. From thence they went over Tearlach to Mhic Coinnich, on which a new and direct route was found by King. They returned by the Mhic Coinnich-Dearg col, round by the head of the Coruisk glen, and over the Druim na Ramh ridge to the Gory Stone, and so to bed.

...On the 15th, Naismith, with the two last-mentioned climbers, ascended a 'forked chimney' in the Bhasteir Corrie side of Sgurr nan Gillean. The divide occurs 100 feet from the start, and the left-hand (true right) branch, which overhangs, was climbed for 25 feet by 'back and knee'; an interesting, and at the same time, safe climb.

Not content with this, they went on to the Bhasteir Tooth, and our worthy Treasurer, who, it seems, when not engaged in collecting subscriptions must be 'bagging' something, proceeded to pick up the last part of the Coolin Ridge that required 'straightening out.' Assisted by Mackay, from the col (A) below the overhanging part of the Tooth, some ledges were followed along the south-western face. From the termination of one of these a sort of open chimney runs up about 15 feet to a higher ledge (with a large stone lying on it), which leads to the bottom of another short and rather indefinite chimney. The hand-holds in the latter are not too large, but there is a good hitch 20 feet up. A few feet above that, the chimney narrows to a crack and divides, one portion going up vertically, and the other, which was followed, running obliquely across a nearly A.P. face to the right. This crack gives splendid hand-holds and ends on the edge of a good platform (B), 6 feet or so below the line of the back of the Tooth, and about 80 feet from its summit. Before doing this climb the party had inspected the upper part with a rope from the top. The crack was first pointed out as a possible road up the Tooth by Douglas, while camped near the Bealach a Leiter, and engaged in demolishing a jam piece. Though sensational, as any climb on an open face of such steepness is bound to be, the route described is not really difficult, and it has the advantage of saving the long descent by the Lota Corrie screes involved in the old route.

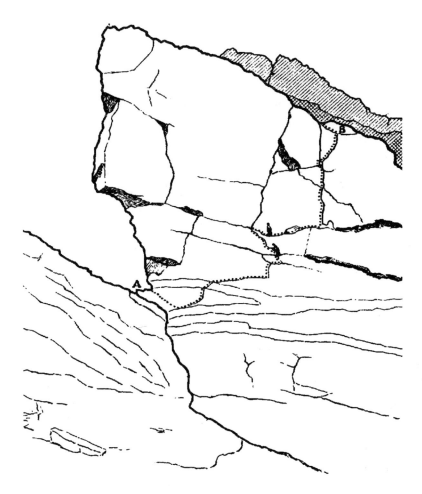

NAISMITH'S NEW ROUTE ON BHASTEIR TOOTH.
FROM COL. A TO PLATFORM B

A'CHIOCH IN APPLECROSS
Vol. XI (1910)   by Geo. T Glover

> This article well illustrates the problems of getting about in the Highlands of the
> period. Presumably the keeper encountered near the end was protecting the deer
> calving.

One hears a great deal from time to time of the pastimes of celebrated people. Some
royalites collect stamps (a dull pastime for a sometimes too strenuous life), the Home
Secretary collects first editions, and to come nearer home, an eminent mountaineer, as
a contrast to peaks upwards of 15,000 feet or so that he has already bagged, is forming a
collection of cabinet-stucke in the form of prominences in North Britain styled A'Chioch.
According to the manner of the true collector, after he has captured the specimen, it is
given to the world at large to admire, and to him we are indebted for this gem.

W. N. Ling and myself, from sundry hints that there was a first rate A'Chioch on the
Scottish mainland, in Ross-shire, not on Beinn Bhan, and not marked on the One-Inch
Ordnance, came to the conclusion that it must be somewhere in the Strathcarron district,
so Friday, 5th June 1908, found us en route for Strathcarron Station. We arrived at mid-
day, and after lunch set out for a walk past the Ballachulish-like Janetown*, of one long
street, then up the hill at the back of the village, and over to Kishorn. The road after
ascending 400 feet descends for about a mile through a fine glen beside a burn. On leaving
this glen we saw in the far distance two magnificent hills. In 1908 it is too much to hope
to find anything good and new in the hill line, but all the same, we felt disappointed when
we simultaneously cried "The Red Coolins". We got some glimpses of crags in the
Applecross district, though the sun was too much behind them for us to make sure of any
detail; but all the same we altered our plans for the morrow, and agreed to make for
Applecross instead of Fuar Tholl. Our way back was cheered by the sight of a very fine
buzzard wheeling about, but after we reached the summit of the road, real rain, a present
from Skye, pursued us the whole way home, which was considerably shortened by keeping
a bad path across the moors, avoiding Janetown, and coming out near Strathcarron
Church.

Next morning was fine, and we rose at 6 a.m., and after some delay drove away at 7.45,
through Janetown and across to Kishorn, seeing the buzzard again in the rocks above the
stream, probably it had a nest there. The sun this time was shining into the Applecross
Forest, and we got a fine view of magnificent rock scenery, big bastions of sandstone rising
in tiers from the usual horizontal terraces. About eight miles away we passed Courthill,
a very southern-sounding name for a very Scottish lodge, situated where the finest views
of the hills opposite can be obtained.

---

* An old name for what is now Lochcarron — Ed.

Just beyond here, and up the hill are the ironstone mines which we were popularly supposed to be prospecting, an ice-axe and an excursion in this direction as soon as we arrived being ample reasons to start the locals gossiping. At last our driver had to ask if we were not going to them, adding that if they were only a success a large seaport town might spring up there — there of all places, as seen on a fine spring morning, with as fine a view as there is on the West coast. "But," he said, "they would never have such luck in this glen!"

We drove a mile and a half beyond Tornapress, and left the machine nearly opposite Courthill, waiting a few minutes to watch the time-saving driver take the ford and splash across to the east side.

We then took to the hill about 9.30, turning over the south-east shoulder of Bheinn Bhan, and were soon looking down on to Loch Coire nam Fharadh, with the magnificent bastions of Sgorr na Caorach rising above it. There was no mistake which spur to make for, and we hoped against hope that this was a find, but felt sure that it was the Chioch. We circled round it, like wrestlers looking for a grip, but obviously there was only one spot from which a start could be made on the south-eastern side, and the route to the top seemed likely to be continuous. The north side had a long grassy ledge leading up towards a gap where the first pinnacle gained the main cliff, but as well as avoiding the climb, it looked as though a slabby cliff, such as one finds at the end of some Torridon gullies, might prevent us reaching the gap.

We lunched at 11.45 (1,100 feet), and then set off, keeping always as near to the edge of the rounded first pinnacle as we could, although at first forced a good deal too much in the direction of the big gully. We went up a succession of short chimneys, which a few moments before we had waltzed up in thought. Alas, what a difference when once one tackled them in earnest, and without any slander, the grand old hills of Torridon sandstone are uncommonly deceiving, there being a lack of handhold when one reaches the top of each pitch of rock. The chimneys were lined with steep grass and loose and rounded rock; we went up these, always keeping an eye on our right hand, as we were undoubtedly too far from the magnificent but unattainable face, which is so well shown in the photograph. We turned to our right and made for a steep wall up which there was a narrow crack, but this route was given up as the top overhung, and it is no use hoping for a handhold where you require it on sandstone. We were afraid that we might have to go leftward to the main gully, but to our joy a way was found round a corner to the right, up steep, but good and firm, rock, with a very sensational outlook, owing to our being on the edge of the arete. Above this we took to a belt of heather which led us to a narrow chimney where the rocks need careful handling, and then over slabs and crowberry plants we practically walked to the summit of the first pinnacle, 1,100 feet.

Alas! a cairn. "Collie", we cried, hoping we would still find that it had been some stalker who had ascended the comparatively easy big gully, and descended without tackling the magnificent face of rock in front of us. As a matter of fact, Collie had ascended the big gully on its right (true) whilst Slingsby and his partners tackled the face at about the same line as ourselves. We sat here for some time admiring the perpendicular view below, and the work in front, about 300 feet of it; then we made a start first down across the head of the dividing gully, which reminded me of one or two Lofoden dips of a similar nature; then up a very pleasant staircase of sandstone, with an occasional small traverse — one of about 15 feet to the right remains in my memory — rock good and outlook to match, but no place or need to slip. Above this we are under the final cliffs of the main tower, some 150 feet of slabby rock. When aeroplanes become commonplace, say in three years' time, I hope to possess a 6 Sparrow-power Vol au Vent, or a 60 Eagle-power Soarer (according to the state of my physical and financial nerves), and I intend to circle around some of these towers to assure myself how really easy these cliffs would be to climb straight up. Meanwhile we chose one of the very few routes open to us.

We first of all went to our right along a very sensational ledge about two feet wide, which probably contours right around the face, and is an ideal traverse walk in calm weather, but as we could find no route commencing from this, we went back again southwards, and up an open stretch of heather, etc., to the foot of a big gully. Up this is easy scrambling until a jammed stone pitch is reached. Ling here made good progress and I fixed myself under the stone, whilst he with the usual tactics and a considerable amount of skill wormed himself up on the (true) left side. Once he announced himself firm, I, well aware of his poetical tendences, had to remind him that "hold the last fast, says the rhyme." Once above this a few feet of scrambling took us to the summit of the tower, and we sat a few minutes discussing whether this was the Chioch or not, and we decided, rightly, that it was, as although there was much vegetation everywhere, still there was a suspicious cleanliness about the likeliest handholds.

We then set along the broad summit ridge, a walk, except where intersected by the heads of gully and the small rocks at these places, can be either scrambled over, or turned on either side by descending a few feet, and so eventually reached the summit of Sgorr na Caorach (2,539 feet) at four o'clock. The summit is part of an enormous plateau sloping gently westward. I will not catalogue the view, every S.M.C. man is familiar with it more or less, or ought to be, but I think the picture is hardly so fine as that from the Teallachs, as neither the Coolins nor the Torridons show themselves at their best, but after a good climb on a glorious day, who shall say that the view is not perfect?

After a rest we remembered the sixteen-mile trudge homeward, and reluctantly descended towards the Applecross road which stretched across the plateau. We reached the famous Bealach nam Bo and the hairpin bends, and are reminded of the exploit of our President, G Thomson, who professionally assisted in conducting a Martini car up the same pass. I wish he had left one for our use. The scenery on this pass is very fine, but we could not see much rock of a climbable nature, and we lightened our way homeward by noting how one could ascend some fine cliffs by walking along sloping grassy terraces.

As the tide was out we crossed the loch, about 300 yards from Courthill, at the north end of a small wood, the water was only about a foot deep, and the sandy bottom everywhere firm. The remainder of the day was mere work until we reached Strathcarron Inn at 8.45.

Next day, Sunday, broke grey and cold. I claimed an easy day, and was let off with a stroll of fourteen miles, partly over some of the roughest going I have met with in Scotland. We went to Coulags by as flat a road as any in the Lincolnshire Fens, and from there made up a good deer path past a keeper's cottage, from which we were temporarily followed; but as we had a fair start and the weather was then really moist, the occupant soon returned to his den, whilst we wound up a very Swiss path on a large moraine, until we reached a bealach between Ruadh Stac and Meall a Chinn Deirg — thence across to another dip — whence rise the grey slabs which slope to the summit of Ruadh Stac. Here we were met by a strong south-west wind laden with such chilly rain and sleet that we could see nothing, so we determined to clear out below the mists, and turned down and across the extraordinary slabs at the back of Ruadh Stac: after lunching by a small lochan (crouched behind any boulder we could find), we had a mile of the roughest going, following a stream down the Allt nan Ceapairean, which name, under the circumstances, afforded us an opportunity for much feeble and diluted wit, which the reader may invent for himself if in the same place and circumstances and so minded. Absolutely wet through, we arrived at Strathcarron at three o'clock.

Next day — our last chance for that year — we resolved on an attack or at least a look at the face of Fuar Tholl in the Achnashellach Forest.Being early birds, we took the 6.50 train, and arrived at Achnashellach, on a warm pouring wet day, and inquired for the keeper. We had previously been warned about new brooms, etc., and only too truly, as the keeper objected, averring that not even the owner dare go up to fish in the corrie below Fuar Tholl at this time of year. We tried to impress him by pulling out some very damp visiting cards as a sign of respectability, but our old gaberdines, wet and frayed, were too much for him, and our day's climb degenerated into a twenty-seven miles' walk. First retracing our way along the line for a mile or two in company with a wet but cheery shepherd, then back along the road past Loch Dhughaill on to Craig, we crossed the railway and went a long way up the Allt a Chonais, before we could cross the burn, then turning south we struck a bealach between Sgurr na Fiantaig and Ben Tarsuinn. At the top of this we went off a short way south to look down towards the Morar country, as by this time the rain and mist were away, then down a long glen to Loch an Laoigh, back to the Inn down Glen Udale, nowhere seeing any climbing rocks.

The district round Strathcarron is a glorious one, and given fine weather, the explorer should be rewarded with several more good climbs, although Professor Collie, I expect, has taken the best with the Chioch. I am indebted to him for the photos illustrating this article, and also for originally stimulating my curiosity.

THE MOTOR IN MOUNTAINEERING(extracts)
Vol. VII (1903)   by W. Inglis Clark

A VISIT TO BUCHAILLE ETIVE MOR

For several years my wife and I have visited Ben Nevis in June, and the accounts of these visits have already occupied perhaps too large a proportion of the Journal's pages. Many a time we looked across the gulf of Glen Nevis and across the Mamore Forest, to where conspicuous Bidean formed a rallying point for the various Glencoe peaks; or to Buchaille Etive, with its frowning buttresses merged in its rocky face.But while these Glencoe mountains held out high hopes of virgin routes and scenic effects, our old love held us back to explore further the fascinating ridges and gullies of its northern face. And so the balance remained equal; and the facility of railway and hotel carried the day in favour of Fort William. But "a nod's as good as a wink to a blind horse," and the casual remark overheard at the Club room, "What! more about Ben Nevis, whatever can he have to say?" decided that the camp must be shifted to pastures new. Hailing as I do from Edinburgh, I have imbibed with its east wind an intense dislike of wasting my not too superabundant energy on the mere walk to or from a mountain, and the advent of a motor car into my peaceful home seemed to open up a new era, when we would drive to the foot of our climb and count the miles between Clachaig and Kingshouse as but dust in the balance. If we except the too short visit of the Club to Ballachulish some years ago, the Glencoe Mountains were unknown to me, and Buchaille Etive only lingered as a faint vision from thirty years ago, when, rucksack on back I wandered from John o'Groats to Cape Wrath, thence through Sutherland and Ross-shire to Fort William, and back to Arrochar by way of Glencoe. In those days sturdy mountaineering boots were not so common as at present, and I can recall the following incident on the steamer from Fort William to Ballachulish. A few day's climbing in the Mamore Forest had reduced my boots to the condition of sandals, and as the steamer started at an early hour, I had to continue my journey with the uppers tied on to the soles with stout cord. The better to suit my appearance, I sought shelter in the steerage, where in due course the treasurer of a German band came, cap in hand, for a donation. Before responding, I pointed significantly to my feet; and the noble Teuton, realising that so ill-shod a creature must be in dire straits indeed, held up his hands, groaned, and refused to accept even a humble coin of the realm.

After much heart-searching regarding the reliability of a motor car for mountaineering, we decided to chance it and make primarily for Kingshouse Inn, later on moving to Clachaig if the roads seemed practicable. But lest any may consider that motor-driving will cause a degenerate race of mountaineers to arise, I would warn them that I have distinctly lost weight as the result of my enterprise. What with dangerous corners and alarmed horses, and the physical exertion of starting the car as often as, through carelessness, one lets it stop on a hill, motor-driving may be recommended for those troubled with embonpoint. Then, perhaps, one of the greatest risks the mountaineer runs is when his petrol won't flow, and the precious hours are lost in trying to find the obnoxious particle of dust which lies low when you are looking for it, and emerges as soon as you start again to shut off your motive power with a malicious cackle. One terrible experience I had, the memory of which well-nigh eclipses the dangers of purely climbing experiences, and which nearly brought the credit of the S.M.C. to naught, and the honorary office of Secretary to shame and confusion. I had fortunately narrowly escaped taking our Editor for a drive in the country, and was hurrying home for dinner by a short detour of 25 miles, when 'the beastie' struck work and refused to go up the slightest hill. It was dour, and no coaxing or drinks of water from a cottage near by would induce it to move. My experience being but limited, the 'deevil' in the petrol was undetected, and when the shades of night came down a sorry nag was procured, harnessed to the car with ropes, and amid the jeers of passers-by I rode into Edinburgh in state. It was past 11 p.m.as we slowly paced through Princes Street, and suggestions to send for the officers of the Society for Prevention of Cruelty to Animals received no countenance from me.Fortunately a Secretary is never without resource, and with the aid of chauffeur's leather cap and prominent goggles, the writer passed off as Count Sokoloffski, the eminent chauffeur. Besides such nerve strains as these, the terrors of the Crowberry Ridge and Chasm seem trifling.

> With his wife Clark went off to Kingshouse on 12 June and after a day on Sron na Creise were joined by Raeburn who led them up the new Direct Route made by the Abraham party in 1900. They were very impressed by the crux...

A few words will suffice to describe the nature of this formidable pitch.Stepping off the ledge, the left foot seeks for a 2-inch foothold round the corner.This consists of a narrowing ledge sloping steeply upwards and outwards, and affording further out grip for the nails only. The right hand retains a rough grip, while the left is rested on a slender pinnacle projecting some 1/2 inch from the face. Having fairly balanced on these slender supports, the body is taken round the corner, and the fun begins. The nearest available hold was some distance from our leader's reach, and he had to forego the little pinnacle and trust to mere hollows for support. An anxious and silent interval was only broken by the slow movement of the rope, but soon it moved more rapidly, and after 35 feet were out my wife followed out of sight to take her turn. With the confidence of the rope I was able to balance myself with the right extremity of the ledge, to reach sufficient holds to prevent falling backward; but for some 8 to 10 feet higher I was not ashamed to call out, "Hold me firm," and to feel gratified at the response from above. The climbing is not over even then, but pales into insignificance before this momentous corner.

> Clark was a keen photographer but unfortunately left a lens at the summit cairn. They had to retrieve it so...

Next day, instead of going up by the easiest way, what should Raeburn suggest but that we should endeavour to ascend by the Chasm, a huge gully on the east side of the mountain, and one, moreover, which had already baffled a strong party. But we had looked into it during our descent, and seen a 100 feet pitch apparently impossible, and which we believed to be the 'ultima thule' of former expeditions. With commendable prudence we decided to start our climb above this pitch, as the most casual glance revealed sufficient difficulties remaining to satisfy even an ardent Ultramontist.

Climbing up past the impregnable pitch referred to, we descended by the northern wall into the Chasm, and were immediately introduced to a succession of water-worn difficult pitches, alternating with snow bridges, snow seracs, and many of the characteristics of an Alpine ascent. The left branch of the Chasm held a prodigious quantity of snow, the thickness possibly at parts being 50 feet. To detail the various pitches and difficulties encountered would be impossible and wearisome, but the climb up to the branching of the Chasm was extraordinary and weird in the extreme. Now we were cutting steps or treading cautiously the sharp seracs, or crossing by tottering snow bridges. Anon hemmed in by vertical walls, we traversed in a crouching position perhaps 50 feet through a snow tunnel. Above, the roof was moulded into numerous arches, and a constant rain of water falling cooled the air.Emerging, a forbidding pitch confronted us, and often only succumbed after a severe struggle. It was indeed a most strenuous climb, and demanded constant strain. Our time was already far spent, for Raeburn had perforce to catch the evening train at Tyndrum. When, therefore, we came to the two last severe pitches, leading into the cauldron, and saw a final triple pitch of at least 150 feet, well decorated with waterfalls, we decided that an escape must be made on the left. Here at the forking of the Chasm rises a magnificent 200 feet pinnacle, the angle very steep. A huge snow mass below left sufficient space for foothold, and with back against the rock, we were able to reach the bottom of a severe but splendid chimney, leading up some 40 feet. Above this the difficulties do not slacken till a grass ledge is reached overhung by a difficult and dangerous wall, resembling strongly the Pinnacle Arete of the Trident Buttress of Ben Nevis. The ascent of this very slightly overhanging portion proved difficult, the numerous holds being unreliable for a leader. Above this another wonderful chimney led to the top (2,500 feet), which is separated by a neat little col from the mountain. We raised a small cairn, christened the pinnacle the 'Lady's Pinnacle,' and were glad to relax our muscles, which for four hours had been put to so hard a test. Looking back on this climb, I regard it as the most prolonged piece of difficult climbing in my British experience. Moreover, in variety, in beauty, and charm, it has few rivals. Bidding farewell to Raeburn, we watched him scamper down the screes like a chamois, and hastened to the summit, where, being 'deil's bairns,' we found the missing lens intact. There on a sheltered ledge we watched the motor, like an uncanny spirit, emerge from Kingshouse, and pick up our friend at Etive Bridge to speed him on his lonely journey to Edinburgh. We ourselves were bound for Clachaig, and after unsuccessful attempts to glissade down the too hard snow of Corrie Tulachan, joined the motor at Altnafeadh, and enjoyed by the roadside the luxury of afternoon tea.

Our stay at Clachaig lasted but two days, during which we seized various excuses for doing nothing striking. The weather, however, was unpropitious, and an attempt on the Stob Coire an Lochan cliffs was cut short by mist and rain after we had ascended Aonach Dubh by the easy gully. The ferry at Ballachulish proved too small for our motor, and we had perforce to return up Glencoe. As evidence of the mountaineering ability of the motor, we climbed about 3,000 feet on the road home, and covered 125 miles on the one day, our route including Tyndrum, Crianlarich, Glen Falloch, Tarbet, Balloch, Buchlyvie, and Stirling.

WIND PHENOMENON ON GOATFELL
Vol XVI (1923)   by W. Inglis Clark

At the recent New Year's Meet, at Brodick, a succession of hurricanes rendered mountaineering difficult. Among other excursions was one to the summit of Goatfell, when a series of wind vortices swept down the slopes, tossing members here and there. Owing to the slight sprinkling of snow, the passage of these cyclones was made visible, each circle of wind raising a margin of snow like a wall some feet in height. But the most interesting thing was that each large circle, revolving, say, at 40 miles per hour, had on its margin five vortices, as shown in the diagram, where the velocity seemed more like 100 miles per hour, and at each of these a pyramid of snow was raised to a height of perhaps 30 feet. The whole circle with its satellites had a rapid movement down the mountain face. To those who were able to look, the sight was an awe-inspiring one. Some of the members were in advance of the writer and, as the circle bore down on them, one could see them brace themselves to resist it; but if by chance they encountered a secondary vortex, resistance was in vain, and they were tossed about with resistless force. No doubt these wind movements accompany every violent storm, but in this case the whirlwinds were rendered plainly visible owing to the snow. The writer could easily recognise the part of a circle in which he chanced to be, but when in the secondary vortex, he was thrown certainly more than 20 feet in a fraction of a second.

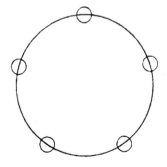

TRIBALISM

Inter-regional and inter-city rivalries are a recurrent aspect of mountaineering as they are in other activities . They can readily be identified in a number of places in this anthology, including these extracts. First, the Glaswegians extol the delights of the Whangie

PRACTICE SCRAMBLES (extracts)
Vol. II (1892)   by Gilbert Thomson

There may be some members of the Club who are in the happy position of getting away for a climb as often as they have a mind to, and who have no need to consider carefully how to make the most of their chances. But there are doubtless more who find that their desire for climbing and their opportunities for doing so are in a sort of inverse ratio, and that often a most desirable expedition - even a Club meet sometimes - has to be given up for want of the necessary time.

The writer and his trusty ally Naismith, pondering over these sad facts, came to the conclusion that if large game could not be had, there was at least small game to be got at, and that half a loaf was better than no bread. Some Saturday afternoons and summer evenings (or mornings, sometimes) might well be spent, not in roaming over roads or even moorland, but in hunting up dainty bits of rock climbing and the like where there was sufficient difficulty to keep the faculties up to the mark. A precipice 20 feet high does not sound very serious, but there may be more fun and real climbing in getting up or down such a place than there is in ascending the 4,406 feet of Ben Nevis.

Keeping our eyes open, and occasionally making a special exploration, we have found many places where good scrambling can be done, these varying from the prosaic quarry face to some of our most romantic glens...............

and in the next issue, in Notes and Queries:, again by Gilbert Thomson

THE WHANGIE

On Saturday afternoon, 9th July, Maylard, Naismith, and Thomson visited the Whangie. As previously mentioned (p.8, et seq.), this ridge had been traversed from north to south with the exception of one point, referred to as 'a sheer drop without any hold whatever.' The special object was to go from south to north, and to get both up and down the part which we have since dubbed 'the pinnacle'. The south and middle sections were easily done, and then the pinnacle was attacked. Two ropes, each over forty feet, were joined together, and thrown over the thin edge. One end was made fast to a big stone on the inside of the gully, the outside one was held round the face so as to give a curved handrail. By its assistance, after dislodging a mass of loose stone, it was found quite possible to get up or down the face, a particularly good bit of climbing, about thirty-five feet high. The rocks throughout are rather treacherous, many being shaky; but although in this respect they are inferior to those of Skye, they can fairly compare with them in their power of producing 'lines of cleavage' in the nether garments.

The Edinburgh response came in Vol. IV (1896)

ARTHUR SEAT AS A SCRAMBLING CENTRE (extracts)

by 'Auld Reekie'

Dear Author of 'Practice Scrambles,' — Your paper upholding the Western Metropolis as a climbing centre for a half-day's amusement has too long remained unchallenged, and I now take up cudgels for mine ain romantic town. The Cartland Crags, the Whangie, and the Devil's Den may be all that you say of them, but what are they when compared with that vast and mighty range of precipices that rejoice in the name of the Salisbury Crags, or the soaring bald pate of the Lion's Head, that delights the eye of every visitor to Edina, Scotia's darling seat?

Come with me, my friend, and I will show you, within a few minutes of Princes Street, as fair a field as was ever presented to man to keep his iron muscles from rust or his wind and nerves from becoming flabby. I promise you that there you will find no 'lack of opportunity to test the accuracy of your spring, your skill in discriminating between fixed rocks and shaky, or the grip of your hand and foot.' Those frowning battlements that front the Castle Rock and throw the venerable old Palace of Holyrood into the shade have untold treasures that will only reveal themselves to the faithful.

There follows a description of the 'treasures' to be enjoyed and the next issue brought a reply.

Dear 'Auld Reekie,' — Have you ever attended a New Year Meet of the Club when the weather was 'seasonable' and when the voice of the enthusiasts had prevailed in fixing the hour for the morning start? If so, you can recall the feelings, not over friendly, with which the voice announcing 'seven o'clock' was regarded. But these feelings, I am persuaded, never last long. Why then do you nurse your wrath against the unfortunate individual who four years ago made a mild endeavour to rouse you to appreciate the climbing blessings at your doors? For, sad to say, the whole of the first volume of the Journal had passed without any reference to Arthur Seat, and with only a casual one to the Salisbury Crags — as possessing a talus slope. The first suggestion that either might provide good climbing was in an article published in the first number of the second volume, dated January 1892, under the heading of 'Practice Scrambles'. Amid the somewhat belated indignation which this has called forth, and that Arthur Seat is thought worthy of better things than to be a racecourse, to be accomplished from and to the G.P.O. within forty minutes. One lives and learns. After realising that the climbs of Edinburgh are within a few minutes' walk of Princes Street, one understands how it is that at a meet the Edinburgh contingent looks so anxiously after means of conveyance, whenever the hill happens to be more than half a mile from the hotel. — Yours retaliatorily,

THE AUTHOR OF 'PRACTICE SCRAMBLES.'

AONACH EAGACH (extract)
Vol. XII (1912)   by Dr W. Inglis Clark

Some years have passed since the 'Motor in Mountaineering' (S.M.C.J., vii. 313) raised a mild protest. But if the objectors or scoffers (and some have even hailed from Glasgow) had kept a note of the proceedings in Glencoe this year, they would have found that that lonely region had been the rendezvous of the S.M.C. on many occasions and that the motor was the means by which such unofficial meets were possible. In fact an entent cordiale between Glasgow and Edinburgh is an accomplished fact, and the young blood of the two cities disport on the Crowberry Ridge or call on Ossian in company. I am not the chronicler of these meets, but I think not less than five of them have taken place since Easter. It may have been due to the fact that one of us hailed from the west and the other from the metropolis, that H. MacRobert (Sub-Editor of the Glencoe district) and I had never climbed together.

PROCEEDINGS OF THE CLUB (extract)
Vol. XIX (1930)

Before passing from the consideration of the Hut business, J.A. Parker raised the question as to whether a key might not be kept in Aberdeen for the use of the Aberdeen members. R.R. Elton stated that the Committee had given favourable consideration to this question, and agreed to the request that a key should be kept at Aberdeen. It is necessary in order to borrow the Hut key at Fort William to produce to the local custodian, Mr Nicolson, a Club Button. The SECRETARY therefore suggested that no key need be kept at Aberdeen if the Aberdeen members would only club together and purchase a button for exhibition when the key was required.

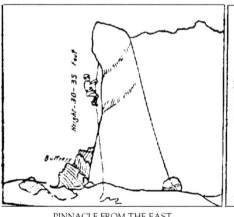 

THE WHANGIE

PINNACLE FROM THE EAST   VIEW OF SOUTH END

A SHORT HISTORY OF SCOTTISH CLIMBING - 1880-1914 (extracts)
Vol. XXII (1939)   by H. MacRobert

...The first ten years of our Club, coincided with the rise of guideless climbing in the Alps.

These guideless pioneers played an important part in developing Scottish climbing, and the most prominent names were J.H. Gibson, J.N. Collie, Chas.Pilkington, and G.A. Solly, who all became members of the S.M.C. in its earliest years. Pilkington had visited Skye as long ago as 1880, and made the first ascent of the Inaccessible Pinnacle along with his brother Lawrence, who is happily still with us. In 1888 he climbed Clach Glas, and in 1889 his article on climbing in the Cuillin appeared in the Alpine Journal. Gibson from the very first took an active part in the affairs of the Club, and his early ascents include the Black Shoot, the north-east face of Ben Lui, and A'Chir in Arran (on which a piton was used!). In 1892 the brothers Hopkinson climbed the Tower Ridge and N.E. Buttress of Ben Nevis, and in 1894 Collie, Solly, and Collier made the famous onslaught on Glencoe and Ben Nevis, their bag including the north-east face of Buachaille Etive (Collie's Route), the face of Stob Coire nam Beith, Collie's Pinnacle and Gully on Bidean nam Bian, the cliffs of Stob Coire nan Lochan, the north and west faces of Aonach Dubh, Ossian's Cave, and the Tower Ridge...

These exploits by Alpine-trained men had an immediate effect on the local talent led by W.W. Naismith. Naismith, of course, had had considerable Alpine experience, having amongst other expeditions climbed the Ober Gabelhorn in 1892 without guides.He and Gilbert Thomson, James Maclay and Douglas, W. Tough and W. Brown, J.H. Bell, Napier and Green, and many others started a thorough exploration of the climbing possibilities of our Scottish hills, which extended for some ten years to 1905. In 1896 Harold Raeburn appeared on the scene, and his remarkable skill and dominating personality may be said to have moulded the subsequent pre-war climbing activities of the Club.

During the first few years the Club's activities were mainly devoted to the exploration of the main ridges and easy snow-fields of the wonderful array of Scottish Bens whose existence was only then becoming known, thanks largely to the labours of Sir Hugh Munro whose famous Tables had appeared in Vol. 1. of the Journal.Professor Ramsay, our first President, was a member of the Alpine Club, and Naismith, Maylard, R.A. Robertson and Munro had some Alpine experience. These were all active members of the Club, but probably J.H. Gibson was the man with the greatest experience in the early days of the Club. Naismith, however, almost at once came to the front, and for the first ten years was undoubtedly the leading force in Scottish climbing. J.H. Bell and Harold Raeburn joined the Club in 1894 and 1896 respectively, and the former for four or five years was the most enterprising of the younger brigade, but Raeburn soon established himself, and for twenty years was our leading Scottish mountaineer with a reputation extending from the Alps to Norway and the Caucasus.

With Naismith one associates, of course, Gilbert Thomson, and those two, sometimes with James Maclay or William Douglas, and later with J.H. Bell, were largely responsible for the development of snow climbing in Scotland. Although Naismith and Maclay were both fine rock-climbers, it must be admitted that it was Norman Collie's exploits in Glencoe and on Ben Nevis in 1894 that gave the first real stimulus to rock climbing in Scotland...

In the year 1895 the Club were at Fort William for the Easter Meet and the Castle Ridge and several gullies were climbed, and also the N.E. Ridge of Aonach Beag by Naismith's party. In May, Tough and Brown cycling from Dalwhinnie climbed the N.E.Buttress of Ben Nevis under the impression that it was a new climb. In August the same party made their famous route on Lochnagar — the Tough-Brown Ridge, and also the fine climb up the rocks to the east of Ossian's Cave in Glencoe. J.H. Bell's party climbed the very difficult B-C rib on Cir Mhor, and made several routes on the Cobbler and on Buachaille Etive. 1896 was also a good year. Tough, Brown, and Raeburn climbed the cliffs of Coire Ardair. Naismith made his historic ascent of the Crowberry Ridge, and also of the Castle of Carn Dearg (Ben Nevis). The Douglas Boulder at the foot of the Tower Ridge was climbed by Brown, Raeburn, Hinxman, and Douglas. The exploration of the gullies and ribs on the north-east face of Ben Lui was completed by Maclay and others. In Skye the 2,500 foot climb on the Coruisk face of Ghreadaidh and the north-west climb on Alasdair were done by Collie's party, and J.H. Bell completed the climb of the famous Water-pipe Gully on Sgurr an Fheadain.

In 1897 the second ascent of the Black Shoot was made by Bell's party, and a third ascent on the following day by Raeburn and Maclay. This is not an easy climb, and conditions in the Shoot are usually foul. It was at this time (Vol. IV., P. 347) that Bell carried out his interesting experiments in regard to the strength of the standard climbing rope. In his report he states that the deadweight supported by the rope with a bowline knot was 1,456 lbs., and that a weight of 11 stone falling clear through about 9 feet would break a 20-foot rope suspended from a rigid belay.

1898 was a specially good year. The cliffs of Coire Mhic Fhearchair and the Chasm of Buachaille Etive were explored. The Church Door Buttress on Bidean nam Bian was finally conquered by a party led by Raeburn and Bell. Raeburn's Gully on Lochnagar was climbed. Naismith found a route up the Carn Dearg Buttress of Nevis and named it the Staircase. He also, with Mackay, made his famous route on the south face of the Bhasteir Tooth. King's Chimney on Sgurr Mhic Coinnich and the Bhasteir Nick Gully fell to W.W. King, who also climbed the S.W. Crack on the Inaccessible Pinnacle safeguarded by a rope from above.

For ten years, therefore, climbing in Scotland had made steady progress and might almost be said to have reached its "peak" in 1898. Thereafter the initial impetus gradually slackened and almost died away in spite of sporadic outbursts until 1908, when a new enthusiasm arose and spent its energy mostly among the wonderful chimneys and faces of the Cuillins. This period, of course, came to an abrupt end in 1914.

15. *On the Salisbury Crags, Edinburgh*

16. *The Great Tower, Ben Nevis, seen from above*

17. *The Great Tower and the summit cliffs of Ben Nevis*

18. The great ridges on the north face of Ben Nevis

It will be seen, therefore, that mountaineering in Scotland has had perfectly natural periods of ebb and flow, and that throughout the first twenty-five years of the Club's existence the active rock climbers were comparatively few. The standard of climbing, however, was steadily improving and members were gradually acquiring a "hill sense", and a knowledge of mountain craft which stood them in good stead when they went farther afield to try their skill in the Alps, in Norway, in Canada, and the Caucasus. They could find their way over difficult ground under the worse possible conditions; they could cut steps in snow and ice, and could appreciate the holding qualities of snow on steep rocks or the probabilities of avalanches from these rocks. But the Club had not specialised in rock climbing, and compared with some of the English Clubs might almost be said to have neglected it. One reason for this neglect, and probably the principal reason, apart from the fact that during the summer months most of the best climbers in the Club were in the Alps or in Norway, must be attributed to Scottish weather. During the usual climbing periods, New Year and Easter, most of the principal rock climbs are plastered with snow and ice or running with water. Difficult rock climbing under such conditions is almost impossible, and so the more popular routes were on the great ridges under snow conditions, routes which under dry summer conditions would be the easiest of scrambles. The Tower Ridge of Ben Nevis, for instance, presents no difficulty in summer, but under severe winter conditions in March or April may defeat the strongest party. The Church Door Buttress for years withstood all assaults, but the first determined attack under summer conditions was successful. It is this variation in climatic conditions which makes it almost impossible to grade Scottish climbs (Probably the great variety of rock structure in Scotland is also responsible - Ed.), and this has not seriously been attempted except in the case of the Cuillin climbs. In Skye, unlike the rest of Scotland, almost all the climbing is done in summer, and here we have conditions more approximating to those prevalent in Wales and the English Lake District, and to climbers from these districts is mainly due the credit for the rapid development of the sport in Skye in the years just before the war.

The above advertisement appeared at least twice in the Scotsman in June 1914. The German has a flattering idea as to the height of the Scottish Highlands, but we are afraid that the selection of places over 3,000 feet would not be sufficiently inviting to the distinguished stranger to warrant more than a bowing acquaintance.

THE ADVENTURE OF THE MISPLACED EYEGLASSES*
Vol. XXXI (1979)   Edited by Robin N. Campbell

I rose to stretch my legs and to afford some relief to my digestive organs, which had been doing stout work with Mrs Hudson's afternoon tea. Holmes was sitting in his armchair, smoking and reading a monography concerning Oriental poisons. I moved to the window overlooking Baker Street and stared out at the mournful fogs of a January afternoon.

'We should get out of Town more often, Holmes,' I remarked. 'These damnable fogs will be the death of us.'

As I spoke these words a figure on a bicycle materialised below the window, dismounted, and moved towards our door. A moment later Mrs Hudson's boy entered with a telegram.

'Perhaps your prescription will soon be administered, Watson,' said Holmes, ripping open the telegram. 'Yes, indeed. And a fairly heavy dose at that. We must catch the Night Mail to Glasgow.'

I picked up the telegram and read as follows: 'NEED YOUR HELP, COME IMMEDIATELY. RAEBURN WILL MEET AND ADVISE. NORMAN.' The telegram had been issued from Fort William Post Office.

'Good gracious, Holmes?' I exclaimed in some dismay, 'Not Scotland surely!'

'I fear so, Watson. My cousin Norman† is a most considerate and courageous man. He would not trouble me over a trifle. I deduce that he has been falsely arrested and charged with murder. Come, we must make some purchases.' Holmes brushed my queries aside and swept out of the room. When I reached the street he had already found a cab. We sped through the murk to Marble Arch and alighted at a tiny dingy shop, Lawrie's by name.

'This gentleman requires a pair of your best Alpine boots,' said Holmes to the shopkeeper, indicating myself, 'and he needs them by nine o'clock this evening. Is it possible?'

Mr Lawrie, if indeed it was he, made some discreet measurements, consulted his watch and replied affirmatively. Holmes and he then embarked on some further exotic negotiations after which we returned to Baker Street. After dinner Holmes packed an extraordinary assortment of articles into his largest trunk before we rattled off to Euston.

---

* The manuscript of this story was prepared by me from a bundle of case notes signed by John H. Watson, M.D., which I discovered in the bottom of a box of lantern slides in the old Clubroom. Examination of the slides made it seem likely that they were donated to the Club by Norman Collie. It is, as always, a hazardous matter to assign a date to Holmes' cases, since Watson was (almost certainly deliberately) lax and, indeed, wayward in giving such indications. Early January 1896 seems the most probable date, shortly before the case of 'The Missing Three Quarter.'

† There seems little doubt that Collie is intended. The photograph recording the Inveroran Meet of 1894 (Club Archives), which shows Collie on the extreme right, makes his resemblance to Holmes very evident.

At the station we took possession of an unwieldy parcel from Lawrie's and soon we were speeding northwards in a comfortable sleeping compartment of the London Midland and Scottish Railway Company. Very early next morning we passed through Glasgow where our coach was transferred to a train of the West Highland Railway Company. Eventually we took morning tea and gazed out at sullen hills around a grey 'loch'. The tops of the hills were wreathed in snow and curling mist.

'Cheer up, Watson,' said Holmes. 'In thirty-three minutes we shall be in Crianlarich. The attendant has promised us a capital breakfast there.'

'Porridge, I'll be bound,' I remarked sadly. 'But Holmes, tell me about your cousin Norman. Who is he and what is he doing in Fort William, of all places?'

'There isn't very much to tell. He is a research chemist at present engaged in secret work for Government, thanks to my brother Mycroft's influence. He visits Fort William regularly in order to practise the art of mountain-climbing with his friends in the Scottish Mountaineering Club. Ben Nevis is there, you see. A mountain, Watson.'

At Crianlarich a surly youth entered our carriage with a hamper. It was indeed an excellent breakfast. We ploughed our way through kippers, bacon and eggs and hot bread rolls while the train chugged up yet more dismal valleys surrounded by still higher mountains. Finally we crossed an endless waste of bog and water before careering down a series of giddy inclines to Fort William. On this last section of the newly-opened line Holmes pointed out Ben Nevis to me - a huge boss of ice and snow with black crags menacing the northern approaches. It was unthinkable to me that a man could derive pleasure from looking at such an ugly mountain let alone from climbing up it.

Soon we were lunching at the Alexandra Hotel with a small stern-looking young man with impressive moustaches and the carriage of a guardsman.

'I am Harold Raeburn,' he had said when he met us at the station. 'Your cousin Norman is in grave danger and has asked me to inform you of the details of his case and to help in whatever way possible.'

After we had completed our meal, we took some brandy in the lounge. Above the fireplace there hung an enormous panorama showing every shoot and precipice of the northern face of Ben Nevis. The remaining furnishings consisted of a few rough pine tables, several massive and evil-smelling armchairs and a menagerie of stuffed carnivores and raptors each of which seemed to have been caught by the taxidermist at the very moment of predation. An admixture of damp logs and peat smouldered fitfully in the cavernous hearth. While we applied ourselves to the brandy Raeburn told us the depressing history which now follows, illustrating his narrative with the help of the large panorama and a scale model of the mountain in "papier-mache".

'Two days ago Norman set off to climb the Tower Ridge,' pointing to the largest and most repulsive of the precipices, 'with a Mr Willoughby - an acquaintance of his from the Foreign Office. It was a fine day but they were held up by the heavy accumulations of ice on the Ridge. At the Great Tower, the crucial part of their climb, Mr Willoughby fell, the rope parted and he plunged to his death in Observatory Gully below. Norman continued to climb with great difficulty to the summit. There he enlisted the aid of a student from Edinburgh, one James Moffat, who was temporarily in charge of the summit meteorological observatory. The two men descended to the Halfway Observatory where Norman recuperated while Moffat continued to fetch the police and a party of Club members attending the Meet here, myself included. By first light we had reached the body. There was of course no hope that he would be alive. However, worse was to follow. Examination of the rope showed that it had been partially cut through by some sharp instrument some six feet from Willoughby's waist. The suspicions of the police immediately fell on poor Norman. The question naturally arose why Willoughby would not have noticed this defect of the rope. Whereupon someone remarked that he was very short-sighted. Despite careful searches, no trace of his eyeglasses was found. However, while returning with the corpse, the police searched the Halfway Observatory and discovered the eyeglasses there together with a small patent pocket knife. Norman was immediately taken into custody. The theory of the police is that Norman contrived to dislodge and remove Willoughby's eyeglasses somewhere on the Ridge, then sabotaged his end of the rope. On the Great Tower there is a steep part where Willoughby would inevitably have put his full weight on the rope.' Raeburn gestured in an unmistakable way to indicate the result of this misadventure and went on. 'At the moment they are seeking the motive in collaboration with Scotland Yard in London. I surmise that, since Willoughby was employed as a secret agent in the Foreign Office, they are looking for some connection between his security activities and Norman's secret work on disabling gases.'

At the conclusion of this dismal speech Holmes congratulated Raeburn on his orderly presentation of the facts and lay back in his armchair, sunk in thought. In the ensuing half-hour he asked Raeburn only two questions. The first was to ascertain whether there were any footprints in the snow around the body when the rescue party arrived. Raeburn had been first on the scene and was adamant that there had been none. The second question concerned the location of the village fruit shop. As we had just consumed a vast dish of brandied plums I could make no sense of this at all. Holmes then left us to make some enquiries in the village. Raeburn had been sent to the police station to arrange an interview with the prisoner for six o'clock, so I had leisure to turn over the facts of the case in my mind. It seemed to me that the case was practically hopeless. If Holmes' cousin had not cut the rope, then who else could have possibly done so? Willoughby? Only if we suppose that he committed suicide in this horrible manner with the purpose of implicating his companion in a murder charge! Surely a fantastic notion! Moreover, how could he deposit the eyeglasses in the Halfway Observatory? So I ruled out Willoughby. It did not seem possible that some third person could have lain concealed on the mountain to spring out with his knife at the ready at the critical moment. And then again there was the curious and damning circumstance of the misplaced spectacles. Since no footprints were found beside the body, this imaginary assailant must have found time to whisk Willoughby's spectacles from his nose before severing the rope and then, somehow on the following morning have left knife and spectacles in the Halfway Observatory. Incredible as it might be, this seemed to me to be the only conceivable solution to the case. No doubt we should have to examine the ground tomorrow for traces that might favour this outlandish hypothesis. I gazed at the panorama before me and gave a shudder at the prospect, I was still transfixed in the same posture when Holmes returned, slapping his arms to restore the circulation.

'Well, Watson, I imagine you have solved the case. Everything you require is in front of you! You know my methods well enough to settle such a simple problem, I'm sure.'

Staring dully at my friend I told him my thoughts about the case.

'Excellent, Watson, excellent!' he cried. 'But if there is no third man, what then?'

'Then the only person who could have cut the ropes is your cousin and he is doomed, Holmes. He cannot escape the gallows.'

'Precisely, Watson, the only person who could have done it would then be Norman and of course we assume that he did not. Surely that suggests a conclusion? No?' I shook my head in bewilderment. 'Well, we shall find out soon enough tomorrow. Let us hope that it does not snow before we reach the vital spot.'

When Raeburn had also returned we took afternoon tea and then set out for the police station. Sergeant McDonald welcomed us warmly, remarking that he was himself a student of Holmes' methods, and showed us into the interview room. Holmes' cousin bore an extraordinary resemblance to my friend, with the same finely-cut features and air of asceticism very apparent. After some preliminary remarks of a personal nature they fell to discussing the case. I will mention here only those parts of their conversation which add to Raeburn's narrative.

Holmes had just asked for a description of the crucial section of the route, the direct ascent of the Great Tower.

'Well, Sherlock,' said the prisoner, 'the difficulties began above a small platform some sixty feet below the summit of the Tower. I was able with the assistance of footholds on Willoughby's shoulder and on his ice-axe, which he had jammed in a crack at arm's length, to reach good handholds and pull myself onto easier ground*. After this, the angle and the difficulties decreased towards the summit of the Tower. Then I called out to Willoughby and took the strain on the rope. You see, he could not follow without the assistance of the rope. At this point I heard a cry from below and the rope went slack in my hands.' On saying this, he plunged his head on his hands. 'I shall never forget his scream of horror as he plummeted to his death on the rocks below. It was ghastly, inhuman.'

---

* Evidently the same route as that later followed by Parker & Inglis Clark (see S.M.C.J., 1897,iv,222).

After a brief interval Holmes asked, 'Did you see anything of this, Norman? Did you notice anything unusual whatever at the time of the accident?'

'No, nothing. I could not see Willoughby because of the convex curve of the ridge, nor even the place where he landed.'

'And how do you account for the discovery of Willoughby's eyeglasses and the penknife at the Halfway Observatory?'

'I cannot account for the spectacles at all. He was wearing them when I last saw him below the Tower. As for the knife, it is mine. I always carry a pocket knife while climbing they are often useful. I'm afraid I have given you a hopeless task, Sherlock. The evidence against me is too strong.'

'Nonsense, Norman!' Holmes retorted. 'I understand everything about this case except the motive. Your next night in this miserable gaol will be your last. Count upon it.'

At this display of confidence the prisoner visibly brightened and we left a much happier man behind us as we trundled back to the hotel in our dogcart. However, as I looked up at the great dark mass of the mountain I could think only of the rigours of the morrow. I could not recall a stronger feeling of apprehension since my time of service in Afghanistan. On that appalling march to Quetta each sunset had brought the same feeling of boneless dread as the mountains darkened around us and the night filled with the alien cries of the pursuing Afghanis as they settled round their campfires.

In the morning we were roused at six sharp and had soon joined Raeburn in the breakfast room. I had little appetite for the greasy slabs of bacon which were put before us. Holmes, though normally a late riser, seemed fully alert.

'What a splendid day it is, Watson,' he ejaculated. 'We shall soon discover whether these small Scottish hills can rival the Alps for beauty, as my cousin would have it.'

Indeed, my spirits lifted a little when I saw the dawn striking the hills on the other side of the 'loch' with tints of rose and purple. And I felt more confident when we assembled in the stable yard. Raeburn and Holmes cut most impressive figures in their hard black Norfolks, heavily nailed boots and murderous pickaxes, girt about with ropes and rucksacks. I hoped that I did not disgrace them with the newness of my own equipment. The cloth of my suit was so stiff and rough, the boots so hard and heavy, the axe so alarmingly sharp that it was only with difficulty and some considerable trepidation that I was able to move at all. However, I managed to mount my pony without mishap and soon we were off, plodding through the village and then along a fairly decent track slanting up the flank of the mountain. At the Halfway Observatory we stopped for a pull at our flasks and a bite of breakfast, then continued past a frozen 'loch' and over some hard snow patches which the ponies negotiated with complete indifference. Eventually we halted at the edge of an abyss and dismounted. Raeburn instructed the groom to return with the ponies to the Observatory and to wait for us there, then set off over the edge of the abyss, with Holmes and myself hard on his heels. Although the ground dropped with alarming steepness, the rescue party of two days ago had cut out large steps in the snow and so we were able to descend without much difficulty. We then began a long level traverse below appalling black cliffs festooned with frozen waterfalls and colossal stalactites of ice. At about ten o'clock we reached the base of the 'glen' at a point where a side valley opened out to the south. The precipice had assumed the hideous appearance of the panorama in the hotel lounge. Our climb began here in earnest. We proceeded up an extremely stiff slope of snow passing the base of the so-called 'Tower Ridge' on its left hand side. I found it very tough going and on several occasions appealed to Raeburn and Holmes for some respite. Holmes offered me a handful of coca leaves to chew (Raeburn and he had been munching them from the outset) but I thought it a disgusting and unhealthy practice and declined *. After an hour of this purgatory we reached an area heavily marked by footprints surrounding a depression in which I remarked the presence of what were undoubtedly blood-stains. Holmes made us stay back while he scurried about, comparing footprints with drawings he had obtained from Sergeant McDonald. Raeburn commented on the agility with which my friend moved about on the steep snow, using his pickaxe purely for balance and rolling his ankles over so that all of his bootnails were always dug into the snowcrust.

'Ah, yes,' said Holmes abstractedly, 'I learned this method from a Swiss colleague of mine, Monsieur Phildius of Geneva. I shall write a letter of introduction for you so that you may study with him on your next visit to the Alps †'

Suddenly Holmes pointed to the ground and cried out, 'Raeburn! What do you make of these marks?'

We moved up and peered at a spot close to the bloody hollow. I could see two marks each shaped like an X with deeper indentations at the extremities of the cross-pieces and about four or fives inches across.

'Well, sir,' said Raeburn slowly, 'that's very strange indeed. They look like these new-fangled instep climbing-irons that Eckenstein has been trying out. Perhaps his friend Crowley wore them - he was with the party - but it's odd that we didn't see them lower down. They may have been obliterated by other tracks, or perhaps he wore them only for this last steep section. After all, most or our members regard their use as illegitimate.'

'I see,' said Holmes. 'Then we shall discuss the matter with Mr Crowley at the hotel. In the meantime we must record the marks for I suspect that they may be vital evidence.'

To my astonishment, Holmes rummaged in his rucksack and withdrew a foot rule and a small camera.

'I borrowed this from Dr Inglis Clark at the hotel,' he explained. 'He is an electrochemist as well as a mountain-climber. He was given this pocket camera by the

---

* The use of coca leaves by Victorian walkers has been explored in a recent issue of the 'Journal' (see S.M.J.C.,1971,xxx, 385). Raeburn's ready adoption of the habit suggests that the practice was not unknown amongst the early Club members.

† Holmes was apparently as good as his word (see Raeburn's 'A Scottish Ice Climb' in S.M.C.J.,1907,ix,153).

famous photographer Stieglitz. A wonderful addition to the armoury of the consulting detective, don't you think? Now, Raeburn, we must proceed to the scene of the accident. How shall we do that?'

Raeburn unwound a rope and tied one end onto his waist, myself in the middle and the other end to Holmes. Then he began to cut a ladder of steps up the steep snow above us. We continued in this way until the crags began to close around us, whereupon we embarked upon a tiny ledge leading onto and across the right-hand crag. This was a most ticklish manoeuvre and only one of us could move with safety at a time. I will spare you a description of the horrors of this passage. Suffice it to say that it surpassed in awfulness the traverse of the ledge above the Reichenbach Falls which I made on that fateful day when Moriarty fell to his death. Eventually we stood poised on the crest of the Tower Ridge at a small uncomfortable platform. Immediately above us the ridge reared up perpendicularly. I recognised it as the last bastion of what Raeburn had called the Great Tower.

'This is the exact spot where Willoughby fell?' asked Holmes.

"Well, perhaps a few feet higher,' said Raeburn. 'He began to climb from this ledge and we may suppose that he fell almost as soon as his weight came on the rope.'

Holmes began to make a minute examination of the traces in the scraps of snow and ice adhering to the backbone of the ridge. After a moment he cried out in evident satisfaction and turned to face me. 'Now, Watson, I have established to my satisfaction that no third person was here. There is no place where he could have been concealed save on the ledge by which we arrived and that bore no traces of previous visitors. Do you recall your own analysis? If the rope was not cut by Norman or Willoughby, then someone else must have cut it. But there are no traces of any third individual. Willoughby and my cousin are eliminated from consideration, the former because of the strange migration of the eyeglasses, the latter by hypothesis. What can we now conclude? Recall my maxim: when you have eliminated the impossible, whatever remains, however improbable, must be true.'

I could think of nothing except the inane remark that the deed must have been done by a person who left no traces.

'Outstanding, Watson,' he cried. 'And so?'

But here Raeburn stepped in, 'By a bird!' he exclaimed. 'Perhaps a large macaw or a Philippine Monkey-eating Eagle?'

'Precisely so,' said Holmes, somewhat discomfited - or so it seemed to me. 'My own preference is for the Hyacinthine Macaw of Brazil, "Anodorhynchus hyacinthus". But you know your birds uncommonly well, Raeburn! Philippine Monkey-eating Eagle indeed! I had not thought of that. You see, Watson, the hypothesis of a large and powerful bird explains everything. It swoops from its lair, bites through the rope - a trifle to such a brute descends to the corpse and returns with the spectacles to its trainer. Moreover, the assumption that it was a macaw is favoured by the hideous screech which so affected my cousin and by the curious traces which I photographed. Not instep climbing irons, but the characteristic talon-print of a large psittaciform! And, look here!' Holmes pointed to a group of four tiny punctures in a patch of snow. 'Here once again is the bird's spoor!'

'But who is the trainer and why did he do it, Holmes?' I expostulated.

'I think we shall find the answers to these questions by asking Mr Moffat in the summit Observatory, Watson. Let us be off now, Raeburn. The day is wasting!'

We retraced our steps along the ledge and after a tiring climb up a steep funnel of snow broke through a cornice formed by action of the wind to reach the final bare slopes of the mountain. The Observatory, a squat structure draped in frozen crystals of fog and of a very sinister appearance, crouched beside the summit. Holmes pushed in the outer door and lit a small paraffin lamp hanging on the inner door. We removed our boots, opened the inner door and climbed down a ladder into the Observatory. We found ourselves in a sparsely furnished room containing a small library and a collection of curious scientific instruments. Raeburn and I were content to sit while Holmes searched the building with customary meticulousness. It was plain that Moffat was no longer resident. When Holmes had concluded his researches he seemed rather disappointed.

'Moffat is undoubtedly our man, gentlemen. My enquiries in the village revealed that on his journey here his luggage contained a large wooden crate which surely concealed the wretched bird, drugged I suppose, and that throughout his stay here he has bought uncommonly large quantities of fruit - its natural diet. The needs of the Philippine Eagle would have been somewhat harder to supply, Raeburn! But there is no trace of the animal here; no feathers, no droppings, nothing. Moffat has been most admirably thorough. We must have physical evidence of the bird to convince the police.'

'Perhaps he threw such things away along with the ordinary rubbish,' remarked Raeburn. 'I will show you where the rubbish is usually deposited.'

We resumed our boots and followed Raeburn out onto the summit. He led us to a point on the cliff-edge which protruded to the north and pointed down into a deep and narrow chasm. My stomach lurched at the sight of it. An apparently perpendicular snow funnel, topped by an enormous cornice led down to a slight bay before plunging downwards once more in the form of a frozen blue waterfall. In the bay we could see a smudge of colour where the rubbish had accumulated.

'Gardyloo Gully. It is named after the old Edinburgh street cry which accompanied the throwing of rubbish from high windows,' explained Raeburn.

'There is nothing else for it,' said Holmes. 'We must investigate these traces.'

With a heavy heart I paid out rope as Raeburn kicked and hacked his way down through the cornice. Despite all the trials of the day I had borne up well, so well that I had surprised even myself. However, I had thought our efforts to be at an end and this unexpected further encounter with the precipice quite unmanned me. I begged Holmes to be left behind, but to no avail.

'No, Watson, you must remain with us. You are safer on the precipice with us than wandering alone on the summit. I dare not leave you.'

I was so dispirited that I failed to react to the aspersion of incompetence cast by this belittling remark. I abandoned myself to my fate and thrust myself over the edge of the abyss enjoining Holmes to keep the rope taut. Remarkably, I did not fall. I kept my eyes firmly fixed on the next step downwards and dug my pickaxe deeply into the snow. Soon I had joined Raeburn just above the slight hollow where the rubbish lay and could watch Holmes' fearless descent of the funnel with astonishment. On the final manoeuvre to gain the hollow Raeburn proceeded very cautiously, prodding the snow ahead of him with his axe. 'This hollow is the outlet of an ice cave,' he explained, 'and we must take care that we do not fall through.' Just before reaching the base of the hollow his axe passed easily through and in a moment he had excavated a circular aperture something like a London manhole. We moved gingerly around this and began to examine the pile of rubbish. It was immediately plain that our search was ended. On top of the pile lay the wreckage of the crate and underneath was the body of the bird, a formidable beast about a yard in length from its poll to the tip of its tail. Holmes seized it to place it in his rucksack and then gave a cry of surprise. Pinned to the breast of the bird was an oilskin packet. The bird once safely stowed away, he carefully opened the packet. It contained a single sheet of paper addressed to Mr Sherlock Holmes and bearing the following sensational message;

'I, James Moriarty, known to you as James Moffat, the son of Professor James Moriarty whom you foully murdered, have taken my revenge upon you. Your cousin Norman will be hanged for murder. Your brother Mycroft will be disgraced and barred from public office. Knowing that your infernal meddling would bring you here, I have mined the cornice of the Gully. You and your wretched accomplice will shortly be crushed beneath tons of snow. A fitting irony that your cleverness should be instrumental in your death! Hail and farewell!'

'So, gentlemen,' said Holmes, 'now we have the motive. I had forgotten Moriarty's spawn.'

He then looked up to the edge of the precipice. I followed his gaze. On the very point where we had stood some minutes before we could see the figure of our executioner, observing us in perfect stillness and silence as if we were already dead. This ghoulish apparition was rendered still more frightful by the circumstance that the face was almost completely covered with a black Balaclava helmet and a smoked-glass visor, recalling a mediaeval headsman. After a while the figure stirred, raised its arm slowly in salute and disappeared.

For the second time that day we had cause to be impressed by Raeburn's presence of mind. Immediately, he seized hold of Holmes, pushed him through the manhole and lowered him into the cave by using his firmly-embedded axe as a pulley. When the rope slackened I was dispatched into the bowels of the mountain with equal lack of ceremony. The cave was illuminated by faint and eerie blue light transmitted through the waterfall. As I fell beside Holmes in the soft snow there was a tremendous explosion from above whereupon Raeburn leapt down through the hole to lie at our feet. The din of the explosion was followed by an ear-shattering rumble as huge blocks of snow cascaded about our prison, blocking the entrance hole and extinguishing the feeble supply of light. The rumbling continued for what seemed like several minutes, shaking the entire mountain to its foundations. Finally, it stopped. Holmes was the first to recover from the shock of this terrific avalanche. His gropings produced a small pocket lantern from the rucksack and when this was lit we could take stock of our situation. Poor Raeburn was our first concern. However, the man was evidently constructed of iron. Thanks to the softness of the snow here, his fall of some forty feet had only winded him and he was soon on his feet again. It was evidently impossible for us to escape upwards. The hollow would be filled with heavy debris. Our only chance was to cut through the waterfall at its steepest section, that being both the thinnest part and most likely to be free of accumulations of snow. We took turns to hack at the ice with our axes at arms' length above our heads - an unbelievably exhausting business. But everything has an end and after an hour we reached snow and were able to push an axe-handle through to the outside world and thus ensure our supply of air. We ate a little and emptied our flasks. With the aid of shoulders and the rope we soon found ourselves perched above the wreckage of the avalanche which stretched far down the mountain towards and beyond the place where Willoughby's body had lain. It was now going dark and we wasted no time in our descent *. However, seven o'clock came and went before we reached the Halfway Observatory and were able to rest — if that is the word — on the broad back of our Highland 'garrons'.

At Fort William we presented our evidence to Sergeant McDonald who took immediate steps to secure the prisoner's release. I was so tired that at dinner I could hardly raise my fork to my lips and, were it not for the need to maintain certain standards, I would have eaten from my plate like a dog. My final thought before I sunk in deep slumber in my unheated bed was that of all the cases on which I had accompanied Sherlock Holmes, none had exacted such a heavy toll of strength and spirit as this extraordinary case of the Secret Agent, the Observatory and the trained Parrot†.

Two weeks later Holmes and I were seated by the fire admiring the beautiful stuffed Hyacinthine Macaw which the police had brought round that morning, when the boy entered with the evening paper. Holmes, as always, began to read it from cover to cover. I could see that an item on the home news page had caught his attention.

'Watson, Justice has been done. Most apposite justice. Moreover, we should have anticipated this turn of events.'

---

*As this descent of the gully is earlier than that of Hastings and Haskett Smith (1897) it is clear that current guidebooks stand in need of revision. Moreover, Raeburn's exact knowledge of the gully's topography suggests that this was not his first descent (or ascent).

† I think that this case must be identical with the one referred to by Watson in 'The Veiled Lodger' as the case of the Politician, the Lighthouse and the Trained Cormorant. The disparity may be due to the well-known deficiencies of Watson's memory or to deliberate concealment. After all the Cormorant - a bird of invincible stupidity - would be anything but an apt pupil.

He handed the paper to me. The item read as follows:

'*UNUSUAL DEATH IN EDINBURGH The death has occurred in Edinburgh Royal Infirmary of James Moriarty, alias Moffat, a student of zoology at the University and wanted by the police in connection with a recent fatal accident in the Highlands. Moriarty died as a result of respiratory complications following contraction of 'psittacosis', the highly infectious disease transmitted by tropical parrots......*'

'Indeed Holmes, he deserved no better fate. But how could we have guessed?'

'The smoked-glass visor that he wore, Watson, and the black helmet. It was not a bright day, nor painfully cold. He had photophobia, which — according to Dr - - - -, your erstwhile colleague — is a common and distinctive symptom of the disease.'

Holmes permitted himself the merest suggestion of a smile, 'Elementary, Watson, I should have thought.'

ON THE TOWER, BEN NEVIS OBSERVATORY
BREAKING THE ICE OFF THE ROBINSON ANEMOMETER

THIRTY HOURS ON BEN NEVIS
Vol. X (1908)   by Charles Inglis Clark

This tale describes mistakes and misjudgements which were often to be repeated on
Ben Nevis. Perhaps the most impressive aspect of the adventure was the way this party
coped with the results and emerged unscathed.

Macintyre, Goodeve, and I found ourselves the sole occupants of the Alexandra Hotel on
Friday evening, 27th December, being the first arrivals of the Club at the New Year Meet.
Macintyre had been up to the Allt a Mhuillinn that day prospecting, and reported the
rocks in bad condition, being plastered with snow. The weather being fairly good and
settled, it was planned to make an early start and attempt something difficult next day on
the "Ben." Leaving Fort William at 6.45 on Saturday morning in the best of spirits, we felt
that we had the exclusive use of Ben Nevis. This was due to the absence of the Hon.
Secretary and other habitués of the Ben, who might forbid an attempt at anything difficult
under the prevailing conditions. It was an exhilarating morning, the keen frosty air causing
a most delightful sensation on the face, especially refreshing after so many months of town
life.

At the first blush of daylight, Stob Ban proudly pushed its snowy summit through its
nightcap of mist, and saluted us in welcome after many years' absence. Good time was
made up the footpath and round to the Lunching Stone, which we reached at nine
o'clock. Both Goodeve and I, although not having had a climb since August, felt
extremely fit after a good season's dances and other energetic amusements. At the
Lunching Stone, after the customary second breakfast, votes were taken regarding what
was to be attacked that day. It was decided to make for the Tower Ridge, as not one of us
had climbed it, and all were desirous of doing so. To our eyes, the Tower Ridge did not
seem to carry so much snow as the North-East Buttress, but I afterwards learnt that the
latter was in better condition. We believed that we could find the ledge to avoid the
Tower, should we be in difficulties, but, as the sequel will show, we failed when the
necessity arose.

These reasons may partly neutralise the reader's idea that we were all absolutely mad,
when we started on the climb without any of the party having previous knowledge of the
Ridge.

Whilst we were cutting steps up the steep snow slope which leads to the bottom of the
couloir between Douglas' Boulder and the Ridge proper, an amusing incident occurred.
Goodeve and I had been having a rather heated discussion on the relative advantages of
his woollen helmet and a leather motor cap which I wore. I was just proclaiming that its
chief advantage lay in the fact that it never blew off, when a fierce blast of wind tore it
from my head, and whirled it high up in the air. We gave up all hope of ever seeing it again
and climbed up the slope. Five minutes later Goodeve gave a shout, and I saw a black

object swirling round his head, and supposed it to be a buzzard or some other bird. He then struck and apparently killed it with his ice-axe. To my great surprise he handed back my truant motor cap. A halt was now made to put on warm clothes and gloves, and rope up. Although we had both an 80 and a 60-foot rope, we stupidly put on the latter, which is rather cramped for a party of three. The cold afterwards was so intense that we did not change the rope during the whole climb, and in consequence much valuable time was lost owing to being constantly hindered by a short rope.

About ten o'clock the party started the climb in earnest. Goodeve led up the gully between the western side of the Tower Ridge and Douglas' Boulder. I followed second, and Macintyre brought up the rear, and this order was always maintained. As the snow was hard and icy, this meant that our leader was continuously cutting steps for thirteen hours, with no relief whatever. I have heard of people swinging Indian clubs for twelve hours at a stretch, but in my opinion, they should take a back place after this feat of endurance. The Gap between the Ridge and the Boulder was reached without serious difficulty, but soon afterwards we were confronted with an almost vertical face of rock above us, shaped somewhat like a mantelpiece. Owing to all the holds being glazed with ice, and having to be cut out, a long time was taken in attempting to force a way up the centre and at both sides. This proved unsuccessful at first, and from the last point reached, Goodeve was lowered down to the right (west); he then made his way along a narrow ledge. After disappearing round the corner, he was stopped by an icy chimney about 30 feet high. A long time was spent cutting steps up the face of this, but, as the second man had no first-class hitch, and there being a big drop below, it was decided to be too unsafe to persevere.

A return was now made to the mantelpiece mentioned before, and after the leader made use of my cranium as a foothold, he managed it in the centre, traversing up to the right by a narrow sloping ledge. There was then a very sensational corner where one could only get foothold on a small ledge which was slippery with ice. While standing on this, the body had to be swung out and round the corner. So far we had all enjoyed the climb immensely, as it was of a first-class order, our only anxiety being regarding time, mid-day was now past. A narrow arete was cut up to the foot of the Little Tower. This arete, which is fairly wide in summer, was not more than two feet broad, owing to the action of the wind on the snow. It was a highly sensational passage, as there was a drop of several hundred feet on one side, and violent gusts of wind threatened to blow one over.

Being now confronted with the Little Tower, we had a consultation how best to surmount it. Macintyre thought that the route led up on the eastern side, while Goodeve and I imagined that the west was the only possible way. As the "ayes" had it (unfortunately as it turned out), we decided to try it on the right. I let Goodeve out on the rope round a narrow ledge on the right, and he reported that it might go. After some considerable difficulty, a way was forced up a narrow chimney which had a long slab in it. A tiny crack in this afforded a small finger-grip, which was the only available handhold. Without this, the pitch would have been impossible. Once again, I had ample time to gauge the leader's weight accurately, and it seemed to me that the Club song might well have an additional verse appropriate for such occasions. The refrain, "Oh, my big hobnailers!" would bring back the joyous memories of crushed-in shoulder blades and aching cranium, N.B. - Club poets please take note.

At last, after much cutting of steps, and after great care had been taken, the foot of the Tower was reached by a snow arete. We were dismayed to find that darkness was rapidly setting in, it being now about four o'clock. Another consultation was held, and in consideration of the late hour, we decided to avoid the Tower if possible, and to make the straightest possible line for that dinner waiting us at 7.30 p.m., at the Alexandra. Easy as it is to suggest such a course of proceeding, we found it a most difficult one to carry out. We had a hazy impression that an easy ledge ran round the west side, enabling one to reach the Gap, without climbing the Tower itself. Certainly, when we looked to the east, there seemed no feasible ledge, as all the rocks were plastered with ice. Acting on this impression and seeing a way which looked possible in the dim twilight, we went along a snowy platform on the western side of the Tower, and encountered occasional rocky pitches which had to be avoided. As we progressed, our route became more difficult. Often much valuable time was wasted owing to our becoming landed in cul-de-sacs which from a distance looked feasible in the semi-darkness. A slight haze also complicated matters, causing extraordinary optical illusions. One might see perhaps a snowy ledge offering tempting foothold. On cautiously stretching out the ice-axe to test its strength, one found a yawning chasm, the patch of snow being in reality, hundreds of feet below. After a couple of hours of this groping in the darkness, we imagined that at last we were secure. Stretching far below, there seemed to be a splendid snow gully to descend, which we could follow with our eyes about half way down to the Coire na Ciste. The first few hundred feet were easily descended, the end men of the rope alternately anchoring and glissading down. Presently, however, the slope became steeper and steeper, until at last we were cautiously cutting steps down very steep snow. Our hopes were doomed to disappointment as an almost perpendicular icefall was encountered. We lowered Macintyre down this for twelve feet, and there he found a small standing space of about three feet. I then went down, cutting large steps for the last man. As this pitch was slightly overhanging at the centre, the problem was, how the last man was to get down. Macintyre and I anchored securely, so that in the event of a slip, Goodeve would not fall very far. He descended with great care, and safely arrived at our platform. Twenty feet lower, we encountered a terrible-looking icefall which was absolutely impossible, having a tremendous overhang. We now realised that we were in the Tower Gap Chimney, and that this icefall was the waterfall described on page 205, Vol. VII. of the Journal, in the account of the original ascent by Glover and Clark.

In this predicament, we had nothing for it but to climb up to the Ridge once again.

To do this, we ascended the steep rocks on our right hand side of the Tower Gap Chimney, keeping practically parallel to it. This part of our route is not shown in the sketch, being lower down in the chimney.

The going was not so fast as earlier in the day, the party being fairly exhausted. After many difficult pitches, icy chimneys, and what not, we arrived about eight o'clock at the same level which we had left with buoyant spirits several hours previous, but this time on the opposite side of the Chimney.

Hitherto, a moderate amount of light had been obtained from the stars, but owing to intervening clouds, we could now see nothing clearly. We then traversed along the west side of the Tower Ridge, keeping under the vertical rocks, and above the icefalls which are found on that side, steering for a snowy ledge which appeared to be the only way by which we could progress. We took some food here, being the second meal that day, as we had never found any suitable place for food. As it was, we had to rope to our ice-axes dug in the snow, to prevent ourselves from slipping.

In the far distance, the lights of Banavie and Corpach twinkled mockingly at us, looking so near, but alas! so far. I experienced a most curious optical illusion, when first I saw the cornice at the summit of the Ben. To my tired eyes, it seemed to be about a rope's length above Goodeve, with an easy snow slope leading up to it. Accordingly, I shouted to him to bring me up on the rope to where he stood, so that I could be of assistance with a back to surmount the cornice. Much to my surprise, although we climbed steadily for half-an-hour, we never came any nearer. In reality, it was still far above our heads with much more formidable ojects to traverse than easy snow slopes. Owing to the darkness, I have no very clear recollections of what difficulties we encountered, except one or two pitches which can never be blotted out of one's memory. At one place, after cutting up an exceptionally steep slope, we were faced by a rocky pitch which was impossible. So steep was this slope, that one looked almost vertically down on the head of the man below. There was a ridge of icy rock on our right hand side, and this had to be traversed. For the first three feet there were some fairly good holds, but after that a distance of about ten feet had to be done practically by friction alone. The rock was deeply undercut at the level of the feet, and one had to take a tremendous stride on to a slippery surface. Holding on with the left hand, the leader had to lean over and cut steps with the right, and then pull himself slowly across by means of a very small finger-grip. We all took a sigh of relief when the party got safely across. An absolutely new route was now made to the cornice at the summit. In daylight, and with plenty of time, one might not have attempted it, but in our case, we either had to go on or else be frozen to death. A rib of rock rose above us, perhaps twenty feet in height and nearly perpendicular. As the ice slope here was almost vertical, it would have been impossible to have made progress, but for the friendly help of this finger of rock. Just in the corner, between it and the ice, there was a little hard snow, and by means of this, the leader was able to worm his way up to a small ice arete, which connected the top of the rock and the ice slope. When it came to my turn, I found the snow practically all kicked away, and I could not have managed the pitch but for the friendly assistance of the rope. As my frantic struggles had effectually removed every trace

19. *The Mitre Ridge of Beinn a' Bhuird; the upper towers seen from the west*

20. *The first pitch of the Direct Route on the Mitre Ridge*

21. Builders at the CIC Hut in 1928

22. An early party of visitors to the CIC Hut in 1929

23. The interior of the CIC Hut

24. Robert Elton, the first custodian and later President of the Club with the 50th Anniversary Plaque, April 1979

25. The CIC Hut

of snow for the last man to get foothold on, there was nothing for it but to lift him bodily by the rope. Goodeve and I sat stridelegs on the ice-arete before mentioned, and at a shout from below, with all the speed of our tired muscles would allow, brought Macintyre up, struggling and kicking like a fish (if I may be permitted the simile). Half-an-hour of step-cutting up a terribly steep ice-slope brought us to the cornice.

At 4 a.m., on Sunday morning, the Secretary's rescue party lowered a lantern over the cornice at the place we cut up, and reported that it did not touch the slope below for an almost incredible distance. So steep was it, that they would not have believed it possible for any party to have climbed it in safety, but for our tell-tale footsteps, and the groove made by the rope on the edge of the cornice.

When I stood vertically in my steps on the slope leading up to the cornice, my face was only a few inches from the ice, so that this gives an unexaggerated idea of its steepness. Happily, the cornice proved not very difficult, and soon after midnight we were all merrily shaking hands at the top of the Tower Ridge. I can honestly say, that during the whole climb, not a single slip of the foot was made by any of the party, owing to the excessive care which we all exercised. On account of the hard state of the snow, it always took a considerable time to get the ice-axe driven right up to the head, and as there were always two of the party thus hitched, this may partly account for the long time taken. We were fortunate as regards weather conditions, as there was not a very high wind, and as we usually were free from mist. As it was, the cold was terrible, both Goodeve and Macintyre receiving frost-bites on their hands and fingers, so that slightly more cold would have spelled disaster to us. In every way we congratulated ourselves as being exceptionally lucky in getting off as we did. Our only anxiety now was for the other members of the Scottish Mountaineering Club, who would have grave doubts of our safety, and who might be organising search parties at the Alexandra. Owing to the Observatory being closed, we were unable to send a message to Fort William to relieve their anxious minds. As a strong gale was blowing on the plateau, we were unable to get a light to take compass readings, and in consequence, after some wandering in the mist, we descended the wrong side of the mountain, having lost sight of the posts which mark the footpath. After cautiously descending for a considerable distance, we found ourselves on very treacherous snow, where steps had to be cut for many hundred feet. We had hopes, however, that we would strike the path, as we did not then know how far we were out in our bearings. On descending a very treacherous pitch, Macintyre slipped his foot, and this gave the rope a pull. Goodeve's hitch stood our combined jerk for a second, and then gave, being unable to stand the strain of two men. At the next instant, both Macintyre and I managed to stop ourselves, but not without previously causing Goodeve to slide down the snow. Unfortunately he struck his head against a rock and received a bad cut. Owing to his exceptionally strong constitution, after a few minutes, he was the most active member of the party.

It was now about 4 a.m. on Sunday morning, and the party being thoroughly tired out, very slow progress was made. Presently, as light increased, we recognised Scuir a Mhaim directly opposite us, and then knew which direction to take. Tracks were made for the col between Carn Dearg (above Polldubh) and the western side of Ben Nevis. Whilst resting here about nine o'clock on Sunday morning we saw an active figure bounding down to us at a very rapid pace. From his speed, we surmised it could be none other than Raeburn, and a few minutes later he was heartily shaking hands all round, acting the kind Samaritan with sandwiches and other dainties. He told us that he was in one of the many search parties which had been scouring Ben Nevis practically all night. Under his kind and able guidance, we were piloted through the difficult and narrow gorge which leads down into Glen Nevis, and after an easy walk we reached Fort William about one o'clock on Sunday afternoon.

I take this opportunity to cordially thank, in the name of the party, all those members who so willingly sacrificed their own arrangements, and gave up their sleep to searching the Ben.

EXPOSTULATION WITH CRUACHAN
Vol VI (1900)   W.P. Ker

Tune: Into thir dark and drublie dayis

OF Crechanben the crewilté,   Quhair is thy lown illuminat air,
The driftis dreich, the hichtis hie,   Thy fre fassoun, thy foirheid fair?
It sair wald tene my tong to tell;   Quheir is thy peirles pulchritude?
Quha suld reherss thy painis fell   Quhy stayis thou nocht as anis thou stude,
Forgaitheris with the frenesie.   Quhy girnis and greitis thou evirmair?

With fensom feiris thou art forfairn,   Return agane fra drowpand dule!
Ay yowland lyk and busteous bairn;   Restoir thy pure wayfarand fule,
With mauchie mistis thy mirth is marrit,   And lat him se thee quhair thou smylis,
With skowland skyis the spreit is skarrit,   With Mul, Arane, and the Owt-Ylis,
And seitis ar cauld upon thy cairn.   Into the lufsom licht of Yule

                                                                Quod KER

THE MIDDLE PERIOD

Mountaineering in Scotland suffered like other activities from the disruption and casualty toll of the 1914-1918 War. This, together with a succession of poor snow winters meant the SMC Journal lost some of its sparkle until the 1930's when Scottish climbing was to revive in new style.

THE RAIN OF PEACE
Vol. XV (1918)
by G.E. Howard

This was written in the dark days of the 1914-18 War

All day long the rain has teemed down on the grey roofs of the factory; all day the wind has moaned. Muddy roads, vistas of murky east London streets, a sodden feeling of dirt and endless work, and over all the dull pall of war, doubly drab on this drab day.

And yet when one thinks of other drab days, of rain to which this is but a faint dew, and of great winds roaring among the glens, one glories in the memory. Indeed it is just those memories which keep one alive and working nowadays - magic memories of the hills.

I remember a day from Kingshouse: a great hurtling wind, an endless roar of rain. We packed into a wagonette and drove to the head of Loch Etive. We had planned an attack on Ben Starav, but nothing would go in such a gale, and rumour had it that the bridges on the south-east side of the loch were washed away. So we set outselves against the wind and walked to Bonawe Ferry. The spume on the loch was whirled hundreds of feet up, and here and there a gleam of sun turned it into fugitive rainbows. The ferryman hesitated to cross in such a sea, but we managed it.

Another wild day saw Unna and me marching from Tyndrum to Ardlui over Ben Lui. It was bitterly cold, and the mountain was a sheet of ice. After a while even crampons would not go, and we had to traverse and walk up the shoulder. The gale was blowing great guns, and you could not see a yard for snow, but we ran down the south-west ridge, just keeping the cornice in sight on our left, till we lost ourselves on that God-forsaken moor below. It is a place of big "shell-holes," now full of snow and water, and we floundered on by compass, praying that we might strike Glen Falloch and not Glen Fyne. After two hours we looked down into a green valley. Where was the railway? Not a sign of it! Therefore it could not be Falloch. However, we slithered down and suddenly saw a deep cutting and the road. We changed our sodden clothes in the train, in an agony of fear at every station lest some one should intrude.

I remember an amazing day of wind in Glencoe. We went up Cam Ghleann, where its numberless little waterfalls were being blown straight up into the air like a girl's hair. It was extraordinary to look up the narrow gorge and see nothing but whirling clouds of spray. Dr Clark was wearing a helmet, and yet his spectacles, ear-loops and all, were caught by a gust, torn off, and carried away beyond recovery. The top of Clachlet was comparatively calm after the funnel of the gorge.

Seton Gordon describes in 'The Charm of the Hills' a fight we once had to get up Coire Etchachan in a blizzard. The wind roared down from Ben Muich Dhui in one staggering, screaming blast of snow. Of course there was not the slightest point in going to the top, which was precisely why we insisted on doing so. The loch was entirely frozen and snowed over, while we were in like case, nearly two inches of ice encasing us from head to foot in heavy armour.

Another time when I was similarly clothed in ice was on an eastern climb up Cairn Toul from the Corrour bothy. It was raining heavily in the glen, with wild roars of wind tearing down from the Pools of Dee. Up on the ridge the rain turned to snow, and we could only move by clinging to the rocks. When we got to the bothy again we lit a fire and scraped off the scales of ice with our ice axes. That day's work gave me a fine dose of bronchitis which lasted me for a month.

I think the only occasion when I did not actively and vehemently enjoy the wildness of the weather was one of my first in the hills — the first of many trips through the Lairig. Dear old Donald Fraser at Derry was pessimistic: no one had got through before, that year, and it was a dirty day of cloud and wind and sleet. I was a little faint-hearted myself, but started off alone, and made good progress till I rounded Carn a Mhaim and turned up the main glen. I have never encountered anything to touch the wind that met me (except once in Skye); certainly I have never before or since been repeatedly lifted clean off my feet and ignominiously dumped down in a heap on comparatively low and level ground. Up by the Pools in the narrow funnel of the Pass, I could never have got through had not the drifted snow anchored me to above the knee at every step. I did not enjoy that day - I felt rather frightened and unspeakably lonely. I did not realise the existence of the Pools till a later visit, for on that day they were all entirely obliterated by snow, a thing I have never seen again.

Later, when I dropped over into Speyside, I got into more trouble through missing the path and keeping, for safety, close to the stream. After three or four hours of struggle along its most unaccommodating margin, I finally found myself on the wrong side at its junction with the burn from Loch Eunach. It was flowing very deep and strong, and I had a nasty time fording it. Finally I lost myself thoroughly in Rothiemurchus, and was lucky to find myself at Aviemore just before nightfall. It had taken me nearly eleven hours from Derry

Lodge. My best time for the Lairig is six hours from Aviemore to Derry, with good hard snow for some distance each side of the summit.

That was a perfect walk. I left the station at one o'clock with a gentle wind behind me. The tops were covered in snow, and a keen frost had polished the surface till it shone again. I realised the appositeness of the name Angel Peak, which was white from its sharp top to the shoulders, and stood out a miracle of shining purity. A marvellous sunset gilded my path to Derry, where Donald was standing on the bridge to welcome me.

Oh those good evenings with the Frasers! The shrewdness, the knowledge of men and things, and endless flow of hill-lore from the old man, and the affectionate solicitude for one's comfort of Mrs Fraser and Mary.

Now I come to think of it, I cannot look back upon many fine days in the Highlands. There was one in the Cairngorms with a beautiful snow surface, when we walked from Aviemore over Braeriach, Angel Peak, Cairn Toul, The Devil's Point, and so down into Glen Geusachan and on to Derry.

Another found me with nothing more attractive than a stroll on Ben Ledi, while a third was sacrificed to the journey from Fort William to Glasgow, with marvellous views of snow peaks, and Goggs to name them for me. This, of course, after five days of hopeless rain on and around the Ben, every one of which was a joy too deep for words.

Once at Kinlochewe we went up Slioch in a drenching storm, and on beyond towards Sgurr an Tuill Bhain. The sun came out, and I shall never forget that strange plateau with its tarns and flat sand and rocks, looking like an early Italian desert landscape with a sky of heavenly blue above. I do not recollect any bit of Scotland quite like it.

Skye has bathed me fairly freely in its time, and I still regard a certain tramp from Coire na Creiche down to Glen Brittle as the apotheosis of the wetness of clothes.

Why it is positively delightful to get wet in Scotland and entirely loathsome in London I cannot tell! How I enjoyed a day at Lochearnhead walking over the sodden ridge of Meall an t'Seallaidh and down Kirkton Glen, with six inches of water flowing over the path all the way, and Raeburn springing along in front as though walking on a cinder-track! Rain and wind always bring me a happy vision of Harry Walker looking like a Norseman in his sou'wester, and that peculiar and serviceable short slip-on overall he affected; his face always radiating good comradeship and optimism. We shall never see his big smile again, but it abides with us as one of our best and cheeriest memories.

I wonder if the war will ever end and give us leave to walk among the hills again. I want to feel the good Scottish rain running down my neck; I want to feel great screaming winds roaring down the glen; I want to hear Willy Ling say for the ten thousandth time, "It's a fine day, but saft"; I want to see that ridiculous little woolly cap on the back of Goodeve's head. In a word, I want a big Easter Meet in peace time, and I want — but there, the rain has stopped, and the evening paper has come, and the war and its work are still our masters.

A SHORT HISTORY OF SCOTTISH CLIMBING
From 1918 to the Present Day
Vol. XXII (1939) (Extracts)   by E.A.M. Wedderburn

This article refers to most of the significant new climbs done in Scotland between the wars. As such it is too detailed for full reproduction here. However, an outline of its most important features follows. Sandy Wedderburn was one of the best climbers and most articulate members of the S.M.C.. Sadly, he did not survive the 1939-45 War.

During the war of 1914-18 there was naturally little time or inclination for climbing. In the summer of 1918, however, a party consisting of L.G. Shadbolt, D.R. Pye, and G.H.L. Mallory set the ball rolling with vigour in Skye, making several fine new routes, including the Crack of Doom and the Slab and Groove climbs. In the same year E.W. Steeple and G. Barlow were back making new conquests, and the work which they did in preparation for the Skye Guide Book, which appeared in 1923. ....

Much of the rock climbing exploration in Skye continued to be done by climbers from England and its focus was Sron Na Ciche.

While in the early twenties much was going on in Skye, Ben Nevis was neglected. The first Nevis Guide Book was published in 1919, but there was little to record about the Ben in summer until 1929. The opening of the Charles Inglis Clark Memorial Hut in 1929 gave a certain stimulus to winter climbing, but the only new winter climbs up to that year were made in 1920 on the Observatory Ridge by Raeburn, Goggs and Mounsey, and on Raeburn's Easy Route by an anonymous S.M.C. party. These winter climbs were the sole Scottish contributions to climbing on Nevis for ten years after the war, and during the same period new climbs by Scotsmen over the whole of Scotland numbered only about a dozen. But 1929 saw a revival on Nevis.

Wedderburn goes on to mention most of the new routes done on Nevis over the next ten years, including the very important contribution by G.G. Macphee. He goes on to mention new climbs in Arran, Harris, South Uist, Creag Meagaidh and occasional explorations north of the Great Glen. The Cairngorms are briefly mentioned, including the notable ascents of Mitre Ridge on Beinn a Bhuird in 1933. Some prominence is given to Lochnagar and its development by Cairngorm Club members, particularly R.G. Symmers, and later by J.H.B. Bell and his associates. The "enthusiastic exploration" of the Arrochar hills by J.B. Nimlin and his friends receives comment but it is Glen Coe which is seen by Wedderburn as the most important arena for the development of Scottish climbing between the wars.

Like Nevis, Glen Coe for many years after the war was seldom visited unless by those who, after a period in which no climbing was possible, were naturally content to repeat the old climbs. When one considers how unexplored even the most prominent cliffs in Glen Coe remained until 1928 and how easy of access they are, it must be concluded that the decade following the war of 1914-18 was one of those periods of ebb which Harry MacRobert mentioned, although the excessive popularity of the Crowberry Ridge, which persists, is also to blame.

> But better things were heralded in 1928 and 1929 when a number of new climbs were done on Buachaille Etive Mor and on Bidean nan Bian.

In 1930 J.H.B. Bell and C.M. Allan were active, climbing the hitherto unexplored Diamond Buttress, which gave a very difficult climb, and making new routes on the Central Buttress of Buchaille and on Stob Coire an Lochan. The Diamond Buttress illustrates the development of a new and unorthodox type of climbing, other examples of which are the Cuneiform Buttress, the Pinnacle Buttress of Cor Arder, and the Parallel Buttress of Lochnagar. Steep grass, moss, and heather, instead of being regarded as dangerous and as spoiling the climb, begin to take their place in Scottish climbing as media to be cultivated and wooed in order to give the best the Scottish hills have to offer. The development, which should influence the future of Scottish climbing considerably, is largely due to the researches of J.H.B. Bell, although Welsh climbing some time before showed signs of developing along similar lines.

> The J.M.C.S. was founded in 1925, and within a few years its members began to make their contribution to Scottish climbing.

In 1934 the Central Highlands Guide Book was published, and that summer saw the start of the present alarming series of climbing accidents in Glen Coe. More pleasing was the Rannoch Wall climb made by Williams, G.F. Todd, Macphee and Jack, which under the influence of the Macphee climbs of the previous year, pointed the possibilities for short severe routes on the east side of the Crowberry Ridge. Such possibilities, of course, exist on many crags in Glen Coe, and if they are keenly pursued we shall undoubtedly see as many guide books published about the climbs in Glen Coe as there are about climbs in Lakeland.

The Rannoch Wall was climbed by a party of the old school. 1935 saw the rising of a new movement in Scottish climbing, in which are prominent what I can only call the "Glasgow ginger group". Most of the members of this group are members of the J.M.C.S., but many are members of one or other of the numerous small clubs of climbers and hill-walkers, notably the Lomond Mountaineering Club, which have sprung up so rapidly in the last ten years. This group brings into Scottish climbing an element, hitherto not prominent, of youth and relative poverty. Scottish climbing has survived in the atmosphere in which it was started longer than has climbing in the Lakes and Wales. It was regarded until about ten years after the war of 1914-18 mainly as a training for larger mountains and as a practice ground in off seasons for members of the Alpine Club. Such an atmosphere naturally tended to make climbing a sport for the wealthier classes, and the new group of climbers thus find themselves not so much the heirs to a tradition as the discoverers of a secret hitherto kept hidden from their class. This has, as is obvious, both advantages and disadvantages. Before the war, if photographs and contemporary articles are any criterion, the typical Scottish mountaineering party would start from some convenient hotel which they had reached the previous evening in comfortable time for dinner. They would be met with on the hills in groups of five or six, several of them membrs of the A.C. and S.M.C.. Some at least, clad in caps, tweed knickerbocker suits, and sometimes gaiters, would wear beards. With 30 feet of Alpine Club rope between each pair of climbers they would be intent on the conquest of some famous route, discussing the while the latest bits of Alpine gossip.

More typical of to-day is the youthful pair starting out late, after making breakfast, from their tent or Youth Hostel which they had reached late the previous night. Some are members of the J.M.C.S. or of the Lomond or Creag Dhu Clubs. They probably wear ragged Grenfell breeches and a miscellaneous and historic array of sweaters, and are all beardless - though probably unshaven. They may be met wandering up with coils of Alpine line, a hatchet, a few spring-clips, and probably a ring spike or two, " just in case", to have a look at some secret project of rock or ice which still awaits solution. Jimmy's exploits of last week-end or perhaps dialectical materialism are probable topics of discussion. These youthful climbers are, of course, not an entirely new phenomenon, nor are they the only ones on the hills, but some of them climb every week-end of the year. They appear to me to have the future of Scottish climbing in their hands.

> In 1936, 1937 and 1938 a number of very important routes were made, mostly by members of this new generation of climbers. The climbs included Agag's Groove, Raven's Gully and Clachaig Gully as well as some fine winter ascents such as Garrick's Shelf. Among the climbers involved were some whose names were to become very well known; J.F. Hamilton, W.H. Murray and W.M. Mackenzie among them.

This brief history has necessarily made no mention of the many steady climbers and hill-walkers who do not strive to be the first to pass. Nor have the small band of winter climbers, whose every ascent is a new route, been given the prominence they deserve. With their seed, however, shall remain continually a good inheritance.

The standard of climbing in Scotland appears to be higher now than ever before, although the average standard of ability is possibly lower. The great increase in the number of Scottish climbers is reflected in the growth of the S.M.C. (182 in 1919, 307 in 1939) and of the J.M.C.S. (founded in 1925 - now 210), but there are many hundreds more of Scottish climbers and mountain goers outside these clubs, many outside any club and as yet inarticulate. The period reviewed in this article is largely one of recovery from the war of 1914-18. Not until its last years do we find climbers who may be said to carry the sport beyond its achievements in 1914. Now it appears that a further setback is to occur. The hills will remain.

THE C.I.C. HUT ORIGINS AND OPENING
Vol. XXXI (1979)   by R. R. Elton

This series of short articles appeared in the Journal in the Jubilee Year of the opening
of the Charles Inglis Clark Memorial Hut on Ben Nevis.

The thought of having a climbers' hut on Ben Nevis arose at Easter Meet 1925 in Fort
William when Maylard in conversation with George Sang (Hon. Sec.) suggested the idea.
Sang had as his guest the factor of the Nevis estate.

Dr William Inglis Clark heard of this from Sang and became engrossed with the idea.
He had climbed for many years, and was not only an authority on the hill, but had through
the Club Journal made his reputation by many climbing articles and by what became the
first guide book on Nevis. This was further emphasised by his continued mourning for the
loss in 1918 of the son Charles Inglis Clark who was killed on active service in
Mesopotamia during the 1914-18 war and by his anxiety in 1908 when his son had a 30-
hours expedition on Nevis (see P73-78).

In 1927 with much work by Sang negotiations for the hut building were completed and
a small group including Sang and Sandy Harrison (now Hon. President) selected the Hut
site along with owners, architect and builder.

The architects were Mears-Wilson in Edinburgh, and the builders W. T. Gibson & Co.
of Glasgow. The former were found by W. W. Naismith, the father of the Club, and whose
indirect descendant is still with the firm. The builders were found by A. E. Robertson
(later President) who knew well Tom Gibson who became the construction builder. Tom
was a complete enthusiast. I met him sometimes during 1928 when he lived on the hill
in tents and later under cover, from his work. He climbed Nevis many times, and latterly
joined the Club I think as an Honorary Member. Unfortunately he died a few years later.

The building work was all done without any record but goods taken up were all carried
on horseback. Furnishings were arranged by Club members and by November 1928, the
position was explained at the Club's A.G.M. and I was appointed Hut Custodian. In the
1929 New Year I spent the weekend with J. H. B. Bell at the Hut, when after 18 inches
of snow in Fort William and an hour digging out the Hut door, we gained access. Hut
usage was rather slow to develop, but access to the J.M.C.S. and guests from kindred clubs
brought an increasing use, which will be dealt with below.

THE C.I.C. HUT — 1930's   by W. H. Murray

When I first went to the hut in the mid-1930's it was the only club hut in Scotland, yet
was still little used. The new Glencoe road had opened only in 1935. One could be sure
of getting in. But already it was playing its part in a new exploration of the cliffs. Macphee
was working on his rock-climbers' guide and without the hut could probably not have

written it. His parties and Bell's were the chief users. Except in thick weather, their every visit either produced new routes or gathered ideas for them. Bell's game was to put the guide out of date, and climbers arriving at the hut always had this immediate excitement of opening the climbs book to read what new thing had been done, tried, or repeated.

The eight bunks were the best sprung and most comfortable in which I ever slept. One could lie there on a winter's night and watch the iron stove glow red-hot in the dark. These comforts of hut-life made a lasting impression on me. Still more could be made of them with forethought. Since my early visits were usually made with Mackenzie, MacAlpine, and Dunn, I rapidly learned the finer tactical points: such as, to carry the keys on the way up, and so without loss of decorum be first through the door to get a bunk by the fire; or be prompt in putting one's blankets into the oven, while it was warming; yet not be forward in the morning, but rather watch over the edge of the bunk to note if the first riser's breath smoked in icy air, and if so, wait till the primus was purring, porridge on the boil, and the raw edge taken off the new day. Fast as I learned, I could not expect to compete with masters, and had to reserve my lore for later deployment in more innocent company. ·

The scenes that spring to mind from early days are those that gave a lift to the spirit on wet or windy nights: that first sight of the hut's beckoning light far up the glen; the warm, wholesome fug when the door swung open; the steaming mugs of rum punch, the brewing of which was always the first move on arrival; and the coal fire in the big iron stove.

It was at the C.I.C. that I first met Dr J. H. B. Bell. I arrived with Mackenzie and MacAlpine late one April night to find him there with three Englishmen — Jack Henson, Dick Morsley, and Percy Small. They were up to make the first ascent of Green Gully (not knowing of Raeburn's climb thirty years earlier). The bitter cold of that night was banished by the welcome he gave us — mugs of hot soup before a blazing fire. I had my first lesson on the follies of 'volunteering' when I went to fetch a bucket of water for the rum punch. After digging through feet of interminable snow I found the burn frozen solid. My principal lesson came in the morning, when I watched Bell make breakfast for his own party. Porridge, sausage, and kippers were all stirred into the one pot. As a practical chemist, he was imbued with the truth that a meal was a fuel-intake, therefore its separation into 'courses' was an auld wife's nicety, and not for climbers. He later persuaded me to share his burnt toast, on the grounds that charcoal was a bodily need. He expounded equations of chemical change, and showed how charcoal absorbed the troublesome gases of stomach and gut, to our mutual benefit. Bell when cook could talk one into eating almost anything. But not even that toughest of characters, Dick Morsley, had a palate tough enough for Bell's porridge. After one spoonful, he strode to the door and flung his plateful out on the snow. The hut for me was a school of further education.

When I began climbing with Bell he made occasional concessions to my weakness for high cuisine. He introduced me to Hell's Kitchen at Fort William. This underground vault had sawdust on the floors and bare wooden tables. It was frequented by fishermen off the boats and by the Lochaber underworld. Fish and chips and black puddings, if too fastidiously cooked apart in two pans, were sensibly served on one plate. After an evening there we could better face dirty nights in the Allt a'Mhuilinn.

I can see from an old diary that my opinions of the hut were not always complimentary. 'The S.M.C. must have been mad to put so foul a building on so foul a hill' is an excerpt of 20th February 1938, wrung from me one black night on the path up. The right bank of the Allt a'Mhuilinn was coated in ice. A dismal mist hung low on the Ben. Beyond the deer-fence were scattered countless thousands of stones and boulders. We seemed to have stumbled over every single one, until at last we abandoned the path for the ice-bound bed of the burn which was easier to find and follow. The toils of ascent with a heavy load will live strong in every hut-user's mind, and probably so does that first sight of its light. But no light shone that night.

My companions on this visit were again Mackenzie and MacAlpine. MacAlpine was the devil's own fire-stoker. He had genius. When he was present, I never tried for the bunks by the stove. His finishing touches last thing at night induced a heat through which Satan Himself could not have slept. And He it was who now saw to MacAlpine's punishment. Inspired by a heady brew, he had stoked the stove to an unprecedented red-hotness, forgetting that his blankets were in the oven. When this was shortly discovered, Mackenzie and I basked in a glow of moral righteousness, the more keenly enjoyed for being so unaccustomed, while MacAlpine debated whether to confess their incineration to the hut custodian or to claim more plausibly that Bell had eaten them for breakfast.

The night outside looked so grim that we believed the next day lost and stayed up until 2 a.m. We rose to a blue and cloudless sky. There was no wind, the sun blazed, and the tight-packed gullies glittered icily. We went for Observatory Ridge, of which no second winter ascent had been made, and had one of the best climbs of our lives. We finished up Zero Gully by torchlight. A high bitter wind flailed us on top. In these days the Observatory still had its roof. It made an excellent outpost for the C.I.C. We wriggled through the upper half of a window to a big snow-grotto inside. MacAlpine had carried up a medicinal bottle of rum. Our festivities lasted till midnight. By the time we had kicked and cut our way off the Arete to the hut it was two-thirty. My previous night's thoughts on the C.I.C., when all looked hopeless, were not only revised but reversed. And so with many of our best days on the Ben. Without the hut we should not have had them.

THE MYSTERY OF THE TOWER RIDGE
Vol. XX (1935)   by G. R. Roxburgh

A pleasant fug filled the Hut, the stove glowed merrily and cast little leaping bursts of light upon the four pairs of boots gathered snugly round its base, whilst a kettle and four large curling-stone hot bottles sitting on top suggested that the occupants were taking no risks of being cold. Outside a silvery moon shone coldly down on the cliffs and snow which glittered and scintillated in the grip of a biting frost. From the Allt a Mhuilinn came little furtive cracks as the water strained against the clutching sheets of ice.

It was New Year's Eve and the four occupants of the Hut, having spent the day in a long and strenuous ascent of No. 2 Gully involving much step-cutting and consequent cold feet in the sunless depths of the cliffs, were pleasantly drowsy after a magnificent dinner carried up with much labour. There now remained nothing to do but to fill the bottles, open a crack of window, and tumble between the blankets for a blissful slumber in preparation for what promised to be a glorious morrow.Reluctantly the last cigarette end was thrown into the stove, the bottles were filled, and before long deep breathing alone broke the stillness of the Hut. Outside the moon shone coldly on the frost-bound world.

I awoke with cold sweat pouring off my brow. The moon was still shining, but now it leered in at the Hut window, and the frost seemed to have stilled even the Allt a Mhuilinn. It wasn't the moon that had awakened me, it was something else which had left a vague feeling of fear behind. Suddenly it came again, a soft low moan gradually rising in tone till it became a shriek and then fading into a bubbling gurgle of despair; and it didn't come from near by, but from away above in the cliffs where no human being had any right to be at that time of night. My blood turned to water and my courage faded away to nothing. I pretended it was imagination and that I had really heard nothing, turned over and closed my eyes, but I knew deep down that it was not so, and I scarcely breathed waiting for it to come again. Silence reigned, then it came - penetrating, despairing, nerve-shattering. I leapt out of my bunk, threw on some clothes, pulled open the inside door and fumbled with the key in the big outside door. As it opened I was met with that heart-rending wail: it echoed round the cliffs, quietened, and then re-echoed off Carn Mor Dearg until the whole amphitheatre seemed filled with shrieking voices, so that the ensuing silence was like the grave. Then I saw a sight which made me gasp. Half-way up the Tower Ridge was a light; it shone clear and bright against the inky shadows on the rocks and looked yellow and warm compared with the cold silver moonshine, and the light was moving, some one was climbing the Tower Ridge with a lantern. And as I watched, that soul-destroying wail commenced again; it rose in fiendish crescendo and faded down to a deep resonant rumble so deep that I felt the ground beneath my feet shiver and shake in unison with it. The light was swinging from side to side now, as though the midnight climber had struck an unclimbable pitch, then it steadied and commenced to move slowly upwards; I could almost feel the fingers groping over the icy rocks for a hold. For an age that slow upward movement went on, then suddenly the light commenced to hurtle downwards and at the same minute that blood-curdling yell burst forth in full volume. Down the light shot, and as it rebounded off the rock there came a series of ever-increasing crashes. Finally with a terrific detonation, it disappeared into the rocks at the foot of the ridge. The impact seemed to shake the whole hill, a violent shiver ran through the ground and, to my horror, I saw the North-East Buttress move. A great gaping crack appeared in the black silhouette and then with a roar the whole ridge crashed into Coire Leis, blocks of stone as big as houses ground and smashed into each other, and the night was made hideous with the rending groans of the tortured rock.

So intent was I on the cataclysmic upheaval at the North-East Buttress that it was only when I felt a gust of air on my right cheek that I turned to find the Tower Ridge dissolving into ruins before my eyes. I stood rooted to the spot — the Douglas Boulder had broken loose; like some unleashed monster it leapt into the air, bounced once, twice — and I shut my eyes to await the third bounce which must be right on the Hut. Came a crash — and my hot-water bottle hit the floor a resounding blow. We had forgotten to open the window and, coupled with a New Year Dinner, the frowst had done its work.

THE
SCOTTISH MOUNTAINEERING CLUB

SPECIAL HUT DINNER
Palace Hotel, FORT WILLIAM
MONDAY   1st APRIL 1929

GEORGE T. GLOVER, PRESIDENT
In the Chair

INITIATIVE IN CLIMBING
Vol. XXI (1937)   by J.H.B. Bell

"He who climbeth on the highest mountains laugheth at all tragic plays and tragic realities.... The atmosphere rare and pure, danger near and the spirit full of a joyful wickedness: thus are things well matched." - ZARATHUSTRA

In this number we publish a brief review of a handy little book of climbing technique * ("The Technique of Alpine Mountaineering.") which has given rise to much controversy amid the great ones of our Craft. We are not here concerned with the points at issue, but we have been moved to some reflections on the attitude taken up by several of the greatest mountaineers towards climbing rules in general.

If climbing mountains were on a par with many other sports, a precise code of rules would, no doubt, be highly important. But, for most of us, mountaineering is much more than a sport. It boasts of a philosophy and of a literature of its own. When our greatest Scottish mountaineer, Harold Raeburn, was writing on the technique of climbing he instinctively recognised this, and entitled the work "Mountaineering Art." A careful perusal of this too-little-known book would well repay the attention of our younger members. In its "General Guide Book" the Club has taken the same line. It has recognised the diversity in character of Scottish mountains, where one may find all sorts of snow and ice, all kinds of rock with and without vegetation, and all sorts of weather at all seasons of the year; so the Club has never issued over-concise regulations as to climbing procedure, but has dwelt on general ideas as to what should be done in varying circumstances.

The Editor recently spent an enjoyable and instructive day on the face of the Pinnacle Buttress of Coire Ardair. This is quite a sound climb for such as have taken the trouble to master the technique of vegetatious mica-schist, a most venerable and ancient rock formation, to which the Central and Northern Highlands owe a great deal of their distinctive character, and one, moreover, which is usually devoid of such modern innovations as belays, or even cracks for the insertion of pitons. Again, the flanks of the North-East Buttress of Ben Nevis abound in smooth porphyry slabs, alike intractable to nailed boots and to the rubbers so favoured by our English climbing brethren. Only stocking soles or certain types of felt soles, much used in the Eastern Alps, would seem to be of value on such rock. Finally, Dr G. Graham MacPhee in our last number put rather a new complexion on some of the climbing problems of Scottish snow and ice.

The greatest mountaineers, like the greatest artists, scientists, and men of action, worked out their own way of perfection: in fact, they broke most of the rules. Years

---

* This review comments adversely on a number of recommendations made in a book published by the Uto Section of the Swiss Alpine Club. No wonder! Among other things it appears to advise that handholds on rock should be taken as high as can be conveniently reached and the body should be kept as close to the slope as possible! — Ed.

afterwards they became canonised; the rules, perhaps somewhat modified, went on. The only trouble with great mountaineers is that many of them, despite everything that one might expect, live to a healthy old age. They tend to become conservative and to insist on the observance of many of the rules which they themselves cheerfully disregarded in the fiery days of youth. To such men we listen respectfully in public, for we know that in private there is always a humorous twinkle of the eye and a tolerant smile for the younger men who go to the mountains in the true spirit of adventure, so long as they are free of the foolhardy pride of self-glorification.

What then is to be done about this business of rules in climbing mountains? Read them through, of course, to begin with, but far better learn the craft on the hills themselves from some experienced climber. Paradoxical as it may seem, there is little doubt that the best time to study a manual of technique is in retrospect, when the doings and experiences of a climbing holiday are still fresh in the mind. That is really the only time when technical advice has any chance of making a deep impression. Rules are very good if they embody the gist of the experience of the best mountaineers, but hardly so useful if the rule book becomes so detailed and complicated that the very effort of scrupulously following it out breeds a false sense of security. As Leslie Stephen has pointed out very justly, it is impossible to lay down any simple code of rules which will provide for security in all cases, and that "Nothing, in fact, is sufficient except skill, activity, experience, and presence of mind."

This point is brought out very forcibly by that great mountaineer, Mr A. F. Mummery, in the final chapter of his book, "My Climbs in the Alps and Caucasus," perhaps the best essay in mountaineering literature on the subject of safety in climbing, an essay which has recently been incorporated in its entirety in a foreign textbook of climbing technique. Concerning the use of the rope, Mummery says, "There is, however, some danger of its being regarded as a sort of Providence, always ready to save the reckless and incompetent, no matter how slight their experience, no matter how little they may be fitted for the expeditions they undertake."

Vigilance and mountain-sense can never be adequately developed, however, unless expeditions are undertaken which, with a becoming humility of judgement, are such as will stretch the climbing powers at least a little more than anything which has gone before. Throughout all this, to quote Mummery again, "The first lesson the novice has to learn is to be ever on his guard, and it is one that the oldest climber rarely fully masters . . . it is a habit which must be acquired, and to which no road, other than constant practice, will ever lead him. It wants long experience to impress upon the mind that the chief danger of extremely difficult climbing is to be found in the easy places by which it is followed."

So much for the spirit of liberty in the matter of climbing rules: unfortunately there is another insidious threat to the true spirit of Scottish climbing, and many of us must plead guilty as aiders and abettors. The reference is to the growing mass of minute detail in the description of new climbing routes. The disease is not yet widespread, but it is growing. Already the western buttress of Sron na Ciche in Skye is becoming nearly as complicated as the east peak of Lliwedd.

These remarks are prompted by a recent communication received on the subject of the notorious Rannoch Wall route on Buachaille Etive. At the crux of the climb is to be found a piton. Should one go straight up from this piton "or move out left on the open face on small but positive holds"? Fortunately, the Editor had been up six weeks previously, and his reasoned conclusion is that Scotland is still a free country, where competent climbers should be able to decide the point for themselves: if they cannot do so they should not lead up Rannoch Wall. This also serves as a rather brusque answer to the latter part of the communication, which cited two cases of parties, who, after experiencing great difficulty at the crux of the climb, were finally extricated with the assistance of the spectators. A great deal might be said on the subject of the use of pitons on Scottish mountains, but it would take too long. This particular one was probably firm to begin with, it was reported to have been quite loose in May of this year; but was quite sound in July. Perhaps it should not be trusted out of season.

The distinctive excellence of Scottish climbing that gives it the character of true mountaineering is surely that much is still left in the matter of route-finding to the initiative of each succeeding party. It is a false sense of progress which would give a detailed description of each pitch, or worse still, of each handhold. The ideal account of a new climb should, in the first place, be accurate about the topography of the start, general line, and finish. Any places of special difficulty, picturesque charm, or distinctive features are worth recording. Beyond this, all that is necessary is an idea of relative difficulty, of time taken, and of the prevailing conditions during the first ascent. It is far too often the case that more detailed descriptions are so confusing that successive parties fail to identify the route.

Action and reaction are usually equal and opposite. There is already the rumour of the formation of a Gadarene society among some of our English climbing friends. It is reported that this society functions in two ways. By day they pull down cairns on routes and mountain tops; by night they prowl around with pots of paint, blazing trails which lead to the disintegrating crest of precipices. Who can say what will be the end of it all?

26. J.H.B. Bell

26a Bell on the first ascent
    of the Long Climb,
    Ben Nevis

27. *One of the most formidable climbing teams of the thirties: (left to right) Bill Murray, Bill Mackenzie, Archie MacAlpine and Kenneth Dunn*

28. Ian Ogilvy (right) and Alex Small
    on an early reconnaissance of
    the girdle traverse of Rannoch
    Wall, Buachaille Etive Mor, in
    1940

29. Alex Small on the girdle
    traverse of Rannoch Wall

30. Hamish Hamilton and Jim Wood under the Shelter Stone

THE FORMATION OF THE JMCS (excerpts)
Vol. XXX (1975)

To mark the Jubilee of the Junior Mountaineering Club of Scotland a large part of the 1975 Journal was given over to a series of articles recounting the history of the JMCS and its Sections in Glasgow, Edinburgh and Perth. That of the Inverness, Lochaber and London Sections came in the next volume. It is all good stuff but space constraints mean that only a selection can be included.

THE BEGINNING OF THE JMCS   by A.G. Hutchison

Two days on the still war-scarred battlefields of the Somme were enough for us and it was with relief that Rutherford and I returned to Amiens where we had arranged to meet Arthur Rusk.

It was July, 1924, and our meeting point marked the start of a mountaineering holiday in the Bernese Oberland.

As the train bearing our friend swept round the steep curve in the station, we suddenly became aware of an excited figure leaning half out of the carriage window and wildly waving its arms. This turned out to be Rusk. He was bursting with a new idea.

'A NEW Mountaineering Club' - that was the theme. An association for mountaineers in which they might meet kindred spirits and find among them those who could teach them the rules of the game. It would be a Club in which the members would learn the rudiments of mountain craft and it might also become a 'feeder' for the senior club which required conditions of membership.

The three of us talked over the project long into the night and next morning our reflections were considerably heightened by the prospects of the Bernese Alps, themselves brilliant in the sunshine. They made a glorious back-drop viewed across the central plains of Switzerland, as the train thundered its way down the Aar Valley.

Our next few days were fully occupied as we prepared for arduous things to come by several days preliminary training.

Later, having crossed the Balmhorn, and en route over the Petersgrat towards the Bietschhorn, we became stormbound for a day in the Multhorn Hut at the head of the Lauter Brunnen Valley. It was here, in that hut, that the constitution for the new club was hammered out and agreed upon. I think we also decided on the name then.

The first meet of the J.M.C.S. was held at the Narnain Boulder in the corrie below the Cobbler, Arrochar. Here is an extract from Rutherford's diary on the event, noted at the time -

Saturday, August 29th, 1925 Left Queen Street (Glasgow) Station by the 5.55 a.m. for Arrochar. Reached the Narnain Boulder by 9.25 and put in some good work with plenty of hands to build up the shelter wall. We stopped at noon and were back by 2.40

p.m. having traversed Jean and the Cobbler. Arthur (Rusk) arrived in the evening. It was poor weather. That night there slept seven under the Boulder, Eddy (Andreae), Waddington, Robertson, A. Hutchison, Arthur, Parry and the writer. A. J. Stevens and the Speirs emulated the coneys farther up the Narnain.

Sunday, August 30th The morning was bad so the inaugural meeting of the Junior Mountaineering Club of Scotland was held with Arthur and Parry still in bed. Arthur made a good outline of his aims for the Club and Eddy was elected Glasgow President, and W. Speirs Secy. E.C. Thomson and Elton came up from below. The whole party then went up Ben Arthur in mist and rain.'

It might therefore be fair to say that it was in the hills of the Arrochar Alps that the J.M.C.S. came to birth. Rusk died in 1965. Looking back, it is possible to recollect something of his philosophy of life, one result of which being the idea which led to the formation of the J.M.C.S. Rusk looked on mountains as a challenge. Many do. But, to him the challenge did not only provide an opportunity in which he might express himself. He looked on mountains from a wider angle and felt the challenge as something more subtle. They were not chance phenomena. They were there for a purpose and had a part to play in the scheme of things. They influenced the lives of men and pointed a way, endlessly, up and beyond the low levels where, for the most part, man's course is run. Metaphysically speaking, mankind need not live in the valleys. The mountain vision could and should have a wider implication in human events. So, he had a burning urge that men and mountains must meet. I think if he were living now, how much he would rejoice that more and more they do. Over the door of the Town Hall in Sacramento, California, a Legend is engraved - '*Give me men to match my mountains.*' Those who go on the mountains might well ponder these words in respect of our responsibilities in today's world. Still more widely, they might provide a clue on how to restore the sense of purpose which the world needs so much.

THE JMCS EARLY DAYS   by C.E. Andreae

Proceeding out from Glasgow on the humble push-bike we always camped at the same spot above Sugach farm at the head of Loch Long, and at the time we felt like pioneers, for camping was in its comparative infancy and we never saw a tent north of Luss. On the ascent from the loch it became a ritual that we should stop at the two large boulders at the foot of Narnain, where one of the two provided good scrambling exercise, but the other held no such attraction except for a large overhang. Thence we proceeded to the Cobbler - the traverse of Jean, the airy arete to the Cobbler himself and the descent by the big gully at the back of the north peak, with variations. That first week-end was the first of many such that for me was to last for four years. The regular pattern was to camp at Arrochar in the summer, while at Easter, during a break after the University term, we went to Crianlarich where we were royally looked after by a Mrs Buckingham in her minute cottage - we called it Buckingham Palace! From there we explored the feast of snow-covered Munros that were within walking distance and with the aid of the trusty bicycle we covered the Beinn Dorain group and Stob Ghabhar.

At Arrochar it was generally misty and wet and I remember about that time the fickle weather produced eleven fine Fridays in succession followed almost invariably by a poor week-end. But there was always the companionship and understanding born of the hills and many are the happy times that we spent on the Cobbler, the Spearhead and Jammed-Block Chimney of Narnain and others, though the Right Angle Gully of the Cobbler took a while before yielding to assault.

Our expeditions were, of course, not confined to Arrochar and Crianlarich, and among others, three in particular might briefly be mentioned. First there was a long week-end in Arran where, after a late evening climb along the A'Chir Ridge, a hurricane suddenly blew up at midnight and flattened our tents. We spent the rest of the night acting as tent poles and were glad at least that it did not rain. Next day we recovered ourselves and our tents and in any case it was far too wild to be on the tops. On the day following, in quieter conditions, we managed a climb on Cir Mhor before rushing for the mid-day boat from Brodick. Then there was a glorious spell of five days after taking our degree in March 1934 when Rutherford, Hunter and I stayed at the old half-way hut on Ben Nevis. After various climbs in misty but dry conditions we had an epic day in bright sunshine when we crossed the Ben, followed round the Carn Mor Dearg arete and across the col to Aonach Beag. The panorama all round was superb with Goat Fell plainly visible eighty miles away. The return was made round the north and east side of Carn Mor Dearg finishing up with an arduous toil of a thousand feet up from the Mhuilinn glen to the hut in pitch darkness. Never did a camp dinner taste better! Lastly, we four spent two weeks in Glen Brittle in summer 1924. We covered a lot of ground in that time in reasonable weather, climbing anything between Sgurr nan Gillean and Sgurr Alasdair, but one of my clearest recollections was the limpet-like behaviour of my clothes to the rough gabbro rock — perhaps showing how *not* to climb.

CLIMBING IN THE 1920's   by William B. Speirs

Transport was the main consideration in arranging climbing expeditions in the 1920's — there were no jet flights to the Himalaya and the Andes, and even the Alps were only for those with four or more weeks holiday. Cars were few in number and for most people bus, train and cycle were the means of travel.

Our first expedition was to what was then the far north in June 1925. Five of us joined the 4 a.m. train to Inverness, and went on to Lairg where a hired truck awaited us. We loaded on our cycles and large rucksacks and climbed in ourselves, and did the 21 miles to Altnaharra by truck to help us on our way, and managed to reach Tongue by cycle before dark. The holiday was mainly fishing, but we climbed Ben Loyal and Suilven. The roads were very bad, tarmacadam having not yet reached beyond the Great Glen, and in most places there were two stony tracks made by the wheels of the motor vehicles and carts, with grass in the middle. We cycled slowly south down the west coast, and as the road made a detour round the many sea lochs, we used all the old ferries which were still operating, and this saved us about ten miles in most cases. Some of the ferry boats were little better than large rowing boats, and with five of us, two ferrymen, five cycles and large rucksacks leaving little freeboard, we were glad to reach the far shore! The expedition finished at Achnasheen where we joined the train for Glasgow.

We had the use of motor vehicles in 1927 and set off for Torridon in June 1927. Three of the party travelled in a new Austin 10 h.p. car, and two on a motor cycle and side car. Unfortunately the weight of passengers and luggage was too much for the car and a rear spring broke at Fort Augustus, and we had to leave the car at the local garage and the three passengers travelled by bus to Inverness and then to Kinlochewe, where they met up with the motor cycle party. We camped at Bridge of Grudie, and climbed all the tops of Beinn Eighe, and also Slioch which was reached by crossing Loch Maree in a hired boat. After five days there, I returned to Fort Augustus by bus and came back with the car and we all went on to Gruinard Bay. Camping was prohibited there but we found a hollow out of sight of the road where there was room for the tents, the car and motor cycle and side car. The weather was very bad for several days, but it cleared up one evening and as there were no radio weather reports in those days we had to rely on our hunch, so got up at 3 a.m. the next morning and were rewarded by a day of glorious sunshine and were able to cover all the tops of An Teallach, and again we did all our climbs without seeing another person. The weather broke again that night, and we returned home next day.

THE JMCS 1935-1940   by W.H. Murray

I discovered mountains in 1934 and had been hill-walking for nearly a year before I joined the Club. The occasional rock-scrambling I had enjoyed by the way had whetted my appetite for more. But 'more' demanded company. I knew no one who climbed. I had heard of the J.M.C.S. from passers-by on the hills, and so, in 1935, I went to see Rob Stewart the secretary. I went with trepidation — mountaineers experienced enough to climb rock would have no time for a walker. To my great relief my wasted years were overlooked; welcomed though prodigal, I learned to my delight that the Club met twice a month, indoors and outdoors. My first meet was at Arrochar, and a lift by car given. It was a grey, windy November day. In icy drizzle, John Brown led me up the Spearhead Arete, Jammed-Block Chimney, and Right-Angled Gully. My first rock-climbs disclosed no talent, yet the bareness of rock and its upper airiness exhilarated me; for years thereafter I missed no meets.

The indoor meetings were as valuable as the outdoor. Since the Club was small, they were held in members' houses, where a room was big enough to hold 20-40 men. The first was Fred MacLeod's near Charing Cross. He was one of the Club's 'characters' and once turned up at a meet direct from an all-night party, still wearing his dinner jacket, in which he climbed. Later we moved to Archie MacAlpine's house in Ibrox. One thing about mountaineers that first astounded me was their improbable appearance. The hard men took no trouble to act up. When Graham Macphee came to give a talk, he was turned out like Beau Brummel, resplendent in white spats; another was George Williams, a top rock-climber of Rannoch Wall fame, yet slight with beautifully wavy hair and spectacles. I had been expecting muscle-men, and their rarity cheered me. (Kenneth Dunn was one exception. I prized him as a car-companion, for I ran tyres down to the canvas and when I had a puncture he could lift the whole side of the car clear of the ground to save jacking). The lectures given by eminent climbers were the least important part of meetings. A lecturer was anti-social if he spoke over one hour, for the more valuable hour was the one that followed, when members had tea and talked. It was then one came to know members, to exchange ideas, to start making friends, and to arrange climbs for the next weekend. That was a main purpose in joining a club; and the best service a club can give its members is the provision of such opportunities. When the Club grew bigger after 1937, the indoor meetings had to be held in a hotel in Bath Street, but there again tea was laid on and members given time and chance to meet and talk and make up parties. I make this point because it was so important to the development of climbing at that time, and appears now to be lost.

The main changes in equipment we introduced were the slater's hammer and long ropes. Our ice axes had 33-inch shafts. The wrist-strain of prolonged one-handed cutting above the head was severe, and a slater's pick with a 14-inch shaft eased it greatly. Climbing times were almost halved. The first man I knew to use a very short axe was Douglas Scott in 1936. He had it made by a blacksmith for his Crowberry Gully climb of that year. Whenever I heard of it I went out to the ironmonger and bought a slater's hammer for 10 shillings, and had the side-claw cut off. That was the best-spent money I ever laid down on a counter. I have rarely enjoyed anything in life more than cutting up a long high-angle ice-pitch where balance was delicate. The craft used varied according to the quality of the ice: black, white, green, blue, brittle and watery, they all had their quirks, which had to be learnt until one could tell them apart at a glance and cut accordingly. We still used the adze of the long axe to cut handholds on white ice, for that could often save minutes.

It has to be remembered that climbers wore tricounis, therefore never carried crampons. They all had ten-point crampons for the Alps or Norway; at home they weren't reckoned worth their weight. The tricouni-clinker sole gave a non-slip grip on hard snow, allowed much neater footwork than crampons on snow- and ice-bound rock, and allowed too an occasional 'miracle' to be pulled off on thin brittle stuff that ought to have peeled. I used to call such moves levitation, for want of any other word — nothing so crude as a step up, but rather a float up, with no weight placed anywhere so far as humanly possible. It worked if you hit top form, and got Mackenzie and me up some nasty places on Garrick's Shelf, Deep-Cut Chimney, and the like.

When I joined the J.M.C.S. the accepted rope-lengths between each man were 60 feet and 80 for the leader. We doubled the first and carried more in addition for winter. The opening up of Rannoch Wall by George Williams of the Edinburgh S.M.C., and by Hamish Hamilton and Ian Ogilvie of the J.M.C.S., equally required long run-outs, which were freely accepted by leaders on exposed climbs without feeling need of intermediate runner-belays. Rannoch Wall was a big break-through at the time, especially Hamilton's route on Agag's Groove, in which Alec Small and Jim Wood participated, for rock so steep and exposed had hitherto been avoided. All the climbs there were being done in rubbers (plimsolls) except when Mackenzie, Dunn and I climbed Agag's in the winter of 1937 (hard frost) wearing nails. Severe summer climbs were nearly always done in rubbers unless the weather were bad.

The great increase in standards, both summer and winter, and in Club membership, was undoubtedly due at this time to motor-cars and improved roads, as well as to the rise of a new generation. The new road to Glen Coe opened in 1935. Second-hand cars were cheap. I paid £8 for a 500cc Norton, which achieved 80 m.p.h. across the Moor of Rannoch. One snowy winter cured me of that. Thereafter it was saloon cars only. For £30 I bought an oil-eating Morris Minor that ran like a Rolls Royce until the door handles fell off. At such prices, one could afford to climb. Much use was made of hotels in winter, for the only hut was the C.I.C. Clachaig Inn charged 5 shillings for supper, bed and breakfast, and the rats in the wainscot lent atmosphere; Kingshouse and Inverarnan, 7/6 (1935) rising to 9/6. Inverarnan in Glen Falloch virtually became the J.M.C.S. winter base. When we ran out of money, or were saving up, we literally hit the hay at Danny's Barn at Altnafeadh, or camped. On good weekends we camped in high corries or up on the mountain-tops. A spin-off from Everest expeditions had been the production of mountain tents (£6), eider-down bags (£2/10/-), and windproof anoraks. A three-weeks' camping holiday in Glen Brittle cost £10 for two men all in. It was a golden age, and even felt like it at the time. Good snow years come in cycles; we had an unbroken run.

The J.M.C.S. had a marked if delayed effect on the future organisation of the S.M.C. Our members declined to leave a club running monthly meets and fortnightly talks for one running only two meets in the year and no indoor meetings at all bar the Dinner. Our membership mounted to nearly 400. The committee in 1938 (when I was secretary), passed these ill-tidings to the S.M.C., who did not take the news at all well. A brass-hat fixed me with a steely eye and barked, 'We don't want climbing gorillas in this club!' But given cause, the S.M.C. never fails to update opinion and practice, which it did as soon as Sandy Harrison became President.

The JMCS 1940-1950   by A.C.D. Small

A detailed account of the history of the various sections would be an involved task possibly beyond realisation, but on a personalised level (mostly Glasgow based) I have graphic recollections of the many changing activities of the different sections during this decade. The onset of war and general uncertainty of conditions made it a reasonable assumption that the J.M.C.S. would more or less cease to be active. However, as anyone connected with the Juniors will be all too aware reason wasn't a factor to bother them much and although organised meets as such were rare a surprisingly large amount of climbing continued to be carried out in the intervals of the other pressing duties.

Naturally club functions varied in attendance, sometimes there would be only a handful present, sometimes upward of fifty. There were even 'Lantern Lectures.' The Glasgow Section had a Slide Collection, the old-fashioned glass type, the very devil to humph about and to store, and over the years several lectures were given using them to entranced audiences. In contrast, some innovators did have modern colour transparencies and in April 1942 the section held a lecture at the Grand Hotel no less, given by Anne Sheriff which attracted 56 people. Hamish Hamilton had taken up 35mm photography and his lecture artfully entitled Elmar and I set a new pictorial standard for Junior lectures. The commentary naturally was unique. Punctiliously we held A.G.M's at appropriate times but progressive decisions were largely acts of faith since the future was highly conjectural. Despite which, to our surprise, the number of members continued to rise even when it was decided to resume the payment of annual subscriptions.

This growth of interest was a surprise and encouragement to the committee although its causes were almost inexplicable when everything seemed to point to curtailment and decline. Not a bit of it. In the south the London Association propelled by Teddy Zenthon and E. C. Pyatt were driving to become a full section. To the north Lochaber were demonstrating that there was more around Ben Nevis than the C.I.C. Hut. Instead of despondency Club affairs were strong and encouraging. So much so that notwithstanding severe pruning of dead wood the Glasgow Section numbered 115 in 1945 and we could return to the normal ambiguous tactic of practicing independence, freedom, or as others viewed it — general bloody mindedness.

> A historical review of the climbs and climbers of the period cannot be attempted in these notes but some comment, inadequate as usual, can be given. Small goes on to mention the outstanding contribution to climbing explorations made by Ian Ogilvy, Brian Kellet on Nevis, Hamish Hamilton (Agag's Groove and the South Ridge of the Rosa Pinnacle) and by Curtis and Townend in Arran, all with the omniscient father figure of J.H.B. Bell in the background.

Came the New Year Meet of 1946, a combined S.M.C. and J.M.C.S. affair, normality had returned or something like it. It was a wonderfully cheerful re-union for most, we even had to turn out a search party for latecomers. Above all there was the warm feeling that the way ahead was clear.

THE JMCS 1948-1953 by Stanley Stewart

With petrol still rationed and cars for most of us just a future hope, the late forties and early fifties were the years of the bus meets. These took place fortnightly from September to June, and were run by the J.M.C.S. though shared with the S.M.C. The bus did help to keep the Club cohesive. We ranged far and wide, but Glencoe was the most frequent objective.

Trying to focus my recollections, I picture such a Glencoe meet. After a morning at the office (every second Saturday) I would leave home for the 3 p.m. rendezvous at St. Enoch's Square. A rope of honest hemp crowned my Bergen rucksack. In season I had my ex-W.D. ice-axe, or 'mountaineer's rockpick' as fellow-passengers on tram or subway were wont to refer to it. The tricouni nailed boots were a problem; fastened outside the rucksack they could cause alarm and injury to the Saturday crowds, but on the feet were a hazard to the wearer, due to their propensity to skite on smooth cobbles and pavements. I always reckoned this was the most perilous part of the weekend.

Those assembled at the rendezvous fell into two categories, or at any rate there were two extremes; young men with big packs, balaclavas and windproofs, much camouflaged as for jungle warfare, and senior citizens, more respectably dressed in collars and ties and soft hats, with small rucksacks and suitcases. Each group derived amusement and a sense of superiority from the odd appearance of the other, but with friendly tolerance. As well as our main pursuit, a bond we had (albeit unconsciously) in common was that all of us shaved and had our hair short at back and sides.

Off we thundered in our great grey Northern bus, with Clubfoot our regular driver, at the wheel. This name did not derive from any physical deformity. The Loch Lomond road with its Corners flashed past. Despite the bus, some of us were also experimenting with our own or hired transport, and to the original Hamish's Corner at Inverbeg soon were added others — Slesser's Corner, Harrison's Corner, etc., etc., each the occasion of some experience usually of a centrifugal nature. These incidents were not allowed to be forgotten, particularly if the person concerned was now with us on the bus.

At Inverarnan we halted for a light refreshment of tea and as much home baking as we could eat. The meringues with fresh cream were especially delicious. I think 1/6 per head, amazing value even then.

And so to Glencoe: Lagangarbh, or doss, or camp for us, and Clachaig Hotel for the aristos. Lagangarbh had a coal stove and calor gas, but was otherwise much as originally designed. This was before the era of quinquennial improvements. Primitive, but we felt at home.

On the Sunday we climbed. We did the classic routes and some of the new ones, and ticked them off in Bill Murray's new Guide Book. The standard attempted and attained was less than it would be now: Clachaig Gully was an enterprise for which one prepared physically and mentally and awaited suitable weather and omens. But this is well known. Fairly soon we did get on to nylon ropes and vibrams, though not without anxious discussion and sage warnings.

I myself climbed regularly at that time with a mad Englishman, Gordon Lillie, now in U.S.A. Whilst some try to push up their own standards, we modestly try to push up each other's, particularly when a crux loomed above. The case for the superior security of tricounis on slimy rock would be forcibly put by Lillie, shod in his new vibrams whilst I still had nails. 'It's the essence of *teamwork*, Stan, each leading where he's best equipped.'

Lillie used to travel on the bus wearing a bright orange T-shirt, which he bought especially 'to shock some of those old S.M.C. members.' Today such a garment would suit someone who likes to merge in with the background, but then it was quite something, and eyebrows did rise a little.

MAY THE FIRE BE ALWAYS LIT (Extract)
Vol. XXVII (1963)   by John Nimlin

A gallon-size community tea-can bubbled between the logs. Someone threw a handful of tea into the can and pointedly remarked at the newcomers that the can had been a Rodine container. We were not impressed, we used the Rodine half-gallon size ourselves, and we confidently dipped our mugs into the cauldron. Thus we joined the Boys, and the Boys joined us. They represented, rather vaguely, organisation, and we in a relative way represented experience.

In time faces became names. Christian names, nicknames, but rarely surnames. Through the years came a great roll of names, some forgotten, some unforgettable. Starry, Bones, Sparrow, Peaheid, Scrubbernut, where are you now? Simple-lifers. Not for them the Ramblers' Federation and the Youth Hostels. *Under the wide and starry sky. There's the wind on the heath, Brother.* We quoted Stevenson and Borrow at length. We had an analytical appreciation of Stevenson's *Night Under the Stars*, which expresses the very essence of sleeping out. Only the aboriginals lived a simpler life than we. Our gear was carried in ex-army knapsacks, for rucksacks had not then appeared.

Back to history. There was still an intermingling of Creag Dhu and Lomond activities. Before the coming of the Club Bus, it was common for combined groups to hire lorries. The lorries were of the covered-wagon type, murderously cold in winter, always overloaded and not entirely legal in this use. Innocent-looking lorries would roll out of Glasgow crammed to the shutters with suffering climbers. There was a time when one such wagon came to a stop on the tramlines of a busy street. The driver could not wake it up, but after some minutes it began to move in a series of jerks. Someone peered out between the tarpaulins and saw a group of tram-drivers, conductors and policemen bursting their braces to get it clear of the lines. He signalled for silence, but a whisper came from a dim corner 'If the polis ask what's in the lorry, make a noise like sheep.'

MOUNTAIN HOWFFS
Vol. XXIV (1948)   by John B. Nimlin

The proposal to build more climbers' huts is a natural outcome of the discussions by the British Mountaineering Council, and, eventually, we may see a proportion of these huts appearing in the Scottish Highlands. What form the huts will take, plain structures offering simple amenities or luxury buildings with h. and c. and electrically heated bed-quilts, will in time be debated by the ascetics and the sybarites. It would also be reasonable to assume that the huts will serve as bases for the widest variety of mountain excursion; and the people who felt the lack of climbers' accommodation in the past should welcome the idea.

What, to me, seems more questionable is another proposal to erect huts on the mountains themselves, one suggested site being the corrie between Ben Narnain and the Cobbler. For this proposal I cannot find a spark of enthusiasm. I keep remembering that the ascent and descent of either hill could be made — if one lacked any imagination — in less than three hours, and that all the peaks in the group, A Crois, Ben Ime and the two already mentioned, could be traversed in a moderate day's outing from Arrochar. Indeed, my one regret — hardly excusable in the face of such mountain perfection — is the comparative smallness of the Arrochar Alps.

On aesthetic considerations my lack of enthusiasm is even greater. Until man can develop the architectural ability to enhance a mountain landscape his activities are better confined to the landscapes he has shaped for himself in the valleys. Already, in the good cause of national economy, Scotland must face some destruction of her mountain scenery by hydro-electric operations; may we, without any such impelling need, presume to aggravate the situation? Would people like myself, in the storm and stress of a winter gale, eschew the mountain hut? Who can say? The spirit is willing, but spare us from temptation!

Another consideration, perhaps the most important of all, is the need to guard against that ever-present urge to modify difficulty. Organised society habitually seeks the smoothest way. With mechanisation and labour-saving devices life has become so smooth that some of us seek a necessary corrective in grappling with rough, undisciplined crags, but we sometimes carry our habits into the mountains. Are huts the beginning of a movement to make the mountains fit for climbers rather than the climbers fit for mountains? It seems more than likely that the modification of much Alpine climbing started with the erection of huts: first the base hut, then the half-way hut and finally the summit hut, and in between, the fixed ropes, the ladders, and the permanent pitons — for pitons, too may serve that urge towards modification.

For me, climbing has always seemed to embody some immutable principles: something stable in a changing world. I like to think that even today my only advantage over

Mummery and his contemporaries is the possession of better climbing-nails, an advantage soon cancelled by the wear and tear of climbing. I like to think that I meet the crags on the same terms and without the aid of modern weapons like pitons, which, if properly used, will enable me to defy even gravity! I also know that mountain huts, guide books, mountain view indicators and all the rest cannot make climbing any more enjoyable than the things Mummery knew. A *gite*, in the shape of a howff or a mountain camp, may well serve the twentieth-century Scottish climber as it served Mummery. The hills are ever open to the climber who seeks them on their own terms — which brings me to this pet subject of mountain howffs.

The best known example of a mountain howff is the Shelter Stone of Loch Avon. Quite distinct from Corrour Bothy, which I would call the first unofficial climber's base hut in Scotland, the Stone is a natural shelter improved by man. The use of a howff is strictly in line with the ascetic nature of mountaineering. While living there the climber accepts the austerity of mountain life until his return to the flesh-pots. No other approach gives the climber such close communion with the hills. Mummery, although he preferred a tent, says this of Alpine bivouacs: "In no other way can one see such gorgeous sunsets, such 'wind-enchanted shapes of wandering mist,' such exquisite effects of fading light playing amongst fantastic pinnacles of tottering ice. To watch the night crawling out of its lair in the valley seizing ridge after ridge of the lower hills till the great white dome of Mont Blanc towers alone above the gathering darkness, is a joy that is hidden to dwellers in inns, and is never dreamt of amidst the riot of the table d'hote."

Mountains, when viewed through the lounge window of a hotel, are not always seen in true perspective. The whole scene may be coloured by the size of the fire in the grate or the relaxing properties of an arm-chair. The rain looks wetter, the mists look clammier and the question of venturing out becomes a matter for debate. But in the mountain howff, with boots on your feet and a wind-breaker on your back, you have no such hard decision to make; no need to test the water with your toes. I have known howffs, in the days before I learned the simple principles for improving their amentities, where it was a positive relief to step out into the blast, straighten the back and relax! However, a few practical touches will transform the average howff into a comfortable base for the better enjoyment of climbing.

There is a model howff — a show howff — in the lower corrie of the Brack some 1,200 feet above the Glencroe road. This howff came in very useful to Ben Humble, myself and the few climbers who helped in the investigations for the Arrochar Guide. Only three hours were spent on its construction. Fortunately, the original cavity had the essentials for a good howff, the main feature being a huge block of mica-schist resting on several square-sided rocks so as to form a sheltered recess with an exposure to the driest and calmest airt. In this case the base of the roofing block, the ceiling, was inclined downwards towards the entrance. This is a big advantage in a howff, as it removes the chance of drips running along the ceiling. As is usually the case, the formidable-looking rocks on the cave floor were loosely bedded and easy to remove. The best tools for this work are ice-axes or hand picks. Having neither implement in the Brack howff, we improvised with flattened soup-tins which made quite efficient soil-scrapers.

Many of the rocks thus excavated weighed several hundredweights, but gravity worked on our behalf. Adopting back-and-knee positions and pushing all together, we soon levered them to the doorway and toppled them down a short slope to the heather. Having thus cleared a space for five or six sleepers, we levelled off the floor, sealed up the apertures at the back of the cave and laid in a foot of heather and moss for bedding. The secret of a draught-proof howff is to baffle the air currents by allowing only one ingress which should be as small as possible. A ground-sheet hung over a wedged tree-branch or ice-axe will then seal the entrance against driving snow or rain. This howff, 'Cobbler View,' was well tested for structural defects that same night. A thunderstorm travelled over Glencroe, and we lay securely in our sleeping-bags as the blades of lightning flashed against the dark mass of the Cobbler.

There is another fine little howff overlooking Glen Loin — I give no other clue to its location — and, strange as it seems, this howff is rather too comfortable. This criticism, which is, naturally enough, not too strongly pressed, comes from our Hon. Secretary, who spent some bed-nights there in testing weather conditions. Two reasons may be given for this unusual situation. The first is a deep bed of dry heather; the second is a turbulent burn which cascades a few feet from the entrance. The monotone of rushing water, by absorbing all other sounds, seems to lull the senses into a deep, almost hypnotic sleep, which invariably means a late start on the morrow. The service of a loud alarm clock is indicated here. This howff may well remain on the secret list, as sabotage by jealous hotel proprietors is not out of the picture.

Comparing mountain howffs with mountain camps, I think the howffs have some advantages. An obvious one is the opportunity to dispense with the weight of a tent. Another is the feeling of security afforded by a well-built howff in bad weather, although this may be a personal opinion arising out of my early experiences in mountain camping.

Among several camping mishaps on the hills is one which I shall never forget. Two of us were camping near the crude shelter which lies under the smaller of the Narnain Boulders. It was a March night with a half-gale blowing from the south-east, but we crawled into our sleeping-bags in a rich, warm fug. The knowledge that nothing but a skin of canvas lay between us and the icy wind only emphasised the comfort of our position. Then, at the outrageous hour of 4 a.m., we were rudely exposed to a nightmare of swirling snowflakes. Alas, it was no dream, for the tent, still anchored to the leeward guys, was flailing about like a kite over the deepening snow. The seconds which elapsed as we danced a barefoot jig and fumbled for our most essential gear are the longest I have ever known. We spent the rest of that long night crouched under the Shelter Stone waiting for the tardy dawn. The phobia born of that incident still overshadows my full enjoyment of mountain camps, and this in spite of sewn-in ground-sheets, anchoring boulders and a necessary improvement in my camping technique.

Wild weather makes little difference to howff-dwelling. Temperature variations are never very drastic in a cave, and the odd snowdrift which might invade a high-level howff is more of an ally than otherwise. When the floor is cleared and all displaced snow is packed against the inside walls the howff is much more draught-proof than in summer. This is an experience I have often had at the Shelter Stone of Loch Avon. On a windy July day draughts will invade the Stone from all airts, but on several New Year visits, with plenty of snow to pack against the walls, I have found nothing more to contend with than low temperatures - no great hardship. On the New Year of 1936, when I had cut down load-carrying to the exclusion of a sleeping-bag, five of us slept at the Stone in a sub-zero temperature. With two men on either side encased in eiderdown bags, I slept in coat and sweaters with feet stuffed into a rucksack. True, my teeth were chattering when I wakened, but I had enjoyed eight hours' sleep, and four other sets of teeth were chattering in unison. True, again, I have to confess that our nightcap was a peculiar mountain brew, potent as heather ale.

Another time when snow befriended us was in the New Year of 1939, when six of us lived under the snow-cap of Ben Nevis. On that occasion the Observatory ruins were snowed-up to roof level, but we dug down to a window, cleared out one of the rooms and lived for two days of ceaseless blizzard completely insulated from the hurricane which raged above us.

Loath as I am to exploit the other man's misadventures, I am tempted to reveal that two members of the Club had preceded us to the summit on the previous day, and there brought in the New Year in a tent. Some time later I learned that the campers had withstood the first night of a blizzard and then beat a hurried retreat. As it happened, their tent had been pitched on the spot we chose for our entrance tunnel, and the spade we were using dug up quite a story. One did not need the sign-reading gifts of a Red Indian to follow that story. First we came on a knife and spoon, then a slab of cake and finally a sonsie specimen of a haggis — the cumulative evidence of a retreat not only hurried but headlong. We carried the food into our lair and devoured it with all that relish which is usually accorded to the spoils of the chase.

Summer or winter, howffs may well have a place in Scottish mountaineering. They can be built on any hill where rock debris is plentiful. Once built they are practically indestructible, and material for repairs is always at hand. The list of sites which offer facilities would fill a book. In Arran the corrie floor below the north face of Cir Mhor has very promising material, and so has upper Glen Rosa. In Glencoe a natural choice would be the upper corrie between Bidean nam Bian and Stob Coire nam Beith, and at the lower end of Coire an Gabhail there are several useful caves just ready for the finishing touch of a howff-builder.

Skye has probably the widest scope for howffs. Harta Corrie, Coire Lagan, Coire na Creiche and Coruisk are all natural sites where howffs might encourage more intensive exploration. In Coruisk especially, a howff would make a valuable base for the investigation of many remote crags, and suitable material is at hand for howff-building. In July 1946 Ben Humble, David Easson and I crossed into Coruisk from Glen Brittle, and on our line of descent, we found a giant boulder perched conspicuously on a mound. The recesses under this boulder would make a fine roomy howff which could be reached in three hours from Glen Brittle over the Banachdich Col. A climbing party with 20 to 25 lb. rucksacks of food, sleeping-bags, stoves and cooking gear could live here for two or three days and climb to their hearts' content.

By the side of Loch Coruisk there are two howffs already built up and ready for occupation. One of them, which lies east of the little copse of wind-stunted oaks and hazels on Coruisk's northern side, has a steep and promising crag springing from its doorstep to the crest of the Druim nan Ramh.

There is another cave on Loch Scavaig, a few hundred yards south of the Mad Burn, which we used as our bivouac during the trip already mentioned. It is little more than a slit in the base of a crag not far above sea-level, but it does not rank as a model howff. When we crawled inside a gusty wind from Coruisk was whistling through it. We did make a half-hearted attempt to build an inner wall of stones and turf, but darkness and fatigue - we had been bog-trotting and climbing for nearly nineteen hours - made us abandon the job. Unfortunately, I was lying at the unwalled section, exposed to a powerful draught which made me feel like an obstruction in an air-pipe. Another trial was the huge fire which had been lit inside the cave to compensate for our lack of sleeping-bags. At unexpected moments its flames would make sudden darts in our direction, blinding us with smoke and sparks. This was trouble enough, had not the man in the outside berth - safe behind his break-wind - kept nagging me to move farther in. My one bright moment was when his heather pallet went on fire and he took a header at the gabbro roof. If I visit this cave again I shall either complete the break-wind or induce someone else to take the inside berth.

There is a deep satisfaction to be found in howff-building, a sense of conformity with the primal nature of the mountain scene. No guilty feeling of spoliation when you move a few rocks and uproot a patch of turf which will in time renew its contact with the parent soil. Should any climber allow himself a greater liberty? In the mountains we find the last relic of the primeval in an otherwise ordered landscape, and this is their greatest attraction. Beside this simple sanctuary on the mountain's breast what deeper imprint would the climber wish to leave but a cairn of stones and a signature of white nail-scars upon the crags?

THE CONQUEST OF BUACHAILLE ETIVE
or
THE ORRA LADS' TALE
Vol. XXII (1934) by the Ancient Scottish Bard, Aodh Macbaph

This engaging tale — the well known party-piece of a senior SMC member — first
appeared in Cambridge Mountaineering

When wintry blizzards come and go
Aboot the peaks o' drear Glencoe,
And guid folks huddlin' roond the peat
List tae the blatterin' o' the sleet,
It's then ye'll hear the story told
Hoo long ago in days of old
Twa orra lads, sae rins the tale,
Did michty Buachaille Etive scale.
God kens the stock frae which they sprang
But they were souple lads and strang,
For no anither since that day
Has ever climbed yon fearsome brae.
The first ane's name, or sae I'm told
Was John MacSnorrt, and he was bold,
A tall, camsteerie, ugly chiel
Wha's temper was the verra de'il.
The ither's name was Wullie Flyte;
A little man wha's build was slight,
His shanks were thin, his hands were wee,
An inconspicious lad was he.

At Kingshoose Inn they spent the nicht
And started off at dawning licht.
Eh, man! but it was sad tae hear
Hoo yon MacSnorrt wad curse and sweir;
"De'il tak ye, Wullie! Hurry up!
Ye're like a muckle daunderin' tup.
Ye're no tae taigle us, d'ye see,
We maun be back in time for tea.

So off they went wi' highest hopes
And sune had climbed the gentle slopes,
And as they left the darksome glen,

Before them rose the michty ben,
Steep precipices, fearfu' chasms,
Eneuch tae gi'e the bauldest spasms.
"D'ye think," speired Wullie, "we micht
fa'?"
MacSnorrt, he answered nocht at a',
Juist boond a rope about his wame
And made puir Wullie dae the same.
They made quite sure it couldna slip,
And, each an ice-axe in his grip,
They started up, hand owre fist,
There was nae crevice that they missed,
Nae handhold but was firmly grasped,
Nae slabs but they were safely passed,
And mony a steep and icy gully
That put the fear o' God in Wullie.

At length MacSnorrt got on a ledge
Abune an awfu' chasm's edge,
And Wullie, scramblin' doon beneath,
Cried up tae him through chatterin' teeth:
"I hope that ye've belayed yersel'."
But bauld MacSnorrt juist answered: "Hell!

Man, but ye're gettin' awfu' saft,
The folk that use belays are daft,
Belays, ye ken, can only gi'e
A sense o' fau'se security."
Wullie replied: "Well, if I fa'
It's your fau't." John said, " Not at a',
It's yours for bein' sic an idjut,
Noo be a man and dinna fidget."

Sae Wullie, baith his e'en shut ticht,
Climbed up the rope wi' a' his micht.
And wi'oot further hesitation
Achieved at length his destination,
And clung there safe wi' pantin' breath,
His cheeks were white wi' fear o'death.

And noo sae far up had they come
There nocht was left but an easy lum,
Up which they went wi' ne'er a slip
Tae reach the mountain's lofty tip.

They sat them doon tae rest a bittie:
Says Wullie: "Man, isna that pretty?
Peak upon peak sae fair and grand
Like elfin towers in fairyland."
MacSnorrt said: "Dinna be sae fulish,
There's naethin' there but Ballachulish,
For God's ske dinna get poetic,
It acts on me like an emetic."

Tae a' guid things there comes an end,
The 'oor has struck, they maun descend.
MacSnorrt, for tae show off his skill
Sets oot glissadin' doon the hill.
But pride aye comes afore a fa'
For what he thocht was frozen snaw
Was really ice, and sune he slippet
And lost the ice-axe that he grippet.
Upon his back at furious pace
He shot twa hundred feet through space,
And on his doup he landed fair,
Eh! but yon dunt maun hae been sair.
Wullie cam clamberin' doon richt fast
And reached the stricken lad at last.
Man, but it gi'ed him joy in troth
Tae hear MacSnorrt bring oot an oath,
And then in muffled accents ask

If Wullie had the whusky flask.
He seized upon the braw Glenlivet,
And though I ken ye'll no believe it,

He didna draw his breath nor stop
Until he'd finished ilka drop.
It filled puir Wullie wi' vexation,
He got quite red wi' indignation.
MacSnorrt juist wiped his muckle mou'
And scrambled up. Man, was he fu',
He clutched at Wullie lest he fa'.
He couldna stand his lane at a'.

Puir Wullie didna breathe again
Until they reached the level plain,
But noo the world was lost tae sicht
In darkness o' approachin' nicht,
And mony weary miles were passed
Afore they reached the door at last.
The landlord welcomed them wi' joy
Tae see them safe frae sic a ploy,
The guidwife sune was on her feet
Tae get them a' a bite tae eat.

Oh happy man am I tae tell
That merry evening a' was well.
The table sune was neatly laid,
And steaming dishes were arrayed,
And though MacSnorrt declined a seat -
He took his supper on his feet -
His aches and pains were quickly drooned
As bottles travelled roond and roond,
And Wullie sune was heard tae say
Hoo much he had enjoyed the day.
But ane and a' agreed tae this:
While perfect rock is perfect bliss,
And ringing axe is music sweet,
The simpler joys are hard tae beat.

31.... mony a steep and icy gully
    That put the fear o' God in Wullie."
    Reg Pillinger in Crowberry Gully, Buachaille Etive Mor

32. Rob Anderson and Bill Murray on Sgurr Alasdair, looking towards Gars Bheinn

33. The Rosa Pinnacle - insets: Hamish Hamilton (left) and Bob Grieve (right)

34. *Looking up Glen Etive to the Buachailles, mountains bought for the nation as a result of the foresight and generosity of Percy Unna*

HIGH COOLIN DAWN
Vol. XXI (1937)

by B. H. Humble

Bill Murray had been in Skye for a week, but had not visited Coruisk, so I planned a journey there — and by the best possible route. At 10.30 p.m. on 23 June we left our camp in Glen Brittle and trudged up Coire na Banachdich. At midnight we bathed in a pool about the highest point of the burn, then zig-zagged upwards over broken rock. At 12.40 a.m., in mist and darkness, we were over 2,000 feet up, and arrived at a sloping ledge with a rock wall on one side and an impressive drop below. We donned extra sweaters, lay down, dozed, and slept. So passed the darkest hours.

At 2.05 a.m. we awoke and moved off. There was thick mist around us and rock to negotiate; with sleep not yet out of our eyes we had to tread carefully. Soon we reached the main Coolin ridge, and it was an eerie business finding our way along it in the grey ghostly hours before the dawn. Rock towers loomed up out of the mist, and were climbed or turned. The scratches of hundreds of hobnailed boots showed the way unmistakably.

On, over the two tops of Banachdich, over Thormaid to Ghreadaidh. I commiserated with Murray that, on this, our long excursion, we should see nothing but mist. He grunted and pointed to the south. It was strangely light now. We were among clouds, not mist! Away to the south a sharp cone of rock appeared. That was but the beginning, and the wonder of it all is still with me. The clouds sank slowly. Peak after peak came into view. It was fascinating, and not at all easy to pick them out and name them when detached from their connecting ridges and divorced from their corries. The sun was now up although hidden in clouds. Sgurr nan Gillean appeared quite black, while its outline was tinged with the rose flush of dawn. Am Bhasteir was unmistakable, and, as the clouds sank lower, we could trace the whole serrated range from north to south. To the west, white clouds stretched out as far as eye could see. To the east, great masses of clouds rolled over the bealach between Bidein Druim nan Ramh and Sgurr a'Mhadaidh and poured themselves down to the abyss, where lay Coruisk.

Suddenly a tremendous peak appeared in the east. It could only be "Blaven, mighty Blaven," a very Everest that morning. For two hours we watched, fascinated by the glory of the cloudscapes, then, in brilliant sunshine, moved on over the four rock tops of Sgurr a'Mhadaidh. Still the clouds swirled below us; from camp they saw nothing but mist at a thousand feet till early afternoon. We were truly "in the higher, purer air."

The heroes who first did the main Coolin ridge in one day took an hour and a half from Banachdich to Mhadaidh. We took six hours, and are not ashamed. Haste would have been sacrilege that morning.

At 9.30 a.m. we started downwards from Bealach na Glaic Moire, and at 11 a.m. had the bathe of a lifetime in a transparent green-blue pool, where the burn enters Loch Coruisk. "Grim and awesome," "Gaunt crags rising from the water's edge," "Dark ledges of barren rock" - these terms occur in the usual descriptions of Coruisk. That was not the Coruisk we saw! It was bright and welcoming that summer day. The ling, the true Scottish heather, was only in bud, but the bell heather was in full bloom. We trod through ferns and young bracken. We saw wild roses and a solitary rowan tree; the brambles tore our legs; the sundew flower glinted in the bogs, and butterwort, and heath dog-violet grew in profusion.

Our arrival was well timed. We had the loch to ourselves for an hour before the tourists arrived. Then MacBrayne's *Loch Nevis* steamed into Scavaig and dropped anchor. Murray said it never occurred to him, but at once I thought — a ship! passengers! food! An obliging boatman took us out, and we caused something of a sensation as we drew up at the side of the ship. Murray had a straggling growth of a week's duration on his face, while the adhesive gabbro had claimed a good deal of my trousers. The steward rose to the occasion nobly — a four-course lunch, two helpings of everything, and as many cups of coffee as we could drink.

Back ashore, and how different Coruisk! Tourists were scattered all over the southern shores of the loch. Some never managed that stony half-mile of path, while others were staggering along on high-heeled shoes. Wild men of the mountains they took us for, and we had to run the gauntlet of their cameras.

At 4 o'clock we started up the glaciated slabs of Sgurr Dubh Beag. The weather was tropical now, and that eastern ridge was sheer delight. Far below lay Coruisk with gulls wheeling around its islands. Beyond were the lighter waters of Scavaig, the green Isle of Soay, and laughing summer seas, extending out to the cloud-shadowed Coolins of Rhum.

That steep ridge was much longer than we thought. And how we suffered from thirst! A drop to the bealach — the only place where we used the rope all day — then on to Sgurr Dubh na Da Bheinn. What took us up that mountain was the thought of our last tin of grape fruit, which we had reserved for the top. Each particle of it I consumed slowly, rolling it round my mouth to savour the full relish of it and moisten my parched throat. Oranges were as scarce as gold in Glen Brittle last June, and we went through twenty tins of grape fruit in ten days.

At 9 p.m. we were on the summit. Our plan to cross the Thearlaich-Dubh gap and descend to Coire Lagan had to be given up, as we had told camp that we would be back about 10 p.m.

A rush down to Lochan Coir' a' Ghrunnda, a last meal there — sardines — and a fast walk over the moor, took us back to camp at 10.30 p.m. exactly, twenty-four hours after leaving. Murray agreed that I had shown him the best route to Coruisk.

A GREAT DAY
Vol. XXVII (1963)   By Robert Grieve

> The South Ridge of the Rosa Pinnacle still holds its place among the truly great classic
> Scottish rock climbs.

One of the great things about having climbed for more than 30 years is that one can look
back over a long series of Great Days. Some are greater than others, and this one day
during the war - and that, I begin to realise, is a long time ago. At that stage I had a very
young family who loved Arran because there they got everything they wanted - freedom
of movement, fishing, the hills, all that. We were staying, on this particular September
weekend, in a cottage, isolated, and standing at the foot of a little rock face beside the sea
near Pirnmill. The weekend was that of the Glasgow Autumn Holiday and Hamish had
asked me to phone from Pirnmill to his hotel at Brodick when he arrived on the Saturday
afternoon. I did so from a lonely roadside kiosk a mile north of the cottage. A cruiser was
moving at full speed down the other side of Kilbrannan Sound, a great wave at its bow and
firing shells over the Mull of Kintyre to a hidden target out on the Atlantic, and this
somewhat interrupted the ebullient one-sided conversation. The substance was that there
was a great climb to be done. It had to be straightened out. It was the south face of the
Rosa Pinnacle of Cir Mhor. "So," said Hamish, "I'll see you at Brodick to-morrow
morning, early, and we'll bash our way up Glen Rosa." For the first time I got a word in.
"There are," I said, "no buses on a Sunday." "Oh," said Hamish, only momentarily
dimmed, "well, you can walk across." "Walk across," I said, "what do you mean, walk
across?" He said "Walk across the island, of course, there are only two mountains in the
way." A very persuasive character, Hamish. I agreed, and only later that evening did I
realise what I had taken on, what in fact I had to walk across. But there it was; I had
contracted to meet him at 11 a.m. at the head of Glen Rosa next morning.

Next morning was dull and misty. The start at 7 a.m. was miserable and my mood was
not the best. However, out I went from the back garden straight on to the rocks. And then
as I mounted the slopes I saw the great north-west ridge of Beinn Bharrain looming up.
My spirits rose and paid no attention to questions of time. I dropped into the corrie and
climbed up this well-remembered ridge. A good scramble but time-wasting, and as I came
up on to the top of the mountain I realised that I would have to move very fast to get to
the head of Glen Rosa so many miles away at 11 o'clock. So I ran down the steep slopes
of Loch Tanna in a series of great leaps through weather which was still misty and dull,
but which had bred a fine free wind now beginning to thin and scatter the clouds that
hung about the great ridge of A'Chir. So I came to Loch Tanna and skirted its northern
end.

Then came the long slopes down to Glen Iorsa and when I reached the Iorsa I had
made enough time to look, in a relatively leisurely manner, for a point of passage where

I could jump from stone to stone and keep my feet dry. Then the long grind up the Garbh-choire Dubh to the northern end of the ridge of A'Chir and down again, leaping, slithering and jumping and recovering myself, to the head of Glen Rosa in the birth of a perfectly magnificent day.

And here was one of these rare conjunctions because I saw Hamish in golden sunshine, a small black figure, moving up the upper part of the Glen and allegedly yodelling. I yodelled back as he approached. He looked as though he had never realised it sounded like that and it stopped him for a while. The Glen settled into its mountain silence. We sat in comfortable companionship and ate. He talked and told me about his first attempt on this great face with George Roger a year before. We lay back on the heather in the sunshine, soaking up the warmth, and regarded the soaring ribs of the pinnacle with delight.

We rose, then, having taken off our boots and replaced them with rubbers. It was rubbers, be it noted; there were then no vibrams - certainly, we hadn't heard of them - and I think that climbing on rough rock in thin rubbers is an exquisite joy which is probably not so often appreciated by the highly technical and meticulously-equipped younger climbers of to-day.

What a superb climb that day was the Rosa Pinnacle! Rough clean granite, sparkling sunshine and dazzling clouds. This is not intended to be a technical account of that first ascent; even if I wished it to be, I couldn't write it. I never remember the details of climbs. So I will only say that I remember with particular delight the long layback with its tremendous impression of under-hanging space and only the strength of arms and the friction of feet holding one from the long drop down the immense spread of slabs and rocks. And, of course, I remember the crux where there appeared to be only two little grooves, one at the extreme stretch of the right arm and the other of the left. It couldn't have been like this but feeling is everything in memory. I remember, too, the overhang on which one lay and only managed to move up by means of the changes of position of one's fingertips and the snake-like undulations of one's belly over the rough rock. No footholds, and always, during the struggle at this point, the tremendous impression of exposure beneath. And, of course, I remember Hamish's splendid lead — that marvellous elan which he always displayed and which I always associate with his lively dark eyes and his black moustache. So, then, the summit, and the glorious half-hour which we all know, after a great struggle of this kind — a perfect miracle of beauty and the relaxation which permits one to know it. I can understand W.H. Murray's comment as he stood looking at his first mountain prospect - "I thought of the shortness of life with a pang."

But Hamish's thoughts were far more earthly. "Boy," he said, as he looked over the vast prospect of my return to Pirnmill, "it must be great to be tough." His relish was not entirely free of a touch of sadism. An exquisite refinement struck him: "And you've got to go right down again for your boots, too." This consideration afforded him extra pleasure, and me some bitterness at a lack of forethought. He talked about the nice stroll down to Brodick and dinner. And what nice dinners they had in his hotel, he said. He talked about the short hands-in-pockets saunter down the delightful Glen of Rosa (how right he was) and about a swim in the Rosa at some convenient and leisurely time during his dander. I was not amused at all. For a short time the brightness of the sun was dimmed and I hated him. I hated his little black moustache. I said abruptly and brutally that he looked like an unfit version of Tommy Lorne.

We made friends again and started the long scramble down to the right of the Rosa Pinnacle, walking down steep rough granite slopes to the Glen like apes with our legs bowed and our rubbers biting into the roughness. Then a short seat on the heather, the sun beginning to set, and we put our boots on again. And shortly after that there was Hamish, again a little black figure disappearing down the Glen, again making his Alpine noises and rendering the beauty of the Glen nugatory.

A'Chir once more, the passage of the ridge, the long corrie down to the Iorsa and, this time, I went straight through the water. The edge of condition was off me and the struggle was beginning to make itself felt. Of all the elements in that day of 17 hours I suppose the worst was the hellish grind up from the Iorsa to Loch Tanna. Some will understand my use of the technique of 1000 paces. You decide to walk 1000 paces. You achieve that target and you either set your teeth, and try another thousand, or you fall flat on the heather and relax for 5 minutes before attempting the next thousand, or two thousand, or three thousand. During this purgatory, clouds were rolling across the mountain tops and pressing down closer and closer to the surface of the earth. The day was going and thousand paces succeeded thousand paces. Grind, grind, grind. And now the wind was coming in great uneven buffets that sent me reeling from side to side over the heather. There is no indignity, to a tired man, like the indignity of punishment by a great wind, and I was full of hatred of it.

At last, Loch Tanna; and the dusk and the waves and the gathering wind and the great steep slopes of Beinn Bharrain. I could not face them or the struggle in darkness and wind over the tops. It was arguably foolish but I decided to come down Glen Catacol, thereby adding some 6 or 7 miles to my journey. Down, then, I went, down the steep slithery slopes of the path from the Loch. I can remember the reeling miles of bog and slough with the gleaming burn on my left in the darkness of the night and its various sounds - some beautiful, some frightening, but always a kind of companionship in them. And the wind and again the wind, throwing me about, forcing my feet to go where they would not go.

When I arrived at the road to Catacol and felt its calculable texture beneath my boots, I felt that the journey was virtually over. I could not resist sitting under the parapet of the bridge over the Catacol for half an hour, smoking a pipe, secure against the wind and waiting for some transport. But, of course, there was no transport, not during the war, not in Arran, not at that time of night. So eventually I arose, faced into the soaring south-westerly gale, now in its fullness of strength, and beat back down the road to Pirnmill, the whole 6 miles of it, lying against and struggling into the wind. Again the technique of the thousand paces.Thousand paces after thousand paces. Now and again the devilish wind would momentarily stop and let me fall, an undignified bundle, on to the road. It would wait till I rose, with rubbery legs, staggering, and would then throw me down on my back. I heard all the time, on my right, the roar of the waves. Sometimes when the road touched the sea I saw the 'white breakers wander in the dark.' When I reached the house at 11.30 p.m. I was hardly able to recognise it or to appreciate that it was there at all.

I came into the lamp-lit cottage and the roar of the waves came into it with me.My wife at the fire turned to the opening door with a degree of apprehension warranted by the hour, and the place. She looked at my face and then at my clothes."Did you have a good day of it?" she asked. I found my lips stiff and reluctant. "A Great Day," they said. But I was thinking — as so many times before and so often since — of the difference between the black jolting hostility of the mountains at night, of the intractability of boulders, peat-hags and rivers, and the warm, lighted, comfortable precision of a human dwelling.

THE KINGDOM OF THE SNOW.
Vol. XXV (1954)   D.J. Fraser

LEAVE the road where motors
          shuttle,
     Climb the slopes an hour or so;
Coming by gradations subtle
     To the kingdom of the snow.

Enter, for you need no permit,
     But a little strength and skill
To defy the hoary hermit
     Who is despot of the hill.

You will find a host of wonders,
     Forces that can overwhelm,
Cold that stabs and wind that
          thunders
     In his brittle, brutal realm.

Yet the fury of the weather
     Can achieve the sheerest grace.

See, a perfect snow-goose feather
     Modelled on each boulder's
          face.

All is new and unexpected
     In the kingdom of the snow:
Nothing here that seems connected
     With the world you left below.

Men have dreams of lunar
          landing,
     Nightmare journeys into space,
Flights beyond our understanding,
     Hazards few would care to face.

But the Scottish mountain lover,
     All within his week-end range,
Winter wonders can discover
     Every bit as rich and strange.

P.J.H. UNNA AND THE MOUNTAINOUS COUNTRY TRUST
Vol. XXX (1972)   by Alex Harrison

At the last A.G.M. of the Club a request was made of us that we reprint Unna's edifying 'Rules' once again. Happily, our Honorary President, Alex. Harrison, has provided us with a fascinating account of Unna's extraordinary generosity to the nation in helping to secure so many outstanding tracts of mountainous country for the benefit of the Common Weal. We print Harrison's account below and follow it with the letter to the National Trust in which Unna laid down his 'principles for the management of mountainous country for the use of the public.'

We are glad to reprint these 'rules' since it seems to us that, if preservation of the wild character of these regions is the aim, then they could hardly be bettered. Unfortunately (in our view) they have not always been strictly adhered to — paths have appeared in Torridon, bridges in lower Glencoe. It should perhaps be pointed out, however, that not all mountaineers agree that the Rules should be given a stringent interpretation. Harrison himself argues that 'under the changed circumstances (here he is referring to the increase in mountain accidents — Hon. Ed.) if paths and signposts will assist in certain cases in the prevention of accidents and in enabling the public to enjoy low-level walks there should be no hesitation in providing them.' Whatever one thinks of this argument, it seems to us that it would be mealy-mouthed to appeal to a more liberal interpretation of Unna's wishes in support of such a flagrant breach of the letter of the Rules. If 'changed circumstances' can justify such a breach, then what breach can they not justify?

"Unna was a realist," writes Harrison. Here, then, is the story of the realist who gave away a fortune to preserve a wilderness....

After the 1914-18 war the creation of a war memorial for Mountaineers was considered and I understand that an offer was made to buy the Cuillins. The reply was that they were not for sale but the mountains would always be open to mountaineers.

In 1935 Lord Strathcona decided to sell his estate and the Scottish Mountaineering Club decided to raise funds to buy the portion which included the north side of Glen Coe as far east as the Study and also a small strip on the south side of the river which included the summit of Bidean nam Bian. The area has 2,600 acres and this was accomplished. P.J.H. Unna was active in this.

In 1937 it was learned that the Forest of Dalness was in the market and Unna, who was President of the Club, took action and with the assistance of James M. Wordie (later Sir James) issued an appeal to the members of the British Mountaineering Clubs to raise £9,000 to buy the forest of 11,600 acres. Unna himself was a most liberal anonymous contributor. Thus an area of 22 square miles of mountaineering country was made available to mountaineers at all times of the year.

Unna, realising the importance of maintaining the wild nature of the country (probably from his experiences in the Lake District), addressed the letter of 23rd November 1937 to the Chairman of the Council of the National Trust for Scotland giving the views of the subscribers to the appeal regarding the making of footpaths and the erection of sign posts and other matters. Mindful of the necessity of providing a fund for the upkeep of the area he executed 7-year covenants which produced a fund of £20,500 known as the Mountainous Country Fund for upkeep and further purchases, and at the same time appointed a small committee to advise on further purchases.

In 1943 the Forest of Kintail came into the market and the committee advised that it was a suitable area and Unna put the N.T.S. in funds amounting to £12,500 to purchase it (again anonymously).

In 1951 the committee advised the purchase of Ben Lawers and adjacent summits for £8,000 and this sum was drawn from the Mountainous Country Fund, and in 1958, £5,000 was contributed to make the purchase of Goat Fell possible.

Late in 1950 Unna handed over to Trustees an investment in an engineering company worth approximately £6,000 with instructions that the Income and Capital should be given to the National Trust for Scotland for such use in connection with mountainous country as the Trustees thought suitable. This again was anonymous. The payments made from time to time included £3,500 for the purchase of Loch Skeen or the Grey Mare's Tail and in 1967 the balance of the Fund of approximately £17,000 was given to the N.T.S. to form an endowment fund to enable the Trust to take over Torridon Estate for the Mountainous Country Fund.

Unna died early in December 1950 and as residuary legatee the Trust received £83,000 after payment of duties. The interest from this fund has been used to maintain and improve the Properties which he donated. The Trust have very wide powers in the use of capital. The present value of all the Unna Funds is approximately £300,000.

Such is the story of the munificence of Unna which has been of inestimable value to climbers and hill lovers.

Letter from P.J.H. Unna, Esq., President, Scottish Mountaineering Club to the Chairman and Council for the National Trust for Scotland, dated 23rd November, 1937.

Dear Sirs

As the movement initiated by a group of members of the Scottish Mountaineering Club to acquire Dalness Forest and hand it over to the National Trust for Scotland, to be held for the use of the nation, so that the public may have unrestricted access at all times, has now materialised; as subscriptions to that end were invited not only from the members of the Scottish Mountaineering Club, but also from the members of all the other mountaineering clubs in Great Britain; and as the fund so subscribed enables the forest to be handed over free of cost to the Trust, together with a surplus to be used as an endowment fund - it is considered desirable that what are believed to be the views of the subscribers as to the future of the estate should be expressed in writing, and recorded in the Minutes of the Trust. This is all the more necessary, as in the attached circular which was issued for the purpose of inviting these subscriptions it was stated that the land 'would be held on behalf of the public and preserved for their use' and 'that the Trust' would 'be asked to undertake that the land be maintained in its primitive condiiton for all time with unrestricted access to the public.' The views in question are:

1. That 'Primitive' means not less primitive than the existing state.

2. That sheep farming and cattle grazing may continue, but that deer stalking must cease, and no sport of any kind be carried on, or sporting rights sold or let; any use of the property for sport being wholly incompatible with the intention that the public should have unrestricted access and use. It is understood, however, that deer may have to be shot, as that may be necessary to keep down numbers and so prevent damage, but for that purpose alone.

3. That the word 'unrestricted' does not exclude regulations, but implies that regulations, if any, should be limited to such as may in future be found absolutely necessary, and be in sympathy with the views expressed herein.

4. That the hills should not be made easier or safer to climb.

5. That no facilities should be introduced for mechanical transport; that paths should not be extended or improved; and that new paths should not be made.

6. That no directional or other signs, whether signposts, paint marks, cairns or of any kind whatsoever, should be allowed: with the exception of such signs as may be necessary to indicate that the land is the property of the Trust, and to give effect to the requirement in the Provisional Order of 1935 that by-laws must be exhibited.

7. That should a demand spring up for hotels or hostels, it is possible that it may be satisfied to a limited extent. If so, they should only be built alongside the public roads, and should be subject to control by the Trust; and it is suggested that no hotels or hostels should be built in Glencoe itself, or on any other part of the property, except, perhaps, in the lower reaches of the Trust property in Glen Etive. It is hoped that the Trust may be able to come to an understanding with neighbouring proprietors as to corresponding restrictions being maintained in regard to land near to that held by the Trust.

8. That no other facilities should be afforded for obtaining lodging, shelter, food or drink; and especially, that no shelter of any kind be built on the hills.

9. It is hoped that the design of any buildings which may be necessary will be carefully considered by the Trust; and that, where possible, trees will be planted in their vicinity.

10. In conclusion, it is suggested that the whole question of the management of the Trust properties in Glen Etive and Glencoe should receive special attention, in view of the possibility that the policy adopted by the National Trust for Scotland in the present instance may create a precedent for similar areas in other mountainous districts, not only in Scotland, but also in England and Wales.

Yours faithfully, P.J.H. Unna.

THE LATER YEARS

WE HAPPY FEW
Vol. XXVII (1960)   by R.W. MacLennan

The epic story of the creation of the Clubrooms

Number 369 High Street was discovered by George Ritchie. He had it inspected by two members who belonged to the architectural profession. They were elated. It was great. Wonderful. Just what we required. It only needed....

It consisted of three ex-slum houses — early nineteenth century — knocked together to form the unprepossessing premises of a rather primitive printer. Floors and ceilings had been hacked about to house his cumbrous machinery and everything expressed the debility consequent on generations of heavy thumping. His policy as regards repairs and maintenance had obviously been 'Apres moi — the demolishers.'

However, lay members in the face of such informed enthusiasm could only endeavour to hide their ignorant apprehensions. Misgivings there were, but somehow they never managed to rise quite to the level of consciousness. If you met George Ritchie anywhere near the High Street he would press a rusty key on you and insist that you have a look. When you returned he would cast a quick glance over his shoulder — to make sure that neither Haig nor Marshall were on the horizon — and ask anxiously what you thought of it. You would say that it was great and he would agree and the conversation would trickle to a dispirited ending.

However the die was as good as cast. Authority was impressed also. The professional pair measured the place and produced a plan — an officiously technical looking thing, very suitable for bandying about at meetings. A plausible spokesman was briefed and primed. That apathetic hum, following a brisk secretarial suggestion and known as 'Committee assent,' was duly secured.

First steps and the mood of the time are best shown by the following quotation — which, of course, betrays its origin: that bombastic yet nauseatingly ingratiating style remains peculiar to the East of Scotland circular, a publication which could justly be described as 'the yellow press of the mountaineering world.'

NEW CLUBROOM

The last circular contained a rather cryptic note about new clubrooms. Those members who have attended recent lectures will have heard more about this and may have accepted the invitation to inspect the premises and see the work in progress.

The remaining 95 per cent may now like to be put in the picture.

The locus is 369 High Street. Two floors above the shop front of Stewart the draper, five dirty windows (one of them a dummy) mark the spot. A common (extremely!) stair leads directly to the second flat. The landing door opens on to a large room (36 by 15 ft.) where the said four windows give a fine view of the north buttresses and curved ridges of St Giles'. This will be the lecture room and/or Club lounge, the transformation being effected by drawing a dual-purpose curtain.

Off this and facing north are two smaller rooms (about 11 by 13 ft.) destined to serve as library and kitchen respectively. In addition, a lavatory and wash-place.

The rent is extremely modest and for a very good reason. The place was in appalling condition - no electric light, scabrous plaster falling off everywhere, a floor of unpredictable contours and an all-pervading, unmentionable smell.

However, to a Club able to substitute unpaid labour for tradesmen's bills, this is a decided opportunity. Similar property in good condition rents at four times the figure asked for here.

We have to thank George Ritchie for its discovery and the professional acumen of I. D. Haig and J. R. Marshall for seeing its possibilities. (This notice is intended to discourage any further remarks anent 'wir fees.')

Thereafter we are indebted to the President and the Hon. Secretary of the Club for coming through, inspecting and sponsoring the project in Committee.

(Those who were privileged to see it will not easily forget the sight of Ross Higgins standing in the midst of the aforesaid squalor, peering into the cobwebby gloom, lit only by a single flickering torch - and, with the rapt look of the visionary, talking grandly of public receptions and Festival exhibitions.)

The Club Committee, who also viewed the premises, took the generous view that this could be the National Headquarters and agreed to back us on the tentative cost put forward to them.

This cost, however, presupposed a large amount of voluntary, unpaid labour. Some of this has been forthcoming already (including J.M.C.S. members), but all additions are welcome. Tuesdays and Thursdays from 7.30 to 10 P.M. are the usual work parties, but any alternative times can be easily accommodated. Work is under the undisputed supervision of I. D. Haig (Dean 3266), who is only too willing to hear of any offers of labour, material, transport, etc.'

The history of the clubroom, it will be noted, resembles that of mankind. After unrecorded tribal confusion the first written document shows a servile state with an absolute ruler firmly established, and the final result is similarly a monument which is the expression of the ruling personality made permanent by the anonymous industry of his enslaved fellows. The lower classes contributed their quotas of dogged labouring and generous pilfering and inspired wire-pulling but were denied any share in the management of affairs. Little sympathy should be given them on that account, however; the astute reader may even detect a note of relief in the subservient reference to 'undisputed charge.' Reacting to the horrible prospect of a Clubroom embodying all the varied prejudices of our untrained tastes, it had been decided to give Haig his head. As he later discovered, the aches went with it. The lower orders became rather adept at loyally passing all difficulties upwards.

Haig was therefore called upon to produce — or rather to generate — at considerable cost to himself — the key processes required for an enterprise based on the shaky chassis of voluntary labour and powered by the uncertain fuel of nebulous funds. Tyrannical gaffering was a first necessity and considerable art is required to inject the necessary urgency. The 'jolly-good-show, go-to-it chaps' atmosphere just won't do.

Equally imperative was an ulcer-courting devotion to logistics and economy, astonishing to those who, with every bright suggestion, added hopefully 'The Club's got the money.' The cost of these rooms if a greenhorn had been in charge can be guessed at from an incident involving a display of ungovernable rage from Haig on learning that one of his deputies had actually made some purchases at normal retail prices.

Thirdly — and most unpalatable of all perhaps — he even developed an Oscar-earning ability to cajole and bully the plausible but dilatory donors of essential goods and services.

These are the tributes that would appropriately be awarded by an impersonal narrator. The writer in this case, however, can draw on his own worm's-eye view memories of this sterling character in action, and is in fact grateful for the opportunity to offer such a 'profile'. Dipping his pen in vitriol he hastens happily on.

The Hon. Architect has never been described as the most genial of men. His normal expression is admittedly astringent. His manner, some might say, is forbidding. A kinder word has been 'off-taking'. Among his friends it is alleged that his characteristic activity is sitting in a corner, quietly hating. His mere presence it is said, has blighted the evening of more than one cheerful novice venturing innocently into Lagangarbh when Haig was in residence.

He was therefore a personality well suited to cope with the types of volunteers who presented themselves. Many of those were sufficiently well known to him to make any pretence at politeness unnecessary. Any of their helpful suggestions, their lengthened sage advices, could be answered, if at all, by his customary stock of four-letter or five-letter words.

The nucleus of the work party was formed by a group of ill-assorted individuals who had frequented a Hanover Street howff with weekly regularity. They now found their Thursday night conviviality transformed into penal servitude with Tuesday night added for good measure. The service they were able to give was varied in quality, the attendance often uneven, but they were apparently the best that could be got.Little attempt will be made here to evaluate their several contributions. Those mentioned directly or by implication are presented because some handy insult is available to drape like an albatross around their necks. Those inadvertently omitted require not apologies but congratulations. In more or less the order in which they came under the hypnotic domination of the Hon. Architect they were:

MacLennan — an individual with a great deal to say but little of it as a rule to any point. As a worker, utterly handless. An indefatigable destroyer of tools and waster of energy. Tolerated mainly for his contacts with the underworld of the building trade and his open-sesame to an Aladdin's cave of disused furniture (library table, kitchen door and cornice, etc.). Even in these directions he was handicapped by his intrinsic lack of common sense. 'What,' thundered Haig repeatedly, 'is the use of leaving messages with you when you never remember them properly?'

Russell — a man of some skills certainly, but most ambitious when practising those he knew least about. Like Haig, another little Caesar — vociferous, venomous, usually to be found working vigorously at the origin of a spate of abuse. A generous provider when this lay in his power — stole and installed the clubroom radio.

Stirling — at that time doppellganger to Russell, a lean, silent, sinewy object with a withering stare. Drifted in unfailingly every night; laboured morosely with ill-concealed scorn for others less skilfully engaged. Much given to Rembrandt-like touchings with the paint brush; after which he would descend to contemplate them soulfully from a distance.

Stewart (J.M.C.S.) — Adam ('Cannon Ball Heid'), a much-maligned dignitary from the days of the cable cars, also highly regular and conscientious (or — according to Russell — given to malingering in quiet corners).

Gordon (J.M.C.S.) — the second of the 'Glen Grant' twins. Dave was a tower of strength and a repository of skills. He could do anything with trademen's tools except explain what he was doing with them. The fairy godmother of the squad — any passing wish for special tools or fitments and next evening Dave would turn up with a huge brown paper parcel containing the lot. Any enquiries were met with a heavyweight wink and 'Eh?' delivered with the same volume of sound as the one o'clock gun. These generous but mysterious benefactions, which overwhelmed even the greed of the Hon. Architect, were eventually received with as much apprehension as gratitude (see end of paragraph on Russell).

George Hood — an obnoxious presence, who, as one of nature's anarchists, could hardly resist the opportunity of paying with some attempt at work for the pleasure of taking part in so perfect a shambles.

A sane man, G. Scott Johnstone, the sole hero who appeared straight out of the alien tracts of the membership list and, working in this half-witted medley, survived uncontaminated (perhaps) until spring and geology bore him away to the North.

J.R. Marshall came in like a lion and went out like one addicted to architectural competitions. His raucous, meteoric presence always gave at least an illusion of rapid progress. His undoubted talents as provider of building materials had their drawbacks. The phone would ring in the middle of a busy office afternoon.

'Boab?'

'Yes, James?'

'Lorry coming with battens, bricks, three hundredweight of sand. You'll have to give the man a hand up.'

'But I'm tied up. I've ...

'It'll be there in half an hour.'

'But how can I ...?'

'So long!'

George Ritchie, on the other hand, gave ample warning of the supplies he procured for us. Seven to eight weeks in one case — a never-failing source of surprise to him — 'What! It hasn't arrived yet? I'll get on to him immediately!' However, for that marvellous toy, the sanding machine, alone he deserves his niche. George also did some florid work on the lavatory door. This was for the record, with the Hon.Architect standing grimly over him.

Haig failed utterly in his ambition to get a stint out of a less busy but equally elusive character allergic to manual labour. A half-promise had been obtained, so when this unsullied individual happened to appear, Haig proferred a paint brush. 'A' (nothing would make us reveal the surname) considered it with a wan sneer. In elegant distaste he murmured, 'Which end do I hold?' And there the prospect faded.

Apart from those still to star in these pages, mention shôuld be made of those who were able to contribute an evening (or perhaps two) and of those unfortunates who, calling up on other business, found themselves press-ganged on the spot.

However, on the basis of the awkward squad aforementioned, the work-in-progress referred to began in the first days of 1958. True, the Hon. Architect had already had a lordly walk round, with slaves attendant, wrenching off a shutter here, tossing a gas bracket over his shoulder there, and so on. But by mutual revulsion the place was left at peace during the festive season, its unredeemed squalor appropriately dishonoured by the graffitti now discovered on the walls: 'G. Caius Ritchus 51 B.C.,' 'Martialis illegitimus est.' (The riposte of the maligned 'M', calling attention to the characterof one Maclenicus, is unprintable even in Latin; he was undoubtedly the ignoblest Roman of them all.)

When the work at last started in earnest it did so in spectacular fashion: walls were attacked with hammers and chisels and ice-axes; the sordid old plaster evaporated in explosions of poisonous dust; laths were gouged out; fireplaces gutted; piping disembowelled. The talents of those engaged were obviously stimulated by the opportunities presented here for wanton destruction (J.R. Marshall was outstandingly brilliant). The nightly scene was one of noise and confusion with the clouds of volatile stour lit only by a temporary electric lead.

The results of all this enthusiasm had to be shovelled off the floor and put into sacks. The sacks had to be tied and piled up in odd corners to make room for a new rain of rubbish. Occasionally somebody gave a half-hearted sweep round but a fresh tide would then engulf everything. When the accumulation became unbearable a lorry and man would be commissioned from Jock the blacksmith and for a glorious evenng or two there would be a yard or two of space.

The said Jock was reduced to a state of wonder and dread by our activities. It was probably seven times that he carted away what he was assured was the very last load.

The neighbours were rightly alarmed. But here we were fortunate. Of the two families in the stair, one was stone deaf. The other consisted of a lady of robust character (when she and Gordon were passing the time of day it could probably be heard out at Fairmilehead), and her husband, who looked in on us every Thursday evening, after his weekly tank-up, to give encouragement and historical background in a state of bemused benevolence. His final benediction was always 'Ye're daein fine, lads ...' as he was helped up the stairs by Haig. From the small hall below a deputation of diffident but resolute old ladies sometimes came up to point out that our knockings interfered with their meeting — a spirtualists' seance!

By the time the preliminary dust had settled, something else was as plain as the bare walls. No more members would arrive. Of the imposing membership list some were over-age, some overworked already, no doubt. Some had more urgent or more vital business and some, we assumed, had a higher I.Q. or a lower opinion of the advantages of a clubroom.

Taking our cue from the Hon. Architect, we lost no opportunity of brightly introducing the subject of the clubroom in any chance encounter with a stray member. We heard with sympathy many stories of incredibly crowded lives. Some of these used to begin spontaneously at the mere sight of one of us. The Hon. Architect even reported that he had seen vaguely familiar shapes hurrying past with averted faces — but he was always one for seeing the worst side of human nature.

However, another and more peaceful phase had now commenced. The ribald song of the blow-lamp made resonant music, and in every corner intent rooted figures with one hand aimed up and down and along, with the other scraped and scraped. It was slow, unsociable work and sometimes, over the welcome break of refuelling, a couple of heads came together in muttered rebellion. But even the most oblique conspiracies for moving on to more interesting tasks were ruthlessly suppressed. "Any instructions?" snarled the Hon. Architect. "Until further notice there is only one instruction. Remove all paint."

So the squad scorched wearily on. MacLennan could be observed expertly cracking window panes with a confidently directed jet of flame. While passing from one glass to another he did occasionally dislodge some paint, no doubt by accident.

The presence of 'Cannon Ball Heid' could be deduced from the polyglot repertoire proceeding from his corner, 'Ich hatt' einen Kameraden' alternating with 'An t-Eilean Muileach.' Gordon was still shouting, as offensively jovial as ever, Stirling still bleakly staring, Russell still fulminating.

Organisational worries now began to beset the Hon. Architect. He began combing the membership list again, impatiently flicking over useless pages of bankers, lawyers, civil servants, M.D.'s, seeking out a peerage of joiners and plumbers, or — most daring hope of all — the princely presence of a plasterer. Having marked down the few strands of gold in this array of white-collared dross he disappeared on mysterious visits. From these he returned in one of three moods — (a) radiant and relieved, (b) sceptical and suspicious, (c) abusive and blasphemous.

However, a new era was casting its shadow. While the proletariat bungled steadily on, a series of star performers from the trades began to tread the boards.

First to appear was our genial Fred Mantz, from the J.M.C.S., following promptly upon a delivery of the bricks that make up his daily work. The effect on the workers hitherto present was like that of the Colonel's visit to the cookhouse or the minister's appearance at the whist drive. For Fred is notoriously gentlemanly, apparently devoid of malice and incapable of satire. In his sunny presence the numbed rabble were for the time being, deprived of their crude nightly orgy of gleefully baiting each other to the raw. Visibly deflated, they watched Fred, on arrival, graciously accept the stack of bricks and the mix obsequiously prepared for him and, before starting to work, don a pair of gloves! Worse was to follow. No four-letter witticisms. The click of bricks falling professionally into place was accompanied by dissertations on the Haydn quartets or whistled illustrations from Gluck's Orphee. The rabble, muck to the eyebrows, worked around on light tasks, while Fred — spruce, white-shirted, gloved — built up fireplaces. The debacle was complete.

This might have made a lasting transformation. But Fred is a man with many calls on his violin and it appears, like most of those addicted to culture, blessed with supreme absence of mind. With half a fireplace left to do, he disappeared, leaving the door unlocked, and we saw him no more. The Hon. Architect, gratified but shaken, completed the job, gradually recovering his venom in the process. The rabble, no longer inhibited by good manners and opera, took to abuse and scurrility again.

Second performer and Joiner No. 1 was R. Brown — another man with many calls on his time. Richard, obviously marked out for a contribution, had, apparently in advance, selected his sphere of activity and calculated to a nicety the appropriate number of man-hours due. He appeared with tools and, taking Gordon in tow, proceeded to conduct a blitzkrieg in the side room, as a result of which the desired library fitting arose magically completed. A fine piece of work, and 'Good old Dick' was the cry of the moment.

But a sad sequel illustrates the transient nature even of deserved fame. The said Richard's evening employment left him with about 15 minutes to spare on certain work nights; these minutes he elected to spend in the Clubroom, strolling happily up and down, humming or whistling, the very image of idle privilege as he treated the bent backs of the labourers to carefree renderings of Mackintosh's Lament or Cha till MacCrumein. Gibes about 'well-dressed gaffers' and offers to lend scrapers or sandpaper brought only a tactful about-turn or an ostentatious switch from urlar to crunluath. And one of those who may have cried 'Good Old Dick,' now standing with a chisel in hand, looked perhaps for a moment at a spot between the shoulders of the slow-marching pibroch whistler — and, with an effort, resumed using the chisel for its proper purpose.

With Joiner No. 2 there were quite different tribulations. R. 'Secundus' Marshall had apparently been awarded the honour of laying the new floor. It is doubtful whether his consent was formally sought, but nevertheless he turned up for the task, imperturbable as ever. Gordon was enlisted as skilled labourer, and plank by plank a new wooden skin began to form over the ocean waves of the old floor.Noisy progress seemed assured. Then

35. *We Happy Few. The SMC New Year Meet at Newtonmore, 1953*
Back Row, left to right: R. Buckland, J.R. Marshall, J. Douglas, K. Armstrong,
D.Mackenzie, J. Kerr.
Front Row, left to right: I.D. MacNicol, R. Jeffrey, J.S.M. Jack, W.N. Ling

36. Tom Patey

37. *Jerry Smith on the first winter ascent of Parallel Buttress, Lochnagar*

38. Iain Brooker on the first pitch of Eagle Ridge, Lochnagar

a sudden stop. Tuesdays, Thursdays followed each other, but no Secundus. He was 'wrighting' ships being drydocked in incredible numbers at Leith. The Hon. Architect danced about, frantic. Gordon wandered disconsolately about the unfinished works. At the pitch of blackest despair Secundus unexpectedly walked in, and resumed as if from yesterday. This pattern repeated itself more than once. In fact, it persisted almost to the very end. There was one long-standing gap in the new floor which no one believed would ever be closed — not until Secundus one evening clouted in the last nail, with an expression of mildly astonished reproach at our impatient anxiety.

There was also the entertaining cross-current of Architect v. Tradesman, a traditional duel in which both sides are as convinced of infallibility as Rome and Avignon. Tactfully, at first, but gradually becoming more barefaced, each protagonist began to employ measures designed to minimise the effect of the other's unfortunate aberration. The result was a masterly contest in floormanship in which considerable resources of guile and obstinacy were called up on either side.

Haig was progressively, helpfully suggestive, pointed, blandishing, darkly authoritative. Secundus, who at best has only about four different facial expressions, none of them particularly communicative, switched them all off and contrived to indicate a mood of faintly amused neutrality — a performance at which he has probably no equal.

Their campaign ranging up and down the floor, and into every corner, whetted their every suspicion of each other. They even took to appearing on alternate evenings — Secundus working with stealthy diligence on Tuesday, Haig marching bands of witnesses over the same ground on Thursday — Down there was where he was to have been working. He only came up here to finish it off his way before I could stop him.'

On the whole, Secundus seemed to have the greater stamina. In their last head-on clash, when Haig pointed an accusing finger at a floor finishing and recalled his minute instructions to the contrary, Secundus considered the evidence, and then Haig, with robust sangfroid: 'It seems, then,' he confessed comfortably, 'that I've made a - - - - - - of it"; his tone was one of cheerful satisfaction.

In the plumbing trade all seemed set fair. D. Lamont (J.M.C.S), a small, youthful, almost spherical object, was mild and obliging. He looked worried as he worked. And he actually changed things at the behest of the Hon. Architect. This was a model assistant, a credit to the ranks of the whippersnappers, and it was considered fortunate that during his stint the S.M.C. Committee would break off from their meeting across the square to call in and inspect progress. Lamont would be on hand, attentive and diffident, handily placed for a Presidential pat on the head.However, when the Committee arrived Lamont was making a joint. This involved looking very worried indeed. It also involved making occasional fast runs along a line between the gas-fire and the kitchen sink. During a lull the Committee entered and took up positions at various points along this line. There was a minute or two of lordly appraisal. Then the next run started. A worried-looking, overalled object took off from the gas-fire with something red-hot in pincers.

Attitudinising members were knocked sideways, Vice-Presidents and Secretaries nearly flattened. An Edinburgh dignitary got as far as 'This is young La . . .' as the latter handed him off, burst through a loose maul into the kitchen and got down to it without a backward glance.

The Committee pretended they hadn't seen anybody.

The foregoing events were not, of course, neatly consecutive. Some idea of the orderly progress of achievement in it will be obtained only if it is remembered that they occurred simultaneously and were telescoped with floor-sanding, Snowcemming, reception of furniture and all sorts of other ploys simple enough to mention but each a crisis in itself.

It was soon summer and barely half-way to any hope of completion. 'I don't know how you fellows have the heart to go on holiday,' commented Haig bitterly to three who had already booked and paid for Austria. And certainly with such upsets things lagged even more. There were spells of near mutiny and the Hon. Architect had to go round mollifying and peacemaking; the rhythm reasserted itself and without enthusiasm work went on. We were scraping the bottom of the barrel for assistance now. There was patching to be done on the door and Haig conjured a joiner out of nowhere to do it. There were tiles to be laid round the fire — a baffling thought until Gordon produced 'the brother' out of thin air and he rattled it off with professional ease.

There was an interminable amount of painting. There was the ceiling to be papered by Haig and Russell (custom-built for this particular height). They got up on a skaky batten, facing each other with hands aloft holding up folds of pasted strips and performed a sort of Balinese dance to get it correctly applied. Neither being of a phlegmatic disposition, this performance was generally highly rewarding to the audience, particularly on the occasion when one of the strips turned out to be a yard short and the dance ended in outstanding tantrums.

Eventually, almost before we noticed, it could be said that the worst was over. The library arrived. The slide collection was moved in. Wondrous light fittings, stimulating aesthetic discussions, made their appearance — the straw cigar in the library and, in the main hall, the spotlights and the two dull opaque spheres that were instantly christened 'The Brothers Stewart.'

An opening day was eventually fixed. But true to experience, work and muddle continued almost up to the very opening hour. On the Saturday forenoon in question the carpet was being sewn together in situ. The curtain thankfully arrived, no more than comfortably anticipating the opening ceremony.

And the writer's experience of Clubroom construction ended, more or less as it began, with the raucous commentary of J.R. Marshall, who was engaged in fitting up the curtain rail. The thing doesn't work properly to this day.

CAIRNGORM COMMENTARY
Vol. XXVII (1962)
Tom Patey

'Any fool can climb good rock,' said Dr J H B Bell, 'but it takes craft and cunning to get up vegetatious schist and granite...' 'We were bound for Lochnagar, the greatest citadel of vegetatious granite.' — W. H. Murray (Mountaineering in Scotland).

It was the opinion of most climbers of the thirties that no worth-while routes had been recorded on Cairngorm granite. This was not misrepresentation but fact. With the exception of a few classic climbs (such as the Mitre Ridge of Beinn a'Bhuird or the Eagle Ridge of Lochnagar) exploration in the Cairngorms before 1946 had not gone beyond the Gully Epoch.

Most gullies are unpleasant. A Cairngorm gully is doubly so. It is the sort of place you would incarcerate your worst enemy; a dank gloomy prison where moisture seeps from every fissure and 'all the air a solemn stillness holds' — save for a constant drip, drip from many a greasy moss-enshrouded chockstone and the occasional dull thud as another ledge sloughs away in a welter of slime and rubble.

The early mountaineers, who revelled in the false security of gullies and chimneys and spurned the hazardous freedom of the open face, must have found the Cairngorms a veritable Mecca. Here were any number of holdless muddy walls against which to erect a pyramid of stout fellows in tweed jackets, greasy constricted chimneys where they might squirm and wriggle to their hearts' content, and improbable through-routes streaming with icy water and black as Old Nick himself which 'would just admit a cragsman of average girth.'

It is a pity that so little exploration was carried out by the mud-bespattered pioneers, for their accounts in epic Victorian style would have made splendid reading. In fairness it could be pointed out that the few climbs they did pass on to posterity earned a notoriety out of all proportion to their number.

There was Raeburn's Gully in Lochnagar which on the first ascent in 1898 harboured a great block 'surmountable only by the aid of an ice-pick hung from the upper edge.' On the second ascent 30 years later, the main obstacle had become 'an imposing two-tier pitch some 70 feet in height.' Unhappily the famous Double Cave pitch was not destined for longevity, and following a rock fall in 1940 'not a vestige of it remained.' The Editor of the Cairngorm Club Journal sang its requiem: "I regard this as a catastrophe of the first magnitude...fitting to be classed with the fall of Constantinople, The Union of 1707, Hammond losing the toss at Sydney, and things of that kind." A few years later I was one of a large party that had a grandstand view of the collapse of yet another entire pitch near the top of the gully. We had a special interest in this pitch because we had descended it only 10 minutes earlier in order to attack the unclimbed chimney on the right wall of the gully. At least two of our number had come along merely to watch or pass ribald remarks, but by the time the echoes had died away and the clouds of dust had settled we had suddenly become a united party of six. Thus was made the first ascent of the Clam.

There was also the Douglas-Gibson Gully of Lochnagar. Like Raeburn's, 'it changes its character from year to year' — to borrow a phrase from the pioneers. Raeburn himself made several unsuccessful attempts between 1897 and 1901; ultimately, he was lowered from the top and was 'sufficiently discouraged by what he saw not to try again.'

Up to the early 1940's the Cairngorms retained the aura of inhospitality ascribed to them by these early climbers. in 1941, however, a worthy champion emerged in the familiar colour of Dr J.H.B. Bell, who may be regarded as the patron saint of granite climbers and the first prophet of the true Gospel. None of us had ever met Dr Bell: to us he was merely a voice, thundering out a clarion call from his distant S.M.C. editorial chair. Yet he seemed to feel much as we did about the Cairngorm granite, describing the Eagle Ridge of Lochnager, his favourite route, in fine authoritative vein as 'for difficulty, narrowness and steepness altogether superior to any of the well-known Nevis ridges.' His two companion routes on Shadow Buttress 'B' and the Tough-Brown Ridge served to illustrate that there was no lack of sound climbing rock in the Cairngorms for those who had the initiative to find it.

It had been amply proved that the Cairngorm gullies had little to recommend them, but Bell was the first to demonstrate that the more exposed ridges, faces and buttresses of rough weathered granite had as much to offer the rock specialist as many more highly rated Scottish crags. His researches were to inspire young Aberdonian climbers after the war, for here a school sprang up owing little to any pre-war group. Many of its early struggles took place in that notorious Douglas-Gibson Gully, whose first ascent had in fact been made in 1933 by one Charles Ludwig (the first man to attach a skeleton to the spire of Marischal College and to cross the "Blondin" wires above Rubislaw Quarry).

Ludwig in fact set little store upon his Douglas Gully adventure, and described the route as 'perhaps unjustifiable.' Such a qualification had of course the unintended effect of securing for the climb the attention of successive generations of young aspirant V.S. men who may be relied upon to accept any open invitation to deride their elders. So for a time in the bad old days 'before the dawn of reason,' many young tigers were blooded in 'Gibson's', often literally, so that the gully gained quite a reputation for itself. The more loose rock they pulled away, the more they uncovered, so that the standard varied from V.D. to V.S. in successive weeks.

It was not until 1949-50 that the winter ascent which had eluded Douglas and Gibson in 1893 was again seriously considered. Abortive attempts followed — probably the most spectacular being that on which George McLeod plummeted from the cornice almost to the lochside, a vertical height of some 800 feet. He had been turned back at the last pitch and, while roping down in the approved fashion, suddenly found that he was no longer able to maintain a grip with numbed fingers and slid down the length of the rope, rocketing off the end like a small shooting star. Deep powder snow saved him from annihilation; he escaped with bruises, and climbed up again to safeguard his companion's descent.

On 30th December 1950 'Gogs' Leslie and I emerged, shaken but triumphant, from a hole in Douglas Gully cornice, thereby ushering in a new era of winter expeditions on routes which had hitherto been regarded a solely within the provinces of the rock specialist. It was also our first premiere and earned grudging recognition from our more talented contemporaries together with admission into the select conclave that gathered in the Fife Arms, Braemar, on a Saturday night. We did not broadcast the principal factor in our surprise coup — that having climbed well beyond the point where we could have safely withdrawn and finding no belays for an abseil we had little option but to continue climbing. In the long run we both profited from this good fortune, and learned several important lessons. I cannot recall ever again suffering such agonies of apprehension on a climb.

Leslie and I had thus dramatically elevated ourselves to a peerage which I had first encountered two years before in rather humiliating circumstances. I was one of a motley collection of Gordon's College schoolboys who had chosen to spend Hogmanay in the Cairngorms, using as our base camp Bob Scott's bothy at Luibeg. We discovered that more than 40 climbers were housed in various outbuildings and that we had been relegated to the stick shed as befitting to our lowly station. Minor snow drifts formed inside the building and an indoor thermometer recorded 40° of frost. Next door in the bothy, which was reserved for the hierarchy and where the heat from a blazing log fire drove one back to the farthermost corners, were two very celebrated mountaineers — Bill Brooker and Mac Smith. We soon guessed their identity by the excited buzz of conversation that signalled their return from a climb, the sudden hush as they entered the bothy, and the easy grace with which they accepted the seats of honour nearest the fire. Mac Smith was then (and still is) the chieftain of the Luibeg Clan — an all-round mountaineer who had taken part in almost every important summer or winter ascent in recent years. He knew the Cairngorms better than any of his contemporaries, and they would have been the first to admit it. The bothy armchair, which has only recently been vacated and converted into firewood, was Mac's prerogative — a rustic throne. Bill Brooker, 'the young Lochinvar,' cut a more dashing figure, the complete counterpart to Mac's slightly reserved manner. To all outward appearances he was merely another pimply-faced schoolboy like ourselves, full of wild talk. But then who could forget that this was the same young heretic who had but recently burst into the climbing arena with a series of routes which had defied the best efforts of preceding generations? With such a wealth of mountaineering experience behind him, you could overlook the lad's extravaganzas.

These were the real mountaineers — not mere 'hill Bashers' like ourselves who had that day tramped many an endless mile in search of a minor 3009 foot Munro top away out in the middle of the Great Moss. We had built a little cairn on what appeared the most elevated undulation and been well satisfied with our day's achievement. These men spoke of icy vigils and gigantic ice falls; routes that finished long after dark; remote bivouacs in faraway corries, riotous nights in bothies, late-night dances in Braemar, and brimming tankards in the Fife Arms. Adventure, unconventionality, exuberance — these were the very elements missing from our scholarly conception of mountaineering which had led us with mathematical precision up and down the weary lists of Munro's Tables.

I do not know what impressions we left behind. A few of our number were kilted and this earned us the title of the 'Horrible Heelanders,' a name which stuck. I remember listening with envy to the two demi-gods as they planned the first winter ascent of Crystal Ridge, success already a foregone conclusion. Late next night when they did not return at the appointed hour, we spoke hopefully of a search party, but this merely earned for us the derision of the company. Their confidence was soon rewarded by the arrival of the victors, eyebrows caked with frozen drift, faces glowing with the heat of battle...

A year later, in my first year at University, I became part-owner of a climbing rope. After some preliminary experiments, we started cautiously feeling our way up the well-trodden Mods. and Diffs. of Lochnagar and the Sputan Dearg.

At that time it was impossible to climb for long in the Cairngorms without becoming aware of the diversities of opinions, and ideals that characterised the bothy set and stamped each of its members as a genuine eccentric, uninhibited by the conventions of society. Even the names by which they were know invited a wealth of conjecture - Sandy-Sandy, Ashy, Chesty, Dizzie, Sticker, Esposito, the Hash Kings...

The Hash Kings might have been a Secret Society. Their hashes, which were compounded of every conceivable ingredient known to man, were justly famous. I never learned the names of the founder members, but on one of my early bothy weekends I met a character who introduced himself with simple dignity as 'Apprentice to the Hash Kings.' Sad to relate, the Hash Kings have faded into obscurity, and the name itself has become abbreviated to Hasher, which is synonymous with bothymonger or nignog, and this is a very low order of animal life indeed.

Of a later vintage were the Boor Boys, a group of unruly youngsters from Aberdeen Grammar School who terrorised the bothies; among their numbers were Kenneth Grassick and Graeme Nicol, later to become respected sons of the S.M.C.

Then there were the individualists, although every man in that company wore the hallmark of an individualist. One remembers Stan Stewart who strummed his guitar on the back seat of the Three Fifteen. (The Three Fifteen from Bon-Accord Sqaure was a special bus tactfully set aside for climbers by Messrs. Strachans Ltd., following incidents in which old ladies had been isolated at the back of the bus by a mountain of rucksacks, only effecting an escape, several miles beyond their destination, by a desperate hand traverse.) There was Charlie Smith, brows furrowed in concentration, whistling some obscure aria; Mac Smith and Kenny Winram arguing about the early New Orleans trumpeters; Jamie Robertson engrossed in Marx; Freddy and Sticker, the inseparables, plotting new routes in Coire na Ciche; Alex Tewnion, with binoculars and camera, in quest of some unsuspecting dotterel; Chesty Bruce resplendent in tartan shirt and wide toothy grin, with his band of camp followers; Bill Stewart, who thought nothing of cycling out to Lochend Bothy for a day's climbing on Lochnagar, a round trip of 100 miles; and Ada Adams bound for Derrry Lodge, to supervise the weekend 'work party' from the Cairngorm Club.

There were three clubs in Aberdeen: the Cairngorm, the Etchachan and the University Lairig Club though, by and large, more reputable climbing was done on impromptu bothy weekends than during organised meets. Only a few regular week-enders were active club supporters and perhaps most of these owed allegiance to the Etchachan Club, a splinter from the Cairngorm Club. The latter club, though nowadays flourishing and not lacking in initiative, seemed to us then rather moribund. Most of the members were keen hill walkers, but there was a notable lack of rock climbers. Even the club circular had an archaic quality, describing club meets as 'motor coach excursions' and ending with the solemn injunction 'Members are requested not to ring the Meets Secretary at his residence.' We later found that the wording of the circular could be adapted with only minor alterations to a West Indian Calypso tune, and the song enjoyed a fair measure of popularity among the nonconformists.

The Etchachan Club was in many ways the antithesis of the Cairngorm Club. The latter wined and dined in the Fife Arms, the Etchachan Club merely stopped for a half-hour break at any convenient pub; their meets were less expensive, but there was a certain air of austerity, not to mention frustration, in leaving a half-pint standing on the bar counter to sprint for a bus which moved off punctually on the half-hour.

The University Club, like most clubs of its kind, enjoyed an ephemeral existence. Certainly its most flourishing period was during the reign of Ken Grassick. It was his policy that a mountaineering club should not solely depend on the support of accredited mountaineers. A club could be run on popular lines if it supplied suitable entertainment for its members, not only in the mountains, but also in the valleys. His recruiting campaign was initiated by an advertisement in Gaudie, the students' newspaper. 'Qualified climbing instructors, including some of World Repute' (this phrase was masterly) 'will be glad to show newcomers the ropes…climbers (of both sexes) welcomed…no mountaineering experience necessary! The bus will stop at the Inver Inn for refreshments, singing, etc.' The response was more than gratifying. Instructors were soon able to select their 'clients' from a large number of applicants and bus meets were attended by upwards of 70 members. Not all came to climb, though nearly all enjoyed a little fresh air prior to the evening's entertainment. Thus it came about that a day meet to Lochnagar cost merely 5s. a head, and the end justified the means.

We saw very few climbers from farther afield: it was left to local climbers to reap a weekly harvest of new routes. Most visitors to the Cairngorms came only to collect Munros, sleep a night at the Shelter Stone or pass through the Lairig. The few who sported nylon ropes, pitons and P.A.'s almost invariably courted asphyxiation in some foul enclosed chimney, or lost themselves in a vegetatious jungle on what should have been an honest straightforward line, misled by ambiguous descriptions in the existing Guide Book.

There were, of course, the Great Unwashed — itinerant, bearded Englishmen usually unemployed or unemployable, all of them friendly fellows, particularly when the scent of food was strong. They could be distinguished by their Mancunian accents, a preference for Glen Brittle Youth Hostel, and an enthusiasm amounting to adulation for a certain Joe Brown, then an unknown name in these remote parts. "'E's incredible!...like a yuman spider!...'e doan't cut 'and-'olds and feet-'olds on t'ice...'e cuts a thin groooooove and lie-backs oop it!' (whistles of incredulity).

These hairy vagabonds were legion in the Cairngorms. One remembers Droopydrawers (an apt name this) who could imitate all the instruments in a jazz band and invariably did just that within seconds of introducing himself to a company of total strangers. His equal in megalomania was the man Bob Scott recalls as the 'Birmingham Highlander.' This gentleman wore his kilt in the manner of his professedly Scottish ancestors, i.e. in modo naturae. He took pains to advertise this, and it was therefore all the more ironic that it should have led to his undoing. One day when walking near the lip of a steep snowfield, he lost his footing and set off upon a long involuntary sitting glissade. Most of us are aware of the heat that can be generated through thick corduroy trousers. This gentleman had no such protection. He has not been seen around much lately.

Among other immigrants were the 'Be Prepared' types, not all of them Scoutmasters. I once accompanied such a man. After relieving him of his pack for a short distance I was curious to discover its contents. The following items came to light — one hemp rope (for use in mist), Guide Book, Maps, Compass, Protractor, Torch and Spare Batteries, one Do-it-Yourself First Aid Kit, one Sleeping Bag (against possible benightment), and a small tent (for indefinite benightment). He told me that the Cairngorms were dangerous mountains, and that it was unwise to take liberties with the elements.

This motley influx certainly added colour to the climbing scene, yet one could only deplore that so many were profoundly ignorant of the vast rock climbing potential. The existing S.M.C. Guide was partly to blame for this, the descriptions of routes being so inexact that in one instance a single route was described three times under different headings. Another route, hallowed by tradition — the Married Men's Buttress of Sgoran Dubh — has never in fact been identified since its inauguration in 1906 'when snow masked the lower rocks.'

It was not until 1954 that plans were formulated for a new Rock-Climber's Guide to the Cairngorms under the joint editorship of Mac Smith, Mike Taylor and myself, the three of us having received official S.M.C. sanction for our labours. Later on several other Etchachan Club members took an active part, but the main burden was shouldered throughout by Smith who had to compile a readable Guide Book from the various sources of information. He devoted six years of his life and a few grey hairs to this worthy cause.

Thus, should the new Guide appear to be too partisan or too well laced with Vallot-type superlatives — (une des plus belles, des plus difficiles, des plus importantes escalades etc., etc.) — then this is only to be expected from such a fervent disciple as Mac, who cannot have missed more than a few weekends in the hills for sixteen years. No local climber past or present could pretend to claim such kinship with the Cairngorms.

Nor is Mac's enthusiasm so grossly unwarranted. It cannot be disputed that a lot of Cairngorm granite would benefit from a liberal application of weed killer; on the other hand, the North-East climber finds more exhilaration in opening up an exciting natural line on a 600-foot unclimbed buttress than in subjugating 150 feet of unscratched vertical outcrop. The latter calls for nerve and high technical skill but makes little or no demands upon the climber's route-finding ability and gives no expression to his imaginative talents. To my mind the magic of a great route does not lie in its technical difficulty or even the excellence of its rock but in something less readily definable — atmosphere is the term generally applied. A route should fulfil an honest purpose: it should follow a natural line of weakness of a natural obstacle and reach a logical conclusion. There are many so-called routes whose conception would not tax the mental faculties of an ape. They start from cairns set midway between existing cairns and follow straight lines up the cliff to other cairns at the top. Such routes portray complete lack of purpose, imagination or logic on the part of their creators. In the Cairngorms the climber's mental horizon is fortunately wider.

There is some loose rock in the Cairngorms. So much the better. Personally, I detest rock which is intrinsically rotten and whose security can never be accurately assessed, but loose rock is a natural hazard which may be safely negotiated by a leader not lacking in guile and judgment. I must confess to finding the impeccable gabbro on Sron na Ciche pretty dull fare. The rock is too good. It is so riddled with holds as to be climbable almost anywhere and it demands no more of a leader than an average athletic physique and some technical ability.

In case this may seem to be a tirade against accepted values in rock climbing, I admit that the Cairngorms do not offer the same scope for severe face climbs as do the playgrounds of the West, Glencoe and Ben Nevis. The Cairngorms are now firmly established as a reputable rock climbing centre and it took several years of campaigning among the infidels to achieve this; hence it may now be freely conceded that Cairngorm Granite does not measure up to Chamonix Granite or even to Glencoe Porphyry for difficult sustained face climbs. If this appears to be a deliberate volte-face then it should be remembered that to destroy a myth you have to create another myth. The sober truth seldom satisfies, for most mountaineers are sceptics by adoption, if not by nature. The net result has been satisfactory and the Cairngorms are now accredited with no more than their fair share of glory. The winter potentialities should be assessed in altogether different currency. In snow and ice climbing, the Cairngorms and Lochnagar yield to none. Their only rivals are Ben Nevis and Creag Meaghaidh, where snow conditions are infinitely more variable, and inconsistent. Glencoe can be discounted right away; the first prerequisiite for winter climbing is a modicum of snow, and the recent mild winters have produced nothing worthy of that name below 3000 feet in Glencoe, thus dealing a death blow to its traditional reputation for ice climbing.

The North-East climbers of the early fifties were all individualists but never rock fanatics. There are no crags in the Cairngorms within easy reach of a motorable road and a typical climbing weekend savoured more of an expedition that of acrobatics. If the weather turned unfavourable, then a long hill walk took the place of the planned climb. All the bothies were well patronised - Luibeg, Lochend, Gelder Shiel, Bynack, the Geldie Bothies, Altanour, Corrour and of course the Shelter Stone. At one and all you would be assured of friendly company round the fire in the evening. Everybody knew everybody and formal introductions were unneccessary.

It was a sad day for Lochnagar when, in August 1953, Bill Stewart fell to his death on Parallel Gully 'B'. Although his initial slip was a mere six feet, the rope sliced through on a sharp flake of rock and he fell all the way to the corrie floor. It was a cruel twist of fate to ovetake such a brilliant young climber, and for many of the 'faithful' it soured the love of the hills that they had shared with him. The numbers dwindled on the Saturday bus and the crags shed much of their glamour; the majority of the old brigade took to hill walking and ski-ing, where they could forget unhappy memories and still enjoy the camaraderie of the hills.

It was not long however before two new groups emerged from the crucible. The first were the Boor Boys, now masquerading under the more genteel title of the Corrour Club and including the aforementioned Nicol and Grassick. The flame of adventure burned as brightly as before. Nicol had read so many books about the Munich climbers of the avant-guerre that he had himself become pseudo-Teuton and spoke of all-night bivouacs on minute ledges 'contemplating his destiny' like a Buhl. History records that after hurtling 120 feet to the Lochnagar screes before a large, impressed audience his first words to his rescuers were as follows:— "Turn me over and let me see the place where I fell. It wasn't V.S.," he cried bitterly, "only Hard Severe." He lived to redeem his lost honour and despite the trifling inconvenience of several cracked ribs was none the worse for his accident, being left without so much as an honourable scar.

His comrade, Grassick, had already fallen off once in the process of testing the security of a large block to which he had conscientiously belayed himself. Unhappily the block was loose: when it fell, Grassick fell too. He wasn't a dangerous climber in the accepted sense of the term — merely 'accident prone' as they say in Industry. This was borne out a fortnight after his first ascent of Polyphemus Gully, scene of previous marathon bids by Brooker. Grassick had just joined the short axe school but failed to realise that the new weapon had only limited application in the art of glissading. The Left Hand Branch of the Black Spout held only a fraction of its seasonal snow build-up, and lower down the gully quite a few sharp rocks protruded from the hard icy surface. Into one of these Grassick cannoned at high velocity, shedding his axe on the impact and finally coming to a halt on the pile of big boulders at the gully entrance. Several relays of stalwart climbers carried him down the mountain and the incident is still commemorated by two brief entries on the wall of the Gelder steading: K. Grassick — climbed Polyphemus Gully — 6 hours, and the postscript in different handwriting K. Grassick — carried down — 5 hours.

An even more colourful occasion followed, on which Gordon Lillie dislocated a shoulder while seconding Kenneth on another Lochnagar climb. They made their way down to the nearest roadhead and were rescued by none other than Princess Margaret. Lillie sat miserably beside the chauffeur; while Grassick in the back seat made intelligent conversation with Royalty. Next morning the press reported the rescue on the front page and Grassick, never slow to seize his share of the limelight, was quoted as saying — "She was radiant...I never knew anyone could look so beautiful...Her pictures just don't do her justice." — a graceful tribute from a commoner of Grassick's lowly station. We looked in vain for his name in the New Year's Honours List.

The Kincorth Club under the joint leadership of Freddy Malcolm and Alex 'Sticker' Thom were formidable rivals. The majority of their new routes were located in the Coire na Ciche of Beinn a'Bhuird, which came to be regarded as club property. The Club Headquarters was sited at the Howff, the exact location of which is still a secret for the excellent reason that the head gamekeeper turns a blind eye to its occupants. The construction is partly subterranean and is the eighth wonder of the Cairngorms, with a stove, floor boards, genuine glass window and seating space for six. The building materials were brought from Aberdeen to the assembly line by the herculean labours of countless torchlit safaris which trod stealthily past the Laird's very door, shouldering mighty beams of timber, sections of stove piping and sheets of corrugated iron. The howff book records the inaugural ceremony — 'This howff was constructed In the Year of Our Lord 1954, by the Kincorth Club, for the Kincorth Club. All climbers please leave names, and location of intended climbs: all female climbers please leave names, addresses and telephone numbers.'

'Freddy and Sticker's Howff' was not unique. It stood in a small village of howffs, three in number and together capable of accommodating an entire climbing meet. There was 'Charlie's Howff' which had lock and key, a tiny door of Alice-in-Wonderland proportions, and a skylight — until some misguided individual fell through the latter, deceived by the almost foolproof camouflage. 'Raymond Ellis's Howff,' the third of the group, was entirely above-ground, with no attempt made at concealment. Five miles farther, and three thousand feet up on Beinn a'Bhuird, you may still stumble upon 'Mac's Howff,' a cave of the Shelter-Stone variety, made habitable only by the extraction of a giant rock tooth which yielded to the combined efforts of 'a drill and a mason's four pound hammer.' 'Mac's' was the first of the howffs, dating back to 1949, and it had been inspired by Jock Nimlin's article in the then current issue of the S.M.C. Journal. It did not enjoy any lasting popularity because of the marathon hike that it demanded after closing time in Braemar — 13 miles via Invercauld Bridge or 9 miles if you chose to ford the Dee, waist deep in icy water.

More new routes were recorded in this period that ever before, though proportionally fewer climbers participated. Nor indeed was the exploratory trend due to any significant advance in skill or technique, because excellent climbs of Very Difficult standard or less were still coming to light. On the other hand, an early sign that the boom period was nearing or past its zenith was the relative increase in the number of first winter ascents, scope for which was still enormous. Developments had proceeded at such a pace that occasionally the first winter ascent of a route followed almost immediately the first summer ascent, and in a few cases actually preceded it, as with 'The Scorpion' on Carn Etchachan. As potential Guide Book Editor, Smith's resources were severely taxed in keeping abreast, and those of us engaged upon checking route descriptions found it more profitable to anticipate new routes than fulfil our obligations with less glamorous second ascents. We had already agreed that any new route worthy of inclusion in a climbing guide covering such a wide area should at least exceed 200 feet in height and should follow a logical line up a recognisable feature. Without these limitations, guide book descriptions would have become hopelessly bogged down by technical data.

Eventually and inevitably, the first invaders began to arrive, precursors of a new regime, which was to challenge the Aberdeen climbers for the leading role in the development of Scottish ice-craft, and whose elite were to make even more exacting winter climbs, routes such as the Orion Face Diretissima and Minus 2 Gully on Ben Nevis.

In these final years of isolation, two further outstanding climbers appeared: Ronnie Sellers, who did many routes of the highest standard, along with Jerry Smith, a likeable Englishman naturalised in Aberdeen. Two accidents in the same summer cost us these two friends.

For 10 to 15 years, the Cairngorm fraternity had existed as a closed community uninfluenced by the traditions of other clubs or denominations. During these years they had perfected a new brand of ice climbing by adapting Alpine snow techniques to the requirements of their native crags in winter. Virtually their only contact with the wider world of mountaineering was at holiday periods when a few enthusiasts reached the Alps, while others hitched a lift to Skye, the Lake District or Wales. Weekend exploration was curtailed by the shortage of car owners. Much more could have achieved, but it would have lost the group its individuality.

Nearly all recent exploration has been from the Braemar side of the Cairngorms. Despite the wholesale exploitation of Aviemore and district as a summer/winter sports area and the seething hordes of humanity on the Speyside hills, very little has been recorded from that airt. Aviemore is too far from the main climbing crags to be of any value as a rock-climbing centre. The northern corries of Cairngorm and Cairn Lochan offer only scrappy climbs and the buttresses of Sgoran Dubh, though impressive as a whole, disappoint individually. Among the popularly acclaimed climbing crags only the Shelter

Stone cirque is more readily approachable from Aviemore than from Derry Lodge, and this only since the new Ski Road was constructed.

Because they have no vested interests in the northern sector of the Cairngorm massif, North-East climbers generally have been indifferent towards the new chair-lift on Cairngorm, which might seem to pose a remote threat to their privacy. The chair-lift might unleash hordes of souvenir-hunters and salvation-seekers over the central Cairngorms: of these perhaps quite a few would come to an untimely end. Against this is the complete lack of inspiration and the gregariousness that characterises the modern tourist.

Ten years ago Coire Cas was as dreich a place as you might find anywhere in the Cairngorms. As a corrie it was wholly devoid of character. At the time of writing it contains one large continental-type chalet (with the hint of more to follow), a chair-lift which works occasionally, and on an average weekend in February, upwards of a thousand skiers of all shapes and proportions. I must confess that I now find Coire Cas more stimulating. Even for the mediocre skier there is a Milk Bar selling hot coffees and no lack of gullible young novitiates upon whom to practise one's skimanship. Knowledge of a few basic terms (mambo, wedln) and a nodding acquaintance with some of the Austrian and Swiss instructors is an undoubted asset. Skis may be carried or occasionally even worn; although in the latter case the least embarrassing course is to continue steadily ascending till out of sight (langlauf). Coire Cas is undoubtedly a colourful scene nowadays, and it owes this to superimposed humanity and not to the landscape.

Nevertheless the danger in the Coire Cas scheme is that it may be the forerunner of others which would threaten the finer and more remote fastnesses of the Cairngorms.

The peculiar fascination that the Cairngorms hold for so many climbers cannot be ascribed to any one special feature. Different facets of the mountain scene have their own appeal for different people. For myself I have always held that it is impossible to dissociate mountains from those who climb upon them. The Cairngorms are a compact group of mountains. The Cairngorm climbing fraternity has always been a closely-knit community, linked by similar ideals and aspirations. Good climbing and good company often go together: each is essential to the enjoyment of the other.

In the Cairngorms they are inseparable.

ON ANCIENT HILLS
Vol. XXV (1954)   Jeff Mason

> TEN thousand thoughts with pendent intent fade,
> Of previous men who on these tops have strayed.
> And suddenly the small
> Tinkle of a mountain stream floats up, to recall
> Wind thoughts, guardian of secret things,
> Offering the fragrance of which it sings.
> 'Tis here, 'tis here,
> Ten thousand memories linger near.

THE PINNACLE AGAIN
Vol. XXVI (1958)

by W. D. Brooker

The Black Spout Pinnacle was the last of the great Lochnagar buttresses to be climbed. Its first ascent by D A Sutherland and myself in 1949 had marked the beginning of a surge of rock-climbing exploration in the Cairngorms. Our original route has long since fallen into the "easy day for a lady" category, but for me, at any rate, the Pinnacle has always proved a fertile field both for conjecture and activity.

The towering 600-foot wall of the Pinnacle is cut at about one-third height by the Springboard ledge system. Above, the buttress rises in two sections. The left flank is a curving sweep of slabs, easing off towards Pinnacle Gully 1 and curling round beneath the Springboard to form a steep smooth barrier extending to the Black Spout. The right half is a very steep wall rising from the Springboard and narrowing to an overhanging nose from which an arete leads to the summit. This wall is sharply terminated on the right by the huge gash of the Black Spout and Left-hand Branch and had remained untouched until Tom Patey's Route 2 was made, traversing across the face, 100 feet beneath the Nose, to reach the slabs of the left flank. The original line, Route 1, follows the roof-like curve of the left-hand slabs and then breaks back to the right to join the summit arete. The bottom 200-foot girdle of slabs was unclimbed until Jerry Smith made his Pinnacle Face Route late in 1955. This climb has a high reputation for difficulty and interest and slants left until it is possible to traverse back to join Route 1 about 100 feet above the Springboard.

However, the Pinnacle, I felt sure, had even more to offer the inquiring climber; and was not its choicest prize of all, an ascent in winter, yet to be awarded?

To the small band of worshippers who seek their Nirvana on the winter cliffs of the Cairngorms, the start of each season brings a hubbub of armchair discussion on the prospects and possibilities of the coming months. Optimistic waves of debate sweep to and fro across the tables of cafes and saloon bars; angles recline, cornices shrink and calloused fingers trace improbable straight lines on glossy photographs. For the moment enthusiasm reigns, for memories of last winter's sojourns on insecure icy stances have been washed away by weeping summer skies. So dawned the 1955-56 season, and hopes were high, the winter sanctity of some of the most promising of Lochnagar routes being, as yet, inviolate. Week-end after week-end the faithful congregated at their shrine, and time and time again they were denied their communion. It was not until the 4th of March that Parallel Buttress, the most illustrious and sought after of the "icy virgins," yielded to persistent wooing.

The following Sunday saw Jerry Smith, Dick Barclay and myself toiling up the snow slopes leading to the Black Spout Pinnacle. Conditions had changed since the ascent of Parallel Buttress the previous week-end. The large quantities of powder snow had shrunk to crisp frozen sheets lying on the ledges and holds. Steep rock surfaces were bare and dry; ice gleamed cold and grey in cracks and was smeared here and there like black varnish. As I slowly worked the treadmill of the Black Spout slopes in my usual position well to the rear, I was galvanised into action by the need to field a rucksack, which came bounding towards me, disgorging various items of food, clothing and less respectable implements of the climber's trade. Heavily laden and bursting with reprimands, I joined the others below the first pitch of Route 1.

Jerry had already donned the rope and was making a few tentative swings with his axe. He moved easily on to the initial slab and worked his way towards its upper margin. Here he stopped. I could appreciate his problem: 8 feet above him lay a recess, which was topped by a slight overhang leading to an upper sheet of slabs. To gain the recess he required two sets of footholds, handholds being lacking. The slab was really a kind of shelf with an enclosing wall on the right. Close to this wall the ice on the slab was thick and satisfying, but farther away it thinned and petered out. The footholds could not be placed in the thick ice because the wall was too close to allow the retention of balance. Carefully Jerry chose a spot where the ice had thinned to about half an inch, delicately carved a pair of slender notches and eased himself upwards. For a critical moment his centre of gravity teetered on the precarious limit of stability, his anorak rasped slowly up and across the wall and with an audible sigh he stepped up to the recess. This recess is an insecure place, even in summer, and the climber savouring its grudging amenities cannot even stand in balance. I did not envy Jerry's position as he extended a gloved hand beyond the roof and pushed a piton into a crack. With its aid, he cleared a large hold of ice, grasped it and swung on to the upper slabs and the comforting security of two good footholds, previously prepared in ice nearly two inches thick.

At this point Barclay raised his head from his hands, blinked a bloodshot eye and announced that, to his great regret, the effect of his carousals the night before would prevent his sharing our day's sport. Jerry rested for a moment and began to hack a line of holds diagonally leftward towards a bulging nose of rock. Beneath the bulge he encountered exactly the same problem as on the slab below and, very carefully, employed the same tactics.

It was my turn and, with the dubious comfort of a sympathetic glance from Barclay, I set off on the stimulating journey to Jerry's stance, extracting the piton en route. We were on a ledge crowned by a wave of hard snow. From the head of an ice-axe plunged into its crest, I launched on to a 6-foot wall and clawed my way ungracefully through a tiny cornice to the blissful security of the Springboard.

In our position we enjoyed the transitory warmth of the sun, shortly to disappear behind the upper battlements of the Pinnacle. The air sparkled with just sufficient frost to keep the crust on the snow. Stately galleons of cumulus sailed across a blue sky and the snow-flecked winter moorland rolled away from the shores of the frozen loch to the Deeside forests. Previous attempts on the Pinnacle in winter had failed on the first pitch, and we felt sure that the hardest part of the climb lay beneath us; at any rate we nursed the hope that nothing quite as hard lay ahead. Our spirits rose to the extent of lobbing an enormous icicle into the Black Spout in the hope of rousing Barclay from his torpor.

Full of eagerness, I began to climb up the right hand of the two lines of weakness that slant up to the left above the Springboard and was abruptly brought to a halt by a vindictive little chimney, which jeered derisively at me from beneath its armour of grey ice. Three times it bested me, and in the end, hot, bothered and very snowy, I worked past it by a zig-zag movement on some small ledges to the right From a sizeable recess I summoned an impatient Jerry and despatched him round a corner to the left, with simple instructions to traverse down a flake to a chimney in the other line of weakness. He disappeared, and after a short silence came a disturbing series of curses and protestations, tinged with strong disbelief. I insisted, and after some rope tension, accompanied by most alarming scraping noises, the rope ran out steadily and I heard the pleasant hiss of pieces of snow and ice on their way to the corrie floor. I moved round the corner to find the familiar flake buried beneath a substantial bulge of ice, and the downward traverse an exciting creep on my edge nails.

Jerry's stance was at the spot where in 1949 a small incident had nearly brought my climbing career to a premature end! Above him an inset corner had to be climbed, a good coating of ice rendering the swing up on to its left wall a straightforward and satisfying movement. Immediately above this came a short steep wall, and after a tentative inspection I made all secure at a handy belay and invited Jerry to join me. He solved the problem by an extremely gymnastic movement, which I later found myself quite incapable of emulating, and worked his way along a great flake to the right.

At this point a pleasant diversion from the exigencies of our climb occurred. A large caravan appeared, working its excessively cautious way across the snow slopes beneath the central cliffs. From our eyrie they looked like ants crawling across a flat white sheet. One of them slipped and rolled towards the loch. Now slowly and now swiftly, he inexorably neared the outcrops above the loch, and we took a sadistic interest in his progress, even making a hurried wager as to whether he would reach the foot. Just short of the outcrops he came to a halt, upside down on the snow, and from the leader of the caravan a stentorian command, "Everyone stand where you are!" echoed round the corrie. I looked up at Jerry inquiringly, but he reassured me that we were not included.

From the end of the flake an awkward mantelshelf rises from a recess to a sloping turf ledge. This is a mauvais pas which I am accustomed to pass by means of a shoulder, for a succession of desperate knees have long since removed all turf from the lip of the ledge, exposing a depressingly naked sheet of granite. Jerry, however, has the Englishman's abhorrence of combined tactics and had ostentatiously belayed well away from the recess. Resignedly I cleared away large plates of snow, studied the obstacle and optimistically notched a handhold in the thin lower tongue of turf, which grudgingly offered its support. I kicked a foot as high as possible and pulled. The hold snapped off and my stomach

39. Tom MacKinnon (above) and
    Bill Murray (below). Young
    activists in the nineteen
    thirties, Himalayan explorers in
    the fifties and Club Presidents in
    the sixties.

40. Rebuilding the bridge over the River Carnoch, June 1981

41. *Ken Johnstone on The Cough, north face of Aonach Dubh*

42. *The Great Stac of Handa*

experienced a disturbing sensation until I re-established myself on the flake. In the end, I swung high and hard with the pick of my axe and rapidly performed what is known in some mountaineering circles as "a Knubel" to gain the ledge above. From here I climbed a wall and a heavily iced chimney, through which ran a vein of sustained difficulty making me oblivious to everything except the task of worming my way through those joints in the upper armour of the Pinnacle. At length I became aware of the heavy drag of the rope and of the fact that I hadn't seen a belay since leaving Jerry. A troublesome gusty wind sprang up and gave me some concern, as I edged along a delicate icy traverse with my chest pressed to a wall and my heels projecting over a 400-foot downward plunge of roof-like slabs. My 120 feet of rope just allowed me to reach easier ground and reel in an impatient Jerry, half frozen by his long wait.

A few more feet brought us to the crest. The ensuing 100-foot arete to the summit was delightfully airy and just hard enough to demand our concentration. In many respects it had been a unique climb for, although we had had five hours of sustained difficulty, sometimes reaching Very Severe level, the perfect conditions and the fact that the first pitch is normally the crux, had resulted in a climb largely free from the mental and physical strains usually inseparable from climbing of this type. We shook hands and grinned happily, for the holiday spirit had truly been abroad that day; the Pinnacle had bestowed its finest gift and we had been its fortunate recipients.

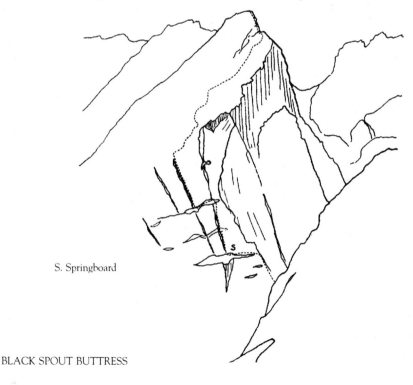

S. Springboard

BLACK SPOUT BUTTRESS

THE INITIATION
Vol. XXXIII (1984)

by J.R. Marshall

Ravens Gully: 135m Very Severe ......It is a distinctive route with character and atmosphere. The standard has not been lowered by rock boots in summer, nor by front pointing in winter. There are eleven pitches. A spell of drought is desirable.
— S.M.C. Rock & Ice Guide

Years ago, as uncouth youths, we had the temerity to take up residence in that haunt of Glasgow's elite, Jacksonville; at the time a stygian hollow beneath a few old pauchled haps.

Out on a stolen week, we diligently polished off the norms of the glen till the weather broke, then we retired to the gloom of the doss. High water came and went, leaving us in its aftermath, perched on narrow planks, sorting ourselves out in a fastidious attempt to avoid contact with an unspeakable mire, masquerading as a floor.

Thereafter, we festered twenty four hours in the pits, till a darkening doss indicated the arrival of owner representation, fortunately in the form of big Smith. 'Aye lads, what are you doin' here, hardly your style is it?' he queried, casually staking a place in the mire. However, our luck was in, Wullie was the most tolerant member of the eclectic group, kind hearted forbye and it wasn't long before we enjoyed the fruits of his seemingly bottomless bag, all conjured with effortless bludging.

Suffused with goodies and camaraderie, the fester continued into the night, with one signal comment of Wullie's echoing into sleeptime: 'Aye, Raven's is good for a wet day.'

Breakfast was well underway when he queried from the pit 'Any tea, where are ye gaun?'

'Raven's' we replied.

'Hmm, no a bad day for it,' as the shining eye took in the dreich drizzle at the door. 'no a bad day, mind and keep your strength up for the Cork pitch.'

We hung about for our breakfast supplement, then having exhausted Wullie's hospitality, moved off uphill, eventually to stop for a breather under Great Gully.

The black impending slit of Raven's Gully showed fleetingly through dark cloud, doubts stirred, then a cheerful 'Hello there!' split the gloom, it was Wullie, sharp cadie and all (looking like a Scots Dick Tracy!). 'Raven's a sociable climb, can I join in?' Such moral support is hard to beat, so we moved uphill at a more enthusiastic pace.

From close quarters, the gully was more inviting and before long the introductory pitches were below us as we roped up under the notorious chockstone of pitch four.

With a knowing smile, Wullie proffered the wall. 'Just up there, tae a big grip, then pull yourself ower.' High with the tradition and grandeur of our situation, I started up past the roof, grabbed the big grip and thought, not so bad.

Advice percolated up through the crack, 'That's it, now just pull.' Easier said than done,

I heaved and stuck, tried leaning out, pushing with left hand, squirming and jamming but to no avail! Fright set in, a clattering retreat saved me but lost the day. I was shattered; to be stopped was a new experience, so back onto the wall, again and again, each time with diminished gain but increased hazard. Frustrated, I acknowledged defeat, our middleman declined and Wullie took over.

Nonchalant, he latched onto the wall, big boots sticking to the rock like magic: then with an imperious doff of the cadie and 'Haud this, Jimmy' he disappeared over the roof like smoke. Christ, that put us in our place and like to disappear into our boots, we followed up on taut rope and nerve to join a tactful Wullie, promising the rest of the climb would be great.

Above, in a hall of rivulets, the chockstone pitch salved our pride, in the glorious struggle to overcome its dank walls. The sheer delicacy of pitch six held me enthralled, but reduced Olly to tatters as he swung off, again and again. What a climb! the easier, tottering upper wall gripped us in awe at the silver-grey, slime wall's plunge into the misty void in frightening exposure.

Thinking all we required was to romp up uninterrupted, we came together under the innocuous looking chimney which Wullie introduced as the 'Cork'. I ferretted up into the thing but stuck fast, descended, stripped off some clothes and tried again. I tried so hard I could feel the ribcage flatten, but to no avail, there was no way I would get up the bloody thing! Olly was demolished, so Wullie doffed the cadie, stripped off his jacket and wriggled his way up and over. We followed unashamedly leaning out on the rope, patting the rock for appearances, to emerge from the Raven's maw, one hundred percent impressed! In retrospect, I know we'd been 'taken' by Wullie, I've often done the same to others since, we didn't know it then but we could not have picked a better man for the initiation.

However, at the time, I didn't give a damn, what a fantastic climb it had been. I resolved I'd get back into the gully again but now it was great to be out of that hole! Off we went into the drizzle and down, burning off the adrenalin with delighted release. In the doss our elation dissipated under increasing pressure from the multiple owners, in an introduction to unimagined depths of ribald coexistence, far beyond the wildest dreams of our hitherto protected environment.

Twenty four hours on, deep in wet and windblown contemplative escape from the harsh reality of a lift by open lorry, and still pondering on the power and grace of these same men on the rocks of Buachaille Etive, it came to me that we had partaken of the height and depth of experience, but more significantly, had been shown the way and the light by Glasgow's Ullysean crew, to a new and vital life style waiting to be enjoyed in our Scottish mountains.

ACH, MEIN GROSSEN BOTEN
Vol. XXVII (1960)   by T.W. Patey

(A spurious Teutonic version of the S.M.C. perennial 'My Big Hobnailers')

Oh the Marteau-Piolet it hangs on the wall,
The hammers and the slings and the drills and all,
But we'll scrape off all the mud, and we'll polish off the blood
And go up to the mountains in the snow!
Let the pitons rattle, as we go to battle,
Sound the ever-ringing peal of steel on steel!
Let the happy chink of the old snaplink
Echo o'oer the mountains and the snow!

Chorus: Ach! Mein Grossen Boten!
         (Auf! Mein Kletterschuhen)
         Ach! Mein Grossen Boten!
         How they speak of frozen feet, and lengthy stride o'er
         Bergschrund wide—
         Ach! Mein Grossen Boten!
         Ach! Mein Grossen Boten!
         Memories raise of hellish days upon the Eigerwand.

Then our V.S. men will assault the Ben,
Profanities will echo up and down the glen,
And every little Tiger will be training for the Eiger
When we go up to the mountains in the snow.
Then our cragsmen bold will swarm down the shoots
And avalanche the tourists on the tourists' routes,
While others, never flagging, Munro-baggers are debagging
When we go up to the mountains in the snow!

In the grim grey dawn, we struggle ever on
Though the nights are long in the Pied d'Elephant,
Though the heartbeat quickens, and the stonefall sickens
When we go up to the mountains in the snow.
We cut no tracks with the 'good old axe,'
We discard the rope on the frozen slope,
In the black Cagoule of the Munich School
We go up to the mountains in the snow.

Minor key:

But - at the last bivouac, when your toes turn black
And the snowflakes whiten the Horeschowsky (sleeping)
    sack....

Major key - triumphantly:

Let the vultures in the valleys hear the Deutschland uber Alles
Faintly wafted o'er the mountains and the snow,
And when the grim day's done, and the victory's won,
We drink a Tutti Frutti to Giusto Gervasutti,
All the Bergkameraden will return to Inverarnan
Descending from the mountains through the snow!

Last chorus: Ach! Mein Grossen Boten!
            Ach! Mein Grossen Boten!
            How they tell of days of Hell, with Tommy Weir or Doktor Bell
            (or, Dreams arouse of the old Kingshaus, and ringing cries of
            'Rauss, Rauss, Rauss!' (shouted or screamed)
            Ach! Mein Grossen Boten!
            Ach! Mein Grossen Boten!
            Throes disclose of toes that froze upon the Eigerwand.

THE C.I.C. HUT (continued) - 1950's and '60's
Vol. XXXI (1979)   by James R. Marshall

My first sight of the C.I.C. was well over 30 years ago, during a stop on Carn Mor Dearg arete to watch the incredible, unassailable looking Great Buttress, materialise through dark, rolling, storm clouds. Then the wet hut roof caught the light and I was appraised in somewhat dramatic emphasis by a learned colleague: 'the men of the S.M.C. reside there when intent on tackling these formidable crags.' On I stumbled, humbled, conjuring visions of Wagnerian heroes sallying forth to great deeds on that sombre frightening crag.

A couple of years later, from a camp below the hut I made a tentative approach thinking (as the whole climbing fraternity seemingly still do) 'maybe a cup of tea or even an invitation to climb with these legendary beings,' but it wasn't to be. I just got a nose in the inner doorway when some specky weed bawled from his bunk 'bugger off' and being a well brought up lad, I did just that.

Strangely in my experience, this is a not unfamiliar introduction to the paradox of the C.I.C., a hut uniquely placed to enjoy the greatest climbing area in the country, yet damned difficult to gain access, tactical not physical. Terms of access require one to be either, a member of an 'acceptable' club, or a guest of a member. Is the former a subtle coercion to club membership? The latter isn't easy either, not many members go to the hut; then find one that deigns to fraternise, not easy! e.g. that famous-infamous old Glasgow club find it hard to qualify, they even have a complementary hut, well a sort of...

No doubt S.M.C. members feel they have the right to be selective, indeed they do, the hut is uniquely theirs, as intended by the original founders, who specifically stated it was for members and friends. What is remarkable, perhaps even shameful, is the S.M.C.'s apparent disregard of the situation (in their unique knowledge of the demand for winter bookings at the C.I.C.). As the senior club in Scotland they should have as far back as the sixties alerted the climbing community to the need to raise funds and construct alternative accommodation, in the form of a mountain bothy or better, wherein overcrowding, non-booking, etc. could be indulged in 'ad nauseam,' leaving the S.M.C. to indulge in the luxury of a Club Hut with selective occupation as their historic right.

Though unfamiliar with present-day statistics; new ascents and the disturbing number of climbers seen daily, in full winter, would indicate a continuing, if not increasing, demand for additional accommodation. As I see it, there is a need for a non-payment, mountain bothy for the young or parsimonious in conjunction with a hut similar to that of the C.I.C. for the more affluent, both to be built on the upper edge of the plain below the present hut (in suitable deference to station!). The whole project should be funded by the national bodies which spawn a proliferation of mountain bureaucrats. In turn, they, having little more to do than endlessly debate the good or evil of mountain educational policies, can be given a more meaningful purpose of life in the responsibility, management and maintenance of the new huts. Surely therefore, the most appropriate means whereby climbers can celebrate this 50th year would be to emulate the founders of the C.I.C. and initiate such a project to end the lottery of place bookings and pressures on over-zealous C.I.C. wardens.

By 1950, though reasonably acquainted with Ben Nevis, my first actual stay in the hut was on a memorable September meet of the Edinburgh J.M.C.S., when we all fought our way against a tremendous gale, which had us shattered long before the hut was reached. High up the wind literally bowled us over, sacs and all, one collapsed but was assisted to our goal. It was the first experience of that sheltered, secure sensation, so much a part of the hut. Outside, the great roar of the wind hammering the cliffs, the endless rushing vibration of the river in spate and the intermittent clatter, as the wind hurtles against the hut on its way down the glen. Soaking in this ambience and great mugs of tea, we realised one of the party was missing, so off we went again into the screaming night to search. Down on the slabs, the gale blew us off our feet several times (no sac ballast) but eventually we found him, sensibly down among boulders in his sleeping bag and got him back to the C.I.C. and recovery, though he must have been up half the night from the volumes of sweet tea forced on him.

In these early years, little was done other than the established classics, the Ben had not yet come to the attention of the post-war, avante garde, so busy in the Cairngorms and Glencoe (one exception being Hamish Nicol who survived a long fall from high up the steep ice of Zero). The neglect was understandable, why toil up Ben Nevis? with so much at easier reach; even though strong, regional competition existed between areas, it was rarely overtly expressed, with so many good routes available for the making.

Then, in a frustrated rebuff from winter climbing, Whillans and Brown put the boot in and climbed Sassenach (1954). Up to that point, a new line could be left till later; no more, if the line was big it had better be climbed. Coupled with this event, progressive climbers became aware of the limitations of a winter Glencoe and naturally turned their attentions to the great crags of Ben Nevis and Creag Meaghaidh.

As new interest developed, the hut was at its lowest ebb, the old stove had had it, the interior was black with soot from dirty primus stoves and when busy the floor swam in meltwater and ooze, giving the place a dank, dingy, uncomfortable air. Help was at hand however, some member recommended a Swedish barrel stove, smoke ring and all, which worked wonders, the interior dried out, it was actually possible to see the floorboards, the blankets stopped growing fuzz and the hut became very popular. (The original stove landed on the refuse pile, duly to be rescued by the Creag Dhu to give long, honourable service in Jacksonville).

The rehabilitation was too attractive, with attention focused on the great gullies, regular occupation was the thing, legitimate or not and certain Glasgow climbers were seen in the city bars suffering 'C.I.C. stoop' a chronic condition from using the 'wee door,' i.e. window access for excessive periods. Ian Clough and colleagues took to occupying the hut mid week then week-enders, booked and non-booked would pile in until the hut was crammed to the door. All this activity drove the hut committee spare; how could it be controlled? Stronger defences just produced greater technical achievement in enforced entry. I had some kind of responsibility role at that time but believed in the 'open' hut concept and participated in over-crowding sessions with a will, once with 32 persons in the hut! Indirectly this had a good effect, in that it was grand to escape onto the cliffs in the morning, besides, C.I.C. crowding came nowhere near that of certain French huts of the period, the only difference being they had a hut guardian to collect!

A great deal of reprehensible behaviour occurred during this era, stemming principally from the Edinburgh 'youth movement,' self-help was rife, sassenach baiting a duty and avoidance of hut chores a must. It was hell when an extra day or two was available and you ended up with all the week-end debris. Yet it was very entertaining and in retrospect hard to decide whether the night life or the crag was the main attraction, e.g. J. C's. (not the one that walked on water) full hut game was typical, in an already warm hut and clad only in underpants, he would complain of the cold then stoke the stove until temperatures soared into the 80's and inmates' faces matched the cherry red chimney of the stove.

Despite the frenetic numbers, surprisingly few new ascents were made during the decade mid 50's to 60's. On the northern cliffs, about 125 new summer and winter ascents were recorded, i.e. little over 12 per annum on average but that distorts events; for in fact the years 58-61 account for more than half that total. Then even more significant, Ian Clough and I account for about 60% of the total, showing I think quite clearly how little exploratory climbing was engaged in by others during the period. (Quantity of course is no indicator of quality!).

By the sixties, the dominant hut abusers had grown old, tired or dead, a new force in the form of The Squirrels emerged, a little more subdued and responsible, to mop up the few remaining old style lines. A new warden took over, one who was aware that 'climber' did not necessarily equate to 'gentleman.' The hut interior was adapted by contractor Clough to take a few more 'herring' and gas was introduced as fuel. Ludicrous password systems were evolved and the hut defences strengthened to a point of paranoia! (futile, the enlightened can still enter).

But the boisterous days were over anyway, the main wave had washed on, the next generation flexed their muscle on the new classic climbs, thrashed times on the big routes, looked tentatively at the unclimbed walls between and continued the vituperative action with over zealous warders on the vexing, access problems. Then came the enlightenment of front point technique, the pick and stick brigade took off, swelling to the second wave, but that's another story and not mine to tell.

THE JMCS (continued) '60's and '70's
Vol. XXX (1975)   by James G. Messer

THE 1960'S AND 1970'S

Aye, indeed. The swinging sixties. Mini-skirts, cheap petrol, climbing glossies and T.V. spectaculars. In many ways I feel that the early sixties were the last halcyon days before climbing became the 'in' thing. It was the twilight of an era when mountaineers were relatively anonymous, little being known about their activities outside a small group of kindred spirits. In those days it was difficult to find out about climbing clubs unless you were visiting the main climbing areas regularly or happened to know a member of a club. I found out about the J.M.C.S. via a friend of mine who knew Jimmy Simpson. I wrote to Jimmy and received the address of Tom Murray who was then the Secretary. Three weeks later I left Ayr on the 5.30 train feeling very self-conscious with my ice axe, rope and tricounied army boots (ex-W.D. of course). People tended to regard climbers with that mixture of embarrassment and curiosity reserved for lunatics.

The J.M.C.S. was very gregarious in those days, we tended to attend meets much more regularly than has been the case recently. No matter what the weather everyone on a meet would go out and do something. I remember the 1963 Coruisk Meet. It wasn't a very good weekend, in fact the weather was atrocious. The trip in from Mallaig was quite rough. On the Sunday a large party set off along the Druim nan Ramh ridge to go up to Bidean. Bill Watson who had been ill most of the way into Coruisk had brought two cases of Carlsberg Specials with him. These he sold (at a vast profit!!!) to the soaking and cold members returning off the ridge. After one or two Specials a lemming-like wave of bodies hurtled across the bog towards the landing stage and literally hurled themselves headlong into Loch Scavaig. Seconds later a mass of naked, blue and sober mountaineers gasped and fought desperately to climb up the landing stage before exposure and unconsciousness made it impossible. I doubt in the long run if Bill made much of a profit, he didn't join us as he couldn't swim and in fact hasn't been to Coruisk since. Mind you he's now the Treasurer.

These were great days, usually finishing up with swims in the nearest river, whether it was the clear greeny/blue waters of Glen Rosa or the Rannoch-impregnated Etive. Silhouettes in the gloaming briskly towelling themselves, hopelessly swatting at the inevitable clouds of midges. We rarely used huts then. The C.I.C. in winter, Coruisk in May and at New Year and rarely Lagangarbh, but usually the meets were held under canvas.

The J.M.C.S. is a great Club. Its future? Who can say. I only hope that I am still around in 2025 when we celebrate our Centenary. I may not be doing much climbing then but I'm sure I'll still be wandering around somewhere between Clachaig and Kingshouse.

THE C.I.C. HUT - BEN NEVIS IN THE 1970's
Vol. XXXI (1979)   by M. G. Geddes

The last decade has brought great changes to Ben Nevis. The introduction of better ice-climbing equipment and the increase in popularity of mountaineering and associated activities throughout Britain have produced a startling increase in the level of winter activity. Summer climbing limps along behind, largely because of the weather conditions, I suspect.

In the early seventies, the great ice climbs of the fifties and sixties were climbed with increasing frequency and those which had remained inviolate for ten years or so were first repeated.

Inclined picks, the moveable hooks, have made steep ice climbing faster and less strenuous, and Zero and Point Five Gullies, Gardyloo Buttress and the Orion Face Direct became classics within a few years. The opinion was even voiced that the new tools would *retard* Scottish winter climbing by diverting attention from the 'real' problems, the buttresses. To some extent, development in that direction was blown off course, but climbers did return to the buttresses and will continue to climb there, better equipped and more capable now that thick ice pitches have been relegated to a minor place in the difficulties of a mixed climb. It is interesting to note, in passing, that the adoption of a different pick is but a revival of an old idea; Welzenbach sported a steeply curved pick on the Oberland north faces, while an Alpine Journal of that era scathingly records a German note on smaller hooks, used for serac climbing, as 'yet a further development of modern mountain-madness!"

The number of climbers visiting Ben Nevis increased dramatically until about 1975, and has continued to increase, although more slowly, since then. While Point Five Gully had only been climbed by about seven or eight parties in the 12 years preceeding 1971, it can currently entertain this number *in one weekend.* The climbing jet-set, and more genuine travellers, even come half way across the world to be blasted by the mountain's winds, buried in its spindrift, and bewildered by the plateau. French, Americans, Canadians, Australians and New Zealanders are now to be spotted regularly. One party of Italians had been particularly well prepared, doubtless by an English party. They managed to wriggle their way through the defences of the hut, without a word of English and liberal use of 'Non Comprendi,' before proceeding to cook their pasta. The occupants tried their best to establish some mode of communication, to no avail until they asked the visitors where they had been. 'Point Five Gully - piece of duff!' was the only English they had been taught!

The use of the C.I.C. hut has been a contentious issue throughout these years. On the one hand there are those who wish the hut to be treated as the private house of the occupants, and on the other there are those who wish it to be used as an Alpine refuge.

The increasing numbers passing the hut each year has exacerbated the conflict; angry and at times violent scenes have resulted. It would seem that both parties are dissatisfied with the current situation. The scene which I personally find most unsatisfactory is when enthusiasts camp for days of rain and storm in the Allt a'Mhuilinn, and the hut remains half empty because the occupants, club members or others, are adhering to the 'private guest house' policy. This is particularly bewildering to foreign visitors, and, I believe, contrary to the spirit with which the bequest was made. To quote MacRobert, describing the opening (Easter) weekend in the *Journal*: 'Soon a stream of visitors arrived, mostly en route for the summit, some bringing their lunch, and enjoying it in the comfortable shelter of the hut, for a piercing wind prevailed.'

The increase in climbing activity has brought with it an increase in misfortunes, although probably not a proportionate one, perhaps because of better belay material and techniques. The scene on a busy day can be not unlike a clip from the climax of a cops and robbers thriller. Shouts are drowned in the chop of a helicopter as it swoops into the corrie, and hats and ropes are whipped about in its wake. Files of orange or khaki cadets stretch down the glen, snocats wail as they sink deeper into the ever widening swamp, and rescue men are lowered from the summit on spidery threads.

To get back to the climbing itself, the development of fine new winter routes, both on ice and mixed terrain has continued abreast of these unfortunate side issues. To list the good ones would take a page, for they are nearly all good. The most notable, for length, 'line-appeal,' independence and sustained difficulty include Minus One Gully and Buttress, Astronomy and Route II. Whether or not these will ever come into vogue depends partly on the degree of winter conditions which the future climber finds acceptable. More likely to attain the popularity of the 'golden oldies' are routes such as Astral Highway, Slav Route, Albatross, Rubicon Wall and Lobby Dancer, which are more often in currently acceptable condition. Summer activity has seen the development of rock climbing on Central Trident Buttress and the North wall of Castle Ridge, and several high standard routes, including a free version of Titan's Wall, and Caligula, the groove right of the Sassenach chimney.

As for the future, I hesitate from suggesting where 'the next great advances,' etc. will take place. Further improvements in ice tools could lead to a burst of activity on the icicles, or development may continue on powdered and verglassed rock climbs. Perhaps the European visitors will lead the way with a few extreme ski descents - Ledge Route, the North Face of Castle Ridge, and the Little Brenva Face seem likely candidates. The most futuristic scene of the decade was witnessed last winter by some friends passing the foot of Green Gully. A lone body rolled out of the mist, shot down the lower reaches of the Gully, and stopped in the snow near them - it was a four-foot badger. The beastie gave them a scowl, shook the snow off, and set off up the Gully on another attempt!

A BRIDGE FOR TROUBLED WATERS
Vol. XXXII (1982)   by Philip Gribbon

I was the gaffer idling on the buttress. A mate was drilling holes on the line of planks. The heavies were carrying masonry on to the pier, and a paddling fisherman was tossing wet stones on the bank.

A clutch of oystercatchers came a-pleeking up the river, and two deer, with their antlers held high, struck across the moss in their bewilderment.

I turned with my hammer to thump the nails into the masticky sandwich of planks that was shaping into a soft bed for the cables. I was engrossed with a craft on a peaceful morning with the Carnach River murmuring its way towards the sea.

It had been a busy week from the moment that we had stumbled ashore over the wrack on the ebb tide. I was under orders to see that the materials were on site from the hi' heidyin, and that the pits, precise in plan and position, were placed to await his coming. I toiled laden up the track from the shore and mulled over our incapability of transporting sacks of cement and loops of steel across squelchy bogs and furrowed hills. I staggered to the site in a trail of hoof prints. There was a mystery mound under a blue sheet with a smell of cement seeping out to the damp air of dusk. Wild garrons, panniered with bags had walked their Rough Bounds of Knoydart, and had saved us not only time and effort, but also the disdain of our hi' heidyin: his haulers and packers would never have met his tight timetable.

On an evening flood they arrived, phutting up the loch. A familiar silhouette in his flat duncher was bowspritting in the gloaming. In greeting I doffed my Hemingway check cap and tugged my forelock, 'Dr Bennet, Sir.'

I smiled graciously to the Gorrie, C.C., the King of the concrete mixers, and was introduced to a Man from a Trust. I offered a strong arm over the slippery seaweed, but in return I was given a box, heavy with turnbuckle screws, spanners and angle irons, all hiding some unknown delicacies, the essentials for a well-equipped engineer, his techbits over his mealkits. Unwittingly a docile sherpa shouldered the DJB box and marched off afar, unaware that only the Injuns lived at Carnoch while the Chiefs dossed at Camusrory, that delectable social centre of the heavenly loch, ping pong tables, beds an' all. So deep in the dusk the master builders sat on the steps, waiting long for their supper, waiting to be sure that a muttering minion returned the box and that there would be a breakfast ahead on the big day.

At the edge of the pit, the duo of poised heidyins made instant and independent proposals on how it should be done; a stuffing of claggy boiled brain oozes, aggravated with gravels sized in abstract ratios, pummelled, pomandered and belted with splatting boulders. I, a progenitor of the pits, found it impossible not to throw learned irrelevancies into an intellectual creativity that involved filling a hole with concrete. Everyone was an expert, self-styled, but a mere gaffer should have known that the engineers were stuck together on a constructional high that didn't tolerate flippant remarks. I dropped rank down to the mixers, with their buckets, by their sand-piles, leaning on their shovels, joyfully waiting in the rain for a decision, any decision, from the heidyins.

A plastic sheet liner to staunch the water seeping out of the walls sank ceremoniously to the bottom of the pit under the first gooey splodges of the mix.Buckets of sand rattled across the aerial twin wireway spanning the river whose level was rising quickly towards the bottom wire. As wet workers, skilled in pacing a day's effort, drifted off for their lunch, the management mumbled disparagingly about those whose enthusiasm for sustained work left something to be desired.Diplomatically I agreed, but notwithstanding nonetheless and all that, where was their lunch? Oh, they weren't having any! Yes, they'd like a cup of tea thanks. It was raining heavily.

We sidled back like wet vermin nailed on wires to the pit on the far bank to find a glutinous dark hole spurting with peaty water. Some frantic bailing lowered the level by a fraction. Gorrie was telling what had to be done to Bennet, who was suggesting his alternative strategy and instructing Gribbon how to do it, thus leaving him in his turn no option but to query both of them: a discordant triumvirate professing and proffering academic gems and quirks of fantasy as the chill waters lapped round their ankles. The mixing shift wielded their shovels at full speed, and batches of concrete streamed inside the pit. The two anchor beams were plunged downwards, striking a finis, git the buggers in, twist 'em, turn 'em, tap 'em. Admiration beamed from faces seamed with riverlets,· while the swollen stream poured into the flood channel, breaching a protective dam, encircling the main pier, taking away in a rushing swirl both boards and tools, and threatening to drown the mix in vortices curling to the sea. Work was abandoned; the heidyins agreed to allow the soaked workers to return to their cold damp tents. Slow and cautious it was, clipped to the top wire and protected by safety ropes, spanning the sprung cables and swinging like marionettes, with the waves tearing, buffeting and sucking like a writhing nest of slavering kelpies waiting for their victims.

Today all was at peace. I was hypnotised by the swirl of silky water and watched the ripples play a pattern on the stones, but in the corner of my mind there was an alien feeling to the quiet valley. Two walkers and a dog were moving purposefully up the far bank of the river. On coming closer I recognised the well-kent stravaiging guardian of the wilderness, with a bunnet, a sweep of the kilt, a whip of a fishing rod and a stab of a black beard giving him away. Whiffs of controversey had become reality. This was no visit of homage: here was the bee's knees, bearding a lion in the den an' all that. His companion was wiry and elfish, unknown, behind dark glasses and beneath a keel-up deerstalker. Cor, I thought, it's our bête noire, the slayer of bridges and his dog come to toast us to shreds.

We turned to the work, watching our visitors out of the back of our heads.They reached the bridge site and their cameras snapped for evidence. We gave them a quick flash. Spurning the wires they paddled a ford to the feet of a startled Man from a Trust returning from a nap at the camp in the ruins of the clachan of Carnoch.They wrung their fingers in friendship and their socks from necessity and ambled towards our apprehensive dithering work crew. Propping a cromach and taking care not to snag a rod they sat down at a discrete distance for their al fresco lunch. Not being able to endure a sudden strain in my cold shoulder, I walked over with conscious nonchalance. The wee dog was slurping his chunky bits out of a plastic dish.

"Hullo, Phil, how are you?" We could be anywhere but where we were.

"Fine," I answered, non-committal, giving nothing away. We passed a few pleasantries, then he played an ace.

"This is Christopher Brasher."

"Who? Oh, I know." I was overwhelmed with confusion, tongue-tied and caught in full view, conniving in man's nefarious anti-wilderness activities by the media's foremost observer. "Pleased to meet you."

"Care for a dram?" he asked, pouring a good measure from his hip flask.

It was an offer I couldn't refuse, no way.

"Cheers, Sandy," a gulp of drambuie, "an' may your boots never get wet." Back at the bridge, with the people's friend padding on my heels, I turned to a poised pencil.

"Yes, it's a bridge repair not a rebuild, an' sure, there's been objections, as you know well enough. Everyone has a right to his opinions an' no one would deny that, but it's those who write articles about remote areas, an' publish 'em, an' write guide books, well, I'm agin them. You've seen what Big Walks has done for Carnmore, with distances, times, an' all, an' you better than most know all about that 'cos you called it the Sanctuary and tried to hide where it was in your articles. If only people would keep quiet about what they go an' do. A wilderness is where no one goes 'cos he's never been told about it, like ... well, y' know." I was mesmerised, a mere pawn, rabbiting on, looking for a diversion.

It came on the bank with a barking dog at heel, brisk and authoritative, in sweater and green wellies, the Factor of the Estate, to see his bridge on his river.What a perfect coincidence, a more uncannily predestined meeting couldn't have been better arranged even by the' diel hisself. Builder, watcher, tinker, spy ... and factor. Oh, if only the two heidyins B & G were here we'd have hit the magic number seven at the scene of the crime.

"This is Sandy MacDonald. He knows all about the bridge. I'm the gaffer."

I was smiling on the wings, and a lark was singing in the blue sky.

PARK RANGIFER VOL XXXII (1981)

At the end of January a party of three were joined by a reindeer as they left the Cairngorm car park en route for Coire an t-Sneachda. The friendly quadruped was rewarded with a sandwich and responded by staying with them all day. This included the ascent of Fiacaill Couloir (Grade II/III). This was done unroped and although in fairly easy condition, was not made any easier by the occasional attempt by Rudolph to take over the lead, punching his forefeet into the soft ice. The day was ended by an impressive ungulate descent of Fiacaill Coire Cas with all four legs splayed out in a controlled slither. If the M.C. of S. can be persuaded to provide the right training for further development along these lines, potential is clearly considerable. Willing trail-breakers and load-carriers are always an asset and their availability could lead to a considerable increase in the use of the C.I.C. Hut by senior members of the Club.

EXTREME ROCK — A REVIEW
Vol. XXXIII (1987)   by D.D.

DD' is here unveiled as that frequent contributor to Cairngorms New Climbs and
Notes in the Journal, Douglas Dinwoodie. Notable for the duration of his experience
in the upper standards of climbing. DD makes some interesting observations about
aspects of the hard rock climbing scene in recent years.

*EXTREME ROCK — Compiled by Ken Wilson and Bernard Newman (Diadem Books, 1987,
numerous illustrations, £27.95)*

Another big Ken Wilson book and the formula is becoming a bit stale and predictable.
Word of this latest venture first got round in the late seventies. In the years to follow great
material advances were made in British rock-climbing and the book was inordinately
delayed as the compilers struggled to keep up with events and include the outstanding new
routes. Added to the problems of press-ganging the various contributors, the organisation
of this book can have been no easy task. Nevertheless, at so many years in the making,
and with such a price-tag, we might have expected something special, and this is not the
case.

The book has been well enough gathered, as is to be expected from its main editor. As
boss of Mountain (the magazine everyone is seething about, as Patey put it), Ken Wilson
often seemed intent on bringing out the worst in us, propelling climbing into a striving
rat-race (now in full flight as men in funny troosers try to outclimb each other for money).
In spite of this the early Mountain was a first-class creation, badly missed in the morass
of hype and rubbishy reportage of today's magazines. This awareness and authority shows
through in the preface and introductory history where various influences and trends are
well-defined and the current 'bold or be bold' dilemma clearly explained. The Scottish
section is perhaps the weak point in this short but excellent introduction and could have
been more discerning even in the brief space allotted. Cubby's clutch of advanced Cave
Crag routes are surprisingly not deemed worth a mention. Also unchronicled is Spence's
remarkably bold lead of The Hill, way back in 1967. The same goes for Dubh Loch's
Gulliver, which (like Haystack) was an outstanding piece of cragmanship. The committing
nature of such strenuous journeys into the unknown is easily underestimated by today's
fitter, better-equiped, and less alcoholic climbers. Nicholson and Carrington were
probably climbing as well as anyone down south at this time, in an environment much less
favourable for hard climbing.

The most serious oversight in the historical section in general is the mention of the
abandonment of bold on-sight leading of this type. Cleaning by asbeil has become a
necessity as routes have got harder e.g. Whillance got nowhere reconnoitering Flodden on-
sight. It is a sad fact that all the excitement and interest of exploration now comes while
dangling on an abseil rope, where it is easy to succumb to the temptation of trying out

moves and protection. This matter of prior knowledge is glossed over in many histories and the importance of many ascents is questionable and needy of qualification. Many of the gritstone and limestone routes were in fact rehearsed on abseil or top-roped first. *Bitter Oasis* and *Footless Crow* are relevant studies on a bigger crag, in that Livesey considered them comparable in standard, no doubt an indication of the relative familiarity gained en rappel. Few of us can be free from guilt in this respect, and a time-machine would be useful equipment for future historians, zapping around the crags to see what tricks the explorers got up to.

Scotland apart, there is not much else to quibble about in the history. I suspect, however, that some of the Northumberland climbs deserve credit alongside some gritstone ones. There is a whiff of chauvinism as the conspiracy to ignore Henry Barber's influence continues.

The choice of routes and areas is as always open to controversy. An enigmatic decision was made to 'concentrate on areas of national interest'. This means including Swanage and Gurnard's Head, and missing out Cheddar and Northumberland. They seem to have got their islands outside-in, because the Outer Hebrides are in, and absurdly, Arran not. The other most notable omissions from Scotland are probably Lochnagar, Carnmore, and Coire Mhic Fhearchair. I suspect that 'to concentrate on areas with eager contributors' might have been a more accurate description.

Readers automatically scan their own stamping grounds for inaccuracies, and a couple of comments on the Cairngorms are called for here. On Shelter Stone Crag the *Needle* is unjustly slighted. It is no more disjointed than the routes to its left, and just as sustained in its grade. Also the *Haystack* pioneers seem to have been libelled with the suggestion that they took the *Steeple* ramp on the first ascent. At Dubh Loch *Naked Ape* is gaining celebrity, and rightly so, but at the expense of *The Ascent of Man*, which is a more natural line, in fact arguably the most challenging unclimbed line in Scotland at the time. This was the first route up the big 'impossible' wall, and as such deserved at least a mention in history or text.

In their parting comment on Scotland, the editors express concern that the Creag a' Bhancair bolts will initiate bolting on the other mountain crags. Such fears are probably unfounded, at least for the time being, since the Tunnel Wall is a unique case and the old aid-bolts provided some excuse. This spread of guilt back through time also applies to Cave Crag, where *Marlene* is perhaps a more dubious case, because this is a line which could have been climbed with the usual pegs, nuts, and Friends. Yet later ascensionists chose to add bolts, not eliminate them.

The history is only a brief section at the start of the book but I think it would have been better if the compilers had responded to the 'desperate need for really authoritative national climbing history' and produced this scholarly work themselves. They are after all Editor and Past-editor of our main climbing magazine. Some of the essays in 'Extreme Rock' are commendable (the Creag Dubh one for example) but many are only worth

43. *The Crowberry Tower, Buachaille Etive Mor*

44. Colin Stead on The Hammer, Etive Slabs

45. *Gordon Townend on Cubic Ridge, Cir Mhor*

46. *Dave Cuthbertson on The Clearances, north face of Aonach Dubh*

reading for information on the particular routes, and surely the guide-book tells us enough on that score. A historical work would have spared us much of the repetitive tedium while still including worthwhile sections from chosen writers.

These criticisms I feel also apply to the photos, which make the main impact in a book of this type. Many of them are in colour and the initial effect is pleasing to a reader expecting the usual black and white of Hard Rock and Cold climbs. This impression is not sustained however, since many of the shots are the routine stuff which has already become over-familiar in the magazines. The editorial decision to concentrate on 'action shots that depict important technical detail' can't have helped in this respect. This approach reaches a nadir in the *Right Wall* sequence which more or less shows how to climb the route's crux. Some of the most accessible of crags have inspired mediocre camera-work. It might be something of an expedition to gain good photos of Creag Dhubh Dhibadail, but we might have expected better at the likes of Almscliff or Curbar. The stunning shots of *Beau Geste* only underline what could have been achieved elsewhere. If the photos lack any one quality in particular it is atmosphere. John Cleare's sole studies on the Cromlech bring on nostalgia for 'Rock Climbers in Action in Snowdonia'. Climbing photography in Britain has stagnated for many years now. Distance shots are often the most evocative, bringing out not only the grandeur of a cliff but also its essential character. Classics from the past which spring to mind are O'Hara's well-known *Dragon* portrait, and the one of Brown attempting *White Slab*. The Lakes section is particularly disappointing in this respect, where spectacular routes such as *Cumbrian* and *Bitter Oasis* are rendered anonymous by lousy photography. Surely shots of Dove Crag would have been better than Langdale's measly Raven Crag, depicted here. The opportunist shots at Dubh Loch show what might have been achieved on other crags by single-minded professionals. (And Dubh Loch is not very photogenic).

What the best photos do display, however, is the dismaying level of strength and fitness which will be required from tomorrow's hot-shots. The limestone shots are among the better ones in the book, and those of German strong-man Wolfgang Gullich at Kilnsey well demonstrate the heinous steepness and strenuosity of the futuristic route. Young hopefuls would best benefit by defecting to the apes of the jungle at a tender age, or else live the life of an ascetic, like that other Wilson (of 'The Wizard', not 'Mountain') and set up home in a cave out on the moors.

Finally, there remains the big question as to whether we really want books of this sort, and many climbers in Scotland have their doubts. We are used to a reasonable amount of peace and quiet on Scottish cliffs but you never know what you've got till its gone, as the song says. Down south they are so used to crowded crags that it is accepted as the norm. Some of the gritstone and limestone routes in this book are already so polished as to bear little resemblance to the original experience. Why funnel mobs of climbers onto our best routes? The walking books are even worse in this respect. The obvious results are loss of seclusion, crowded bothies, and erosion. Hair-raising stories circulate about the antics on Ben Nevis in winter, and Lochnagar is getting just as bad. How much to blame is 'Cold Climbs'? The classic retort to this argument is that there are still plenty of quiet hills and crags for the lover of solitude. But I don't think John Muir would have happily watched the ravages of Yosemite just because there remained tranquil (but lesser) places over the head of the valley.

It is obvious that the commercial success of these books is dependent upon the great numbers of us now going to the hills, so it is not surprising that the media-men stay quiet about the attendant drawbacks. We can be glad about the areas missed out, while no doubt the Irish will sigh with relief over the neglect of Fair Head and the rest. It is this outlook which, in Scotland, Extreme Rock refers to as 'a curious strain of perverse romanticism!' Clearly this is a perversion worth encouraging, if only to irritate Ken Wilson!

THE TERRIBLE MODERN HORRORS OF GLENCOE, 1946

ON THE ROCKS

THE GREAT STACK OF HANDA
Vol. XXXIII
by Hamish M. Brown

Handa is one of those places that vaguely rings a bell - but only one in a hundred could site it correctly. It is a well-hidden island off the Sutherland coast and its Great Stack was the scene of an ascent a hundred years ahead of its time.

We are constantly told in historical works that rock-climbing in Britain began with this or that ascent in the 19th century but this is quite wrong. In 1876 the men of Lewis 'raided' Handa and 'conquered' the Great Stack, an event paralleling Sassenach on the Ben, except the players were obscure peasants and the event only just recorded! But their forebears were the first British climbers — with cliff-scaling deeds on Sula Sgeir, North Rona, St. Kilda or Handa recorded long ago. The men who led the first ascent of Stac Lee (photo in SMC 1981) may have had ulterior motives (the capture of birds) but it was a rock climb of some skill. This was Britain's first real rock-climbing.

Some would detract by saying these climbs were not done for sport .but that is misleading. The main objective was food-gathering but young men are young men and climbs were done purely for fun and kudos - just as first ascents today. Nor did they carry pitons and chalkbags, and I doubt if their horse-hair ropes would appeal to our jangling heroes today. To prove their worthiness as prospective husbands, lads on St. Kilda would perch on a jutting rock hundreds of feet above the sea and there go through dangerous balancing feats. All males climbed and some climbed better than others - human nature has not changed. The ascent of Handa's Great Stack was the result of just such a bit of showing-off.

The men of Noss (in Lewis) regularly culled the birds of North Rona. They do so to this day, by a special clause in Bird Protection Acts, though they no longer row there (North Rona is 45 miles north of the Butt of Lewis and can just be seen from Cape Wrath on a clear day). They had no need to head for Handa to collect birds - but it was a good excuse. It had probably been planned and talked about for long enough.

Donald Macdonald was probably a bit of a rebel. He had character enough to fall out with the local church the year after the Handa raid and took himself off with a friend, to voluntary 'exile' on North Rona. They stayed on after the cull but the following summer when the men of Noss returned they found both men dead, for reasons which will now never be known.

But before considering the climbs of the Stack, a few words on Handa itself. I first read about it in the Victorian memoir of its then laird, Evander Maciver of Scourie. He wrote 'Handa is composed of sandstone and rises gradually from the sea to attain a great height on its north and west side, where the cliffs are perpendicular. It is the resort of myriads of sea-birds. When I came here in 1845 I found Handa occupied by seven crofter tenants, with a queen amongst them. They lived comfortably, and grew large crops of potatoes on its sandy soil, when top dressed with seaweed. When the potato disease broke out in 1847 the crop failed in Handa completely; the people's source of support was gone. They said they were willing to emigrate to America if the Duke of Sutherland would pay the expense of sending them there. The result was that not only were the tenants of Handa, but a very large number from Assynt and Eddrachillis sent to Canada and Novia Scotia during the next two years - in all exceeding 500 people.'

Handa is a bird island now, a reserve of the RSPB. From April to September it is wardened and visitors come out with one of the local crofter-fishermen. It is not an island of bird rarities but shocks with numbers instead. The red sandstone sweeps up gently from machair-edged silver sands facing the port of Tarbet on the mainland then suddenly finishes on the sea-sliced precipices facing the Minch. Here there is an urban bedlam of birds, an ornithological tenement-life, with the Great Stack the high rise of them all. Nobody can fail to be impressed by the Great Stack. It stands in the mouth of one of the many geos with the highest point of the island not far off (406 feet). It is a bold ledge-banded monolith of rock, riddled with sea-level tunnels, capped with rank gull-manured vegetation and, in season, every ledge crowded with guillemots, razorbills, gannets, puffins and shags. Ten thousand or so of these at a time is a memorable sight, sound and smell.

Two of us who spent a month last summer as voluntary wardens on Handa (there is a fine bothy) were lucky to visit the Great Stack with Robert, one of the boatmen. We chugged off, east-about, along the coast. The cliffs steadily grew in scale, geos and caves honeycombed the coast and we dodged flat islets, bases of long-fallen stacks. The north reach of coast is a massive 400 foot blank 'curtain wall' which has resisted the attacks of the sea. At its west end the attack had been more successful with a chaos of broken pillars and crags. The Great Stack so fills the mouth of its geo it cannot visually be separated from the land. With necks craning up at the whitewashed ledges (empty with the lateness of the season) we passed its outer bastion. Robert turned the bows in towards what seemed no more than a doorway in the rock. It was a doorway that reached to the sky however. Shags crashed out about us as we chugged through the gloomy corridor while the sea surged and gurgled in and out of the many holes and tunnels The Great Stack is a huge tooth with rotten roots.

Before we could take it all in we were round and out again to the sunny sea. We shook our heads in wonder that this 'impregnable' tower had been climbed. Climbed is used loosely. The techniques were slightly unusual.

There is a certain confusion about the first and/or second climb and having read all the accounts possible I'm not too clear either. Harvie-Brown (writing of 1873-1876) says the first was by a Uist party (why from the other end of the Isles?) called in at the laird's behest to clear off the summit-nesting black-backed gulls. (Why?). They were supposed to have thrown a line across (80 feet), caught it round something firmly (what luck!) and sent a lad out with a heavier rope - which sounds highly irresponsible. Perhaps this account has been mixed up with the other, better documented and thoroughly proved ascent, by the group of skilled Lewis men I've already mentioned. They were thoroughly familiar with cliffs and rope-handling. An ascent from sea-level was rather discouraged by the bird-crowded ledges, a fact re- discovered by Tom Patey long after, but they won their summit by a piece of bold simplicity. They walked the ends of a long rope out both arms of the geo until its central length between came to rest on the Great Stack!

The rope was then tied or anchored firmly and 'ace climber' Macdonald swarmed along the rope: a feat, simple perhaps, but of staggering boldness for there was no security as he cat-crawled out 400 feet above a crashing sea and with birds shrieking round. A sort of pulley system was then rigged up and the birds were culled. Stakes, stuck in the middle of the green cap of the Stack, remained visible till after the last war - as challenging a sign as a peg in the middle of a big face.

On the first of July 1967 Tom Patey, with henchmen Chris Bonington and Ian MacNaught Davies, arrived on the scene. They repeated the Lewismen's raid on the Stack but even with all the aids of modern mountaineering found it no easy task. Nylon rope stretches more than natural fibre so as soon as the fixed line had Tom's weight, it sagged. He was sitting in harness, suspended from jumars, and these proved frustrating and exhausting for Tom's parabolic route. Birds cannoned into the rope and Tom noted, while dangling like a spider in the middle, that a guillemot 'was pecking thoughtfully at the taut rope' where it crossed its territory.

A few days later this gang were off for the Orkney Isles and the tele-spectacular of the Old Man of Hoy. Tom Patey was killed in 1971 when abseiling off another stack by Loch Eriboll. Macdonald died on North Rona. It seems a rather chancy game.

The Great Stack was finally climbed from sea-level by Hamish MacInnes, G.N. Hunter and D.F. Lang on the first of August 1969. They also climbed the obvious Stack in the bay (Puffin Bay) where the path across the island reaches the cliff edge.

There is room for more though — and many other unclimbed stacks and cliffs. My eye of faith noted several as we returned from our circumnavigation. If only I was twenty years younger.

Postscript: This letter appeared in the 1985 issue of the *Journal*.

Dear Sir,
In the article on Handa last year I said that Donald Macdonald who made the first crossing to the Great Stack later on fell out with the kirk and went off to North Rona; which

information I have learnt to be untrue, though so repeated in most sources. The exile was a Malcolm Macdonald. He actually initiated the Handa raid, but being too old, got Donald Macdonald, then 26, to lead it in 1876. It was Malcolm Macdonald who went off into self-imposed exile and died, aged 67, in 1885. Tom Weir, who passed on this corrected information, noted the graves of the two shepherds on a visit in 1984 — 100 years on from their luckless landing. Bill Murray, in the 60's, met a retired schoolteacher in Dunoon, who was the son of Donald Macdonald, and heard from him the story of his father's climb. Just as errors became accepted (like the Ben Alder Cottage myths) or Caulfeild always gets spelt Caulfield, there has been this mix-up of Macdonalds. The above I hope sets out the truth of the personalia involved.

Yours etc.,
Hamish M. Brown.

LANDING PLACE ON STAC LEE

THE BLACK SHOOT

This gully is the subject of the following comment by Peter Hodgkiss in the SMC District Guide to the Central Highlands:

'At one time Beinn Eunaich was best known for its 'Black Shoot' and a train of aspirants attacked it, and were usually repulsed, in the years about the end of the last century. There are no fewer than 21 references to it in the first 8 volumes of the SMC Journal and any climber contemplating an ascent could prepare himself by reading accounts by two of these ancients and one modern whose wit is well seasoned with awe. The climb is up a series of chimneys, well vegetated and seemingly always wet. It is at least severe in standard'

THE BLACK SHOOT OF STOB MAOL
Vol. II (1892)   by W.R. Lester

The Black Shoot has now succumbed to patient and persistent attacks, the last of which was made by four members of our Club on the Queen's Birthday holiday of 24th May this year. This party consisted of Messrs Gibson, Naismith, Douglas, and myself; and as I have taken part in all the four attempts which have been made, I have been asked to give a short account of them.

It may as well at once be stated that the climb is a pure piece of mountaineering gymnastics, and is a case of seeking out a difficulty for its own sake. There are, of course, perfectly easy ways up the mountain by other routes.

The Black Shoot was first noticed by J.R. Robertson and myself, while coming down Ben Eunaich in December 1889. It forms a large deep fissure in the face of an almost perpendicular cliff to the left of the glen, looking up, and it is not noticed from below until the pedestrian comes directly opposite.

The Shoot then presents almost the appearance of an elongated cave, beginning about 300 feet above the glen, from which it is approached over a steep slope of fallen stones. Above this slope the Shoot proper begins, splitting up the face of the cliff for another 300 feet until it debouches on the hillside above.

On the occasion referred to, being struck by the very unusual appearance of the Shoot, Robertson and I decided to go up and prospect as far as was possible under the circumstances, which circumstances were not very favourable for a climb of the sort, all the rocks being coated with snow and ice, and we being equipped with nothing more formidable than walking sticks.

However, after a stiffish climb over the lower slope of stones and heather, in some parts of which real care was required, owing to the covering of snow which lay on the steep grass and moss immediately below the Shoot, we arrived in the Shoot proper, and Robertson leading, at once set to work to find foot and hand hold in the ice-covered fissure which from this point upwards divides the face of the cliff. This proved no easy matter, as, in the absence of axes, and Robertson's stick having meanwhile disappeared into the depths of the glen below, we were reduced to finding holds in the rock, by picking out or melting the coat of frozen snow and ice with our finger tips. Progress, in these circumstances, was neither speedy nor agreeable; and after mounting some hundred feet of the Shoot it was decided to beat a retreat.

On return to the Dalmally road, two of the natives whom we met gave the Gaelic name of the place, with its English equivalent; and on inquiry as to whether any one had ever been up it, the reply was, "No, neither man nor beast!" which information was distinctly consoling after our defeat.

Attempt No. 2 was made the following Easter, by Campbell and myself. This time we had the rope, but no axe, and all the winter's snow had disappeared, and was replaced by slimy moss and trickling water. The Shoot was therefore easier, but quite as disagreeable as before.

We passed the place where Robertson and I had previously stopped, and clambered some thirty feet higher, over rock which approached nearer and nearer to the perpendicular as we proceeded. We then came to a stop, feeling very doubtful whether it was possible for us or any one else to go higher. All that could be seen above was an exceedingly steep and smooth chimney, which had to be approached over wide slabs of rock equally steep and smooth. From where we stood it was impossible to say whether or not there was any exit to the Shoot above on to the face of the mountain; and in fact this was a disputed point to the very end, — to within a few minutes of the time that the exit was actually found on a later occasion. We therefore descended, having, as I say, reached a point some thirty feet higher than before.

The next time a party went to the Black Shoot, snow and ice had again covered up foot and hand holds — such as they are. This was on New Year's day of the present year and Gibson, Naismith, Thomson, and the writer had come to Tyndrum to make the third attempt. Our old enemy was found to be in a very bad condition. Such parts of the rock as were not under ice ran with water, or were covered in moss like a wet sponge.

This, it will readily be understood, was extremely trying, especially in a chimney which has to be climbed with back on one wall and knees on the other. The whole party being roped at the mouth of the Shoot, rapid progress was made with the help of the axes, until the point was reached at which Campbell and the writer had previously turned back, i.e., where the vertical chimney begins. The writer had the honour of leading; and up this chimney, which is in reality a small waterfall, and as wet as anything could well be, he and Gibson made their way for some thirty feet till a large boulder, fallen from above and jammed in the chimney, was arrived at overhead. This obstacle, coated as it was with ice, proved beyond my powers to pass. It was also impossible, owing to the narrowness of the chimney, for any of those below to take my place, unless I first descended to the bottom of the vertical part (where there was standing room for more than one) and, as by this time we were all thoroughly wet and cold, it was once more reluctantly decided, after a climb of about three hours, to give it up.

The following 19th of May found four of us again at Dalmally, with the avowed object of doing the Shoot, or once for all proving it was impossible. Gibson, Naismith, and the writer were again there, while our editor had taken the place of Thomson.

Gibson was unanimously voted leader; and on arrival at the Shoot we once more roped, and quickly reached the bottom of the vertical chimney above referred to.

It has seemed to me remarkable how, on each attempt, we, with perfect ease, reached the highest point previously gained, surmounting without difficulty obstacles which before had taxed us severely. It was only after passing these points that difficulties seemed to begin. The unknown above seemed to magnify the obstacles, as no doubt it does in every first ascent.

The top of the chimney having been gained, it was now the turn of Gibson to try his skill on the boulder which blocks the exit.

We had previously decided that if this boulder could be turned, few difficulties would remain between us and the top, and the party were therefore doubly anxious to get past it. This belief, however, proved to be a mistake.

Gibson, apparently with great ease, got round the boulder, and we three followed with the help of the rope. We were now on a ledge, with just room for the four of us to stand, and a choice of several routes higher up presented itself. For the better part of an hour, Gibson with indefatigable energy, tried two of these ways, but could make neither of them go. During this hour the rest of the party had no choice but to stand on the ledge under a small cascade, which empties itself from above.

Finally, Gibson was successful with a third route, and the others again followed.

The angle of the face was now easing off, and the Shoot was gradually merging itself into the cliff, which was here strewn with loose stones on the very point of falling. One of these, several pounds in weight, unfortunately was dislodged, and fell at a bound some twenty feet, striking the shoulder of the last man, — happily, however, without worse consequences than a bad bruise.

The Shoot had now finally merged into the hillside, and we at last stood on the top, having taken two hours and a half to do the 300 feet. Feelings of exultation were, however, considerably damped by the thorough soaking we had got. We stayed but a few minutes at the top, and it was decided not to try the descent by the same route.

A quick scamper over the hills to the top of Ben Eunaich helped to bring back our normal temperature, and the evening saw us safely again at Dalmally.

As to the Shoot, on one point we were all agreed, viz., that it would never see any of us again. It had given us enough, and to spare, of its water and its mud, of which my clothes bear traces to this day.

In summer or dry weather the place may possibly be improved, and should any one foolishly decide to follow in our steps, they would be well advised to choose such a time and no other.

THE BLACK SHOOT IN WHITE (extracts)
Vol. VI (1901)   by Harold Raeburn

My acquaintance with the Black Shoot was made during the Winter Meet of 1897 in company with Maclay, a member well known for his love of steep, slimy, and difficult cracks and chimneys.

We took it in turns to lead up the various sections of the climb, and I noticed, not with too much regret, that M. arranged it so that the steepest and wettest portion fell to his share.

From the description of former explorers it is clear that they had omitted the lower part of the gully below the Shoot. This is a somewhat ill-defined waterslide, a mossy luzula-bedecked wall, of very considerable steepness. The original route goes up the buttress on the north side of this, and traverses into the gully just where it becomes better defined, and the angle eases off for a while very considerably.

Maclay and I, however, tackled it from the very bottom, and found this lower portion — perhaps 50 feet in height — if not the most difficult, the most disagreeable and dangerous part of the ascent, on account of the treacherous nature and abundance of the vegetable covering, and the necessity of standing in and seeking handholds under the stream of icy water that trickled down the slide. As showing the changes that may occur in climbs in the course of a few years, I may mention that the boulder which stopped the earlier explorers, and which was at last surmounted by Gibson had now disappeared, and we found the chimney quite unobstructed.

The foot of this chimney is the spot where, if hitherto a wetting has been avoided, a shower bath appears in ordinary circumstances inevitable — a jet of water usually shooting down the crack of the chimney and distributing its chilly favours with impartiality upon the up-struggling face, body, and limbs of the climber. Above this, though the climbing is actually more difficult, the chimney is much drier.

Maclay and I emerged on the summit on this occasion certainly pretty wet, yet after all Bell and I got even wetter next day in merely walking from Loch Awe Hotel to the summit of Eunaich and back again.

> Raeburn goes on to describe the ascent after a snowfall but not in full winter
> conditions. But let us look at this gully through a more recent account
> by a modern whose wit is well seasoned with respect.

PINK ELEPHANTS IN THE BLACK SHOOT
Vol. XXX (1972)   by R.N. Campbell

"The Black Shoot of Ben Eunaich?"

"You're right in tune," said the Old Man past his umpteenth pint.

The Squirrels' Annual 'Dinner' was going its pleasant predictable way. Another year and another place, Oban, but the bar atmosphere and long-familiar faces open a door down through the years and we remember old heroic drinking bouts and I forget my present rust-clogged thrapple and founder in a Corryvreckan of weak liquor. But the memory of the Old Man's words is locked fast.

Not only the morning is grey. Heavy clouds blanket the tops of men and mountains impartially. As we lurch up the Glen Strae track the Old Man tells a Story from his Young Days. In 1950, he had been walking up the same track with a companion, whiling away the dreary miles by playing a form of cricket with his ice axe, when he met Willie Ling returning from the scene of Unna's accident the day before and naturally in a somewhat sour humour.

"Young Man," said Ling sternly, "that is an Ice-axe, not a Cricket Bat. Treat it with the respect it deserves."

Ling then gave the Young Man some instruction in the Proper Way to Carry an Axe and passed on down the track. The Old Man in his morbid way points out that the approximate site of the Unna accident and acts out this pointless story with enthusiastic cover drives and towering six-hits over Beinn Lurachan. Fortunately he doesn't have his ice-axe with him so that no graves are disturbed.

We plouter up the corrie towards Beinn Eunaich, fouling the air with our stale breath. Over on the left there's a scruffy crag peeping through a shroud of vegetation. This seems to mean nothing so we thrash on into the upper corrie to stare in disbelief at the Salvationist summit slopes.

"It must go up that scruffy little crag back down there. Imagine. Bell made a *rock climb* there."

The significance of its name, the Beaver Buttress, sinks in as we picture the Subtle Doctor gnawing his way from branch to branch.

Soon the Black Shoot presents itself. The first pitch, a concoction of greasy flakes and saturated curtains of turf, flavours our light-headed mood with a pinch of anxiety.

"It was your idea," says the Old Man, proffering the end of his appropriately ancient rope.

We stumble about for a bit, fumbling grannies into bowlines, shaking fuzzy heads over the topological puzzles presented by the rope. Eventually all is prepared and I kick my way ponderously up the turf, pushing-not-pulling past the greasy flakes. As the Old Man grumbles up it starts to snow heavily and soon we see nothing but the black slit of the Shoot twisting up above us.

"A real period piece," says the Old Man with relish.

Greek meets Greek as he sloshes off up the Shoot, digging mitten and boot deep in the snowy mush. I find him again sniggering below the first chimney pitch, going on about how funny it is climbing when you are drunk, how you don't really worry about the climb, how you can't see the simplest little move and so forth. My Sense of History is much stimulated by this pitch. The climb itself is like an old book, long unread, its covers mouldering, its binding cracked. The chimney's walls and chockstones wear a thin coat of soft green lichen. A tiny stream gurgles and drips melancholy accompaniment to my staccato dither and lurch. Here the early Ultramontane chose to make their first mainland foray. For two years their stout attacks were beaten back by the twisting chimney, their tweeds torn and muddied, their pipes comprehensively extinguished, their hip-flasks mangled and crushed deyond all hope of repair, but their spirits undamaged.

There are really two chimneys: the first is commodious, well furnished with chockstones and stances, but dies at an overhang; above and to the right the very narrow second chimney starts abruptly. The intervening ten feet or so provides the crux of the pitch. I poke and prod at it while the time goes by. I cannot see the simplest little move, though naturally I'm not at all worried, not even by the sniggering Old Man down below. At length the scales fall from my eyes and the narrow chimney is gained by an impressive pull-up with the right knee. Above this a chockstone, garnished with a malodorous hemp sling which parts at a touch, gets in the way and the pitch ends with a mantleshelf onto my rump to gain a large ledge on the left. Here, as we discovered later, the intrepid Gibson, making the first ascent in 1892, had thought that the Black Shoot had finally shot its bolt but soon found that the easy-looking wall behind was most deceptive and after many vain attempts led his party back into the disgusting chimney and on to victory.

The Old Man joins me on the large ledge and fixes the wall behind with his somewhat bloodshot Eye of Faith.

"Up this easy wee wall, eh?" he says, moving purposely up the lower holds.

Time passes and the light grows dim, while History Repeats Itself as the Old Man moves like a crab across the wall, looking for a line in the snowy swirl. Sure enough, down he comes and puffs and grunts his way up the chimney and out of sight. The chimney is almost a sobering experience as sloping greasy mantelshelf follows sloping greasy mantelshelf, each one knocking the breath in and out of us in great gulps and whoops. The climb finishes as it began, with a wall of turf and loose flakes now buried in snow and dark inscrutability.

Down the long complicated slopes to Glen Strae we stagger, jumping small cliffs and sidling round the bigger ones.

"Unna fell over one of these. Probably in the dark, too," says the Old Man.

"Treacherous stuff, this new snow lying on grass. There might be patches of old ice, even," he adds hopefully.

But all is well and we are soon zipping down Strathfillan in his sporty little Alfa, roaring round the bends and careering past fish-lorries. He takes time off driving to enliven the long dull straights with more tales from his Young Days about how he almost hit this bridge and how he bounced off that boulder trying to take the bend at eighty and so on.

"I don't feel very well," I venture tentatively.

"Never mind," he says, "We'll stop off at Strathyre for a few pints and you'll be as right as rain again."

THE SQUIRRELS RIGHTS
Vol. XXX   from Letters to the Editor

Sir

We in the Squirrels is objecting to your snidy remarks about our manuscrepts and taods and princesses. Just because old Dutton hasn't got a plate in his head is no reason for going on about our writing. If we was good enough to write our S.M.C. application forms we are good enough for to get our articles published and another thing all that poetry and capital letters and 'we' stuff doesn't go down a bundle in the Dray - no wonder that old Dutton ———— that you couldn't understand got the old heave-ho, why couldn't he call a spade a spade, and it looks like the new man wont be any better. Some of our lads even stopped climbing so they could get married and its hard enough paying the mortgage and looking after the kids never mind writing articles which is why we never get up to Glencoe anymore, trying to be respectable like you S.M.C. smart alecs that we are just as good as. Anyway who's interested in your rotten journal when we can write for Mountain and Ascent and the Alpine Club and climb the Eiger and Mount Everest and North America Wall first British ascent, because you dont have to be a good writer to climb all them things only a good climber which is more than all youse old ————s is even if you can write, though none of us is getting any younger. Youse should ask yourselfs how many good climbers has never been heard of because they couldn't write good over the years since you started, what makes you think its the S.M.C. that's done all the climbing its not everybody likes to write their own trumpet?

Yours, etc.

The Squirrels

BUACHAILLE ETIVE MOR - THE CROWBERRY RIDGE
Vol. IV (1896)   by W. W. Naismith

Although Buachaille Etive Mor has figured considerably in the Journal, climbers who know it will agree with me that it well deserves all the attention yet bestowed on it, and a great deal more. An English climber lately offered to negotiate for a transfer of this mountain to Wastdalehead in exchange for Great Gable. Perhaps we might have "a waur offer", for the Gable is no mean mountain; but where's the Scot who would entertain any such proposal? I have therefore no compunction in asking permission, encore une fois, to say something about a section of this glorious cone that has not been described. I refer to that part of the east face between Dr Collie's and Mr Tough's routes (see Sketch, Vol IV, p. 100). The accompanying view, which is reproduced from a photograph taken at Easter 1893, by Mr Rennie, from the Glencoe road, two miles west of Kingshouse, shows this aspect of the mountain in greater detail. On the extreme right is the big gully, often ascended in snow. Next comes the huge rounded ridge climbed by Messrs Brown and Tough. Then a long gully, narrower than the other. It has probably not yet been done; but judging from the glimpses we had of it, and the fairly continuous snow in the photograph, it may be expected to offer no serious difficulties.* Bounding this gully on the left is a prominent ridge, shown in the view as almost directly under the top of the mountain. This was our climb. Then comes a shallow gully, evidently quite simple, and, I fancy, the quickest route to Buachaille Etive from Kingshouse, though no ascent is yet recorded. Further to the left is a curved ridge, ascended by Mr G.B. Gibbs in July 1896, and described by him as not difficult. Then a straight little couloir, with snow in it, and a short ridge beside it, guarded by tremendous cliffs on the left. Neither of these possible routes is believed to have been tried. Dr Collie's route — the earliest ascent of the east face — is still more to the left.

On the 3rd August 1896, Mr Douglas and I met at the Bridge of Orchy, the Editor having bicycled all the way from Edinburgh in two stages of about sixty miles each. We rode to Kingshouse in an hour and a half, leading our machines for less than a mile out of the thirteen. At Kingshouse we were welcomed noisily by a Skye terrier and two young collies, who in doubt whether we were friends or foes, and divided between the conflicting claims of duty and natural affability, compromised matters by barking vigorously and at the same time wagging their tails. On explaining the object of our visit the barking subsided, and we invited them all to dinner at nine p.m., though only two doggies were able to accept. After making some change in our garb, we proceeded on foot to the junction of the roads, waylaid Her Majesty's mail coach, seized the mails, and abstracted a rope and a pair of climbing boots. That highway robbery accomplished, we made a bee-line for "the Shepherd", the river Coupal being low and allowing us to cross dry-shod.

This is Crowberry Gully ! — Ed.

The ridge we were aiming for looks appallingly steep from the road, but we had been deceived once before by the inaccessible appearance of those Buachaille Etive crags, and were not to be "done" again. This particular portion of the mountain is certainly steep. The contour lines on the 1-inch map indicate that the upper 2,000 feet are inclined at an average angle of 45°, and the last 1,000 feet rise at an average rate of 11 in 9 - that is about 50°. We reached the foot of our ridge in rather more than an hour from the road, including the ascent of some easy broken rocks. The writer's chief difficulty so far had been to get his companion past the clumps of ripe crowberries growing everywhere, and this circumstance has suggested a name for our climb. The forbidding aspect of the ridge was now somewhat mollified, though its ascent still promised to be stiff enough without looking for difficulties. Both sides of the ridge, as far as we could make out, were sheer walls, so that there would be no escape into either of the gullies in the event of our being "pounded". At its lower end also, the rocks which formed the crest of the ridge are hopelessly steep, and nearly unbroken for some 300 feet. The photograph shows that no snow lies on them. I will not prophesy that that cliff will never be scaled in a direct line, but before then I think mountaineering science will have to advance to a higher state of development. It is conceivable that a line might be chosen up those rocks, any part of which could be climbed if it were, say on a "boulder", or even if there were a reasonable number of platforms or anchorages. But in the absence of these, a continuous steep climb of 300 feet is at present generally regarded as "impossible", because it would make too great demands on nerve and muscular endurance. In this connection I cannot help thinking that what may be termed the psychological influence of platforms receives inadequate acknowledgement in most descriptions of rock-climbs. A brick wall ten feet high, with all the joints between the bricks open, is an easy climbe; if twice that height, a desperate feat; while a chimney stalk, 100 feet high, in similar condition, would be "impossible" without a steeplejack's apparatus.

But I am wandering from the "Crowberry Ridge", at the bottom of which Douglas and I are putting on the rope, while we scan with eager anticipation the mighty rocks above us, hitherto untrodden by either man or beast. To the right of the high cliff the rocks sloped upwards more gently, abutting against the loftier portion of the ridge like a lean-to-shed against a higher building. The two sections of the ridge appeared to unite above, and a shallow gully or groove, that ran up the middle of the lower rocks, evidently offered the best prospect of success. After proceeding gaily for a short distance we came to an overhanging part, where we were forced to leave the friendly groove, and go up ten or fifteen feet of a vertical rock ladder, with a horrible drop below into the chasm on our right. The highest step of the ladder was several feet short of the top of the pitch, and the only obvious handhold within reach was a big block, which swayed ominously at the first touch. Seeing that we were both directly underneath this gentleman at the time, we begged him earnestly not to disturb himself on our account — until we got past — when Douglas, in the interests of future climbers, tipped him over into the gully, with a clatter that woke all the echoes of the surrounding crags. Above that difficulty we passed two minor obstacles, and got to a tolerably level place, where we thought we could, by turning to the left, reach the crest of the ridge. In any case there seemed to be no alternative route, for the moderate slope we had been following ended abruptly, a short distance ahead, at the foot of an impossible precipice, with a huge spike of porphyry projecting from it. Starting with a climb up a wall ten feet high, where we both found it difficult to keep our balance owing to a slight overhang, we had to mount a rather troublesome slope of slabby rock. There were few good grips, and no anchorage for the leader till he reached the crest. The whole of our sixty feet rope was needed at this place, and it would not be particularly delightful to go down. From this point onwards we followed the crest of the ridge, which is fairly narrow, and allows one to look down into the abyss on either side — always a pleasurable sensation. It is quite an easy scramble, and we rose rapidly, although we encountered one or two steep bits, and some more crowberries. On approaching the top we saw that our ridge terminated in a pinnacle, detached from the mountain, the gully on our right (N) side running up to the gap behind the pinnacle. As our side of the gully appeared to be still very precipitous, we were in happy uncertainty whether, when we got to the top of the pinnacle, we should not find ourselves, as an Irishman might say, in a hole. However, on getting to where we could look into the gully, we saw that we could readily reach a little grass ridge connecting the pinnacle with the rest of the mountain. The pinnacle rises about forty feet above the saddle, and on the top of it we found the first sign of visitors we had observed - namely, the cairn built by Dr Collie's party, who had ascended it from the saddle in snow.

The ridge was vanquished! It had given us a thousand feet of interesting climbing, and had occupied just two hours. On the way up we had left one or two stone marks along our track. The porphyry of Buachaille Etive is an honest, downright sort of material, nice to climb. If a fragment is loose, it tells you so at once; and if in situ, you can usually trust your whole weight to the tiniest flake - not like some rocks, which seem to be firm to the hand until a strain is put on them, when they suddenly fail you.

Ten minutes more took us to the summit of the mountain. There we sat down and feasted our eyes on the wide panorama on one of the loveliest evenings it has ever been our fortune to spend on a hill top. All the giants round about were clear, except Ben Nevis, which alone had a cap of cloud. To the west Loch Linnhe was crossed by a broad belt of gold; while down below, on the other side, we saw the conical shadow of our mountain mapped out on the level moor.

We left the cairn at six o'clock, to descend the big gully beyond Tough's ridge. In such weather one would suppose it to be an easy matter to find this gully, but in some inexplicable way we followed the wrong ridge, and only pulled up on the brow of the Tulachan Corrie, a quarter of a mile away! Several other climbers have, strangely enough, been baffled in their efforts to hit the big gully, and one is almost forced to explain the phenomenon by concluding that this place is the "sanctuary" of the mountain elves and

47. *The top of Observatory Ridge, Ben Nevis*

48. *Carn Dearg Buttress, Ben Nevis*
   Inset: Robin Smith

49. *Alastair Walker on Minus One Buttress Direct, Ben Nevis*

50. Bill Brooker on the final tower of Mitre Ridge (Bell's Route), Beinn a' Bhuird

fairies, who, to prevent the impious invasion of its solitudes, are wont to employ all their harmless arts to lure the unwary stranger into other gullies, which are, so to speak, open to the public. Their usual dodge is to conceal their ravine under a veil of mist, but on this summer night they tried a different plan, and made the atmosphere so unnaturally transparent, that objects a mile off looked close at hand. We at last discovered the gully despite its witchery. It follows the line of a dyke of reddish igneous rock, less durable than the porphyry. Its descent is by no means a simple walk, as it contains several steep pitches. One place, about half-way between the top and the waterfall, took up a good deal of time. We had there to descend a hundred feet of wet rock, garnished with water cresses and other aquatic plants, among which it was not easy to find and test the footholds. There would be no such difficulty when ascending. It was quite a revelation to us to compare the August condition of the gorge with is appearance at the snowy Easter of 1893. Then it presented a broad, smooth, and, except at one point, an unbroken slope of snow, rising at an almost uniform angle. Now that the snow was gone, we noticed that it had hidden a perfect chaos of rocks, caves, trenches, cascades, and what not. The depth of the snow at one or two points must have been as much as forty or fifty feet.

As we were enjoying ourselves we did not hurry down, and by the time we reached the road the stars were twinkling in the southern sky.

ROUTE
Vol. XXXII (1984)   by G.J.F.D.

we made a route on last night's mountain.
from the ruin picked out
a single buttress, set it,
twelve hours' rock and ice,

white from the ruck of the dark.
can now look back and trace it,
drifting star to star
across the cold lumber,

committed, all construction over.
can enter the hut and close the door;
beside the fire
rejoin the peace of transience.

GIANT
Vol. XXXII (1983)   by A.J. Hastie

A thousand metres sheer,
Diamond buttressed, mammoth shouldered,
Dagger at the stars,
He shrugs presumptuous climbers off in avalanche
As stallions switch flies from their flanks,
And endures perennially battering blizzards.
Epochs ago when mountains were holy -
Not playgrounds but temples -
They named him,
Those dawn-men who danced in his shadow,
'Sentinel', 'Shepherd' and 'Giant'.
They knew he was old then,
Even as he was old when Megalithic Man
Set stones on the moor,
Aligned to him,
When sighting setting suns;
An eternal solstice recorder,
Recorder of Time itself.

Eternal?
His body built of sea-snail shells.
He is a tower of ancient bones
Folded and piled when continents collided,
Churning Everests out of abysses.

And he rots at the edges!
Dissolves by drips from leprous ledges,
Crumbles like cheese from frost-shattering ridges.

A stone falls from the face,
Clatters and claps down the screes
To the well-heads of rivers
That grind rock on rock
And roll all their grist to the sea.

... Till the snails grope again where the giant stood,
Under yellow water, feeling flat, blue mud.

THE OBSERVATORY RIDGE, BEN NEVIS
Vol. VI (1901)   by Harold Raeburn

Insatiable is the appetite of the modern, even of the modern mountaineer, for novelty. When one centre becomes exhausted, or he considers it so, he flies to pastures new. Latterly our Scottish mountaineers have apparently been falling into the belief that Scotland is one of these exhausted centres. We hear of their doings in Switzerland, the Tyrol, Dauphine, or even in remote western lands such as Canada or Kerry. Desolation meanwhile has fallen on such exhausted centres as Skye and Arran. No more are the wondering and disgusted fishers in the smoke-room at Sligachan swept out by a spate of mountaineering maundering — as they consider it — and their fishy tales forced to hide their heads before the mute eloquence of the "big hob-nailers" and the long yarns of the 60-foot rope. No more do we read of doughty deeds done on the faces and in the gullies of the slabby granite peaks of Arran, and even Nevis is becoming deserted for lowly and obscure English or Irish rocks, with such outlandish names as creeks or reeks, arks and rakes, or similar harshly sounding titles. That Nevis at any rate is not quite yet an utterly exhausted centre it is the purpose of this paper to show.

True it is that all the main ridges and buttresses have long been climbed and re-climbed up and down, traversed on to at various points, and ingenious schemes evolved for evading their main difficulties. Still, in the lower corrie are numbers of ridges and buttresses, not to speak of chimneys, left, each one of which looks capable of affording a good climb; and in the upper corrie two long ridges, the lower very little shorter than the North-East Buttress itself, afford interesting variations to the direct climb of the great north-east face.

The objection may be urged that these routes are not the plain and obvious ones to the summit of Nevis. No more they are — the obvious route is the path; but the objection is of no value to the genuine climber. One might as well say that the Zmutt or Furgg Ridges were not the obvious routes up the Mattehorn, but are they any worse as climbs for that?

At Easter this year a party of four S.M.C. members made an attack on the upper of the two; but after a three hours' contest, during which they mounted a bare 300 feet, were forced to beat a retreat. The conditions were certainly adverse. Deep loose snow in the corrie was replaced by slabby rocks covered with a glaze of ice, over which swept hissing streams of loose snow from the upper regions. The steepness was such that in places handholds as well as footholds had to be cut in the ice. Such climbing may not be very difficult, but it becomes a question of time and endurance, and the party decided that neither commodity would hold out. As it was, through various little circumstances, they did not dine that evening till 11 p.m. As one of the party on that occasion, the writer came to the conclusion that the lower or North-East Ridge would give later on not only a better climb, but one considerably longer and better defined.

On the 22nd June the opportunity came of testing this theory. I was trysted to meet that evening on the summit of Ben Nevis, Dr and Mrs Inglis Clark. They had come fresh from battling with the elements on the rugged ridges of Skye, and flushed with the conquest of a new route on the "blue-grey stone" of the Eastern Coolins, to finish their trip by doing the most of the Nevis climbs in two days.

Thanks to the new Mallaig Railway, a train now leaves Edinburgh at 4.30 a.m. which deposits one at Fort William before 10 o'clock, so that by 10.30 I had left the Alexandra Hotel behind and had set face towards the familiar slopes of Meall an t'Suidhe.

I had failed on short notice to find a companion for the day, so was forced to go solus. One advantage of this, however, is that there is no one to force the pace, so that rests can be indulged in as much as one is inclined, and leisure afforded to study the natural surroundings. Deviations from the direct path are also permissible, and accordingly I deviated in order to visit the nesting rock of a pair of buzzards which earlier in the season were building here. They were unfortunately not about today, but I hope may have escaped the fate too often meted out to these interesting and practically harmless birds at the hands of the £.s.d. game-trader. The weather, which had been close and warm in the morning, became threatening as I entered the great corrie, and soon after down came the rain in real Nevis style. It did not last long, however, and as I gained the foot of the Observatory Ridge, the mists began slowly to roll up their filmy curtains - magnificent transformation scenes of gleaming snowfields, jagged ridges and pinnacles, black frowning cliffs, and long white deeply receding couloirs, coming into view as the visible circle gradually widened.

In my opinion these is nothing finer in all 'braid Scotland', lovely Lakeland, or rugged Skye, to surpass or even equal the splendid north-east face of our highest mountain. There was still an immense amount of snow in the corrie, and my way lay for a time over the rugged miniature seracs of old avalanche remains; then slanting upwards I traversed a steeply sloping snowfield which abutted against the foot of the ridge.

The bergschrund here was fortunately neither deep nor wide. Had it been of a similar character to that which our party encountered on the following day, 30 to 40 feet deep and 8 to 10 feet wide, it would have proved impassable in the absence of an ice axe and required circumvention.

The climb begins at no very severe angle, but on rocks distinctly slabby, and poor in holds and hitches. It almost at once becomes a well-defined arete, and higher up is bounded on both sides by very fine almost A.P. precipices. Throughout its whole length it affords less opportunity of deviation from the exact ridge than does its north-east neighbour. Perhaps at no point does it offer such an awkward bit for the solitary climber as the 'man-trap' of the North-East Buttress - which can be escaped by descending a little on the right, or up a rather difficult chimney on the left — but I remember three distinctly good bits on it. First the slabby rocks near the foot. Then a few hundred feet up an excellent hand traverse presents itself. It is begun by getting the hands into a first-rate crack on the left, then toe-scraping along a wall till the body can be hoisted on to a narrow overhung ledge above. This does not permit of standing up, but a short crawl to the right finishes the difficulty, at the top of an open corner chimney, a more direct and possibly preferable route.

The third difficulty, and the one which cost most time, is rather more thatn half-way up, where a very steep tower spans the ridge. I tried directly up the face, but judged it somewhat risky, and prospecting to the right, discovered a route which after a little pressure went. This is a slightly sensational corner, as the direct drop, save for a small platform is several hundred feet. This part occurs a few hundred feet below the termination of the back portion of the ridge.

The ridge now eases off and traverses show up as possible, either on to the North-East Buttress on one's left, or to the upper or South-West Observatory Ridge to the right. The gully on the left now holds heavy snowdrifts. The climbing, however, is far from over, numerous steep or slabby bits engage the climber's vigilance; but at length the last rocks are gained, where the crest of the ridge plunges under the great snowfield that girdles this face of the mountain, still at midsummer presenting in places icy cornices 20 feet high.

Here I sat down after building the usual cairn — time 4.30 P.M., three hours from the bottom — to bask in the sun, which had been shining gloriously for that last hour and to drink in the grandeur and beauty of the surroundings. These I fear are apt to be missed by the climber during the actual climb, especially if engaged by the problems that confront him when engaged on a new ascent.

But what is that note? A bird song strange and new! What could it be? There is only one possibility — it must be the snow bunting; and there sure enough it was, a splendid male in full summer plumage, singing sweetly, with utterly unbunting-like notes, from a rock projecting from the snow below the brow of the cliff.

But one must be an ornithologist to appreciate the pleasure of hearing for the first time the song of a bird hitherto only familiar as a winter visitor.

Though it would be rank heresy to write so in these pages sacred to the cult of the mountains as 'haunts of scansorial feet' of men, yet I fear that if asked to say which of the two I would sooner have missed, the climb or the song, I might be tempted to say the first. However, no such invidious choice was forced on me, and the snow bunting's song was an additional pleasure to a most enjoyable scramble.

THE GREAT GULLY OF SGOR NAM FIANNAIDH, GLENCOE
Vol. XXI (1938)   by W. H. Murray

First Ascent. - 1st May 1938 Party. - W.H. Murray, W.G. Marskell, A.M. MacAlpine, and J.K.W. Dunn (all J.M.C.S.).

> Better known as THE CLACHAIG GULLY this is now a classic climb and probably the best known and most frequently climbed summer gully in Scotland. The first ascent described here was immortalised in a song by Tom Patey in The Ballad of Bill Murray which went:-
>> "It was in the Clachaig Gully that young Murray rose to fame
>> On the slabs of the Great Cave Pitch"
> and later...
>> "On the Wall of Jericho, when they shouted 'Will it go?',
>> As he hung from a hair trigger hold.
>> But he answered not a word as he rose like a bird
>> Through the mud and the slime, and the cold."

This gully, hitherto known as "The Unclimbed Gully at Clachaig," is the finest and longest climb of its kind in Scotland. The gully starts on the open hillside in front of Clachaig Inn, and splits the mountain from top to bottom. The walls are deeply cut, and for the main part vary in height from 100 to 300 feet. Unchecked readings by altimeter give the start as 400 feet, and the finish as approximately 2,500 feet. Surprisingly few climbers have any idea of the real character of the gully, although its history is a long one.

The Great Gully may be divided into two distinct sections -

(a) The first 800 feet. A forest of small trees sprouts from the high walls amidst a profusion of luxuriant vegetation. It is a mistake to imagine that one climbs over such stuff. When the walls approach the bed of the gully they come fairly close together and the bare rock is exposed. Only a few of the pitches are vegetatious; for the main part the climber goes up on sound interesting rock through exotic jungle scenery. At about 1,200 feet lies the Great Cave pitch, which marks alike the limit of the tree zone and of previous exploration.

(b) The final 1,200 feet. Above the Great Cave the character of the gully completely changes. The walls become bare and narrower, the rock scenery stern and more majestic, and the climbing harder. At perhaps 1,700 feet the gully narrows to a rocky trough - one may touch both walls at once - and with a sharp double twist develops into a mere chimney before widening again. This upper section harbours many fine pitches, and three of these approach the standard of the Great Cave.

One of the main difficulties of the gully is route-selection at stiff pitches. The climb is too long to allow much waste of time through misjudgment in this matter. The Great Cave pitch is a notable example, and our first visit there, on the previous week-end, was devoted solely to finding a possible line of attack. There is an escape below the pitch on the left wall, but higher up in the gully Jericho Wall (described below) presents a similar stumbling-block with no escape, and we were fortunate to solve the problem at the first attempt.

There is no pitch in the gully so fierce of aspect as the Devil's Cauldron in the Chasm. On the other hand, the standard of difficulty is greater than in the Chasm, and the climb is longer with fewer chances of escape. There are about 40 pitches, varying in height from 15 to 80 feet, with very few stretches of "walking" relative to the length of the gully. From the Great Cave onwards one pitch seems to follow hard after another, happily on good clean rock.

It is well to observe that the gully might be dangerous for a mediocre party with a good leader, for there are two severe traverses where the last man would have a long swing against slabs if he came off. Combined tactics are nowhere required, and the best size of party is two, or preferably four climbing on two 100-foot ropes, the ropes being joined only where necessary. Rubbers should be carried. The gully should always go after a fortnight of dry weather. The time for the first ascent was nine hours fifteen minutes.

The weather conditions on 1st May were excellent, and no rain had fallen for three weeks. A fair amount of water was running down the lower part of the gully, but only at one difficult place — the Red Chimney, which is placed high up before the water gathers in volume — does the route lie up the actual watercourse. We climbed on two ropes; Murray led the first and MacAlpine the second, the ropes being joined for each of the four main obstacles. A detailed list of pitches would fill the entire Journal, and although many are notewothy only the four most important and difficult ones are described below.

(a) *The Great Cave*: at approx. 1,200 feet. The gully is fairly wide here and is barred by a wall of rock 50 feet high. The left-hand half of the wall is a shallow cave, which rises 40 feet and ends in a vertical 10-foot chimney. The chimney is the watercourse and is probably impossible. The right-hand half of the wall is a sheet of discouraging sleek slabs, leading up to a grass corner near the top. The corner is the key to the problem; it is bounded on the left by the slabs and on the right by an exceedingly steep wall. This wall is only 6 feet wide, and is in turn bounded by a steep rib. To reach the foot of the rib one climbs up to an enormous slab on the right wall and traverses leftward on its lower rim. Some delicate hand-balancing is required near the base of the rib in order to effect lodgement. Small holds then assist one upwards for a foot or so until it is possible to make a short but exhilarating traverse on exposed rock into the grass corner, which slopes steeply outwards and should never be used when damp. It is safe when dry and affords difficult access to the top of the pitch. The pitch is severe in rubbers and cannot be avoided. A steep and unpleasant escape may be found on the left wall of the gully.

(b) *Jericho Wall*: at approx. 1,500 feet. An immense shallow cave blocks the gully and looks more hopeless than (a). No direct route up the watercourse seems possible, the left wall overhangs, and there is no escape. The right flank appears at a first glance to be perpendicular, the lower part quite smooth and the upper deplorably loose — so loose that we imagined a loud shout might bring down the upper wall about our ears — and the place was named accordingly. The route goes up this wall by way of a very smooth corner that finally merges into the upper face. A steep upward traverse then goes leftward to the top, where there is some difficulty in finding a suitable stance in a wilderness of slabs. The upper part of the wall is quite safe when treated properly. Most of the loose rock was removed, revealing sound holds underneath. We all found Jericho Wall severe in rubbers, but it may well prove less awkward for future climbers. 100 feet of rope is required by the leader.

(c) *The Red Chimney*: at approx. 2,000 feet. Here we have an excellent 70-foot pitch on dark-red rock. An imposing shallow cave rises to a height of 30 feet, and from the outside edge of the roof there springs a 20-foot chimney, which overhangs the base. The chimney leads to a steep 20-foot slab. One climbs up the right-hand wall of the cave on the outside, until one arrives at a small ledge level with the foot of the chimney and only one foot to its right. The crux of the pitch is the step into the chimney, an exposed movement on smooth wet rock with awkward holds. The rest of the chimney is strenuous. There are two small chock-stones; the upper one is loose and must be used cautiously. There is a good stance above the chimney from which to tackle the final difficult slab. The pitch as a whole is an amiable severe. (Climbed in boots.)

(d) *The last pitch*: at approx. 2,500 feet. The gully ends in grand style on good red rock. The last pitch of 30 feet is severe in boots, and is climbed on its right-hand side. The first 15 feet are obvious and easy; the last 15 feet call for a difficult movement towards the centre of the pitch up steep red slabs with minute footholds, which bring a thankful climber to the end of all further difficulty.

The best route of descent goes down the true right bank of the gully.

THIRD ON THE ROPE
Vol. XXV (1953)   by Graham S. Ritchie

Gardyloo Buttress on Ben Nevis was to see several attempts before it was climbed in
July 1944 (see below). This is the story of one of these attempts (by a Dundee party).

It was two o'clock in the morning one day in July 1941. A final nightcap had been brewed
and conversation languished. A warm, companionable silence reigned in the Hut, now
the roar of the primus stove was stilled.

Then, quite unobtrusively, the faintest sound broke in upon our private musings. It
came from nowhere, lingered a moment and was gone — only to force itself upon the ear
again as the all-too-familiar throb of aircraft engines. "Hope he remembers to keep above
4,406 feet," John remarked disinterestedly. The throbbing drone drew suddenly very close
then, as suddenly, was blanketed by the hills. "That sounds awfully like Jerry," said
someone; "let's have a look outside."

Steaming mugs of tea in hand, we moved out into the night where the great cliffs of
the Ben towered jet-black against a dark sky. No sound came to us save a soft rustle of
wind. Yet we lingered expectantly. Then lazily, so lazily, converging streams of red tracer-
shells rose from behind Carn Dearg and mounted the sky. Two great flashes lit the horizon
and the hills stood revealed for an instant. But not a sound was heard. It was all rather
eerie and exciting, yet peaceful and strangely beautiful.

....

That afternoon something of the wonder of the scene was still at work in each of us. An
elation of spirit demanded a fitting climax. We were a little above ourselves. At that
moment the serpent whispered "Gardyloo Buttress."

So it came about that we three, Sydney, John and I, found ourselves on the Eastern
Traverse regarding, without marked enthusiasm, the grand sweep of the buttress - a superb,
challenging mass, with scarce a visible chink in its armour of slabs. Nevertheless we
traversed the snows of Tower Gully to the base of the rocks and surveyed the scene. From
a depression high up between the ridges of the buttress a snow-patch mocked us. It was
quite plainly the key to the climb. Could we but reach it there seemed to be no great
difficulty beyond. But between us and that promised land stretched the most hostile rock.
Two long grooves slanting down from the high funnel were very promptly dismissed from
mind, and we turned our attention to the left-hand ridge. This was crowned by most
alluring towers, set askew; and siren-like they sang to us. The sight of an ominous grey
wall, well above mid-height, should have given us pause. For, should we succeed in
climbing so far by our selected route and then be stopped, a traverse to the snow-filled
depression might well be impossible. Such was our mood, we gave it scarce a thought; and
it was now 6 p.m.

Sydney led off from the bergschrund below the rocks, leaving John and myself contemplating a litter of Observatory rubbish, prominent among which were unmistakable portions of a certain china article which caused quite disproportionate mirth, as such things do on such occasions. Our leader meantime was not on difficult looking rock: yet, after a paltry 30 feet, there he was calling for ironmongery, and in particular for a variety referred to as "wee beauties." "John," I said, "nip up and give Syd a hand; he's off form." After 'nipping up' some 10 feet he descended precipitately upon me, lit a cigarette and commented shortly, "Syd's doing O.K." Thereafter we both sobered up considerably.

Sydney placed a piton before crossing a steep groove to a slab on which we all forgathered. I found the climbing hard as third man. By common consent boots were removed at this point, and we proceeded in stocking-soles. We moved right round a corner, then up left to a ledge where we found the first of the only two rock belays which we were to encounter on the whole expedition. Beyond this, easy climbing took us to a ledge overlooking the head of a slabby groove which dropped clean into the 'schrund below and merged above into two thin chimneys, at the top of which were some insecure-looking blocks. We eyed the chimneys with distaste and cast about for some less loathsome line of ascent. We decided that the wall of the buttress overlooking Gardyloo Gully held out the best hopes for some distance — and there, for the evening, the matter rested. In the absence of any rock belay to safeguard our descent, a piton was hammered home. The rising note of each successive blow of the hammer was sweet and reassuring to the ear. We then roped down to the 'schrund and returned home by Tower Ridge, leaving an ice-axe high up on the Little Tower just to ensure that we *did* return on the morrow.

The following morning a rather more realistic outlook was to be discerned in the party. Prior to starting out we made due obeisance before the small bottle of a liqueur which we had brought in the hope of celebrating the first ascent of Gardyloo Buttress. This done, we sallied forth and, after a period of time which shall remain unspecified, we stood at our highest point of the previous evening, roped in the same order.

My special care this day was the 'boot-rope,' a 50-foot length of line to which were attached all our boots, our ice-axe and our one rucksack. This tail-piece was left hanging down the cliff face most of the time, so that we could climb the pitches unencumbered and keep the stances clear.

Sydney started out on the Gardyloo Gully face and then moved back on to the true ridge after 40 feet. There he encountered a huge, unstable block which had to be passed. It proved to be so insecure that he decided to dislodge it before venturing further. John and I tucked ourselves and the rope out of the line of fire, and then the block was sent down. Observatory Gully was still filled with snow, and down this funnel that boulder rolled. From one side to the other in turn it weaved its way in great sweeps, its momentum just insufficient to surmount the snows banked against the gully walls. Finally it came to rest by the Allt a'Mhuilinn.

After climbing another 30 feet of steep but delightful rock Syd called down in high glee that he had found our second belay, a most satisfying bollard on a very samll ledge which just accommodated the three of us sitting close-packed. There we sat, feet dangling in the void, for all the world like the Three Wise Monkeys. The 'boot-rope' was made fast and then hauled up. Some food was extracted from the rucksack, the luggage was lowered down the cliff once more and we lunched in our strange eyrie, savouring the situation to the full. The day, which had begun dry but sunless, now broke up beautifully; but where we sat no sun could reach. The downward view, however, put us in good heart, for we felt that we were beginning to make height on the rocks. On the other hand, there was precious little chance to relax, and so we soon resumed the attack.

To the right of our perch a large semi-detached flake offered an easy ascent for some feet. The others shinned up in turn and disappeared, taking with them plenty of spare line, and I was left to admire the scene. The eye travelled straight to Carn Mor Dearg. This complete absence of foreground made me feel distinctly isolated, so I sought solace in tobacco.

Meantime, the others seemed to be making very little headway. The rope was almost static. A lengthy conference was in progress, for I could hear voices without being able to distinguish the words. Soon the sound of hammering drifted down, followed by two coils of rope, which I was adjured to look after most carefully, these being additional safeguards on the succeeding very exposed climbing. Precisely what was going on above was only made clear to me later that evening. But plainly the crux of the climb was at hand, so I sat at the ready. The complex system of ropes made me feel like a bell-ringer, and I hoped that, in an emergency, I would not get myself 'imbrangled' like Wally Pratt in 'The Nine Tailors.'

Time passed swiftly and inexorably. The evening shadows began to lengthen in the corrie. Then a glorious light flooded down Gardyloo Gully, suffusing the rocks with an unbelievable purple glow which slowly paled and suddenly was gone. Still the contest, for such it had become, went on somewhere above me. An hour fled by while the ropes moved spasmodically upwards, never more than a few feet at a time. The tension never relaxed, but rather grew with the passing of the minutes. No verbal communication was possible, owing to the configuration of the crag; and when, at length, the ropes began to swing down like the cables of a lift I could only assume that our attempt had failed. I could not truly say that I was sorry, and when two dejected climbers came warily down to rejoin me it was with a feeling of relief that I greeted them.

For them, too, the zest of the game had for the moment departed. They told of steep, holdless grooves and ribs and continuous exposure. They had forced a way over such rocks until it became plain that further direct progress was highly problematical and a traverse to the snow out of the question. John summed it up: "There ought to be a sign up there, 'Cyclists, this hill is dangerous!'" A deeply rusted karabiner and a weather-faded belay-loop were produced - evidence that they had passed the highest point reached by a previous party who had been forced off by bad weather. We had no such excuse, if any were needed. Sydney and John were convinced that both parties were not on the correct route, which lay almost certainly between our ridge and the grooves draining the snow-filled recess.

And so we prepared to descend. The necessary preliminary was to don our boots; no mean feat in our cramped quarters. In the event Sydney was grabbed, just in time to prevent him toppling off head-first, as he struggled into his hob-nailers. So, to restore his morale, we generously allowed him to test the belay for a long, airy rappel by sending him down first. A series of descents on the rope took us to the snows of Observatory Gully, down which we glissaded merrily. Soon the Hut was before us.

We felt no pricking of conscience as we ate our gargantuan meal and relived the climb. We simply hoped that Lord Woolton's slumbers would be as sweet and deep as our own.*

As the three of us tumbled into bed the bottle of liqueur stood unopened on the table. No dull opiate was needed that night, and as I sank lethewards my drowsy mind recalled and re-echoed the words of Slingsby, "We'n powler't up an' down a bit an' had a rattlin' day."

---

* Lord Woolton was Minister of Food at that time of severe food rationing

The 'Sydney' referred to above, is Sydney Scroggie a Dundonian climber who was blinded and lamed at the close of the Second World War. Despite his afflictions he is yet a familiar figure on the hills. He wrote the following poem especially for this book.

> And some that stand upon the Ben recall
> Who mark the melting cornice in the sun
> How legend says Locheil shall lose his all
> Should ever summer's dwindling drift be done
> And boulder-naked Nevis stand at last,
> Stark in the trembling stillness of July.
> Locheil shall lose his all? That doom was passed
> Upon Lochaber in the days gone by,
> But now the drifts depart and now they stay,
> And still the stubborn ghost of long ago
> Melts in the alien sunshine of today,
> But leaves some residue in doing so.
> And legend lies, for life its fortunes owes
> To something deeper far than Nevis' snows.

Sydney Scroggie

GARDYLOO BUTTRESS — from
'A Record of Ben Nevis Climbs'
Vol. XXIII (1946)   by B. P. Kellet

Brian Kellet carried out a brilliant series of explorations on Ben Nevis while engaged
in forestry work in the area during the war years. The climb described is now known
as Kellet's Route, Gardyloo Buttress.

 The account is taken from the personal notebooks left after a fatal accident on Ben
Nevis in September 1944 in which Kellet lost his life.

This buttress consists of two ridges, of which the left hand is fairly well defined, but with
a very shallow depression between them. The upper part of this depression opens out into
a wide funnel with what is almost a gully at the back; most of the water from this gully
drains down two long grooves slanting down from left to right, very steep and smooth and
probably unclimbable. Between the lower part of these grooves and the left-hand ridge is
a very steep face of over 100 feet, and above that three more grooves running parallel to
the two long grooves, and having slabs on their left, walls on their right; they end after
about 100 feet at the same level as the foot of the funnel.

 Below the steep face and stretching right across the foot of the buttress is a 150-foot
band of easy-angled rocks climbable almost anywhere. On this route serious climbing
began at the top of this easy-angled section up two parallel cracks about half-way between
the left-hand ridge and the foot of the long grooves. They face towards the Great Tower
as they are on the right wall of a tiny subsidiary buttress standing out a little from the main
face; they should be unmistakable, as they are narrow at the foot but become broader
higher up where the wall between them is made up of splintered blocks. At the top, where
the wall bounding the left-hand crack is formed by a semi-detached flake, they curve over
to the right.

 The start from the broad shelf between Gardyloo Gully and Tower Gully was made in
a straight line below the foot of these cracks. If the climb is started from the broad shelf
up the left-hand ridge, then the foot of the cracks is reached by making a 50-foot traverse
right, when a piton with two rope slings is found at an easy-angled part of the ridge. It is
not certain if this is the highest of the four pitons left by previous parties; probably not,
as the ridge appears to be climbable for some distance above this, and, indeed, is at a much
easier angle than the face on its right; the trouble is that higher up it becomes unclimbable
at a place where it would be difficult, perhaps impossible, to traverse right.

 These twin cracks have good holds and are fairly easy, though near the top one has an
uncomfortable feeling that the semi-detached flake might suddenly remember that it had
a pressing appointment down in Observatory Gully. For this reason it would probably be
better not to use the small sloping stance at the top, especially as the belays are all rather

doubtful. From here a short traverse right is made beneath an overhang and then a little overhang is climbed direct to a very small stance; here again it would probably be better not to bring up the second man, as the only belays are small, insecure-looking blocks on the floor of the recess. Possibly the best plan would be to use a 150-foot rope and to climb the whole of this very steep section in one run out.

The 15-foot corner starting on the right of the recess was very strenuous and proved to be the crux of the climb. The left wall is perpendicular, the right wall slightly overhanging; handholds on the left wall, though well placed for climbing straight up it, are not well adapted for preventing the body being pushed off to the left by the overhanging wall. The key to the pitch is the large spike handhold facing horizontally left; this was used by the left hand and had to take most of the weight of the body, while the mossy holds above were cleaned and tidied with the right hand. The higher holds had to be groped for as they could not be seen from below, and the whole process proved to be very strenuous so that numerous descents had to be made for rests, and this short pitch took nearly an hour to climb. Once preparations were completed the right hand was shifted from a flat press hold to a much higher hold (rather unsatisfactory) and then the left hand unwillingly left the beautiful spike for another hold, also much higher. This was really the hardest movement as both feet were on very poor holds and the body was being pushed off left all the time by the overhang. Once both these higher handholds had been reached there was no further difficulty in stepping up on to the large flat hold previously used by the right hand and then climbing the remaining few feet of the corner. This led to a series of small broken ledges running below the three parallel grooves already mentioned. The foot of the right-hand groove was slightly undercut and proved to be a little strenuous; delicate climbing, mostly up the slab on the left of the groove, but using also holds in the crack at the back of the groove, then led to a small stance below a 15-foot right-angled corner. This was quite hard, and from its top a step left led to another shorter and easier corner, above which easy ground was reached, with a way-off up the upper part of the right-hand ridge. However, to preserve the central character of the climb the gully in the upper funnel was climbed; this proved quite easy as most of the wet, mossy holds could be avoided by bridging.

The standard was Very Severe owing to the continuously steep and exposed central section of about 250 feet. Climbed in rubbers (socks for the gully). Conditions excellent on the sixth day of a dry spell. The climb would only be feasible under reasonably dry condition. Time about three hours.

THE BAT AND THE WICKED
Vol. XXVII (1960)   by Robin Smith

You got to go with the times. I went by the Halfway Lochan over the shoulder of Ben Nevis and I got to the Hut about two in the morning. Dick was there before me; we had to talk in whispers because old men were sleeping in the other beds. Next day we went up *Sassenach* and *Centurion* to spy on the little secrets hidden between them. We came down in the dark, and so next day it was so late before we were back on the hill that the big heat of our wicked scheme was fizzling away.

Carn Dearg Buttress sits like a black haystack split up the front by two great lines. Centurion rises straight up the middle, 500 feet in a vast corner running out into slabs and over the traverse of Route II and 200 feet threading the roofs above.Sassenach is close to the clean-cut right edge of the cliff, 200 feet through a barrier of overhangs, 200 feet in an overhanging chimney and 500 feet in a wide broken slowly easing corner. At the bottom a great dripping overhang leans out over the 100 feet of intervening ground. Above this, tiers of overlapping shelves like armour plating sweep out of the corner of Centurion diagonally up to the right to peter out against the monstrous bulge of the wall on the left of the Sassenach chimney. And hung in the middle of this bulging wall is the Corner cutting through 100 feet of the bulge. Dick and I lay and swithered on a flat stone. We wanted to find a way out of Centurion over the shelves and over the bulge into the Corner and up the Corner and straight on by a line of grooves running all the way over the top of the Buttress, only now it was after two in the afternoon.

But we thought we ought to just have a look, so we climbed the first pitch of Centurion, 50 feet to a ledge on the left. The first twisted shelf on the right was not at all for us, so we followed the corner a little further and broke out rightwards over a slab on a wandering line of holds, and as the slab heeled over into the overlap below, a break in the overlap above led to the start of a higher shelf and we followed this till it tapered away to a jammed block poking into the monstrous bulge above. For a little while Dick had a theory that he felt unlike leading, but I put on all the running belays just before the hard bits so that he was in for the bigger swing away down over the bottom dripping overhang. We were so frightened that we shattered ourselves fiddling pebbles and jamming knots for runners. We swung down backwards in to an overlap and down to the right to a lower shelf and followed it over a fiendish step to crouch on a tiny triangular slab tucked under the bulge, and here we could just unfold enough to reach into a V-groove cutting through the bottom of the bulge and letting us out on a slab on the right just left of the Sassenach chimney.

And so we had found a way over the shelves, but only to go into orbit round the bulging wall with still about 40 feet of bulge between us and the bottom of the Corner now up on the left. The way to go was very plain to see, a crooked little lichenous overhanging groove looking as happy as a hoodie crow. But it looked as though it was getting late and all the belays we could see were very lousy and we might get up the groove and then have to abseil and underneath were 200 feet of overhangs and anyway we would be back in the morning. We could just see the top of the Corner leering down at us over the bulge as we slunk round the edge on the right to the foot of the Sassenach chimney. A great old-fashioned battle with fearful constrictions and rattling chockstones brought us out of the chimney into night, and from there we groped our way on our memory of the day before, leading through in 150-foot run-outs and looking for belays and failing to find them and tying on to lumps of grass and little stones lying on the ledges. When we came over the top we made away to the left and down the bed of Number Five Gully to find the door of the Hut in the wee small hours.

We woke in the afternoon to the whine of the Death Wind fleeing down the Allt a'Mhuillin. Fingery mists were creeping in at the five windows. Great grey spirals of rain were boring into the Buttress. We stuck our hands in our pockets and our heads between our shoulders and stomped off down the path under our rucksacks into the bright lights of the big city.

Well the summer went away and we all went to the Alps. (Dick had gone and failed his exams and was living in a hole until the re-sits, he was scrubbed.) The rest of the boys were extradited earlier than I was, sweeping north from the Channel with a pause for Wales in the Llanberis Pass at a daily rate of four apiece of climbs that Englishmen call X.S. (X is a variable, from exceptionally or extremely through very or hardly to merely or mildly severe) From there they never stopped until they came to Fort William, but the big black Ben was sitting in clouds in the huff and bucketing rain and the rocks never dried until their holidays ended and I came home and only students and wasters were left on the hill.

Well I was the only climber Dougal could find and the only climber I could find was Dougal, so we swallowed a very mutual aversion to gain the greater end of a sort of start over the rest of the field. Even so we had little time for the Ben. We could no more go for a week-end than anyone else, for as from the time that a fellow Cunningham showed us the rules we were drawn like iron filings to Jacksonville in the shadow of the Buachaille for the big-time inter-city pontoon school of a Saturday night. And then we had no transport and Dougal was living on the dole, and so to my disgust he would leave me on a Wednesday to hitch-hike back to Edinburgh in time to pick up his moneys on a Thursday. The first time we went away we had a bad Saturday night, we were late getting out on the Buachaille on Sunday and came down in the dark in a bit of rain. But the rain came to nothing, so we made our way to the Fort on Monday thinking of climbing to the Hut for the night; only there was something great showing at the pictures and then we went for chip suppers and then there were the birds and the juke-box and the slot machines and we ended up in a back-garden shed. But on Tuesday we got up in the morning, and since Dougal was going home next day we took nothing for the Hut, just our climbing gear like a bundle of stings and a bee-line for Carn Dearg Buttress.

51. *The Foreign Connection. Russian climbers on Great Gully Buttress, Buachaille Etive Mor, in June 1960. On the left Robin Smith leads July Crack*

52. Stuart Smith on Pinnacle Buttress, Aonach Dubh

53. *Dougie Niven on the North Face of Central Buttress, Buachaille Etive Mor*

54. Ken Crocket in Vanishing Gully, Ben Nevis

This time we went over the shelves no bother at all, until we stood looking into the little green hoodie groove. It ran into a roof and from under the roof we would have to get out on the left on to what looked as though it might be a slab crossing to the bottom of the Corner. I was scheming to myself, now the groove will be terrible but nothing to the Corner and I will surely have to lead the crux, but Dougal shamed me with indifference and sent me round the edge on the right to find a decent belay under the Sassenach chimney. There it was very peaceful, I could see none of the tigering, only the red stripes down the side of the Carn Mor Dearg running into the Allt a'Mhuillin that was putting me to sleep if there hadn't been odd faint snarls and scrabblings and little bits of rope once in a while tugging round the small of my back. But once Dougal was up he took in so much slack that I had to go and follow it myself. Half-way up he told me, you lean away out and loop a sling over the tip of a spike and do a can-can move to get a foot in the sling and reach for the sling with both hands as you lurch out of the groove and when you stop swinging climb up the sling until you can step back into the groove; and his sling had rolled off the spike as he left it, so I would have to put it on again. I came out at the top of the groove in a row of convulsions, which multiplied like Asdic as I took in the new perspective.

Dougal was belayed to pitons on the slab under the Corner. The slab and the left retaining wall went tapering down for 20 feet till they merged and all heeled over into the general bulge. Above, the Corner balanced over Dougal like a blank open book with a rubber under the binding. The only big break in the bareness of the walls was a clean-cut black roof barring the width of the right wall. The crack went into the right wall, about six inches wide but tightly packed with bits of filling; and thus it rose in two leaps, 35 feet to the black roof, then out four horizontal feet and straight up 35 feet again; and then it widened for the last 30 feet as the right wall came swelling out in a bulge to meet the top of the great arc of the sky-line edge of the left wall. And if we could only get there then all the climb would surely be in the bag.

Well I had stolen the lead, only some time before I had been to a place called Harrison's Rocks and some or other fellow out of London had made off with my P.A.'s. Now P.A.'s are the Achilles' Heel of all the new men, they buckle your feet into claws and turn you into a tiger, but here I had only a flabby pair of kletterschuh with nails sticking out on both sides of the soles, and so I worked on Dougal to change footwear at which he was not pleased because we stood on a steep slab with one little ledge for feet and a vision before us of retreating in our socks. We had two full-weight ropes. Dougal had one rope that was old before its time, it had once been 120 feet long but it lost 5 feet during an experiment on the Currie Railway Walls. (This last word to sound like 'Woz'.) A Glaswegian who was a friend had one day loaned us the other, and so it was even older, and he mentioned that it had been stretched a little, indeed it was 130 feet long, and so Dougal at the bottom had quickly tied on to an end of each rope which left me with 15 feet on the one to get rid of round and round my middle to make the two ropes even. This was confusing, since I had a good dozen slings and karabiners round my neck and two bunches of pitons like bananas at my waist and a wooden wedge and a piton hammer swinging about and three or four spare karabiners and a big sling knotted into steps.

But I could still get my hands to the rock, and I made slow progress as far as the black roof. I left about six feeble running belays on the way, mainly so that I would be able to breathe. And as there seemed little chance of runners above and little value in those below and nowhere to stand just under the roof and next to no chance of moving up for a while, I took a fat channel peg and drove it to the hilt into the corner crack as high under the roof as I could and fixed it as a runner and hung the knotted sling from it and stood with my right foot in the sling. Thus with my hands in the crack where it came out horizontally under the roof, I could plant my left foot fictitiously away out on the left wall and peer round over the roof into the Corner above. Deep dismay. The crack looked very useless and the walls utterly bare and I shrunk under the roof into the sling. Shortly I leaned away out again to ponder a certain move and a little twist and then something else to get me up 10 feet up, but what would I do then, and then the prepondering angle sent me scuttling back like a crab into shelter. In a while I got a grip and left the sling and heaved up half-way round the roof and sent a hand up the Corner exploring for a hold, but I thought, no no there is nothing at all, and I came down scarting with a foot under the roof feverishly fishing for the sling. And there I hung like a brooding ape, maybe there's a runner 10 feet up, or a secret keyhole for the fingers, but how are you ever to know for sitting primevally here, so for shame now where's your boldness, see how good your piton is, and what's in a peel, think of the Club, think of the glory, be a devil. I found a notch under the roof in which to jamb the knot of a sling which made another runner, and I tried going up a few more times like a ball stopping bouncing until I realised I was going nowhere and trying nothing at all. So I jacked it in and left all the runners for Dougal and Dougal let out slack and I dribbled down to join him on the slab.

Here I sat a while and blew, then I took my coat of mail and put it on Dougal and Dougal wanted his P.A.'s back and we untied to swop our ends of rope so that Dougal could use my runners and I tied myself on to the stance while Dougal rotated into the tail end of the longer rope and the time went by. But Dougal caught it up a little by rushing up to the black roof while I pulleyed in the slack. And here we had a plan. Just above the lip of the roof, the crack opened into a pocket about an inch and a quarter wide. There should have been a chockstone in it, only there was not, and we could find none the right size to insert. If there had been trees on the Ben the way there are in Wales there would have been a tree growing out of the pocket, or at least down at the stance or close to hand so that we could have lopped off a branch and stuck it in the pocket. But here we had a wooden wedge tapering just to the right size and surely it once grew in a tree and so maybe it would not be very artificial to see if it could be made to stick in the pocket. Blows of the hammer did this thing, and Dougal clipped in a karabiner and threaded a sling and the two ropes and pulled up to stand in the sling so that he could reach well over the roof and look about at ease. And sure enough he could see a winking ledge, about 25 feet up on the right wall.

Now Dougal is a bit thick and very bold, he never stopped to think, he put bits of left arm and leg in the crack and the rest of him over the right wall and beat the rock ferociously and moved in staccato shuffles out of the sling and up the Corner.I shifted uneasily upon my slab which tapered into the overhangs, making eyes at my two little piton belays. As Dougal neared his ledge he was slowing down but flailing all the more, left fingers clawing at grass in the crack and right leg scything moss on the wall. I pulled down the sleeves of my jersey over my hands and took a great grip of the ropes. Then there came a sort of squawk as Dougal found that his ledge was not. He got a hand on it but it all sloped. Rattling sounds came from his throat or nails or something. In his last throes trying to bridge he threw his right foot at a straw away out on the right wall. Then his fingers went to butter. It began under control as the bit of news 'I'm off,' but it must have caught in the wind, for it grew like a wailing siren to a blood-curdling scream as a black and bat-like shape came hurtling over the roof with legs splayed like webbed wings and hands hooked like a vampire. I flattened my ears and curled up rigid into a bristling ball, then I was lifted off my slab and rose 5 feet in the air until we met head to foot and buffered to a stop hanging from the runners at the roof. I could have sworn that his teeth were fangs and his eyes were big red orbs. We lowered ourselves to the slab, and there we sat in a swound while the shadows grew.

But indeed it was getting very late, and so I being a little less shattered heaved up on the ropes to retrieve the gear, leaving the wedge and the piton at the roof. We fixed the sling to one of the belay pitons and abseiled down the groove below with tails between our legs and a swing at the bottom to take us round to the foot of the Sassenach chimney. By now it was dusk and we thought it would be chaos in the chimney and just below it was very over-hanging, but I knew a traversing line above the great roof of Sassenach leading to the clean-cut right edge of the cliff.My kletterschuh kept slipping about and I was climbing like a stiff and I put in two or three tips of pitons for psychological runners before I made the 50 feet of progress to peer around the edge. But it looked a good 200 feet to the shadowy screes at the bottom, and I scuffled back in half a panic out of the frying pan into the chimney. Then two English voices that were living in a tent came up the hill to ask if we were worried. We said we were laughing but what was the time, and they said it would soon be the middle of the night, and when we thought about the 700 feet of Sassenach above and all the shambles round the side to get to our big boots sitting at the bottom of the cliff, we thought we would just slide to the end of the rope.

So I went back to the edge and round the right angle and down a bit of the wall on the far side to a ledge and a fat crack for a piton. By the time Dougal joined me we could only see a few dismal stars and sky-lines and a light in the English tent.Dougal vanished down a single rope while I belayed him on the other, and just as the belaying rope ran out I heard a long squelch and murky oaths. He seemed to be down and so I followed. Suddenly my feet shot away and I swung in under the great roof and spiralled down till I landed up to my knees in a black bog. We found our boots under Centurion and made off down the hill past the English tent to tell them we were living. When we hit the streets we followed our noses straight to our sleeping-bags in the shed, leaving the city night life alone.

The next Sunday we left a lot of enemies in Jacksonville and took a lift with the Mountain Rescue round to Fort William. They were saying they might be back to take us away as well. We had thick wads of notes but nothing to eat, and so we had to wait in the city to buy stores on Monday, and we got to the Hut so late that we thought we would house our energies to give us the chance of an early start in the morning. Even so we might have slept right through Tuesday but for the din of a mighty file of pilgrims winding up the Allt a'Mhuillin making for Ben Nevis. We stumbled out rubbing our eyes and stood looking evil in the doorway, so that nobody called in, and then we ate and went out late in the day to the big black Buttress.

This time we went over the shelves and up the hoodie groove no bother at all. It was my turn to go into the Corner. By now I had a pair of P.A.'s. I climbed to the black roof and made three runners with a jammed knot, the piton and the wooden wedge and stood in a sling clipped to the wedge. Dougal's ledge was fluttering above but it fooled nobody now. At full stretch I could reach two pebbles sitting in a thin bit of the crack and pinched them together to jam. Then I felt a lurch in my stomach like flying through an air pocket. When I looked at the wedge I could have sworn it had moved. I seized a baby nylon sling and desperately threaded it round the pebbles. And then I was gracefully plucked from the rock to stop 20 feet under the roof hanging from the piton and the jammed knot with the traitor wedge hanging from me and a sling round the pebbles sticking out of the Corner far above. I rushed back to the roof in a rage and made a strange manoeuvre to get round the roof and reach the sling and clip in a karabiner and various ropes, then trying not to think I hauled up to sit in slings which seemed like a table of kings all to come down from the same two pebbles. I moved on hastily, but I felt neither strong nor bold, and so I took a piton and hammered it into the Corner about 20 feet above the roof. Happily I pulled up, and it leaped out with a squeal of delight and gave me no time to squeal at all before I found myself swinging about under the miserable roof again. The pebbles had held firm, but that meant I hung straight down from the lip of the roof and out from the Corner below so that Dougal had to lower me right to the bottom.

By now the night was creeping in. Peels were no longer upsetting, but Dougal was fed up with sitting on slab and wanted to go down for a brew. But that was all very well, he was going home in the morning, and then coming back for a whole week with a host of terrible tigers when I would have to be sitting exams. So I was very sly and said we had to get the gear and climbed past the roof to the sling at the pebbles leaving all the gear in place. There I was so exhausted that I put in a piton, only it was very low, and I thought, so am I, peccavi, peccabo, and I put another and rose indiscriminately until to my surprise I was past Dougal's ledge and still on the rock in a place to rest beside a solid chockstone.

Sweat was poring out of me, frosting at my waist in the frozen mutterings flowing up the rope from Dougal.Overhead the right wall was swelling out like a bull-frog, but the crack grew to a tight shallow chimney in which it was even blacker than the rest of the night. I squeezed in and pulled on a real hold, and a vast block slid down and sat on my head.Dougal tried to hide on his slab. I wobbled my head and the block rolled down my back, and then there was a deathly hush until it thundered on to the screes and made for the Hut like a fire-ball. I wriggled my last slings round chockstones and myself round the last of the bulges and I came out of the Corner fighting into the light of half a moon rising over the North East Buttress. All around there were ledges and great good holds and bewildering easy angles, and I lashed myself to about six belays.

Dougal followed in the moon-shade, in too great a hurry and too blinded and miserable to pass the time taking out the pitons, and so they are still there turning to rust, creeping up the cliff like poison ivy. Heated up by the time he passed me, Dougal went into a long groove out of the moon but not steep and brought me up to the left end of a terrace above the chimney of Sassenach. We could see the grooves we should have climbed in a long line above us, but only as thick black shadows against the shiny bulges, and so we went right and grovelled up in the final corner of Sassenach where I knew the way to go. The wall on the left kept sticking out and stealing all the moonlight, but we took our belays right out on the clean-cut right edge of the cliff so that we could squat in the moon and peer at the fabulous sights.When we came over the top we hobbled down the screes on the left to get out of our P.A.'s into our boots and back to the Hut from as late a night as any, so late you could hardly call it a bed-night.

Some time next day Dougal beetled off and I slowly followed to face the examiners. The tigers all came for their week. On the first day Dougal and the elder Marshall climbed Sassenach until they were one pitch up from the Terrace above the chimney, and then they thought of going left and finished by the new line of grooves. Overnight the big black clouds rolled over and drummed out the summer and it rained all week and hardly stopped until it started to snow and we put away our P.A.'s and went for hill-walks waiting for the winter. They say the grooves were very nice and not very hard. All that was needed to make a whole new climb was one pitch from the terrace above the chimney, until we decided that the way we had been leaving the terrace as from the time that Dick found it when we first climbed Sassenach was not really part of Sassenach at all. By this means we put an end to this unscrupulous first ascent. The next team will climb it all no bother at all, except that they will complain that they couldn't get their fingers into the holds filled with pitons.

THE UGLY SISTER
Vol. XXVIII (1964)   by Robin Campbell

> Aonach Dubh, the westmost of the Three Sisters of Glen Coe, has some of the best and
> most challenging rock climbing in the Glen. This deals with the notable phase in its
> development which took place in the 1960's.

One of the principal foci of development in recent years has been Aonach Dubh. For some
reason, however, it has not received the attention of the climbing world at large to the
same extent as, for instance, Carn Dearg Buttress on Ben Nevis or the Slabs of Beinn
Trilleachan. This may well be due to the Club's regrettable failure to produce a guidebook
to the area. In this article I hope to remedy this to some small extent. There are two cliffs
whose development I intend to trace, the North Face, a classic crag, and the South Face
of 'E' Buttress on the West Face, a completely new cliff which holds three routes, each as
good as any in Glencoe.

For a long time the North Face was synonymous with Ossian's Cave, and if a climber
braved the terrors of the path to its foot, it was for one reason and for one reason only; to
visit the Cave and sign the Book in the Box. This tradition was started by Godfrey Solly
in the year Dot and has since been continued by such well-known mountaineers as Kilroy,
Yogi Bear et al. On the last occasion that I visited the Cave, the Book in the Box had
disappeared, and must therefore have been stolen. Vandalism is everywhere.

However, in recent years, a few climbers have managed to resist the attractions of the
Cave, and consequently some fine new routes have been made. The fall of *Deep Gash
Gully* to Cunningham, Rowney and Smith of the Creagh Dhu M.C. in 1951, and *Fingal's
Chimney* to the ubiquitous Mr Brown and Lovat in 1955, marked the end of the Gully-
and-Chimney era on this particular pile. Neither of these routes has had a second ascent
in summer, but another Creagh Dhu party, Cunningham and Noon this time, climbed
Deep Gash Gully again in the winter of 1957. Apparently they climbed part of it feet-first,
which is no surprise to anyone. Then in April 1959 Smith and Haston gave us a foretaste
of what was to come with *Stook*, a 400-foot Severe corner which springs up from the right-
hand end of the face. The next big route to fall was *Yo-Yo*, the vertical corner in the centre
of the cliff which slices for 300 feet through rotten overhanging walls to Pleasant Terrace,
the which must have been named in a spirit of pure sarcasm. Whillans had a stab at it in
1958, but, unaccountably, turned back after passing the first overhang. Then in 1959
Smith and Hughes climbed it in two days. Smith spent something like four hours hanging
on the bottom overhang, wiping the rock dry with a towel, before he eventually won
through. To date the climb has had only three ascents, the second by Jimmy Marshall and
Moriarty and the third by Macniven, Ronnie Marshall, and Holt. This route must rank
with the best in the country.

The stage was now set for what must be the longest one-man siege in Scottish mountaineering history. After Yo-Yo, Smith spent most of his weekends in Glencoe trying to work out a *Girdle* of the cliff. In 1960, with Haston, he struggled all day long across the white wall to the right of Ossian's Cave and then up a staircase of noxious turf before escaping via Fingal's Chimney. Later in the same year he returned, this time with Wightman, added another staircase of turf, this one downwards, and crossed a steep loose wall to a corner, up which they retreated to Pleasant Terrace. Then, in 1961, he and Haston added two more long pitches before coming to an abrupt halt at a terrible-looking pitch, which they christened the Barrier. This impasse seemed to end all hope of making a Girdle, since it stretched throughout the entire height of the cliff. It was as if the cliff was in two parts which overlapped, with the Barrier forming the overlap. It looked like pegs and Smith didn't like pegs. It took him another year to swallow his distaste. Then, in May of 1962, the brothers Marshall repeated what had already been done, but they too could make nothing of the Barrier. When they returned to Lagangarbh, Smith had just arrived from Edinburgh, and, perhaps out of perversity, went right back to the Barrier the following day with Ronnie Marshall and climbed it in a good eight hours, using only three pegs. The Girdle was all over bar the shouting, and Smith, Haston, Macniven and myself shouted all the way across to Deep Gash Gully the very next day.

To turn now to the South Face of 'E' Buttress on the West Face, it is not altogether surprising that this cliff remained untouched until 1959, for it has the most forbidding aspect of any cliff in Glencoe, Slime Wall not excepted. Furthermore the approach to its foot is a formidable undertaking; many crags are less steep than the grass slopes beneath.

In 1959, Haston and Moriarty arrived in the bed of Number 4 Gully with that sly old man, Marshall, and his wee brother. Jimmy pointed to a 500-foot pillar on the right-hand side of the face, said what a marvellous line for a rock-climb, and moved further up the Gully to do a new route called *Stickleback*. Nothing daunted, Haston and Moriarty climbed the pillar by the best possible line, a real tour de force, for the cliff was nowhere less than vertical throughout the first 400 feet, and the rock was rotten and scaling in parts. However, the holds turned out to be more like amphorae than jugs and Youth had scored a victory over Crabbed Age. They called the route *Hee-Haw*, which was a very graceless thing to do to such a graceful climb.

Still, every dog must have its day, however aged or crabbed, and Marshall got his own back in 1960 with *Trapeze*, which is the natural line on the crag, starting off up a hard corner well to the left of Hee-Haw, and crossing some pink slabs before wriggling summitwards through the overhangs. Then, in 1961, Smith put up his *Big Top* with the assistance of Moriarty, and Gardner of the Creagh Dhu. This route, of similar length and veriseverity to the others, follows the left-hand arete of the face for 200 feet before cutting in right and finishing via a monstrous object, described by Smith as a flake.

What remains to be done on these two cliffs? Well, on the North Face there are the right and left bounding walls of the Cave. Although Haston towed me up the bottom half of the right-hand wall last October, the worst is yet to come, if it is to come at all. As for the left-hand wall, apocryphally named Abortion Wall, it is a terrifying spectacle, towering sheer and ledgeless for 300 feet, and bleeding silent slime. The man who climbs it will need as much iron as courage, and he'll need plenty of that.

On 'E' Buttress there is room for two more routes or, at least, two more starts.Between the Big Top and Trapeze there is a 200-foot wall which will give someone a dreadful fight, and, between Trapeze and Hee-Haw, there is a quite feasible line of short walls and cracks leading up to the top overhangs, where a modicum of imagination might be required.

To give a somewhat distorted picture of what climbing on one of these cliffs is like, I have appended a description of the North Face Girdle. I make no apology for the imitative style in which it is written, since it dates from the time when the Maestro was still alive, and being sincerely flattered.

NORTH FACE GIRDLE

I don't know why it is, but I seem to do girdles all the time. Three years ago a frivolous trot round the Rosa Pinnacle, and two years ago a conducted tour across the longest, grimmest, hardest, blackest cliff in all Glencoe. Anyhow, the late Neil Macniven and I found ourselves committed to following the late Robin Smith, alias Wheech, and Dougal Haston (still extant) to the foot of Aonach Dubh on a Monday morning in May when it was far too hot to climb, when we'd run out of fags, and when all the decent hard-working men had gone back to Edinburgh.

The whole route had been done, but not in one, all except the last 500 feet, which were rumoured to be a doddle anyway. However, on a visit to the Barrier the day before, Wheech had taken all day to climb it, and the Baron, alias Ronnie Marshall, who was with him, didn't fancy climbing across it and taking all the gear out, all in ten minutes in the dark, so the gear was left in; a magpie's dream of glittering metal and shining white nylon. So we had to go and do the route, if only to get Wheech's gear back.

Dougal and Neil were first away, through the river and up the terrible path into the shadows, slime, and vertical rubbish which is the way up Aonach Dubh, so that Wheech and I wouldn't have to wait at belays.

We two were making little piles of gear on the grass when Wheech found he'd got no P.A.'s. I lied about the size of my feet so that he wouldn't knock mine, but he had an idea he might have left them up the mountain somewhere, so he charged off up leaving me to bring up the rear and the gear. At the foot of the Cave he reappeared with no P.A.'s and the news that Dougal and Neil had cheated and gone straight on to the Barrier by a roundabout route, leaving the first 500 feet of Ancient History to us, since somebody had to do it.

Since we were going very fast to catch up, and my memory of all but a certain pitch is indistinct, I won't bore you with the details (you can read about it in the Guidebook, if it ever comes out), but we bumbled across creaking walls and cracks, and a particularly noisome grass ledge, from the Cave to the Barrier.

The Barrier is the right-hand wall of the big corner to the left of Yo-Yo. Two monstrous overhangs with a lesser one in between about sums it up. You go swinging across the lesser one in slings or etriers, from peg to spike to peg to spike to peg, then make a last big reach to a last big spike and after that it's only desperate to belay right out on the edge of everything. When we got there, the others were still sweating it out so we had a seat. Dougal was at the belay, but Neil was just leaving the last peg, lurching about in his etriers and fouling the air, until eventually he grasped the big spike with a gasp of relief and staggered on to the belay.

Now, my brain was working overtime through all this, because I saw that some poor sucker was going to have to take the etriers with him, and that was going to be me, so that I would never reach that last big spike, so I got Wheech to give me a crash course in prusikking and he tied the loops on for me, one on each rope. Wheech sauntered across the pitch in his great clumsy boots, finding difficulty only in deciding what gear to leave in place for me and what to take with him. Then he fixed a huge peg belay and grinned across at me encouragingly. Off I went, grunting and sweating, to the last peg, no bother at all. Then Wheech tied a great knot in the rope behind the peg so that he wouldn't have to hold me. I took off all the gear but a tiny sling, which I threaded through the peg for a foothold and tried to reach the spike, but I'd nothing to hold on to with my left hand while I groped with my right, so I gave it up, sat in my prusik loops feeling very scared indeed, for the rope was an old one of Neil's which he'd used to tow cars and things, and jumped off.

A ghastly pendulum took place, away out and up into the sky so that I could see all the great grinning faces and the horrible drop to the screes 300 feet below. Then back and forward until I stopped swinging. The rock was still about ten feet away and I was just bracing myself for the next bit of fun and games when I started to revolve around the axis of the rope. Twist, twist, twist. Stop. Twist, twist, twist, back again. Stop. And so on ad nauseam! Very soon my eye-balls were twisting in sympathy. Everything merged into a dizzy swirl. Wheech's horrid prune-face, the mountain, the sky and the Glen chased each other round the rope like some sort of hellish kaleidoscope, and all the while fiendish laughter echoed from above, across and below. Raucous bellows from Wheech, horse-laughs and screams from Macniven, and, away to the right, graveside chuckles from Haston every five seconds, when he could just see the tips of my P.A.'s on the way round.

Sooner or later it all stopped, the nausea passed and I was able to look in one direction at once. The rope was twisted all the way up, so that my loops were all useless. I took two more from the festoons round my neck and, after various failures, managed to tie the things on. Then I fought my way up to the belay. This took ages because every time my weight came off the bottom loop the rope sprang into a Gordian knot, the untying of which necessitated all sorts of contortions; hands below feet, head between knees, and worried sick all the time about falling all the way down to the end of the rope. I got there in the end, feeling not too bad, since it gave the boys a laugh, and some of us have got to be buffoons.

By this time Haston was having a ball in terra incognito, hurling down giant blocks and screaming it was in the bag and what a climb and so it was. There was only a wee move out of Yo-Yo, or so we thought until we caught them up in a recess on a terrible belay. We sat on ledges and waited. Wheech sang all the four parts of the Hallelujah Chorus at once, to pass the time and because he was chuffed, blasphemous croaks and screeches which must have loosened a big stone, because it dropped away from beneath Haston and smashed the ledge where I'd been sitting not so very long ago.

However, Dougal found the way to go across the next bit very quickly and it wasn't really at all bad. We split up and we found a better finish than they did, right across to the bottom end of Pleasant Terrace. We ran away down the rubbish in the dark, and back to Lagangarbh, where we wrote it all up in the Book, and, lo and behold, when the pitches were all added together they came to 1000 feet exactly, which made everyone very happy and we all went to bed.

SMALL WOMAN, BIG BREATHS
Vol. XXXIII (1984)   by Bob Duncan

I often used to wonder why I took up rock climbing in the first place. Okay, I was useless at football, worse at rugby and the kiss of death with girls, but I really can't see the relevance of such minor failings. Uncharitable hypotheses to the effect that it was all some misguided effort to prove my masculinity I consider beneath contempt. Did Mallory and Irvine have to suffer such slanders?

Still, I suppose it is necessary to acknowledge my physical (and, some say, mental) unsuitability for such a demanding pastime as (relatively) modern rock climbing. Now, genetically it is quite possible to have a few characteristics of either parent, so it is quite unnecessary to speculate, as some have done, on some fantastic and improbable liaison between my dear mother and a decrepit version of Charles Hawtrey in order to explain my physique. It must have been a continuing shock to her, and my father, when, as their firstborn grew older, his build remained essentially that of a malnourished infant.

However, when I wasn't recovering from over indulgence in shandy, or from muggings at the hands of penniless pensioners, I worked at developing my puny frame. Torrid sessions in the sweatshop of Meadowbank, rubbing torsos with latter-day Greek gods, had their effect. The spring of 1982 saw me depart the Meadowbank Wall for the last time until October — sporting what, to the untrained eye, looked like a body a ten year old would be proud of. I strutted out, unassisted through the revolving doors, to the unashamedly admiring glances of a Brownie hockey team.

That summer saw me and Jerry (the Blob) hammering the soft touches round the country. His greater technical expertise meant that I was employed mainly as the powerhouse for those strenuous leads which seem to figure so prominently in modern routes. This did result in rather a poor tally of strenuous leads and quite a lot of abseiling to retrieve runners, but I did get up the odd route and began, foolishly, to think I was going pretty well.

Then the summer holidays ended and Spider suggested we made a foursome to split costs on weekend jaunts to Derbyshire. I was happy to say yes. Travel on the bike had yielded less in the way of weak-kneed women than I had secretly hoped. The prospect of being chauffeured over long distances held more immediate appeal.

And a very pleasant change it made too, but it wasn't all roses. Apart from the endless playing of 'Bat Out of Hell' on the car stereo, the biggest problem was the climbing. Derbyshire is not crammed with soft touches, and we worked them out pretty quickly. Then I at least was forced to face reality. Jerry played about on micro-limbs, kidding himself that he was doing his technique a tremendous amount of good, but I could scarcely leave the ground on such 'routes' and was compelled to continue working out on the strenuous stuff. This didn't go much better, and Derbyshire weekends began to give me nightmares, thoughts of unprotected exhaustion haunting my sleep.

Much of this nocturnal petrification concerned one climb in particular. 'Wee Doris' is no longer a super-route, dating as it does from the late sixties, but neither is it a complete stroll, not if you haven't done it before.

A word of warning. Watch some bronzed youth cruising some limestone horror, casually remarking how reasonable it is, forcefully expelling breath just after the crux. Impressive, isn't it? But the chances are that he's done it before, and not just once. A touch of cynicism is in order if you're not to be psyched out before you start climbing. Time enough for that on the route.

As the weekends passed and I gradually failed on, or frigged, all the alternative possibilities, it became apparent that I could no longer put off my date with 'Wee Doris' without losing face. Was I man enough? This weekend would surely tell. I didn't see how I could avoid it. But age has its compensations. Experience, for one. An idea took shape in my head. The usual sequence of events was to have first choice of route every alternate day, and really it was my turn. But I had managed to cram my climb for the weekend in the previous day, after an unheard-of piece of efficiency on the part of the Blob in not requiring all the daylight hours to achieve his ascent. So, trying hard to sound nonchalant, I suggested that it might be fairer if he did his route first.

To my amazement, he agreed — and so, breathing more easily, I settled down for a pleasant day belaying. 'Bubbles' may not be the Eigerwand as far as length is concerned, but neither, as I have implied, is Jerry a second Messner.

Devious and unreliable as ever, the Blob firmly extracted his finger for the second successive time that weekend. Not only that, but from somewhere he appeared to have acquired a little 'bottle', to judge from the way he seemed to be pushing the boat out as he neared the horizontal break just below the top. I began to take more interest in the proceedings, and was rewarded almost immediately by the terrifying sight of the Blob taking flight. Terrifying, not because of any misplaced sense of affection for the body now darkening the sky as it accelerated towards me, but because it was my job to stop it. Worse, rather careless positioning had left me very vulnerable should runners or ropes fail (not such a remote possibility considering the mammoth forces about to be generated as I attempted to halt the Blob's dynamic descent).

Fortunately, both gear and second man proved equal to their mighty task, and after a period on the ground to recuperate, Jerry returned to complete his ascent, with one fall for aid, and the onset of his grey hair advanced by a couple of years. There was no question of my seconding the route: I wanted to save myself for the horror I knew awaited me a short thrash away through the undergrowth.

And so it was my turn. By modern criteria (admittedly, not always rigorously applied except to donglers like myself) any ascent I made of 'Wee Doris' that day, or any other, would have already been flawed. I had belayed Le Miserable on one of his numerous attempts the previous year, and, apart from watching him climb the crux, had actually stooped as low as to use the rope through his runner as a top-rope in order to have a half-hearted bash myself. It wasn't really a serious effort on my part, but I had been emphatically and repeatedly told that this was no excuse. I suppose I inwardly agreed, but I certainly had no intentions of admitting it. Let them play their silly games. Feeling that strange, familiar mixture of fear and eager anticipation I chalked up and touched rock. The first few feet of 'Wee Doris' actually follow 'Medusa', a Hard VS, unless you're simple enough to take in the 'Direct Start', a ridiculous and pointless little boulder problem quite out of character with the rest of the climb. At least, that's how I justified missing it out!

A few easy moves on extremely polished holds land one on a neatly sawn-off tree stump, where it is traditional to place a pointless sling. From here the route goes left, along a good foot-ledge with fine holds, but an unfortunate bulge between the two, making a prolonged stay rather energy-intensive. Then the first real climbing, a few feet up twin cracks to the 'roof'. All this went fine; it's really quite easy, I suppose. Placing runners at the roof used up a fair amount of my miserable reserves of strength, so I scurried back to the stump for a breather. One of the problems with 'Wee Doris' is the polished state of the holds, caused by the number of top-rope ascents it receives for training, owing to the bulk of the climb remaining dry for quite a long time after rain starts to fall. This does make the climbing less pleasant, if that description could ever be applied to such an experience, and makes things even more strenuous, as fingers hang on while feet skate off greasy holds.

I knew, as I started again, that once over the roof I would be committed. The adrenalin surged and my stomach churned as if I was ascending to some insatiable courtesan's boudoir. In some ways that simile was to prove more apt than I might have cared to imagine.

The crux is getting stood up above the roof. It's not too hard, really, although it does require a little power. Just a little, thank God, otherwise my attempt would have foundered there and then. But technical difficulty is not what 'Wee Doris' is about. No, the successful suitor must husband his (or her) strength, there being no rests between the stump and the top. Oh, we've heard how so-and-so hung about above the roof for hours, but his arms don't look like the legs on an underfed sparrow. Despite my rigorous training regime mine do, so I threw a runner into the bomb-proof crack and kept going. For a millesecond. Then primordial instincts took over. I knew that this was the last place I would be able to get runners, so, on the belt-and-braces principle, I stopped and put in a wire. Well, ropes 'have' been known to break.

I think it was then that I knew I was going to yo-yo it. I half-heartedly tried the next move, getting from one huge solution pocket to another, but all the time I was thinking about how attractive the ground looked, how restful it would be to be down there. And how safe. After a few minutes of this I sank onto the rope and the Blob lowered me in disgrace to the ground.

I sat feeling sorry for myself for ten minutes, letting the blood drain back into my forearms, kicking the rock, and hating all those people who had managed the climb in good style. Then I tied on again, resigned to just getting the thing out of the way.

The moves from my previous highpoint to the next pocket turned out to be fairly straightforward with reasonably fresh fingers and forearms, and the holds above looked as if they got better. Time to GO FOR IT. After a few more moves I could reach from a flat horizontal break to the final little wall. I got some slimy flat holds, pulled up, and came to a halt. A quick search for better things above proved fruitless, and I began to sweat. So far, my mental condition was quite normal. Many - not all - of my successful ascents have involved periods when the likelihood of a fall has seemed quite great. Now worried, but not desperately so, I made my second big mistake. (The first was being within a hundred miles of Stoney Middleton). I brought my feet up so I could reach further.

All that happened was that I could no longer take either hand off the rock, the holds were so flat that one by itself was inadequate. Neither could I reverse the last move, my balance being so precarious. I really began to sweat. I looked down , down, down to my runners, now nearly twenty feet away. I looked up, to the top of the climb. Five feet above my head? not much more, anyway.

It was then, with my fingers tiring rapidly and my brain able to think of nothing to do to improve my position, that an icy hand ran down my spine as I finally truly realised what was about to happen to me. There was nothing in the world except me, the rock in front of my nose, the hole at my feet, and, thank God, some bomb-proof runners so far away that they looked closer to the ground than my heels. The last strength trickled out of my forearms, now swollen to a ridiculous mockery of their true worth. It was time, no point in (no way of) postponing the inevitable. I swallowed nervously, grunted to Jerry (mentally blessing his vast bulk), thought fleetingly and tragically of the legions of sophisticated women whose future happiness lay in the balance, and let myself go.

I appeared to accelerate in two phases, the second coinciding with me passing my top runners. Even reaching them had seemed to take an age. Only half way, boy, still the other half to go, the world spinning crazily and the ground and the Blob's anxious face getting rapidly closer.

When am I going to stop? Oh, mother!

And then, almost too late, all the breath was knocked from my body as the ropes whipped tight, slapping the rock noisily in their fury at being so ridiculously overworked. My head carried on a little further and I ended upside down, oscillating gently, and looking into Blob's ashen features. I had come to rest at about the level of the stump, so one advantage of the length of my plummet was that at least Jerry didn't have very far to lower me.

That was it for that weekend. Further excitment seemed superfluous. I thought I could just about cope with lying in the back seat of the car for a few hours.

I went back and settled the score the following weekend, belayed by another friend (Jerry having seen enough), and wearing my crash hat for a change. Despite my extensive first-hand knowledge of the route, still things didn't go totally smoothly. As I neared the point of the previous week's take-off I was shaking so much that I could hardly see the rock. Fortunately I was able to beat a hasty retreat to the Runners, was lowered ignominiously to the ground yet again, and, after at time spent calming myself down, and wishing I smoked, I returned for the fifth, thankfully successful, attempt.

As you can see, I didn't do too brilliantly on 'Wee Doris'. I know I should feel absolutely terrible about it, but, to be honest, I actually prefer it the way it was. Daft it may be, but forgettable it wisnae.

THE WALL
Vol. XXXIII (1985)   by Gary Latter

The first moves come easy, though they should do as I've done them often enough. At about 15ft. an arm lock provides a rest of sorts, feet bridged wide apart and the first runner is placed - a bombproof hex. - in a shallow quartzy scoop.

A dip in the chalkbag, ten deep breaths to get the blood pumping the essential oxygen to the muscles, and the previous high point is reached. The moves themselves prove to be not over technical, but following in rapid succession as they do, trying to rest on 6a moves, place runners, even chalking up becomes a fight against gravity and muscle fatigue. Another 10ft. or so and a second runner is rather hastily placed. By this time sweat is starting to flow readily and it becomes almost essential to chalk up between almost every single move, such is the fingery nature of the climbing.

Unsure of the last runner placement, or perhaps a lack of the total commitment required on such a hard and sustained route, forces me to 'take a flyer', though fortunately the runner is a good one and a great deal of relief shows in my face when a possible thirty footer (and near groundfall) turns into a mere slip. A lightning fast lower to the ground, back to the horizontal world and a short rest, both physically and mentally, allows the fingers a chance to straighten out and the heart to slow down to a more realistic rate.

I am confident that I can do the moves, at least up to the halfway point, where the short slanting crack will definitely provide some good nut placements and a comparatively good resting sport. At about 40ft. a fearful glance downwards sends a shiver up my spine - the last runner has come out, and the result of a groundfall from this height does not bear thinking about. I decide to go for it, though I get a touch of the shakes on the way, and at one point a fifty-footer looks so close - too close for comfort! After what seems like a million moves (more like a dozen or so), the foot of the crack is eventually reached.

First one Friend is thrown back as far as possible, then another, closely followed by three or four really god nuts. I'm definitely taking no chances now that I've got this far.

I let go of the rock, not caring, knowing that the runners will hold. Once again solid ground is reached and I just 'flake out'. Totally spent, I don't even possess the energy to utter a word! After what seems like an eternity I open my eyes to see the progress that I've made - the ropes thread up the apparently holdless and featureless wall, hanging free about ten feet from the base of the rock. My forearms feel like lumps of lead, and I've lost the feeling in my fingers altogether.

I decide that a good rest is on the cards before I give it another attempt. Recuperating and 'psyching up' for what, for today anyway, has got to be the final attempt, I try to work out in my mind the next series of moves.

I set off again, the moves firmly implanted in the grey matter, together with the presence of chalk on all the proper holds and the added advantage of what is effectively a top rope, making it a real pleasure, a total physical workout, no overloading of the nerves with the fear of taking a monster fall. Powering up the rock, feeling in complete control, getting all the sequences right, continuing unfaltered, really getting the rhythm going now, a fluid and dynamic approach, pausing only intermittently to ensure a liberal coating of chalk on the fingertips, which by now are sweating profusely.

In no time at all the top runners are reached and easily by-passed, the crack providing a few meaty jams and a welcome rest for the fingers, though the arms still have to do their stuff. A rock-solid stone is slotted in at the top of the crack, but I can't hang about here all day, so with a final dip in the chalkbag, which makes the sweet smell of Friar's Balsam pervade the air, I push on.

The difficulty continues unabated, the rock still as steep and unrelenting as ever, the moves more akin to a climbing wall situation, though somewhat steeper and in a much more compromising position. The sharp knobbly holds are by now starting to shred my fingers to pieces, and I realise I've got to step into overdrive, with no chance of a second try should I mess up in the moves or burn out. A distant voice from below urges me on, coming from my patient and ever alert belayer. Not that it makes all that much difference anyway, as I really am determined to get up this route, having put this much effort into it, not to mention months of hard training.

By now I'm looking at a thirty footer, with no runner placements in sight. Should I try to reverse the moves, or bail out? Nah, keep going, nothing to lose. After a particularly hard and problematic section a thin hairline crack appears, something to go for. When I reach this, I find I can't take either of my hands from the rock in order to place a wire or two. A couple of feet more and a comparatively good hold is gained, from which I select a couple of 'tinies' and eventually manage to wangle them into the crack. Psychological runners in the truest sense of the word. They might slow me down but its extremely doubtful if they would hold a fall, even a short one.

Putting such thoughts to the back of my mind and instead concentrating on the rock ahead, I'm really pushing the boat out now, at the limit of my endurance, really can't hold on for much longer. Quickly trying to shake some more blood into my fingertips, I really give it my all. So near and yet so far. Twenty feet of easy though fingery climbing to go. Gasping for a breath of air, I've never done anything as strenuous or sustained as this before, and probably never will. Fast and furious now, not even stopping to chalk up, putting all my energy into getting to the top. Just about there. Hand finally grappling for something to hold on to. Anything. A large clod of that ubiquitous Scottish heather provides the final and much sought after handhold. A last desperate struggle and I'm up.

55. An early SMC party in the Centre Gully of Ben Lui

56. Mike Thornley on the Eastern Traverse of the Great Tower, Ben Nevis

57. Chris Gilmore on Harrison's Route, Carn Dearg

58. The winter cliffs of
    Lochnagar

59. Graeme Nicol on
    Parallel Gully A,
    Lochnagar

MIDS'T SNOW AND ICE

WINTER ASCENTS (extracts)
Vol. I (1890)   by H.T. Munro

".... while protesting against the calumny on our climate which credits us with no summer at all, we must admit that for purposes of mountaineering, 'winter' often extends over a far longer period than the traditional three months assigned to that season by the calendar. Winter may be defined by the mountaineer in Scotland, as that portion of the year during which the higher ranges are more or less continuously covered with snow.

In these high latitudes snow may occasionally fall in any month of the year, even at a comparatively low elevation. It is usually, however, well on in November before the mountains permanently assume the aspect of glistening whiteness, which often does not leave them until the spring is far advanced. Our heaviest falls of snow often occur in March or April, and even in May the mountains are commonly covered to a great depth. On the 28th April 1886, I stood on the snow above the 'hotel' on Ben Nevis, of which there was not as much as a corner of the roof visible. To the mountaineer, winter ascents offer many advantages. In the first place, the interest of the walk itself is much increased. The snow is often so hard as to present all the features of the upper part of a Swiss glacier, rendering the ice-axe almost indispensable, and even the rope sometimes necessary. If the weather happens to be fine — and there is at least a good chance of fine weather in winter as in summer — the atmosphere is generally far clearer, and the views therefore more extensive and more distinct. Even should the day prove foggy, a climb on the mountains is of far greater interest in winter than in summer. A grass slope which ordinarily is easy often becomes perilously steep when covered with hard frozen snow, and rocks which are child's play in their normal condition are frequently quite impracticable with a coating of ice over them. In fog, the climber, being unable to see ahead, cannot pick the best ground, and often has these obstacles to encounter; he has nothing but the map, the compass, and the aneroid to steer by, and very possibly a piercing wind and a blinding snowstorm to add to his difficulties.

In the more remote districts the winter traveller has often to put up with somewhat primitive fare at the inns, but, on the other hand, he runs no risk of finding all the rooms engaged, and he is sure of a kindly welcome and attention. Moreover, the keepers or caretakers of the shooting-lodges are generally glad to give accommodation, which cannot of course be looked for in the shooting season. It cannot be denied that some few disadvantages attend winter and early spring climbing, but I am sure that all who have tried it will agree that the pleasure derived is more than ample compensation."

SNOWCRAFT IN SCOTLAND (extracts)
Vol. II (1893)   by W. W. Naismith

As the pursuit of 'Alpine work' is one of the main objects of the Club, it may interest any members, who as yet know the mountains only in their summer dress, to glance at the subject in somewhat greater detail; at the same time noticing some points of resemblance between winter climbing in Scotland, and summer mountaineering in Switzerland. There may be difference of opinion about one or two matters to be alluded to, and the writer would here disclaim the least desire to pose as an authority.

The use of the ice-axe was unknown in Scotland till about ten years ago, when it was introduced by a few climbers, who had served an apprenticeship in the Alps. These pioneers were commonly regarded as eccentric persons, hardly accountable for their actions: so much so, that they fain, when plotting a snow ascent, to conceal their intentions from kindly innkeepers, who would have sought to dissuade them from their hazardous enterprise. At Dalmally, and one or two other climbing resorts, an ice-axe is now (thanks chiefly to the Scottish Mountaineering Club) almost as familiar an object at Easter as a salmon rod. Since 1889, when the Club was founded, a great many of the mountains have been climbed in snow, for the first time in their history so far as we know, and much valuable information bearing on snowcraft has appeared in this *Journal*.

> Naismith goes on to point out that Scotland offers plenty of places where winter ascents can vie with Swiss peaks where the 'stiff climbing' is often confined to between 1000 and 2000 ft. He lists twenty bens as a few examples which offer suitable faces. He then discusses.........

WHEN TO CLIMB — Among the higher summits snow may fall in every month, and winter reigns for the half year; or, roughly speaking, from November till May. Climbing may be had during the whole of that period, but the months of March and April — the season of dust and east wind — are generally regarded as 'par excellence' the time to practise snowcraft. For mountains above 3,500 feet, I should give the preference to April. The snow is then at its best, and extends down to about the 2,000 feet contour, at least on the colder sides of the hills. Above that temporary snow-line, one can count upon frost every clear night, and frequently in the shade all day as well. At Christmas there is nothing like so much snow, and besides more rigorous weather, the days are six or eight hours shorter.

The April climber has the benefit of a temperature not only cool but equable, and can indulge in severe exercise with comfort, even in the glens. He has nothing corresponding to the enervating grind under a sub-tropical sun, so often undergone in the Swiss valleys. The result is that the pace on the lower ground is faster, and if it were not rank heresy, I should say the air is more uniformly invigorating than in the Alps.

BAD WEATHER — The moistness of Scots weather is an unfailing source of innocent hilarity to our friends from the south, which we need not grudge them.

Let us suppose that you get caught in a storm, or that, despising 'sage advices', you deliberately sally forth to do battle with the elements. You find yourself in the midst of a howling tempest — a veritable Alpine *tourmente*, — the level snowstorm tearing along as though it were 'the wind made visible'; the fallen snow drifting like smoke from the ridges. You can hardly see your companions, much less make them hear. With hair and clothes hard frozen, you stagger on with a list to windward; crouching down at times and holding on with your axe, when a more furious gust strikes you. 'Where does the pleasure come in?' somebody asks. *It is all pleasure!* If the nature of the ground allow the whole party to move together, the fight with the wind quickens the circulation, and puts you in a glow of exuberant health and high spirits. When at last, after doing your climb, you get out of the clouds and down to the road, you are as jolly as possible. You are wet through of course, for on the lower slopes the snow has changed to rain, and it may be your boots keep up a conversation; but a hot tub and dry garments await you, and at night, round a roaring fire, you fight your battle all over again.

CHARACTER OF SNOW — Among the Alps, where the snow is exposed every fine day to a broiling sun, the climber must get up in the middle of the night, to make sure of a moderately hard surface during a long ascent. In the Grampians about Easter, on a mountain face of the kind before described, snow will probably — in frosty weather, certainly — be in good condition throughout the day. In fact it is, so to say, more Alpine than in the Alps. The advantage will be appreciated by every one who prefers to breakfast at a later hour than one a.m.! On plateaux and slopes facing south or west, the character of the snow is more variable, and after the sun gets round, it is apt to become soft. In warm cloudy weather also, *any* slope may be in bad order. *Powdery* or granular snow does not appear to retain its distinctive character for long after it falls, but quickly alters and unites with the old snow. At any rate one rarely comes across it in April: about as seldom as in Switzerland in August. At Christmas, and in the early months of the year when the heavy snow-falls occur, the mountaineer may expect more trouble from it.

In cold weather one occasionally sees steep snow, with a ripple-marked surface, which while keeping the texture of snow, is frozen so hard that a large number of strokes are required for each step. The axe is extremely liable to stick in that sort of stuff.

Now and then snow is covered with a *crust* of ice, or there may be several layers of crust, with soft snow between. On a level field a thin crust makes walking most fatiguing, but on inclined snow it is sometimes a help to the climber, and enable him to kick a series of *pigeon-holes* with great rapidity.

SNOW RIDGES AND CORNICES — Knife-edges of rock are rare among the central Grampians, and narrow snow 'aretes' are still more uncommon. The writer has never succeeded in finding a satisfactory specimen in Scotland. At the same time it seems likely that a heavy snow-fall might cause any narrow ridge to have for a time a crest of snow. Ridges with one precipitous, and one flat side are common enough, and if the wind has been blowing towards the precipice, the edge is sure to be corniced — the cornice often projecting several feet. The mountaineer has of course in such places no object in approaching the dangerous edge.

SNOW GULLIES — These are numerous among the higher mountains, and many of them offer grand sport to the adventurous climber. They have most of the characteristics of Alpine snow *couloirs*, and may even terminate in a small *bergschrund*. If the gullies have perpendicular walls, between which the sun's rays seldom penetrate, combined with a north-easterly aspect, they are generally filled with solid snow far into summer, or in rare instances all the year round. It should be borne in mind that gullies are liable to be swept by falling stones, as scores and gashes in the snow sometimes indicate. The chance of stones falling from above is too often ignored by climbers at home, but there is no doubt it constitutes a real danger.

FROZEN TURF — SNOW ON GRASS — A variety of ground peculiar to winter climbing, and demanding special care against a slip, consists of ledges of frozen turf or moss on a rock face. The turf may be nearly as hard as trap rock, and then the axe is of little or no use. If there is any old snow lying about, the climber will generally find good footing in it.

Steep grass or heather, covered with new snow, is a very slippery combination; but there, in the writer's opinion, the axe may be used as an anchor; practise enabling one to feel when the pick is firm enough to stand a moderate strain - more strain than he means to put upon it.

ICE-GLAZED ROCKS — The Scottish mountaineer does not meet with any formidable slopes of grey or black ice, like those his Alpine confrere encounters late in the season, denuded of snow. He is more likely to find ice in gullies than on open slopes, owing to the former being usually covered-up water-courses, or possibly to their containing avalanche snow, which has packed and congealed. After fresh snow caution would have to be used.

Anywhere, in the vicinity of rocks, small patches of ice may underlie the snow. Smooth rocks also, over which water has trickled from melting snow above, are often covered with ice, thick enough sometimes to cut steps in.

If the climber should come across a piece of 'unmitigated ice', where it is preferable to prevent a slip, than hope to check it after it has occurred, I believe it is better to hold the axe as if glissading, and dig the *spike* firmly into the ice about the level of the thigh, before each step, rather than to use the pick as an anchor — the proper method on hard snow, or ice covered with frozen snow.

This advice gave rise to the spike v pick controversy that raged for some time after. None other than Harold Raeburn was later to support Naismith on the grounds that in 'unmitigated ice' even the pick gave no security and 'the fundamental secret of safe climbing' lay in 'balancing out' which was most easily maintained by use of the spike.

AVALANCHES — Dangerous avalanches occur ordinarily where fresh snow lies on top of ice, and are not likely to be encountered in Scotland.

Naismith went on to qualify this comment but it was left to Raeburn, writing twelve years later, to give a more accurate and developed picture of this aspect.

GLACIERS — It seems necessary for a paper on Snowcraft to contain a reference to Glaciers. While there are plenty of disused moraines, there are no glaciers in the Scotland of to-day, and the branch of mountaineering which deals with *crevasses, seracs* and *ice-falls* must therefore be studied elsewhere. Half a century ago, when the mountain fastnesses of Inverness and Ross were absolutely unknown, and very vague notions about the height of the peaks prevailed, the idea is said to have been entertained in some minds, that hidden away in the inner recesses of the glens, there might still exist the last shrunken remnants of the glaciers of the Ice Age. The idea was not so absurd as it appears at first sight. Considering the moderate elevation of the Norwegian Folgefond and Jostedalsbrae — the former in the latitude of the Shetland Islands, it is reasonable to suppose that the upheaval of the Cairngorm range, by about a thousand feet, would once more adorn the flat tops of Ben Macdhui and Braeriach with permanent ice-caps, with small glaciers radiating towards Loch Etchachan and Glen Dee.

Before concluding, perhaps I may be permitted to say a word to the younger readers of the *Journal*. If the knack of climbing rocks, neatly as well as safely, can best be acquired by a boy in his teens, it is equally desirable, in order to attain that easy confidence upon snow, which young Swiss porters show so markedly, and which is purely the result of practice, that the practice should begin as early as possible. The obvious moral is to invest in a good ice-axe at once, and learn how to use it at home; and not to wait, as most people do, till they visit the Alps.

The subject was pursued further by Harold Raeburn who had become the authority on these matters during the Edwardian period.

SCOTTISH SNOW (extracts)
Vol. VIII (1905)   by Harold Raeburn

Among the epoch-marking papers which have been written for the Journal, the admirable article by Mr Naismith on 'Snowcraft in Scotland' occupies an important place. This paper was published in the number for January 1893.

Since that date twelve years have elapsed, the number is now long out of print, and possibly some new members have not had an opportunity of reading it. In any case sufficient time has passed to render it interesting and useful to sum up the results obtained from the lessons and maxims therein contained, and at the same time to summarise the twelve years' extended experience of the members of the Club, of snow work and snowy conditions to be found scattered through the articles and notes published in the *Journal*.

Mr Naismith in his paper did not adopt the apologetic tone visible in the Badminton volume on Mountaineering, and even in that of Dr Claude Wilson with regard to this country as a possible school for real Alpine climbing. He boldly claimed for British winter climbing that it approached in many respects to good summer work in the Alps. The present writer goes further, and considers that winter mountaineering in Scotland is in many respects a better training and a more strenuous sport than most of the ordinary Swiss work, where one plods behind a guide up a well-known route by what is often a plainly marked track. Here we can still find unknown ground and new routes, and exercise our exploring faculties — by far the most important part of mountaineering — for ourselves.

I may state at once that this is not written for the expert, nor do I desire for a moment to pose as a dogmatic authority on the subject, but there are now a considerable number of young climbers who 'go to the mountains in the snow', and who often do not know what can and what cannot be attempted with safety on the snow-clad face, or in the snowy and icy gully.

The terrible accident of Easter 1903, by which a glissader of such a gully lost his life, shows the necessity of caution in dealing with such places. Though there are no records of fatal accidents through the breaking away of cornices in this country, still we have heard rumours of narrow escapes due to this cause. To attempt the ascent of an avalanche-grooved gully, known to be overhung by huge cornices, on a warm, muggy mid-day in late spring is not an advisable proceeding, and in fact is directly contrary to the canons of good mountaineering.

It may often happen, in winter, that the gully we are ascending becomes the gathering and stream-bed, as it were, for a perfect cataract of hail or snow, blown into it from the cliffs or plateaux above, but this is quite different from the case mentioned, and though perhaps unpleasant is not at all dangerous, though it may render step-making or cutting excessively laborious.

As someone who once had the unpleasant experience of being swept off an ice pitch by a torrent of spindrift the Editor does not agree with this assessment. However Raeburn goes on to describe a condition which has caused many serious winter accidents. The Perthshire Ben More has been the scene of more serious accidents to ice-axeless hill walkers than any other mountain in Scotland, excepting Ben Nevis.

There is one condition, not very common maybe, that renders almost any steep Scottish mountain difficult and even dangerous to an inexpert or ice-axeless party, and it was probably this condition that caused the fatal accident to an ice-axeless tourist on Ben More ten or a dozen years ago. It is brought about thus. After a spell of wet weather comes a sharp frost, rendering the turf and earth as hard almost as rock; then comes a slight fall of snow, a partial thaw immediately after, followed by hard frost again, with a final powdering of loose snow. Even the ascent of an easy angle becomes under these circumstances difficult, and if the angle is steep the climb becomes well-nigh impossible. This brings us naturally to the main object of this paper, the collection of the combined experience of the whole Club, and we shall first see how it answers the question of what we mean by a steep angle.

Angle. — In collecting information on this and other points, I have carefully examined and read every article and note published in the pages of the "Journal" since its commencement. Averaging all the recorded angles of snow slopes, on faces and in gullies, after rejecting several obviously exaggerated, brings out the figure of 47°. This, I think, we can therefore look upon as the average angle of a steep snow slope. This angle would probably be estimated by an inexperienced party, without a clinometer, at 57° or 60°. I do not think snow will stay long on any extent of slope at an angle exceeding 55°. Under a cornice, or in a narrow chimney, the case is different, and any angle up to 90° may be found, but only for a few feet.

Avalanche. — There is frequent mention of avalanches in the various numbers of the "S.M.C.J." Naturally not very many members of the Club have actually seen these in the act of falling, but there are nevertheless accounts by several climbing parties of falls seen. That large and dangerous avalanches do often fall is patent to any one who visits the great north-east corries of our higher mountains in late spring. In the upper corrie of Nevis, the avalanche debris at the beginning of June cannot be much less than 100 feet in depth. I well recollect on the occasion of my first ascent — in mist —of the Tower Ridge, at Easter 1896, hearing the roar of several very large falls off the Observatory cliffs, and a couple of weeks later the gullies of Creag Meagaidh were quite unapproachable, constantly swept by large falls of snow, ice, and rocks.

On the Ross-shire Beinn Dearg (Vol. VI., p.159), 'a great fall, with a width of over 100 yards,' was seen by one party. Carn Dearg (Nevis), 'a huge avalanche fell 1,000 feet off buttress' (Vol. V., p.289). A formidable fall was seen by another party on 12th June 1904 (Vol. VIII., p.180) to fall 'from gully between Observatory Ridge and North-East Buttress of Ben Nevis. Many large falls observed on Aonach Beag, April 1904. These large and dangerous avalanches are, of course, usually caused by the breaking away of the cornices, but sometimes a surface layer of the snow will suddenly peel off a face. One such instance is given in Naismith's personal experience. Another was that of a party of three, of which the writer formed one, at New Year 1904. Ascending the Observatory Gully on Nevis, the snow was found to be very hard. Higher a layer of powdery snow, with a slight surface crust, lay on the hard. Shortly after adopting the precaution of cutting right through this upper snow, and making steps in the solid underneath, and when at a good height above an unpleasant iced wall, the whole upper surface suddenly cracked right across the gully, here about 40 yards wide, just above us. It did not at that time move farther, but the precaution of cutting into the under layer was a very necessary one, and should invariably be adopted in like circumstances, even though it involve considerably more labour.

Bergschrund. — There are of course no ice bergschrunds in Scotland, but very colourable imitations, in snow little less hard than ice, may be met with in May and June in the Nevis corries and elsewhere. They exist in just such places as we find them in the Alps, and are due to a similar cause — where the snowfield, or glacier, slopes against the rocks, the melting of the snow, or ice, in immediate contact with the heated rocks. The writer has seen one (Vol. VI., p.229) at least 40 feet deep, by 8 to 10 feet wide, in Nevis Upper Corrie in June, between the snowfield and the foot of the Observatory Buttress.

Cornices. — These, of great size and exquisite beaty, may exist on any Scottish mountain possessing a steep rock face. The size of these will vary according to the height and aspect of the mountain and character of the snowfall during the winter and spring.

An analysis of the occasions when figures are given in the *Journal* regarding size, of course estimates only, gives 20 feet in height and 10 feet overhang as about the maximum. It is possible that these figures may be found to be exceeded on special occasions. A cornice of the above dimensions may, however, be considered as rendering an ascent impossible. We have the record of two Alpine pioneers who, on the occasion of the first ascent of the Tower Gully on Nevis, actually burrowed through the great cornice at the top, taking two days to the task — the intervening night being spent at Fort William — but such a feat is too heroic for most.

One of the observers at Ben Nevis Observatory, however, informed the writer that he had measured a cornice at the head of the Observatory Gully which was 40 feet in height.

Glissade. — Within the letters of this word are contained some of the most subtle and fascinating joys of the snow-climber. Why the apparently simple and childish pastime of sliding down snow should possess such fascinations is difficult to explain to the unelect.

Let one of those, however, be but persuaded to try it, and explanation is no longer asked for. He straightway joins the inner circle and requires none. It is the same with regard to tobogganing, and with the highest development of the glissade — skiing.

Glissades are of two kinds, sitting and standing. Of the former variety, the attitude may vary from bolt-upright to lying at full length, according to the angle and condition of the snow.

The standing glissade requires more skill and balance than the sitting. It is more comfortable as regards after conditions of person and garments, but requires special conditions of snow and a considerably steeper angle to make it go well.

Personally speaking, I have seldom obtained any very long standing glissades in Scotland. Perhaps the longest was about 700 feet in Coire na Ciste of Nevis in July 1903.

In that late and snowy year, however, during a short Norwegian holiday I glissaded standing an aggregate of over 10,000 feet. One does not get glissades like these in the Alps in the ordinary climbing season. A common error of the novice in standing glissades is to lean too heavily on his ice-axe, which is extended behind like a third leg. This is excessively fatiguing to the arms. More reliance should be placed on balance and on rising on the heels to check and regulate the pace. Given favourable angle and snow, it is quite possible to glissade standing for long distances without touching the snow with the ice-axe at all. The writer has covered hundreds of feet at a stretch in Norway in this manner, and has seen young Norwegian ladies gliding down a steep snow slope on their feet, with ease and grace, with nothing at all in their hands. This, of course, is the result of long practice on ski.

> Sadly, the standing glissade has almost disappeared from mountaineering art today, along with the long ice axes and nailed boots which were its accessories.

The beginner at glissading ought to select easy places at first. An easy place may be defined as a steep slope of fairly soft snow on a face, or in a wide open gully, which is seen, or known, to take off to an easy angle before coming to an end. It should be remembered that the snow in a narrow gully is in late spring usually hollowed out in the centre by the stream below, and even if open pitches or bergschrunds do not exist, the place where the snow roof will be the weakest will be just at the top of a steep pitch or concealed waterfall.

In glissading down an unknown gully, if glissading is permissible at all, it should be done only in rope lengths. The first man drives in his ice-axe, using it as a hitch, while the other or others slide past him, keeping good control of course on pace. The last man, who is now first, drives in his axe in turn, and the process is repeated. Even gullies so steep as those on the great east face of Buchaille Etive Mor may be safely glissaded in this manner, if the snow is in good order and deep.

Many and varied are the methods of braking adopted by the sitting glissader. There is no doubt that as in standing glissades, the main control should be by the feet, but this has often the unpleasant effect, if the pace is good, of driving a perfect stream of snow into one's face. In using the ice-axe as a brake, different methods are adopted. The best, in the writer's opinion, is to grasp the shaft near the head with one hand, the palm of this upper hand turned up; the other hand is placed on the shaft with the palm down.

Putting the ice-axe now behind one, with the spike dragging through the snow, immense brake power may be obtained by widening the space between the hands, and raising the body on the lower arm. A very bad method, but one often adopted by beginners, is to take the ice-axe by its lower end, and brake with the pick, or over the blade. This acts all right as long as braking is only a little, or not really necessary at all. Whenever a real emergency occurs, and it is desirable to stop suddenly, this method fails, as the ice-axe is invariably wrenched out of the slider's hands, and he is left helpless. If in glissading down a steep slope or gully one finds that, owing to the avalanchy condition of the snow, we are bginning to ride upon the top of a large pile of snow, it is advisable to get off promptly sideways, before the pile becomes too thick to be penetrable by the ice-axe, and all control lost.

With regard to the length of glissades to be obtained in Scotland, these are often better and longer than can be obtained in the Alps in summer. The longest recorded is in Vol. VI., p.198, when a party 'estimated that they glissaded 2,500 feet on the descent of Ben More.' Other records are - Easter, 1895, on Nevis, 2,000 feet; Vol. III., p.80, Ben Dorain, 1,000 feet; Vol. II., p.83, Ben Ledi, 700 feet; Vol. VIII., p.147, Aonach Mor, 1,500 feet; and numerous instances of from 500 to 800 feet.

Ski. — No mention of Scottish snow-sport would nowadays be complete without inclusion of this.

I consider ski will but seldom be used in Scotland with advantage and enjoyment. The condition and amount of snow even on our hills is not often likely to be suitable. On the low ground, at any rate in the neighbourhood of Edinburgh and Glasgow, we have many winters with practically no snow. On the hills it is usually, if not soft and sticky, hard and icy. Seldom do we find the compact dry white powder characteristic of the Norwegian winter snow. In exceptional frosts in exceptional seasons, such as occur at intervals of ten years or so, we may have opportunities of safe practice, but to become adepts, and to enjoy this most interesting and fascinating sport to perfection, we must visit countries less under the influence of Atlantic mildness and moisture than is our native land.

We have seen from the foregoing what a wide field our Scottish fells present for the education of the snow climber. For six months in the year he may there find practically Alpine conditions. Indeed, if attempting some of the highest north-east gullies, the ice-axe will be found indispensable at any season of the year. If after an experience gained here, he goes to the Alps, he will find that his expeditions on his native hills will stand him in good stead. His ice-axe is a familiar and trusted friend, not an uncouth weapon, dangerous to himself and others. He will have learned, if at all observant, a good deal about snow conditions on steep slopes, only he must remember the hotter sun and slighter adhesion of snow in the Alps. Above all he should have learned, if he is capable of learning, the great lesson of balance, to stand up straight and to plant the feet firmly in the steps. He must also remember, however, that though his conquest of the snowy gully, with its 10 or 20 foot ice pitches, is probably a more difficult and risky bit of climbing than almost anything usually done in the Alps, still there everything is on a much greater scale, and endurance of long-continued exertion is much more valuable than any other climbing qualities, except balance and caution. Balance is the most valuable quality because it in reality doubles at least a climber's endurance. All three qualities spell safety on long and difficult expeditions, and safe is the highest qualifying adjective we can bestow upon the mountaineer.

The cultivation of coconut-like biceps by any of the modern methods of muscle growing may possibly be of some use to climbers. But man after all is not a monkey, and if an army may be said to travel upon its stomach, the mountaineer travels, even though the angle approach 80°, mainly by means of his feet. It is to the education of the feet therefore, and incidentally of course to the education of hand and eye and brain, that mountaineers should devote their attention. There is no better field for this education, apart altogether from the aesthetic joys to be obtained, than our Scottish Bens in their wintry garb of snow.

Vol II (1892)

MEASURING SNOW GULLY ON BEN VORLICH

THE FIRST SCOTTISH ICE CLIMBERS
Vol. XXX (1972)   by R.N. Campbell

.At the Coming-of-Age Dinner of the Club, in 1909, Professor Ramsay (our first President) remarked that the Club had 'come into the world nearly a hundred strong, starting full-blown like 'Athene from the head of Zeus'..

Whatever one thinks of this startling simile, it is certainly true that the late Victorian pioneers showed extraordinary enterprise and competence and that in one particular sphere, ice-climbing, they immediately established a standard which endured until very recent times. Most of us who have come to mountaineering in the last 20 years or so can fumble our way back through Brooker, Marshall and Patey to the great pre-war ice-climbers — Bell, Macphee and the well-known Glasgow group of Mackenzie, Murray et al. Knowing that the ice-climbs of the former group were in certain ways an advance over those of the latter often engenders the assumption that the climbs of the pre-war group were similarly superior to those of their great predecessors, the Victorians. In fact, with the exception of Bell's partial ascent of Zero gully in 1936 (see S.M.C.J., 1936, xxi, 200) and Mackenzie & Murray's ascent of Garrick's Shelf in 1937 (see S.M.C.J., 1937, xxi, 237), the pre-war group's main achievement was to re-establish ice-climbing in Scotland at the former high standard attained by the Victorians. This is not, of course, in any sense a criticism of their efforts: from the Ultra-montane viewpoint, Scottish mountaineering in the late twenties and early thirties was enjoying a veritable Dark Age — there is no doubt that the pre-war ice-climbers were regarded by the bulk of their contemporaries as the most Desperate and Dangerous Radicals — and that they achieved as much as they did under the circumstances was remarkable.

We are now in the throes of another Great Leap Forward on ice-climbing. That bugbear of the fifties and sixties, the Unmitigated Ice-pitch, has been divested of most of its terrors by a new technique, sprung on the unsuspecting Cairngorms by that ageless Lion of the Creagh Dhu M.C., John Cunningham.

Lest this new advance (if that is what it is) delude us into supposing that we are now remote from our ancient predecessors in technique as well as time, let us Cut a Retrograde Step and remember the incomparable Victorians....

First and most illustrious was Collie, who blazed a trail of fine climbs through Glencoe to Ben Nevis from the Inveroran Meet of Easter 1894. The culmination of this fortnight of effort was his two ascents of Tower Ridge, the first with Solly and Collier, the second with Hastings. The first ascent occupied five hours and Dr Collie thought that it 'resembled the Italian side of the Matterhorn, and was the best climb he had ever had in Scotland.' However, his account of the climb in the Journal was cloaked in pseudonymity and took the form of a third-person report of a quasi-religious Quest.

After some preliminary meanderings, the Allt a'Mhuilinn is reached and Ben
Nevis described.

'Across the valley they see the great Mountain, the Immensity of Greatness, the majestic
Silence, the prodigious Dampness, the Height, the Depth, in shape like a great Dome....
Before them rose hugeous rocks and bulky stones standing on end facing to the north,
where the ice and snow tarry from one winter even until the following, for in these places
the sun shines not, neither are found the comfortable soft and juicy breezes of the south;
there the brood of the black Crow and the white vapours and comprehensive congelations
of the Mistus Scotorum are produced. So were the three Brethren sore amazed, but as yet
could not see even the first matter of the Work.'

But the Eye of Faith soon detects the Tower Ridge.

' "See," said one, "the way leadeth upward, for doth not a mighty petrolific ridge, full of
points, towers and pinnacles, descend from above, whereon the pursuit may be pursued,
the operation of the great work may be begun? First must we fashion in the snow and ice
great stairs of steps, by the aid of which, through prolongation, extension, reduplication,
and multiplication, shall we be brought on to the ridge, even at the beginning".'

This is soon done and the ridge is followed with little comment until the Great
Tower is reached and the Western Traverse assailed.

'But presently came they to a great rock, a majestic tower; here were they perforce
compelled to depart to the right hand, placing themselves in steep and perilous positions
on slopes of ice, which downward seemed to end in the empty air, even in the great void.
Still all things have an end at last — good Wine, Pinnacles , Spires, cabalistic Emblems,
and oromaniacal Wanderings.... So did the Three find the perilous passage across the
headlong steep finish. Then did they pass onwards to the Labyrinth, the rocky Chaos, and
greatly did they marvel at the exceeding steepness thereof; so that only by great
perseverance, turning now to right and now to left, were they able to break themselves
free from the bonds and entanglements, and climb sagaciously upwards to the summit of
the great tower.

Here they stop to look back on their journey and survey the difficulties ahead.

'Behind, and far below, imprinted in the snow were the steps by which they had mounted
upwards, winding now this way and now that, looking like scarce seen veins in finest
marble. But before them lay the narrow Way, the Ridge, the Cleft, and the white Slope,
leading even unto the utmost height, the sovereign summit of the mighty mountain.

These delights are soon disposed of and the Quest is satisfactorily ended when the travellers gain admittance to a Temple on the summit.

'So were they shown by the dwellers in the Temple many and marvellous wonders. In the centre stood a furnace for all the transmutations and agitations by heat; whilst on shelves did they see divers bottles, pans, boxes and bags, wherein were stored succulent sauces and philosophical essences to the end that the delectable concoctions of the pious might be completed. Likewise great store of books. In some could be found treatises of the true science, also devices, hieroglyphic interpretations, and perspicuous renderings of great wisdom, in others histories of joyous diversions. Also were there curious and ingenious engines for all sorts of motions , where were represented and imitated all articulate sounds, and conveyed in trunks and strange lines and distances. Likewise mathematical instruments, exquisitely made, for the discovering of small and minute bodies in the air. Also were shown many and marvellous things pertaining to the harmony of the heavenly spheres.

'Then did they drink the mixed draught, the comfortable potation, joyously, philosophically, and with discernment, for they had attained to the divine Secrets of the Philosophers, even unto the mystagorical Delight, the great Fulfilment of the spagyrick Quest of devout Oromaniacs.

Dr Collie's description of the technical problems presented by the climb is not illuminating.

'And what joy, think ye, did they feel after the exceeding long and troublous ascent? — after

Scrambling,slipping
  Pulling,pushing
    Lifting, gasping
    Looking, hoping
      Despairing, climbing
        Holding on, falling off
          Trying, puffing
          Loosing, gathering
            Talking, stepping
              Grumbling, anathematising
                Scraping, hacking
                Bumping, jogging
                  Overturning, hunting
                    Straddling, —

                    for know you that by these methods alone are the most divine mysteries of the Quest reached.

Snow and ice climbing in Scotland, then, began with the ascent of a route which even now enjoys a fair reputation. Nor was this an isolated ascent: J.H. Bell, Napier and Macgregor climbed it the following winter and at the Easter Meet of 1896 the ridge was climbed by at least five parties. Reporting the Meet, William Brown remarked that, under winter conditions the Tower Ridge affords a most respectable climb and no one can complain that the passage of the Tower is devoid of interest or difficulty. In September of the same year W. Inglis Clark and J.A. Parker visited the Ridge expecting, of course, a summer climb. However,

'we were surprised to find the cliffs plastered with snow for 600 ft. below the summit, so we made for the Observatory to borrow an ice-axe. We encountered a heavy snow-storm... and on reaching the top found icicles three feet long hanging from the doorway. The only available axe was one of which the pick was partly broken, and the handle had no point. Leaving this at the halfway Observatory, we returned home to prepare for a winter ascent. Retracing our steps to the Hut, where we recovered our axe, and striking round by the screes of Carn Dearg, we were not long in reaching the scene of operations. Out of the sun it was very cold, and ice encrusted the ground.

The climb is begun and in the early stages the borrowed axe is something of an encumbrance.

The chief difficulty encountered was in taking the ice-axe along with us, and we found it often profitable to send it up on a spare rope. At one very steep pitch a ledge had to be followed round a corner to the right, and here the axe was a regular obstruction.

However,

Until we reached the Tower proper we had no real difficulty.

This statement, implicit in the earlier accounts too, will ring strangely in the ears of those many of us who have spent anxious hours on the Little Tower...
    Later on, the ice-axe comes into its own, even the lack of a spike proving to be an advantage

'On reaching the Tower itself we found all the holds covered with hard snow or ice, and even the preliminary climb up the lower walls required careful treatment. Reaching a narrow ice-covered platform, a great wall of rock towered above us for about sixty feet. On this the holds were very few indeed, and our hopes centred in a shallow recess or gully which, starting about twenty feet up, led to the top. A narrow ledge, four or five inches wide, crossed the wall about fifteen feet up, but terminated about five feet from the lower end of the gully. Up to this ledge there were but suggestions of holds. A narrow crack, sufficient to admit the pick of the axe, went vertically up the face. To make a start, it was necessary to step off the platform on to a projecting knob on the right, where you overhung the precipice descending far below. The only available hitch is about three feet up, and from that point Parker, who led in excellent style, virtually took his life in his hands. Progress was very slow, and the horizontal ledge could not be reached until the leader had obtained two steps for his left foot — one on the ice-axe, the handle resting on my shoulder; the other on the ice-axe held up at arm's length in my left hand. In each case the pick was placed in the narrow crack already mentioned. The ledge proved to be covered with ice, and had to be cleared before a foothold was obtained on it.... The gully itself was filled with ice, and being at a very steep angle, afforded no safety. Leaving the axe here, Parker crept cautiously to the right, where a projecting knob vertically above me afforded the first and only safe hitch.'

The Victorians, then, made of Tower Ridge a winter Trade Route — it was climhed by all and sundry, in all weathers and with the most primitive equipment.

Another great winter pioneer was William Naismith, one of the Club's founders. His retrospective article in the Journal of April 1925 recalls his youthful beginnings.

'Professor Ramsay gave his Junior Latin Class a fascinating lecture on Alpine Climbing in 1872, and showed us his ice-axe and how to use it. About the same time there fell into my hands Whymper's "Scrambles" and I devoured it with the most intense delight.... In 1880 I took part in a first ascent of Ben Nevis for the year on 1st May with two friends. The conditions were wintry, and we got good practice in glissading, with the help of stout walking-sticks, on the slopes above Lochan Meall an t' Suidhe. The upper 2000 feet of the mountain being in cloud, we steered almost entirely by map and compass, but found the top all right.

There were then no buildings on the summit — only a big lonely cairn, the top of which was just visible above the snow. This ascent was regarded as sufficiently unusual to be referred to in several newspapers'.

Four years later he visits Ben More, Perthshire, in March.

'Staying overnight at Luib Inn, I asked the inn-keeper whether anyone had climbed Ben More yet. His reply was emphatic that it would be quite impossible at that season, and if anyone were foolish enough to try it, he would likely lose his life; "and besides,"he added, "if a man did get to the top he might see ghosts"

This good advice is of course ignored.

In the morning I started early, carrying an alpenstock... I first approached the north-east

60. The Centre Gully of Ben Lui

61. *Looking down Crowberry Gully, Buachaille Etive Mor*

62. *Douglas Scott at the Junction Pitch of Crowberry Gully*

63. *The Ben Nevis cliffs in winter. A solo climber approaches the foot of
Gardyloo Gully*

base of Ben More, but found the slope too formidable. So a traverse was made to the left above the Allt Coire Chaorach, until below the col between Ben More and Stobinian — the V-shaped gap as it is often called. There an easier snow-slope presented itself, and was mounted with little difficulty. From the col to the top of Ben More was, however, a different story, for the snow was covered in most places with a sheet of ice, the surface having evidently melted and frozen again, and my alpenstock was, of course, useless for making steps. Fortunately, however, the angle was not severe, and by going now to the right and now to the left one could often avoid the most slippery parts. There were also rocks and stones projecting from the ice, and so, by dodging about from one rock or platform to another, the cairn was at last reached without any mishap.

Or, presumably, sight of ghosts ! However, Naismith draws a moral from the day's experiences.

'In winter and spring the higher Scottish mountains ought to be treated as seriously as Alpine Peaks — with the same equipment of axes and a rope.'

In the early days of the Club, Naismith took part in a number of fairly modest winter climbs such as the Upper Couloir of Stob Gabhar and the North Coire of Beinn Dothaidh, but under Collie's influence his record blossomed with ascents of Castle Ridge and the North-East Ridge of Aonach Beag in April 1895. However, his greatest achievement was the first winter ascent of the great North-East Buttress of Ben Nevis on 3rd April 1896 with Brunskill, Kennedy, King and Squance. Something of Naismith's well-known self-effacement and of the Victorian climbers' attitude to winter climbing is shown by Brown's matter-of-fact report, 'The N.E. Buttress was only ascended by one party. It held a good deal of ice, and was reported to be in a rather difficult condition. The gully above the first platform was paved with blue ice, and had to be left severely alone. Higher up also, below the last 'peeler', the summer route was impracticable for the same reason, and a new line had to be struck out up the rocks on the left.' Thirty years later, Naismith 'admits' that it was he who made the ascent.

'This was a long day, for we were on the buttress for nearly seven hours. The party was a jolly one, but rather large for speed. The rocks were plastered with ice and snow and distinctly difficult. At one or two places the route followed by the first climbers (here Naismith is referring to the first summer ascent) was impossible and had to be varied. Until we actually reached the summit, there was a slight doubt as to whether the top would 'go' or not, for a pitch that Brown had climbed with difficulty was now found to be iced and hopeless; but by crossing to the left side of the buttress, we followed a narrow gully, at first hard ice but afterwards good snow, which led us past the last obstacle. It was pitch dark long before we arrived at the Alexandra Hotel.

In fact, this astonishing early ascent was so little noted at the time that our present guidebooks either fail to mention those responsible for it or list them as 'unknown'. Collie and Naismith, despite their great achievements, were, however, no more than Minor Prophets of the New Faith. The greatest of the Victorian ice-climbers, beyond any doubt, was Harold Raeburn, who burst upon the scene in 1896. In the ensuing twenty-five years or so, Raeburn was responsible for a glittering constellation of ice-climbs which spanned the winter-climbing firmament from Ben Nevis in the West to Lochnagar in the East. Many of these climbs, such as the Central Buttress of Stob Coire nan Lochain and Observatory Ridge on Ben Nevis, stand comparison with the great ice-climbs of the late thirties and forties and the early fifties. In our current guidebooks these fine routes are credited to Raeburn but some were formerly credited to other, later, parties. The first of these was Crowberry Gully on Buachaille Etive Mor. Discussing the climb in the *Journal* of June 1911, Raeburn remarks.

'So far as is known only three ascents of the gully have been made. The present writer has had the good fortune to be in all three. The first two were in spring with the assistance or otherwise of ice and snow. The third, that of last year, was a summer climb.

The first ascent was made with E.B Green on 10th April, 1898.

'The season had been a snowy one. Vast quantities of snow lay in the gully. The smaller pitches were completely obliterated, the larger, greatly diminished in height. Long tongues of hard snow and ice, behind which dark and gloomy caverns stretched far into the heart of the mountain, reared themselves high in the air. From their summits it was usually possible to affect a lodgement, after some cutting, on the north wall of the gully and then contour in above the pitch. The only serious difficulty, according to the writer's recollection, was encountered at the last great pitch not far from the summit. Here the gully forks, or rather there branches out of the main gully a comparatively short, but deeply cut and overhanging chimney.'

Raeburn attempts this but is soon discomfited,

The leader, by back and foot wedging, climbed the lower pitch to a far out chockstone. Above, the far projecting top pitch looked horribly uninviting. To settle the matter a fierce blatter of hail came on, and a stinging mitraille of cataracts of ice-pellets poured down upon the uplifted countenance of the leader.'

However, the right fork was then attacked and proved not too difficult. On this ascent the rocks were more or less free of snow but on his second visit at Easter 1909 'The Crowberry Ridge was sheathed in masses of new ice.' Raeburn was acting as host to a party of English climbers who had been expecting a rock-climbing holiday. Two decided to remain at the hotel, being 'lately recovered from influenza' but the others, Brigg and Tucker, were safely manoeuvred to the Gully.

'After lunch we attacked it. There was less snow in the gully than in 1898 and the first great pitch was very stiff. Fortunately the thick glaze of ice on the right wall allowed of steps and handholds being cut and it was eventually overcome. At the great pitch below the fork we were forced to make a long traverse out on the north wall, rather nasty with ice, and slippery with new snow.... The summit was gained at 3.30, after a tough struggle of four hours and twenty minutes. Here the furious blasts of wind laden with hail proved an unwelcome change after the peace of the gully.

However, although expeditiously completed, the climb had not been without incident, thanks to the frequent spindrift avalanches.

'At one pitch, where the gully narrowed, and the only possible route lay up the fall, the party was struck by a larger rush of new snow than usual. The leader was buried to the shoulders as he held the second's rope taut round the perfect hitch of his well-buried ice-axe.

The second, who at the time was occupying the position of a chockstone in the pitch, was completely snowed over, while the third man, at the foot of the pitch, was overwhelmed, and went off down the gully till brought up by the rope.

Raeburn's second great forgotten ice-climb was Green Gully on the Comb, described in the Journal for January 1907. The climb was made in April 1906 with a Genevese gentleman, a member of the Swiss Alpine club, Monsieur Eberhard Phildius, who was staying at Fort William and who proved a pleasant companion and a keen and capable climber. The mountain was clearly in splendid condition.

'Many feet of snow lay in the deep chasms below the Tower Ridge, and sheets of snow-ice covered the roches moutonnees below the glacier-planed lip of the Lochan na Ciste. Above us rose the jagged arête of the Tower Ridge, but how different from its summer aspect! Just like a great iceberg it was, or perhaps more like a mass of rough marble, all the dark rock hid by a plating of ribbed and embossed dull white snow-ice, with here and there streaks, ribs and columns of pale green water-ice from a few inches to several feet in thickness'.

Raeburn's intention is to climb not Green Gully but the Comb, using the gully as a link between the lower diagonal ledge of the Comb and the upper arête. This ledge is traversed and the foot of the gully reached.

'Now we found ourselves looking up, so far as the mist and the descending cataracts of snow dust would permit, the steep gully which should give access to the ridge. Then began the real struggle. Keen frost reigned, and a biting wind moaned among the icy battlements impending over the great moat of the Coire na Ciste. We two, stormers of one of the salient towers, felt the blast strike us now and again as it swept round the angle of the Comb.'

Nor is the wind the only problem,

'The worst was that the snow batteries were opened on us from above and below. From above one could, to a certain extent, take cover beneath the shield of our cone-pointed, brim-turned-down felt hats, but occasionally the snow that fell mixed with the seldom ceasing stream that poured down the gully, was caught by the powerful ascending eddy and rushed up, thus taking us behind our defences. The pain of a stream of icy snow in the face is so great that work must stop, and the face be covered till breath is regained. Fortunately those underhand tactics were never long continued, and the interrupted sapping and mining was soon renewed.'

The gully puts up a stubborn fight,

'Two of the pitches we now encountered, if we make a distinction in what was practically one great pitch, were what is usually known as perpendicular, i.e., probably 70° to 75°, with small portions approaching 90°.

'It was of course only due to the peculiar tough quality of the snow-ice curtain hanging down these steeper portions that they were climbable at all. At angles such as these it is impossible to remain in toeholds in ice without holding on as well, and it is impossible to hoist the body up unless the handholds are cut so as to give a "pull in." These icy curtains allowed of this being done; frequently the pick broke through to soft snow or black vacancy, hacked with green bulbs of ice, and "pigeon-hole" holds resulted.

'Ice-work of this kind is, however, particularly cramping and exhausting, and progress was slow. To hang on with one hand, while that long two-handed weapon, the modern ice-axe, is wielded in the other, is calculated to produce severe cramps in course of time, and did so now.'

Raeburn now makes a futuristic suggestion.

'I suggest for climbs such as this our going back to the original Swiss icemen's tools, the iron-shod straight "baton," the light tomahawk-like hatchet stuck in the belt when not in use. The second of these pitches almost stumped us, but yielded at the third attempt, and the reserves, in the person of M. Phildius, were now brought up, and took their place in the van.'

The way to the arête is now clear, but it looks so heavily corniced that they press on up the gully, passing the cornice by traversing to the right.

'Obviously our only chance… was to traverse out on the right where a rib of ice-covered rock ran up to meet the cornice, reducing it to half-height, and where it was only slightly over-hanging. This way eventually "went", but the Comb was game to the last, and I must confess to a feeling of helplessness for a moment as I stood on my ice-axe, driven horizontally into the vertical snow wall, some hundreds of feet of little less than vertical ice-plastered rocks stretching away down into the depths of the mist beneath, while my fingers slid helplessly from the glassy surface of the cornice neve, in the vain endeavour to find or make a hold by which I might haul myself up. The problem was solved by a retreat, until Phildius was able to pass me up his axe. Then the ice-plating was quickly shattered, and with fingers well crooked in the tough neve, a steady drag landed the body over the cornice lip, and Phildius soon followed.'

Raeburn now forestalls a strange objection,

'Objections may be made to this climb that it is not the actual climb of the Comb. This is true, for we were never once on the exact arête. But what does that really matter? Phildius and I came out for a climb, and we got one, up one of the steepest cliffs on Nevis, in as icy condition as I have ever seen the old berg. We were both pleased and enjoyed it every bit, except perhaps when under the "hottest".fire of the rear batteries.

It seems that by pretending to have climbed the Comb poor Raeburn was later deemed not to have climbed Green Gully!

(The early articles from which this 'memorial' was culled are Divine Mysteries of the Oromaniacal Quest, by Orlamon Linecus, Volume Ill; Lochnagar and Ben Nevis by W. Inglis Clark, Volume IV; Early Winter Climbing by W. W. Naismith, Volume XVII; The Crowberry North Gully, Buachaille Etive by Harold Raeburn, Volume XI; and A Scottish Ice Climb by Harold Raeburn, Volume IX; I am indebted to J.R.Marshall for pointing out the shortcomings of our current guidebooks, those which are relevant being fully or partly his responsibility! - R.N.C.)

DEFEAT (A December Night on the Crowberry Ridge)
Vol. XXI (1936)   by W.H. Murray

It is the custom of mountaineers to set on record their most successful climbs, but to say nothing of their reverses. The custom is an unfortunate one; there can be no doubt that one may sometimes gain more genuinely valuable experience from defeat than by virtue of the most brilliant series of first ascents. This consideration, supported by the Editor's invitation, persuades me to set down in writing an unsuccessful attempt, on 13th December of last year, to make the first winter ascent of the Crowberry Ridge by way of Garrick's Shelf.

Dunn, MacAlpine, Mackenzie, and myself (all J.M.C.S.), after an unfortunate series of delays, set off from Coupal Bridge at 10.30 a.m. The hour was late; yet we adhered to our original plans, although a defeat high up at dusk on a rock-snow-ice climb could hardly be contemplated with equanimity. However, the route was well-known to us and we felt confident of success. We were all in excellent physical condition, exceptionally well equipped, and yearning for a first-class climb. These factors overcame our good judgment. The morning was cloudy, with the wind in the west-south-west. New snow had fallen overnight, but was not lying in sufficient depth to impede our progress to the foot of the Crowberry Gully, where we encountered a short difficult pitch that whetted our appetite for bigger and better things. Never was an appetite destined to be more harshly glutted.

We now left the gully and moved up to the first pitch of Garrick's Shelf by traversing a ledge of steeply shelving snow on the northern wall of the Crowberry Ridge. Here we found a cave large enough to accommodate the whole party, and we gulped down our second breakfast hastily before roping up.

The construction of Garrick's Shelf is peculiar. It is a narrow gully or trough running up the northern wall of the Crowberry Ridge parallel with the Crowberry Gully. The Shelf itself, which is punctuated with steep pitches, terminates in precipitous rock some 250 feet below the crest of the Ridge. This last section, very difficult in summer, ends in a steep scoop that debouches on the Crowberry Ridge near the base of the Tower.

We found the rocks well plastered with snow, but ice was present only in small quantity - too small quantity as we discovered later. The snow-covering on steep rock was not sufficiently frozen to hold, and had to be cleared away as we advanced. Our progress was much hindered by fierce blasts of wind from the south-west, which swept down the Crowberry Gully and Shelf, bearing great clouds of powder-snow that completely filled all the holds after each of us had passed upwards. Woollen gloves froze to the holds, and were sometimes difficult to disengage.

Four hours of continuous climbing on the Shelf found us at the top of the fourth pitch. The Shelf now began to narrow and steepen, while the snow was thinner and in poorer condition than ever. The sun had already set and the upper reaches of the Shelf were pervaded by a grey and gloomy twilight. The need for haste had become urgent, yet the next 50 feet of plain, straight-forward gully occupied no less than twenty minutes. The difficulty lay simply in persuading the snow to hold. There was no danger of its avalanching.

Garrick's Shelf now ended and merged in the steep face of the final rocks. On our right the Shelf fell perpendicularly into the depths of the Crowberry Gully; on our left rose the vertical wall of the Crowberry Ridge; before·us the rocks swept up in a steep pitch some 60 feet high. A small tower, rectangular in shape, stood at the top of this pitch and lent distinction to the place.

The first problem was a narrow crack set in a corner and packed with snow. The first two attempts on it failed, but a third and more determined effort proved successful, and the crack was climbed by the lay-back method to a small ledge. The time was now 4.30 p.m. The usual route into the square recess at the base of the tower was unjustifiable, and an attempt was therefore made to force the rocks on the left. After a great deal of manoeuvring for position, an outward-tilting mantelshelf plastered with snow lying on ice was laboriously overcome. For a moment the position looked promising; on the left only a short wall barred the way to easier rock running east of the tower. But the first movement to the left would of necessity be made without handhold, a "down and out" strain being placed upon the feet, the foothold being a sloping slab coated with verglas.

The party consulted. The time was now a quarter to five; the weather was rapidly deteriorating; to retire now would spell immediate benightment with the whole of Garrick's Shelf below us. On the other hand, only 6 feet of rock barred the leader from almost certain triumph. The decision we had to make was a grave one. Should or should not that next, very dangerous step be taken? We decided that it should not, and the leader retired.

The wall of the North Buttress was now growing steadily dimmer in the gathering darkness; already the rising storm was roaring across the upper rocks of the Crowberry Ridge. Snow was falling steadily, and this was reinforced from time to time by sheets of drift-snow that were hurled upon us from the rocks above. The situation appeared to be sufficiently desperate, but the party had climbed too long in combination to entertain any doubt of a satisfactory issue. We carried with us 330 feet of rope, a torch, spare batteries, and sufficient food. We resolved therefore to continue to climb downwards rather than bivouac.

The descent of the steep section in the snow-gully to pitch four was less hazardous than we had expected. The first three, secured by the rope, enjoyed a comfortable passage and cheerfully assured the leader of their ability to field him if need be. But to the real chagrin of the party, number one declined to enliven this passage by any of the horse-play commonly attendant on glissades, involuntary or otherwise, so the party moved down in strictly text-book style to pitch four. A wide, square-cut chimney, all three walls of which were vertical, now presented an interesting problem, largely complicated by its invisibility.

The solution taxed us for two hours but we finally succeeded in roping down from a spike of iced rock.

We were now enveloped in darkness. The snow on the Shelf and on the surrounding rock could be dimly discerned as a dull grey mantle, far too obscure to afford any indication of the route. We progressed slowly by torchlight. Creeping circumspectly down the Shelf over snow and broken rock, we descended as much as 150 feet in one and a half hours. Above the uproar of the wind could be heard a torrent of bizarre noises which, had we not known each other better, must have sounded suspiciously like profane language. At 9 p.m. we reached an open corner at the top of pitch three.

Here we were unable to rope down. There was no rock-belay, and the snow was too unsound to take an axe, but we contrived a good belay by jamming our axes in an angle of rock. Thus protected we climbed in turn down steep snow to a point near the base of a rock-face. A distinctly tricky traverse to the right then led, after one and a half hours, to soft snow below the pitch. The leader was coached over the traverse in brilliant style by the second, who employed the effective though inhumane device of ruthlessly skewering his victim with the spike of an axe.

We were now back in the gully, hard against the wall of the Crowberry Ridge, and descended very slowly to a short pitch that we failed to remember climbing on the way up. A little disconcerted, we climbed down from axe-belays and found ourselves in a very fine, narrow cave. This was the most comfortable spot on the whole route, and we felt loth to leave it. The place was hailed with great joy by the leader, who, after ejecting the rest of the party, urged disingenuously that any haste in accomplishing the next section would be particularly unadvisable. From the narrow recesses of this cave the leader could speculate as to what was happening below, while he watched, with a certain measure of perverted pleasure, the swirling snow pour in hissing cascades over the roof and down the Shelf, where his more energetic companions would literally "get it in the neck."

Time sped on. For over an hour there had been a great deal of shouting below and singularly little movement. But at long last a faint call from number two summoned the leader downwards. Sixty feet below we all congregated on what appeared to be a broad horizontal ledge running against the Crowberry Wall. An 80-foot rope had been fixed round a spike on the Wall itself and number four, after prospecting the route at the far end of the ledge, had just announced that further advance was impossible. He was faced, or seemed to be faced, with a bottomless abyss. We had lost the route.

A good twelve hours had now elapsed since our last meal, and the thoughts of the party turned to hot soup and roast pork. Plum pudding and brandy sauce were also considered, although a majority protest vetoed the actual sauce in favour of its more potent ingredient.

With freezing fingers we then extracted from our rucksacks the handfuls of sodden crumbs that had formerly been jam-sandwiches. We reviewed our position as we ate, and came to the conclusion that we were now above Garrick's Shelf on a ledge ending in a cul-de-sac. The torch-beam was therefore directed downwards towards the Crowberry

Gully. After some prospecting a lower route was pronounced practicable.

Our principal concern was whether the fixed rope would reach to the foot of the pitch. Number four, belayed by the others, set off downwards; he went leftward down steep snow and then swung into the mouth of a vertical shallow chimney. A long period of suspense followed. In half an hour there was still no movement of any kind from below. The party above gradually realised that it was being kept waiting - a strange presentiment, never absent during the entire descent — and wrathfully inquiring howls were directed downwards. Several minutes later a muffled "What?" drifted upwards, followed after a while by "Yip!" — whatever that might mean. We gave it up.

Quite suddenly a shout, redolent of triumph, assured us that our proper route had been regained below pitch two: the vertical chimney was, indeed, on pitch two itself. In half an hour we were all down. The fixed rope refused to run round the spike and was left behind. A further hour of vigilant toil took us all to the top of the first pitch, where an outcrop of rock presented a rectangular face to the lower regions of Garrick's Shelf. We edged carefully round the right-hand corner of this rock, and near its base discovered an excellent spike-belay. The snow here was firm but rather steep, so we stood face-in during the hours that followed.

Our plan was to attach a 30-foot loop of line round the spike, to rope down on 120 feet of rope, which we hoped fervently would reach the foot of the pitch, and to secure the first man down with 100 feet of line. This 250-foot maze of rope and line was thereupon possessed by an evil spirit and became tangled in the darkness. The whole Shelf resounded with the most powerfully expressive oaths know to the human tongue. Incredible delays occurred. Violent bursts of wind-driven snow still came lashing down the Shelf, and the last battery in the torch was fading. By wriggling our toes continuously during these halts we contrived to avoid frostbite.

At four o'clock in the morning everthing was ready. One by one we roped down a narrow chimney on the left flank of an overhanging bulge. This was appallingly difficult, for the rope declined to run, and our descent resolved itself into an exhausting struggle against friction. The torch was now out of action, so a fitting climax to this pitch was provided by an awkward right-hand traverse round the bulge, which led us into the cave below the Shelf. Upon reaching the foot of the chimney, the last man found himself unable to persuade the now obstinately vicious rope to run through the loop. He left it behind with emotions closely akin to pleasure. When the leader at length joined the party in the cave, he at once remarked in the bearing and attitude of his companions a striking complacency, the source of which was speedily betrayed by the crumbs adhering to their now incipient whiskers. Thus gorged, these callous people had yet no scruple in demanding bites at the leader's one remaining apple, on the pitiful plea that all their own food was finished.

We now roped up on 100 feet of line. The absence of a torch was a serious handicap, and we experienced no little difficulty in the traverse along the Crowberry Wall, where drift snow had piled up on the ledge at a high angle. Shortly afterwards we gained the lower part of the Crowberry Gully, where we found our difficult pitch of the previous day miraculously transformed into an easy scramble, but on leaving the gully we unfortunately lost all trace of the usual line of descent.

An hour of prospecting, both up and down, resulted in our finally defying orthodox tactics by committing ourselves to the mercy of an unknown gully, which led us with unexpected ease to the moor. The latter imparted some wholehearted if concluding kicks, and we were all, at one time or another, immersed up to the.thighs in bogs. We reached Coupal Bridge at dawn, safe and sound, if not precisely hale and hearty. We had been out for rather less than twenty-one hours, of which fourteen had been spent on the descent.

The moral of this is only too plain, and is appreciated by none more fully than by those most closely concerned. Our defeat had in no way discouraged us in our determination to make a second attempt under more favourable conditions, when the Shelf would be more heavily plastered with ice. By the end of March such conditions obtained and the route was climbed in its entirety.

The successful ascent of Garrick's Shelf was made by W.M. Mackenzie and myself on 28th March 1937. We left Coupal Bridge at 8 a.m. on a perfect morning, and reached the Shelf at 10 a.m. The first three difficult pitches were heavily iced. The vertical chimney at pitch four was lightly iced, and although not exposed, was severe. At 12 noon we reached pitch five, the crux of the climb. This pitch had shrunk to 50 feet. The ice-coating was light; axe-cut holds to the square recess below the pinnacle were painfully minute. Our escape from the recess, made on the pinnacle's right-hand edge, was extremely delicate. Splayed out on this bulging corner we had to change feet on a small sloping hold without handhold, and with a sheer drop below into the Crowberry Gully. The pitch was very severe and occupied two hours. In the scoop above the pinnacle were two sensational and very difficult ice-pitches, each 50 feet in length, from which we saw our steps immediately under pitch one. We reached the crest of the Crowberry Ridge — a razor-edge of transparent ice — at 3 p.m.

FROM THE BALLAD OF BILL MURRAY   by Tom Patey
Vol.XXIX (1970)

In that tournament on Ice, Death or Glory was the price
For those Knights in shining armour long ago —
You must forage for yourself on that ghastly Garrick's Shelf
With every handhold buried in the snow.

There was green ice in the chimneys and black ice at the crux
And not a single piton or a screw —
Murray did his Devil's Dance on each microscopic stance
Recording his impressions of the view.

THE ZERO GULLY AFFAIR
Vol. XXVI (1957)   by Tom Patey

At the time when this ascent took place crampons had generally been adopted for winter climbing in Scotland. The 'Aberdeen School' had continued to favour tricouni nailed boots, well suited to the Lochnagar winter buttresses. They regarded crampons as cheating and in turn were looked on as being hopelessly behind the times. As usual, the rivalry was friendly but spirited.

"Still plenty of time to get up before dark," observed Graham Nicol. It was two o'clock on a February afternoon, and he was gazing wistfully at the 1,000 feet of vertical ice which constitutes Point Five Gully on Ben Nevis.

On such occasions there is nothing for it but to humour my fellow Aberdonian's enthusiasm. These brain storms only occur periodically. A well-thumbed copy of Anderl Heckmeir's "Derniers Problemes des Alpes" is ever on his bedside table, and on the night before a hard climb he is accustomed to search for inspiration in selected readings from the text.

An hour later the argument was renewed. I had climbed the first 100 feet of 70 degree snow-ice and been swamped by several powder-snow avalanches before taking advantage of a sheltering bulge of green ice to insert a peg and rope down. As a consolation I diverted him round the foot of Observatory Ridge for a brief inspection of Zero Gully, also unclimbed, vertical, and bulging with overhanging ice. It formed the perfect counterpart to Point Five.

Between them these two gullies had aroused more interest among post-war climbers on both sides of the Border than any other ice climb. Zero had always seemed the more likely of the two to go, if only because Point Five was so seldom in climbable condition. A mere sprinkling of fresh powder in the upper couloir of Point Five would fill the vertical lower cleft with choking clouds of spindrift — the latter a virtually uninterrupted ice-pitch of 500 feet. We had visited Ben Nevis six times in recent winters with intentions on Point Five but had not succeeded in leaving the ground. Always there was the threat of avalanche. The only serious attempt had been made by a Rock and Ice party, and this had ended in a spectacular exodus from the gully when the leading pair were held at full stretch by the last man on the rope.

Zero Gully, on the other hand, had survived several attempts, although the upper 500 feet had often been climbed by parties engaged on the winter ascent of Observatory Ridge. The real problem is the direct ascent of the lower icefall, and on the most successful attempt by Bell and Allan in 1936 this had been avoided by an excursion towards Slav Route on the left. A further tour de force by an O.U.M.C. party in 1950 ended in disaster. They were near the top of the difficult section when the leader fell, ripping out several ice-pitons and dislodging the second. By a miracle they both survived the 400-foot fall.

Subsequently Zero Gully became linked with the name of Hamish McInnes, of whom more anon. The climb had now withstood several McInnes blitzkriegs: numerous ice-pitons and an ice-axe marked the site of the battle. Perhaps inspired by Hamish, the Creag Dhu entered the lists in 1956 with summer ascents of both Zero and Point Five Gullies. They found neither gully a satisfactory summer climb. There was far too much unreliable rock, but no one doubted that in winter conditions they would provide ice routes of unique length and difficulty.

"Sans competition pas de sport" wrote Alain de Chatellus. Perhaps that explains why no less than a dozen climbers from Aberdeen and Glasgow were due to congregate at the Clark Hut that week-end in quest of Zero and Point Five Gullies. There had been a mutual agreement among all the interested parties. Nicol and I had inadvertently broken faith by arriving one day in advance, thanks to an impromptu lift in a cement lorry. We had therefore to await the main body with patience despite all Nicol's protestations. His argument that the premature bagging of Point Five would leave us all free to concentrate on Zero was hardly adequate.

Len Lovat was the first on the scene next morning - quite out of breath after a furious chase up the Allt a' Mhuilinn. We had written him to say we might be a day late, but his jubilation had turned to dismay on finding fresh tracks in the snow. There followed at a more leisurely pace a succession of the Glasgow "faithful" — Malcolm Slesser, Donald Bennett, Douglas Scott and Norman Tennent.

The cast was complete, but the stage was not yet set. Ben Nevis is notoriously temperamental on important occasions, and a strong south-west wind was already whipping the spindrift off the Observatory and drenching the north-east face in dense white clouds. A gully climb was out of the question — today at any rate. Len joined forces with Nicol and myself, while the other four set off towards North-East Buttress. We watched them proceed smoothly up Slingsby's Chimney to the First Platform, and then transferred our attention to the left-hand flank of the Buttress which fronts Corrie Leis. Bill Murray had drawn our attention some time before to the possibilities of this fine 1,000-foot face. Although a rock climber's midden in summer, like many similar faces it seemed to offer glorious winter climbing — a miniature Scottish Brenva, in fact. We picked the easiest route, a central line up a long snow couloir. This ended about 600 feet up, below some overhanging ice, where a long traverse rightwards involving a 120-foot lead-out provided the highlight of the climb. All the party were in good fettle, and we reached the top in three hours from the corrie floor. The Cresta Climb seemed to be an apt name for the new route, in view of the Alpine nature of its environment. During the descent we observed that another and more exacting line existed between our couloir and the edge of the North-East Buttress. It could provide one of the longest ice routes in Britain.

Back in the hut we had visitors — two climbers, whose characteristic patois, coupled with a distinct air of authority, stamped them as members of the Creag Dhu Club. They were, in fact, Johnny Cunningham and Mick Noon. They mentioned casually that they expected to climb Zero Gully on the morrow, without apparently noticing the disquieting effect this had on the rest of the company.

We remarked upon the absence of Hamish McInnes. "He doesnae ken we're here, and furthermore we're no tellin' him," said Cunningham. However, he had apparently underestimated Hamish. Scarcely were the words out of his mouth when the door crashed open and the self-appointed guardian of Zero Gully stood before us in a state of wild disorder.

The news of our arrival had reached him at Steall Hut, where he was acting as instructor on a Mountaineering Association course. He had set off immediately across the Carn Mor Dearg Arete, delaying not even to collect provisions for the trip. (Hamish makes a habit of travelling "light.")

It was impossible to remain indifferent towards such a man: his appearance alone invited controversy. A great rent extending the whole length of one trouser leg had been repaired unsuccessfully with string. In his hand was the famous all-steel hammer-pick, named affectionately by the club "The Message".

Cunningham challenged him gruffly, "Just where do you think you're goin'?"

"Zero Gully, of course."

"Solo?"

"I suppose I might allow you two along as well."

"That's very generous considerin' we're goin' anyway."

So the composition of the party was settled to the chagrin of the rest of the company, who had not allowed for such formidable competition. We reflected sulkily that there was always Point Five.

Around midnight some conscientious person drew attention to the fact that the North-East Buttress party were "rather late back." With some grumbling a search party was organised, but before we could leave the four absentees staggered in, mumbling excuses about "Two feet of ice on the Man Trap." It was easy to commiserate with them on their misfortune, as they would now be unable to rise from their beds before noon, certainly too late for serious climbing.

Nicol and I were up at the crack of dawn, but only in time to witness the departure of the Creag Dhu who had already breakfasted. "It's a great day for avalanches," Hamish declared enthusiastically as he opened the door to a full-scale Ben Nevis blizzard.

At other times I would have returned to sleep with an easy conscience, but Graham Nicol was bursting with impatience and would brook no delay. The distant roar of avalanches was a sufficient contra-indication to an attempt on Point Five, and we left without any fixed intentions. A momentary clearing in the mist revealed our rivals at the foot of Zero Gully, where a minor altercation seemed to be in progress. The tall figure of Hamish kept pointing insistently skywards.

I don't know why we finally selected Comb Gully. It would seem in retrospect to have been a most inappropriate choice. Not only did it enjoy a considerable reputation for difficulty, but we had just witnessed a fair-sized powder avalanche issue from the gully. However, Graham inclined to the view that all the unstable snow must now be swept clear, and we scuttled up the first three pitches with great abandon. Despite the blizzard and a steady stream of spindrift we could not complain about the quality of the snow. It was ideally suited to step cutting, with a fine hard crust as a legacy of the recent avalanche.

Along came the crux, a 30-foot vertical ice-pitch, above which the angle appeared to relent. It was not a pitch to linger over, as the streaming drift found its way into our windproofs, rapidly numbing wrists and fingers. I crouched for a minute's respite in the lee of the top overhang and knocked in two ice-pitons for security. The next few feet were the worst. At this point the falling spindrift met a violent upblast of wind going straight up the gully, and the result was a regular maelstrom. Eyes crusted over and holds refilled as fast as they were cut. I fought for breath, almost choking with the snow going into my mouth. There was little finesse in the climbing, and I was extremely thankful to get out of the place without literally suffocating. Above this there were no further difficulties as the cornice had come away in the avalanche, and we reached the top in little over an hour after starting the climb.

We cut our way down North Gully of Creag Coire na Ciste, feeling very pleased with ourselves at disposing of Comb Gully in such a short time, and returned to the hut in time for a second breakfast. We were soon followed by the Creag Dhu who had turned back with reluctance in the face of several avalanches. The weather had now deteriorated further, so Cunningham and Noon decided to return to Glasgow on the motor bike that evening. Before he left Johnny asked us about our plans for tomorrow. We had been offered a lift back to Banff by Norman Tennent and it seemed too good an opportunity to miss. "But what about Point Five?"

"It'll wait," I replied.

"It'll no wait for ever," he countered with a grin.

"Neither will Zero, come to that," rejoined Nicol.

Hamish suddenly came to life. "Are you guys interested in Zero tomorrow?"

Fate was obviously taking a hand, and I recalled that the best climbs usually arrive unexpectedly. Leaving Aberdeen that week-end we had spoken little about Zero Gully; our hopes were all for Point Five. I thought for a moment of Norman's cosy van and yielded. "O.K. It's on." In vain did Johnny remonstrate with Hamish to keep it in the club. Hamish was unyielding. It was his climb, he pointed out; and it was his gear that was on it. Indeed, few men would dispute his ownership. He had earned it, if only by reason of a recent solo winter ascent of Observatory Ridge, undertaken merely to inspect Zero Gully! We parted with good wishes on both sides, but it was satisfying to deduce from the heat of the argument that the climb must be in excellent condition. The other five were remaining an extra day, and Len Lovat was undecided whether to join us; but the prospect of a possible benightment and the absolute necessity of returning to Glasgow for the following afternoon tempered his enthusiasm.

Next morning we rose at 6 a.m. to find a clear sky and hard frost. Over breakfast Hamish disposed of the climb as if conducting a business transaction. "You can lead the first four hundred feet and above that it's just a steady slog. I've led it once, so I'm satisfied. It took six and a half hours," he added as an afterthought.

"Then why didn't you get up?" I inquired.

"There was a wee avalanche."

Probably quite a large one, I thought, if they had decided to retreat so high up.

We ploughed up to the foot of the cliffs through 3 feet of new snow. Our luck was in. The recent powder had failed to adhere to the almost vertical snow-ice of the gully and conditions were ideal. It was Zero hour.

Whoever christened it a gully was an optimist. For 400 feet it is no more than a vertical corner bulging with overhangs, but Hamish's eye of faith could detect a route. The first pitch was obvious. A shallow trough ran up the centre of the 85-degree wall for 100 feet to peter out below a fair-sized overhang. By cutting handholds on the side wall of the trough it would be possible to climb in balance despite the extreme angle. A line of steps terminated abruptly at 20 feet. I looked at Hamish inquiringly.

"That's where Long John got hit on the head with some ice," he answered. "It's a pity because he was going fine."

My fears that I might emulate Cunningham were unfounded. For once Ben Nevis was tolerant of Hamish's presence and no debris fell. It was a model ice-pitch and the security astonishingly good despite the exposure. I straddled the side walls of the trough, unable to resist a morbid satisfaction in noting that the rope hung absolutely free from my waist to the two at the bottom. They seemed strangely remote and not very interested in my progress, though Hamish would occasionally stir himself to shout "Straight on up" whenever I stopped for a rest.

I halted below the overhang with 120 feet of rope run out and still no stance worthy of attention. "There's a bit of nylon cord sticking out of the snow here," I yelled.

Hamish was delighted. "It's attached to Hope's ice-axe," he roared. "That's your first belay."

I ventured to say that it was "quite steep up here." "Don't worry about that. You've done the worst bit and it's just a doddle now."

Leaning backwards on the frozen cord to inspect the overhang I came to the conclusion that Hamish was either a superlatively good climber or a fanatic. Watching him climb neatly up the first pitch I decided that he was probably a bit of both. Nicol, not to be outdone, came up with equal nonchalance, but spoiled it all by dropping his axe at the top. It plummeted down without striking the face and impaled itself in the snow at the bottom. Fortunately for him we now had a spare axe. This had been left by Hamish and Bob Hope when they ran out of ice-pitons during the disastrous retreat of the previous month. On that occasion Hamish had made the dramatic entry in the hut log book - "This climb is not possible in one day."

I started on the overhang with some misgivings, convinced that the best route lay to the right, hard in by the corner; but Hamish assured me that he had tried this himself and the overhang was the only way through. Fortunately the ice was deep enough to take pitons, and for 20 feet I was very glad of their assistance. The technique is to take tension through an ice-piton placed as high as possible above the climber until the next few handholds have been cut. Then, hanging on with one hand, a higher piton is inserted and the one below removed for further use. This is all very delicate work, as any outward pull on the piton will have the maximum result. The other two inclined that I would profit from a couple of etriers, but I assured them without any real conviction that I was quite happy.

Half an hour later I crouched in another miserably cramped stance above the overhang. I couldn't find Hamish's ice-piton which was buried somewhere in the vicinity, but had hammered an ice-axe well in, using the "Message" for the purpose. Its owner now had nothing to assist his progress. He dispenses with an axe on ice climbs and only uses the hammer-pick. At last a shout came from below. "Keep the rope tight and I'll come up on the Prusiks."* At another time I would have enjoyed the joke, but I was beginning to realise the range of this man's enthusiasm.

"Stop!" I roared, as he prepared to launch out into space. There followed a short pause and the rope started hesitantly to come in.

Hamish appeared to be rather disgruntled. He claimed we had lost a full three minutes. Personally, I couldn't see the importance of this as we had already put 300 feet behind us in one and a half hours, and this section had taken four hours on the earlier attempt.

Now the route went rightwards towards the corner, at the point where it bends out of view as seen from the foot of the gully. The traverse led along a narrow strip of high-angled snow between two overhangs, with some quite superb exposure. For the first time we could progress without the constant support of a handhold or ice-piton.

At the end of the traverse I stepped on to an easy snow slope running back at 50 degrees into the face. This was the limit of the McInnes-Hope tentative. It was difficult to conceive how they had considered themselves above all difficulties, even allowing for the prevailing snow-storm and limited visibility. For the next 80 feet the route had some of the characteristics of a gully climb, hemmed in by smooth ice walls. Then a gigantic ice-pitch soared up vertically for 100 feet seeming to seal off all access to the upper gully.

From round the corner came the familiar shout, "He's up - no bother at all now."

I smiled sardonically. This joker must be held to his promise. "Hamish, it's your lead — there's still a wee pitch left."

Nicol and I belayed at the foot of the wall to two ice-axes and three ice-pitons. On the

---

* Prusik Knot technique for climbing up a fixed rope, held from above, used in Alps for rescue from crevasse, etc.

right an easy snow shelf led on to Observatory Ridge, but since any avoidance of the direct line would amount to sacrilege, nobody dared draw attention to it. In went the first ice-piton, and with a violent heave Hamish got a crampon level with where his nose had been. The only indication of his passage was a large bucket hold every 6 feet. The urgency of his climbing indicated that this pitch was to be a vindication of the use of crampons for the benefit of the tricouni-favouring Aberdonians. However, we were satisfed to observe that his initial impetuosity soon waned, and presently the rope came to a dead stop. All that was now visible of Hamish was the soles of his boots outlined against the sky — an apparent contradiction of the laws of gravity, until you relised that his weight was supported by the angled spikes on the front of his crampons.

"Let's sing him a song to cheer him up," suggested Nicol. He broke into the traditional New Orleans funeral march, "Oh, didn't he ramble?" I joined in on the chorus, which ends triumphantly with the line, "Yes, he rambled till the Butchers cut him down."

Hamish, whose preference is for chamber music, was rather nettled. "There's a lot of loose stuff up here and some of it's going to come down."

Nicol failed to heed the warning and jerked his head back in time to catch the full force of the avalanche. When the debris cleared he was bleeding from a cut above the eyebrow, but otherwise intact as his spirited rejoinder demonstrated.

More and more snow came down as the minutes ticked past. Hamish was now out of sight, and we wondered if he was tunnelling the overhang. Every now and then we heard a gasp, "Thank God for a piton," but that was all. Two hours elapsed before the signal came to follow on.

I won't attempt to estimate the diffculty of the pitch, as I did most of it on a tight rope, and the steps seemed designed for a yeti. Suffice to say that it was quite up to anything else on the climb, which indeed had seldom varied below Very Severe. Hamish was satisfied with his "shift" and prepared now to rest on his laurels. "It's the interesting stuff that gets me, I'm afriad. I'm not much of a hand at the step bashing," he said, indicating the rest of the gully with a lordly gesture.

It was true. We had at last penetrated the forest of ice overhangs, and the way was clear to the top cornice. All the pent-up energy of the last two hours exploded in a frenzy of activity. We moved together, the pace of the party (contrary to the textbook) dictated by the fastest member. Nicol was the most exhausted; he carried the pitons. The slope eased off all the time, and the few minor pitches passed almost unnoticed. Fifty minutes later and five hours from the start of the climb we emerged into the warm sunlight of the summit plateau.

Nicol's yell of ecstasy was intercepted by Tennent and Slesser, who were completing the second ascent of the Cresta Climb. They shouted their congratulations, and the knowledge that a lift home was still in the offing completed our jubilation. We wished Len Lovat had been with us, but he too had enjoyed an excellent first winter ascent of No.3 Gully Buttress in company with Donald Bennet. It was one of those rare days on Ben

Nevis. Everyone satisfied, perfect climbing conditions and an unlimited vista as far as Sutherland and the Wetern Isles.

"A great climb!" Hamish declared, "Up to Raven's Gully standard."

"In fact, it might even hold its own on Lochnagar," added Graham with patriotic fervour. They were still arguing as we reached the hut.

....

The sequel to that eventful week-end merits a full article.

How Cunningham and Noon, thirsting for revenge, attacked Point Five Gully in appalling thaw conditions and almost carried the day against all odds till the collapse of 20 feet of waterlogged ice enforced retreat. How Hamish returned alone to the Ben, dragging 600 feet of Alpine line which he attached to an ice-axe at the top and descended the gully till the rope gave out, dangling like a yo-yo over the abyss. His climb back to the top, unaided by the rope, left much less virgin snow for future pioneers.

But these are stories that will be better told by Hamish or John Cunningham when they finally succeed in their campaign, as I have little doubt they will.

> In fact Point Five Gully was to yield to siege tactics applied over five days by a party led by Ian Clough. Nowadays, with the application of modern 'pick and stick' ice climbing techniques it has become something of a trade route.

TOBOGGANING ON BEN NEVIS

LOCHNAGAR
Vol. XXVII (1960)   by Tom Weir

A March night in Glen Muick. Snow sparkling in the headlights, and the green eyes of hundreds of hungry deer luminous in the woods. 'How far would we be able to get?' Norman Tennent, Graham Nicol and I wondered as we bumped through the drifts, giving thanks to the unknown vehicle that had broken a trail up the glen. We were heading for Lochnagar, with sleeping-bags and food for two days, hoping to get to the bothy at the end of Loch Muick. No hope of getting there when the tracks stopped and we saw before us nothing but snowdrifted mountainside, impassable to anything but a 'weasel.' We found that the vehicle tracks turned up to a house, and there we were invited to stay in the adjacent barn for the night, so we were cosy despite the unseasonable temperature of 20 degrees of frost which sent us into our sleeping-bags the moment we had tossed down our scrambled eggs.

One of the advantages of going to bed with all your clothes on is that it makes it easier to get up in the morning, and Nicol was determined we would not sleep in by asking me the time at 5.45 a.m. We rose at 6 and were away by 7.45, into a dull morning of lowering mists and a soot-and-whitewash landscape, enlivened by the crowing of grouse and the chuckling music of a water ouzel singing its heart out from the stones of a black burn in the snow. It cheered us up as we took turns at breaking a trail, sinking up to the calf at each step and going over the knees in the deeper drifts.

We were wishing we had brought skis, to slide easily over this tiring surface, but as events were to turn out in the hard fight for that summit we could not have used them in the darkness of the desent. With three of us breaking the trail the work was not too exhausting, and as always the snow became firmer as we climbed, though it was not until we were nearing the col beneath the Meikle Pap that it would bear our weight. With lightness in our step we looked over the narrow barrier to the frozen loch and the icy rampart of cliffs we had come to climb.

The Aberdeen climbers sing a song which compares Lochnagar to the Himalayan giants. It goes something like:

> Gasherbrum, Masherbrum, Distighil Sar,
> They're very good training for Dark Lochnagar.

Never having done a winter climb on these cliffs which they regard as the finest in Scotland, superior even to Nevis, it was a thrill for me to see the cirque in its most Alpine form, buttresses submerged in frost crystals and couloirs showing the bottle-green of ice; the huge finger of the Black Spout Pinnacle looming dimly through a scarf of mist twining its jagged top. The walk to the corrie had taken us twice the normal time, so the reward was great when suddenly the sun burst through the lowering cloud, sparkling on summit cornices and giving texture to everything, while across the Dee peaks appeared one by one until the huge range of the Cairngorms floated through a curious haze which gave a violet light to the snow.

Now we asked Nicol what he thought we should climb, with the emphasis on 'nothing too hard.' Nicol is a disciple of Patey. With Tom he made climbing history doing Zero Gully of Nevis in winter, following it up with Sticil Face on the Shelter Stone Crag on Christmas Eve and then climbing Polyphemus Gully on Lochnagar during February of 1958, a route much coveted by tigers of Aberdeen for it had been done only twice before.

"I'm just wondering what Patey would take you up if he was here," said Nicol. "The mountain is in terrific condition and you don't want to waste it by doing anything too easy." It was at this point I was foolish enough to ask him if there was any route he had not done, so that we could all have something new. "Yes, Parallel Gully A," he said. "There it is!" And following his finger I saw the narrow thread of a shallow scoop winding out of sight between the iced rocks to appear again as the merest channel in the very steep summit crags.

"Looks hard to me," I said.

"And to me!" exclaimed Tennent.

"Now, Graham, I don't want to spend all day in a gully when the sun is shing on the tops, so let's hear your estimate of how long it's going to take." "No more than three hours," answered Nicol, so positively that the two old-timers of the party felt slightly ashamed as we followed the younger generation to the foot of the gully.

I wore crampons on a Scottish climb for the first time in my life that day. Nicol advised it and was himself equipped with twelve-pointers. Only Tennent wore tricounis. Carrying 240 feet of rope, two ice-axes, a piton hammer and a jangle of rock and ice pegs, the leader advanced to what he called 'the easy lower rocks.' We said they didn't look easy to us, but Nicol was confident in his opinion even when it took him half an hour to advance 20 feet, and by the time another hour was past we were beginning to have misgivings about this 3-hour climb for he had not yet reached a belay.

There were diversions, however, in the squeals and clockwork creakings of ptarmigan, suddenly silenced when an eagle swung into view over the cliffs and sailed round, lifting one broad wing, then the other, as it rocked on the updraught, wheeling in tight spirals. Not until five minutes after it disappeared did the ptarmigan start up again, like the switching on of a machine, and we could see them fly over the loch like white doves.

Then came another sound, the ring of the piton hammer, as Nicol battered a peg into a crack, and with numb hands I started up a horrible pitch of powder snow lying on a slippery mixture of verglas and frozen turf. The leader had fought for every inch of the way up this abominably dangerous 100 feet, the only positive holds being little notches cut in the turf; otherwise it was pressure holds on the glazed rock, with crampons scraping.

We were not yet in the gully, but separated from it by a bulge of mountain wall over which we had to edge a delicate way by cutting hand and footholds round an awkward corner. The first sight of the gully came here, and it was a shock, rising as a cascade of ice stretching as far as the eye could see. Luckily the ice was so deep we could hammer in an iron spike a foot long and so provide anchorage for the next pitch.

Nicol wasted not a moment in getting hammering with his hand-axe, and in 35 minutes had climbed 110 feet, cutting the absolute minimum of hand and footholds and using the points of his crampons to bridge the gaps. It was the ideal place for claws, but I hammered out intermediate steps on the way up for the man who was not wearing them. Above our heads Nicol was flimsily anchored to another ice-peg and, while I brought up Tennent, he raced ahead on the only easy ground we were to meet that day, about 200 feet of it.

Now we were faced with another ice-wall, steeper than anything we had met so far and compressed between two slabs of granite sheeted in ice and powder snow. Just where we would go at the top of this ice-wall we could not imagine, but Nicol was not going to put off time thinking. Balanced on his lobster points he was making do with the very minimum needed to keep balance when a foot slipped and for a moment his body hung uncertainly. Somehow he arrested the slip, looking down at us with a cheery grin, and then after some difficult moves he was hard against the barrier rocks and hammering in a belay.

Our situation was now rather desperate. The time was 5.30 p.m. It would be dark in less than 2 hours, and looming ahead of us was the hardest climbing of the day, 200 feet of it with no possibility of escape. The normal route was out of the question, on exposed ice-glazed rocks overlaid with powder snow. I favoured an attempt on the direct line to the summit, beginning on an ice-chimney. Nicol favoured that line also, and Tennent was in no position to see it. In 1 hour Nicol had climbed only 30 feet; with little perceptible movement in the next half-hour, as the clouds came down to envelope us.

Feet and hands senseless with cold in a misty world, there was nothing I could do except advise the leader to retreat if it looked hopeless above. The reply 'To retreat is to die!' not delivered as a joke, was enough to convince me that a life and death struggle was going up there, but a cheery voice shouting "Don't worry, a few hard moves and I think I'm up," was reassuring. Next moment an axe and a shower of ice-blocks came shooting over my head, not followed by Nicol as I half-expected, body braced to withstand the jerk of a 70-foot fall.

A short silence and I heard the scrape of his second ice-axe. Tennent, a rope-length below, was stamping his feet and waving his arms to restore circulation, but on my minute ledge cut in the ice I could do no more than just stand and watch the rope snaking out inch by inch. It was nearly all out when I heard that ringing music of the hammer which meant some respite from a desperate lead sustained heroically.

Then I brought up Tennent, clipped him into my piton and took off myself on what I believe to be the hardest pitch in my experience, made harder by fingers and toes without feeling. The difficulty was the slippery nature of the ice-glazed granite and the smallness of the holds for climbing rocks at such a high angle. For Nicol, who had to uncover such holds as were now available, it must have been a lonely fight, and I saw why there had been such a long pause at 30 feet, at an overhang demanding a pull-up on a rock knobble and a delicate squeeze with the left foot to jam it sufficiently long to transfer the right hand to a higher and better hold.

Very Severe as that move was, there was still another bulge which at first sight seemed impossible because it had a horrible projection forcing the body outward with little to support it in space. The technique was to by-pass this bulge by climbing parallel to it, then so twisting the body that a foot could be placed on top of the boss. Then with the body in precarious balance over a 70-foot drop you had to traverse in a sidling motion to get your hand on a clean edge of rock that gave a solid pull-up to another overhang.

This last move was an ugly one, with an icy roof overhead and the blessed haven of a safe snow slope leftward, only 2 feet away, but to reach it meant another awkward edging round a vertical corner where the proverbial well-directed push with a straw would have sent you plunging into space. Thirty feet above me I found Nicol anchored to a pair of pegs driven into shallow cracks in the rocks, a belay which was to prove a life-saver in the next half-hour.

"We are as good as up," he said. "You bring Norman and I'll go on as hard as I can to get this over before it becomes really dark." And as he spoke, as if in augury of success, the enveloping clouds swirled open, revealing the oval of the frozen loch against the dark glen out of which I had been hearing the bubbling of the blackcock for the last hour, a strange link with the outside world. Then the hostile mists closed again, and a voice floated up faintly, asking how we were getting on.

How are we? Fine, as far as I could tell by the showers of ice-chips flying past my head and the rope going straight into space. I told Tennent to begin climbing, and he must have been numb with waiting. Anchored to the two ice-pegs and with a good stance hacked from the snow, I felt well placed to hold a slip, but so fiercely did the rope jerk when Tennent did come off that I was torn from my stance and had to take his weight hanging from the pegs. I heard him shout for a pull, and I gave him all I could, praying that the pegs would not come out or all three of us would be toppling down that face. All was well, he had found his feet again and performed with marvellous speed on a tight rope, which was more important than anything else at this moment. The lack of crampons was an impossible handicap on this pitch, and his performance was all the more amazing.

The final pitch up 100 feet of untrustworthy snow could have spelt disaster to a man less experienced than Nicol, with a surface just hard enough to take your weight without cutting through to the ice beneath. A novice would probably have trusted it and slid to his death, but he, a veteran at 22, had cut deeply through to the ice at every step, right up to the curling cornice where he stood, a dim shape in the night, as I joined him. Very soon the flicker of Tennent's head-torch emerged from the jaws of the gully and we were united for the first time in 9 hours. It was nearly 8 o'clock, and as we foregathered in the bitter cold and mist to munch chocolate our feeling was one of joyous deliverance from the Pit itself. Now we would be able to move frozen limbs, and even if we had to take care not to go over the north-eastern cliffs, we each had a torch. Graham knew the mountain intimately, and off we went, contouring to find the easy slope that leads to the Meikle Pap.

We had hoped the snow would bear our weight, but it did not. Our feet broke through as in the morning, but our tired labours had the merit of thoroughly warming us up and making us thirsty for the tea which tasted like nectar 3 hours later. It would have been nice to crawl into our sleeping-bags then, but Tennent had to be home that night, and so we faced the long drive to Aberdeen and on for another 40 miles to Gardenstown in Banffshire, reached at half-past three.

It was an exciting drive with an incipient blizzard blowing as we contoured the narrow roads that lead down to the sea from Turriff. Through the flying snow we were aware of a strange paleness like moonlight — hard to understand unless it was mist. When suddenly the snow ceased, Tennent stopped the car exclaiming "The Northern Lights!" — And there, in front of us, streaming over the whole Moray Firth were pinkish searchlights and green curtains making day of the night, and we were not too tired to appreciate it. But bed was a pretty good place to crawl into.

Marvellous to be alive next morning in the warm sunshine, listening to the hedge-sparrows and rock pipits singing as I took my cameras high above the village to try to capture the turquoise blue of the sea and the snow headlands shining above the fishing village tucked into the red cliff. Everything seemed to have a new and unexpected beauty, but I expect the rebirth was in myself, the enjoyment of relaxation and the freshness of spring after the death struggle of yesterday.

This was the first winter ascent of the Right Fork of Parallel Gully A.

LOCHNAGAR CLIFF

THE ORION FACE
Vol. XXVII (1961)

by James R Marshall

Sheets of flame reveal partner Wheech (otherwise Robin Smith) doing a dervish dance round the hut's mangled old stove; his fat-fingered fumble provides an amusing ten minutes of cosy reflection before the soothing hiss and familiar gloom swallow the hut. But thoughts of prolonging the horizontal are rudely thrust aside as his hacked and filthy visage, that could frighten lesser men, peers over the bunk to pronounce the day 'the mostest fantabulous' of the week.

An hour later, bellies filled with rich greasy omelettes and all goodies that happened within reach, we are toiling towards the tall white face of Orion, intent on making a superb Diretissima by the great ice fall which pours from the 'Basin' to the floor of Zero Gully.

By the time we have staggered to the base of the wall, the route is dissected into his and mine sections; so Wheech leads off, up a pleasantly fat ice slope, whilst I sort out the many slings, hammers and karabiners from the bag.

At 50 feet Wheech's tour had misled him on to a thinly iced slab, where it was obvious he would either waken up or roll back down to the hut; his bow-legged bumbling at the foot of this great ice wall seemed as out of place as a can-can in the Swan Lake; however, by performing an exciting traverse of crampon scarts to reach thick ice, the rapid progress is resumed and a large ledge reached 150 feet higher; joining Wheech after being truly stung by his mauvais pas, we searched for a peggable crack with delayed success. The situation was magnificent : above us a great groove, rich with ice, swirled into obscurity; rightwards, Zero Gully took on the air of an escape route, whilst the great iced slabs to the left promised future 'joyous days upon the mountainside.'

Fully whooped up and anxious to reach passage to the wall which we both felt was somewhere about 100 feet above, I climbed over Wheech into the groove and hacked and whooped the way up over grand bulges, howking immense jug-handles in the ice; an ice column runner gave joy at 90 feet, then a little higher the angle eased, and a small hole under a rock roof 40 feet above promised security. Gaining this hole, I hacked away a curtain of icicles and squeezed in like a frightened ostrich, to manufacture a belay on an inverted channel piton in the rock roof; this didn't instil a sense of security so with an incredibly awkward manoeuvre the axe was driven into the floor and a cowardly sprauchle backwards performed to stand secured by slings above the void. Feeling brave once more I took the rope as Wheech came on, babbling back and forth about character, quality and senility.

We were now at the question point of the route; to the right, the difficulties were obvious and in sight, whilst above nothing could be seen but a steep icy rib and a skyline begging the question; naturally the unknown appealed, so the bold climbing machine hacked away up and round the rib out of sight, but unhappily not of sound. A few minutes after he moved from sight, a horrible flow of oaths seared down the sterile slopes; I thought he was in a cul-de-sac, but no, he had climbed into easy ground, with the way to the Basin clear, and the share of labour too small for a step-hacker of Wheech's calibre. With an added sense of satisfaction, I watched the rope snake out at an increasing pace and soon the ostrich act was repeated, as I removed our comforting anchorage. The climbing above was delightful and somewhat reminiscent of the slabs of the Crowberry Gully junction, but continuing for greater lengths.

A short wall above Wheech led on to a long snow rake, where a quick cramponing crawl brought us to the snowfield of the Basin. From a rock belay on the right edge of the depression, Wheech cut up an ice slope for 100 feet, then made an icy 50-foot traverse rightwards to belay at the foot of the Second Slab Rib of the Long Climb. Standing at the belay in the Basin I couldn't help recalling the last visit, when Patey and I had made the girdle traverse of Ben Nevis; there had still been traces of the Smith-Holt rope leading out by the 'V' Traverse to the North East Buttress, from their ascent of the Long Climb one month earlier which unfortunately, owing to lack of time, stopped short at the Basin. It was this sense of the unfinished that was partly responsible for our very presence on the face at the moment. However, Wheech was finished with the work above and I hastened to join him, where I was rather disappointed to find the rib above too thinly iced for comfort. An exploratory traverse 10 feet round the corner disclosed a well-iced wall, shining green in the evening light and perched over the now impressive drop of the wall beneath: 130 feet higher the hunt for peg cracks failed in the gathering gloom of night and a belay in powder snow brought the sharp edges of frost and fear into the struggle: Wheech came and went, swopping wet gloves for dry, trending left and up by shallow grooves, over treacherously difficult breaking snow and verglassed rocks; night was fully launched when the rope ran out, but the moon stayed sly behind a blanket of cloud. Following up was like walking on eggs, the dark pit beneath our heels sufficient warning to take care; a short step of ice above Wheech led on to the high snow slopes which form beneath the terminal towers of the Orion Face. Here the expected respite failed to materialise; knee deep and floury, they whispered evil thoughts, threatening to slide us into the black void and extinguish the winking lights of the C.I.C. Hut. Floundering up this snow, doubts plagued the mind; our original intention to spiral up rightwards round the towers lost its appeal on the face of such threat; perhaps a move left would bring us on to the crest of North East Buttress? But again the snow. Great shadowy forms confused the issue, so we persisted with the straight-up as being mentally the least trying.

A yell from above lit the night; Wheech had found a rock belay. A jumble of talk awakened vague morning memories of the face, then by right of sequence I deprived partner Wheech of his dry gloves, leaving him to fight the cold war whilst I tackled the obscurity above. A scrabble up a cone of snow above the belay led to a well-iced groove; it was necessary to feel the angle ahead with the hands, as up here everything was whitened by fog crystals and in the misty gloom distance was incalculable. Up above there appeared to be an immense cornice; the thoughts of an enforced bivouac beneath the icy beak passed absently through the mind as I chopped away at the ice. About 40 feet up, the groove steepened to a bulge; finding the holds with the cramponed feet was extremely awkward at times, and often moves were made hanging from the handholds whilst the crampons scarted about in search of the 'buckets' cut below. Above, the bulge loomed more ominous, so a trouser-filling traverse was made on to the right wall, along a short ledge; then a frightening move, leaning out on an undercut ice hold, to cut holds round a rib on to the slab wall of a parallel groove. The ice here was only about an inch thick and moving into the groove was very difficult; the cat crawl up the thin ice remains imprinted in the memory, for at this 'moment of truth' strains of an awful dirge came up from the Blackfoot 90 feet below, "Ah kin hear the hammer ringin' on somebody's coffin...' Other ditties may have followed, but that particular one registered and stimulated progress across the slab to a comforting snow-filled groove, where the calf muscles could recover.

At last things were beginning to take shape; a large cornice at my level closed the top of the first groove, and above me was a steep wall, thick with ice. This looked the way and, having no desire to freeze, a short traverse was made up the thinly iced slab to an accommodating ledge; then the great hacking resumed. Strain on the back of the legs was becoming very trying, and I had to cut a deep step occasionally to stand on to relieve the calf muscles. I began to worry about the length of rope, feeling much more than 140 had passed; the thought of having to continue without a belay gave further chill to the night; then suddenly there was no more ice to cut, and in front a gentle slope catching the cold filtered moonlight shone in a heart-warming scene. Whoops of delight went down to thaw out Wheech, then up a couple of feet to discover the rope was out, a retreating belay from the edge as Wheech came up the snow cone enabled me to take an axe belay 10 feet back. It was grand to be able to sit down and relax. A whooping session began as Wheech came up in a series of frozen jumps, purring about quality and character. "What a climb!" was our chorus, then his amorphous shape appeared over the edge, covered in snow, ironmongery clanking, like some armoured beast from the underworld. Gathering up the rope, we rushed up to the plateau, to arrive at the point where the North East Buttress branches from the summit plateau. Then stowing heaps of rope, slings and snow into the frozen sack we pushed off across the misty plateau making for the hut, heat and the big sweet brew, occasionally stopping to howl into the night what a 'mostest fantabulous' climb we'd had.

THE FIRST WINTER TRAVERSE
OF THE CUILLIN RIDGE
Vol. XXVIII (1965)   by Tom Patey

It was a frosty moonlit night in February this year, and snow lay deep on the hills around the head of Loch Broom. I had just finished my evening's work when the phone rang. Anticipating a late-night visit, I lifted the receiver with weary resignation.

'Hello there! Is that you, Tom?' said a familiar voice. 'I was thinking of pushing over to Skye tonight for a look at the Ridge. Naturally I thought you might like to come along.'

The enthusiasms crackling along the line soon left no doubt as to the voice. Who else but Hamish MacInnes would phone at this hour with such a preposterous suggestion?

'It's great to hear from you again, Hamish,' I replied cautiously. 'Could I perhaps phone you back in an hour? I would need to make a few trifling arrangements, you know.'

'Of course, of course,' he conceded magnanimously. 'Perhaps an hour would be sufficient , and if I haven't heard from you by then I'll just set off.' Sixty-five minutes later I rang him up. 'Hello again, Tom, I thought it might be you,' he bellowed cheerfully, 'you're just in time. We're about to leave.'

'We! — Who is we?' I asked suspiciously.

'Davie Crabb and myself, who else? Didn't I tell you? Oh, of course, you wouldn't know. Well, when you didn't phone back I asked him to come instead. It's unfortunate that you've got everything fixed up.' His voice took on a sententious tone. 'Three is a bad number for the Ridge — far too slow and they eat too much. Why don't you find a fourth? Anyway I can't stop to talk now. See you tonight at Sligachan The last ferry from Kyle leaves in three hours, so you might just make it, if you hurry.'

I swore violently as the line went dead. My mind went back to the occasion several years ago when I had received a postcard which briefly announced, 'Meet me at Molde on 25th June at 3 p.m.' Molde is a tiny place somewhere up a Norwegian fjord. I already knew of Hamish's violent fits of enthusiasm, so I had thought of phoning him at his home in Glencoe on the appointed day and announcing my arrival in Molde. I had abandoned the idea. He would have commiserated briefly and then asked about the snow conditions …

I remember, too, the scraps of information scattered haphazardly through Hamish's letters, that had a simplicity often shattering in its impact : 'If you receive no reply to your next letter you will know that I have gone up the Amazon in search of a new species of long-tailed monkey. It promises to be a really interesting project.'

It was eight years since our last climb. That was a red-letter day in February 1957 when with Graeme Nicol of Aberdeen we made the first winter ascent of Zero Gully on Ben Nevis, at that time the most difficult winter route on the mountain (S.M.C.J 1958). It is curious why we had never joined forces again.

My annoyance at MacInnes' premature departure for Skye was eased the next day by the news that he had stuck in a snowdrift near Cluanie and retreated to Glencoe to carry out essential repairs on his car.

Meanwhile I had been phoning up various likely partners. Eric Langmuir, the Warden at Glenmore Lodge, was immediately enthusiastic. Eric was an old friend and a very experienced Alpinist. It so happened that another mutual climbing acquaintance, Graham Tiso, was visiting the Lodge when I phoned so that he too became entangled in the plans.

The same evening a small wiry individual wearing a climbers' safety-helmet arrived at our door looking for a 'doss.' It was none other than Brian Robertson. He had hitch-hiked from Fort William in a fish lorry and wore the keenly expectant look of a man who has wandered many days in the desert and suddenly stumbled upon an oasis. His arrival could scarcely have been better timed.

The following evening found us at Sligachan. We had chosen to attempt the Ridge Traverse from the North because this would enable us to abseil several sections where the reverse direction would involve very severe ice-climbing. Langmuir and Tiso had left immediately on receiving our S.O.S. Tiso's van was piled high with every possible item of climbing equipment.

We phoned MacInnes in Glencoe and told him snow conditions appeared excellent and we would be starting at dawn. If he hurried he could just catch the late night ferry. It says a lot for his superb sang-froid that he was able to accept this information with no show of emotion and to inform us in a detached tone of voice that he would be unable to leave for several days due to previous commitments. On the other hand, he could well have been clairvoyant.

. I had already made one attempt on the winter traverse of the Main Ridge, and I knew of at least a dozen others, including six made by Hamish himself with different companions.

It was three years almost to the day since my own visit. On that occasion Richard Brooke and I arrived in Skye together with the worst blizzard of the winter. Between Sligachan and Glenbrittle our car stuck in a snowdrift. There was a dance on that night and we were joined by several car loads of frustrated merrymakers. This was fortunate because we soon found ourselves at a hastily arranged Ceilidh in the kitchen of the nearest croft.

Next day we staggered to Glenbrittle through two feet of newly fallen snow. Getting from there to the summit of Garsbheinn, the southernmost point of the ridge, was even more harrowing. In summer this is an easy three-hour walk. It provided us with six hours of undiluted misery floundering in snow seldom less than thigh-deep. On the ridge itself we were due for further disillusionment. Through its entire length the Cuillin Main Ridge had been stripped of every particle of snow by the westerly gales. It was, in fact, the only area of bare ground in Skye. There was no point in tackling it under what amounted to summer conditions.

We could have completed the climb in less than twelve hours from end to end, but we would seldom have to cut steps and there was no advantage in wearing crampons. We found the harder pitches little more difficult than in summer. Our retiral disappointed the locals, for whom the Winter Traverse had become something of an out-of-season attraction when so many rival groups of climbers were vying with each other for the honour of being the first.

I was rather disillusioned by this visit. It began to look as if the Cuillins, because of their proximity to the warmer Atlantic, seldom if ever come into condition for winter climbing. The essential ingredients for success appear to be a nearby snowfall without an accompanying wind and followed successively by a quick thaw and an equally rapid freeze. A further essential is that the weather must remain favourable for at least two days. All these conditions seldom concur during the course of a Skye winter. It is hardly surprising that I had had to wait three full years, after my first attempt, before returning to the fray.

On this occasion, as events were soon to prove, it was the climbers and not the Cuillins who were out of condition. In direct contrast to my previous visit there was no snow at all below the 2000-foot contour but above this level the fantastic jagged skyline of the main ridge was crusted as white as a Christmas cake. The conditions were perfect — iron-hard neve, ideally suited to front-point cramponing. We intended to carry two ice-axes per man. An ice-pick in either hand as additional points of contact would serve to narrow down any element of risk involved, since we planned to climb up rope for most if not all of the way along the ridge. Without twelve-point crampons we would have needed to cut thousands of steps and might easily have spent the better part of a week on the climb.

Because of an unduly late start we did not reach or first objective, the top of Sgurr nan Gillean, until midday. All four of us carried heavy rucksacks full of bivouac equipment.

We traded valour for discretion by ignoring the challenge of the direct route via the Pinnacle Ridge — a jagged crescendo of glistening ice-towers — Himalayan in its unaccustomed winter garb. Instead we climbed the Tourist Route which spirals up the back of the mountain. This was a much longer approach and I am not convinced that we saved ourselves any time.

Near the top we were suddenly enveloped in dense cloud that had been building up over the Sound of Sleat all morning. Big flakes of snow began to fall — sporadically, but with ominous insistence. We began the tricky descent of the West Ridge believing that the weather was going to deteriorate further and any subsequent effort would be merely a formal concession to the occasion, calculated to save face on our return to Sligachan, Consequently there was little urgency and we indulged our fancy by finishing of the delicacies which were to have soothed our bivouac.

Soon we came to where the ridge narrowed in a jagged sword-blade of gabbro. Here we were forced to rope up. Half-way along the icy tightrope the snow-encrusted Gendarme held us up for half an hour. Eventually we discovered that a double rope reached the snowfield below on the north side. It was then simple to by-pass the Gendarme by an abseil and an easy horizontal traverse, regaining the Ridge at the next col.

Here, Robertson and I reverted to climbing solo. Langmuir and Tiso had roped up at the start and were already far behind. Although we sympathised with their conscientious approach we considered that the traverse would take three or four days if we were ruled by traditional precepts. We had only enough food for two days and in any case only a rapid optimist could expect Skye weather to remain fine any longer than that. The first instruction in the climbing manual is to 'climb as if the rope wasn't there.' We had no need for pretence. Anyone who has made a regular practice of climbing solo over a period of years must of necessity be a competent climber. If such was not the case, he would be dead. Nature has effective methods of eliminating the unreliable individualist. I am not making a case for solo climbing — merely pointing out that most solo climbers are not the unprincipled fanatics that some authorities claim but are essentially dependable and well-adjusted companions.

Time was once again important. As if to mock us, the cloud barrier had dispersed and the afternoon sun lit up a dazzling panorama of snow-capped peaks from Ben Nevis to Torridon. There was no longer any possible justification for giving up.

A long abseil from the top of the next peak landed us on the Bhasteir Tooth — a clean-cut prow of black rock starkly outlined against the universal snow blanket.

Descending the Coruisk side of the Tooth we eventually reached a point where a 300-foot rope, doubled through a piton of doubtful integrity, just reached the foot of the cliff. The abseil was largely free and because of a slight bulge half-way down we could not verify that the rope in fact reached the bottom. I offered Robertson the privilege of the lead. Some time after he had disappeared from sight, the rope suddenly went slack. As there was no simultaneous scream I gathered he had reached the bottom under control.

The Ridge was now easy for a long way. The other two had just arrived at the top of the Tooth but we decided not to wait for them as we intended to stop at least an hour before dark, to prepare a communal bivouac. This would let them catch up.

Only now had we begun to move at a respectable pace, as muscles became attuned to the rhythm of front-point cramponing. A quick stab with the crampon, a punch with the ice-axe spike — right foot — right hand — left foot — left hand — so on it went, hands and feet like pistons, pricking out a thread-like tattoo-line across the glistening neve. We could count from memory the rock holds we had used since Sgurr nan Gillean. These were the climbing conditions which one dreams about, but in practice seldom encounters. In sixteen years' winter climbing in Scotland I have never found better. The creaking of crampon points was sweet music to the ear.

Two hours later we came upon a perfect site for the bivouac — a curving snow wreath directly below the west peak of Bidein Druim na Ramh. To-night there was the merest breath of wind, but no sooner had the sun sunk behind the Hebrides than it became so cold that we were forced to excavate a 3-foot deep trench, wide and long enough to accommodate the four of us.

We were so preoccupied that it was dark before we realised the second string was considerably overdue.

'A bit odd.' I ventured after a long silence. 'When did you see them last?' 'Not since the Tooth,' Robertson confessed. 'You don't suppose there was any particular reason for all that shouting an hour ago?'

'I could only just hear it,' I said, 'so it could hardly have been anything too drastic.'

'On the other hand that sound must have carried quite a distance,' commented Robertson gloomily. 'At least two miles, I'd say at a guess.'

I had been thinking the same thing, but not wanted to say so.

'Anyhow,' I remarked with a feeble attempt at optimism, 'they must have bivoacked by now because it's so dark they wouldn't be able to see their own feet, far less climb. In any case I haven't heard any shouting for a long time.'

'There may be a very good reason for that,' he observed drily/ 'It's a bit of a bind, after digging such a flaming big hole ... Still, you never know — it might make a fabulous grave for Tiso ... Perhaps he's gone and hanged himself,' he suggested brightly.

Robertson must have the Second Sight.

The next time I opened my eyes it was broad daylight and the sun must have been up for over an hour. Once again the weather was beyond reproach. I levered myself out of my ice-encrusted cocoon and peered blearily over the rim of the snow-hole. Our bivouac site commanded a view of the whole ridge back to the Tooth. It was as empty as the back row of a cinema during the national Anthem.

With a resigned gesture I switched off the torch, pathetic little beacon that had shone bravely but to no avail throughout the night. 'I'm afraid that's it, I remarked tonelessly. 'I suppose we ought to go back and look.'

Robertson was visibly depressed. 'Remember that bit in Gervasutti's book where the German fell off the overhang for the third time? What did Gervasutti say? "Though my heart was near to breaking I let him down." 'You can understand how he felt,' he said bitterly.

We split up, Brian retracing our tracks along the crest of the Ridge while I descended into the western corrie to search the base of the cliffs. It pays to be realistic on these occasions.

About an hour later the corrie resounded to a volley of oaths.

'What are you doing down there?'

'I — am — looking — for — dead — bodies.' I replied spitefully, giving every syllable its last ounce of venom,

'Sorry — can't make out a word you're saying. Why — is — Brian — up — here? Did — you — fall — off?'

I gave up and sat down on the snow in an attitude of despair. Getting no further reply to their shouts they all eventually descended the corrie.

It was an exotic story. Told against the background of a cloudless sky and the Cuillin

Ridge in unique winter conditions, it sounded like a bad joke.

The trouble began because Tiso was too conscientious. Having abseiled down from the Tooth and thus tested the piton to most people's satisfaction (he was the heaviest member of the party) he took an extra precaution. He knotted a loop on the double rope, stepped into and swung with his full weight on the rope. This would have been all right if it had not been for three significant factors. The rope had reached him at a slight angle; and he was wearing crampons. When his gyrations ceased he found himself 5 feet off the ground with one crampon entangled in the loop. In an effort to free it he turned upside down ...

He was now hanging by one foot with his head caressing the snow. It was a unique and quite irreversible position. Physiologists have stated that a man hanging freely in space from a rope around his waist expires from suffocation in somewhat less than twenty minutes. (I can't imagine how they arrived at this hypothesis). Probably no one has calculated the life-span of a man hanging from one foot, but it is reasonable to assume that his condition will steadily deteriorate. Hence it was not surprising that Tiso's initial distress signals had carried a distance of two miles.

Up above, Langmuir was in an unenviable position. It was obvious that some stirring drama was being enacted at the foot of the cliff, but the bulge concealed it from view and also distorted Tiso's colourful commentary. There was only one way to find out. This was to descend the fixed rope which was stretched taut as a guitar string. He had no spare rope to rig an abseil and it would have been suicidal to try to climb down without protection. He used the only safety device available - a thin nylon sling which he attached to the main rope by a Prussik knot. Every time he adjusted the knot to a lower position, his other hand clutching the rope had to take his full body weight. Where the rope ran over a projection, the situation became even more hazardous. His downward vista centred round the upturned sole of a Tiso Special Climbing Boot, behind which he could see the congested features of its leading Scottish distributor.

Half an hour later, his herculean task accomplished, he unhooked the unfortunate Tiso, with a flick of the ice-axe and both collapsed on the snow in utter exhaustion.

Not surprisingly, they had been unable to get much further along the ridge before darkness forced them to bivouac.

We had been prepared to be critical. Instead we had to admit that they had done extraordinarily well to extricate themselves from a nightmarish situation. It could have happened to any of us and in retrospect had its lighter moments, but at the time the outcome could have been serious.

So ended our first Cuillin adventure. I might not have been so despondent had I known that we would be returning to Sligachan before the week was out.

I 'phoned MacInnes, as I had promised, with the news of our defeat.

'So you didn't get up,' he remarked before I had even spoken

'How on earth did you know that?'

'Well I heard that conditions were almost spring-like, so I knew you wouldn't bother

64. *A.E. Robertson, the first Compleat Munroist*

65. *Sir Hugh T. Munro, the author of Munro's Tables*

66. An Teallach from Toll an Lochain

67. *A Highland keeper and his family at Strathmore at the head of Glen Strath Farrar, 1905*
68. *Looking from Strathmore south to Pait Lodge across a glen now flooded by the waters of Loch Monar*

pushing on with it. Quite right. it would have been daylight robbery to claim a first winter ascent.'

'What do you know about it?' I replied huffily. 'You weren't even there.'

'Ah, you forget that friend of mine, Peter Thomas, lives at Glenbrittle,' said Hamish in his 'matter-of-fact' voice.

I returned the gauntlet. 'If that's what you think, go over and see yourself.' 'All right,' he said thoughtfully. 'I think I will. I'll find Davie Crabb and we'll be on the road in an hour. See you at Sligachan...'

From the road outside the hotel, MacInnes was prepared to admit he was wrong. That was about all he was prepared to concede. 'Tom — this idea of yours of getting Peter Thomas to carry the bivvy gear up to Sgurr na Banachdich is all very well, but Davie and I have been thinking and we reckon it's cheating. You know, of course, what everyone will say?' he added darky.

'You think it's cheating? Well, look at it this way — I've already carried a heavy rucksack as far as Bidein and that's almost as far as Banachdich. I'm damned if I'm going to do it twice in a week merely to keep the records straight. I want to enjoy the climb — so does Brian. If we happen to find a couple of rucksacks on top of Sgurr na Banachdich just before dusk we shall accept their existence as an Act of God and put them to good use. Peter Thomas is agreeable?'

'Oh yes, he is quite willing to help out but wonders if you are happy about the ethics of the thing.'

'Overjoyed.' I said, ' and so will you be when we take your packs off you after you've collapsed with exhaustion ...'

Once more we stood at the top of the abseil from the Bhasteir Tooth. The weather was perfect, the snow beyond reproach — only the time of day differed from the last visit. It was merely 11 a.m. Our rapid progress was due to two factors. We had our own recently made tracks to guide us. There was also a hint of rivalry between the two pairs of climbers - the merest suggestion, but sufficient to cause a gradual and insidious acceleration in the combined speed of the party. All the way from Sligachan we had been forced to put up with MacInnes's Lifemanship gambits. He appears to be entirely unaware of his talents in this field, so that his comments are usually unanswerable.

'That was a tricky bit, eh, Davie? The boys made it look quite easy! It only shows how carrying a pack can upset your equilibrium. Makes an easy pitch into a Very Severe.'

Or again...

'Please don't let us hold you up, lads!' He was hammering along like a steam engine at the time. 'It's going to be a terrible cold night for you if you don't reach Banachdich to-night. I know quite well you're both keen to get ahead.' We were in fact finding considerable difficulty in keeping up but we had a measure of excuse for our poor showing. MacInnes and Crabb had gone religiously to bed at 9 p.m. the previous evening. Robertson and I had stayed up until 2 a.m. at a Ceilidh, exchanging stories with mine host,

John MacLellan, former Scottish Champion Athlete of the Heavy events. Several other convivial Sgiathanchs had joined the group around the fire. An accordion, a mouth-organ, a tape recorder and a bottle of whisky were ideal ingredients for an impromptu Ceilidh. The whisky circulated briskly. I am not hang-over-prone — Robertson unhappily is. He had been unable to resist the fiery creutair and the temptation of getting something for nothing. We had got up at five, roused by an alarm clock. I could barely convince my self that we had slept at all. On the way up the mountain Robertson had been stopping every half-mile to be sick, and I imagined he might give Sgurr nan Gillean a miss since he had climbed it only a few days before. I soloed up the gully leading to the final col on the Pinnacle Ridge and then made my way with some difficulty up the most direct route to the top, being forced to cut steps for the last 400 feet. Despite this I arrived a little in front of MacInnes and Crabb who had climbed the West Ridge, finding the Gendarme tricky.

The four of us were climbing unroped and Robertson and I were ahead of the others by about ten minutes when we reached the crucial abseil, the scene of Tiso's solitary penance. History almost repeated itself. I was half-way down the aerial section when a freak knot appeared on the rope below me. Next minute it had jammed squarely against the karabiner at the waist and I was left spinning round and round on the rope like a frustrated marionette. Desperate situations call for desperate measures: I eventually solved the problem by hammering the knot through the karabiner with my ice-axe. Surprisingly the rope was undamaged.

It was only when we were about to retrieve the abseil that I realised that the knot was on the 'wrong' half of the doubled rope. Sure enough, it jammed again in the eye of the abseil piton. There was no easy solution this time. We would just have to wait for MacInnes and Crabb to free it.

Then I noticed they were preparing to abseil down an altogether different part of the wall somewhere in the neighbourhood of Naismith's Route.

'Climb down a bit this way. that's the wrong route,' I called up persuasively. 'It looks O.K. to us,' said Hamish, ' and will save five minutes in any case.'

'You realise that if the rope's only 150 feet long, it won't reach the bottom?'

'Of course it will. I happened to measure this pitch last summer. It is exactly 135 feet top to bottom.'

MacInnes has such an impressive array of facts and figures at his fingertips that one occasionally doubts their authenticity. However, his voice carries such conviction that one hesitates to argue.

'Actually it would help us if you could come down the same way; our rope is jammed, and you could chuck it down to us.' I felt the small boy who asks for his ball back from the next-door garden.

The practised Lifeman never exploits such an obvious confession of failure. Instead he pretends to ignore it altogether, although his face shows that he has had to make a conscious effort to do so.

'Pity about that,' remarked Hamish, in an abstract way as he handed us a neatly coiled rope. 'We must have lost at least ten minutes on that little mishap. Can't be helped, of course. These things do happen.'

We mumbled our apologies and offered to take our turn of carrying packs.

'I'm feeling fine,' said MacInnes, who indeed looked it. 'How about you, Davie?'

'Never felt better,' replied that stalwart with his usual loyalty.

'Thanks all the same, Tom,' the gallant hero continued, 'but you have to get to Banachdich for 4 o'clock and we'll manage to struggle along.'

I was beginning to question which pair of us was labouring under the bigger handicap. Without rucksacks we should have been half as fast again as they were, but with Hamish in his usual superb physical condition this was an impossibility.

I must admit too that we were dismayed to discover how effortlessly Davie Crabb was keeping pace with MacInnes. For a man who had only recently entered the limelight he was making light of snow and ice problems that would have caused most veteran Alpinists to demand the protection of a rope. I had always understood that although reigning tigers might surpass their elders on short routes of extreme technical severity they lacked experience to move fast and competently over average difficulty. I was now finding out, like many others, that this is another myth as ridiculous as the tale that our modern climber only betters the achievements of his forefathers by excessive use of pitons and slings. In climbing, as in any other competitive sport (which climbing most certainly is), a man's ability and achievements must only be measured against the yard-stick of his contemporaries.

We passed the site of or previous bivouac shortly after midday, a much-improved performance. At the tip of the snow gully between the central and west Peaks of Bidein we grappled with our first pitch of actual rock climbing. Even so the vital holds were hidden under blue ice and had to be bared with the axe. Although merely a 'muscle-loosener' in summer this was now a pitch of severe standard. Having duly appropriated the Central Peak we abseiled back to the col, passing the other pair on the way up.

From here to Sgurr a' Mhadaidh was no more than a walk. That is to say, you could have fallen and escaped with your life. This could not be said of any other part of the Cuillin Ridge in the condition we found it. There was a sufficient depth of iron-hard snow on most of the ledges to incorporate them into the uniformly steep slopes which fell away from the ridge — itself a tortuous knife-edge of snow. We could never hope to find more perfect climbing conditions.

Two successive abseils from the twin towers of Sgurr a'Mhadaidh launched us upon the long middle section of the Ridge Traverse which leads successively over the summits of Sgurr a'Ghreadaidh and Sgurr na Banachdich. Here are no outstanding rock problems, but in winter a steady succession of minor difficulties which would greatly reduce the pace of a roped party. Fast progress on this part of the Ridge is absolutely essential if one is to complete the traverse in two days. Indeed if a climber has not the confidence and experience to cope with this section unroped he would be ill-advised to attempt the Ridge Traverse in winter.

There are climbers who advocate moving together, carrying coils, on this kind of terrain. My own view is that in these circumstances the rope is rather a hindrance and a hazard than a means of protection: if no belays are taken then any protection is largely illusory. Quite apart from this, very few climbers climb with the same margin of safety if they are clutching a coil of rope in one hand.

Although now enveloped in mist the party continued to advance in loose order. Robertson was still vomiting periodically, about twenty minutes behind me. I could gauge his progress from the occasional sounds of ice-axe or crampon. At least half an hour behind him were MacInnes and Crabb. Why they were no longer challenging was not obvious. Later it transpired that a most disastrous thing had happened. Davie Crabb had broken a crampon. For a time, MacInnes even considered abandoning the attempt. In effect, Crabb was climbing with one foot and a heel, the toes of his unprotected vibram-soled boot stubbing uselessly against the glassy surface. He roped up behind MacInnes.

I knew nothing of this and by the time I reached Sgurr na Banachdich sounds of pursuit had long since faded. Visibility was down to ten yards and I was aware of a gnawing doubt whether we would ever be re-united with that all-important rucksack containing the bivouac gear and food rations for the next twenty-four hours. Supposing Peter Thomas had left it at the wrong place? We had only an hour of daylight to seek our salvation.

Suddenly and quite unexpectedly I came upon the tracks of a dog. A few yards further were more dog tracks and a trail of clearly defined footprints leading towards the summit of Banachdich. I heaved a profound sigh of relief.

The supply party — consisting of Catherine MacInnes, Peter Thomas, and Hamish's two Alsatian dogs — had passed this way an hour earlier. A few more steps and I came upon the rucksacks, neatly stacked against the summit cairn. It was a poignant moment.

Here, too was a cryptic message scratched on the snow which read, 'A 1 MET.' I decided that MET must be Peter Thomas's initials. Perhaps he preferred to be called Peter just in order to be complicated (some people do). In that case A 1 would be a symbol of self-congratulation, like patting oneself on the back. Why shouldn't he congratulate himself on his hard work — perhaps nobody else would? It seemed a logical explanation. Only afterwards did we discover the significance of this message left by Catherine MacInnes for her unpredictable spouse. De-coded it meant 'Weather forecast — continuing fine.' Characteristically, he was no wiser than we were.

As I had not seen anyone for several hours I was quite relieved when Robertson appeared about twenty minutes later. By this time I had discovered a well-protected ledge for a bivouac and half an hour later when the other pair dropped in we had already excavated a level platfrom capable of holding four in some discomfort.

'It looks a bit cramped,' MacInnes remarked critically, 'I rather fancy digging a snow hole. How about you,Davie? It would be good practice if nothing else.'

I waited with interest to see if Hamish intended to carry out such a prodigious threat. In the end he settled for another smaller ledge a few feet to the side.

A vague element of insularity still coloured the remarks that wafted across the icy no-man's land between rival bivouacs.

'This is excellent soup, Davie. What's it called?'

'What's after the baked beans, Brian?'

'I don't know whether I could eat any more if I tried!'

'This is a palace!'

'I could live here quite happily for a week!!!'

'I reckon the packs were worth the effort. Makes you sort of feel that you have earned it all.'

'That was a great idea getting the packs sent up. Organisation — Pity we had to stop! — I could have gone on for hours!' Etc., etc.

In fact, the organisation was far from perfect. We had assembled the contents of Peter Thomas's rucksack in a hurry on our return from the Ceilidh. Our choice showed little discrimination and a lack of consideration for our porter's feelings. Catherine MacInnes told us later that he had eventually opened the rucksack out of curiosity and asked with disgust, 'Is this a bivouac or a birthday party?' There was some truth in his complaint. The contents included three packets of margarine, a large tin of salt and a half-gallon can of water. We had selected a fine vantage point for our bivouac. Anchored by ropes and pitons, and secure in the warmth of duvets and sleeping bags, we could pass away the evening by identifying the numerous lighthouses off the west coast of Skye. Nearer at hand the lights of Glenbrittle beckoned like a friendly beacon. How easy and pleasant it would be to glissade down the long slopes of Banachdich! In an hour we could be sitting by a warm fire. In the morning if we rose early we could be back on the top by dawn and nobody would know we had deserted our posts...

At some unearthly hour I was awakened by a light fall of snow and the dawn ushered in a cheerless morning. Grey tentacles of mist clung to every cranny on the Ridge and fresh hoar-frost covered the rocks. It had been one of the coldest nights of the winter. Although I had fallen asleep in comparative luxury, I woke in misery. Condensation inside the polythene bivvy-bag had soaked inexorably through sleeping bag, duvet and trousers. As soon as I got up, my clothes became as stiff as cardboard. The primus refused to work in the cold and we had to borrow Hamish's butane stove. It was almost 9 o'clock before we finally got under way. We climbed with the agility of four knights in full armour.

Fortunately it was an easy start to the day. At the col between Banachdich and Sgurr Dearg we jettisoned all the spare rations and bivouac gear. MacInnes, ever cautious, placed his rucksack under a prominent boulder: I slung my own with utter contempt in the direction of Glenbrittle and watched with gay abandon as it finally disappeared from view, 1500 feet below, in one final gigantic arc, Robertson followed suit, although with mixed emotions. It was the first time he had wilfully abandoned his precious ironmongery and there was a nostalgic look in his eyes. (Both rucksacks were recovered intact the following morning, less than an hour's walk away from Glenbrittle.)

We now had to keep our first appointment of the day. The Inaccessible Pinnacle of Sgurr Dearg was an unpleasant customer to meet in the morning. Easily the most impressive summit pinnacle in Britain, it is considerably more intimidating in mid-winter. We began by examining the north end of the Pinnacle — the so-called 'Short Side.' It was plated from top to bottom with black ice. The ascent can be quite awkward on a wet day in summer, yet Hamish was confident that he could force a way up even in these conditions.

It promised to be a long teethy struggle, and I do not enjoy watching life-and-death drama for the same reason that I would not pay to watch circus acrobats: I become too personally involved. Suddenly, I had an impulse to investigate the 'Long Side'. Consequently, I left the other two spectating and walked round towards the other end of the Pinnacle. Although reputedly a much easier climb than its counterpart, it is at least twice the length and might now present similar technical difficulties, for the angles of both routes are roughly comparable. After fifty feet of climbing, undertaken purely for reconnaissance, I became unpleasantly aware that I was now committed to the climb. After 100 feet, I would have given a great deal for rope protection and a belay. There was little time to cut extra holds. The edge of the arete had been denuded of snow by the sun., but even so there was less than half the summer quota of holds. When I came to the short vertical step where one usually pauses before stepping up onto a rather thin bracket, I decided that it was time to enlist Robertson's assistance. Unfortunately he was out of sight and apparently beyond recall because nobody appeared to investigate my shouts. There was no sense in hanging on indefinitely for a last-minute reprieve, so I chose to continue while I still had some strength. As so often, no sooner had I made this resolution, when everything suddenly clicked. Crampon points bit tenaciously into thin wafers of water-ice, woollen gloves clamped down firmly on rounded verglassed holds and before I even had time to consider the penalties of failure, I was already over the difficulty and scrambling up the last few feet to the top. Total time for the ascent — ten minutes — Standard — a good Severe — and I had to suppress an urge to dramatise my sudden appearance on the top of the Pinnacle. It was gratifyingly effective nevertheless, as MacInnes was at grips with the 'badstep' and in a position to appreciate a top-rope. (Although, knowing Hamish, he would obviously have fought his way up in time.)

I pulled up an extra length of rope from the base of the Pinnacle and belayed MacInnes from one rope, leaving the second for use as a handrail.

'This fixed rope isn't much good, Tom. It will swing off the rock. Can't you flick it across to your left?

'All right. I'll do that,' I said, 'but I'll have to let go your rope. O.K.?'

'No! Not on your life. I'm relying on this rope for support.' Most odd, I thought. I am obviously belaying him with the wrong rope. By ordinary standards, Hamish ought to be in mid-air.

After jugglery, we had a second rope secured top and bottom, and the rest of the party made free use of it to clamber up and down the Pinnacle. (We were not to know that merely forty-eight hours later the second victorious pair to complete the Traverse of the Cuillin Ridge would be persuaded by our tracks into tackling the Short Side of the Pinnacle. One was the indefatigable Tiso: the other the formidable J. Moriarty, the Not-So-Gentle-Giant, 'Big Elly' himself. This was a sterling performance as our quartet would be the first to confirm.)

The first of the two redoubtable strong-points of the Cuillin Ridge had been out-manoeuvred and overcome. Now only the Thearlaich-Dubh Gap remained. The early morning mists were dispersing rapidly, the sun shone on a dazzling landscape and for the first time we dared to contemplate success. If the weather was not going to stop us nothing else would.

We glissaded down the long snow chutes of An Stac and climbed the twisting aerial stairway to Sgurr MhicCoinnich. From the summit eyrie, one after another we spun down the 150-foot abseil which hung clear of the cliff like a spider's thread. So on to Sgurr Thearlaich by a left-flanking traverse on 100 yards of creaking snow that threatened to avalanche but held firm. At the top of the Great Stone Shoot we turned aside to pay homage to Sgurr Alasdair and a magnificent viewpoint.

We were impatient to come to grips with the last difficulty on the Ridge — the Thearlaich-Dubh Gap. It needed only a few seconds' inspection to confirm that its ascent under present conditions would be exceptionally 'thin' — corresponding to a summer grading of 'Very Severe' and rating high in that category. An evil veneer of ice obscured every wrinkle on the wall. Without crampoms any ascent would have been out of the question, but where were there big enough incuts to support the front points of a crampon? I did not fancy peeling off backwards. Someone did this some years ago and paid for it with his life. A glance at the jagged boulders which lined the floor of the Gap recalled this incident.

Moriarty and Tiso must have come to the same conclusion two days later. Although they had already dealt with the difficult 'Short Side' of the Inaccessible Pinnacle they failed to climb out of the Gap and had to abseil all the way down to the corrie floor, only regaining the Ridge after a slight detour.

We were most reluctant to take diversion from a Ridge Traverse. Robertson therefore prepared to hurl himself at the last hurdle in a fervour of martyrdom.

At that moment MacInnes, who had yet to descend into the Gap, made a novel suggestion. 'If you just hold it a minute, lads,' he shouted, 'I might manage to get a rope over to the other side.'

Surely, I thought, someone would have discovered this solution ages ago, if it existed?

However, there are few who can rival Hamish's flair for improvisation. 'The fact is, I've been here investigating in the summer,' he confessed (familiar phrase, I thought) 'and there's a pointed rock on the other side that will take a direct pull from below, supposing I get the rope to lie behind it.'

With the very first cast his rope wrapped neatly round a projection at the top of the wall. Most men would have sweated blood and tears to achieve this. Only one thing troubled me. It was obviously not the same projection that Hamish had aimed at.

'How do you know this rope is safe, Hamish?'

'I don't,' he replied in his abstract way.

'Well how are we to find out whether it's safe if you can't tell us from there?'

MacInnes was the model of patience. 'Try climbing up the rope,' he remarked encouragingly. 'I'll be most surprised if it comes away.'

'You won't be the only one,' I thought.

Now followed the Moment of Truth, beloved of mountaineering chroniclers — the Throw of the Dice that was the difference between success and utter disaster. Even if the whole of my past life did not flash across my subconscious mind as is supposed to happen on these occasions, I still remember the enormous relief when I pulled myself over the top to find the rope securely jammed. We had broken the last Barrier. Success was assured.

One abseil remained. Then we coiled up the rope for the last item and each of us wandered silently and independently along the final mile of scree-speckled ridge to Garsbheinn, the final outpost of the Ridge. Beyond lay the blue Atlantic, warm and inviting in the afternoon sun. Down there by the shore a different world awaited us — a world of colour and contrast. In one searing whooping glissade of 2000 feet we returned to it. It was indeed good to be back. Our two-day journey in the winter Cuillin and the twelve-hour 'tarantella on ice' when crampon tips and ice-axe spike were our only contacts with tangible reality, now all seemed a strange and wonderful fantasy.

A little older in wisdom, a little younger in spirit, we marched back over the moors to Glenbrittle. Down there in Cuillin Cottage, Mrs Campbell would be waiting for us with supper. It was a long-standing invitation that we fully intended to keep...

There are many ultimates in mountaineering and every generation finds its own Last Problem. The five others who shared the first winter Traverse of the Cuillin Ridge probably feel the same way as I do. There are are many harder and more exacting routes, and many more still to be explored, yet I feel confident that the Winter Traverse of The Main Ridge will always retain its place as the greatest single adventure in British Mountaineering.

It would be presumptuous to be conceited about the success of our own exploit. We can only be grateful that we were lucky to find this superb climb in superb winter conditions. If any individual honours are awarded they should go to Davie Crabb and Brian Robertson who completed the Ridge on half a crampon and half a stomach respectively, thereby revealing — in Hamish's own phraseology — 'a determination that is truly Scots.'

COOL ON THE CUILLIN
Vol. XXXII (1981)

The traverse of the Cuillin Ridge is a winter route badly out of condition in the summer when drinking water is scarce and scree unprotected by neve. This is the opinion of S. N. Smith who presents the winter passage as a mere dawdle. He writes: 'There have now been well over half-a-dozen winter traverses of the Ridge and most find the excursion to be most enjoyable, in fact so much so that one party bivouacked three times; this seems to be taking hedonism to rather great an extreme. The best plan seems to be that adopted by Colin Grant, Ian Fulton and myself in February '79. We pitched our tent at Sligachan and set off early the next morning so that the summit of Sgurr nan Gillean was reached at dawn. From here the Ridge can be admired while you get your breath back.

'Abseiling down Naismith's Route on The Bhasteir Tooth is always fun and is no less so in winter. There follows various interesting Grade III pitches which, like all the other steps should be soloed, the ropes only being used for abseils. This plan means that three is a good number because two men can each carry 150 ft of rope while the third carries the stove and a few packets of biscuits.

'We bivouacked at Sgurr Thormaid which is a reasonable half-way point although other parties have gone further.

'Most parties (ourselves included) miss out the Inaccessible Pinnacle to get to grips with the sections that lead to the King's Chimney abseil and later the Thearlaich-Dubh Gap. At the T-D Gap forget MacInnes's rope tricks and just scramble down the gully into Coir a'Ghrunnda and then back onto the ridge and so eventually to Garsbheinn. The B.M.C. hut can then be reached in time for tea.

'On returning to our tent at Sligachan, we discovered the police had removed the entire contents to Portree. Since a note of our intentions had been left behind, the reasons remain obscure'.

This incident illustrates that although we may enjoy better protection on a climb than our predecessors, off it there are new hazards of which they never dreamed.

THE LAST OASIS
Vol. XXXII (1982)   by Andrew Nisbet

Before you ask, it's a route on Creag an Dubh Loch, named because a steady stream flows over its pink walls and slabs even when the rest of the cliff is dry and baking under a relentless sun (it used to happen when I first started climbing, but that's not so recently). The walls stay pink because even the grey Dubh Loch lichen can't survive such permanent submergence. A good summer route when dry; consequently it's rarely climbed.

You might think it would have had a winter ascent years ago but it's one of these routes where the feeding spring seems to freeze up and disappear in winter. Not that there hadn't been intentions. A notable Etchachan Club pair (this famous phrase makes them easy to identify in previous Journals) once went to climb the Oasis, found good conditions but had forgotten one of their ropes, so had to be content with a snow desert instead. The inherent steepness of the route was sufficient to put off contenders when conditions were anything less than ideal.

When Neil Spinks and I went up there for a look last winter, it was predictable by the perverse laws of opinion that conditions would be good - that is, everyone else had dismissed the weekend as being too warm/too dry/too late in the year/or were just too apathetic. Mind you, April on the Dubh Loch is optimistic. But as we had hoped, it was a frosty morning with not a cloud in the sky as we walked up from Glas Allt, and on arrival we found the route was smothered in ice from top to bottom. The sun was starting to angle up out of a clear blue sky as we approached the cliff — no walking on the loch this time.

"Climbing in April is really pleasant," I remarked as we put on crampons in the sun. (At this point the discerning reader might anticipate a small problem which would crop up.) A good covering of crisp snow made the walk over the boulder field towards the start easy but we were sweating under a heavy load of ice screws, even though we had chanced to leave our sacks by the loch on such a fine day.

On the cliff the frost had been less active and the snow was soft under a thick crust. Our feet kept breaking through unpredictably so we put on the rope for the scramble up to the start of the Broad Terrace Wall. The sun was higher now and sweat was running down my brow from under my helmet as we plodded up deep soggy snowfields. I was hoping the snowfields wouldn't slide off a lubricated grass surface as the start of the route is rather too high for a surfboarding descent. My vest was clinging to my back now under six layers of clothing and a baking sun, which shines directly on to this part of the face in the morning. Sheets of snow were slithering ominously off the slabs around us.

The introductory gully was almost in the shade. But suddenly I broke through the temporary neve and water oozed out of the hole made by my axe. As it flowed, the neve turned to slush for Neil to wade up. He was unhappy.

"It's a bit warm." Then after a pause during which I failed to take him up on his disguised suggestion, added, "I think we could abseil in one into S.E. Gully." I took this simply as an interesting observation. He joined me on the first stance. I quickly set off up an ice bulge, made a delicate move up a slab of ice backed with water which threatened to peel off when I kicked my points into it, and managed to place a good axe over the lip. I had struck a spring again. Water streamed down my arms, poured off my elbows, eventually penetrated my whole body and dripped off the soles of my feet.

"Hold it — I must take a picture — nobody will believe this" and Neil shrieked with laughter. Moving off the bulge was awkward and took time (unfortunately for me). All the ice above was slush except a thick band in a groove which slanted abruptly right above the bulge. I kept the good placement in and mantelshelfed into the puddle over the lip.

The amount of climbable ice was rapidly shrinking so I was forced left away from the summer route into a cramped stance under a small roof. At the back of this recess seemed a good place to stay. The stream flowed over the lip in front of us and the icicles which were crashing down off the main icefall to the right would miss us, even if they came unnervingly close. Neil was still unhappy. "The sun will be away soon," I suggested. This wasn't a lie, it just turned out to be not quite accurate. The more the sun moved south, the higher it became and it neatly traced a line just above the outline of S.E. Buttress. We were so wet by now that we needed its warmth.

We chatted for a while behind our curtain of water but I couldn't bring myself to agree to a retreat. It might be ten years before there would be climbable ice on this route again. The crashing of icicles seemed to have eased a bit. In fact, most of them had already fallen, so I gingerly edged out across a slab aiming for the main icefall, diagonally over a bulge and across the other side of the ice. I knew if I dug deep enough in the slush there was an odd fixed peg and a good chock placement, an advantage of having been here before in summer. I needed the reassurance, it looked very steep and serious above. I didn't even try putting in ice screws, in slush like this they would just fall out. A double bulge loomed up above but the axes were going in up the shaft. It was still worrying in case one pulled right through so I rested on my axes between the bulges, not because I had run out of strength but so that I was fresh if anything unexpected happened (such as the whole pitch collapsing). Sixty feet above the good Moac runner and increasingly nervous, I came across the direct continuation of the ice, a forty foot plumb vertical screen of soggy icicles, but there was no way I was going up there without runners. The only ones possible were slings round icicles, just a wet joke in these conditions, so I slunk off sideways into a cave behind the ice, battered a number ten hex sideways into a slush-filled crack and pegged up the summer route. I feel apologetic about the aid now but I was under some strain at the time. Just to emphasise the point, Neil followed without using the aid.

Now we were faced by the last twenty feet, a straight pull-up on to a slushy ledge, which could be awkward in these conditions. But we hadn't noticed the sun had gone behind the hill. The snow was rock-hard to finish!

MUNROSIS

MUNRO'S TABLES (extracts)
Vol. I (1891)
by H.T. Munro

When the TABLES GIVING ALL THE SCOTTISH MOUNTAINS EXCEEDING 3000 FEET IN HEIGHT were completed by Hugh T. Munro and published in The Journal, the intention was to catalogue the mountain resources of Scotland. At the time it was not generally known how considerable these were. In doing so Munro never realised that his name would enter the English Language and foster an activity now pursued by hundreds—thousands? It has been called 'The Scottish Disease!' Munro listed 283 separate mountains. The most recent edition of the Tables (1984) contained 276 mountains and 516 Tops, but one further Munro has been added to make the current total 277.

In the Preface to the first number of the *Journal* it was correctly stated that there are more than three hundred mountains in Scotland whose height exceeds 3,000 feet. The exact number cannot be determined, owing to the impossibility of deciding what should be considered distinct mountains. For instance, Braeriach and Cairn Toul are always counted as separate mountains, and so are the various peaks of the Cuillins, in Skye; and yet they are no more distinct than are Sron Isean or Stob Daimh from the two main peaks of Ben Cruachan, one and a half and two miles to the west. The names of these peaks, though, are not even given on the Ordnance sheet, but are generally included under the name Ben Cruachan.

In the following tables, therefore, it has been thought best to include every Top which attains an elevation of 3,000 feet; while in the first column only such as may fairly be reckoned distinct Mountains are numbered.

From the tables it will be seen that there are in all 538 Tops exceeding 3,000 feet in height. The whole of these are situated in the Highlands, and all — with the exception of Ben More, in Mull, and the Cuillins and Blaven, in Skye — are on the mainland. The southernmost is Ben Lomond, in Stirlingshire; the northernmost is Ben Hope, in the north-west of Sutherlandshire; the easternmost is Mount Keen, above Loch Lee, between Forfarshire and Aberdeenshire; and the westernmost is Sgurr na Banachdich, in the Cuillins, Skye; while on the mainland Ladhar Bheinn, in Knoydart, Inverness-shire, is the westernmost.

Various explanatory notes follow, before the Tables which are divided into 16 sections by area.
Munro concludes...

Every endeavour has been made to secure accuracy and completeness. It is inevitable that there should be some mistakes, but it is hoped they will not be found very numerous. The decision as to what are to be considered distinct and separate Mountains, and what may be counted as Tops, although arrived at after careful consideration, cannot be finally insisted on. I have only to add that, when first this work was commenced, I had little idea of the enormous amount of labour and research which it would entail — a labour which, even if it had not been altogether abandoned, would have been vastly increased but for the invaluable assistance given by Mr Colin Phillip, whose extraordinary topographical knowledge of Scotland has probably never been equalled.

THEORETICAL MUNROOLOGY: THE METAPHYSICAL APPROACH
Vol. XXXII (1981)

Counting a set of semi-magical entities such as the Munros is a metaphysical problem as an arithmetical solution cannot be arrived at without destroying the magic. Consider the following parable about the magic pigs of Cruachu by an Irish research worker of the ninth century. '... out of Cruachu came these pigs. Wherever they would be counted, they would not stay, but if anyone tried to count them they would go to another land. They were never completely counted; but 'There are three,' said one,; 'More, seven,' said another; 'Eleven pigs,'; 'Thirteen pigs.' In that way it was impossible to count them. Moreover, they could not be killed, for if they were shot at they would disappear. One day, however, Queen Maeve counted them and they were never seen again.'

: THE STATISTICAL APPROACH

In recent years it has become apparent that the Munros go up and down and have lateral movement, ie they change their heights and map references. The summit of a Munro therefore probably traces a sub-circular path over the years, perhaps linked in some way with the erratic wanderings of the magnetic poles. Those near the boundary of 3000 feet, therefore, are constantly entering and leaving the Tables. Thus the number of Munros is a statistical concept and there never will be a final perfect *Table*, only a series of *Tables* constantly brought up to date by indefatigable Editors. Indeed it may not be possible to do all the Munros unless you do the Tops as well, for the first Munro that you climbed when young may have dropped out of the Table valid at the time of your final ascent and have been replaced by one or more summits that were only Tops in your youth . . . . .

THE "MUNRO'S" OF SCOTLAND
Vol. VII (1902)

by A. E. Robertson

By December 1988 over 600 have recorded their 'Compleation' of the current list of Munros. In the early days mobility and access were less easy and A. E. Robertson was the first only Compleat Munroist for over twenty years. The feelings written below were typical of those to be expressed repeatedly by his successors in the future.

Peak-bagging and record-breaking are somewhat, I fear, looked down upon by the members of the S.M.C. And outside of the Club they are as a rule regarded in the same unfavourable light. The other day, when telling a friend some of my experiences in endeavouring to climb every hill over 3,000 feet in Scotland, he could not see the point of it at all. "Why should you want to climb every hill?" he queried, and then irreverently added, "no one has ever kissed every lamp-post in Princes Street, and why should any one want to?" Yet it must be confessed that the writer has never looked at it in this profane light, and that for many years past he has very much wanted to kiss every summit that finds a place in the historic Tables. And in a word be it said, after many vicissitudes and exertions, he at length, last September, in Glencoe, wiped out the last of the 3,000 footers, some 283 separate mountains in all, according to Munro's list.

The Editor, has asked me in view of this to give some of my impressions of the hills of Scotland as a whole, and I gladly respond, though I must say his request has been found far from easy to fulfil.

The campaign has been a desultory one, and has occupied about ten years. It was begun with no thought of ever climbing them all, but simply from a desire to obtain a general knowledge of the Highland hills. In this way about a hundred, scattered up and down through the country, were climbed. In 1898 a three months' holiday added some seventy-five to the list. The thought then occurred to me that the thing might be completed, and another three months' holiday in 1899 in which some seventy-two new hills were 'bagged,' brought the goal in sight, which was at length attained this autumn.

The first thought that strikes one in looking back over the hills of Scotland as a whole, is that there are almost none that have not some fairly easy route to the top — and I regret to say it. For although the most incorrigible of peak-baggers I love a climb as well. Like the keeper I once asked if he would have a dram or a pint of beer, I most emphatically reply, "Both is best!" I only wish I could tell the Club of some far-away unknown peak bristling with difficulties on all sides, but the fact is there are none. The only hills where there are no easy ways to the top are certain of the Coolins in Skye, Sgurr Dubh for example or Mhadaidh and perhaps Sgurr Alasdair, though on Alasdair you have got the Stone Shoot which leads to within 125 feet of the top.

When one asks what are the best climbing hills, provided you are willing to seek out difficulties, the list widens at once. First and foremost I would place the Coolins, then the north face of Ben Nevis, Glencoe, the Torridon Hills, the Teallachs, for rock work; while as regards snow craft, on almost every one of the 3,000 feet hills one can get excellent climbs provided the north or north-east face be taken and there be frost to put the snow into proper order. The inland mountains carry the most snow, for example Mam Soul, Sgurr nan Conbhairean, the Cairngorms, Ben Alder, Beinn Heasgarnich.

The difficulty of getting at the remoter hills and securing a suitable base of operations, was often a very serious one. In this connection I found my bicycle simply invaluable, and many of the more distant expeditions which would have involved a night out, or a long tedious and expensive hire, were brought by the aid of the wheel within the compass of a long day from some fixed point. Take for example the districts of central Ross-shire and north-west Inverness-shire. One can cycle up Glen Strathfarrar as far as Monar Lodge, up Glen Cannich as far as the west end of Loch Mullardoch, and up Glen Affric as far as Affric Lodge; in this way all the remote summits at the head of these glens can be reached in the course of a long day from Affric Hotel or Struy Bridge Inn. Likewise Glen Quoich can be got at from Tomdoun, and the head of Glen Lyon from Bridge of Balgie. Don't be afraid your bike will run away, or be stolen in your absence! Turn him loose to browse in the heather, and he will be waiting for you when you return. For the few up there who could ride away with him, would not!

But there are regions where neither trap nor bicycle are of the least avail, and where hotels are gloriously conspicuous by their absence — and long may such regions exist. When you go to Glen Dessary, to Loch Hourn, and to the more distant parts of Kintail, you have to renounce all ideas of cycling or driving, not to speak of the Capuan luxuries of a roadside inn. There is nothing for it but to tramp it, carrying your all in your own rucksack, taking your chance for quarters at the shepherds' shielings, or keepers' houses passed on the way.

What delightful weeks I have spent in this manner. The long fine spring and early summer days, the loneliness and the wonder of the world and unknown country; no trains, no coaches, no villas, far out of the track of that baneful and vulgar modern product the guide-book tourist. You set forth to traverse your peak, and the only house within fifteen miles is that keeper's there, where you must be put up for the night. You sight it with your glass as you lie away up among the tops far down in the glen below. Towards evening you approach the house not without apprehension, the dogs rush out barking vociferously, half in welcome, half in anger. You knock at the door, there is a parley. You are admitted, and once admitted, treated with all the courtesy, dignity, and hospitality that are the prime characteristics of the Celtic nature. In all my wanderings I have never been refused a night's shelter. The Highlander is nothing if he is not hospitable. Of course this has to be gone about in the right way. If a man comes up to a keeper's house and demands a bed in the same tone of voice as he would engage a room at the Metropole, he will be refused — and quite right too — for even a Highland keeper's house is his castle. But if he approaches his would-be host and hostess with fitting politeness, with a certain sense of obligation in his voice and bearing, he will certainly be received and welcomed and given the run of whatever is in the house.

What fine characters these shepherds and keepers are, well read, well informed, intested, capable, God-fearing.

And what lonely lives they lead, an isolation scarcely credible in these railway days. In one family that I know well, the eldest girl though fourteen years of age, had never seen a church or a school in her life, yet for all that, quick witted, intelligent, far more truly educated by nature and the occasional visit of a peripatetic teacher, than the many town sparrows, crammed with superficial smatterings in our city Board Schools. And what naive ideas many of them have! I well remember the air with which one good woman opened the door of a tiny room in which was a sitz-bath standing up on end, and the pride with which she exclaimed, "This is the bath-room, if such a thing should ever be required."

And what pawky humour too. There is more sly fun in the Celt than he gets credit for. I could fill pages with their stories, but let one reminiscence suffice. "Well, Donald," I remarked one evening as we sat with our pipes over the peat fire, "this must be a wild place in winter." — "Oh, yes, sir, a wild place in the winter time." — "Big storms, I daresay." —"Hoo, yes, storms." — "And wrecks?" — "Ach, aye, wrecks, the weemans will be taalking about them wiles; but it will be years since she didn't see any." — "And strange animals, perhaps?" — "Heuch, aye, strange beasts and wild beasts." — "Serpents?" — "Yes, serpents, aye and sea serpents, great sea serpents. There was waane, it wass two years ago, her heid cam thro' the Kyle on the 7th of June, and it wass the 12th of August before her tail passed oot. I wass tired waatching her."

In the interest of sporting rights, most, if not all the hills under deer were climbed either in spring or early summer. This time of the year has many advantages. The days are long, the high ground is all under snow, the weather is generally settled, for May and June are undoubtedly the driest months in the Highlands, and last but not least, one is free to move where'er he please without let or hindrance.

In conclusion, let me say that I look back upon the days I have spent in pursuing this quest as among the best spent days of my life. Amid the strange beauty and wild grandeur of rock face and snow slope, scaling tops where literally almost foot hath never aforetime trod, I have indeed come face to face with the sacred sanctities of Nature, and he would be indeed dull of heart who could see her beauties thus unfolded, feel her hand on his brow, her breath on his cheek, who could see and feel that unmoved. When I call to mind the cast-iron peaks of the Black Coolins, the ridges on Ben Nevis, the gullies on the Buachaille, the rich and varied hues of the Lochinver and Assynt hills, the sea-scapes from the Torridons, the wild, lonely, rolling uplands of the Mam Soul range, or the region in and around Ben Alder — the memory of these things is a priceless possession.

Nor is it altogether retrospect, Othello's occupation is not gone! and to the silly people who ask me, "What will you do now since you have no more worlds to conquer?" I can only say, "I am going to climb them over again."

A NEW 'MUNRO' (extract)
Vol. XVIII (1929)   by J. Gall Inglis

When Munro drew up his Tables he used the existing O.S. maps which did not show
the altitude of all summits. Amendments to the Tables were made in succeeding
years. J.Gall Inglis with J. R.Corbett were checking up on suspected Munros in
Fisherfield Forest area.

Beinn Tarsuinn next claimed attention. In the 1927 November Journal, Parker drew
attention to the climbing possibilities of this hill, and certainly from where we stood it was
a remarkable sight. The whole of its north face — crescent-shaped and about a mile in
length - was in deep shadow, so that details could not be made out very well, but it seemed
mostly precipitous, and cut up with gullies, in which a few patches of snow lingered. The
top of the ridge itself was of a very unusual nature, being a succession of long, narrow, flat-
topped blocks with deep gashes between: one of these, near the northern end, had a very
curious outline, resembling the purple flower of a thistle; its sides overhung greatly, and
the top was perfectly flat.Towards the eastern end the ridge swelled out into a great
perfectly flat circular plateau with steep, rocky sides, much resembling the similar
formation of the Quiraing in Skye. Altogether it looked a formidable ridge to tackle, but
Corbett said he had been along it, and all difficulties could be avoided.The top of the hill
was at the extreme eastern end of the ridge: after that it fell in easy, grassy slopes to the
col between it and the "hump" of Mullach Coire Mhic Fhearchair.

As the ascent of Tarsuinn from the east was so easy, and would take us little out of our
way when going back to the hotel, we resolved to bag it, and see if our aneroids would
confirm the visual observations. So we retraced our way to the col, repeating, when we
were 260 feet below the summit, and thus about level with the Maiden and Sgurr an Tuill
Bhain, the comparison of Beinn Tarsuinn with these hills. Tarsuinn was well above the
line joining them and must therefore be not far short of 3,100 feet, so it had evidently a
good margin to work upon in its claim to be a "Munro." On reaching the col we skirted
the rocks on the western side of the hump, which involved some further descent, and after
a fairly easy traverse reached the col of Tarsuinn, which is about 2,430 feet. After that was
an easy ascent over grass, with a snow-field or two by way of variety, up to the top, where
we eagerly consulted our aneroids.

"What do you make it?" said Corbett, who, as the strong man of the party, had got up
first.

"260 feet below Mullach; that is, 3,067 feet, using the reading when we left the top,
but 3,077 feet if we take the reading when we arrived." (According to Whymper, the
latter reading is the most reliable to take.)

"I make it 3,100," said he, "but as your graduations are wider than mine, I daresay yours
may be the more accurate."

The Ordnance Survey give 936m (3,071 ft) as the height of Beinn Tarsuinn on current
maps.

MUNROS, BEARDS AND WEATHER
Vol. XX (1935)   by J. Dow

The Editor has suggested to me that following precedent I should let him have some notes on the 'Munros'. I am not sure that I have much to report which is in the least degree new, but I shall try to avoid repetition.

Subject to my remarks below, Robertson's pioneer work in ascending for the first time all the 3,000-foot mountains of Scotland was certainly a feat. Again, subject to my later remarks, to cover all the subsidiary tops as well as the main mountains, as Burn and Corbett did, was also somewhat of a feat, and similarly to ascend all the 3,000-foot mountains in Great Britain and Ireland as Parker has done was a very meritorious performance; but when I have said this I would like to make it quite definite that to complete the ascent of the 277 Scottish Munros under modern road and transport conditions is very far from being in the slightest degree a feat. This will be very clearly seen when I have to admit that never once did I fail to return to a hot bath and a comfortable bed, and very rarely did I even miss dinner, so that in actual fact the whole affair was in my case pretty much of a luxury progress. Fifty-five of the hills were climbed on day excursions from my former home in Edinburgh, and in every other case the return was to a fully equipped and licensed hotel* (the latter adjective is inserted, I should explain, for the benefit of other Club members). If nowadays any kudos is to be obtained by ascending all the hills on the Munro list it will, I fear, have to be earned by climbing them all on dates between, say, 1st December and 31st March, or in some such fashion.

I am not prepared, however, to be too modest about the matter, and I would therefore quote two points in my favour. The first is that the hills were all ascended by me after the age of forty-five, though this is a very trifling thing in these days of longevity; when someone does the lot after he reaches sixty I shall be willing to take off my hat to him. The other point is, however, much more important — that no one before me has climbed the 277 mountains without the assistance of a beard. I do think that this is a really vital consideration; and indeed one might argue with considerable force that bearded men cannot, in a civilised society, be reckoned, and that therefore to me belongs the glory and honour of being the first to count as a conqueror of the Munros. While I would not be prepared to press this contention to the bitter end, or even to go to the length of arguing that to call in the extraneous assistance of a beard is as illegitimate from the mountaineering point of view as would be, for example, the making of all the ascents seated in a caterpillar tractor, I am still strongly of the opinion, however, that it is not quite playing the game; and when one contemplates in particular Robertson's conduct in

---

* These conditions are now known as Dow's Principles and have been adhered to by some Munroists - (W.D.B.)

this connection it is difficult to find suitable language in which adequately to describe it Burn, Parker and Corbett, while they certainly completed the list in each case with the aid of a beard, have had the grace not to play the hypocrite in the matter; but Robertson, after making no doubt full use of this artificial and (I repeat) semi-illegitimate aid, most basely and callously after his performance sacrificed that which I have no doubt really made the performance possible. I am content to draw attention to this, and to leave judgement to others, but a more lamentable example of sheer ingratitude I should have difficulty in conceiving.

One more word before leaving this subject of beards. Those who have had may I say the pleasure and privilege (please do not insert a query, Mr Editor) of ascending Munros with me may, on occasion, have marvelled somewhat at my solemn and respectful demeanour and behaviour when at the summit cairns. I should therefore explain that at these supreme moments there was always in my mind the thought that on this peak four grave and reverend men have at one time stood, and that over this cairn, on four great days of the past, four dignified and (more or less) flowing beards have wagged. Such thoughts, it will be admitted, would induce awe and reverence even in the most frivolous, and I hope that I am not of the most frivolous.

On the question of transport one point might be mentioned. I find that 214 out of the 277 hills were ascended with the help of a motor car — somebody else's when available, or my own in the last resort. These cars were left lying, generally for many hours at a time, here and there all over the Highlands without the slightest precaution ever being taken, and not only was there never any theft, but never once was anything even disturbed unless on one single occasion in Glencoe when the road reconstruction work was in full swing there. I do not think that a higher compliment could be paid to the people of the Highlands of Scotland than merely to state this fact; and I do not believe that in any other country in the world could such a record have been possible. Coming to statistics, I find that the ascent of the 277 Munros and of 153 of the subsidiary Tops in the Tables, most of which Tops were taken as being either on the route or reasonably near, required a total of 150 days out, spread over 6 years. I have sometimes been asked as to weather experiences, and I am giving a short analysis which may be of some slight interest in this connection. To the 150 days noted other 8 days have been added which were occupied by repeat ascents, and it must further be explained that owing to the necessity in my case invariably of making arrangements in advance none of the days was picked for weather reasons but all had to be taken just as they happened to come. I have assumed the three main enemies to be wind, mist and rain in the order stated, Class 3 comprising days when none of these was troublesome and Class 0 days in which they were all troublesome more or less. The result is as over.

In fully half of the months the totals are, of course, too small for the results to be of any value, but the preponderance of good weather in May and June and of bad weather in August is certainly striking, and the figures for the winter months are also interesting although as noted of little real value. As an interference with enjoyment mist is the greatest nuisance, and out of the 227 Munros 114 were mist-capped when ascended. For a variation of the proverbial pastime of hunting in a pitch-dark room for a black hat worn by a bare-headed nigger who isn't there, I can confidently recommend searching the summit plateau of a flat-topped Munro in thick cloud for a cairn which may not exist! — though in actual fact it almost always does. Only 20 Munros have summits without marking of any kind, and 10 of these are reasonably sharp-topped; but in a fair number of cases the cairn is not on the actual highest point of the hill.

	Class 3	Class 2.	Class 1.	Class 0.	Total.
January	2	2	1	1	6
February	2	2	1	-	5
March	2	1	1	2	6
April	7	6	5	5	23
May	13	15	2	3	33
June	9	7	3	2	21
July	4	2	1	-	7
August	3	4	7	2	16
September	1	-	-	1	2
October	5	8	8	3	24
November	1	1	1	-	3
December	3	7	1 1	12	158

On classifying, roughly, days in Classes 3 and 2 as good and in Classes 1 and 0 as bad, the following percentage results are obtained:-

	Good Per cent	Bad Per cent		Good Per cent	Bad Per cent
January	67	33	July	86	14
February	80	20	August	44	56
March	50	50	September	50	50
April	57	43	October	54	46
May	85	15	November	67	33
June	76	24	December	83	17

With regard to relative difficulty from the point of view of the hill walker, to which class will normally belong the type of man who will desire to complete all the Munros, it can quite definitely be repeated that there is nothing whatever out of Skye which cannot be ascended under normal conditions without the compulsory use of the hands. In Skye the Inaccessible Pinnacle is the only summit for the ascent of which a rope might be desirable, and even here if the hill walker finds, as he probably will, that the ascent of the shorter side is beyond his powers, and has to go up the eastern arete, he may feel that any help he can get from the rope is more moral than physical. None of the other Skye Munros need trouble the hill walker at all provided he goes to them in good weather.

And now, finally, a few remarks with regard to the Tables themselves. I understand that the new edition of the General Guide is to be issued with the Tables unaltered, but as the Club by including them in the Guide is to some extent accepting responsibility for them, more or less, I think that sooner or later their revision will have to be tackled, and possibly in the near or distant future the Club will appoint a Sub-Committee to take the job in hand. I am not personally aware of the rules which Sir Hugh Munro applied in deciding which were separate mountains and which were Tops — if indeed he did apply any rigid rules at all — but my own idea is that a businesslike classification would have to take into account the following factors, of importance in the order names, (1) dip, (2) distance and (3) difficulty. A formula could no doubt be evolved for dealing with the first two factors automatically, and while the third might to some extent be a matter of opinion general agreement as to the facts in each individual case would probably be found to exist. As an example of the changes which might be found necessary were the list to be reconsidered on these similar lines I might mention the following — as examples merely, not as an exhaustive list by any means:— An Teallach and Beinn Eighe might each rank as three Munros; the two Buachailles of Etive, Bidean nam Bian and Liathach might in each case rank as two Munros; Am Bathaich of Sgurr a'Mhaoraich might be a separate Munro; while on the other hand the number of Munros in the Cluny Ridge might be reduced from seven to five; Mam Sodhail might be a top of Carn Eige; in the Ardverikie Forest, Aonach Beag might be a top of Geal-Charn and Creag Pitridh a top of Mullach Coire an Iubhair; Carn Ban in the Monadhliaths might be a top of Carn Dearg; and An Garbhanach and Stob Coire a' Chairn in the Mamores might perhaps hardly be considered as separate Munros. There would also be many possible adjustments in the list of tops, but my notes are lengthy enough already.

Vol IV
(1896)

GARBH BHEINN, CLACH GLAS, AND BLAVEN, FROM SUMMIT OF MARSCO

BEN FESKINETH - A LOST MUNRO
Vol. XXXII (1981)   by J. C. Donaldson

It was impossible to give details of Ben Feskineth in the 1981 edition of The Tables as the information available was very sketchy. The position of this mountain is still not clear, but as rumours of its existence may be circulating it has been decided to make public such facts as are known.

During the summer of 1980 the writer came across a copy of a Guidebook to Scotland published by Adam & Charles Black. This was the 19th edition published in 1872. It contained a page which named the principal peaks of Scotland and, as good Edinburgh men, Messrs. Black had seen fit to include Arthur's Seat in the list, albeit the lowest eminence of all. But, somewhat higher up the list, appeared the entry — Ben Feskineth, Perthshire, 3530 feet and immediately there was the electrifying thought that there might yet be another Munro discovered neither by Munro nor the Ordnance Survey and that not even Colin Phillip or Hamish Brown had come across it during their perambulations of Scotland. Investigation became of the utmost importance.

The book in the writer's hands had belonged to a Mr George Burnet who, it was easily ascertained, died shortly after 1900 at no great age. His copy was the special 'Pedestrian's Edition' and there is a note in it by the publishers that a 'few copies have been printed on thin paper for the use of pedestrians.' From this it seemed reasonable to assume that he was an active mountaineer and as such might well have been an early member of the Scottish Mountaineering Club. A thorough search of the Journals right up to 1900 followed but there was no record of Burnet as a member. However, at the Dalmally Meet of 1894 a guest of the name of Burnett (two T's — but the Journal Editor has never been immune from error — no initials given) attended, apparently as the guest of either Tough or Brown, being out on the hils with one or both of these celebrated climbers on each day of the Meet. He never figures again in the pages of the Journal.

But, like the dog that failed to bark, the significant feature of this Meet may be that Munro himself was not present. Surely, if he had been there Burnet would have mentioned this mountain that was listed in his book but not in Munro's Tables, in which case the mystery might have been solved there and then.

There followed some months of inaction broken only by a moment's excitement when a climber was encountered who claimed to have actually climbed Ben Feskineth. But the euphoria quickly subsided when it was established that he really meant Ben Heasgarnich. Now, the heights of the two peaks are the same, and it did seem possible that confusion might have risen in Black's mind but, as a visit to the National Library Map Room quickly showed, this was not the case. Along with their guidebooks Blacks had commissioned Mr John G Bartholomew to produce a set of maps of Scotland with a scale of 4 miles to the inch. They are beautifully drawn maps and that of Perthshire, while it shows a croft called

Feskinninch at the foot of Loch Lyon, clearly names Benheasgarnich (sic) in its proper place. There is no Feskineth, while the O.S. map for the same period has a different name for the croft.

The next step was to find out what help the National Library itself could give. Two editions of the book were made available for inspection, one being the same edition as had already been seen, the other the 15th edition published in 1861. This earlier edition also mentioned Feskineth but gave its height as only 3521 feet, which was at least evidence that by 1872 recognition that some mountains were capable of changing their height (S.M.C.J., 1977, xxxi, 191) was already established. In neither edition does Ben Heasgarnich appear in the list of principal peaks. In both editions the editors invited corrections, but while in 1861 they offered to send a free copy to anyone returning a guidebook annotated with corrections they did not do so in 1872. One assumes that the offer was withdrawn having been found to be too expensive. But it is reasonable to suggest that someone must have pointed out that they had the height of Feskineth wrong in 1861. Otherwise it would not have been changed. But if the height was corrected why not the name if that was wrong? The index to the guide is no help, although comprehensive it includes neither Feskineth nor Heasgarnich.

The likely explanation of the mystery may well be that Feskineth is really Heasgarnich but as the possibility of another Munro is involved a decision one way or another cannot be lightly made.

Another explanation that has been put forward relates to the astonishing rate of growth of the mountain already referred to - nine feet in only eleven years. Perhaps like a mushroom its rapid burgeoning was followed by a brief maturity and equally rapid collapse. Who knows, perhaps only The Doctor can provide a satisfactory solution to the problem? If he could be persuaded to lead a team of investigators suitably qualified for so important a matter, readers might expect a report in a subsequent Journal.

To finish on a lighter note, Black's Guide provides much practical imformation within its pages. Of particular interest to climbers are the prices charged for coffee and whisky: sixpence for a cup of the former and threepence for a glass of the latter in 1861. But by 1872, while the cost of coffee was unchanged the price of whisky had doubled! - 'O MIHI PRAETERITOS REFERAT SI JUPITER ANNOS'.

AN OCCASION
Vol. XXXII (1982)   by G.J.F. Dutton

'The Doctor' and his hapless associates have been popular denizens of Journal pages for twenty years. Their absurd adventures would fill a book - and have, The Ridiculous Mountains. One example will suffice in this one ...

"Of course we should go," said the Doctor, sternly. "The least we can do. He is a Good Man, and has been kind to us. The Apprentice and I groaned. The back bar of Daddy McKay's gleamed in sympathy. There seemed no way out. Our consciences shared the same rope: the Doctor couldn't go alone. But he frowned. He drank thoughtfully; a good fifty pence of Glen Bogle. "It might even be an enjoyable occasion." He was unconvincing. We stared into our glasses; Glen Bogle stared back.

The occasion was to be the Last Munro of old Zero. Old Zero, alias The Reverend Zoar McKinley McSigh, M.A., B.D., had been a friend of the Doctor's at college. "He always was an elderly-looking youth," the Doctor recalled. Twenty-five years later he resembled a grave and active septuagenarian. He was the respected minister of a Wee Free flock in Glasgow, a staunch teetotaller and tireless campaigner for the Light, a diligent visitor of the sick and uncared-for. Distressingly admirable. He made us fidget. "Excellent fellow," the Doctor would say; and reach for Glen Bogle or its equivalent. The Rev. McSigh had nevertheless one fleshly weakness. He climbed hills. As a student he had climbed Salisbury Crags; but he gave up such doubtful adherences on ordination. A long hill walk inspired a wider view, and he persuaded his congregation that no trespass was involved. Certainly his Saturday excesses brought them fine draughts of fire and resonance the following day, in both Gaelic and English.

The path is slippery, however, and the Devil had whispered 'Munros' .... There was no excuse. True, the first Compleater, No. 1, had been a minister, but the Rev. A.E. Robertson was not of the Evangelical Free Church; and therefore no fit person to emulate. As with lesser men, totals inflated the head of McSigh. Pride lifted him continually above 3000 feet; outlandish hills were followed. Little by little. Until Auld Hornie had sold him the lot, and the last one was coming up this Saturday. It was Carn an t-Sagairt Mor* . Would so auspicious a name avert retribution?

No. To ensure infernal success the Tempter took on the irrepressible and rotund form of A.J. Evergreen Smith, who had completed them all — Separate Mountains, Subsidiary Tops, Eminences Furth of Scotland and the whole litter of Corbetts, Donalds, Dochertys and Maxwells — a dozen times ..... Evergreen, a compulsive organiser, happened to organise the Boys' Brigade in McSigh's district and soon swept the straying minister into

---

Big Hill of the Priest — Ed.

intemperate and brow-knitting enthusiasm: the ascent of his Last Munro should be a Real Occasion.

Not only would the youth organisation of all the kirks in McSigh's district take part, but even the more able-bodied of his own congregation. And also as many as possible of the previous Compleaters would be called out, each identified by the number of his or her position in the Official List of Munroists as published (shame-facedly) by the editor of the *Journal*. All would assemble at the summit, where the Rev. Zoar would exhort them before psalm-singing and descent. Exceptionally blameless, if somewhat Apocalyptic. And the Doctor and ourselves were especially asked to share his pleasure. How could we refuse? Glen Bogle gave no answer. It glumly retreated beneath our eyes.

Well, we were there. At the foot of Carn an t-Sagairt Mor. As expected, mist and drizzle. Last Munros are usually, despite the weather, scenes of alcoholic mirth, often of excess. This occasion would be decorous. At first, no stimulating beverage was considered; but the diabolical inspirer of Evergreen Smith persuaded minister and elders, in view of the cold and exertion, to allow a little weak medicinal wine for those frailer members of the congregation who might need it — no beer, and certainly nothing spirituous. After all, a sip of Bouvier or suchlike celebrated physical thankfulness on these occasions in the old days. He even persuaded, with the extensive nether forces at his disposal, McSigh to agree to savour a touch of weak, very weak, medicinal wine himself at the top. McSigh had never — not even as a divinity student — tasted alcohol; his Communion wine was non-alcoholic; this was indeed a victory for darkness. He had wrestled; but — the Last Munro: just once, just once; to do it 'properly'.

The Doctor had no objection to wine on the hill; he toasted Alpine summits with aluminium and vin-du-pays. But that week a rich and thankful patient had given him a bottle of Lochaber No More, the finest and rarest of malt whiskies, 16 years old and 100 proof . . . . The temptation to alleviate the strain of duty was too great; he brought it with him.

From the busy group round the cars and buses that morning, McSigh came over. As a special mark of friendship he presented us with a half-bottle of wine, wrapped in brown paper. "Just like my own — of course I shall take only a sip — but I expect you fellows will nearly empty the bottle!" And almost a wink from that clear blue eye: then he swiftly returned to the black-coated huddle of elders.

We unwrapped the brown paper, and stared. *Sister McVittie's Medicinal Wine. Extra Weak; Formulated Specially for Invalids and Similar Persons. Sister McVittie*, unexpectedly rubicund, eyed us firmly and therapeutically from the label. She pointed unflinchingly at the small print: *Guaranteed to contain less than 0.5% ethanol.* We unscrewed the bottle and sniffed. Ghastly. The Doctor hurried behind the car. He emptied the bottle, washed it thoroughly, and refilled it with Lochaber No More. He put it in his rucksack for the hill. He did not wish to hurt his old friend.

We relaxed, and set off. As we left, crates of Sister McVittie were being unloaded and dispensed, each bottle wrapped in brown paper, to the many Invalids and Similar Persons of McSigh's congregation; they stuffed them hurriedly away in pockets and bags.

It was no climb. Wet heather and grass, uphill. Visibility, a dozen yards. Interesting yards. Across them passed a succession of improbable figures. Not only the elders and congregation, puffing and mist-dripping, in gumboots, goloshes and steel-rimmed spectacles, clutching black plastic bags and wilting umbrellas; not only the pink and uniformed Youth carrying banners; but also more familiar figures in rock-torn attire, some already well-stimulated and each bearing his number as a Compleat Munroist; the Mark of the Beast, as arranged by Evergreen's Infernal Master. (Prudence compels the narrator to change the numbers here and To State Clearly That they *Are* Changed ....). Several, as a token of respect requested by Evergreen, were repeating for McSigh's Last Ascent, the self-imposed conditions of their own Last Ascent. They paraded like sufferers out of Dante. Number 112 was carrying a set of pipes, No. 105 a folding stool; 125 was burdened with his skis. Number 172 was in evening dress, No. 230 in nothing but a kilt and a false beard. Number 83, who had stepped to his summit cairn carrying his fiancee, a wee smasher, in his arms, now followed obediently her matronly shadow; No. 76 experienced similar difficulty with his baby, grown too large for the rucksack, who stalked gloomily beside him, six foot three and desirous of Hampden.

Halfway up we came across Sir Hector Macassar — No. 56, an old vintage — sprawling on a plastic Inverness cape. Unashamedly, he was enjoying his whisky. He offered us some. The Doctor slung off his sack and in turn proffered our disguised Lochaber No More (Sister McVittie continued to point, unmoved). Despite Sir Hector's indignant refusal, we poured it out, pressed it within olfactory range. Whiskers twitched. Eyes widened. Mouth opened. Savour. Gulp. Savour.

"Terrific stuff, man, terrific stuff . . . . Where on earth . . . .?" The Doctor signalled silence.

McSigh had appeared. Well ahead of his flock, only the fittest of elders beside him. He came up to us. Sir Hector, also once a fellow-student, welcomed old Zero and offered him a drink.

"No, no. No. But — " and here McSigh glanced most gaily at his elders, who smiled grimly and inspected the turf — "at the top I mean to take a wee mouthful: of weak, very weak, medicinal wine." And he produced his half-bottle. Macassar sat up, unwrapped it and held it at arm's length.

"It's real!" insisted the unbecomingly enthusiastic Zero.

"Disgraceful," observed Macassar. His further remarks were lost in the arrival of others. Among them were those two inveterate old summit-scavengers, Geordie and Wull.

'Awfy wet day," volunteered Geordie. "Could dae wi the sun," suggested Wull.

And of course Evergreen himself, leading battalions of the young, his bald head gleaming with drizzle and pleasure, his twelve cards twinkling. About him dangled also multicoloured buttons, symbols of the various groups of sub-Munros he had conquered and reconquered throughout the four and a half countries of the British Isles.

We extricated ourselves, put Lochaber No More back in the rucksack and steamed on. "Keep it for the top," advised the Doctor.

At the top, there was some delay. The battalions had to be mustered, the flock folded and stragglers accounted for. Number 76 had lost his baby, No. 112 his Low G. But it was a gallant throng. Banners dripped determinedly.

An elbow nudged me, hard. It was Geordie, offering a can of Export. "Aye, doon wi it," urged Wull, holding two. We quaffed. The Doctor was about to open our supercharged Sister McVittie: but the ceremony had begun.

Cries for silence. Banners dipped. The Rev. Zoar McKinley McSigh was balanced on the cairn and about to address us.

"My friends, this is a Happy Occasion. We have taken a rest from our Everyday Toil, and are gathered here together in the Clear Upper Air...."

Geordie, beside me, nodded and wiped froth into his moustache; drizzle beaded his sweating brow. Zero then elaborated the parallels with the Spiritual Ascent — the steepness, the backslidings, the mists, the rewards of perseverance. We wondered how soon he would come to the wine. Quite soon.

"And now we have reached this top. This Earthly Top; that is yet, friends, also a Higher Top. And we shall celebrate that Higher Top shortly, with all our hearts. But before celebrating that Higher Top, let us pause, and celebrate this Earthly Top. In an earthly way: for have we not reached here, friends, by an Earthly Way?" Geordie nodded. Wull drank noisily behind him; too precipitate — steel spectacles turned and frowned.

"Let us celebrate this Earthly Top in an Earthly Way, in the customary manner, before we go on, before we celebrate our greater ascent. Let us drink a toast to the friendly earth and stones that have helped us up, so far, so very far — though not, friends, far enough." Geordie clouted my ribs again — "Man, he gies ye an awfy thirst, ken," he whispered hoarsely, "dither in-datherin awa like yon." But the Rev. Zoar signalled down to his elders. Furtive rustling of brown paper behind the cairn.

"Let us therefore drink a toast. Some may wish water, fine burn water, others the juice of fruits, others, others," — he hesitated — "others may be forgiven, perhaps, a mouthful of weak, weak, medicinal wine, for such an occasion, for such an occasion. O, it is a weakness, a failing of the flesh, for the flesh is weak in climbing a mountain; it is like embrocation for the stiffness or plaster for the blisters, on a mountain .... A weakness, a failing, but" - (he was clearly anxious to get on with the experiment) — "in-human-sympathy-with-those-before-us-who-sought, amidst-all-difficulties-of-stress-and-storm, these-heights-of-our-earthly-kingdom, we-will-celebrate, each-in-his-own-way, our-vouchsafed-and-happy-arrival-here."

He bent down and was handed a large cup (!) by a frozen-faced elder. It appeared remarkably full. It winked over the brim as he stood erect. He raised it to his lips. A hundred other cups, glasses, flasks and bottles of coke were raised also.

"To our Bonnie Caledonian Hills and our climb beyond them to greater and more blessed Heights ...."

He downed it. All downed it. Very felicitous. We were moved. The Apprentice ventured not a joke. We were all brought up in good kirk-fearing households. And old Zero was so excellent a man

He was also a thirsty one. His mouthful drained his cup. He looked surprised. The wine — even under the resolute supervision of Sister McVittie — affected him severely. He was quite unused to alcohol. He coughed, sneezed, grew red and watery-eyed. He swayed, and was helped down. Great applause, rapturous from the like of Geordie and Wull and Macassar, dubiously tight-lipped from the umbrella'd and goloshed throng.

Buzz of conversation. Then a psalm began.

Having no book, the Doctor hauled out our bottle. He unscrewed it and offered it to Geordie and Wull. They read the label, glanced at each other, and shook their heads. The Doctor winked and grinned broadly, poured some into a plastic glass and handed it to Geordie. Geordie tasted it, blinked, and handed it to Wull. Wull sipped it, twice, and handed it back.

"Good, eh?" asked the Doctor, pouring some out for us. "Sixteen years old, 100 proof, and the best!"

"No bad," said Geordie; "but no like whisky, mind."

'Ay, whisky'd be the thing," agreed Wull. "Gey cauld here the now."

We stared uncomprehendingly at their lack of taste. The Doctor shrugged, and swigged his glass.

"Grooogh!" He spat it out. "Wine; damned medicinal wine! Evergreen's damned medicinal wine!" We all spat in sympathy, upsetting the damp-leaved psalmists about us.

'Some swine's switched bottles!" choked the Doctor. But his rage, and the countering belligerence of our shocked and hitherto tuneful neighbours, were lost in a growing tumult.

The psalm had ended. The crowd pushed forward. The Rev. McSigh, clutching his cup, refilled and respilling, was endeavouring to climb back up his cairn. Two elders were trying to assist him, three to restrain him. On hands and knees he reached the top. He was excited and flushed. He perilously straightened and stood, swaying. Then he began to bellow.

It was a rousing sermon, graphically if unconventionally illustrated. More of Paisley than Chalmers. Much was in Gaelic.

McSigh was above and due west of us; it was a westerly wind. We sniffed .... "Lochaber No More, by the Devil!" hissed the Doctor. "He's been drinking our bottle!"

I glimpsed Macassar a little way along, gold teeth filling his whiskers, cigar in hand, gazing happily. It had been him; while we were distracted by Geordie and Wull and Evergreen...

A rousing sermon; but the preacher was profoundly drunk. One hundred proof, 16 years old .... We listened and watched admiringly. He maintained precarious balance, on both cairn and theology. The congregation stood enthralled. Never had flames roared brighter. Calvin stoked furiously, Knox brought more faggots. Heavens! Another gulp from the cup...

The Doctor was about to scramble up and snatch it, risking unseemly altercation; when further fruits of error, rewards of Satan, tumbled to earth. A body of police, waterproofed, radio'd and ominously bulging, pushed amongst us.

The Inspector — our old friend McHaig — seized the Doctor. "Ah, thank heaven, it's yourself, Doctor: what is going on here, now?"

A very puzzled man. We explained. He stopped breathing. Then he stepped back, slapped his thigh and began to curse, most frightfully and unsuitably. Our black-coated neighbours, breathless in their turn, white with horror, turned and engulfed him. One furious lady shook him, another slapped off his cap, another hit him quite hard with her umbrella.

Violence breeds violence. His men breathed deeply, felt under their raincoats, bayed, and likewise surged forward, grabbing most ungently. A regular brawl developed. We saw the helpless Evergreen, betrayed by the False One, delivered to judgement; his glittering badges proclaimed him ringleader. The Inspector ran about trying to call off his keepers of the peace. Scuffles, cries. We began to imagine a CS edge to the westerly drifts of Lochaber No More. Above us, the sermon continued, a uniformed interrupter being disposed of by an accurate kick.

Eventually the Inspector, with the Apprentice's rather too eager help, drove his men out of the fray. Order was more or less restored. Silence fell.

We all looked up. The cairn was bare. No preacher.

He was lying flat beside it. Two elders lay beside him. Uproar again. Hysterics. The Doctor hurried forward. He knelt by the victims, undid collars, felt pulses, listened to chests.

We saw, with relief, the bodies stir, and sit up. They rubbed eyes and groaned. Two fell back and began to snore. The Rev. McSigh, a man of steel, accepted a hand and was helped up. The Doctor, ever sagacious, leapt on the cairn. He called for silence. He explained that Excitement, due to the unfortunate error of our gallant police — who were looking for .... for burglars (unlikely, we thought) — that Excitement has caused Mr McSigh to lose his balance. The fall had stunned him. But no injury whatever; perfectly fit. Though naturally he might be somewhat giddy for a while, with a headache and perhaps difficulty in communication for an hour or two. And the elders? Ah, the elders had also suffered from Excitement, but they were older men, and might take a little longer to regain their feet; but nothing serious, nothing at all. Plenty of willing hands. Let us continue with the service. Not spoil so happy an occasion. Another psalm. Eighty-four? To Martyrdom? Let our good friends the police join in ....

Cheers, clapping. Singing. The Doctor rejoined us through an accolade of black gloves.

"Tight as owls," he said, "all three of 'em. The elders sooked the bottle behind his back. Old devils. Hardly any left. Let's go and finish it."

A hand tapped the Doctor's shoulder. Inspector McHaig. Sad and embarrassed. He drank the proffered glass without a word. Then, nervously, he explained why he had been summoned.

"A damned old fool" — a Major Pigstrap (the name sounded like that, but surely could not be) — had rung him up excitedly. Pigstrap lived just outside Balqueenie and had been taking exercise from his car, near the track up the glen. He had seen strange motor cars, vans and buses arrive. From Glasgow. *Glasgow!* Nosey-like, he had investigated further, with dog and walking stick, and had seen troops of people, some with curious bags, some with badges and numbers pinned on them; some in paramilitary uniform and carrying banners. All disappearing up into the mist. Some secret rendezvous. Many young, many older — old enough to know better, obviously there to lead them on, furtive, desperate-looking dark-clad buttoned-up people, grim-faced, determined — Real Reds they must be, Fanatics. And they were carrying, and trying to hide from him, brown paper parcels that looked like bottles — inflammable liquid? *Petrol bombs!* That's what they would be! Petrol Bombs! And he had heard bagpipes ... - *Nationalists* there as well. He had asked a youth what was going on: the answer was sinister — "A special occasion. Arranged for No. 293. *The Big Event.* Secret, you see. Code. Cells." Pigstrap had crescendo'd by describing it, through foam, as an armed meeting of activist extremists who would afterwards descend on the, on the ... McHaig looked grave. "You ken WHO's staying there the now ...."

The Inspector wiped his brow in anguish. It had *seemed* so genuine. Why, as they had puffed up — too misty for helicopters — they even heard singing. Impassioned singing. The SAS man attached to them (McHaig peered anxiously around) had unhesitatingly identified Old Hundredth as the Internationale ..... "Ye cannae blame the lads, like ...."

Nothing would happen, we reassured him. Errors were too evenly distributed. He came down the hill with us, his men limping behind. He ignored the ribald staggerers to right and left. He ignored the obviously unsuitable would-be drivers singing on the road beneath. He ignored the piper on the bonnet, hugging his recovered low G. It was enough to have avoided arresting the Rev. Zoar McKinley McSigh, M.A., B.D., for being drunk and disorderly and/or inciting to riot and/or civil disobedience and/or armed insurrection on the summit of Carn an t-Sagairt Mor at 13.15 hrs on the 11th October, nineteen hundred and whatever .... A narrow escape. He pressed both the Doctor's hands silently as he left. From high above came wafts of (devoutly-led) thanksgiving.

The Doctor let the clutch in, rather cautiously. In the back seat, the Apprentice and I passed between us the much-diminished but authentic bottle of Lochaber No More. We had left Sister McVittie behind the ditch. We lay back, content.

The Doctor swerved skilfully round an errant sheep.

"Quite an occasion," he said.

IN MEMORIAM

In this chapter are memorial references to a few of those who have played a significant role in the progress of Mountaineering in Scotland which is the theme of this anthology. There are of course many others which available space does not allow us to include. In fact only an introductory extract is given for most of them. Their complete obituaries would cover a substantial part of the Scottish Mountaineering record

JOSEPH GIBSON STOTT
Vol. XXI (1938)   by R.A. Robertson

Every member of the Club will regret the passing of Joseph Gibson Stott, which took place at Melbourne on the 11th of June last, at the age of seventy-seven.

I understand that a short history of the Journal is likely to appear in the Jubilee Number. To all the original members and to many other Joe Stott was the Journal. Its history will be the finest memoir of him, and without trespassing on this it is fitting that in the present number something more than a mere intimation of his death should be noted.

Probably nine-tenths of the members never saw Joe, and these may wish to have a personal description of this "big chiel ayont the seas" over whom there was cast such a spell by the Bens and Glens of Scotland that he wrote of them year in and year out during nearly fifty years of exile. What was he like? He was of medium height, stoutly built, a well-made man with prodigious muscular strength and one of the cheeriest of companions. He was a man to go "tiger-hunting" with. You felt that he would be steadfast and true to the very end. He was a "salvationist," but of a sterner and more robust type than that pictured by Dr Hely Almond, who coined that word. Hill-walking was his passion and the longest of days had no terror for him. Had he had the time and opportunity he would have made a good third to Munro and the Rev. A.E. Robertson in acquiring and dispersing knowledge of the Scottish hills. Perhaps of necessity he had a craze for walking during the night, and he was the ringleader in many mad walks which space forbids me from describing. To him "it was a pleasure sure in being mad which none but madmen know." Those who never knew Joe may understand that those who possessed his friendship have a most affectionate memory of him, and those who were in touch with him during his long exile can realise that his thoughts and dreams were in the heartbreak words of Robert Louis Stevenson:

"Blows the wind to-day, and the sun and the rain are flying,
Blows the wind on the moor, to-day and now.
Where about the graves of the martyrs the whaups are crying,
My heart remembers how."

SALVATIONIST AND ULTRAMONTANE
Vol. XXII (1939) by J.H. Bell

"...The Salvationist takes his pick from the list, And the agile Ultramontane finds the exercise he's wantin'——"

- The S.M.C. Song, by J. G Stott

No doubt many of our members, as well as members of the Junior Club, have sometimes pondered over the origin and significance of these two words as applied to mountaineers. The Club Song itself was composed by J. G. Stott, the first Editor. The first three verses arrived from his place of exile, New Zealand, in time for the Loch Awe Meet of New Year 1892. The lines quoted above are from the fourth verse, which, along with the rest, was printed in the Journal of January 1894. The terms themselves appear to have originated in an article, "Ben y Gloe on Christmas Day," by Hely H. Almond (Journal, Vol. II., p. 235). His dissertation is so humorous and illuminating that we make no apology for including a lengthy quotation.

"Members of the Mountaineering Club may be divided into two classes. There are those whose ambition it is to scale the inaccessible side of peaks with unpronounceable names....I admire these people; I like to dine with them and hear them talk; for the sake of a name I call them the Ultramontanes. It is delicious and inspiring, in these after-dinner moments, to rise to the faith which is beyond reason, and like various kinds of spirits, above proof, and to murmur Credo quia impossibile.

"But let me confess with all due humility and shame, that I have permanently enlisted in the Salvation Army, which is the name I give to the second class of mountaineers. As our name implies, we like to know that we are safe - absolutely safe. We don't like contusions; we would rather go home to dinner than lie on the ground till people came to set our bones, or carry us off on a stretcher; we have no desire to be the conscious element of an avalanche or a land-slip. And yet, like Mark Twain on his celebrated ascent of the Riffelberg, we like something of the pomp and circumstance of glorious war - an alpenstock, a bit of rope, blue spectacles - a good deal of noise and fuss about it when we come home again....Now I am going to make a bold assertion - perhaps too bold. I believe the Salvation Army to be in a majority in the Club..."

Doubtless these are ideal types, and many of us indulge in both forms of climbing. Even so, the comprehensive nature of the Club cannot be better exemplified than by the inclusion in this number of a biographical memoir on the leading historical figure as regards each of these two aspects of Scottish mountaineering.

69. Cairngorm Langlauf. Crossing the plateau from Braeriach to Cairn Toul

70. The Scottish Haute Route. On the ridge of the Grey Corries

71. The Scottish Haute Route. Skiing from Stob Coire Easain towards Sgurr Choinnich Mor

72. Off Piste in the Cairngorms. The run from Ben Macdui down to the Lairig Ghru

First - The Salvationist
SIR HUGH T. MUNRO, BART   by Jas. A Parker

Hugh Munro was an original member of the Club and was, in fact, one of its most enthusiastic promoters. He was one of the strongest personalities in the Club, and probably no one did more for it than he during the first twenty-five years of the Club's existence. It is curious to reflect now that of the present members of the Club 75 per cent. never met him, and to them "Munro" is little more than a mere name for any Scottish Mountain of, or exceeding, 3,000 feet in height.

Munro belonged to Angus where his home was the dower house of Drumleys, and latterly, when he succeeded his father in 1913, the mansion house of Lindertis, about three miles to the west of Kirriemuir. Munro was a member of the first Committee, and served on the Committee until 1915 with only three short breaks, a total in all of nineteen years' service. He was Vice-President in 1893, and President, the third, in 1894-97. He was admitted to the Alpine Club in March 1893, and was a Fellow of the Royal Geographical Society.

Munro is believed to have missed very few of the Annual Dinners of the Club, and at the first one he replied for "The Lairds." He was a most regular attender at the Meets and would return to Scotland from the most outlandish places in order to attend one. Of the fifty-seven Meets that were held from April 1889 to Easter 1916, Munro attended no fewer than forty-one. From Easter 1895 to January 1913 he missed only three Meets out of a possible of thirty-four. Surely this constitutes a record!

Munro always had the intention that when he succeeded his father there would be a Meet of the Scottish Mountaineering Club at Lindertis. As a matter of fact there were two, the first in January 1915 and the second in the following May. The attendance at each was necessarily small; but it is needless to say that the two Meets were most enjoyable, as Munro was a perfect host. The writer of this note attended the second Meet, and on several occasions was a guest at Drumleys or Lindertis.

Munro was a regular contributor to the *Journal*, and altogether about eighty-four articles or notes by him appeared in the first fifteen volumes. His most important contribution was, of course, his famous "Tables giving all the Scottish Mountains exceeding 3,000 feet in height," which were published in the *Journal* for September 1891, the compilation of which involved a tremendous amount of accurate work.Otherwise his most important articles were "Winter Ascents," "Dark Lochnagar," "Ben-y-Gloe," "The Western Cairngorms," and "An Teallach."

As far as Scottish Mountaineering was concerned Munro had three ambitions, viz.: to be a President of the Club, to hold a Club Meet at Lindertis, and to get to the top of every one of the five hundred and thirty-eight 3,000-foot mountain tops that were mentioned in his Tables. He achieved the first two, but the fates were against him as regards the third.

He managed to get to the summits of all the "tops" with the exception of two, these being the Inaccessible Pinnacle in Skye, which beat him many times, and Carn Cloich-mhuillinn in the Cairngorms, which latter he had kept for "the last one" as he wished to invite the Aberdeen members to attend the ceremony!

But it was not to be. His last tries at the Pinnacle were made in September 1915. In the spring of 1918 he went to Tarascon with his two daughters and started a canteen there for the French troops. That done he returned home to attend to his estate. He went back to Tarascon in the spring of 1919, caught a chill, and died from pneumonia a month later at the age of sixty-three. His obituary notice by W.Douglas, with a contribution by Miss A. K. Munro, his sister, appeared in the *Journal* for October 1919.

next - the Ultramontane
HAROLD RAEBURN
by W.N. Ling

As one looks back over the annals of the Club for the fifty years of its existence which we are now celebrating, certain names stand out prominently of those who have done much pioneer work and have enhanced its prestige as a mountaineering club. Amongst these must be counted the name of Harold Raeburn.

He was not an original member, but joined the Club in 1896, and at once began to pile up a formidable list of explorations and first ascents. Gifted by Nature with a marvellous sense of balance, a wiry frame, and an extraordinary suppleness of limb, he added to these a cool judgment, entire fearlessness, and an indomitable will which refused to be beaten. An intense interest in Nature in all her manifestations, in wild life of birds and beasts, in flowers and plants, in rocks and the structure of mountains, gave him that keenness of observation which at once caught the attention of anyone who had the privilege of being his companion.

This keenness of observation enabled him to discover many of the climbs which have become classic in the history of the Club, and in no selfish spirit did he keep his discoveries to himself, but was always ready to place his skill and experience at the service of others less gifted than himself. Many a member of the Club will acknowledge the help and education he received from him, and he was always ready to initiate any keen young novice into the mysteries of the mountains.

As examples of some of his work may be cited the following. Several unsuccessful attempts by strong parties had been made on the Church Door Buttress on Bidean nam Bian from 1894 onwards, bit it was not until July 1898 that the ascent was finally achieved by a party led by Raeburn, who had to remove his boots before he finally conquered the crucial difficulty.

The Observatory Ridge, Ben Nevis (alone), was another of his pioneer ascents, and indeed the mountain was a great favourite of his, both in winter and summer, as climbs on the North-East Buttress, Castle, North Trident Buttress, and others show.There are very few parts of Scotland where some new route or climb was not discovered by him.

The Barrel Buttress on Quinag was another well worked out job which Mackay has graphically described in his article written after Raeburn's death. There were one or two pitches of great severity, and on the first attempt the party was brought to a halt by a pitch which seemed to block further progress. It was decided to prospect the climb from the top, and this was gained by an easy gully between the buttresses.From here the upper part was descended to about 30 feet above the highest point reached on the first attempt. A rope ring and a doubled rope were used to overcome this part, which was overhanging. Then the rope was pulled down and the pitch tackled in earnest. From the shoulder of the second man - Mackay — Raeburn managed to get over the overhang to a good stance. The second man followed from the third man's shoulder. The third man, who was fortunately the lightest, unable to stand on his own shoulder, had to kick off below the overhang and be hauled up, rather breathless, and the difficulty was overcome. This was typical of Raeburn's unwillingness to accept defeat.

He was a prolific writer in the Journal, and in the first ten volumes his name as author appears no less than forty-nine times.

His book, "Mountaineering Art," is a model of what such a work should be, and has doubtless helped many a young mountaineer to grasp the theory and practice of climbing. I remember meeting two young Americans on Monte Rosa, and in the course of conversation asking them what had started them on their climbing career. Their answer was that they had come across Raeburn's book. When I told them that I had been his companion in many a mountain adventure, their interest was almost embarrassing.

His modest accounts of his successes at home and abroad do not give a full picture of his greatness as a climber. I can see him as he fought his way up the east face of Monte Rosa from Macugnaga, up the Zmutt Ridge of the Matterhorn draped in ice, and taking eleven hours from a high bivouac, and in the Viereselgrat of the Dent Blanche, all first British guideless ascents.

I can see him, too, on the seaward face of Slogen in Norway, a climb not repeated for twenty-five years, on the ice-clad cliffs of Tschantschachi Choch, and in a five days' battle with the twin peaks of Uschba, in the Caucasus, where defeat left no bitter feeling, for he had gone to the extreme limit of safety, but no one saw him on his daring, single-handed traverse of the Meije in Dauphine.

His gallant attempts, too, in the Himalaya, in spite of crippling illness, showed the mettle of the man, and acclaimed him one of the foremost mountaineers of his day.It is right, therefore, that on this anniversary in the history of our Club we should honour his memory for the distinction he brought to the Club, and the shining example he gave to all of us, his contemporaries and followers.

IN MEMORIAM (extracts)

Vol. XXXI (1976)   J.H.B. BELL, D.Sc.

It is difficult to know how to commemorate adequately in print a man like Bell. An issue of the Journal could be entirely filled with history and anecdote — but to what end? One might as well make every page a photograph of a Scottish hill, and try that way to memorialise the Highland landscape. He is too big. To those who knew him, Bell will remain a great force quite undiminished by death. We can only address the following lines to those who never knew him, and we hope in some degree they will personalise the man who in his own lifetime passed from mere legend into myth. There is firstly an outline — they can all only be outlines — of Bell's contribution to climbing in Scotland, by a leader of the generation most directly inspired by him; then follow sketches of the man himself in action - in battle, feast and argument — by two of his companions; finally a meagre account of his achievement as Journal editor — and it can be meagre, for is not that achievement, at least, firmly in place between boards? But the anecdotes keep breaking in - as they must, with Jim Bell, for always that irrepressible twinkle, that outrageously pungent humour, lay behind the granite authority of his logic.

W.H.M.

Vol. XXVII (1963)   ROBIN SMITH

In maturity he was one of the hardest climbers I have known. His strength and perseverance were shattering. On one climb he hung on a problem, spending five or six hours to gain some ten feet, whilst using a towel to swab the wet weep from the rock. On his winter ascent of Gardyloo he cut for six hours to overcome the near- vertical 150-foot prow of the ice-plated buttress. Or his ascent, under almost winter conditions, of the Fischer Wand, with several unpremeditated bivouacs, frostbite, darkness, enormous cornices, and hunger; in fact, a typical Smith outing. He delighted in impromptu, unexpected incidents which would carry the adventure far into the night, to impress one's memory indelibly with a sense of satisfying fulfilment and a wild belonging to the mountain world.

But now Smith's gone, killed unbelievably on some Russian mountain. He is, and always shall be, greatly missed by his friends, and can certainly never be forgotten by the climbing world.

His long list of first ascents, both summer and winter, encompass some of the finest climbs ever to be made in this country. Abroad, his seasons, ill-planned and shambolic, naturally accounted for most of the great routes in both the Dolomites and Western Alps.

Undoubtedly the greatest climber of our generation to join the club, he was possibly the most outstanding mountaineer throughout the long and varied history of the S.M.C.

It is hard to avoid the pitfall of remorse and endless eulogies; but he himself would reject these, and we are best to remember him by his wild whoops, the tuneless ballads wailing from some fearful dank wall, the hair-raising climbs far into the night and his wanderings about the moonlit snows of the Highland summits.

J.R.M.

Vol. XXIX (1971)   THOMAS WALTON PATEY

With the death of Tom Patey, the Club has lost a member of outstanding talent and personality. As a mountaineer, he was an all-rounder of astonishing versatility and international reputation, while at home his explorations ranged as widely as those of Raeburn and Bell, predecessors of the same stamp. In purely climbing terms his contribution was enormous; in new routes he was prolific, in directing attention to new climbing grounds and attitudes, equally so. His popularity and influence 'shifted the centre of gravity of British climbing several hundreds of miles northwards.' This achievement was all the more remarkable considering that as an individualist he was far from being an organisation man. He was doctor, musician, writer, raconteur and mountaineer extraordinary. In any one of these roles he could have made his living, and in them all he enriched the mountaineering scene.

In twenty years of continuous and high standard climbing many shared his rope.No one man was closely associated with him throughout the whole period. This appreciation comes therefore in two parts: the first from his Aberdeen friends with whom he climbed during the fifties, and the second from Hamish MacInnes, a frequent companion of the sixties.

W.D.B.

Vol. XXXII (1980)   JOHN CUNNINGHAM

Cunningham was not a member of the SMC and did not contribute any articles to the *Journal*. However, an anthology about a 'Century of Scottish Mountaineering' would be incomplete without due reference to him.

The death of John Cunningham closed a unique chapter in Scottish climbing history. His career was exceptional for he was responsible for a proliferation of new routes over a span of thirty years. John started climbing as a lad of fifteen — on hard routes, and ended as he began, still climbing at a very high standard with a competence which earned him the respect of everyone he knew, and many he didn't. For several decades he was a legend and a driving force in the Creagh Dhu Mountaineering Club.

As a shipwright he served his time in John Brown's, where many other aspiring rock gymnasts germinated and the crags and peaks of west Scotland became his play- ground.

Routes such as Gallows and Guerdon Grooves were far ahead of their time and even later, when Sassenachs in the form of Brown and Whillans stole across the border to do their damnedest on Scottish rock, John still held his own. He must have pioneered more routes than the average climber has had pints of ale. John was difficult to get to know, especially in his early climbing days, but once that barrier was overcome he was a delightful companion. I knew him over a large part of his active climbing life and found him a wonderfully easy person to get along with and also extremely humorous, especially in his early motorcycling days when we used to scare the daylights out of tourists and ourselves on the snakey side of Loch Lomond. I remember he had the record number of falls on a given weekend. On one occasion he fell off his machine and accompanied it in a elegant slide through the wicket gate of a cottage.

He seemed more at home on British hills than on higher mountains, though he had several visits to the Himalayas and to Antarctica as well as spending some time in New Zealand. After his various Odysseys he took a P.E. Diploma at Jordanhill and started instructing professionally. His dedication is well remembered at Glenmore Lodge and his final act was one of dedication in attempting to save a pupil from drowning off the cliffs of Anglesey. In so doing he lost his own life; an end not unexpected when you knew him.

Despite his possibly unmatched record of new rock routes in Scotland, he will be best remembered in years to come as a prophet of hard ice climbing. For it was John who, when in Antarctica, first experimented and developed his 'ballet' on ice (in fact he did study ballet at one time), using his unique ability to climb intimidatingly steep ice with razor keen crampons and an ice dagger. After the coming of age of the dropped pick there was no stopping him and from his base at Glenmore Lodge he raised the art of ice climbing to new dimensions.

John Cunningham may have passed on, but as long as climbers use climbing guides his name will remain.

H. MacI.

Vol. XXXIII (1986)   FOR BRIAN

Gone
The steady hand to guide the rope
The cheery curse to calm the nerves
No more
To breast the crux and see the impish smile
Above.

Remaining
Memories of friendship forged in trust
On Summer rock bright Winter ice
Long aching walks through mud to
Mountain hut.

Gone
Nights of laughter after climbs
Talk of hills, routes and climbs
In high lonely places facing fear
Together.

Those the Gods most love are early called
While we must vainly strive to follow
The light which burns the brightest burns
Not long.

H.H.

ON THE BOARDS

ON THE CAMPSIE FELLS WITH NORWEGIAN "SKIS"
Vol. II (1892)   by W.W. Naismith

For the sake of any uninitiated, it may be explained that skis (pron. "shes") are wooden snow-skates, 7 feet long and 3 to 4 inches wide, largely used throughout the northern parts of Europe and Asia (see Dr. Nansen's "Across Greenland"). The best are made of ash or plane, and cost, with fastenings, about £1, but a light serviceable pair of pine can be had for a few shillings by writing to Messrs Hagen & Co., Bergen. On 12th March, shortly after a considerable fall of snow, M.T.G. and W.W.N. climbed the Campsies behind Milton, and followed the crest of the ridge for two miles to the Meikle Bin. From that commanding point, after a snow shower had passed, a grand view was obtained of the Highland mountains all dressed in white, the Ochils, Firth of Forth, tops of Arran hills, &c., &c.. On the return journey the same route was followed. The skis were not of much use when ascending, but upon level ground, and especially where the snow was soft, better progress was made with their aid than without them, while a very slight gradient was sufficient to get up tremendous speed during the descent. When the angle was too steep to risk, the skis were slipped off and turned into an improvised toboggan. At one long slope, some 300 yards in length, and inclined at a general angle of 15°, an hour was enjoyably spent, the snow being in perfect order for ski-ing — firm underneath, with a powdering of drifted snow on the surface. This snowbed was crossed by one or two small ridges which imparted a switchback element to the sport, somewhat puzzling to inexperienced amateurs. Of course the party came to grief several times, but they returned home well pleased with their experiment. Skis might often be employed with advantage in winter ascents in Scotland, or rather descents, — for although Norsemen skate up as well as down hills, few men in this country are likely to acquire such facility as to use them when going uphill, but they can be easily towed up, as they weigh only a few pounds. In the Alps it is not unlikely that the sport may eventually become popular,

.... INDEED IT MIGHT!

AQUATIC SPORT ON BEN NEVIS (extracts)
Vol. VIII (1904)   by W. R. Rickmers

> Rickmers was a Continental with an evangelical enthusiasm for skiing. He was also
> a master of a particular style of prose writing, the like of which we may never see
> again! It has a certain curiosity value and readers attracted to it are recommended to
> read the complete article.

"Snow is hardly water," said my friend who saw the above headline and thought he knew
the subject. "Snow is hard water," I replied, and he vanished, muttering as he went, "It's
illicit still; his imagination is out of bounds." No doubt he was sorry to leave me alone with
my inspiration. "He meant 'out of bond,' surely," I chuckled, and from its crystal bower with
loving lips I lured the Scottish muse.

The British, the greatest of all seafaring nations, were clearly predestined to be the first
in taking up mountaineering as a sport. Between the Mountain and the Main the
connection is not far to seek. From ice to water is but a question of temperature; from Ararat
to Ben Nevis through the ten lost tribes (who were evidently not competent to go without
guides) to the British Isles stretches one unbroken tradition and from Noah to mountain
dew is one absorbent theme. As a mere Continental I had not until lately quite realised
how important water is to the Nation of the Seas. It is the mainspring of their greatness,
their well of health, and the source of their pleasures. No wonder they worship it to an
extent undreamt of in other countries. They rule the waves, they fish the stream and tread
the snowy crest, they enter into water from their beds, and even mix the omnipresent liquid
in their drinks. Truly, providence favours them and always provides an exceptionally
liberal supply of wet for the holidays, so that these islanders may sail forth and, together
with their favourite element, swamp the playgrounds of Europe. Was it mere idle fancy of
the poet's mind that Venus rose from the foaming waves? I think I see the purpose of the
symbol. From water, the all-pervading, material generator, is born the ideal, the all-
beautifier: She, woman, the giver of life, the inspiration of our work, the companion of our
sports. Though it may be the etymological speculation of one who left out of his glass the
sober fluid of the pump, I revel with unsophisticated joy in the idea that 'she' is the word-
root as well as presiding unit of the triad She, Ship, and Ski. Before I saw this, I objected
to the Norwegian spelling 'ski' (I wanted 'skee') and the Norwegian pronunciation (which
is 'she') being introduced into the English language. But history and providence knew
better, and now I have been taught that the three best things in the world are called 'she.'
True heirs of the chivalrous Norsemen who roamed over the briny and the snow, the
British have the ships and what goes with them, and they were the first to adopt the ski
before any other country outside of Scandinavia.

Reader, if you feel a moist mist gathering round your understanding, if you resent my
flight of fervid fancy (alas! its wings are dripping still), remember that I, a son of the sunny

South, have, before writing this, tried to absorb the local colour of your literature, and among others I perused the book of a former Astronomer-Royal of Scotland, which left on my mind that indelible impress which nothing can wash off. His speculations about the Great Pyramid have a natural attraction for mountaineers, for Cheop's tombstone is high and steep. I have studied the book carefully, and by the clear exposition of the she-symbolism I hope to prove myself as possessing the inheritance of the true spirit of him who did his oriental work in one of the driest regions of the world, who from Auld Reekie to Gizeh joined two contrasts into one fantastic revelry of the imagination, and who must have been instilled with and tried to combine what is most characteristic of the two extremes.

I am still wet with Highland moisture outside and in. That is my justification to the patriotic Scot, who, filled with grief (unless it be something better), bids me hurry to the scene of my exploits. He does not realise perhaps that I am already in it, in full swim, in fact, making headway with a will, and trying to reach the shore. Allow me to say that for eight days I have been the hygroscopic victim drenched between the infinite deluge of a dilute outer world and the concentrated and stronger flood of the limited space within. Small wonder that I was a sodden sponge which would have burst asunder but for the tender care of friends, descendants of the hardy clans of the North, and therefore accustomed to the rough nature of Caledonia stern and wild. They rescued me and sent me to my home, which I reached safely, leaving across France a trail of brownish liquid, defined by a distinguished analyst as moorland water, and which smelt of Harris tweed. After my return the Lake of Constance rose steadily, and the fish died from an epidemic of bacillus peatreekus. But I am glad to say that things are now gradually subsiding into a normal condition. The lake is falling visibly, and I am squeezing over these introductory pages the remnant of my humid recollections, which I offer as a last tribute to the land of the lochs. I am beginning to feel dry, and I hope to remain so ever after. So I need hardly apologise, trusting that I have made it sufficiently clear to you that up to the time of writing this, I was quite full of my subject, and felt no need to refresh my memory, externally or artificially, by the use of either pump or flagon...

...Skiing is to my mind the finest variety of mountaineering. How freely do we breathe the crisp, dry air; how the eye does revel in the scintillating jewellery which the last fall of new snow has thrown over the trees of the mountain-side; and how we delight in the view, so deep and clear, that crystal purity wherein seems to float a distant promise of eternity. Gently rising towards the glorious fields of white we watch the growing splendours of the winter morn, and looking backwards we survey with pride the many windings of the slender track, that clear-cut line of man-made beauty among the unspoilt charms of hill and dale. Then, after pleasant toil the top is gained, and basking in the sun, eating our wholesome food, we rest content, or relish the expectation of things to come. But who can describe with the ink flowing from a sluggish pen the feelings of the downward slide, the exuberant joy of the swaying motion — in short, the whole rippingness of a good run.

No more can I say than that the flood of my tears shed over the brilliant and sunny picture which I have painted of the skisters' joys cannot compare with the rain which mercilessly beat down upon us. But it could not wash out the spirits of the Scotch. There was enough and to spare for Southron and Teuton, and I shall always remember with intense gratitude the staunch will and the bright, brisk, unbroken temper of those whom I had promised much and for whom a sullen sky spoilt nearly all. For eight days we plodded to the mountain, stubbornly intent to frolic, but obliged to snatch from driving sleet and cutting wind a few moments of practice on the fleeting boards. Eight times we climbed, skied on some patch or slope, ate a frugal meal on some spot where the water seemed driest, while our imagination soaring to extremes revelled in orgies of devilled dishes, hot ginger, and "extra dry." Then we went down again, and home, to map out to our patient landlady by a fluid track over hall and stairs a realistic account of the natural beauties prevailing at the time in the neighbourhood of her hospitable roof. Sometimes we enjoyed a sail in our Hon. Secretary's splendid steamboat, thus shortening the daily swim to our playground.

On Sunday we went to see the Meteorological Observatory at Fort William, and I shall never forget the enthusiasm of the venerable man who presides over this admirable institution — an institution which serves to encourage the natives. It was nice to hear him say that a thermometer registers heat, and when he showed us the rain-gauges we stood in awe before the reckless ambition of human genius which attempts to measure the immeasurable. These rain-gauges are metal funnels connected with vast subterranean vaults holding thousands of gallons. A powerful pump empties them when full, which is about twice a day, as I was told. Pathetic above all it was when he, with noble eloquence, expressed his unshaken faith in the existence of a sun, though it was difficult to suppress a feeling of pity and regret when he tried to advance what in childlike zeal he called a scientific proof. His sunshine-recorder, evidently supplied by the S.P.R., was a globular crystal enclosed in a semi-circular arc with cabalistic signs. So crystal-gazing was the means by which he sought to produce a dream of brightness in the minds of the simple Highlanders. Poor man, he does his best and works hard. May the day come when he rests from his labours in a sunnier clime and beholds with wondering eye the glittering orb of which he reads in books.

But one thing always remains faithful to the ski-runner, and that is the snow. It may sometimes be fickle and change its mood from hour to hour, but its one great virtue is that in bad weather it is nearly always good. Last Easter the slopes from the summit of Ben Nevis to within a hundred feet or so above the lake at the col were in fine condition, affording a steep run of over two thousand feet. Such stretches of unbroken snow at stiff angles are by no means frequent, not even in the Alps. This was what I expected, for it is an axiom that the snow at the beginning of spring is the most reliable and promises the greatest chance of good sport. It has settled, does not superficially hide treacherous obstacles, and though hard throughout, is slithery on top, thus making an ideal surface for swings and curves. So the ground and the snow on Ben Nevis were excellent, but the climate was most emphatically not for beginners, being extremely discouraging. That is the only drawback in Scotland as far as natural elements are concerned. The question of good approaches and comfortable lodging close to the snow is also there, but not insoluble.

In fine weather a two-hours' walk to the snowline is a mere nothing to the ski-runner, who is looking forward to the pleasure which he knows he will find above. I do not know how the weather is in May, but I suppose that there is less rain in that month than in many others. For me there is not the shadow of a doubt that enough snow for good skiing lies on Ben Nevis throughout May; and on the first of June, to judge from photographs, the runner can still find snow-slopes of at least five hundred and maybe a thousand feet in height. During winter, skiing is probably very uncertain all over Scotland. The granite blocks or the heather are too much for the soft and unset layer, whereas any patch one sees in April is a sort of solid filling to a hollow in the ground; it is practically neve. Scotland, therefore, is essentially a country for "late skiing" (April and May). Beginners can find tame runs, and experts can be suited with forty-degree inclines, gullies, and block-studded snowfields, to satisfy the most fastidious, without much danger from avalanches. Owing to its height and to its position in the West, which favours great accumulations, Ben Nevis is probably the best, because the runs will also be the longest. But I may be mistaken, and other places may equal it, though one must always consider the existence of railways and hotels. In the winter the far interior is better, but for the reasons explained above (soft snow, &c.) good skiing will not be a certainty in normal winters. The question for skisters in Scotland — their season is the spring — is not one of the ground or snow, which can be guaranteed, but rather of the sky above. Experience will show if the month of May, as I surmise, is on a better footing with the clerk of the weather than the early days of its predecessor.

He who can spare a week during the winter will do best to go to the Continent, and there I can conscientiously recommend the Black Forest, which has a far harder winter climate and more snow than the Alps. Within twenty-four hours from Charing Cross the ski-runner can sit in the warm and comfortable hotel on the Feldberg, more than four thousand feet above the sea, and surrounded by an expanse of fine ski snow which lasts from the beginning of December till the end of April.

Skiing in the British Isles is not an innovation. The more this fascinating pastime steps into public notoriety, the more one hears of localities where the swift planks have been in use for generations. In the Alpine Journal I have repeated Dr Savage's personal recollections. Mr Glover writes to me that at Allenheads (Cumberland) all the village boys still have skis made out of barrel staves, and a newspaper cutting tells me that in some of the dales of Yorkshire and Durham the sport is by no means new, and that fifty years ago the Weardale miners went to their work on skis.

I appeal to the members of this and other Clubs to collect reports of this kind, and to try to obtain "genuine and authenticated old home-made British skis," which cannot be extremely rare if one knows how to look for them, but which will be priceless treasures in the ski collections of the future. They will be witnesses that nothing is new to the ever-wakeful instincts of a sporting race, just in the same way as these lines are a proof that an inclement sky cannot smother its enterprise and dash. Though my wife and I, northward bound as missionaries of the ski, have been drenched to the skin, we have basked in the warm sunshine of friendship, whose glowing essence, added to the great clear stream of Scottish hospitality, makes that true Highland blend which mortals taste with joy.

THE ALPINE SKI

SKIS IN SCOTTISH MOUNTAINEERING
Vol. XXVI (1958)   by Geoffrey J.F. Dutton

Twelve months ago there was unveiled the first permanent ski tow, hoist, lift or sack elevator in Scotland. Temporary contraptions of its kind have often been encountered of late by the unwary climber. The Glen Shee hills in summer hold several small rusted engines squatting balefully in hutches, wired and battened down; and in winter here and there the righteous mountaineer has paused to survey, far below in a corrie, lines of figures hauling endless ropes, and has noted with mild interest the remote fury of those crouched round some similar hutch, now frozen and doubly inaccessible; later he has heard the pop, the splutter and the inevitable malignant and deliberate silence. But such things are comforting, even necessary, to a winter climber in Scotland, providing tangible evidence of a pursuit at times more pointless and frustrating than his own.

This being agreed upon, the writer still thinks the possibility of a successful ski-lift, with its attendant flags, loudspeakers, race-cards and sleigh bells, bang next door to the ascetic recesses of the Buachaille, may provoke wrathful comment on all plank-straddlers from members-who-do-not-ski. So he humbly proposes to take up where Unna left off in that masterly article (Vol. 19, p. 257), not forgetting MacRobert's excellent survey (Vol. 21, p. 379) or Naismith's recommendation of 1892 (Vol. 2, p. 89), and briefly construct an apologia for ski excursions over Scottish hills with fellow-members, far from the Downhill-Only Boys. He may as well state his opinion now: that in reasonable conditions such ski-touring is vastly superior to simple hill-walking, and in unreasonable conditions it elegantly combines, as hinted above, the pointlessness of climbing in Scotland with the frustration of trying to ski there.

Now an added attraction of climbing on skis is that the difficulty is enormously increased. The veriest hump of a sub-Munro arches its back, steepens its flanks and bristles with suddenly bared rocks; all sides instantly face north. Thus what would normally be a saunter becomes, thanks to these artificial aids on the feet, a tricky problem of route-finding and mountain craft, calling for initiative, leadership and all the well-known virtues.

Who, for instance, finding himself accidentally on the top of Ben Chonzie in the summer, amid harebells and bumblebees, could imagine the epic struggle J.R. and the writer had there one February? Merrily they struck up the snow by Invergeldie burn, into the mist and the N.W. wind. When the slope became too steep to point the skis uphill, even with the aid of skins, they side-stepped laboriously, peering about to detect some easing of the slope. It steepened, and the wind howled and rattled through six frozen skins. The writer, faced with some 1,200 feet of side-stepping and conveniently hidden from J.R. by the mist, thought to remove these excellent skis and proceed more easily on foot. He was interested to discover that vibrams were no more comforting on the now very icy snow than were steel-edged skis, and to carry two 6-foot planks in such a hurricane either up or down such a slope by means of steps poked out with two ski-sticks held in one hand was not to be thought of. So he side-stepped up to the top and found a great plateau and a blazing sun. The run down on the south side was pure joy, skating on the level with the wind, tacking skilfully with outstretched anoraks in pterodactylic delight, and then a weaving down from snowfield to snowfield by short steep and narrow bits, a maze of exhilaration. Thus did a humble mound, bad-tempered in a N.W. wind, provide first-class enjoyment and a refreshing change from ascents of the head-down, feet-kick variety.

Then again, there are conditions when it is impossible to proceed on foot. Deep snow fell overnight at Clova, choking all gullies; determined pedestrians accompanied us to the gorge on Jock's Road, before falling back exhausted, engulfed and with oaths. On ski we had a superb day over to Craig Herrich above Caenlochan Glen, a wonderful Arctic day, with blown fine snow streaming across miles of sastrugi (Wave-like formations of icy snow, frequent in Scotland; anything up to a yard high from trough to crest.), the sun low in an icy pale blue sky. After a day such as this the run down in the silent evening, that effortless gliding over packed snow in the corrie, makes for such a sense of physical contentment and of the skier's absolute identification with the scene, that the idea of treading in or clattering down on foot comes as an intrusion, a rude and hearty shattering of the spell. And this spell grows not so much from the stillness as from the silent motion and the gradual unfolding of the picture to a body perfectly relaxed and swaying to the very contours it is watching, like a physical drinking of the landscape.

Truth, alas, compels the writer to record less gratifying episodes, when the jeers of the heathen found justification and nourishment. Late one May he had seen great confident snowfields on Beinn a'Bhuird and had accordingly lured J.R. to Invercauld. The journey up the Slugain Glen was ill-omened: large wet snowflakes fell. The Quoich was full and had to be waded. Then waist-high slush-bearing heather mutely resisted all the way to the Allt an t-Sneachda and its eponymic whiteness in the mist. Through a howling blizzard two figures carried skis up deeper and deeper snow. At 3,000 feet they turned, clambered on to dripping wood, pulled ineffectual straps and lurched down again into the tourmente. Veils will be drawn over the way they swung, slipped, staggered, fell, leapt, bounced, collided, crashed, ploughed, rose, groped, slithered, fell again, smacked, knelt, tottered, sprawled, lost a ski, overtook it, put it on, spun, collapsed, struck matches (no good, skis too wet, wouldn't burn), waded, dived, gasped, blew, dropped, rolled, bounded and finally arrived breathless at the bottom. Then the heather and the (deeper) Quoich. Ski de pied with a vengeance.

It is more comforting to recall the great days, the first runs in October, the last swoops to the loch in June, midwinter days of traverses when new snow had spoilt all other climbing; the crossing from Dalnaspidal to Dalwhinnie, over a great silent plateau looking to an Alder Forest locked and shining in ice; a desolate flat place but noble in winter and where a pedestrian was met, alone and stepping hugely in snow-shoes. Or the Glas Maol ridge, with its plunges from corrie to corrie; or from Clova to Lochnagar and back again to Glen Isla, with those white miles of drifting above a Strath More engrossed in its own spring ..... Such tours only yield their best when the skier is reasonably skilful and is not constantly reminded of the bed of clay; so summer quarries have equivalents in winter golf courses, and many a night and oft did the writer and his cronies ski back from these under the street lamps of Edinburgh and Dundee, wringing the last hour out of each week of snow, and stacking their skis in the drift by a startled tram stop.

So far we have not used the term 'ski-mountaineering'; for whilst ski-touring over the easier Salvationist hills is a most satisfying improvement on walking over them and needs more mountaineering knowledge, rarely could it be called 'ski-mountaineering' in the accepted sense. Skis are sometimes essential for reaching the more difficult Scottish mountains, but actual mountaineering on ski over them (if ever necessary) is extremely uncertain because of the general treachery, iciness or simple absence of the upper snow; it would be foolish to scrape expensively from rock to rock on these hills and neglect the fine foot-climbing they must afford. Such determined efforts should be regarded rather as a means of getting fit for Alpine ski-mountaineering, and are best made on borrowed skis. Delightful ski ascents of the greater Scottish hills may be made, however, in spring up their long snow gullies, with a walk or scramble to the cairn and a sun-bathing, burn-drinking descent on perfect snow, but by such lotus-eating distinctions will be blurred. And with pure ski-ing on Scottish hills, difficult or otherwise, up and down fashionable gullies, the writer does not propose to deal; that delectable pursuit must be sternly relegated to ski-club circles.

Forecasting a drought of Scottish contributions, Unna recommended inclusion of ski-touring notes in the Journal. Certainly, ascents or traverses on ski of otherwise uninteresting or 'exploited' hills offer something both fresh and Scottish for our cataloguing pioneers, heirs of Burn and Philip and other trackers of unrecorded heather; Munros might then tick by unheeded. The working out of long, linked high-level tours, a Haute Route Ecossaise, would seem possible, especially in the east (starting, say, at Mount Battock and arriving at Glen Tilt in time to consider the situation). These journeys would need the highest mountaineering skill and judgment in bad weather, and the ski clubs do not cater for such activities, regarding the hills, as Unna says, merely 'as suitable places for the use of ski'. We would regard skis (along with boots, nails, ropes, axes, crampons, pitons, pulleys, ladders et al.) as suitable things to use on the hill, with the obvious proviso that it depends on the hill. One would not take skis to Glencoe any more than one would carry a piton hammer up Tom Buidhe; but if both these poles were visited with the proper equipment they would be found to offer comparable enjoyment and, should the jungle call, equal opportunities for le Tigrisme.

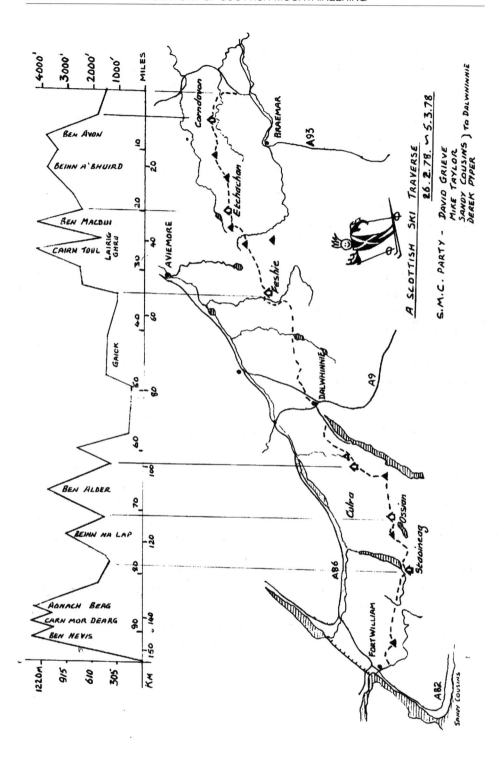

THE SCOTTISH HAUTE ROUTE
Vol. XXXI (1978)

by David Grieve

CONCEPTION

The growth of interest in ski mountaineering as a sport has led to the establishment in several different countries of high level ski routes, e.g. the Classic Haute Route from Chamonix to Zermatt, a Norwegian Haute Route, even a Moroccan Haute Route. The intention of this article is to establish a Scottish Haute Route and to describe what is believed to be its first successful completion.

Previously various attempts to traverse the Highlands on ski have been made but all seem to have been frustrated by bad weather or other factors. One notable effort backed by the B.B.C. is said to have foundered in the fleshpots of the Coylum Bridge Hotel! In general terms any true Haute Route requires to follow an E-W line including Nevis in the West and the high Grampians in the East. West of Drumochter the mountain spine is interrupted by Lochs Treig and Ericht and unless one has a boat laid on these obstacles force detours from the direct line.

East of Drumochter, in the vicinity of Gaick the Grampians divide into two lobes on either side of the Geldie and Dee valleys. The southern lobe extends along the broad ridge including An Sgarsoch, Beinn Iutharn Mhor, Glas Maol, Lochnagar and Mount Keen while the northern encompasses the Cairngorms proper. Either provides a satisfactory high level route but our own choice was with the northern lobe because it took in the Cairngorms, thus not only providing a more challenging route in the technical sense but also incorporating the two highest mountain ranges in Scotland and truly deserving the title of the Scottish Haute Route.

The precise staging and detail selection of the route is open to a good deal of variation and no doubt weather conditions and the energies of different parties would produce differing bags of peaks traversed en route. One factor which dominates however, is the distribution of mountain bothies and the need to base one's plans on their availability. Much of the Scottish character of the whole venture arises from the use of these splendid shelters and we often found ourselves giving a vote of thanks to the Mountain Bothies Association for their efforts in this direction.

Other considerations required, were a line which was as straight and uncontrived as possible, no break in continuity of the route or reliance on mechanical transport, suitable provision for modification or escape if conditions warranted and finally a route which could be completed within the span of a week's holiday, with luck and perseverance.

Our Scottish Haute Route starts in Deeside at Crathie and follows a virtually straight line across the Highlands for one hundred miles (163 km.) to finish at Fort William. It may be done equally well in the opposite direction.

In more detail, there are six more or less equal stages as follows:-

Approach: Crathie to Corndavon Lodge (9 km., 2 km. of which by car if the road is open).

Stage I: Corndavon Lodge — Ben Avon, Beinn a Bhuird — Hutchison Hut in Choire Etchachan (24 km.).

Stage II: Hutchison Hut — Ben Macdui, Lairig Ghru, Cairn Toul, Moine Mor — Ruigh-aiteachan Bothy in Glen Feshie (25 km.).

Stage III: Ruigh-aiteachan — Carn Dearg Mor, Tromie Dam, Carn na Caim — Dalwhinnie (29 km.).

Stage IV: Dalwhinnie — The Fara, Culra Lodge, Ben Alder - Ben Alder Cottage (26 km.).

Stage V: Ben Alder Cottage — Sgor Gaibhre, Corrour Lodge, Beinn na Lap — Staoineag Bothy (26 km.).

Stage VI: Staoineag Bothy — (Sgurr Choinnich Mor) Aonach Beag, Carn Mor Dearg, Ben Nevis — Fort William (24 km.). This was our conception of the Haute Route. In fact, bad weather led to it being done in seven stages instead of six, as will be described.

OBSERVATIONS AND EQUIPMENT

The following comments may be helpful to others who wish to do the Route.

Ideally there should be complete snow cover from coast to coast. In practice this happens rarely and one should be prepared to carry skis across low ground connecting the main sections.

The decision to travel eastward or westward can only be made in the light of weather patterns or predictions. Expected wind direction is a major factor but there is much to be said for a fine weather start from Nevis where ski-ing in bad visibility may be difficult and even dangerous.

Emergencies — Parties should be ready to bivouac if need be and able to provide adequate repairs to ski equipment and first aid for such accidents as a broken leg. The route takes one out of touch with civilisation for up to three days at a time so rapid rescue cannot be expected. In fact firm arrangements may have to be made to avoid alarms being raised and premature rescue being enforced.

Wet Weather probably poses as great a hazard as blizzard conditions so adequate protective clothing is needed. One of our group had a suit of the new Goretex clothing and was able to stay pretty well dry throughout.

Navigation, etc. — White-out conditions were encountered several times and demanded great care. It is even easier to go over a cornice on ski than on foot. We used a Thommen altimeter and found it a valuable aid.

Weight — The need to carry axe, crampons and a lightweight rope (we used 100 ft. of 6 mm.) and to be self sufficient in bothies (food, cooking equipment, sleeping bags and spare clothes) made weight a major consideration. We were unable to get below 30 lbs. (14 Kg.) although we planted several food caches to provide culinary luxury and lighten our packs. A good modern pack frame rucksack sits better when ski-ing downhill, sweats less under the back and has a useful selection of pockets — an improvement over the traditional Joe Brown type sack. Worthwhile extras we carried were a tiny radio for weather forecasts and a 4 oz. handsaw for cutting up firewood.

Ski Equipment — Langlauf skis are excellent for fast cross-country work in good snow conditions but we considered them unsuitable for several sections of our Haute Route where pleasurable ski-ing would only be possible with downhill gear. Heavy packs further reduce the advantages of Langlauf skis. We recommend 'Compact' skis which have the great advantage of being shorter and more easily carried on a rucksack, preferably specialist off piste models such as the Rossignol 'Choucas.'

Bindings such as the Vinersa which give an option of complete heel lift are a substantial improvement on those with a more limited uplift like the Marker. This is especially the case on the flat or gently sloping terrain so typically encountered in Scottish ski mountaineering. Skins which stick on are much better than those with straps, in terms of weight, efficiency in use and speed of handling.

Harcheisen (ski crampons) were a decided asset on steep or icy slopes. Boots should not only give good ski-ing control but also accept crampons and be suitable for walking.

EXECUTION

The idea of attempting the Scottish Haute Route was discussed at the S.M.C. Dinner in December, 1977. During January, arrangements were finalised and late February was chosen as the most suitable time. This proved an unfortunate choice because the first half of February produced a nearly ideal combination of heavy snowfall followed by fine weather. On Sunday, 26th February, four days after the thaw set in, the party assembled at Dalwhinnie. Sandy Cousins and I drove down from Aviemore and Mike Taylor and Derek Pyper arrived from Braemar via Kirkmichael. The weather was discouraging to say the least, with thick mist and penetrating drizzle. At one o'clock, the weather report predicted brighter weather in the East and so it was decided to do the trip from East to West. Mike Taylor's Saab was left in Dalwhinnie with spare gear and food in it. The other car was loaded up and driven to Deeside over the Devil's Elbow. Deep snow still blocked the Gairnshiel road just above Crathie, so this was the enforced departure point. After final packing and distribution of communal gear, the car was driven back to Aberdeen by the support party in the person of Madeleine Grieve.

The expedition then set out on ski, through mist to Corndavon Lodge, arriving there shortly after dark. Although the Lodge is largely in ruins, there remain a stable and bothy in excellent condition. Abundant firewood was to hand and a fine steak supper was shortly washed down by a bottle of claret, in front of a roaring fire. Everyone rated this a suitably auspicious start and Corndavon a five-star bothy.

DAY ONE

Overnight, clearing skies led to a hard frost. When we set off at 7.30 the following morning, the weather was perfect, the snow was crunchy and Glen Gairn was looking absolutely great. Progress up the long shoulder of Ben Avon was slow and laborious due to unaccustomed heavy packs. Once on the plateau progress was easier. The weird summit tors were encrusted with snow and the plateau surface contorted with sastrugi. Descending to the Sneck on excellent snow we had fine views of the Garbh Choire and Mitre Ridge. Windswept slopes above the Col forced a short ski carry and in deteriorating weather, Cnap a Chleirich was skirted on the North side. Map and compass had to be used to locate the North top of Beinn a Bhuird in a surprisingly sudden and complete whiteout. The descent from the summit to the Yellow Moss is three kilometres in length and in clearing mist we had full advantage of this fine run. A motion to climb Beinn a Chaorainn was not seconded and so we crossed the Yellow Moss in a westerly direction before dropping steeply down to the Lairig an Laoigh. From this point a long descending traverse below the cliffs of Beinn Mheadhoin, crossing massive avalanche debris, led without further effort to the Hutchison Memorial Hut in Choire Etchachan. (Ten hours from Corndavon Lodge).

A food bag buried earlier in the season was retrieved slightly the worse for wear. Suffice to say that of Scotland's traditional products, whisky keeps better underground than oatcakes! The Hutchison Hut is a very bare bothy and was by far the least comfortable of all the overnight stops on the trip.

DAY TWO

The next day dawned cold and cheerless and the cliffs of the corrie were veiled in thick mist. We set off at seven o'clock in a persistent drizzle which turned to snow about the level of Loch Etchachan. There was little wind and zero visibility. All our navigational skills were eventually required to locate the summit of Ben Macdui. In this respect, mention must be made of the value of the Thommen altimeter. On this occasion and subsequently it allowed pinpoint accuracy in route finding under the most adverse conditions. From the summit the Tailors' Burn was located and descended in thick mist down to the 800 metre level. This was bad luck, because the snow was superb for ski-ing and the poor visibility prevented full enjoyment of what must be one of the finest ski descents in Scotland. The snow was continous to the floor of the Lairig where we lunched, four hours after leaving the hut. After crossing the Dee on a substantial snow bridge, a long diagonal ascent led through the mist to the lip of the Soldiers' Coire. From this point, a series of steep zig-zags took us to the foot of the South East summit ridge of Cairn Toul. This was ascended on foot, giving an exhilarating and interesting ridge climb. There was perfect snow again for the run off Cairn Toul and this time the weather cleared in time to enjoy it. Direct vision simplified the descent to Loch nan Cnapan and the crossing of the Moine Mhor where the deep trough of Glen Einich and the huge buttressed face of the Sgoran Dubhs opened before us. It was a long slog round the head of Coire Garbhlach and a relief to reach the head of the Allt Coire Chaoil. This was well filled with snow and gave a good run to well below the tree line as darkness was falling. A rather weary party made its way by torchlight through the Feshie forest to Ruigh-aiteachan Bothy. (12 1/2 hours from the Etchachan Hut). This was another first class bothy and before long a roaring fire with food and other refreshments from the second food cache restored us all to high spirits.

DAY THREE

The section from Glen Feshie to Dalwhinnie had been regarded as a fairly easy day on lower ground. Low cloud and rain at 8 a.m. led to the traverse of Carn Dearg Mor being abandoned. Instead the day started with a short walk carrying skis through the woods of Glen Feshie. Then the route followed an interesting glen past Lochan an t-Sluic to the water shed. From here we contoured round the south side of the Tromie basin, keeping above the snow line, to reach the Tromie Dam below Lochan an t-Seilich. Unfortunately as the day progressed, the weather deteriorated steadily. By lunchtime an easterly gale was blowing great sheets of sleety rain across the mountain sides. It was clearly impractical to traverse either Carn na Caim or Meall Chuaich and so an escape route was selected through the pass between them. A snow-filled Land Rover track down the Allt Coire Chuaich gave an excellent ski descent almost to Loch Cuiach. The final eight kilometre walk alongside the Aqueduct to Dalwhinnie was an unpleasant experience. The weight of skis on rucksacks was greatly exaggerated by the gale force wind while the rain continued unremittingly. Darkness fell as the lights of Dalwhinnie appeared in the distance and the final stretch was again by torchlight. (11 hours from Glen Feshie).

The conditions experienced on this section were arguably the most dangerous we encountered. The chilling effect of gale and rain must not be underestimated. Once wet, stops to rest and eat became inadequate because of the rapid chilling. The tendency to press on quickly in order to keep warm increased fatigue and exhaustion/exposure was perhaps already taking effect.

The transport cafe at Dalwhinnie can be given an unreserved recommendation — it is clean, warm, comfortable and cheap and gave us the chance to get all our clothes dried.

DAY FOUR.

There was no change in the weather the following day and no one was keen to set off for

Ben Alder. Thus the programme fell one day behind. This created problems for Derek and Sandy who were obliged to start work on the Monday. Reluctantly it was decided to split the party and Derek and Sandy obligingly offered to drive the Saab over to Fort William. After a large transport cafe lunch Mike and I left at 2 p.m. bound for Culra Lodge. The gale was moderating somewhat and the rain becoming intermittent. A short climb above Loch Ericht led into a snow filled gully taking us into the upper corrie and finally on to the ridge of The Fara. This was a quite delightful ridge, with good snow cover and impressive views into steep corries, with Loch Ericht and Ben Alder Lodge far below. After Meall Cruaidh a good run down stopped just short of the tin garage at Pattack. With firewood from the forest, the sacks were heavy for the last few kilometres across to Culra Lodge, reached shortly after dark. It was well worthwhile however, to have a cheerful fire and dry our clothes again. (5 hours from Dalwhinnie).

DAY FIVE

Friday was once more dull and misty with intermittent showers but with the promise from the Met. Office of improvement. Skis were carried for about two kilometres above the Lodge until the river was crossed. Thereafter progress was on ski through the mist to the foot of the Long Leachas. When the angle became too steep, crampons and axe substituted for skis. The Long Leachas is a most attractive ridge and one of the finest approaches to Ben Alder. With four inches of new snow on top of old and with skis on frame rucksacks the ascent was not without difficulty. However, it was snowing gently and there was thick mist which reduced the feeling of exposure. Once on the plateau, the equipment change was reversed and a careful altimeter setting made. The two kilometres to the summit of Ben Alder were navigated painstakingly - mindful of the heavily corniced edge of the Garbh Choire. For a moment at the cairn, the sun seemed about to shine. Then all was white again. Total white-out, giving rise to acute vertiginous sensations on the descent, due to the complete lack of sensory stimuli. A simple bearing led on to the great west ridge of Ben Alder on splendid snow and the mist cleared at about 900 metres allowing a more rapid and relaxed run down to the Bealach Chumhainn. After lunch on the Bealach, the descent was resumed. The Uisge Labhair was crossed easily on foot and a jigsaw of interconnecting snow patches ran into a long snow-filled gully which gave an excellent descent to the bridge at Corrour Shooting Lodge. (7 hours from Culra Lodge). A food cache was collected from the keeper there and he very obligingly gave us the use of a ghillies' bothy for the night. (The planned over-night stop was Ben Alder Cottage, on a west-east traverse). The arrival from Glasgow of Sandy Cousins an hour later was an unexpected but welcome surprise. He acted as hut custodian and general guardian angel for the next 36 hours.

DAY SIX

Saturday was a clear day with a powdering of new snow on the ground and a bitterly cold north-west wind. It was possible to put skis on at the side of the road and follow the edge of the plantation to the Allt Loch na Lap and thence westwards on to the ridge of Beinn na Lap in the lee of which a well marked windslab was forming. On the summit the cold was very severe with considerable spindrift. Westward, the Mamores and our ultimate goal of Nevis looked magnificent. Conditions for the descent were the best yet — soft powder on a frozen base, extending right down to the Loch Treig railway line. The walk round the head of Loch Treig and up the glen to Staoineag Bothy was quite springlike in the warm afternoon sun, a strange contrast to conditions on the mountain. Nor was there anything springlike about the icy waters of the Amhainn Rath which we had to wade to reach the bothy (71 / " hours from Corrour Lodge). Staoineag was another five-star bothy. Sandy Cousins in his gardien role had preceded us and superintended an excellent dinner which was consumed in front of a crackling fire.

DAY SEVEN

Reveille was 04.00 hrs. An hour later, by torchlight, the river crossing was reversed - no easy task as the stepping stones were glazed with ice and the banks white with frost. Torchlight was necessary as far as Luibeilt. The snowline was reached shortly after a memorable dawn and we donned harscheisen to give a grip in the hard frozen crust. The line of a stream took us to the shoulder of Sgurr Choinnich Mor, which was followed steeply to just below the summit, the last fifty metres being done on foot on account of a slightly unstable wind slab. The scene was superb, a day in a hundred; snow peaks on all sides, sharp ridges, steep rocky corries and over all, a deep blue sky.

A long descending traverse on good snow, skirting the shoulder of Sgurrr Choinnich Beag, led easily to the col below the great Buttress of Aonach Beag. This was turned on the left by ascending delicately to the Sgurr a Bhuic col using crampons. From the col, a long gradual ski ascent led up to the ridge of Aonach Beag and the summit at 12.45 hrs. The run down to the Aonach Dubh col was quick and enjoyable. However the slope leading over to the Carn Mor Dearg col was unskiable. This was disappointing as we had both successfully skied the slope the previous May. In fact, it was quite poisonous, with soft new snow lying on old, and numerous patches of green ice. Not only were axe and crampons required, but the rope was brought into use on the steepest part of the slope. A lot of precious time was lost in reaching the col and as a result lunch was delayed till 14.30 hrs. This unfortunately led to a flagging of energy and spirits on the ascent of Carn Mor Dearg and the day came close to being abandoned on that summit at 16.00 hrs. However strength and reserve returned at the brave sight of Nevis in the late afternoon sun. A few parties were still at work in the gullies. The weather remained very settled and a slight wind had dropped again. Needless to say we carried our skis over the Carn Mor Dearg arete. It was in excellent condition with a generous covering of firm snow and forty minutes sufficed to reach the final slope of Nevis, the summit being attained at 17.20 hrs. as the sun set. No other human was in sight as the water bottles were drained and the last chocolate bar consumed.

The descent from Nevis in the grey light of evening was a fitting climax to the trip. Five hundred metres of perfect powder was followed by a further four hundred metres of variable packed snow, frozen crust and Easter snow. Ski-ing petered out at the bend on the tourist path below Lochan Meall an t'Suidhe. As darkness fell, we strapped our skis on our rucksacks for the last time and began the painfully laborious descent. The final mud slide to the Youth Hostel in Glen Nevis was accomplished by torchlight, arriving at 19.30 hrs. on Sunday night. (14 hrs. from Staoineag Bothy).

This completed a hundred miles of ski-ing across the Scottish Highlands, and a most enjoyable and eventful week's holiday. The car was retrieved from the car park in Fort William, but unable to obtain an evening meal in Lochaber we had to keep the hunger pangs at bay until the chip shop in Kingussie. The Grieve caravan was used for a brief overnight stop before driving back to Aberdeen and Peterhead in time for Monday morning surgeries.

CONCLUSIONS

The map gives a diagramatic representation of the Scottish Haute Route. In comparison with the classic Haute Route from Chamonix to Zermatt the distances involved are generally greater in Scotland but the altitude differences are broadly comparable. The effects of altitude in the Alps are offset by heavier rucksacks in Scotland. A fundamental difference between the two routes is that the Alpine Haute Route generally follows the line of least resistance through cols whereas the Scottish route crosses the mountain tops which is aesthetically more satisfying. Having done the Verbier variant of the Alpine route the previous year, we were agreed that the Scottish hills have demonstrated once again that avalanche hazards must not be underestimated and that it is all too easy to ski over a cornice in a whiteout. One decided advantage of Scotland which has a special appeal to the Aberdonian character is cost. There are no hut charges in Scottish bothies and the party had its cheapest holiday in years.

CAIRNGORM LANGLAUF
Vol. XXVII (1963)   by Adam Watson

It was a Saturday in April 1962, and I'd been burning heather all day on a Deeside moor just below the snow line. We had marched off the hill hot, tired, and thirsty, but a sudden frost soon had us shivering at the contrast from the blazing inferno of a few minutes before. I was looking forward to a long lie in bed next morning. But later that evening I began to wonder. This was the first April since 1958 with so much snow. If I got up early, and the weather held, what a fine langlauf tour could be done on the Cairngorms! I nipped over to the little shop up the road at 11 o'clock, and bought six tins of fruit, knowing I'd crave sweet liquid rather than food the next day.

I rose very sleepily at three, and after breakfast drove swiftly up Deeside. The sky was cloudless and moonlit, and the ground iron-hard, as I set off at 5 o'clock from Invercauld through the pine woods towards Glen Slugain. A frosty mist hung over the Dee, magnifying the craggy low hills and the tall spruces into a landscape more like the Rockies. I was carrying a pair of long narrow skis, weighing only 7 lb., which I'd bought at the hamlet of Kaaresuvanto in Lapland for 50 shillings, and a fairly full rucksack with ice-axe, sleeping bag, camera, binoculars and food. I was determined not to continue with the ski tour any longer than I was enjoying it, and to sleep at Corrour or some other place if the day became too much of a penance.

From the upper Slugain onwards, the snow lay deep and continuous, so hard that it bore my weight with scarcely a mark. On with the skis, and I rattled away at great speed over the icy surface towards Ben Avon. It was already dawn and cock grouse were cackling all around, standing up on every big snow-free patch and shouting defiance to their next-door neighbours — a cheery Deeside morning sound seldom heard in the barren far west. The sun was flooding in a rosy glow over the great bulk of Beinn a'Bhuird and down into the old green mushroom pines of the Quoich. It was good to be climbing at last, up towards Carn Eas. Skins were needed for a grip and soon afterwards a problem appeared. The steep south side of Carn Eas was ringed from end to end by a massive cornice which had been avalanching in yesterday's strong sun. There was only one narrow line of weakness without a cornice - a 45-degree slope which had thawed partly the day before and was now very hard. It was a case of kicking steps in a long traverse below the cornice, then cutting steps straight up over the line of weakness. Having done no climbing whatsoever for four months, I was glad to inch gradually over the bulge and off this icy slope that swept far down into the murky shadows of the Gairn valley.

At Carn Eas I was now on the Ben Avon plateau and looking down over the vast Aberdeenshire grouse moors, mostly covered by an early-morning cloud sea. Up here some of the snow had evaporated in the dry sunny air, exposing bits of green moss and grass, and the golden plovers were back, flying like butterflies in their courtship and piping mournfully - always a welcome sign of spring on the hills of Deeside. I tore on at a great, but jolting, pace over hard ridged snow, and soon the black rocks at the summit loomed up above. An icy east wind blew there, showering the fog crystals from the rocks. There was a view of utter desolation towards Tomintoul, where the bleak flat Banffshire moors were an unrelieved expanse of white almost all the way to the Moray Firth. Through binoculars I watched cars crawling like ants on the road towards Glen Livet. It was 8.30 a.m., and I was 3 hours from Invercauld. Already very thirsty, I sucked fog crystals at the cairn till the cold sent me off. I turned west towards the finer prospect of the Mitre Ridge and Beinn a'Bhuird.

A few minutes and half a mile later, the plateau was behind after a fine run on smooth powder snow. But afterwards the fairly steep descent to the Sneck was slow and tiring on very icy ridged snow, where the long narrow skis were difficult to control. I went down painfully, with a few tumbles and undignified scrapes. Then up the other side, with a spectacular airy view on the right along the great ice-plastered wall of Mitre Ridge.

From Cnap a'Chleirich to the North Top of Beinn a'Bhuird, it might have been an Arctic ice-cap — not a black speck in sight, and psychologically very tiring with the intense glare, flat snowscape and no view. But at last at 10.30 a.m. the tip of the North Top cairn peeped through, and a fine view opened out to the west. The 2-mile descent to the Yellow Moss was the best ski run of the day, with glistening hard-packed powder in every direction. I swooped leisurely from side to side all the way down Coire Ruaraidh, and finally far out on to the Moss in a last straight run. But out on the flat glaring expanse of the Moss I again felt tired, in spite of the perfect snow surface, and started getting cramps up and down my legs. No doubt about it, I wasn't in form, what with no ski-ing at all for over six weeks, and that — of a day yesterday tasting the preliminaries of hellfire hadn't helped. It was tempting to think what a good finish it would make to ski quickly all the way down to Derry Lodge and have a brew of tea over a fire. This was a signal that it was time for a good rest, and I opened a tin of fruit.

Refreshed, I pushed on swiftly and was soon edging down the steep slopes into Glen Derry. Here the snow was very icy, and the endless fast traverses and kick turns brought the floor of the glen up slower than if I'd been on foot. The Derry Burn was showing at one place, the last water I was to see till Glen Dee, and I drank a good quart. Coire Etchachan was suffocating — no wind, blazing sun, a dark blue sky and utter calm. Every step was an effort, relieved only by watching the infinitely more painful progress of two heavily laden parties on foot. As I climbed, a cornice cracked and tumbled down the 500-foot red wall of Creagan a'Choire Etchachan, and the whole corrie had an air of menace. It was so calm that I could hear my heart thumping as if it was outside my body, and the 'silence you 'most could hear' swishing in my ears. Some ptarmigan were quietly dozing on top of boulders in the hot sun, their eyes closing lethargically from time to time. I rested for a while on a boulder near them, feeling quite spent.

There was a refreshing change at last up at Loch Etchachan where a cold wind blew over the flat white invisible loch. I was tempted to go down by Derry Cairngorm, but now felt slightly better, so I plugged on uphill mechanically and took heart when I caught up with two skiers from Yorkshire. The snow was smooth but our pace slow to the MacDhui cairn, where about six people had gathered. For the third time I felt like ending the tour by heading off south, but some food and a rest for an hour in good company changed my mind. Ken Armstrong and a friend appeared from Glen More and shortly after headed back, flashing down at a great speed off the North Top. How I envied their fine downhill technique and the stability of their heavy skis. By the time I had wobbled down unsteadily on my birch boards from Lapland, they were distant specks. Still, the plateau was a continuous sheet of silk smooth snow, and now on the flat, my skis had the advantage, I felt stronger, and soon I'd passed ahead of them. After leaving my pack at Lochan Buidhe I felt like jumping in the air with relief and I now flashed quickly on to Cairngorm, through scores of skiers and walkers thronging the summit and the Coire Cas ridge.

Not long afterwards I was ski-ing gingerly down the top of the March Burn. The slope was now 45 degrees and had softened dangerously in the strong afternoon sun, so I fixed the skis to my pack and trod carefully downwards, shoving my ice-axe well into the snow and sending off minute avalanches all the way down. I skied down the last 200 feet in a glorious steep swoop to the invisible Pools of Dee and suddenly out of warm sun into freezing hard shade.

I ate two more tins of fruit and took stock. It was 5 o'clock and the cramps and weariness of the forenoon had all gone. However, I was now finding climbing very tiresome with the pack but easy without. So — why not leave the pack in the Lairig below Coire Bhrochain, ski round, back a short distance for the pack and on to Corrour? This meant some extra distance and loss of height, but I couldn't enjoy any more climbing with the pack.

The steep climb up Braeriach on skins was easy, on snow so hard in the shade that the skis scarcely left a mark, and yet not so icy and steep that the skins didn't grip. An hour later I was at the top, looking down a Coire Bhrochain precipice heavily sheathed in ice and frost. A bitterly cold breeze was blowing but the few clouds in the sky were all vanishing rapidly. It was good to look away from the glaring snow and ice for a moment, down past the cone of Carn Eilrig to the warm reddish-brown moors of Strath Spey, the green fields of Tullochgrue and the houses at Coylum among the pines.

I moved off in a long run downhill to the plateau, and an easy 50 minutes later I was on Cairn Toul, looking west over the Great Moss towards Glen Feshie. This was obviously the grand finish to my tour — a long 2-mile run down to the Moss, then another steeper 2-mile run to Achlean. But with a pack in the Lairig and a car at Invercauld, I had to turn east. I clambered down the bouldery ridge of the corrie below the summit and soon came on a drift stretching 2000 feet to the Dee. No place for a solitary fast glissade, but the surface was safe enough for a fast trot downhill, and I was at the bottom within 20 minutes.

I had a good rest at my pack and ate the last two tins of fruit. Dark blue shadows were spreading rapidly in the glen and already tiny daggers of ice were visibly thrusting out over the pools of melt water.

It was good to warm up again, gliding quickly down the moraines to Corrour. The last sun rays were burning red on Ben MacDhui. By contrast the bothy was dark and gloomy and I was feeling not at all tired, so I moved on across the snow-covered Dee and up round Carn a'Mhaim. The snow was no longer continuous and many stones appeared, but it was still much quicker to scratch and push forwards with the skis. Finally a last run down to the pines of Glen Luibeg; there was no snow down there, so I had to walk the remaining mile and a half to Luibeg. I was now so used to the ski-ing motion that I felt I could have kept that going all night, but I found the new movement of walking very tiring.

It was getting dark at 9 o'clock as I reached Derry Lodge, where I met Bob Scott and my father. My father had been ski-ing at the Great Moss and Glen Geusachan and wasn't long off the hill himself. Back to Bob's for cups of tea, and then down the road to Braemar where we swung into the welcoming lights of the hotel for a dram and pints of beer with some of the residents. We left after midnight and collected my car in the Invercauld wood at 1 a.m. The greatest mental effort of the day was now required to drive down Deeside without falling asleep.

I'd had a good 24 hours' worth, seeing the whole Cairngorm range and other parts of the North-East from innumerable viewpoints. Time had passed so slowly that it seemed more like a week - a good indication of a day lived to the full.

I worked it out later at about 38 miles, with 34 on skis and 8700 feet of climbing. It is certainly no more than a hard but enjoyable day in good weather to a lightly laden man, and I would carry a lot less if I did it again. Without a push I think I could have done the tour in 14 hours instead of 16, and still enjoyed it.But I don't think the time could be cut much more without making the day a matter of physical effort rather than of enjoyment. It is a grand way of re-exploring familiar hills, and the Cairngorms, noted originally as a paradise for hill-walking and shown by the recent Guide to be equally enjoyable for rock-climbing, should become famed for a third aspect of the sport — ski-mountaineering. Langlauf provides the opportunity, and I'll be back as soon as I can — and this year looks like giving another opportunity.

GRAND PRIX LANGLAUF - Memoires de la Premiere Fois Vol. XXXII (1983)

Adam Watson sends the following meditation on lone ski-ing: The 1981 Journal contained a note from Tim Walker that G. Boyd and G. Keir had gone round the six tops of the Cairngorms on skis (in spring 1980). The note said known previous attempts since my tour in 1962 had 'faltered for lack of a long enough interval of settled conditions whose rarity makes this trip a serious undertaking for the lightly laden skier . . . But more remarkable still remains Watson's solo effort in a faster time, with an earlier mode of cross-country equipment and a heavier sack.' Here are a few comments that may be of interest to ski mountaineers.

1. Settled conditions occur nearly every spring, and you need only one day of them!

2. To a lightly-laden skier the tour is a serious undertaking even in settled conditions.

3. As long as the weather is not downright bad, snow conditions are more important than weather. Even in good weather a tour is difficult on snow too soft, too hard, a continual mixture of both, or too ridged. Snow was good on most of my 1962 tour, but bad on some parts. Much better conditions occasionally occur over a big area and altitude range. In the best conditions, ski-ing is almost effortless, but such conditions are rare in Scotland; I have seen them only on one trip in the last three years.

4. Weather can be too settled. One likely reason why the 1980 tour took two hours longer than mine is that it was too calm. Calm weather makes you sweat and turns the snow soft. On the day of the tour by Graham Boyd and Graham Keir, I went ski-ing from Loch Muick over the hills to Glen Tanar, but it was too calm for fast going. A breeze does wonders for the body and the snow, and even a fairly strong wind drifting the snow can be good as long as it's not in your face most of the time.

5. It costs less energy if you are alone for a long trip on ski or foot. You vary your pace throughout the trip according to how you feel at the moment, not according to your companions' pace at the moment.

6. Equipment is relatively unimportant. In April 1958 I toured from Luibeg by Cairn Toul, Braeriach, Cairn Gorm and Ben Macdui back to Luibeg. Despite having very heavy old skis, at a comparable stage in the tour I was far less tired than in 1962; I was fitter because I had done much more cross-country ski-ing over the previous few weeks. The only reason why I didn't go to the last two, easier, eastern tops in 1958 was that I hadn't risen early enough in the morning; going on would have meant floundering back through deep heather in Glen Quoich in the dark without a torch, and that would have spoiled a good day. On my six tops tour I had light wooden skis, though not nearly as light as some modern plastic skis. Plastic has advantages, and often surpasses wood, but wood in the right conditions gives faster and more secure ski-ing if you are alone. What is the best equipment is a topic for endless inconclusive argument. But whatever equipment makes you feel better will be less tiring for psychological reasons. And on a long day it's how your mind feels that is crucial in deciding how you are enjoying things and hence how much further or faster you want to go.

7. I could have taken less time by not taking photographs, looking at views and wild life, and talking to people. In 1958 I saw only one person, but in 1962 spoke to people on Moine Bhealaidh, Loch Etchachan, Ben Macdui, Cairn Gorm and Corrour Bothy. I could have pressed on and avoided them, but saw no point. Continual checking of time destroys my enjoyment of a hill day. The 1962 tour could have been shorter by starting at Loch Builg, but if I had made too many preparations I would never have done any long tour. The best days on the hill are the ones you snatch unexpectedly, without much planning.

EXTREME SKIING IN SCOTLAND
Vol. XXXIII (1986)   by Martin Burrows-Smith

> In the major continental Alpine journals a significant proportion of the 'new climbs'
> sections consist of new extreme descents on ski.

EXTREME skiing (as it is popularly called) is practised in many areas of the world from cornice jumping in Utah, major mountain descents in Alaska, the Andes and the Himalayas, to the more popular Alpine areas particularly the well known faces, ridges and eponymous couloirs above Chamonix. Whether Scottish mountain skiing is extreme at present is a matter of opinion but nevertheless, there is no doubt that the Highlands provide a wide variety of challenging ski descents and in the future an increasing number of ski mountaineers will be testing their skill and nerve in remote mountain corries.

Some may well doubt the sanity and point of skiing steep and confined ground in an exposed and serious situation and not infrequently I have shared similar feelings myself. However, speaking personally, the challenge has become addictive and I'm constantly searching for the perfect ski descent, hopefully completed in good style and control.

Historically, I have little information on the development of the sport. Maybe some SMC members could add some light here? In the Northern Cairngorms, the new approach was initiated by Nethy Bridge ski instructor, Harry Jamieson. Harry is no climber but clearly a talented, motivated skier with bottle. In the early 70's he made many bold first descents including *Aladdin's Couloir*, the Shelter Stone gullies and the *Couloir* in Coire an Lochan. The rest of us follow in his wake.

Instructors at Glenmore Lodge, with their enthusiasm for off-piste skiing and knowledge of local corries were naturals to follow in his tracks but took their time to become really committed! Aladdin's Couloir became popular and eventually exploration took place elsewhere.

It is not easy to grade or compare difficulty as so much depends on conditions. Thus relatively easy angled gullies such as *Left Hand Branch* Black Spout, Lochnagar, or *No 3 Gully* on the Ben have proved particularly trying because of a glaze ice, whereas others, longer and steeper and with more apparent difficulty, have proved relatively trouble free. The start of the descent is often the crux. Cornices can be cut down, outflanked, jumped or side-stepped with an ice axe for aid. My own feeling is that a rope should not be used unless the descent is really worthwhile — I don't suppose anyone else gives a damn but it seems important to me. I have only used a rope twice, both occasions in *Hell's Lum* in the Loch Avon basin.

Snow quality is everything. Undisturbed (by climbers) hard pack and neve with good surface roughage are the most challenging and least forgiving. A slip could be terminal. Icy crusts and heavy icy rimes are nasty and have provided much soul searching. Windslabs, soft and hard, are pretty good for skiing but obviously there is a concern of avalanche. Here one is constantly test-skiing so if a fracture line is created, one can hopefully drop down onto firmer snow underneath. Powders and deeper snows are perhaps less technically satisfying but feel much safer as an accidental outside edge will only result in a deep crater below. Spring snow on the turn can be delightful as long as it is clean and undisturbed.

The following is a list of descents of which I have personal knowledge. Snow quality on these descents is mentioned and any directions are relative to the direction of travel, i.e. downwards.

Northern Cairngorms:

Coire an-t-Sneachda;

A superb skiing corrie and not just because of its ease of access. The slopes left of *Jacobs Ladder* and around the *Goat Track* give good practice. *Jacobs Ladder* — hard pack. Cornice outflanked by short snow ridge on the left. Usually just a cornice problem with straightforward snow underneath. *Forty Thieves* — spring snow. Upper section serious as it is undercut by rocks above the couloir. Awkward narrow section 200 feet below cornice. *Aladdin's Couloir* - has been skied regularly in a variety of conditions.

Aladdin's Mirror — hard pack. Needs a good cover as there is a low relief rock ridge to cross. Has a serious feel at the start as one is skiing above *Aladdin's Buttress*.

Central Gully Left Hand — hard pack. A fine descent often in condition. Has also been skied in powder on a firmish base.

Central Gully — soft slab. Needs a good fill as there are narrow sections. Cornice can be awkward.

Central Gully Right Hand — powder. Needs good cover. Steeper and more serious than its neighbours.

Coire an Lochain;

Fiacaill Ridge left hand flank on wet slab. Rather pointless. Much better descents are available on the fine slope between the ridge and *No 1 Buttress*.

The Couloir — hard pack/powder on the Great Slab. A very fine excitingly situated descent, 20 minutes from Cairn Lochain summit to Coire Cas car park.

Stag Rocks;

Diagonal Gully — neve, steep bulge at the top. The Descent Gully further to the west also gives a good ski descent.

Hell's Lum Crag;

Hell's Lum — skied on two occasions. The first time was very unsatisfactory with wet snow and falling icicles. The rope was used twice. The second attempt was an improvement, the rope used once at the cornice and the gully was occasionally side-slipped and skied on soft slab.

Atmospheric.

Shelter Stone Crag;

Castlegates Gully — hard pack. Often awkward at start.

Pinnacle Gully — neve. Under good snow both of these provide an excellent introduction as they have width and good scenery.

Lochnagar:

Black Spout — softish neve.

Left Hand Branch — similar but with a glaze of ice. Nasty.

Central Gully — perfect neve. Very fine.

Red Spout — neve.

Creag Meaghaidh:

Easy Gully — relatively straightforward. Can be icy at the start. A good introduction to remote gully skiing but is an awfully long walk in!

Raeburn's Gully — neve. Initial section avoided on right via slopes above

Bellevue Buttress — A superb descent.

Cinderella — wet fresh snow with a crust in places and short icy steps. Good value.

Ben Nevis:

No 5 Gully — deep powder. A fine run once one realised the avalanches weren't going anywhere, although apparently shortly after my descent a climbing party was avalanched 1,000 feet from the top.

No 4 Gully — very icy. A cornice and short steep slope problem. Would be a suitable introduction with better snow.

No 3 Gully — icy, serious at the top. Cornice avoided. Again this could provide a fine, scenic descent with good snow.

My visits to this hill on skis have yet to coincide with good snow. The potential here is obvious for some classic and exciting runs.

Glencoe:

Aonach Dubh;

No 2 Gully — soft slab. Scenic and very fine. Descent curtailed at Middle Ledge due to lack of snow on Dinner Time Buttress. With a rare good cover of snow to the Glen, this would be one of the best.

Stob Coire an Lochain;

Forked Gully — icy crust and many footsteps. A lot of side-slipping required. Disappointing and worrying.

Beinn Dearg:

Cadha Amadan (the Fool's Pass) — well named, — skied on avalanche debris.

An Teallach:

Lord's Gully — soft slab. The gully forks at the diamond shaped buttress of Lord Berkeley's

73. Ben Cruachan from the west

74. *Two early climbers take a fall*

75. *A Glen Coe stretcher party of the nineteen fifties. Donald Duff, SMC member, surgeon and comforter of many a fallen climber, is behind the stretcher in the centre*

76. *Carn Mor Dearg*

Seat. The descent was started from below this rock. Ice and fear prevented the link from the summit of Sgurr Fiona. If good snow were available here, there would be a truly magnificent descent.

Hay Fork Gully — soft slab. Convexity at the top avoided — avalanche risk. Impressive right wall.

In case anyone thinks I've recorded every gully that I've scratched and scraped down in atrocious style, I can only say there have been many other failures, rebuffs and half-started or not finished. For instance *NC Gully* was too tight, *Garadh Gully* too icy, *No 2* too heavily rimed, *Inverlael Gully* on Beinn Dearg avalanche prone, and many others I don't think I'll mention.

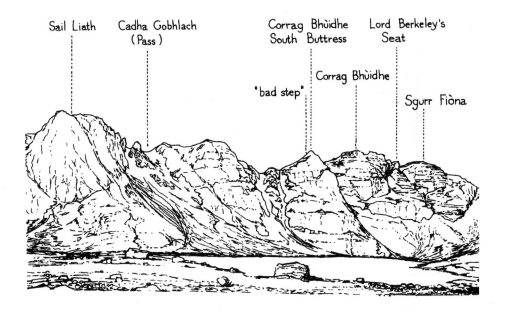

AN TEALLACH FROM LOCH TOLL AN LOCHAIN

MELANCHOLY OCCURRENCES

THE SAME OLD STORY
Vol. XXXII (1982)   by John Hinde

I have been delving in the files of the Inverness Courier *and came across two interesting accounts of early accidents in Lochaber. They are both described under similar headings of 'Melancholy Occurrence'.*

12th October, 1836

Samuel Macdonell of Fort William — 'a fine young man of about twenty years of age' who had 'been frequently upon the hill' — set off for the summit of Ben Nevis accompanied by two young gentlemen from the South. 'They scaled the gigantic precipices with comparative ease, and having satiated themselves with the magnificent prospect from the summit prepared to descend.' On the way back...

'by the time they returned to the point opposite the house of Glen Nevis, it was six o'clock, and the evening was fast setting in upon them. At this place the party had separated, one being in advance of Mr Macdonell, and the other a little behind him. The grass was wet and slippery, and Mr Macdonell amused himself by sliding down parts of the hill to outstrip his more cautious companions. The latter remonstrated with him on the danger to which he exposed himself by such a practice, but he persisted, till at length, the unhappy youth lost the power of stopping himself, and his foot coming in contact with a stone, he was precipitated headlong down a deep ravine. The gentleman in the rear hurried to where he lay, and found him weltering in blood and quite insensible. He lifted him from the ground and carried him to a spot less dangerous in appearance; and then proceeded onwards in search of his companion, whom he overtook at a short distance. He briefly described the melancholy accident that had occurred, and directed him to return back to the place, while he himself made his way to Glen Nevis to procure assistance. About an hour elapsed before he got there, but this being accomplished not a moment was lost in obtaining torch-lights and individuals anxious and ready to render what aid was in their power. Here, however, a most painful cause of delay took place: the young man, not knowing the local bearings of the hill, and being otherwise confused and shocked with what he had witnessed, could not recollect the exact spot where he left his companions — he wandered about in quest of them, imagining every fresh turn or ascent would lead them to the fatal place; and thus four hours were spent in the fruitless and heart-sickening search. At last one of the men heard a faint cry, which the shepherds at first thought was that of a lamb, but which proved to be the moaning of the second of the party, who was lying utterly exhausted, and in danger of perishing from cold and fatigue. He had also been unable to find the spot where their unfortunate young friend lay. Some of the party carried this gentleman to Glen Nevis, where restoratives were promptly administered, and he again revived. A fresh party, now set out to join those already on the hill, and after a long and anxious search of several hours they discovered the body of Mr Macdonell in the place to which it had been carried by his companion, but every trace of life had fled.'

1st September, 1847

Two English tourists (45 and 23) left the steamer 'Culloden' at Ballachulish and walked up Glencoe to Altnafeadh, in stormy weather with high wind and sleety showers. At Altnafeadh they took a piece of oatcake and a glass and a half of whisky - all that this 'humble change-house' could provide, and their only refreshment since breakfasting on board at an early hour. They rested for one hour and crossed the Devil's Staircase to Kinlochleven. They were seen five miles from Altnafeadh between 5 and 6 in the evening, tired and very wet.

They crossed the Leven Bridge at Kinloch and met a girl who pointed out the way to Fort William, which was then a further twelve miles, by the old Military Road. 'They were not seen in life afterwards.'

After walking a total of twenty-two miles, with nine miles still to go, they died three miles beyond Kinlochleven. Their bodies, with knapsacks on their backs, were found lying close together by two shepherds, beside the road, seemingly asleep. Near the bodies were found an umbrella, a walking-stick and a small pocket spirit flask, empty. The gentlemen had become exhausted by fatigue and hunger, benumbed by cold and wet, and benighted they slept 'the sleep of death' where their bodies were found.

Local worthies from Kinloch carefully removed the bodies to the small inn at Larachmore, from whence they were taken to Fort William. They were medically inspected in the presence of the Sheriff, and the doctors agreed that no marks of violence could be found.

'There seems no reasonable ground for doubting, that, exhausted with their long and fatiguing journey on foot, drenched with rain, having encountered the cold blasts of the wild regions through which they passed, and forded deep and rapid mountain streams, the weary travellers at length sat down by the wayside to rest, and fell asleep, to wake no more. Their fate should prove a warning to our southern tourists, many of whom rejoicing in their strength, ascend high mountains and attempt long journeys through unfrequented by-roads, without guides, without clothing suitable to the country and climate, and in the distressing case we have been recording, without adequate sustenance.'

Melancholy Occurrences indeed, and sadly far from the last such.

THE CAIRNGORMS IN WINTER (extracts)
Vol. I (1890) by A. I. McConnochie

"Winter ascents of our Scottish mountains are by no means so popular as they deserve to be, though time and example are gradually popularising them and unfolding their beauties and pleasures. Such ascents, of course, should not be attempted unless one at least of the company has an intimate knowledge not only of the proposed route but also of the neighbourhood, in case of any deviation that may have to be made from circumstances beyond the control of the party.

I have had an experience of over twenty years at all seasons on the Cairngorm mountains, from the Dee to the Spey and from the Feshie to Loch Builg; and after a big fall of snow, followed by severe frost, I know of no excursion more pleasant than a walk across these mountains. Under such circumstances, I hold that the ascent is easier than in summer, for all the little hollows are levelled up, and there is a smooth, dry, and hard surface for walking. As for the safety of such a journey, it is — due care being of course taken — in my opinion no more dangerous than one in summer. There are certain ascents and descents that the prudent mountaineer will eschew at all times; while others which might be made while the mountain sides are free of snow, will, in the winter season, be wisely avoided whatever may be the temptation. For a successful winter ascent, then, considerable knowledge is requisite in the first place, and great prudence in the second."

> Then follow accounts of ascents of Ben Macdui and crossings of the Cairngorms in both directions. They were coloured by no more than the usual wintry hardships but then....

"My next winter expedition had both its comic and almost tragic side. Again Ben Muich Dhui and Cairn Gorm were to be crossed from Braemar, and the weather was propitious, — that is, there was a great depth of snow, and severe frost of some day's duration. The party numbered six, two however only going, by arrangement, as far as Derry Lodge. The drive from Ballater to Braemar was made on wheels; from Braemar to Derry Lodge it was done in sleighs. Bidding good-bye to our two friends at the Lodge, the Lui Beg route was taken. In the lower part of the glen walking was not particularly easy, so thinking to better themselves, two of the party, in spite of my remonstrance, took to the ridges on the right. The consequence was that, getting round Cairn Crom and along the ridge between the hill and Derry Cairn Gorm, progress was at last found by them to be impossible, more especially as their knowledge of the Cairngorms was limited. In these circumstances they returned to Braemar, after making an unpleasant slip on the frozen slope, the consequence of which was rather unpleasant to one of them who wore the kilt. When I, along with the companion who had stuck to me, got to the turn of the Lui Beg (1,536 feet), we found walking easy enough; and after we got into the fork of the burn, at a height of from 2,500 to 3,000 feet, we could discern our two friends away over on the ridge of Derry Cairn Gorm. So steep, however, is the slope there, that a descent, in the snow, was quite out of the question, and, as already stated, and as I had fully expected, they retraced their steps. We reached the cairn on Ben Muich Dhui without difficulty. As might be expected, it was a solid mass of ice, most fantastically shaped on the north side. Here sky and mountain seemed to meet; above, one could only see for a few feet; while a radius of about a dozen yards closed the vision around. After a slight lunch we made for Cairn Gorm, walking by compass. We got as far as the head of Coire Domhain, where the ridge between Loch Avon and Loch Morlich is very narrow and precipitous, especially towards the latter. Somehow or other I slipped here, and slid down the corrie a considerable distance. I managed to stop myself by the aid of my stick, fortunately a stout one, but my thoughts may be imagined as I shot past black bits of jutting rock, contact with which would have sent a bruised, perhaps lifeless, mass into the Maghan na Banaraich. I may tell my feelings. I had no fear — perhaps there was no time; I only said to myself, Well, if my head comes against any of these black rocks, it is all over, but I can't help it. Judge of my horror when, after having succeeded in safely stopping my descent, I saw my companion sliding down at a fearful rate. He had thought my hurried descent was voluntary, and an easy way of getting downwards, so off he went! I tried to catch him as he passed, but he slipped like an eel through my hands (I had on worsted gloves), and, head first at times, did not stop till he was about 200 feet below me. When I reached him — which it was only possible to do by turning over face downards, and making my way step by step with toes and hands dug into the snow — he was minus his hat, stick, and flask, but providentially uninjured. We walked the rest of the way to the Shelter Stone and examined the interior, and thence along Loch Avon, ice-covered, with here and there cats-paws of snow, to the Saddle. Then up the Saddle, and along the Nethy to Nethy Bridge Hotel, eighteen hours after leaving Derry Lodge; but, be it observed, the last four miles were done within the hour. Before breakfast next morning a telegram was received from Braemar, announcing the arrival there of our quondam companions and inquiring as to our safety. As our reply took several hours in transmission, not a little anxiety was evinced on our account. The scene from the moment we left the Ben Muich Dhui cairn was not one which we shall readily forget, apart from the untoward incident of the journey. For mountain and rock, loch and stream, were shrouded in ice and snow; not a water-course visible — in summer we all know how numerous the burns and water-courses are; everything white, except here and there the black top of some great rock. The outlines storm-formed, were weird and grand, though often fantastic enough. The walk along the Nethy, with the slope of Cairn Gorm on the left and Ben Bynac on the right, and their picturesque snow-clad crags, was also one to be remembered for a lifetime. On the top of Ben Muich Dhui we estimated the depth of snow to be six feet, and in the corries often a hundred, but of course we had nothing to test the actual depth. It may be interesting to state that the only deer we saw were between Braemar and Derry Lodge. My friend recovered his cap and stick at the bottom of Coire Domhain, and next summer I found the flask, full and uninjured, on the bank of the burn."

> On his next winter outing McConnochie describes how he and his companion found themselves at Ryvoan bothy after nightfall. The bothy was locked but they were tired after walking in deep snow so ...

"I reluctantly deemed it prudent, in the circumstances, not to proceed further, and accordingly burst open the door of the bothy. Some of the furniture, including a quantity of paraffine, had to be sacrificed to make a fire, and a table formed our couch for the night."

> It seems that bothy vandalism had early and distinguished beginnings!

GRANDPA ON THE MOUNTAIN - A HEARTLESS TALE
Vol. XXXII (1984) by B.S.F.

He checked all our gear and he hushed all our chatter,
For "Climbing a mountain's a serious matter."
Then we lined up behind him while he set the pace,
For "Climbing a mountain should not be a race."
It wasn't a race, but we wanted to know
Why climbing a mountain should be quite so slow,
And I said as I shuffled along in the rear
We'd get on much better if Grandpa weren't here.

As we tramped up the ridge in a long crocodile
With Grandpa in front of the slow moving file
He stepped on a treacherous cornice of snow
Which promptly collapsed and he shot off below.
We watched and applauded this singular trick,
For we'd never seen Grandpa moving so quick.
He crashed to the bottom and lay there quite still;
So we went up for lunch to the top of the hill.
The view was delightful, the company good,
The weather was fine, and so was the food,
And I said as I gobbled up Grandpa's share
"We're getting on better now Grandpas's not there."

A SURVEY OF MOUNTAIN ACCIDENTS IN SCOTLAND 1925-45
Vol. XXIII (1946) (Extracts)   by B.H. Humble

> Ben Humble was a remarkable individual who made a significant contribution to Scottish Mountaineering in spite of his becoming afflicted by total deafness. He promoted awareness of hazards and the improvement of safety standards in mountain activities by exhibitions and educational efforts, by his involvement with the Mountain Rescue Committee for Scotland and by compiling an Accident Report published annually in the *Journal*

This survey is made from accounts of accidents of which particulars are available over the twenty-year period. It includes all affairs which involved search and (or) rescue parties. The particulars have been classified under the headings: Date, name, age, club, nationality, locality, details and references, and an analysis gives information which, it is hoped, will be of use to the First-Aid Committee. Over the entire period notes are available of 90 accidents, involving 106 hill-walkers, tourists or climbers, and there were 45 deaths. From 1930 until the beginning of the war there was a gradual increase, and 1939, with 18 accidents and 8 deaths, was the peak year. During the war years 1940-44 there was an average of 2 accidents per year, while in 1945 the number jumped to 7 accidents with 6 deaths.

A summary of the survey follows;

LOCALITY

Glencoe - 20 accidents (1 death)   Skye - 16 (8)
Ben Nevis - 16 (8)   Central Highlands - 3
Cairngorms - 7 (8)   Angus Hills - 3 (1)
Crianlarich Hills - 7   Lomond & Arrochar - 6 (4)
Arran - 1 (1)   Northern & Western Highlands - 2 (1)
Near Glasgow - 7 (3)   Southern Uplands - 2

SEASON: of the 90 incidents,
under snow conditions - 28
free of snow - 62

NATIONALITY: of the 106 people involved in the 90 affairs, 57 were Scots, 45 English and 4 foreign. Of the fatalities, 25 were to Scots, 18 to English and 2 to foreigners. These figures show that the highest accident rate is to visitors from south of the border, as the number of Scots climbing in Scotland is many times greater than the number of English climbing in Scotland.

AGE: under twenty - 30
twenty-thirty - 54
thirty-forty - 12
over forty - 10

CAUSE OF ACCIDENT

Eight of the affairs turned out to be benightments only, but involved large search parties. In one affair a large party were climbing The Merrick; all gave up except two. Near the summit they separated. Both descended safely, but on different sides of the hill. Both at once organised search parties for the other, an aeroplane and a detachment of troops being called out, and a large number spent all day on the hills. In another case a member of a search party slipped and was killed.

Forty-two of the accidents involved only novices, or those showing complete disregard for all normal precautions (24 deaths). These include such cases as long journeys in the Cairngorms in winter by persons neither suitably clad nor properly shod; traversing snow slopes without ice axes (two slipped to death); Sunday scramblers on friable rock of the Campsies; rock-climbing alone; ankle and leg injuries on tourist paths, etc. One notes several cases of visitors from the south having an accident on a first excursion immediately after arrival, and before muscles and legs were attuned to hill-walking. In about ten cases the cause was a *simple slip*, which usually occurred when descending a hill.

In 5 cases, elderly folk had heart attacks on the hills, and 4 were fatal. One notes that three of them occurred whilst resting at the top of an ascent (2 at top of Ben Lomond and 1 at top of Sgurr Alasdair Stone Shoot).

Of the accidents to experienced climbers, 9 were apparently due to a simple slip on easy ground, and one notes that several of these occurred after the rope had been taken off at the top of a climb. The other causes:— are lost control when glissading (3), avalanches (2), hit by falling rock (2).

Ten accidents occurred when the parties were roped together on a rock or snow climb. In 2 cases both members of a rock-climbing party were killed, and the rope between them was not broken. In 1 case the leader was killed (rock), in 1 case the second was killed (snow), in the other 6 cases the leader was injured.

ACCIDENT REPORTS

Since the late 1940's the SMC Journal has normally listed the accidents for the previous year.

A DIFFICULT RESCUE: from the 1974 List.

February 16 — Two climbers (22 and 24), both from Cheshire started to climb Observatory Ridge but took a westwards line rather than the crest and forced further and further to Zero side of ridge. Leader was just below top of steep section when he fell (about 70 feet) and was held by his second. Unhurt, he started to climb back but fell a second time, getting a bad shaking and bruising his ribs (thought he had broken a rib). There was no spare rope and to abseil from this point would have been very difficult, so they started yelling for help. A party on N.E. Buttress heard them mid afternoon and alerted Rescue Team on completion of their climb. Kinloss R.A.F. M.R.T. also called on. Both teams combined and sent parties to foot of the ridge and to the summit. Police snow-trac vehicle proved most valuable to transport equipment and advance party to half way lochan. At first light next day it was decided to lower two men down from top of Zero Gully. Ian Sutherland and Ian Sykes, as the only men present who had climbed Zero, had this unpleasant job. Weather fine but very cold and windy on the plateau and very chilly work for the lowerers there. They were lowered on two 500-feet pre-stretched nylon ropes, the stranded two being about 1,000 feet from the summit. Lowering was straight-forward with good radio communication and good visibility from top to bottom. They were able to swing across from the gully to the side of the ridge (the only technically difficult part of the job). The two men were very cold but seemed O.K. It was then decided to lower the two to the foot rather than climb back up and three 500-feet ropes tied together used for this. Though lowering was getting hard to control and ropes were getting very elastic, the final section completed without incident and all got to foot after three hours. The longest single lower yet done in Britain.

AN EARLY BLIZZARD: from the 1976 List.

September 8 — Seven Belgians, three men and four women, one of the men a doctor, were in camp at Glenmore Site. They enquired at Forestry Information Centre if there were any high level huts. The clerkess there informed them correctly there were no such huts. She enquired about equipment and clothing. They stated (very incorrectly, as was afterwards shown), that they had such. They did not mention Shelter Stone of Loch Avon. Weather fairly good in morning when they set off. None of them had proper equipment. Footgear included Hush Puppies, Wellingtons and plimsolls, and clothing, jeans and light trousers. They carried no extra gear and but little food. It seems they noted Shelter Stone marked on map and assumed it was an alpine type of hut. Weather deteriorated in afternoon and they arrived at Shelter Stone all cold and wet. Nothing to cook with, and no hot food. Chris Watts, an Outward Bound instructor, and girl friend were in occupation. Both very well equipped and Chris a most experienced mountaineer. The party spent a miserable night under the Stone and overnight a heavy snowfall (first of winter), almost blizzard conditions. Though none of the Belgians were in good condition their leader still wanted to return with them over Ben Macdhui. Chris had some difficulty in talking them out of it. He and his friend gave them hot drinks and realised they would have difficulty in returning and so went with them, to help. Conditions steadily grew worse and by the time they were in upper part of Coire Raibeirt they were in bad condition. Three were showing signs of exposure and one collapsed. Watts got them into their spare sleeping bags and left them in the shelter of a snow bank. After that he and his friend had much difficulty in getting the other four over to Coire Cas, one man almost having to be dragged. Got them all safe down to car park and called on help for the three remaining ones. A helicopter was called on but could not help, due to high winds and thick mist. It required Lodge plus a dog and dog handler in case there had been heavy drifts. The party were found in poor condition and it required a very tough carry of three stretcher loads from Coire Raibeirt to car park. It seems certain that but for the chance meeting with Watts at Shelter Stone this affair may well have ended in a major tragedy like that of the six children in 1971. It also shows how often a good forenoon is followed by a sudden change of weather in afternoon.

A SKYE TRAGEDY: from the 1987 List.

Early 1987 - Loss of a Policeman in the Black Cuillin. Gendarme fell off the West Ridge of Sgurr nan Gillean.

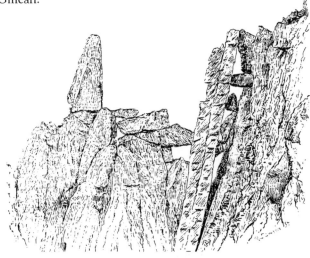

THE TOOTH OF SGURR NAN GILLEAN (LOOKING N.)

AVALANCHED!
Vol. XXXI (1977)
by Sandy Cousins

Thrilling, frightening, comic, tragic — an avalanche is all of these. Due to our misjudgment of snow conditions I was caught in one and maybe the experience will be of use to others.

My tale begins at Corrour Bothy in the Cairngorms. Our party was on a two-day ski tour enjoying good Easter conditions of ample snow cover following the heavy fall of the previous few days. We skied from Achlean to Corrour in sunshine and occasional mist. Next morning the blasts of wind which rattled the bothy during the

'Cousins In Full Flight'

night had died down and we emerged into cold calm sunshine. The Lairig Ghru was carpeted wall-to-wall by firm snow, a joy to ski. We skinned easily up the pass on smooth snow many feet deep over the Pools of Dee and by noon we were passing the March Burn which was completely snowed over. From the top of the Lairig we looked through to the Sinclair shelter and Rothiemurchus forest, bathed in sunshine.

Various alternative routes to gain the west corner of the Cairngorm plateau were discussed and finally we chose to climb out of the Lairig about half a mile west of the March Burn to gain the top of the Allt Creag an Leth-choin and thereby have a fine three-mile run down to the Glenmore forest. There had been no snow for two or three days but the slope above held a lot, the horizontal sastrugi showed there had been some wind-packing, though generally it was soft so that one sank over the ankle without ski. We chose to climb the strips of frozen scree for better footing. Our party was what the Press would call 'very experienced and well equipped,' but there was no mention, or I believe, even thought, of avalanche. Later of course it was obvious the new snow had fallen on old hard snow in freezing conditions with no subsequent thawing and freezing to key the whole thing together. Here was an obvious case for pondering the conditions prevailing for the few days before one's climb and our mistake was in not realising we were 'standing into danger.'

And so we climbed with our ski on our packs. Well up the frozen scree slope half our party took to the snow, plodding deep steps up a shallow gully about twenty feet to the right of the little ridge the rest of us climbed. I led up a short steep section and found the ridge levelling off as the head of the gully swept up in a steep snow-wall. Above the slope rolled back in a series of snow waves. Some of our group seemed to find the steep section a little difficult so I moved right to walk up the deep snow close to the right of the ridge. The first man of the other group was just climbing out the side of the gully up the snowy grass opposite me. His followers were plodding up the gully and mine were close behind me, the last man still on the ridge.

Suddenly I sank back, took a couple of steps up and with a sickening feeling realised that I was on a moving mass of snow — Avalanched!

I learned later that the last man in the gully group had seen a crack open in front of him and away he went thinking he was the only one, so the whole mass had started simultaneously. I remember thinking as I sank into the snow, 'Oh, Christ, you mug, avalanched!' With no time to look round I glimpsed the sunlit crest close on my left leaping away upward as I sagged into a moving snowy mattress. I rammed my ski sticks through the snow seeking a hold but everything was on the move, accelerating fast. My ski were down the loops at the side of my pack, clipped together at the tips above my head. Some had theirs across their packs or up the side and they suffered most damage. Almost immediately I was rotating and tumbling past our steep section. I felt myself falling a short way, then I was on my front, head down, flying in a confusion of snow. Some rasped my throat and I remembered, 'don't inhale snow' so I held my mitt across my face, sucking air through my teeth. Now I was bowling down on my front, sometimes bouncing, in the dark grey world inside the avalanche. I wondered if the others were alright somewhere around me or if I was on my own. Remembering the slope below was an open snow slope, free of pitches and rocks, I thought it might be best to get as far down as possible in case the tons of snow behind should bury me. Some time ago in a winter climbing fall I had done some seven hundred feet down a gully and I hoped my God and my luck were with me again. That time my companions had lost their axes and mine had broken but I was able to stop us all using an ice-spike I had, but this time I knew I was at the mercy of the snow. I paddled with my elbows to keep the snow loose around me and kept my legs together to prevent damage from flailing about. My head was between my ski and thus protected a bit, and I held my sticks across before me to ward off any bumps. I found myself saying, 'relax man, save energy in case a real burst is needed to dig upward.' Since my initial burial I had been almost holding my breath and just as I wondered how long until I had a chance for clear air I burst into white light momentarily and gulped air through my mitts, then I was covered again. Snow was tumbling around me and once I felt it begin to pack so I immediately kicked and elbowed to keep it loose. However, I was still moving, and then, as suddenly as I had slid backwards probably less than a minute ago, I tumbled out into bright sunshine and stillness.

Looking up in case debris was still following I saw a large area of jumbled blocks and the empty swept slope above. I stood up, dropped my pack, noting my ski seemed O.K. (I later found one tip slightly crimped), my limbs seemed alright and glancing at the blue sky I thanked God. Above me figures lay or stood around on the mound of debris. The snow blocks were rock-hard and several rocks had been torn from the gully. Two figures were still high on the hill, the man on the right had been left above the gully as the snow vanished behind him and the other on the left had been finishing our steep bit when he suddenly saw a tangle of arms, legs and ski flash past him in a cloud of snow. I yelled at them to count us and heard seven were visible, so no one was buried. The fracture of the slab avalanche ran right across the head of the gully including some of the slope above the rest we had been climbing. Judging by the figures there the wall was at least fifteen feet high in the gully and some hundred feet across. It had swept the slope clean. One of the party had fallen through the avalanche and had been dumped on the scree after only a few feet. The debris had come to rest about fifty feet above the floor of the Lairig and I estimate our speed was some twenty miles an hour down six hundred feet (vertical) at maybe forty-five degrees, amongst about five hundred and thirty tons of snow.

Knox and Sandy made their way down to us joining Andy in the gully. Hugh lay a hundred feet above me not moving and near him Graham sat holding his head as a large red stain spread down his pullover. I tried to walk up to Graham but my legs would hardly move and I found my elbow becoming warm and sticky from a cut. We all felt we had been through a mangle. Hugh stirred and staggered down with Graham and I bandaged the long cut in his head. Tom came down, blood dripping from his sleeve and Hugh diagnosed a smashed elbow which he bound. Ken was worst hit, head, back and arm being hurt, so Bill, Andy and Knox put him in a sleeping bag in a tent. Three chaps who had seen our slide from the Lairig came across and gave very competent help. Several ski were smashed and packs ripped. We considered a ski-sledge for Ken but our two doctors were reluctant to risk rough handling. Regretfully, I suggested I ski down to call for assistance from the staff at Glenmore Lodge. At this stage we hoped to get a sledge and take our friends down ourselves.

Ski touring is part of mountaineering and as such one must accept its risks, however serious. Rescue is not something one should automatically expect and I feel that self rescue should always be considered first, even though the decision is finally taken to call for outside help in the interests of the casualty

I reckoned on one and a half hours to reach the Rothiemurchus Hut then with say three hours to return we could make it in daylight. Hugh and I set off on ski. One group stayed with Ken and one group walked Graham to the Sinclair bothy — hard going in deep snow. At the Hut Fred Harper's reassuring voice on the phone was welcome. He soon had the information and a chopper was on its way, diverted from another avalanche call which had come earlier from Coire an Lochain. Hugh arrived very tired and the folk at the Hut were very helpful.

In the busy moments spent at Glenmore Lodge as the helicopter was briefly there I am sure our sincere thanks were hardly noticed so from us all I give them again to both the helicopter people and the Lodge staff involved. Soon Ken and Tom were on their way to hospital, young Graham was stitched and we walking cases dispersed to hobble around like old men.

FREE ON SUNDAYS - AT THE BRECHE DE ROLAND
Vol. XXXII (1982)   by Dan Livingston

Down the years, I have made several visits to the Spanish side of the Pyrenees and usually the Breche de Roland has been included in the itinerary. This breach in the frontier ridge, if we are to believe the legend, was cloven by the mighty sword of Roland to facilitate his retreat from the Moor. Each visit seemed to be associated with an unusual incident, always minor but nonetheless memorable in some way. The very first was back in 1956 when Spain required a visa for entry and when John Lowe and myself walked in by the Breche, blissfully unaware of the fact that this route was prohibited. The result — we were confined for two days by the Carabineros, while we were investigated. But this is not the story that I want to tell. The latest incident at the Breche was more amusing.

The party consisted of George Roger, Hugh and Nan Leith, Margo McDougall and myself. We had left Tarla on the Spanish side to prowl around the mountains for three or four days and the journey took in, as usual, Roland's Masterstroke. The snow on the slopes down to the Refuge des Sarradels was quite firm and a bit icy in places. Suddenly, I slipped and fell, putting out my free hand to break the fall. It was when I got up and looked at the right hand that I was astonished to see that the pinkie of the right hand was exactly at right angles to the direction of the other fingers. There was no pain. Had I not looked at it I wouldn't have known.Being a bit dim on medical matters, I assumed that it was broken. Nan, behind me, expressed horror and looked as if she had seen a monster. Fifteen minutes brought us to the Refuge where I asked Madame la Gardienne if there were in the hut any visitors with medical knowledge. No, but she must radio the mountain rescue post down in Gavarnie. After a long exchange with the post, it emerged that an ambulance bearing the letters C.R.S. was going to make for the road end at the col which is called the Port de Gavarnie and I was to descend the 800 feet and rendezvous with it there. It amused me to see and hear Madame gazing at me and reading of my salient features for identification. I was an Englishman, small, elderly, and with white hair. To none of these, although most are true, do I give official recognition. Soon George, Hugh and I set off down to the Port, the ill-directed digit held aloft to prevent anything or anyone knocking it off. When 200 feet above the Port we spied a small helicopter well below us and like ourselves it was heading for the pass. We watched it circle low over the col and head up our own track. Now, knowing, or rather believing, that the French are not so generous in mountain rescue as the British and having already made a hasty mental estimate of the cost of an ambulance, panic entered my mean breast, when I saw the machine heading for us and for such a trivial injury. As he overflew us, he was loud-hailing "Are you the Englishman? Are you the Englishman?" To my credit I didn't say yes but I did hold up my bent pinkie for identification.He turned and landed. A young man nimbly disembarked and wanted to hustle me on board. "Mais je n'ai pas commande un helicopteur et je ne veux pas payer pour un helicopteur." This sentence was processed in the two minutes before landing and I didn't give a damn whether the helicopter was masculine or feminine. "Vite, vite" said the young man who turned out to be a doctor and I allowed myself to be hustled on board, having made my statement in regard to payment. A few minutes took us down to the post of the Campagnie Republicaine de Securite at Gavarnie. Now that we could talk, the doctor told the pilot and the mechanic of the Scotsman who almost wanted a statement before boarding that he should not be billed. The pilot told me that the service was always free on a Sunday — especially for Scotsmen. There was much good humoured banter before the pinkie was straightened — it was only a dislocation.

The arrangement that had been made with George and Hugh was that I should spend the night in Gavarnie and on the following morning about 10 a.m. we should meet at the Port for our return to Spain. However, the advent of the chopper on the scene had advanced events so much that I wondered if perhaps I might be able to walk back up the Refuge before nightfall. The crew thought it not advisable. Then the pilot dropped a bombshell. He would fly me back up to the hut! I gathered from the talk that supplies had to be taken to a hut in an adjacent cirque and that he would be prepared to go out of his way and drop me at Sarradels. After a fantastic flight round the Cirque de Gavarnie he touched down outside the hut and I clambered off amid hasty and unheard words of thanks and farewell.

Nan and Margo were dumbfounded to see me arrive in this way. As for George and Hugh, they were still slogging up the soft snow after their mercy mission. I had two large drams in me before they arrived — aghast at seeing me here.

When I was young, I used to think erroneously that gratuitous meant free.Later, I learned that it meant 'uncalled for'. Now, I know that it can mean both — on Sundays at the Breche de Roland.

FOREIGN CONNECTIONS

THE BIG EYE OF SUMMER
Vol. XXXI (1977)

by I.H.M. Smart

> From the mid 1950s, Scottish climbers were frequent visitors to East Greenland, an area with which a special affinity was often experienced by those fortunate enough to visit it..

In the High Arctic there are long periods in summer when the weather is calm and cloudless. At such times the silence, clear light and brilliant reflections make previous experience unreliable. The detail visible on distant hills is such that twenty miles seem nearer than two. The fjord waters mirror the stone hills and icebergs so exactly that seaplanes coming in to land cannot distinguish the essential interface between reflection and reality. A cry in the lowlands vanishes into the air like a stone disappearing into water without a splash or ripple, while a shout among the hills comes back from the planes of rock in multiple echoes of varying intonation whose loudness is often unrelated to the sequence of return.

The familiar sun, however, remains above the horizon all day, tracing an easily variable circle in the sky. This most reassuring fact is said to be an illusion. Astronomers and their equations seem happier if the moving sun is taken to be stationary and the solid earth rotating. Be that as it may, once during a period of settled weather our boat crossed the inner reaches of Scoresby Sound, threading its way along the narrow sea lanes between the hundreds and thousands of icebergs which are a feature of this area — mansions, palaces, and cathedrals of crystalline splendour daring and original in design and each meticulously repeated by its reflection in the still water, a silent white city fifteen miles across, the Summer Capital of the Winter King, built like others from the resources of its hinterland.

I was left on the shore near Gurreholm at the mouth of the Schuchert River while the boat returned vanishing Lethe-wards among the reflections. For reasons which need not distract us here I had to be 120 miles away as quickly as possible. This was no hardship; a man who finds himself to be healthy, alone, and free to travel lightly laden in the still emptiness of the High Arctic has been granted a high privilege.

The first leg of the journey lay across the level floor of the Schuchert Valley. My initial target was a point which, clearly visible five miles away through cotton grass and haloed against the low sun, induced a liberating tranquility. The mechanism of progress can be left to the spinal cord which enjoys an autonomy it has not had since the introduction of cephalisation. There are no navigational problems and the mind is free to join the landscape. After a succession of these five mile stretches the route left the valley floor and climbed up to the broad saddle leading to Orsted's Dal and the sea. Here I stopped for a few hours' rest while the sun hung low over the northern horizon. The shadow of night lay far to the south with its edge over Scotland. In Greenland, however, it was the time of the union of opposites when there is no today and time hangs between the brocaded richness of yesterday's evening and the brave simplicity of tomorrow's dawn.

I was sitting opposite the broad Roslin Glacier. A dozen years before, the youthful Slesser and I made the first crossing of the unknown southern Staunings Alps and emerged down this mighty glacier after days of crevassed uncertainty and windy camps in the much serrated interior of the range. I remembered reaching the mouth of the glacier on an evening as serene as the present. We had, with growing confidence, become separated. Slesser had wandered off by himself and a mile of flat glacier lay between us, but such were the acoustics we could still argue distinctly by slow shouts. I remember the final shout 'C-a-l-l y-o-u-r-s-e-l-f a b-l-o-o-d-y e-x-p-l-o-r-e-r.' It echoed and re-echoed from the ranks of broken buttresses of bracken-brown granite, returning again and again in the glory of the golden evening, sometimes clear, sometimes fragmented; a scene where only man was vile and he was a mile off the route, too.

A decade later another expedition fought its way up the same glacier through the deep snow of early summer. After three days of heavy-laden struggle they reached their base camp in the promised land of an unknown side glacier deep in some inner sanctum of the range. Four prospectors were already there sitting round a table playing cards in front of a large, well-appointed tent with a helicopter parked suburbanly by its side. They offered these travellers from an antique ideology cups of coffee and kind smiles, fresh rolls and the latest news.

The route now wandered through a pleasant landscape of green meadows and blue lochans. Herds of musk oxen safely grazed among the poppies and sun-caught cotton grass. Skeins of well-rehearsed geese peter-scotted across the dawn sky. Legs, given their head, moved effortlessly, rhythmically, feet rattling against the yellow and white Draba flowers. The soul was free to take down interesting thoughts from the richly-stocked shelves of the mind, throw them up in the air and watch them sparkle in the clear morning light. This exhilaration stemmed from confidence in one's physical and mental ability to travel in empty lands, the perfectly tuned mind in the perfectly tuned body in an aesthetically perfect environment.

This lasted until noon. Time for a short nap. It was then I noticed an impulse to crawl head first into my sleeping bag, easily resisted but an odd desire, nevertheless. After a few hours rest I descended into the middle reaches of Orsted's Dal. But something had changed. The landscape seemed to be taking note. The hills hemming in the valley were no longer mounds of indifferent stone to be patronisingly measured by the mind as being shapely or ugly, but seemed to have usurped the initiative and were taking cross bearings on my slow progress down the long valley.This feeling of being watched grew all afternoon. Every pebble stood out sparkling and crystalline in the clear light, each a cell in the great compound eye of the landscape. If only a tent were available to crawl into to reduce the visibility, or a cave to provide some privacy and escape from the singing breezes. You can't lie down to sleep in a whispering shop window or a room walled with one-way mirrors.

Towards evening the native hills drew back to leave a plain ten miles across.The golden light filled the early autumnal landscape up to the blue shadows of the northern hills. It would soon be time for supper and a relaxing dram before enjoying the ambience of the surrounding grandeur as one dropped off to sleep, tired by an unforgettable day's walk. The mind tried to board up the windows with the old familiar cliches but they kept falling off. Maybe it would be better to cross the Pingo Dal river first, a few miles further on and nearer the hills. It would be easier to relax with this obstacle behind. It was reached effortlessly, passing on the way the gaze of a bright-eyed lochan surrounded by blue eye-bright ("Euphrasia frigidea") and the Argus-eyed inflorescences of the artic primrose ("Primula stricta"), the latter a rare plant in these parts. The river was bigger than I had expected. Its braided tresses sang in the sunlight and the far bank lay in cold shadow. Still, it would go with care and a safe route could be picked out among the gravel banks. The crossing was easy until an irreversible commitment had been made to the last stretch which turned out to be deeper and faster than it seemed. The sunlight shimmered on the dazzling, dancing, trilling water, so much more attractive than the cold gloom of the approaching bank. It would be so reasonable, so interesting, to yield to the eager insistent pressure of the thrilling, lifting water and discover the origin of all the excitement. Legs, however, kept moving ahead, gripping the river bed, unmoved by the heady fire water. Then into the shadow; the jewels turned to lead and the seductive laughter to splashing water.

After the trembling and the cold sweat had passed and the hair on the nape of the neck lay flat, I sat in the shadow of the valley, back against a boulder in the protection of a sleeping bag looking southwards to where the warm brown moorland of Orsted Dal lay combing its golden hair in the sunshine. To the left crouched the lowering pack ice with its wandering bears and unpredictable ways. Behind and to the right the dark and drublie hills still lacked their usual indifference as if they sensed that the action had gone wrong. Nearer hand clumps of 'Saxifraga stellaris' starred the dark tundra — a tenuous link with the past, for they also grew light years away at home. Time to take stock — the cliches were beginning to run out.

The Big Eye is a well known phenomenon in the Arctic, characterised by sleeplessness and the feeling of being constantly watched. The mind usually does a good job to protect its owner from the pressure of surrounding things; the unknown is efficiently silvered over to give comfortable reflections of the familiar. In lonely open places without the constricting resonance of a companion or any sign of human artefact the expected reflections return only weakly. The silvering begins to dissolve, and bright undefined things come through and create a debatable land of possessor and possessed. The searing nakedness of that which is there becomes too much for eye and mind. Exploration of this territory is an unchancy business, and in moments of emergency survival depends on the immeasurably greater experience of sub-cerebral reflexes. It is no time to have a beginner in the driver's seat.

After six hours' rest, the journey continued through a range of Torridon-type mountains into the next broad valley turning red and gold under the first frosts of autumn. Then another night passed in a gloomy pass, but controlled this time with the frontier better defined. Another day in the silent land and I was safely back at the Danish weather station at Mesters Vig, back in the kindergarten again with the old familiar pictures on the wall. The walk seemed to have taken a long time, but measured by the schoolroom clock it had lasted half an hour under three days.

PYRAMIDS - S.M.C. ABROAD.
Vol. XIII (1914)

Mr Naismith was in Egypt in March and April, helping to distribute Testaments among the soldiers. While there he climbed the three Pyramids of Gizeh.

The Second Pyramid (Khafre), 447 feet, is rarely ascended by Europeans, although some barefooted Arabs climb it for money in an incredibily short time. It is a trifle steeper than Cheops, the angle being 52°. In its lower 350 feet the nature of the climbing is similar to its neighbour, but in its final 100 feet this pyramid is still covered with the original casing of polished limestone slabs. Its ascent gives a better idea of what these superb monuments must have looked like in their glory than any of the other pyramids in Egypt.

The slabs, or more properly the outer sides of the huge horizontal blocks comprising the "casing," are fitted together so accurately that a penknife cannot be inserted between them when unbroken. It would be impossible to climb to the top, if it were not that in many places the stones have been splintered, perhaps by lightning, perhaps by weathering.

Mr Naismith was taken up by two Arabs, who, before tackling the difficult part near the S.E. angle, removed their shoes and outer garments, and closed their eyes for a few moments in prayer. They then lead the way along a somewhat sensational traverse to the middle of the E. face, and afterwards zig-zagged upwards to the summit. Some of the top blocks have been displaced, and the apex is now about 8 feet square.

When coming down the guides insisted on rolling their turbans, fastening them together, and attaching one end round their "howajah's" waist. A few weeks later the latter managed to elude the Bedouin, and made the same ascent alone. Some of the holds being overhung are difficult to find from above, and he therefore left some chalk marks on the way up. Having nailed shoes he took them off and went up barefooted, and he came down the top part backwards. This bit would be regarded as a difficult passage if met with on a rock peak.

WELCOME BACK TO TOM MACKINNON
Vol. XXVI (1956)
(recited at the Annual Dinner, 1955, by BOAB)

—on returning from the British Kanchenjunga Expedition

Losh, Tam, you're lookin' fine an' braw
Your naked broo like Rannoch Wa',
An' taw-three hairs mair gane awa'
Frae aff your heid,
Tae mark the frichts an' sterts an' a'
On Himal dreid.

It maun hae been an awfu' fash
Tae scart an' howk' an' kick an' bash,
Whiles listenin' tae the fearfu' crash
O' thundrous snaw.
An' maybe feelin' no' sae brash
At whit ye saw.

Still, Tam, ye ken, ye're jist the same,
Wi' maybe just a wee less wame,
An' maybe just a wee mair fame
Than 'fore ye gaed.
We're thanfu', tho', a Sherpa dame
Ye didna wed!

Man, Tam, it's grand tae hae this nicht
O' Evans and Joe Broon a sicht,
An' a' aroun' the room sae bricht
Wi' meat an' drink,
An' worth it if we a' get ticht
An' land in clink.

So here we pour a muckle dram,
An' haud it oot at length o' arm,
An' raise it up frae oot o' harm
O' graspin' freen.
Then put it whaur it works a charm
An' lichts the e'en.

WEE MALKIE
Vol. XXXI (1978)   by Raymond Simpson

In these days when even minor expeditions to the Himalayas are liable to media-hype,
this account has a certain appeal.

Allan and I found 'Wee Malkie' during a long summer spent walking and climbing in Kashmir. We had been travelling extremely light with a minimum of climbing equipment and few specific objectives during the early part of the summer which had been spent in the high valleys of Indian Kashmir on the borders of Ladakh. The five peaks we had enjoyed there more than satisfied us and when the monsoon winds began to blow we fled to the arid majesty of the Karakorum.

Here, the mountains overawed us with their gigantic scale and we were content to wander their flanks enjoying Hunza apricots. We had not, however, enjoyed the cliff-hanging truck ride up the Indus valley and resolved to return on foot by the old silk route across the ranges to the south of Nanga Parbat. After five days of tranquil walking we came to the first village of any size on the south side of the range. Some hours above this village, we were told, there lay an attractive lake surrounded by snow peaks. Intrigued, we stocked up with food and ascended by a cascading clear burn on a sandy track weaving up through old gnarled pines; dramatically changing in a few hours to grassy meadows framing a long blue glacial lake.

The vegetation here was green and lush, a welcome contrast to the high desert ranges where we had spent the last few weeks. Masses of succulent yellow flowers tumbled to the shores of the lake on the surface of which was reflected a wall of snow peaks. 'High, but not too high' we thought, '19,000 feet at the most.' One dominated the others; its massive bell shaped summit, embellished with graceful flutings of snow, focussed our eyes and aspirations.

We pitched our tent on a flower-strewn bank facing the big peak. A tantalising line led through a hanging glacier, skirting a steep rock band on the right and looked as if it might take us to the summit icefield. We estimated 3,000 ft. of mixed climbing on most of which we should be able to move together, apart from perhaps part of the rock band. The icefield? Well, it looked like just another uniform slope of neve of the type we had become used to ascending and descending without too much difficulty on other peaks.

We cast a not too critical eye over minimal climbing equipment and meagre supply of food. We agreed that at least we could 'have a look at it,' after all it was just another hill to climb with definable difficulties. Or was it? It hung above our idyllic campsite threatening the contentment of yesterday with its challenge, giving nothing away to furtive glances for reassurance. Its face was enigmatic, flattened by the evening light, and as the sunset colours faded our hopes rose and fell as we peered into the shadows gathering across its enormous western front.

Some Gujar children were herding goats down by the lake, and when they collected round the door of the tent we asked them what they called the mountains. Their name for the big one transliterated into something like 'Wee Malkie' and for us this became its title.

A long day was spent mainly in a maze of little buttresses below the hanging glacier which we hoped would provide a route to the summit ice field. The lake grew smaller and smaller beneath our heels and it was with great relief that we threw the sacks down on top of a buttress just below the glacier. There was not really room even for our tiny tent but we contrived to erect it astride the crest. This perch afforded us magnificent views of the jagged brown peaks to the south. The face above us looked like a giant liquorice allsort with its alternating bands of rock and ice. The setting sun caught the undersides of the low creeping flowers which spread their tendrils amongst the rocks, gilding their petals with a brief but lovely luminosity. When this faded, the sudden chill forced us to seek in vain the comfort of sleep on one of those fitful nights where tiredness and excitement battle for control of the consciousness. We were glad when the watch said it was time to brew up and be off.

A living sea of cloud filled the valleys below us, creeping in smoky wisps up the gullies. Rock peaks emerged from the sea to the south and west and were already turning pink with the first sun, instilling a sense of urgency as we fumbled with crampons.

The terminal icefall had looked ugly from below, however a hidden ramp in the ice provided a steep but secure passage and we were soon making our way up the hanging glacier to below the summit icefield. From the top of the glacier a shallow couloir offered a route but we were surprised to find that the ridge on its right was relatively easy. We unroped and delighted in climbing the warm slabby rock, chuckling to ourselves that this enigmatic black patch, seen from afar and obviously the key to the route, could not stop us now and was in fact providing us with an easy line through some incredible rock and ice scenery. To our left the face rose in one great rock step of a thousand feet over which avalanches spewed from the ridge above to the hanging glacier below; to our right a chaotic face of steep ice and seracs tumbled down from the summit.

The sun was already on the summit icefield when we arrived at its foot, small stones stotting down from the ridge to the left, but the centre seemed to be safe enough, at least for the time being. We still did not know how long it would take but as we had climbed almost three thousand feet from our campsite we reckoned that it could not be very much further.

Two hours later we were well beyond the point of no return but were still barely halfway up the icefield, having seriously underestimated the length, steepness and hardness of the ice. Our situation was delicate; for five rope lengths we had been strung out on a slope of brittle water ice, our blunted crampons skating on the glassy surface. Because of a botch boot repair in Hunza, involving a chunk of tractor tyre, I could put no pressure on my front points and was forced into the strenuous contortions at which the

French are said to excel. The brittle nature of the ice and the need for speed ruled out step cutting; even our drive in peg would not penetrate without fracturing the ice so that we could only belay the leader on each run out with our one tubular screw; the second following perforce with a tight rope on a psychological belay. Fortunately at mid-height the slope, being convex, eased slightly and we could traverse by means of frozen-in rocks to the relative security of a ridge where the snow cover was more generous. Thus for another eight rope lengths to the summit dome, where, gasping for breath in the thin air, we collapsed in the soft snow, ten hours from the tent.

By this time in the day the views to the north were obscured by cloud but we could see the lake far below, looking so incredibly small that it was hard to believe that this massive peak and all the others could ever have been mirrored in its tiny surface. We could not afford to hang about however as we were anxious to find a descent route before dark. We groped down a bottomless slope of soft wet snow to a steep little buttress leading to a col on the west ridge.

The brown and gold sunset saw us still high on the ridge, traversing cautiously along an apron of snow which spilled over the huge rock band above the hanging glacier. Unwilling to contemplate the descent of such an obstacle in the dark, we were forced down to a steep glacier on the far side of the mountain. A bivouac was contemplated, the cold however forced us to keep moving down and eventually the moon came out to show us a narrow high angled snow gully leading back up on to the west ridge five hundred feet above. After this heartbreaking effort the ridge thankfully broadened out. We unroped and followed it to the top of a wide couloir running down in the direction of our camp.

By this time we were moving automatically. I fell asleep at one point waiting for Alan and woke with a start having dreamed that he had passed me in the dark. I ran down several hundred feet shouting at rocks till I realised he was still above me and that I could only have closed my eyes for seconds. Realising that we had no hope of finding the tent in the dark, we bivouacked on some rocks by the side of the couloir. I was wakened by the cold just before dawn and was surprised to see the tent on its ledge a little below us. We stumbled down to it, cooked some atta, brewed some tea and flaked out for most of the next thirty-six hours.

Picking our way down to the lake and past the smoky sheilings on the alp, we cast many a backward glance at Wee Malkie. Its fluted summit, half hidden by tails of cloud, wore for us a more benign aspect than it had a few days before. The experience it had given us had intensified our appreciation of the lonely valleys it dominated. We knew nothing of and cared less about its true name, height and mountaineering history (if any). To us its charm lay in its obscurity, together with the knowledge that the world held more interesting and exotic valleys, and more remote and lovely peaks than we could visit in a lifetime.

DEDO DO DEUS
Vol. XXIX (1968)

by Malcolm Slesser

A tendency to indulgence, whether in food, mountains or liquor has, happily, always been a feature of the members of our Club. Never are we better than when flouting danger or offsetting some discomfort with the knowledge that in the valley lie groaning tables and exquisitely distilled malts. Age may alter the relative balance of such immoderation, but the Club spirit is unassailable. It will be perceived, therefore, that I, an ageing member surrounded by the bald granite precipices of Rio de Janeiro with gin at five bob a bottle, experienced little difficulty in fitting into my new environment. It is true that when viewed on a cold winter's night in Scotland, pictures of these sun-drenched precipices draw forth fire and bold talk. But when seen in reality with the sun almost vertically overhead and temperatures oscillating a degree or two about the hundred, the alternative of a Brazilian gin tonic in half-litre mugs seemed the saner course. Nevertheless my S.M.C. conscience would twinge now and again when the sun set behind some glorious vertical precipice, or when one day poised behind a beer on the summit of Sugar Loaf (it has a telepherique) I suddenly saw the Finger of God. I felt an instant admonishment. Moreover, it was an American professor, a stranger to climbing, who brought me to its foot.

The Dedo do Deus (5300 feet), to give it its Brazilian name, is a 600-foot finger of vertical granite set on top of a steep jungle-clad spur, the second of a series of five peaks that grace the east flank of the Organ mountains some fifty miles from Rio city. It was climbed first in 1912 by Aceio de Oliveira and large body of comrades in the days before incoming Czechs and Austrians gave Brazilian climbing the tone it has today. It was time I, too, climbed it, for Brazilians on learning of my pretensions as a climber would smirk and say "Ah, but have you tried the Dedo do Deus? Of course, it is only for experts!".

Harvey's Chevrolet purred its expensive U.S. way through the deserted streets of Rio at 4.00 a.m. with myself and Carlos Costa Ribeiro in the back seats. Carlos, a student of physics, was a renowned climber, having had a go at the recently- discovered highest mountains in Brazil on the Venezuelan border. As a youth in Austria he had been introduced to kletterschuhe and dolomite. Harvey and he talked about the benefits of Communism while I slept.

We parked at a roadside shrine at 2500 feet in the depth of the slowly wakening forest, and looked up to see the momentary sun blush on the Finger, which poked censoriously out of a palisade of trees. One day — I thought in the putting-off frame of mind 6.00 a.m. always instils in me — we must have a go at the east face. Thank God, the normal route is round the other side. For several hours at least one could press on assuming it was easier.

"That's our way" declared Carlos pointing to the east face. "The original route would bore you."

Tamely and silently I followed him as he led into the jungle along a vague trail designed for pygmies. However, five minutes into the jungle and the plants on the floor gave up trying to live. One could stand up without being swiped in the eye by bushes, or throttled by hanging lianas. A prey to fears, I looked anxiously about for anacondas, rattlesnakes or cor-de-rosas, and faced with what strength I could the thought of beating off Oncas. I took it as a matter of course that my skin would be swollen with insect bites, and that the ensuing nights would be spent in mad scratchings.

The first pitch loomed out of the gloom, a sebaceous groove whose crucial move was executed by a monkey-like swing from the fragmentary root of a once-noble Ipe tree. I was soon to learn that were it not for trees, Brazilian climbing would be impossible.

More gloom. Then slabs, and for a moment we broke into sunshine, and saw the north wall dripping with cornices of moss, gravatas, and other nameless growths that lent an air of Fester outdoing Coire Ardair at the height of summer.

Another half hour of gloom and sweat and then Carlos paused.

"We leave sacks here."

Personally, I never felt less like parting with my belongings. Reluctantly I changed boots for P.A.'s, and draped on a few tape etriers, hammer and pegs.

"You won't need these."

I smiled. Reports I had heard of Brazilian belay techniques would have scandalized Tennent, far less the author of a slide-rule work on running belays.

Carlos then led across an avalanche chute. These are common hereabouts, though mud and old trees take the place of snow. The debris is unstable, and often can be jarred into further movements. The consequences are too awful to contemplate. Soon we were on mud of inconceivable steepness, barely held in place by lush growth. With one hand on the north face, we slithered, groped, pulled, yanked, sweated and clawed our way up mossy grooves, rotting trees and holdless chimneys. Harvey did it all on his fingers. Carlos enjoyed antigravity. Then suddenly I was face to face with a mass of deep red orchid blooms, and it was worth it. Soon shouts from ahead spoke of light, and following a tunnel in some dense bushes I found my two companions sitting on a small rock tower looking up at the east face of the Finger of God.

It seemed to be composed of four totally detached pieces of rock that, like some child's puzzle, fitted together into a mountain. What route there was must lie along the interlocks.

The climbing, when it came, was delicious. Here, right on the Tropic of Capricorn, even at 4700 feet there is never any frost. The rock, though the finest granite, is almost totally lacking in incut holds. Nor does it ever have the roughness of a Chamonix slab. Rather, it seems to have solidified from a pitted syrup, and been up-ended. The few cracks lay along the interlocks, or where massive chunks had broken loose. Resolute trees had managed to worm long tough roots far into the interior of the Finger and I found them useful as runners and belays. Much needed too, for my companions showed a complete lack of interest in such procedures. Harvey had no experience, and was in any event by this time utterly exhausted. He had climbed fully 2000 feet from the car largely on his hands. Carlos used ritual belaying. I looked for peg-cracks, and found none. The drop beneath us was impressive; the landing a green umbrella of branches.

By now the nearer of the northern peaks, which stretch for a thousand miles or more, were visible; they included fine summits in a neighbouring valley which contains some virgin walls, and at least one unclimbed peak. We could now look over an intermediate ridge to the National Park of Teresopolis, and the attractive town of that name beyond, sequestered 3000 feet in a knot of little ridges. Harvey was breathing stertorously, and Carlos was lassoing spikes in Whymper fashion.

We reached a cave and thankfully crawled into the shade.

"Up?"

"Out."

Out right under an overhang I saw the first of several bolts. Like half inch carriage bolts, these Brazilian things are made to last, and to take the weight of about ten people. The whole philosophy and safety of Brazilian climbing hinges around them. The rock being holdless, it is their answer, and not a short-term one.

Harvey allowed his eye to dally a moment, and then undid the rope and started down. The Luso-Scottish elements, scandalised, called him back pointing out the commonplace that the party does not split up, adding the rider that the majority were in favour of going upwards. Harvey, no traditionalist, gave way only when he found we wouldn"t give him a rope to rope down. Carlos led, and vanished. Whatever instructions he subsequently offered were lost in the wind, and Harvey was dangling on the first tape before he had time to reconsider. I fear we were brutal. When Harvey wisely announced that he had neither strength nor skill for this sort of thing, and that he would come down, Carlos instantly slackened the rope. Harvey slid wildly to the right, and, being a scientist, was at once aware that gravity was going to spring him out under an overhang, and not back to me.

"What do I do?" he shouted.

"Impossible to get back," I shouted encouragingly.

But Harvey was a U.S. citizen; and Carlos knew how to give a friend a helping hand. The grunts that ensued might have lured a female hippopotamus. And when my turn came I appreciated the difficulty. This pitch, called the 'maria cebolla' was led by a Czech immigrant called Drahomirubas. What he held on to while putting in the expansion bolts is a mystery. The last 20 feet are a slanting crack between an overhang and a vertical wall calling for uncritical faith in hand jams. I found Carlos contentedly gazing at the view, belayed to a cactus whose roots I was able to lift with one hand.

Thereafter we climbed within, not on, the mountain. Often as much as ten feet from the outer face we chimneyed for two long pitches, crept up a slab and reached the top of a plinth. A huge rock crevasse, overhanging above us like a bad rimaye, was all that lay between us and the top. We climbed it the only way anyone has yet found - by a ladder. Half a century's weathering had exchanged iron for rust, but to make sssurance doubly sure, the top was tied with decayed electric flex to an expansion bolt.

The summit is as flat as a navvy's thumb, with a forest large enough to keep visitors in firewood for decades. We all, for various reasons, were very happy.From here one can see some of the superb faces on the north side of the range. Some, like Garafao, are virgin and over 1500 feet high. We dined off gammon (from the PX) and bruised pineapple, and slid down the ladder for the start of the descent by the voie normale: a series of chimneys on the west face with ledges between. Harvey wouldn't climb, so we had to rappel. He lost his spectacles, and their glassy tinkle could be heard from the bowels of the mountain for minutes after. On the third rappel, the steepness of the pitch, and absence of foreground nearer than 1000 feet, caused Harvey to ask for a safety line, and my rope was put in play. I had descended, and was enjoying a quiet contemplation of cavorting mists and mysterious walls, when the rasping noise of Harvey's skin on the rope stopped, and he started gurgling badly. The safety line had jammed in a karabiner

I shouted to him to haul himself up on his arms while Carlos freed it, but his arms were done.

"Cut the rope," he demanded in a high-pitched voice that was not like him at all.

"Wait a minute." One is not born in Aberdeen for nothing. Moreover Tiso's was at least eight weeks postage away. I climbed up and tried to lasso Harvey and haul him onto a higher ledge. However, having discovered a solution he was single minded in demanding it

"Cut the rope" — a cry which, as he slowly went blue, he modified to:

"Cut the rope. I'll buy you a new one. I'll buy you as many ropes as you like, but cut the rope.."

I nodded, and Carlos cut, and Harvey landed drunkenly beside me, while I coiled 40 feet of useless nylon.

There were no hard feelings. The dusk was brief and beautiful, and we groped down the festering jungle on all fours, and made the road three hours after darkness. I had been neither attacked nor bitten. Next day, Harvey, a good colleague if ever there was one, offered to send to New York for a new rope. "Forget it. Just one of those things." We worked on, while his cigar smoke coiled lazily in the cold air of the air conditioner.

"Malcolm, you get whisky?"

"No." To all except diplomats it was £8 a bottle in Brazil.

"A case any good to you?"

If the Finger of God wagged at me, I never saw it.

DEDO DE DEUS - 'HARVEY'S STORY
Vol. XXIX (1969)   by E. J. Henley

Professor Slesser's version of our ascent of Dedo de Deus and of how he transformed an old, frayed, nylon rope into a case of Chivas Regal is badly in need of elaboration. His overly modest account of what surely must be acclaimed as the 'rope trick of the year' hardly makes him out to be the rogue and blackguard he really is. Indeed, the true saga of how a feeble, middle-aged, New York City cliff dweller whose previous highest ascent had been to the top of the Empire State Building (in an elevator) found himself nearly strangled near the end of a tortuous 5300-foot, fourth-degree climb (the great Herzog called it 'very challenging') may be of interest to readers. It may also serve as a deterrent to other novice climbers who may be foolish enough to trust Malcolm Slesser.

I freely admit that I went of my own volition; indeed, it was I who suggested the near fatal climb, and introduced Slesser to Carlos Costa Ribeiro, our Brazilian guide and gracious host. It was, in fact, my second attempt at Dedo de Deus. Ribeiro and Mauro Andrade, who was then one of my graduate students at the University of Brazil, had attempted to yank and shove me up the 'tourist trail' to the top of the rugged peak the previous month. The fact that Ribeiro and Andrade, two of the strongest, most resourceful rock climbers in Brazil, had not succeeded in hoisting me more than 500 feet over the well trodden trail to the summit is an accurate testimonial to my physical condition and skill as a mountain climber. I still recall, with a warm glow, how Ribeiro and Andrade walked over to me as I lay panting and prostrate on a gentle 45-degree slope and said with typical Brazilian tact and gentileza, 'Professor, at times when climbers are faced with insurmountable obstacles, they show more courage by retreating than by going on. '

It was in a naive, American spirit of Rotarianism that I introduced Ribeiro to Slesser and offered to drive them to the base of Dedo de Deus. It was my intention to walk with them to a comfortable vantage point and then enjoy a picnic lunch and a restful afternoon with a good book, leaving the climbing to the professionals. In preparation, I loaded my knapsack with two bottles of Beaujolais, a small roast chicken, biscuits, a package of Gruyere cheese, containers of coleslaw and potato salad, carrots and cauliflower, a tin of Toll House cookies, two pears and an orange, silverware, napkins, and a tablecloth, an autographed copy of Professor Slesser's Red Peak, my camera, a pair of high-power binoculars, sneakers, a first-aid kit, mosquito repellent, an inflatable cushion, a box of Suerdicki cigars, and a flask of Remy-Martin. The cognac wine and cigars were, as I recall chosen with some care since I had to consider the bon vivant tastes of my erstwhile Scottish friend.

The ninety-minute drive behind us, we arrived at the base of the mountain at the uncivilized hour of 5 a.m. I did not partake of the conversation in the car, partly because I was too sleepy, but mostly because it was in a foreign language, mountain-climberese.

There was a certain amount of semi-abrasive, verbal sparring since Slesser had never climbed in Brazil, and he was understandably curious to learn what the Brazilians considered to be a difficult climb, and what techniques were used. Ribeiro responded to Slesser's questioning, as one might expect a proud native of an underdeveloped country to parry the thrusts of a European superman. His general attitude, quite understandably, was that of a confident young challenger who was eager to know how hard the champion could hit. It was the beginning of a friendly rivalry; I was to be its first victim.

We cast a few coins in the fountain next to the shrine in memory of the climbers who had died attempting to scale the formidable peak, and then began the four-hour trek to the base of the Finger. Had I not been struggling unsuccessfully with the tropical underbrush, a heavy knapsack, and a pair of ill-fitting mail-order boots, I would have noticed that we were taking an entirely different route to the one Ribeiro, Andrade, and I had taken three weeks earlier. Adding to my confusion was the fact that I was perspiring so much that my glasses were fogged, and I was suffering from what Jack Benny once called the clothing sickness — my tongue was coated and my breath was coming in short pants.

At approximately 9 a.m. I practically fell into Ribeiro and Slesser who had been racing along ahead. They had removed their knapsacks and were pensively scrutinizing the 1000-foot high rock pinnacle which loomed up immediately ahead. It was an heroic sight; I felt like a roach at the foot of an obelisk.

I was very grateful to Ribeiro for having taken us to see this epic view. After consuming some food and a bit of cognac and snapping some photos, I suggested we move around to the other side of Dedo de Deus, where we could begin our ascent. The conversation, which had previously been carried out in English, Portuguese, or German, in all of which I am relatively proficient, suddenly lapsed into French, leaving me voiceless and voteless. It was apparent, however, that Ribeiro was having a difficult time convincing Slesser that an ascent was even remotely possible. It involved, as it turned out, pulling one's way up about 700 feet of a 90-degree slope, followed by a thumbhold traverse across thirty feet of the exposed face and finally a series of two hundred-foot French chimney wriggles up ten-inch wide, damp openings inside the peak.

There were four reasons why I did not spread my tablecloth right then and there. (1) It was too early in the day; Red Peak could not possibly hold my interest for more than four hours. (2) The first few hundred feet of the ascent promised to be fun, since much of it could be accomplished by climbing up the branches of trees which grew in miraculous fashion in the granite rock (this also made it look deceptively safe). (3) I had already consumed half a bottle of wine in an attempt to maintain my water balance. (4) I had become somewhat emotionally involved in the contest.

There was much talk of the equipment which would be required. The two Professionals donned hand-tooled leather boots and appropriate paraphernalia, and I was outfitted with a pair of canvas-topped bedroom slippers with rope soles called 'alpagadas' which cost 50 cents and are usually worn by impecunious fishermen. There was a long discussion of whether or not Slesser would need expansion holts and pitons, but ultimately he was dissuaded and he set out only with muscatons, wedges, and an old ninety-foot rope which looked suspicously like the one I had seen his wife hang the laundry on. Ribeiro also carried a ninety-foot rope, but for some reason they did not want me to take my brand new 30-meter nylon rope.

By some untold miracle, I managed the first 700 feet. The procedure was roughly as follows. Riheiro would shimmy gracefully up a crevice or tree and then fix a rope so I could pull myself up. My legs never touched the side of the mountain. I was, however, making good use of my knees and elbows, which were a bloody mess. I do not know how Slesser negotiated the climb because whenever I reached Ribeiro, I collapsed in a soggy heap. No one was paying any attention to me at all. Slesser was alternately complimenting Ribeiro on his artistry as a climber and then berating him for his complete disregard for safety precautions. Ribeiro was romantically involved in the thrill of climbing and the glories of the vistas. It took us approximately three hours to negotiate the 700 feet, and to reach our first crisis; we were at the point where it was necessary to traverse the open face.

The 'jeito' for reaching the open face was to crawl along the branch of a small tree. If done properly, the tree bends and drops you against the side of the cliff whereupon is fastened an iron spike. As you clutch the spike and pull yourself out onto a barely perceptible ledge, the tree moves away from you; it is literally a point of no return unless one is wearing a parachute. It was an ideal place for me to settle down with my remaining bottle of wine and hook. Why didn't I?

The traverse, incidentally, is named the Maria Cebolla (Mary Onion is a literal translation). 'Maria Cebolla Day' in Brazil is the equivalent of the American 'Sadie Hawkins Day' where the ladies are allowed to marry any man they can outrun. It is descriptive because the traverse slopes steeply up; hence, it must be negotiated quickly without loss of forward momentum.

When I proposed that I stay and wait for the two protagonists, Ribeiro, who had already negotiated the traverse, argued that it was not safe to descend via the Cebolla. I then offered to meet the duellists at the foot of the mountain, if they would let me borrow one of the ropes for the descent. This was vetoed by Slesser because Ribeiro had fixed one of the ropes for the traverse and had left the other one as a belay (the fixed end of the belay, as it turned out, was tied to a cactus). I was given no choice; I became an unwilling participant in an unscheduled Olympic event.

It took us four hours to climb the remaining 200 feet. Although most of the delays were due to 'Harvey's' cramps, Slesser's desire to recover two 25 cent wooden wedges which Ribeiro and I would willingly have abandoned proved to be a major hang-up. It was almost five o'clock and nearly dusk when we started our descent. The simplest way down would have been to rappel; however, this would have deprived our two adversaries of the challenge of racing down the chimneys, so back into the bowels we went. At this point I had the good fortune of losing my glasses. I say good fortune, because I am considerably myopic and without my glasses the descent was much less terrifying.

It was dusk-turning-to-darkness when the final and fateful crisis came. We were confronted with a forty-foot rappel, the first five and the last twenty of which were free fall, for the cliff had a negative slope. Slesser was the first one down. He eschewed a belay largely, I suspect, because he did not trust either Ribeiro or me to secure it properly.

I followed with Slesser's rope as safety looped round my chest. My rapid, giddy descent was interrupted violently approximately eighteen feet from the bottom. The safety rope had tightened in a vice-like grip around my chest and I was spinning like a top in mid-air. The belayed and the fixed rope (both of which were in the same karabiner) were tangled and knotted!

Despite my total lack of climbing experience, I immediately made the correct diagnosis and with what little wind was left in my crushed chest, I called out bravely, 'Cut the safety rope, Carlos. '

'Don't you dare, ' bellowed Slesser, 'that's my rope. It cost 7 pounds. '

What took place in the next twenty minutes is too bizarre and shameful to recount. It was patently obvious that Ribeiro could not pull me up; I could not detach the safety rope without endangering my life by releasing the rappel; there was no way that Slesser could get to me, since I was four feet from the cliff in mid-air.

I am convinced to this day that had I not offered Slesser a case of Scotch I would still be hanging battered and bruised above the foot of Dedo de Deus. If Malcolm Slesser saw, as he wrote, the Finger of God wagging at him as we left the scene, it was because Deus was saying 'For shame! For shame! '.

(Postscript - Adherents of this divine digit may be interested in the following, kindly sent by Col. Roger North: 'The Brazilian P.O. issued a special stamp in April, 1962, to mark the 50th anniversary of the first ascent of the Dedo de Deus. The stamp is emerald green and white, with a design showing the peak itself behind a rope and rucksack. " 8.00 cruzeiro" is in the top corner and "La Escalada ao Dedo de Deus-1912-9 iv-1962." Execution is rather indistinct, but sufficiently clear to show the formidable nature of the peak. It may be bought for a few pence from dealers.

We regret that the 'do' instead of 'de' in our last issue derived from Slesserian Portuguese — Hon. Editors).

A GUIDED TOUR
Vol. XXIX (1970)

by Allan Austin

It was dark. Heavy rain was falling as we rattled across the bridge. The light in front glowing in the darkness meant warmth and comfort. Just what I needed. Matie was well ahead owing to the fact that someone had inadvertently left a plank off the bridge and I managed to put my foot on it. The rushing water sounded very near indeed, as I grovelled face down on the boards, nose pressed between the gaps, securely held by the heavy sack which had come to rest on the back of my neck. I sighed; it had been like this all day. I managed to reach a position of verticality without losing my gear over the side and set off in pursuit.

Matie had been ready to start first and with practised smoothness had picked up the torch and gone. I was still bemoaning the unfairness of it all and entirely failed to see the hole in the path down which I slid in the direction of the river. It could have been worse. At least I had stopped short of the water. My feet were still dry. This was soon remedied as I plodded dourly on towards the dancing light. It seemed the path had taken a detour over a small bridge; it felt like a drainage ditch. The light stopped. He was waiting for me! Maybe he wasn't so bad after all. But it seemed he was only waiting for moral support. He wanted to be two up when we tried for a night's lodging.

A climber lounged in the doorway propping up the doorpost. He was huge. The doorway was completely blocked. At the sight of the great black-visaged giant I resumed my rightful place at the rear; after all, Matie had the torch and anyway he was bigger than me. Then the incredible happened. The black visage cracked in a smile of welcome. A few words from Matie and the giant waved us inside. 'Be my guest,' he boomed. It seemed they had been on a rescue together in Chamonix.

They were just about to eat. There was a pale thin-faced youth with shifty eyes who seemed incapable of telling the truth. There was a stocky short-legged one with strange round eyes. A short tubby one with thinning hair and an easy-going expression, and his brother, irreverently referred to as the 'Old Man' . The evil-looking curry on the table was for all. I was thankful that 'all' did not include me. Even this strange and motley crew were failing. But our friendly giant didn't seem to mind and ate the lot, emptied the dish and finished with the pan. I lost a bet with him and he ate my biscuits. We retired to bed having lost a shilling at cards, two shillings in an electric meter that didn't work, and with the information that a climb called Hee-haw was a good one for wet weather.

We were up late the following day sluicing pots of tea into a team of Scots idlers living it up in bed. A cunning ploy this. We needed a guide to show us the way. Alas, they all had elastic bladders. No amount of persuasion seemed able to move them from their beds. Appeals to their sense of decency, sportsmanship, etc. , fell on deaf ears. They all slept. We offered to make their breakfast and at once the big man rolled over. 'Aye, ' he

77. SMC in the Staunings Alps, East Greenland. (Above) Malcolm Slesser at the head of
the Bersaerkerbrae, and (below) Robin Chalmers camped on the Lang Glacier

78. *The McCook family at Benalder Cottage, 1905. Does the ghost of McCook still haunt the cottage?*

79. Sgurr nan Gillean

80. Evening on Nevis

announced, 'It's no fair to let you go on your own; I'll come wi' ye'. He stood up and stretched and decided that we needed a fourth member. With an easy, effortless movement he reached a hand under the next bunk and dragged forth a blinking, bleary-eyed youth, the short-legged one. We gave them grapefruit, porridge and bacon butties, and even cleared up for them. And finally when they could prevaricate no longer we set forth for the Clachaig.

I should make it clear at this point that we had entertained some doubts as to the usefulness of their recommendations and had decided on Clachaig Gully instead of some nebulous VS we had never heard of.

I stood there aghast. 'That's it,' they assured me, indicating the foaming torrent rushing down the hill. 'That's the way, just follow the burn. ' There was a certain amount of confusion when they found out I had no boots, hadn't been able to wear any since last year, the results of a wee miscalculation on a boulder. P.A.s wouldn't stand up to it, they insisted. Wouldn't stand up to it? They weren't the only ones. I could see right away that this wasn't the climb for me. I'd made a big mistake coming down here, but there was no point in compounding it. I put on a brave smile. 'Don't bother about me, chaps, ' I said, 'You just go on ahead, I can always do it some other time. ' Och, nae bother at aa,' said the giant, dragging forth a pair of hut slippers from the depths of the van. They were Matie's old kletts, monstrously big with holes in the toes and one sole gaping. 'These'll dae fine.'

I blundered along in the wake of the giant as he ploughed his way up the stream bed, slipping and sliding on invisible boulders and eventually measuring my length in the water. I staggered to my feet to find my finger split across the end and opened out like an unzipped banana. The giant peered at it with interest, snapped it back into place and watched me spew in the burn. By this time Matie and the short-legged one had come back to see what the hold-up was. 'I think you'd better climb with me,' the short-legged one announced, obviously fearing that the giant was too soft. 'Give him the rope.' And a dripping coil of rope was hung about my neck.

He stormed off up the stream, his short, sturdy legs pounding the water to foam, while I vainly tried to instil some power into mine to keep up. Eventually he stopped below a particularly difficult waterfall which fell into a deep evil-looking pool. 'We'll put the rope on here.' I breathed a heartfelt sigh of relief. I could just about second it, I thought.

'You'll have nae bother' he announced, pointing to a red shelving wall on the right. 'There's a tree up there you can use as a runner.' The tree, a ridiculous immature sapling, sprouted from a grass sod about halfway up. If I should fall off, the life expectancy of the sapling would most certainly be severely reduced. I crawled up the wall using to the maximum the friction offered by my voluminous ex-army breeches, rounded the unhappy little sapling and slithered across to a handy boulder at the top of the fall. It was all very insecure, but fortunately the rain lashing down on my spectacles effectively blinded me and the depths of the pool remained out of sight. The short-legged one followed without appearing to experience any difficulty and my hopes of fishing him out of the pool remained unfulfilled.

He disappeared upwards through some minor submerged boulder pitches and when eventually I caught him up he was standing on the edge of a pool below a particularly intimidating fall. 'That's the way' he announced, indicating the roaring torrent, which I now perceived was actually a chimney in disguise. I was beginning to suspect that perhaps this man wasn't a friend after all and it was some time before I was persuaded that salvation really did lie in that direction. Matie and the giant had caught up by this time and all three stood in a semi-circle whilst I advanced, somewhat hesitantly, to battle with the great fall. The only possible way seemed to be to get in there and fight it out. Tentatively I poked my head in, but it was as black as night. The weight of water had washed my balaclava down over my face and I was effectively blinded. Back I blundered, arms waving, tripped on an unseen boulder and measured my length in the pool. I surfaced to the sound of hoots of laughter from the ill-mannered throng, which had the effect of dredging up from somewhere a bit of determination. I felt a definite stiffening of my upper lip. Stuffing the offending balaclava into the short-legged one's hand I stormed back into the fray.

Now I had been thinking about it and had decided on a plan. I would climb as far as I could in the water, then lean out backwards, take a couple of gulps of air and plough on. A reasonable enough theory, one would suppose. The moment arrived when I could hold my breath not a second longer, and so in accordance with the plan I headed out for the light and air. There was nothing wrong with the plan. Superman could have managed it, maybe even the giant below; but a bumbling Sassenach? More hoots of laughter as once again I was fished out of the pool.

This was the end. Whose idea was it anyway? I refused to go back into that maelstrom ever again, and indeed insisted that it was the short-legged one's turn. Whereupon he discovered that a little rib just on one side was a 'variation' . . .would I like to try? It was well scratched and about moderate in standard.

It will be appreciated that climbing in such conditions inevitably subjects one's equipment to undue stresses and strains and my braces were showing every sign of falling down on their job. I was reluctant therefore to place further strain on them, but it seemed there was no way out, the only way was up. Fortunately, they showed an unsuspected tenacity to life and though at times I seemed to be climbing with my knees tied together the worst did not happen and I was saved from an embarrassing situation. Eventually in answer to my monotonous request the short-legged one agreed. We could go home, this was the top, we could go no further. Joyously I passed this bit of information down to the next team. The last bit was a boulder pitch and stimulated by the knowledge that he was almost there, Matie came sprinting up in a flying mantleshelf and with a vigorous heave crashed his head against a protruding boulder. This caused great amusement, and in no time at all Matie's face was all shades of red as blood blended with rain to run from his chin in an impressive flow. The two guides disappeared into the gloom chortling and whooping and leaving us to coil the ropes — our ropes, and follow them down.

We totally misjudged both their fitness and our own, however, for in spite of a five minutes start we must have overtaken them somewhere on the hill, and when eventually I managed to stagger through the bar-room door, I found to my surprise I was the first arrival. 'I' ll have a wee dram' said the voice from the rear.

And so help me! It's all true!

(Readers will recognise characters in the above recalling Moriarty, Haston, Smith and the two Marshalls - Hon. Eds.)

AN EXCURSION IN SCOTLAND
Vol. XXIX (1968)   by Royal Robbins

(For the benefit of our older Salvationists, the author is one of the best-known young climbers in the United States. The exploits of his group on the pitiless fly-frying Yosemite granite have had a great influence on advanced-aid climbing in Europe. His impressions of a snatched, wet and pitonless day in Glencoe are therefore all the more interesting; they include a visitor's glimpses not only of the rock and the weather, but also of the varied fauna haunting the neighbourhood. — Hon. Eds.).

When Chouinard returned to the States from his visit to Scotland, he said he had been treated like a king. He spoke highly of the manly, hardy race from the northern part of the British Isles. I wondered if I would be received the same way. Everyone likes Chouinard.

Impressions...legends...the Scots figure early in the consciousness of Americans — the edifying parables of Robert the Bruce; the great hero, Wallace; MacBeth, a rough but good man gone wrong...an evil woman led him astray...one mustn't get in with bad company; and the other characters in that play — Duncan who was all good, the smooth-cheeked princes, they were Scots too.

When I met the reality I understood more deeply the legends. I visited Scotland while on a lecture tour down in England. It wasn't really a lecture tour. I showed some slides and a movie, and said a few interpretative words. Not really lecturing. I remember the reception at the Alpine Club: exceedingly polite, exceedingly unenthusiastic. One can't blame them. It was mostly the old guard, the conservatives who disdain pitons. And what I offered was mostly American ironmongery, and some monkey tricks on big rock walls, hardly grande alpinisme. They must have felt like spectators at a zoo.

Tom Patey was the cause of of our trip north. He telephoned us while my wife, Liz, and I were in the Lake District, and turned his considerable powers of persuasion to the task of convincing us of the propriety of making what we considered an impossible trip. Patey was enthusiastic. He would come down from Ullapool if we would come up from the

Lakes. Meet us half-way. The time was late afternoon; with a lecture awaiting us just two days away, we found Tom's logic less than cogent. His enthusiasm, however, was so infectious as to be virulent. We caught the bug.

Late that same night we motored north along winding, narrow roads. I was occasionally startled into wakefulness when the car careered around a particularly bad curve. Liz was driving. I remember little except waking up amid amber lights. They were eerie, those long rows of amber lights in the black, wet, Glaswegian night. It seemed not a gay city.

I stumbled into a phone booth and called the number we had been given. Tom came out and led us to Mary Stewart's home in the country. In the morning we awakened to a life which one occasionally reads about in books, but rarely sees in reality, at least in the sedate American sort of reality to which we were accustomed. There were about half a dozen children, robust youngsters, beaming with superb health. Their frontier dress gave a hint of their wild free-spirited nature. The older ones cared for the younger, the strong for the weak. And there were the animals. Mary loves animals. There were dogs and cats of various aspect, goats, a horse, and...a lamb. Behind the house were 200 cats in cages, which Mary used, alas, for research.

Scattered about the house were individuals of widely varying sorts, folk-singers, do-wells and ne'er-do-wells, even a climber or two. All had come to Mary Stewart's pad for a bit of comfort and relaxation, and to escape the cares of the world. Patey insisted we go to Glencoe. I felt more like sitting around Mary's place, taking it all in, but resistance was futile against such a tornado of energy. I can't remember when I first met Tom, but I had long admired him as one of those rare persons who have so much life that it rubs off on those around them. We had recently been involved together in a television stunt on the Anglesey sea cliffs in North Wales.

Tom drove north like he had only a few hours to live, and didn't want to waste a second. He talked continuously, telling Liz and me of this adventure and that, and relating pithy anecdotes of various climbing personalities, and other stories as well — doctor tales of marvellous complications which arise as a result of vaginitis. I couldn't help but suspect that Dr Patey embellished the stories a bit, added a bit of Ullapool colour, as it were. But we didn't mind. As the car rattled north, Tom told us how proud of it he was. It was a red Czechoslovakian crate, and the wonder was, to us, that it ran at all. Patey says he's not mechanically adapted. If true, that car was a fine companion, as it seemed the most ill-adapted mechanical contrivance to which I had ever dared trust my life. But it got us there, and somehow got us back.

As we approached Glencoe, Tom pointed out various areas of climbing interest, and indicated several couloirs from which acquaintances had been avalanched. We bounced to a stop on a gravel lot. Before us stood the Buachaille. In front of it, much closer, was a white building, the S.M.C. hut. As we strolled by it, toward the mountain, Patey, ever anecdotal, told us how naughty Dougal Haston had estranged the leadership of the S.M.C. by painting the interior livid colours because he was bored by its drabness.

We were on our way to the Rannoch Wall, to do Agag's Groove, an easy Very Difficult route, which shows, damn it, how times change. The weather looked terrible, but Tom assured us he thought it would only rain. Only rain? I thought of the white, warm, Yosemite granite, and of the endlessly blue skies of the California summer days. Only rain? But clearly it rained a lot in Glencoe. Every footfall squeeged into the turf. We seemed to be walking on a gigantic sponge. The rock face was a long time getting closer. These hills are bigger than I thought, I thought. It's no wonder that in the winter, with the short days and the fearful Scottish ice climbs — of which we have heard, even in California — it's no wonder the epics occur, and that the stories find their way 6000 miles to the West Coast. But this was to be a fun rock climb, and Tom would take good care of us.

The route was pleasant, but undistinguished — just the sort I wanted. Liz and I roped up at the bottom, while Tom soloed ahead, to show the way. He kept close by, relating how one climber had fallen off here, another there. I can remember little of the route, except that it was enjoyable and just hard enough, considering we used no pegs. I was faced with a series of problems, none fearful, each of which had possibly several solutions, but only one elegant one which, when I found it, gave a feeling of pleasure, when my body moved up — a feeling akin to the thrill of solving a chess problem with just the right balance of simplicity and complexity. That is to say, the possibilities were, or appeared to be, complex, but the solution, when found, was beautifully simple. Such climbing, abundant in the British Isles, is comparatively rare in my country. One needs a steep wall which is rough, textured with small ledges, knobs, holes, jam-cracks, rugosities, bulges, shelves, flakes, horns, corners, ripples and overhangs, so the climber has something of a choice of whether to pull, push, wedge, cling, bridge, straddle, or fall off. In the States, the free-climbing problems, though sometimes very hard, tend to be simpler in terms of intellectual problem-solving. This is particularly true of Yosemite. There, the smoothness of the rock limits the possible ways one can get up a given section of rock. The holds which a cunning mind might ferret out on a British crag often just don't exist in the Valley. I have observed that British visitors to the Valley fare no better than the locals on such walls as the north face of Sentinel Rock, which is 1500 feet of slippery jam cracks. And even Don Whillans had to sweat on the super-smooth Crack of Despair. But on the Crack of Doom, regarded by Yosemite veterans as just as hard, he found a very Whillanesque solution, an ingenious but straight-forward combination which enabled him to pop up a section where I, for one, passed half an hour in intense struggle and finally overcame by dint of brute force and determination. While I am not the cleverest of American climbers, I believe this episode to be typical. And I believe it is at least partly a result of where the emphasis is placed in one's home training ground. In America, stress is on strength, gymnastic ability, and technique, in the sense of making movements (liebacks, jam-cracks, etc.). 'Working things out' is less important partly because of the type of rock we have, and partly because we use a lot of free climbing protection (mostly pitons). With good protection, a leader can afford to go all-out whether he has worked out a solution or not. If his security is middling, then judgment and cunning become his most reliable assets.

Anyway, Agag's Groove made no exorbitant demands upon my physical capacity, but what with those long, pitonless runouts, to err might be human, but it would also be fatal. Yet it was refreshing to climb with just a rope, sans paraphernalia. And I was feeling a bit northwallish clinging to the cold rock which a drizzle was now wetting. Liz came up happily, without apparent effort. It was her sort of climbing, if not our sort of weather.

When we reached the top, the yellow rays of the lowering sun were bursting through new rents in the clouds and lighting the vast moor to the east. My first moor. A moor at last. I had long heard of the great Scottish moors, and here was one for real. It, and the surrounding mountains seemed eerily desolate, and brought to my mind Jack London's tales of the Alaskan tundra. Patey had earlier described a frightful massacre that had occurred here. It seemed a fitting place for dark deeds and heroism.

The descent was a trifle dangerous, with the wet rock, and the lichen, moss, and grass which occasionally covered it. Tom saw us safely off the crag, and then, bursting with energy, ran cross country to fetch the Red Blitz to meet us at the end of our more direct descent. We walked straight down and passed what I presumed was a climber's hut. Some men were in front and one shouted something incomprehensible. But I sensed it was shouted not to us, but at us. Anxious to avoid a situation in which I might be called upon to do something honourable, I light-stepped it, with Liz on my heels, from stone to stone quickly across a creek and reached the safety of the Far Side. And if you think that's easy, try it.

Later, Tom told us we were lucky they hadn't stoned us while we were crossing the creek. And at another time, another place, Davy Agnew, upon hearing me relate the same story, told me exactly the same. Creagh Dhu boys, they were, and tough as they come. Jim McCarthy of Manhattan, no patsy himself, had first told me of this fabulous group, and described them, much to my astonishment as such a rough bunch that they made the New York Vulgarians look like cream puffs in comparison. I didn't really believe this, at first. But now I have heard so many stories that I no longer doubt. Some of the best stories came from Agnew. Davy and I worked together as fellow ski instructors in the Leysin American School, in Switzerland. And as I write this, we are again co-performers in the production of a ski movie. Davy is a burly, strong, smiling man with a generous spirit. He skis like the wind, does back flips off the balconies of Swiss chalets, drinks with his friends, and is capable of slowly breaking the fingers, one by one, of a man who, in a fight, has grabbed him where he shouldn't. So, when Davy tells me of his mates in the Creag Dhu who are really tough, I listen with awe.

As we drove pell-mell and lickety-split back toward Glasgow, Tom told us of Joe Brown's first trip to climb Ben Nevis in the winter, and of how happy the Scottish climbers were when the Human Fly fell several hundred feet down an icy couloir, and all this related in the spirit of good-natured, healthy, competition.

That night I showed the Yosemite climbing film which I had brought for my lectures to a small group in Mary's home. To give the right impression, I presented it professionally; that is, I lectured and played music on a tape while the film wound out its 40 minutes. By the time it was half-way through, I felt a pompous ass treating that small group as an Audience, and my embarrassed voice dribbled off into occasional self-conscious interjections. Later, the party improved as the drink flowed and Patey sang his wonderful songs. Brian Robertson was there. I had first met Brian after the Dru Direct caper that John Harlin and I had cut. Brian had been on the regular Dru west face route at the time and had taken some pictures of us, which he later tried to sell to John. I confess I remember feeling slightly superior to this commercialism, not realising that a poor American climber was affluent compared to a poor Scottish one. I'm less uptight now. (Anyone want to buy some pictures?). Despite Tom's repeated refusals, Brian kept urging him to sing 'John's Song,' a Harlin-deflating ditty in the Patey manner. Considering that John had just died on the Eiger in circumstances prophetically described by Tom's song, and that I, a former friend of John's, was sitting in the room, I thought Brian's repeated insistence a piece of marvellous Scottish sangfroid in the face of that grinning, expectant gloater waiting out there in the darkness for all of us. Finally Brian sang it himself, but rather diffidently, as if he must. I met Brian again in that haunt of the egoists, Yosemite Valley. He came to the Valley camera in hand, with modest ambitions and without fanfare; that is to say, with a sensible attitude, and proceeded to enjoy himself, to do good climbs, and to win the respect of the hyper-critical, snobbish Yosemite climbers. I remember Brian on the Camp 4 boulders: he was at first stopped by their peculiarly rounded and smooth character, but he kept at them with the dogged persistence of the famous Scottish spider, and was soon doing the hard ones.

Next morning, although a bit haggard, we drove south feeling proud and happy to have fitted so much living into so little time. We did not realize then that we had forgotten the lecture film, nor that when I had recorded the singing I had erased the music I used to accompany the film...Mary Stewart saved us in the nick of time - but that is another story. As far as we knew, we were living happily ever after.

ENTENTE CORDIALE
Vol. XXXI (1979)

Miscellaneous Notes

In February, a group of six French climbers visited this country as guests of the British Mountaineering Council. All but one were young professional guides whose main objective was to sample some Scottish winter climbing and to this end B.M.C. officer Alex. McIntyre brought them north. Donald Bennet organised accommodation at Fort William from where they polished off various Creag Meagaidh classics at furious speed, namely Smith's Gully, The Last Post and South Post, the last in the company of Alastair McGregor and Bill Duncan. On Nevis they disposed of Point Five, again in record time.

For their second weekend they moved to the East where Bill Brooker had arranged the Lairig Club Hut at Allt-na-giubhsaich and brought out a representative team from the Aberdeen School to host the visitors.

REFLECTIONS OF THE FRENCH VISITATION

Greg Strange reports as follows:- With a little apprehension a normally reticent group of Etchachan Club members made a rendezvous with the six French celebrities and their English entourage. Could these colourful, friendly, yet unassuming young men really have climbed the most difficult routes in the Alps, skied down major north faces and only a few days ago ascended Smith's Gully in the impressive time of 3/4 hr? At the Spittal car park someone presented Jean-Marc Boivin with a large shovel suggesting that it might prove useful for climbing Lochnagar. This caused much laughter which combined with Alex McIntyre's rock music and a display of Northern Lights set the tone of events for the weekend. From the 5.00 a.m. chaos of an overcrowded Alt Na G. food was produced and snow melted for brews (the pipes were frozen). Despite warnings from Alex the French seemed keen to team up with the Scots so first light saw various international parties heading for Lochnagar and Creag an Dubh Loch. It was a beautiful day. As if by order the view of Lochnagar from the col was as good as ever. A great iced cake set against a blue sky. Hardly a rock was showing. Not unexpectedly, the snow and ice conditions were mediocre; nevertheless Eagle Ridge, Parallel Buttress Direct, Pinnacle Face and a hard variation to Winter Face were all climbed in fast times. The French equipment and technique was very efficient. Using precision-made Charlet or Simond crampons and axes they were able to climb almost as fast as they could walk. Clearly they enjoyed themselves immensely, likening the fantastic snow scenery to that of the Andes. At Creag an Dubh Loch, Labyrinth Edge and a route in the Hanging Garden were climbed. Sunday provided the perfect contrast. A great gale from the south-west beat back several combatants and only three Frenchmen made it into the corrie. Undaunted by the conditions, Rene and

Alex were determined to make up for the previous day's disappointment on a rather bare Creag an Dubh Loch. They polished off Eagle Ridge then Parallel Gully 'B' and still arrived back at the hut before nightfall. Two parties also climbed Shallow Gully. The day was rounded off with pints and pool in the 'Tink' bar followed by a fine traditional Scottish meal of mince, tatties, neeps and skirlie with cloutie dumpling to finish, courtesy of the Pannanich Wells Hotel, and the Mountaineering Council of Scotland. It was a relaxed and homely affair with a kind of fractured franglais circulating freely as linguistic currency. As Derek Pyper said to me afterwards - "Imagine the song Tom Patey would have written to record the occasion when Armand Charlet's grandson climbed on Lochnagar.' It was a remarkable weekend.

THE AIGUILLES DE CAIRNGORM (THE ALPS IN 1954)

Tune: The Mountains of Mourne Words: Tom Patey (extracts)

Oh Chamonix sure is a wonderful sight
With the cafes by day and the pictures by night
They're all wearing duvets and look very neat
And everyone laughed as I walked down the street.
'For Campbell's Tricounis are all very well
But quite out of place here.' remarked Monsieur Snell.
But I told him his Frendos were no use to me
Where the Aiguilles de Cairngorm sweep down to the Dee.

It's a sweat up to Montenvers packed in the train
Where the bloated aristocrats sip their champagne
A telescope stands at the head of a queue
Only ten francs a time for a peep at the Dru.
'Look, Mama, that fellow is surely a Guide!'
I look for another, then tremble with pride
For I'm only a poor Aberdonian you see
Where the Aiguilles de Cairngorm sweep down to the Dee.

Now I've drunk all their wine and it's gone to my head
Now all that I want is to die in my bed
So I'll swap all their Gauloises and garlic and wine
For bridies and chips at the old Bruach Dryne.
So I'll fly through the air like a bright shining star
To the friends who are drinking tonight in Braemar
Wherever I wander my heart it will be
Where the Aiguilles de Cairngorm sweep down to the Dee.

IN REFLECTIVE MOOD

MAINTAINING THE SPIRIT
Vol. XXXI (1976)

by Iain H. Ogilvie

'...*usquebaugh*, at first taste affects all the members of the body; two spoonfuls of this liquor is a sufficient dose; and if any man exceed this, it will presently stop his breath, and endanger his life.'[1]

'He walks into the sea up to his middle with his clothes on, and immediately after goes to bed in his wet clothes, and then laying the bedclothes over him proceeds to sweat....'[2]

Yes! They were a tough lot! But modern technology has improved both the whisky and the bathwater and our lot is a much easier one

Unfortunately our national habit of sinking whisky as if it was beer, has led to technological research being largely devoted to production with the result that some of the finer points of consumption have been overlooked. I am therefore encouraged to hope that this note may usefully fill a gap.

It cannot be disputed that nothing is nicer when one comes off the hill, than a dram and a hot bath; preferably both; preferably both together; in fact, preferably a dram in your bath. There are however snags. For example, the older types of bath, commonly found in Highland hotels so often used for New Year and Easter meets, have curved tops to their parapets and even modern ones, though flat on top, have a ridge round the edge so that a whisky glass placed there, may get upset. In extreme cases, when the bather has actually decided to wash and not just to soak, the whisky may even be polluted by soap suds. This not only spoils the whisky but may result afterwards in a general looseness of the bowels.

Original experiment[3] indicates, however, that, provided you don't propose to make a pig of yourself and that the bottle isn't quite full, it will be buoyant and can be conveniently floated in the bath. It is however important to ensure that there is not too much whisky in the bottle as buoyancy will be close to zero and with the top off, there will again be a danger of dilution[4]. This can be guarded against by having a stiff dram before getting into the bath.

---

[1] 'A description of the Western Islands of Scotland.' Martin Martin. Gent. 1703.
[2] Ibid.
[3] Archimedes. He was a Greek, poor chap, amd must have had to use Retsina or Ouzo.
[4] There is little danger of pollution at this early stage.

As the level of the whisky drops, some bottles will be seen to keel over at an alarming angle but research has shown[5] that, with the exception of Dimple Haig, Antiquary and one or two other types, which become unstable, the bottle will not coup[6] even when empty.

The procedure described above not only ensures that whisky is conveniently to hand at all times but that you can have a hot toddy without all this nonsense of having to dilute it with boiling water.

Specific gravity is also important. For absolute alcohol it is 0.792 and the % age of absolute alcohol in proof alcohol is 57.06, both at 60 F. Therefore, by simple arithmetic, the specific gravity of proof alcohol must be 0.881. Distillers state that it is 0.920 and explain this away by a supposed loss of volume when alcohol and water are mixed. There is no scientific justification for this and it should be ignored as being merely a blind to conceal normal sampling losses.

For easy reference, since not all bathers have a slide rule conveniently at hand, a table giving typical characteristics of a few significant indicator brands is given overleaf.

BRAND	ORIGIN	PROOF	SP.GR.	C[7]
Glenmorangie	Tain	70°	0..917	.99
Glenfiddich	Dufftown	80°	0.905	.75
Smith's Glenlivet	Tomintoul	100°	0.881	.50
Talisker	Skye	175°	0.792	.25
Auchtermuchty	Not known	0	1.000	0
Laphroaig	Islay	200°	N.A[8]	

A warning must be given at this point about the introduction of a chilled bottle into hot water. Senior members will remember all too well an unfortunate incident some years ago, when during an early research programme, a bottle of Talisker had been left[9] on the window sill of an unheated bedroom. Returning late and cold from the hill, the researcher seized it and jumped straight into his bath. The bottle at once shattered and, as the bath was already full the whisky became so severely diluted as to be virtually unpalatable and the programme had to be abandoned

A more recent researcher[10] may have had this incident in mind when he started work on the development of the 'Bather's Liquid Comforter.' This is reported to be a bicompartmented container, one half of which is vacuum insulated and can hold a bottle

---

[5] The stability of a floating body is a function of the draught (Tippler's Law).

[6] Tech:= Go airse over tip, with consequent loss of contents.

[7] Credibility factor.

[8] But ref. Martin Martin above.

[9] Levison-Smith - Crianlarich - New Year 1923.

[10] Unidentified but reported to be a senior member of the Club.

embedded in crushed ice. The other contains a bottle exposed to hot bath water. The whole clamps onto the side of the bath by means of ingenious rubber clips. The bather can indulge in the luxury of alternate drams of hot malt and cold blend[11]. The present author can conceive of no valid reason for drinking cold whisky but this may be a refinement to the self-inflicted agonies ritually performed in the latter stages of a Sauna bath. Research continues.

Ogilvie has applied to the S.M.T. for the Sang Award as a means to futher his work in this field. We regret to report that the Trustees have turned him down on the grounds that his normal life style is well able to maintain his researches at the fullest possible pitch. (Ed.).

[11] 'Bugger up the Blend but don't muck about with the Malt' - Confucius.

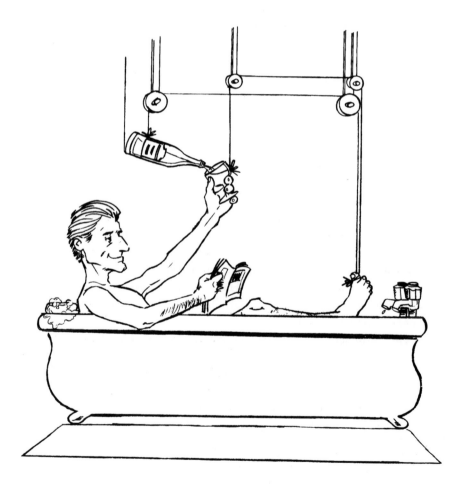

FIVE TIMES LUCKY AT BEN ALDER
Vol. XXXI (1976)   by Philip Gribbon

'Of all the remote unget-at-able mountains in Scotland, Ben Alder ranks among the first.'

This gem, give or take a few inexactitudes, comes from W.H. Murray's classic work, Undiscovered Scotland. I have begun, with hindsight, to appreciate his title from a fresh viewpoint.

Ben Alder lies somewhere amidst the ranges that roll through the hinterlands of the Central Highlands. Ben Alder is 'troublesome to reach.' Choose a loch at any point of the compass: Rannoch, Laggan, Ericht or Treig. Ah yes, it's going to be a fair hike-in, but with some time, energy, ambition, and luck it should be no problem to knock off this lump, a big Munro, 'so shapelessly graceful,' ash-pale under an Empty Quarter of the skies. Just the same as any other Munro. Put it in your mind, and climb it. Nae bother!

Nonetheless Ben Alder threw an indefinable aura around its flanks. There are tall tales about the mountain. People who swam into the frigid winter waters, or strode on frost-bitten feet under the moonlight. Ben Alder, a mystery mountain, a wide land with a jinx.

In the beginning, it was a perfect weekend with the summer sun spitting out of the sky, the gorse burnishing the slopes, the trees splashed green with late spring fever, and the hills a-beckoning. What could be more desirable than a voyage up the entrenched Loch Ericht to the eastern spurs of Ben Alder, camping by the canoe, and even climbing the hill, if the spirit moved us. However it didn't matter how serious, or otherwise were our intentions, because we got no further than a wee glen in the Angus foothills, and that, my friend, is nowhere near Ben Alder. We came over the Dundee hillroad and had a brief glance over the Carse of Gowrie at the Grampian hills spread out sharply across the blue horizon, Beinn-a-Ghlo, Vrackie, Schiehallion, and all that lot, with somewhere Ben Alder, unseen but not unseeing, unknown but not unknowing, its topmost tantalising tip thrust up derisively on a western backcloth. It was a revealing moment, but fraught with inanimate disintegration, because at the sight of our promised land the timing chain jumped joyfully off its sprocket, snarled a nest of links round the driveshaft, and in sheared delight demolished the car engine, once and for all.

Let's try again. Take him stealthily from the back, with gay abandon. We crammed into a tent on the first winter snows beside the concrete bridge near the outlet from Loch Laggan. That's miles away to the north of Ben Alder. Sure, I know that. Now. We were to travel light, to storm over the intervening hills with minimum gear. Some friends agreed to carry our food in to the bothy: some friends could have found less devious means of getting some extra grub. We made such reasonable progress towards the bealach that the dynamic hillbashers decided to take in a Munro. Soon over the bealach we were floundering in a desert of powder snow with all the lee slopes transformed to fluffed meringue pies. The woman was sinking up to her oxters; I was delving even deeper. We hit the stalker's road with relief, and saw the last roseate tinges on the dusken clouds at the same time as we saw the bothy. She thought we had made it, but I knew it was the wrong bothy. Somewhere beyond the sinuous spines of the ridges, further even than the ashen headwalls of the corries, some friends would be sitting comfortably in the other bothy, now lost for the night in a distant valley. Ben Alder had blocked us from our food. Still, Culra bothy accepted us thankfully: we had half a tart and some coffee and there was a wee rodent-ravished clump of solidified sugar on the shelf. We had been on the beds for hours when the straggling crawlers walked through the door: the hill had bashed them. On the morrow I got Geal Charn and Creag Pitridh on the scorecard; perhaps, it was the inspirational brilliance of the successive waves of white hills a-sparkle in a sun-shimmering plaster of snow, with ne'er an icy twist of chill breath to cut the still air, or perhaps, I was hunger-struck, daft, and deranged; it could have been the sun....

All right, let's make a full frontal approach, and to hell with the ghosts. This time Benalder Cottage would be the right bothy, the spirits would ensure we got up at the stroke of dawn.

However, we arrived too late to walk in from the hydro-dam at the southern end of Loch Ericht. We had to use our tents. They were fully aerated, wind-billowed fridges, wistfully sucking in the snow; encouraging shivering submersion in the bags and discouraging disgorgement to face the winter shroud slipped across the pale hill shoulders. Bothy-bound, with the Colonel in his canoe weaving an erratic pewter-boned wake across the loch, and with the wandering walkers trudging disconsolately around the shoreline indentations, we approached the mists in Ben Alder. A curtain of drifting snow, first to mottle, then to scour, came soft-fingering through the desolation, plastering the pines, huddling the deer, burying our footsteps with silent whispers. We found the cottage in the dusk, our firewood in the dark. Our shadows hung flickering on the walls; we basked in the warmth, our thoughts roaming far and wide, no thought for the coming unknown.

Cur—rumble! Its sound was shattering and overwhelming in the deep tangible darkness of a claustrophobically confined space. It was inexplicable, indefinable, all-pervading, nebulous and unnerving. The vibrations ran to their decay out of the floorboards, each to match the awesome tremors of our unmitigated shock. Gone the quiet patterns of half-somnolence, the unconscious beat of tired bodies, to be overtaken by stifled gasps, throbbing hearts, listening, waiting, wondering. Everyone suspended in disbelief, burrowing deeper to limbo within their bags, incommunicado. The tense minutes flew; the slightest creak in the rafters, a dying quiver in the fire embers, and the primitive alert signals flashed up out of our subconscious. Cluny MacPherson perched in his cage, McCook at the front door, I fitfully dozed into a lifeless dawn, awakening to a mouthful of her long silken locks, and the blown snowflakes splattering on the window panes. We never broached our reason for staying at Benalder Cottage: we knew that the highland plateau was a blizzarded whiteout.

We gathered some deadwood under the swaying branches of the larch trees. We were buffeted by the squalls marching down Uisge Alder. We toiled back to the cars. Oh yes, what about the poltergeist? Dammit, but hadn't the Colonel with his last indolent sleepy stretch mischievously tipped with his toes one of the unstable fire-side boulder seats into a rocking, rattling spasm of damped oscillations that had shattered our slumbers? He was quite unrepentant....

My lack of success was becoming noticeable. We tried the same approach in early summer, but we couldn't even get through the locked gate beside Loch Rannoch. She appreciated her afternoon tea, with the rain lashing solidly across the Moor, and a shadowy electronic snowstorm bringing a glorious day on the turf at Hampden Park. We came ashore on an island paradise in the heart of the wilderness, the sunset a-glimmering through the night over the ringing hills, the air scented with bluebell, birch and burning bracken. We steamed beside the fire, while herons slowly wheeled over the waters. Ben Alder was lost in the quiet reflections dancing off the dappled surface of the loch.

The mountain of the rocks and the waters was acting with a coy and hesitant reticence. The game had gone too long. Who wins?

The gates were open, Ben Alder was beckoning in the sunshine. We were sharing our fortune. We walked awash through the crunching sands, following the Culra river to the bothy. We were alone, with the mountain waiting.

Rain belts, ploughing in quick succession down the glen, raced each other on their way. Each northern ridge presented its undoubted charms for our choice and glistened silver-gilt in the late summer sun. The swollen streams, free in their turmoil, rushed from the Bealach Dubh, tumbling below the purple sheen of the ling fields, and the unchastened deer browsed among the blaeberries. We ambled, under the curses of the blackbirds, over the rocky outcrops up the Long Leachas ridge to the bleak undulations of the high plateau; we skirted the lips of Garracoires; we reached the summit of Ben Alder in the mist. Done! She had enjoyed our wee dander...

I had enjoyed the knowledge of the days of failure. I had had to anticipate the inevitable moment of a so-called success. The Ben Alder saga appears to be complete. I harbour still a few regrets....

A CHUILIONN (extract)
Vol. IV (1899)

by Norman Collie

Although Collie's distinguished mountaineering record included climbing and exploration in Norway, the Alps, the Caucasus, the Rockies and the Himalayas, it was to Skye he always returned, and it was at Sligachan Hotel he finally settled in 1939. On his death in 1942 he was buried at Struan beside his old companion and friend, John Mackenzie, the well-known Cuillin guide.

....Fortunately the Coolin are never inferior mountains, unless we measure them by the number of feet they rise above the sea. "Comparative bulk and height," says the late Sheriff Nicolson, "are of course important elements in mountain grandeur, but outline and features are, as with human beings, even more important." Clachlet at Easter covered with snow, and seen from the Moor of Rannoch, towers up into the heavens, at a distance of a few miles, just as grandly as a peak five times its altitude does, thirty miles away in the Himalayas.

It is the atmosphere that adds both dignity and charm to these Scotch hills, making them appear far bigger than they would in the clearer air of the larger mountain ranges, and giving them all the softened colour and perspective so necessary to emphasise the real beauty of true mountains. Their form also helps them in no small degree. The long flowing lines of the lower slopes gradually rising from the moorland below, and the beautifully carved corries that nestle into their sides, all tend to strengthen and serve as a fit substructure for their more wild and broken summits.

At their feet lie no valleys with dirty white streams tearing down between mud banks, their sides are not disfigured with monotonous pine forests of a uniform and dull light green colour, but the heather and the grey rocks, lichen covered, mingle together on their slopes, lighting up with every flash of sunshine or deepening into every shade of brown and purple gloom as the storm clouds sweep over their summits; whilst below brown trout streams wander between the wild birches and Scotch firs, staying here in some dark pool hidden away under the rocks covered with ferns and heather, flashing out again there into the sunshine over the pebbles and across the low-lying moor.

Those who have seen the Coolin from the moors above Talisker in the twilight; or have watched them on a summer's evening from Kyle Akin, rising in deep purple velvet, broidered with gold, out of the "wandering fields of barren foam," whilst

"The charmed sunset linger'd low adown,
   In the red west:"

or lazed away a whole day on the sand beaches of Arisaig Point gazing towards Rum and Skye, lying light blue on the horizon, and across a sea brilliant in colour as the Mediterranean amongst the Ionian Islands; or lingered at the head of Loch Coruisk till the last pale light has faded out of the heavens behind Sgurr Alasdair, and only the murmur of the streams breaks the stillness of the night air — those who have thus seen the Coolin will know that they are beautiful. But to the climber who wanders in the heart of this marvellous mountain land the Coolin has more pleasures to offer. He can spend hour after hour exploring the corries or threading the intricacies of the broken and narrow rock edges that form so large a part of the sky-line. From the summits he can watch the mists sweeping up from below, and hurrying over the bealachs in tumbled masses of vapour, or he can dreamily follow the white sails of the boats, far out to sea, as they lazily make for the outer islands; then clambering down the precipitous faces he can repose in some sheltered nook, and listen to the sound of a burn perhaps a thousand feet below echoed across from the sheer walls of rock on the other side of the corrie; there is always something new to interest him, it may be a gully that requires the utmost of his skill as a mountaineer, or it may be a view of hill, moor, and loch backed by the Atlantic and the far-off isles of the western sea. Nowhere in the British Islands are there any rock climbs to be compared with those in Skye, measure them by what standard you will, length, variety, or difficulty. Should any one doubt this, let him some fine morning walk up from the foot of Coruisk to the rocky slabs at the foot of Sgurr a' Ghreadaidh. There he will see the bare grey rocks rising out from the heather not 500 feet above the level of the loch, and these walls, ridges, and towers of weather-worn gabbro stretch with hardly a break to the summit of the mountain 2,800 feet above him. Measured on the map it is but half a mile, but that half-mile will tax his muscles; he must climb up gullies that the mountain torrents have worn out of the precipices, and over slabs of rock sloping down into space at an angle that makes hand-hold necessary as well as foot-hold; he must creep out round edges on the faces of perpendicular cliffs, only to find that after the perpendicular cliff itself must be scaled before he can win back again to the ridge that is to lead him to the topmost peak. There are many such climbs in the Coolin. The pinnacles of Sgurr nan Gillean, the four tops of Sgurr a' Mhadaidh, and the ridge from Sgurr Dearg to Sgurr Dubh are well known, but the face climbs have been neglected. The face of Sgurr a' Mhadaidh from Tairneilear, the face of Sgurr Alasdair from Coire Labain, are both excellent examples of what these mountains can offer to any one who wants a first-rate scramble on perfect rock. Sgurr a'Coir' an Lochan, on the northern face, gives a climb as good as one could anywhere wish to get, and it is only a preliminary to the giants Sgurr Alasdair and Sgurr Dearg that lie behind.

Yet splendid though the climbing in the Coolin may be, it is only one of the attractions, possibly a minor attraction, to these hills, and there are many other mountain ranges where rock-climbing can be found. It is the individuality of the Coolin that makes the lover of the hills come back again and again to Skye, and this is true also of other mountain districts on the mainland of Scotland. To those who can appreciate the beauty of true hill form, the everchanging colour and wonderful power and character of the sea-girt islands of the west, the lonely grandeur of Rannoch Moor, the spacious wooded valley of the Spey at Aviemore, backed by the Cairngorm Mountains, wild Glen Affric, prodigal of gnarled pines, abounding in strange curves of strength, or the savage gloom of Glen Coe — all these scenes tell the same tale, and proclaim with no doubtful manner that the Scotch mountain land in its own way is able to offer some of the most beautiful mountain scenery in the world. The Highlands of Scotland contain mountain form of the very finest and most subtle kind — form not so much architectural, of which Ruskin writes, "these great cathedrals of the earth, with their gates of rock, pavements of clouds, choirs of streams and stone, altars of snow, and vaults of purple traversed by the continual stars," — but form where the savage grandeur, the strength, and the vastness of the mountains is subordinated to simpler, yet in a way more complicated structure.

Scotch mountains have something finer to give than architectural form. In their modelling may be seen the same beauties that in perfection exist in Greek statuary. The curving lines of the human figure are more subtle than those of any cathedral ever built. The Aiguilles, round Mont Blanc are architectural in the highest degree, but the mighty summit rising up far above them into the blue sky, draped in wonderful and sweeping lines of snow and ice, marvellously strong, yet full of moderation, is far more mysterious, far more beautiful than all the serrated ridges and peaks that cluster round its base.

It is in the gentleness of ascent in many of the Highland hills, in the restraint and repose of the slopes "full of slumber," that we can trace all the more subtle and delicate human lines, and it is due to the strength of these lines that the bigger mountains seem to rise without an effort from the moors and smaller hills that surround them. To many people the Cairngorm Range is composed of shapeless, flat-topped mountains devoid of character. They do not rise like the Matterhorn in savage grandeur, yet the sculptured sides of Braeriach, seen from Sgoran Dubh Mhor, are in reality far richer in beautiful intricate mountain sculpture than the whole face of the Matterhorn as seen from the Riffel Alp.

The individuality of the Coolin is not seen in their summits, which are often almost ugly, but in the colour of the rocks, the atmospheric effects, the relative largeness and harmony of the details compared with the actual size of the mountains, and most of all in the mountain mystery that wraps them round: not the mystery of clearness, such as is seen in the Alps and Himalayas, where range after range recedes into the infinite distance till the white snow peaks cannot be distinguished from the clouds, but in the obscure and secret beauty born of the mists, the rain, and the sunshine in a quiet and untroubled land, no longer vexed by the more rude and violent manifestations of the active power of nature. Once there was a time when these peaks were the centre of a great cataclysm; they are the shattered remains of a vast volcano that ages since poured its lavas in mighty flood far and wide over the land; since then the glaciers in prehistoric time have polished and worn down the corries and the valley floors, leaving scars and wounds everywhere as a testimony of their power; but now the fire age and the ice age are past, the still clear waters of Coruisk ripple in the breeze, by the loch-side lie the fallen masses of the hills, and the shattered debris left by the ice, these harbour the dwarf hazel, the purple heather, and the wild flowers, whilst corrie, glen, and mountain-side bask in the summer sunlight.

But when the wild Atlantic storms sweep across the mountains; when the streams gather in volume, and the bare rock faces are streaked with the foam of a thousand waterfalls; when the wind shrieks amongst the rock pinnacles, and sky, loch, and hill-side is one dull grey, the Coolin can be savage and dreary indeed; perhaps, though the clouds towards the evening may break, then the torn masses of vapour, tearing in mad hunt along the ridges, will be lit up by the rays of the sun slowly descending into the western sea, "robing the gloom with a vesture of divers colours, of which the threads are purple and scarlet, and the embroideries flame;" and as the light flashes from the black rocks, and the shadows deepen in the corries, the superb beauty, the melancholy, the mystery of these mountains of the Isle of Mist will be revealed. But the golden glory of the sunset will melt from off the mountains, the light that silvered the great slabs will slowly fail, from out the corries darkness heralding the black night will creep with stealthy tread hiding all in gloom; and last of all, behind the darkly luminous, jagged, and fantastic outline of the Coolins the glittering stars will flash out from the clear sky, no wind will stir the great quiet, only the far-off sound, born of the rhythmic murmur of the sea waves beating on the rock-bound shore of lonely Scavaig, remains as a memory of the storm.

ON THE RIDGE OF CLACH GLAS — LOOKING SOUTH

The last word will rest with Iain Smart who as Assistant Editor of the S.M.C.J. has been straightening the slumping shoulders of successive Editors for at least twenty years.

A TREE FOR EACH SEASON
Vol. XXXIII (1986)   by I. H. M. Smart

'the best fantasies rest on a sound notion of reality' Andrew Greig: *'Men on Ice'*

Here are four stories about climbs that seemed to reach their main conclusions under trees. They are four similar beads, if you like, strung on the thread provided by the introductory quotation.

SPRING   *The great wood in motion,*
                                fresh in its spirit;'

                          Sorley MacLean; 'Woods of Raasay.'

This tree was a Scots pine great in the number of its branches. I received its hospitality one memorable March night when I couldn't get back to my car because of a swollen burn. The day had begun well enough skiing across twinkling snowfields in clear, still weather. Under such conditions you can travel effortlessly for miles.At the end of the morning, alas, a front moved in bearing cloud and rain on a warm wind. The expected exhilarating ten-mile return run in the evening glory became a slow trudge through grey porridge with a visibility of yards. Eventually the burn appeared; it had been miniscule in the morning but was now huge and frothing at the mouth, tugging at the chain holding it to the hill. There was no way past this man-eater burning white in its cave of gathering darkness. Fortunately some shelter lay nearby in a gloomy forest of the night, a wood of feral pine trees framed, unexpectedly, in fearful asymmetry against the last of the gloaming. The chief tree, the many-armed warrior mentioned in the opening sentence, offered the only escape from the soggy ground. The lowest branch was easily accessible and broad enough to give a perch of reasonable security. It's interesting how these old knacks come back again so easily after millenia of disuse.

Through the long night the overflowing burns roared from the corries. The winter kingdom of a few hours ago had been so peaceful. Now the old regime had collapsed and the restlessness of a new dispensation was in the air. There was life in the warmth of this disturbing wind; things were moving, not least the tree that was taking the brunt of the wind.

Hours later the rain stopped and the cloud started to break, shreds passing from time to time across the moon. Then, moon and clouds stood still and the trees started a headlong rush through the night. It was a misconception of course; the mistake you make when you think the other train is stationary and you are moving when its actually the reverse. Well, either you correct that impression and spend a boring night back home in a damp, wind-buffeted tree or, more enterprisingly, you enter into the spirit of the thing. And so we galloped down the glen, hair streaming moonlit in the wind, gathering reinforcements from the scattered remnants of the old forest until we reached the stockaded plantation of sheep-like spruce trees, the dull usurpers that had driven the unprofitable natives into the upper glen. These boring trees we ravaged, putting them to the blunt axe of the wind. It can't have been all imagination because the next morning a lot of them lay flat on the ground.

SUMMER

'Bacchum in remotis carmina rupibus
Vidi docentem …'

This tree was a birch arching gracefully over a patch of greensward by a purring burn tumbling over and over among bright waterfalls and brown pools. I encountered this spot on a sunny day of high summer after the first of the only two VSs I have ever led in my life. It was, therefore, a long time ago but, nevertheless, clearly remembered. The climb had been delicate and exposed, cruxing in a holdless corner, a veritable diedre of the sorrows with each move more dreadful than the last. In those primitive days we climbed VSs raw; we were too thick to think of using protection, so ascents were complicated by the cold breath of impending dissolution causing ripples to pass unnecessarily often across the nape of the neck.

Leaving the hill afterwards the descent was lightened by the glow of survivor's joy; that feeling of suspended gravitas you get when your appointment with the Great Dentist in the room next door is suddenly cancelled. It was then I encountered the patch of birch-shaded greensward. What an opportunity! The others were away ahead, too far to be consulted, so quick as a flash I was down there supine on the grass, head pillowed on my rucksack. The ambience was too good to obliterate in serious slumber; it was better to hover on the brink aware of the smell of the warm earth, the trill of water and the green canopy of the tree seen through half shut eyes flickering in the breeze as heliographing leaves deflected little bits of sunshine into the restful shade. Then came the powerful sensation of a presence and the sound of something not unlike distant singing coming from some far hinterland of reality. Whatever this strong and disturbing land may be, it is usually kept hidden by a protective screen of suitably opaque metaphors. My old pagan friend Quintus Horatius Flaccus who saw round many an odd corner of the normal world, re-corded the sensation pretty accurately in Book ii, Ode XIX, the introductory lines of which head this section. (Bacchus, by the way, was originally a more general nature God, before he took up drink).

It's all physiological of course. The effects of falling adrenalin levels and the release of dear knows how many curious neurotransmitters, neuromodulators and endorphins by an alarmed nervous system make it relax its guard; flickering light and the melodious trilling of water in this case, confused it even further and generated a bit of wobble in the perceived world. Something similar happened after the second VS I led, so ever since I have stuck to Diffs and V Diffs which produce a lesser effect. Some people I know can climb VSs all day and every day and find it pleasantly stimulating. These are hard men with pieces of fencing wire for fuses in their nervous system. You have to be suitably deferential in their presence; some of them can even construe Horace and must know all about distant singing in rocky places.

AUTUMN

'Sunt lacrymae rerum et mentem mortalia tangunt'

Virgil.

lacrymae rerum - up your jumper'

Sidney Goodsir Smith.

This was a sad sort of autumn day — dark, damp and edgily disagreeable. I left my rucksack under the ghost of a birch, a grey stem ascending to a cloud of leaves drained of colour. The path then led past an abandoned shieling, mouldering under a pall of grey nettles and dun bracken. The reason for treading this depressing place was the crag above. It had looked attractive when first seen weeks ago. A scramble on its rocks had seemed a good way of spending a poor day. This, however, was an unusually poor day. There were tears for things in general and mortal things in particular touched the heart. However, the rock seemed good and in spite of the psychological burden of pervading melancholy, the pitch went well. Thirty feet up after an irreversible move the horizon started to move or, more correctly, although it seemed to take quite a time for the mind to work this out, the slab bearing the crucial holds toppled over and fell. A hand, mine as it happened, clutched at a passing hold and swung me away from the executing crunch of the descending megalithic axe which then bounded on downwards chopping grey scree and sombre bracken with each blow against the passing hillside. It all happened quickly and the avoiding action was calculated and carried out by an efficient subconscious organisation without, it seemed, much help from one's owned dulled persona. This fits what is known about the evolution of the nervous system. Very little is discarded; primeval circuits are retained and underpin the new accretions acquired during slow evolutionary time. In the old days the survival reflexes could get on with the job without extraneous input from higher centres given over to contemplating such absurd notions as lacrymae rerum. Now, in an emergency these ancient survival routines are still able to wriggle out within milliseconds from under a burden of blunting subjectivity and camsteerie logic to look after their owner's immediate interests.

Still, there are advantages. The higher centres after a near miss, seem to celebrate their reprieve by being particularly sensitive to the colour and depth of the world around. This became apparent a little later when the weather turned for the better. In the improving light a colourful landscape of near and far emerged from the flatness. Searchlights of sun came through the moving clouds and scanned the hillside, picking out from time to time autumnal birch trees, bright against the dark heather including, for one exhilarating moment as I retrieved my rucksack, the silver stem and golden crown of the one that had earlier been a grey ghost with colourless leaves.

WINTER

Dispel the cold with amber fire
From logs laid tinder dry upon the hearth
And pour the twelve year old Glenlivet
In generous drams from its earthen jar.

Horace Ode I, ix (after a fashion)

I made camp early in the morning at the head of the glen among the last trees of the old forest. The rest of the day was spent on the ridges above in an uncompromising land of winter where rock and snow were abraded by spindrift driven by searing wind. Travel in this dead land at the edge of survival was exhilarating for a while but as the day waned and the shadows grew it sharpened a hunger for other living things. The last mile back to the camp was made in dying light with the growing loneliness of seeming to be the last man left alive on a dead earth. Usually you have to grit your teeth a little before entering a wood in the twilight. The additional darkness is not easily accepted. This time, however, the old forest offered company and protection from the callous wind and the hard glitter of the stars. As the fire flared up a comfortable room was fashioned from the darkness. Its floor was sheltered and the cold light of only a few stars penetrated the pillared walls and vaulted ceiling. Relaxing after dinner with half a bottle of malt in a comfortable fireside armchair provided hospitably by the thrust out roots of a particularly noble tree was as pleasant an experience as I can remember. The trees gathered round the fire and we communed together in a companionable way in spite of the vast difference in our ages and the divergent paths we had followed in the course of evolution. I thought of other Scots pines I had bivouacked under - in Rothiemurchus and the Derry, around Rannoch, in lonely Barrisdale and over the sea in Norway; then of more distant relations, a pinon in Utah which had shaded me from quiet moonlight and a most ancient bristle cone pine I had snoozed beneath in the noonday heat of sunny California. While we went through all this family gossip the greater darkness waited indifferently outside; in time it would reabsorb tree, man and earth alike and recycle us all into, and maybe beyond, the hadrons and leptons of an indeterminate universe. Meanwhile we living things gathered round a communal hearth, preserved for a time in an amber bubble of firelight, purring contentedly together and enjoying each other's company.

But finally, instead of riding off into the sunset, let us share one more experience from the contact zone between the mineral and the biological worlds. Indeed doesn't all mountaineering belong in this area of encounter?

BEYOND THE DREAMS OF AVARICE
(Extract from Three Immoderate Mountains)
Vol. XXXII (1982)   by I.H.M. Smart

'An t-or is fearr air bith
- the best gold of any.'

The western slopes of the Colorado Rocky Mountains have spectacular Fall colourings. Predominant is the bright yellow of the aspen poplar. This tree is tall, slender stemmed with a terminal canopy of trembling leaves that turn their colours on and off in the breeze. We had climbed a shapely mountain somewhere in the San Juan range which gave a circumferential view of these realms of gold. Near the top, I remember, was a last isolated thicket of low Juniper. Here, under a bough were traces of a twig couch and a very modest fire where some discriminating citizen had passed the night. Had we had the foresight to bring food into this Midas land we'd have done the same. Our improvidence forced us off the top in the late afternoon and the rocks and screes funnelled us towards a steep slope stalked and shared with aspen saplings fifteen feet high. Their thin, whippy stems were ideal for cushioning the descent. I can remember brachiating down the golden brae swinging from trunk to pliant trunk through the wake of currency shaken from the trees by my spendthrift companion. The air was filled with coin of the realm raining down from the blue sky: sovereigns, doubloons, guineas, Kruger rands and gold moidores floated in the air shining as they hit the sunlight, full face and disappearing when they turned edge on. This was copious, innocent wealth you could revel in with a clear conscience — a cloud of gold a hundred yards long you could run through whooping and yodelling and shouting 'Rich beyond the dreams of avarice.' There were banks of it on the ground and as you passed you could kick it back up into the air again to join the gold leaf raining down from heaven. I have always wanted to order a pile of Kruger rands from the bank and kick them up in the air while the tellers showered me with gold moidores: it was every bit as enjoyable as I had supposed .

This experience is clearly recorded somewhere in my mind and I often re-run the episode during boring committee meetings. Up till now it has always been played silently and without movement but I suppose one time I'll forget and start kicking the order papers up in the air, whooping and yodelling all the while. Such behaviour will no doubt arouse criticism.

A SCOTTISH MOUNTAINEERING CLUB.

4 Berkeley Terrace, January 19, 1889.

SIR,—As one who loves and knows the healthy influence of a ramble among the Alps of Switzerland and the mountains of Scotland, I warmly sympathise with the sentiments given expression to in some recently published letters in your columns, and would very cordially support any movement to form such a club as is proposed.

I must say, however, that I should object to the term "Alpine" being applied, especially if such a club were constituted on the lines laid down by Mr Naismith. We should suffer like so many other Scotch clubs by the marked inferiority we should bear to the English corresponding club. England in the south is practically destitute of hills, while we have many, and all within comparatively easy reach. There is therefore little reason why we should wish to form an Alpine Club; rather let us have a club which would be peculiarly our own, and one to which many of our southern Alpine climbers would be proud to belong—which certainly did we term ourselves an Alpine club they would not care to do.

A word as to the initial construction of what I have ventured to term a "Scottish Mountaineering Club." To form a nucleus of the club let such gentlemen as show an interest in the movement, irrespective of their having performed any particular kind or number of ascents, meet together and discuss the matter over.

I may say that in order to give the project a start I should be very willing to receive intimation from any gentlemen (or ladies) who feel interested in the matter, and—if from the opinion of such it seem advisable—to convene a public meeting by advertisement.—I am, &c.,

A. ERNEST MAYLARD.

Glasgow Herald, January 21, 1889.

A SCOTTISH MOUNTAINEERING CLUB.

4 Berkeley Terrace, January 24, 1889.

SIR,—Since my letter on the above subject, which you were good enough to publish on Monday the 21st, I have received so many sympathetic and cordial expressions regarding the matter, both verbally and by letter, that I think I may safely say, for the information of those interested, that there is little doubt but that some such Club as that suggested will be started. I must in the meantime ask those who have written to me, or are yet likely to write, to excuse any acknowledgment of their letters. I hope, in the course of a fortnight or so, to arrange for a general meeting of all who have in any way intimated their interest in the project. I may say that the hope has been expressed that gentlemen in Edinburgh, Dundee, Aberdeen, and other towns may be induced to join us in the matter, so that the Club